Midget & Sprite Owners Workshop Manual

R G O Hawes

Models covered
MG Midget Mk I, II, III and 1500; 948, 1098, 1275 and 1493 cc
Austin-Healey Sprite Mk I, II, III and IV; 948, 1098 and 1275 cc

ISBN 978 0 85733 690 3

J H Haynes & Co. Ltd.
Haynes North America, Inc

www.haynes.com

Acknowledgements

Thanks are due to BL Cars Limited for the supply of technical information. The Champion Sparking Plug Company supplied the illustrations showing the various spark plug conditions. Duckhams Oils kindly supplied the lubrication data, and Sykes-Pickavant Ltd provided some of the workshop tools. Special thanks are due to all those people at Sparkford who helped in the production of this manual.

About this manual

Its aim

The aim of this manual is to help you get the best from your car. It can do so in several ways. It can help you decide what work must be done (even should you choose to get it done by a garage), provide information on routine maintenance and servicing, and give a logical course of action and diagnosis when random faults occur. However, it is hoped that you will use the manual by tackling the work yourself. On simpler jobs it may even be quicker than booking the car into a garage and going there twice to leave and collect it. Perhaps most important, a lot of money can be saved by avoiding the costs the garage must charge to cover its labour and overheads.

The manual has drawings and descriptions to show the function of the various components so that their layout can be understood. Then the tasks are described and photographed in a step-by-step sequence so that even a novice can do the work.

Its arrangement

The manual is divided into twelve Chapters, each covering a logical sub-division of the vehicle. The Chapters are each divided into Sections, numbered with single figures, eg 5; and the Sections into paragraphs (or sub-sections), with decimal numbers following on from the Section they are in, eg 5.1, 5.2, 5.3 etc.

It is freely illustrated, especially in those parts where there is a detailed sequence of operations to be carried out. There are two forms of illustration: figures and photographs. The figures are numbered in sequence with decimal numbers, according to their position in the Chapter – Fig. 6.4 is the fourth drawing/illustration in Chapter 6. Photographs carry the same number (either individually or in related groups) as the Section or sub-section to which they relate.

There is an alphabetical index at the back of the manual as well as a contents list at the front. Each Chapter is also preceded by its own individual contents list.

References to the 'left' or 'right' of the vehicle are in the sense of a person in the driver's seat facing forwards.

Unless otherwise stated, nuts and bolts are removed by turning anti-clockwise, and tightened by turning clockwise.

Vehicle manufacturers continually make changes to specifications and recommendations, and these, when notified, are incorporated into our manuals at the earliest opportunity.

Whilst every care is taken to ensure that the information in this manual is correct, no liability can be accepted by the authors or publishers for loss, damage or injury caused by any errors in, or omissions from, the information given.

Introduction
to the Austin Healey Sprite and MG Midget

The first member of this range of small, two-seater sports cars was the Austin Healey Sprite, introduced in 1958 with its characteristic 'frog-eye' headlamp arrangement, and fitted with the familiar A-series 948 cc engine. This car was identified as the Mk I, and in 1961 the Sprite Mk II was introduced together with its companion, the MG Midget Mk I. These were virtually identical, but the general arrangements of their bodywork had been considerably altered from that of the Mk I Sprite, and this new appearance has been broadly continued.

The first major engine alteration came in 1962 when the larger 1098 cc engine version was fitted. The Sprite Mk III and Midget Mk II appeared in 1964, the major changes being the introduction of semi-elliptic rear springs and wind-up windows. In 1966 the Sprite Mk IV and Midget Mk III appeared with a 1275 cc engine installed.

Sprite production was discontinued in 1971, but the midget Mk III continued to flourish until 1979. A steady programme of improvements has been maintained including, in 1974, the fitment of a specially tuned version of the Triumph Spitfire 1500 engine together with a specially adapted Marina 1.3 gearbox. Although not technically sophisticated, the 1500 engine, like the smaller 1275, has proved itself to be tough, practical and reliable.

Over the many years of production of this economy sports car, many detail changes have taken place, although the original concept has remained basically the same. These changes include specification changes to suit local conditions, mainly North America with its safety and emission control regulations.

The Sprite and Midget models have always sold well, probably because of their relatively low new price, simplicity and economy of operation but, above all, because they are fun to drive. For many, a well-used 'Spridget' will have been their first real sports car. There cannot be many among the ranks of motoring enthusiasts who have not, at some time, owned one of these models.

Contents

Austin-Healey Sprite Mk I

MG Midget Mk I

MG Midget Mk III (USA specification)

MG Midget 1500

Use of English

As this book has been written in England, it uses the appropriate English component names, phrases, and spelling. Some of these differ from those used in America. Normally, these cause no difficulty, but to make sure, a glossary is printed below. In ordering spare parts remember the parts list may use some of these words:

English	American	English	American
Accelerator	Gas pedal	Locks	Latches
Aerial	Antenna	Methylated spirit	Denatured alcohol
Anti-roll bar	Stabiliser or sway bar	Motorway	Freeway, turnpike etc
Big-end bearing	Rod bearing	Number plate	License plate
Bonnet (engine cover)	Hood	Paraffin	Kerosene
Boot (luggage compartment)	Trunk	Petrol	Gasoline (gas)
Bulkhead	Firewall	Petrol tank	Gas tank
Bush	Bushing	'Pinking'	'Pinging'
Cam follower or tappet	Valve lifter or tappet	Prise (force apart)	Pry
Carburettor	Carburetor	Propeller shaft	Driveshaft
Catch	Latch	Quarterlight	Quarter window
Choke/venturi	Barrel	Retread	Recap
Circlip	Snap-ring	Reverse	Back-up
Clearance	Lash	Rocker cover	Valve cover
Crownwheel	Ring gear (of differential)	Saloon	Sedan
Damper	Shock absorber, shock	Seized	Frozen
Disc (brake)	Rotor/disk	Sidelight	Parking light
Distance piece	Spacer	Silencer	Muffler
Drop arm	Pitman arm	Sill panel (beneath doors)	Rocker panel
Drop head coupe	Convertible	Small end, little end	Piston pin or wrist pin
Dynamo	Generator (DC)	Spanner	Wrench
Earth (electrical)	Ground	Split cotter (for valve spring cap)	Lock (for valve spring retainer)
Engineer's blue	Prussian blue	Split pin	Cotter pin
Estate car	Station wagon	Steering arm	Spindle arm
Exhaust manifold	Header	Sump	Oil pan
Fault finding/diagnosis	Troubleshooting	Swarf	Metal chips or debris
Float chamber	Float bowl	Tab washer	Tang or lock
Free-play	Lash	Tappet	Valve lifter
Freewheel	Coast	Thrust bearing	Throw-out bearing
Gearbox	Transmission	Top gear	High
Gearchange	Shift	Torch	Flashlight
Grub screw	Setscrew, Allen screw	Trackrod (of steering)	Tie-rod (or connecting rod)
Gudgeon pin	Piston pin or wrist pin	Trailing shoe (of brake)	Secondary shoe
Halfshaft	Axleshaft	Transmission	Whole drive line
Handbrake	Parking brake	Tyre	Tire
Hood	Soft top	Van	Panel wagon/van
Hot spot	Heat riser	Vice	Vise
Indicator	Turn signal	Wheel nut	Lug nut
Interior light	Dome lamp	Windscreen	Windshield
Layshaft (of gearbox)	Countershaft	Wing/mudguard	Fender
Leading shoe (of brake)	Primary shoe		

Buying spare parts and vehicle identification numbers

Buying spare parts

Spare parts are available from many sources, for example: BL garages, other garages and accessory shops, and motor factors. Our advice regarding spare parts is as follows:

Officially appointed BL garages -- This is the best source of parts which are peculiar to your car and are otherwise generally not available (eg complete cylinder heads, internal gearbox components, badges, interior trim etc). It is also the only place at which you should buy parts if your car is still under warranty; non-BL parts may invalidate the warranty. To be sure of obtaining the correct parts it will always be necessary to give the storeman your car's engine number and chassis number, and if possible, to take the old part along for positive identification. Many parts are available under a factory exchange scheme -- any parts returned should always be clean! If obviously makes good sense to go to the specialists on your car for this type of part as they are best equipped to supply you.

Other garages and accessory shops -- These are often very good places to buy material and components needed for the maintenance of your car (eg oil filters, spark plugs, bulbs, drivebelts, oil and grease, touch-up paint, filler paste etc). They also sell general accessories, usually have convenient opening hours, charge lower prices and can often be found not far from home.

Motor factors -- Good factors will stock all the more important components which wear out relatively quickly (eg clutch components, pistons, valves, exhaust systems, brake pipes/seals and pads, etc). Motor factors will often provide new or reconditioned components on a part exchange basis -- this can save a considerable amount of money.

Vehicle identification numbers

Modifications are a continuing and unpublicised process in vehicle manufacture quite apart from major model changes. Spare parts manuals and lists are compiled upon a numerical basis, the individual vehicle numbers being essential to correct identification of the component required.

When ordering spare parts, always give as much information as possible. Quote the car model, year of manufacture, body and engine numbers as appropriate.

The car number is stamped on a plate secured to the left-hand sidemember adjacent to the inner wheel arch within the engine compartment.

The engine number is stamped on a plate attached to the right-hand side of the cylinder block by the dynamo/alternator upper mounting on all except 1500 models. On these models, the number is stamped on the flange on the left-hand side of the block immediately below No 4 spark plug.

Car number identification plate

Engine number (1275 model)

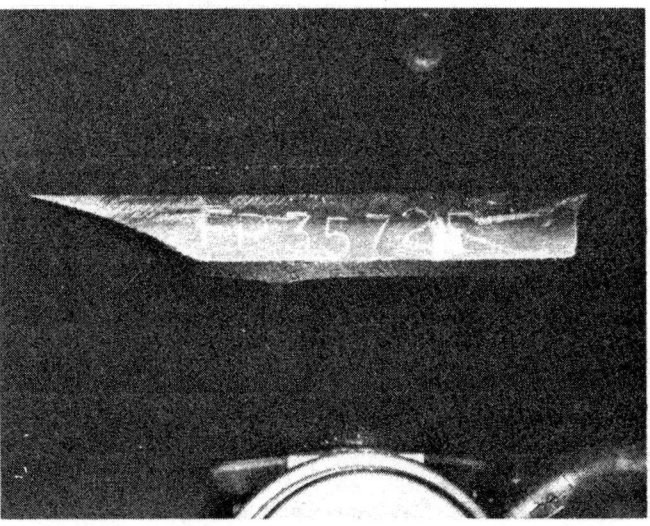

Engine number (1500 model)

Tools and working facilities

Introduction

A selection of good tools is a fundamental requirement for anyone contemplating the maintenance and repair of a motor vehicle. For the owner who does not possess any, their purchase will prove a considerable expense, offsetting some of the savings made by doing-it-yourself. However, provided that the tools purchased meet the relevant national safety standards and are of good quality, they will last for many years and prove an extremely worthwhile investment.

To help the average owner to decide which tools are needed to carry out the various tasks detailed in this manual, we have compiled three lists of tools under the following headings: *Maintenance and minor repair, Repair and overhaul*, and *Special*. The newcomer to practical mechanics should start off with the *Maintenance and minor repair* tool kit and confine himself to the simpler jobs around the vehicle. Then, as his confidence and experience grow, he can undertake more difficult tasks, buying extra tools as, and when, they are needed. In this way, a *Maintenance and minor repair* tool kit can be built-up into a *Repair and overhaul* tool kit over a considerable period of time without any major cash outlays. The experienced do-it-yourselfer will have a tool kit good enough for most repair and overhaul procedures and will add tools from the *Special* category when he feels the expense is justified by the amount of use these tools will be put to.

It is obviously not possible to cover the subject of tools fully here. For those who wish to learn more about tools and their use there is a book entitled *How to Choose and Use Car Tools* available from the publishers of this manual.

Maintenance and minor repair tool kit

The tools given in this list should be considered as a minimum requirement if routine maintenance, servicing and minor repair operations are to be undertaken. We recommend the purchase of combination spanners (ring one end, open-ended the other); although more expensive than open-ended ones, they do give the advantages of both types of spanner.

Combination spanners - $^7/16$, $^1/2$, $^9/16$, $^5/8$, $^3/4$, $^{13}/16$, $^7/8$ and $^{15}/16$ in AF
Adjustable spanner - 9 inch
Engine sump/gearbox/rear axle drain plug key
Spark plug spanner (with rubber insert)
Spark plug gap adjustment tool
Set of feeler gauges
Brake adjustment spanner
Brake bleed nipple spanner
Screwdriver - 4 in long x $^1/4$ in dia (flat blade)
Screwdriver - 4 in long x $^1/4$ in dia (cross blade)
Combination pliers - 6 inch
Hacksaw (junior)
Tyre pump
Tyre pressure gauge
Grease gun
Oil can
Fine emery cloth (1 sheet)
Wire brush (small)
Funnel (medium size)

Repair and overhaul tool kit

These tools are virtually essential for anyone undertaking any major repairs to a motor vehicle, and are additional to those given in the *Maintenance and minor repair* list. Included in this list is a comprehensive set of sockets. Although these are expensive they will be found invaluable as they are so versatile - particularly if various drives are included in the set. We recommend the $^1/2$ in square-drive type, as this can be used with most proprietary torque spanners. If you cannot afford a socket set, even bought piecemeal, then inexpensive tubular box wrenches are a useful alternative.

The tools in this list will occasionally need to be supplemented by tools from the *Special* list.

Sockets (or box spanners) to cover range in previous list
Reversible ratchet drive (for use with sockets)
Extension piece, 10 inch (for use with sockets)
Universal joint (for use with sockets)
Torque wrench (for use with sockets)
Mole wrench - 8 inch
Ball pein hammer
Soft-faced hammer, plastic or rubber
Screwdriver - 6 in long x $^5/16$ in dia (flat blade)
Screwdriver - 2 in long x $^5/16$ in square (flat blade)
Screwdriver - 1$\frac{1}{2}$ in long x $^1/4$ in dia (cross blade)
Screwdriver - 3 in long x $^1/8$ in dia (electricians)
Pliers - electricians side cutters
Pliers - needle nosed
Pliers - circlip (internal and external)
Cold chisel - $\frac{1}{2}$ inch
Scriber
Scraper
Centre punch
Pin punch
Hacksaw
Valve grinding tool
Steel rule/straight-edge
Allen keys
Selection of files
Wire brush (large)
Axle-stands
Jack (strong scissor or hydraulic type)

Special tools

The tools in this list are those which are not used regularly, are expensive to buy, or which need to be used in accordance with their manufacturers' instructions. Unless relatively difficult mechanical jobs are undertaken frequently, it will not be economic to buy many of these tools. Where this is the case, you could consider clubbing together with friends (or joining a motorists' club) to make a joint purchase, or borrowing the tools against a deposit from a local garage or tool hire specialist.

The following list contains only those tools and instruments freely available to the public, and not those special tools produced by the vehicle manufacturer specifically for its dealer network. You will find occasional references to these manufacturer's special tools in the text of this manual. Generally, an alternative method of doing the job without the vehicle manufacturer's special tool is given. However, sometimes, there is no alternative to using them. Where this is the case and the relevant tool cannot be bought or borrowed you will have to entrust the work to a franchised garage.

Valve spring compressor
Piston ring compressor
Balljoint separator
Universal hub/bearing puller
Impact screwdriver
Micrometer and/or vernier gauge
Dial gauge

Stroboscopic timing light
Dwell angle meter/tachometer
Universal electrical multi-meter
Cylinder compression gauge
Lifting tackle
Trolley jack
Light with extension lead

Buying tools

For practically all tools, a tool factor is the best source since he will have a very comprehensive range compared with the average garage or accessory shop. Having said that, accessory shops often offer excellent quality tools at discount prices, so it pays to shop around.

There are plenty of good tools around at reasonable prices, but always aim to purchase items which meet the relevant national safety standards. If in doubt, ask the proprietor or manager of the shop for advice before making a purchase.

Care and maintenance of tools

Having purchased a reasonable tool kit, it is necessary to keep the tools in a clean serviceable condition. After use, always wipe off any dirt, grease and metal particles using a clean, dry cloth, before putting the tools away. Never leave them lying around after they have been used. A simple tool rack on the garage or workshop wall, for items such as screwdrivers and pliers is a good idea. Store all normal spanners and sockets in a metal box. Any measuring instruments, gauges, meters, etc, must be carefully stored where they cannot be damaged or become rusty.

Take a little care when tools are used. Hammer heads inevitably become marked and screwdrivers lose the keen edge on their blades from time to time. A little timely attention with emery cloth or a file will soon restore items like this to a good serviceable finish.

Working facilities

Not to be forgotten when discussing tools, is the workshop itself. If anything more than routine maintenance is to be carried out, some form of suitable working area becomes essential.

It is appreciated that many an owner mechanic is forced by circumstances to remove an engine or similar item, without the benefit of a garage or workshop. Having done this, any repairs should always be done under the cover of a roof.

Wherever possible, any dismantling should be done on a clean flat workbench or table at a suitable working height.

Any workbench needs a vice: one with a jaw opening of 4 in (100 mm) is suitable for most jobs. As mentioned previously, some clean dry storage space is also required for tools, as well as the lubricants, cleaning fluids, touch-up paints and so on which become necessary.

Another item which may be required, and which has a much more general usage, is an electric drill with a chuck capacity of at least $\frac{5}{16}$ in (8 mm). This, together with a good range of twist drills, is virtually essential for fitting accessories such as wing mirrors and reversing lights.

Last, but not least, always keep a supply of old newspapers and clean, lint-free rags available, and try to keep any working area as clean as possible.

Spanner jaw gap comparison table

Jaw gap (in)	Spanner size
0.250	$\frac{1}{4}$ in AF
0.276	7 mm
0.313	$\frac{5}{16}$ in AF
0.315	8 mm
0.344	$\frac{11}{32}$ in AF; $\frac{1}{8}$ in Whitworth
0.354	9 mm
0.375	$\frac{3}{8}$ in AF
0.394	10 mm
0.433	11 mm
0.438	$\frac{7}{16}$ in AF
0.445	$\frac{3}{16}$ in Whitworth; $\frac{1}{4}$ in BSF
0.472	12 mm
0.500	$\frac{1}{2}$ in AF
0.512	13 mm
0.525	$\frac{1}{4}$ in Whitworth; $\frac{5}{16}$ in BSF
0.551	14 mm
0.563	$\frac{9}{16}$ in AF
0.591	15 mm
0.600	$\frac{5}{16}$ in Whitworth; $\frac{3}{8}$ in BSF
0.625	$\frac{5}{8}$ in AF
0.630	16 mm
0.669	17 mm
0.686	$\frac{11}{16}$ in AF
0.709	18 mm
0.710	$\frac{3}{8}$ in Whitworth; $\frac{7}{16}$ in BSF
0.748	19 mm
0.750	$\frac{3}{4}$ in AF
0.813	$\frac{13}{16}$ in AF
0.820	$\frac{7}{16}$ in Whitworth; $\frac{1}{2}$ in BSF
0.866	22 mm
0.875	$\frac{7}{8}$ in AF
0.920	$\frac{1}{2}$ in Whitworth; $\frac{9}{16}$ in BSF
0.938	$\frac{15}{16}$ in AF
0.945	24 mm
1.000	1 in AF
1.010	$\frac{9}{16}$ in Whitworth; $\frac{5}{8}$ in BSF
1.024	26 mm
1.063	$1\frac{1}{16}$ in AF; 27 mm
1.100	$\frac{5}{8}$ in Whitworth; $\frac{11}{16}$ in BSF
1.125	$1\frac{1}{8}$ in AF
1.181	30 mm
1.200	$\frac{11}{16}$ in Whitworth; $\frac{3}{4}$ in BSF
1.250	$1\frac{1}{4}$ in AF
1.260	32 mm
1.300	$\frac{3}{4}$ in Whitworth; $\frac{7}{8}$ in BSF
1.313	$1\frac{5}{16}$ in AF
1.390	$\frac{13}{16}$ in Whitworth; $\frac{15}{16}$ in BSF
1.417	36 mm
1.438	$1\frac{7}{16}$ in AF
1.480	$\frac{7}{8}$ in Whitworth; 1 in BSF
1.500	$1\frac{1}{2}$ in AF
1.575	40 mm; $\frac{15}{16}$ in Whitworth
1.614	41 mm
1.625	$1\frac{5}{8}$ in AF
1.670	1 in Whitworth; $1\frac{1}{8}$ in BSF
1.688	$1\frac{11}{16}$ in AF
1.811	46 mm
1.813	$1\frac{13}{16}$ in AF
1.860	$1\frac{1}{8}$ in Whitworth; $1\frac{1}{4}$ in BSF
1.875	$1\frac{7}{8}$ in AF
1.969	50 mm
2.000	2 in AF
2.050	$1\frac{1}{4}$ in Whitworth; $1\frac{3}{8}$ in BSF
2.165	55 mm
2.362	60 mm

Jacking

All models are supplied with a screw pillar jack designed to lift one side of the car at a time. It is important to stop any tendency for the car to move when jacked up. Get the car onto a firm, level site and apply the handbrake. Chock the front and rear wheels in contact with the ground with large stones, bricks, blocks or similar items. In addition, engage first or reverse gear.

Remove the plug from the jacking socket in the door sill and insert the lifting arm — this might need adjustment of the jack. Make sure that the jack will have a firm footing and that the lifting arm is well home. The jack should lean slightly outwards at the start of the lift to allow for radial movement of the chassis as it is jacked up.

Never work under the car while it is supported solely by the jack. Ensure it is supported securely by axle stands or substantial wood blocks. When using a jack other than the one supplied with the vehicle, this should be placed under the rear axle casing close to the spring attachment points, or under one of the two main chassis members running beneath and either side of the engine. Do not jack under the floor pan or it will probably be distorted.

The screw pillar jack in position

Recommended lubricants and fluids

Component or system	Lubricant type or specification	Duckhams recommendation
1 Engine	Multigrade engine oil, viscosity SAE 20W/50	Duckhams Hypergrade
2 Gearbox Except 1500 models 1500 models (top-up only) 1500 (refill)	Multigrade engine oil, viscosity SAE 20W/50 Hypoid gear oil, viscosity SAE 90EP Hypoid gear oil, viscosity SAE 80EP	Duckhams Hypergrade Duckhams Hypoid 90S Duckhams Hypoid 80
3 Rear axle	Hypoid gear oil, viscosity SAE 90EP	Duckhams Hypoid 90S
4 Tie-rod end balljoints (not later models)	General purpose grease	Duckhams LB 10
5 Steering and suspension grease nipples	General purpose grease	Duckhams LB 10
6 & 7 Handbrake cable and compensator	General purpose grease	Duckhams LB 10
8 Carburettor dashpots	Multigrade engine oil, viscosity SAE 20W/50	Duckhams Hypergrade
9 Steering rack Early models Later models	Hypoid gear oil, viscosity SAE 140EP General purpose grease	Duckhams Hypoid 140S Duckhams LB 10
10 Water pump (early models only)	General purpose grease	Duckhams LB 10
11 Propeller shaft (universal joints on early models only, and sliding joints of 1500 models only)	General purpose grease	Duckhams LB 10

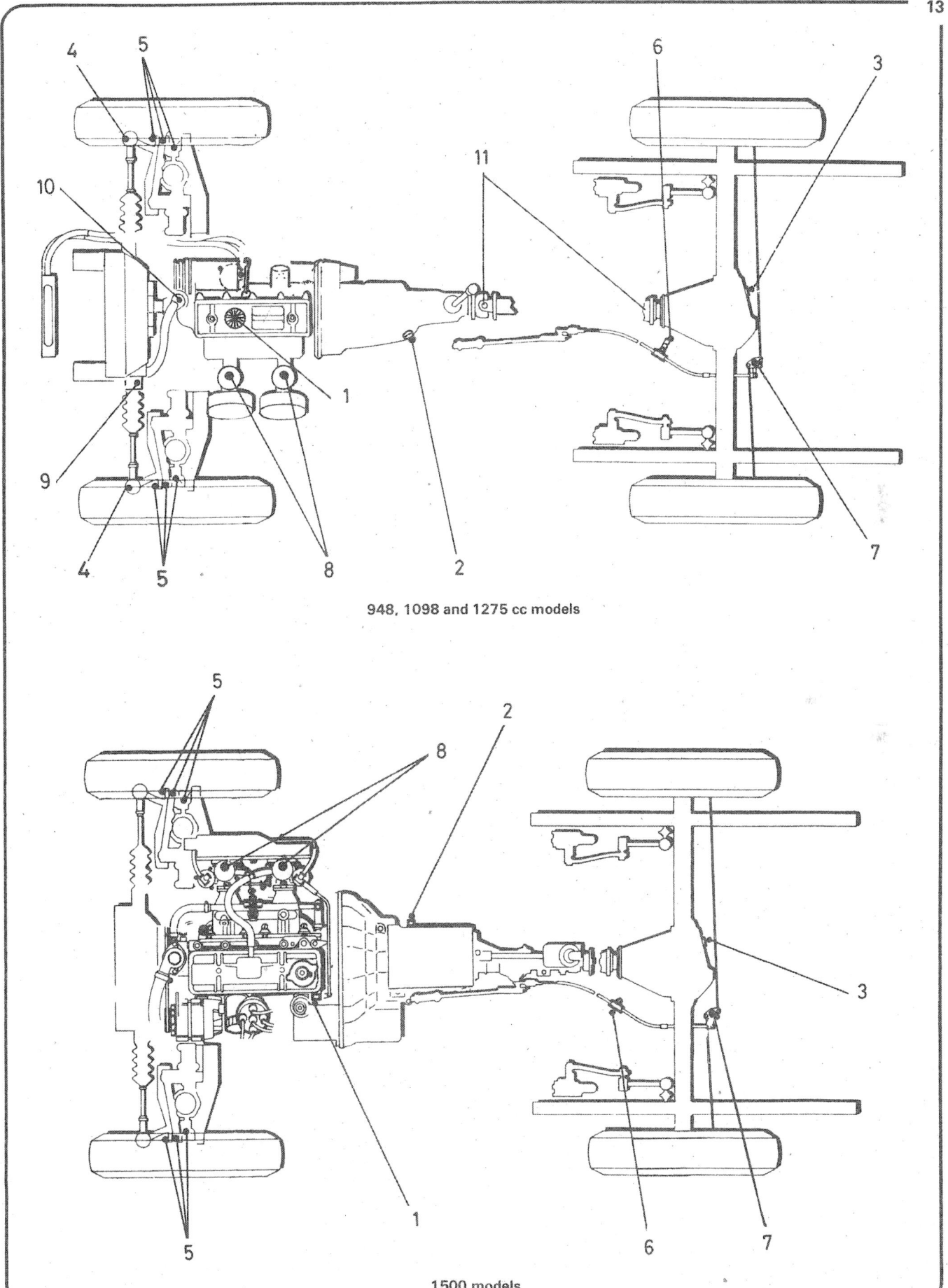

948, 1098 and 1275 cc models

1500 models

Safety first!

Professional motor mechanics are trained in safe working procedures. However enthusiastic you may be about getting on with the job in hand, do take the time to ensure that your safety is not put at risk. A moment's lack of attention can result in an accident, as can failure to observe certain elementary precautions.

There will always be new ways of having accidents, and the following points do not pretend to be a comprehensive list of all dangers; they are intended rather to make you aware of the risks and to encourage a safety-conscious approach to all work you carry out on your vehicle.

Essential DOs and DON'Ts

DON'T rely on a single jack when working underneath the vehicle. Always use reliable additional means of support, such as axle stands, securely placed under a part of the vehicle that you know will not give way.

DON'T attempt to loosen or tighten high-torque nuts (e.g. wheel hub nuts) while the vehicle is on a jack; it may be pulled off.

DON'T start the engine without first ascertaining that the transmission is in neutral (or 'Park' where applicable) and the parking brake applied.

DON'T suddenly remove the filler cap from a hot cooling system — cover it with a cloth and release the pressure gradually first, or you may get scalded by escaping coolant.

DON'T attempt to drain oil until you are sure it has cooled sufficiently to avoid scalding you.

DON'T grasp any part of the engine, exhaust or catalytic converter without first ascertaining that it is sufficiently cool to avoid burning you.

DON'T allow brake fluid or antifreeze to contact vehicle paintwork.

DON'T syphon toxic liquids such as fuel, brake fluid or antifreeze by mouth, or allow them to remain on your skin.

DON'T inhale dust — it may be injurious to health (see *Asbestos* below).

DON'T allow any spilt oil or grease to remain on the floor — wipe it up straight away, before someone slips on it.

DON'T use ill-fitting spanners or other tools which may slip and cause injury.

DON'T attempt to lift a heavy component which may be beyond your capability — get assistance.

DON'T rush to finish a job, or take unverified short cuts.

DON'T allow children or animals in or around an unattended vehicle.

DO wear eye protection when using power tools such as drill, sander, bench grinder etc, and when working under the vehicle.

DO use a barrier cream on your hands prior to undertaking dirty jobs — it will protect your skin from infection as well as making the dirt easier to remove afterwards; but make sure your hands aren't left slippery. Note that long-term contact with used engine oil can be a health hazard.

DO keep loose clothing (cuffs, tie etc) and long hair well out of the way of moving mechanical parts.

DO remove rings, wristwatch etc, before working on the vehicle — especially the electrical system.

DO ensure that any lifting tackle used has a safe working load rating adequate for the job.

DO keep your work area tidy — it is only too easy to fall over articles left lying around.

DO get someone to check periodically that all is well, when working alone on the vehicle.

DO carry out work in a logical sequence and check that everything is correctly assembled and tightened afterwards.

DO remember that your vehicle's safety affects that of yourself and others. If in doubt on any point, get specialist advice.

IF, in spite of following these precautions, you are unfortunate enough to injure yourself, seek medical attention as soon as possible.

Asbestos

Certain friction, insulating, sealing, and other products — such as brake linings, brake bands, clutch linings, torque converters, gaskets, etc — contain asbestos. *Extreme care must be taken to avoid inhalation of dust from such products since it is hazardous to health.* If in doubt, assume that they *do* contain asbestos.

Fire

Remember at all times that petrol (gasoline) is highly flammable. Never smoke, or have any kind of naked flame around, when working on the vehicle. But the risk does not end there — a spark caused by an electrical short-circuit, by two metal surfaces contacting each other, by careless use of tools, or even by static electricity built up in your body under certain conditions, can ignite petrol vapour, which in a confined space is highly explosive.

Always disconnect the battery earth (ground) terminal before working on any part of the fuel or electrical system, and never risk spilling fuel on to a hot engine or exhaust.

It is recommended that a fire extinguisher of a type suitable for fuel and electrical fires is kept handy in the garage or workplace at all times. Never try to extinguish a fuel or electrical fire with water.

Note: *Any reference to a 'torch' appearing in this manual should always be taken to mean a hand-held battery-operated electric lamp or flashlight. It does NOT mean a welding/gas torch or blowlamp.*

Fumes

Certain fumes are highly toxic and can quickly cause unconsciousness and even death if inhaled to any extent. Petrol (gasoline) vapour comes into this category, as do the vapours from certain solvents such as trichloroethylene. Any draining or pouring of such volatile fluids should be done in a well ventilated area.

When using cleaning fluids and solvents, read the instructions carefully. Never use materials from unmarked containers — they may give off poisonous vapours.

Never run the engine of a motor vehicle in an enclosed space such as a garage. Exhaust fumes contain carbon monoxide which is extremely poisonous; if you need to run the engine, always do so in the open air or at least have the rear of the vehicle outside the workplace.

If you are fortunate enough to have the use of an inspection pit, never drain or pour petrol, and never run the engine, while the vehicle is standing over it; the fumes, being heavier than air, will concentrate in the pit with possibly lethal results.

The battery

Never cause a spark, or allow a naked light, near the vehicle's battery. It will normally be giving off a certain amount of hydrogen gas, which is highly explosive.

Always disconnect the battery earth (ground) terminal before working on the fuel or electrical systems.

If possible, loosen the filler plugs or cover when charging the battery from an external source. Do not charge at an excessive rate or the battery may burst.

Take care when topping up and when carrying the battery. The acid electrolyte, even when diluted, is very corrosive and should not be allowed to contact the eyes or skin.

If you ever need to prepare electrolyte yourself, always add the acid slowly to the water, and never the other way round. Protect against splashes by wearing rubber gloves and goggles.

When jump starting a car using a booster battery, for negative earth (ground) vehicles, connect the jump leads in the following sequence: First connect one jump lead between the positive (+) terminals of the two batteries. Then connect the other jump lead first to the negative (−) terminal of the booster battery, and then to a good earthing (ground) point on the vehicle to be started, at least 18 in (45 cm) from the battery if possible. Ensure that hands and jump leads are clear of any moving parts, and that the two vehicles do not touch. Disconnect the leads in the reverse order.

Mains electricity and electrical equipment

When using an electric power tool, inspection light etc, always ensure that the appliance is correctly connected to its plug and that, where necessary, it is properly earthed (grounded). Do not use such appliances in damp conditions and, again, beware of creating a spark or applying excessive heat in the vicinity of fuel or fuel vapour. Also ensure that the appliances meet the relevant national safety standards.

Ignition HT voltage

A severe electric shock can result from touching certain parts of the ignition system, such as the HT leads, when the engine is running or being cranked, particularly if components are damp or the insulation is defective. Where an electronic ignition system is fitted, the HT voltage is much higher and could prove fatal.

Routine maintenance

Maintenance is essential for ensuring safety and desirable for the purpose of getting the best in terms of performance, economy, and reliability from your car. Over the years, with improvements in technology, the need for periodic lubrication — oiling, greasing and so on — has been greatly reduced and, in some areas, eliminated altogether. This has unfortunately tended to lead some owners to think that, because no action is required, components either no longer exist or will last forever without attention. This is a serious delusion.

It follows, therefore, that visual examination plays an increasingly important part in routine maintenance. Whenever it is necessary to do any work on the car, the opportunity should be used to closely examine the area concerned and its near vicinity in a search for any abnormality. Remedial action can then be taken, where necessary, before what might be a minor fault can develop into a major problem.

The maintenance schedules listed below are based on the maker's recommendations. Over the years, and with the different models concerned, these recommendations have changed in various aspects. The various recommended maintenance schedules have therefore been combined and additional items have been added, based on experience, to provide what should be regarded as a list of the minimum amount of maintenance tasks required to keep your car in good condition. Additional information on servicing procedures may be found in the relevant Chapters in this Manual.

Every 250 miles (400 km), before a long journey, or weekly

Check, and if necessary, top up the following:
    Coolant level
    Engine oil level
    Battery electrolyte level
    Hydraulic reservoir(s)
    Windscreen washer fluid
Check tyre pressures when cold, including the spare, and adjust if necessary
Examine tyres for tread depth and damage
Check the tightness of the wheel nuts
Check the steering for smooth and accurate operation
Check the operation of all lights, windscreen wipers and washer, horn, direction and warning indicators
Check the operation of the handbrake

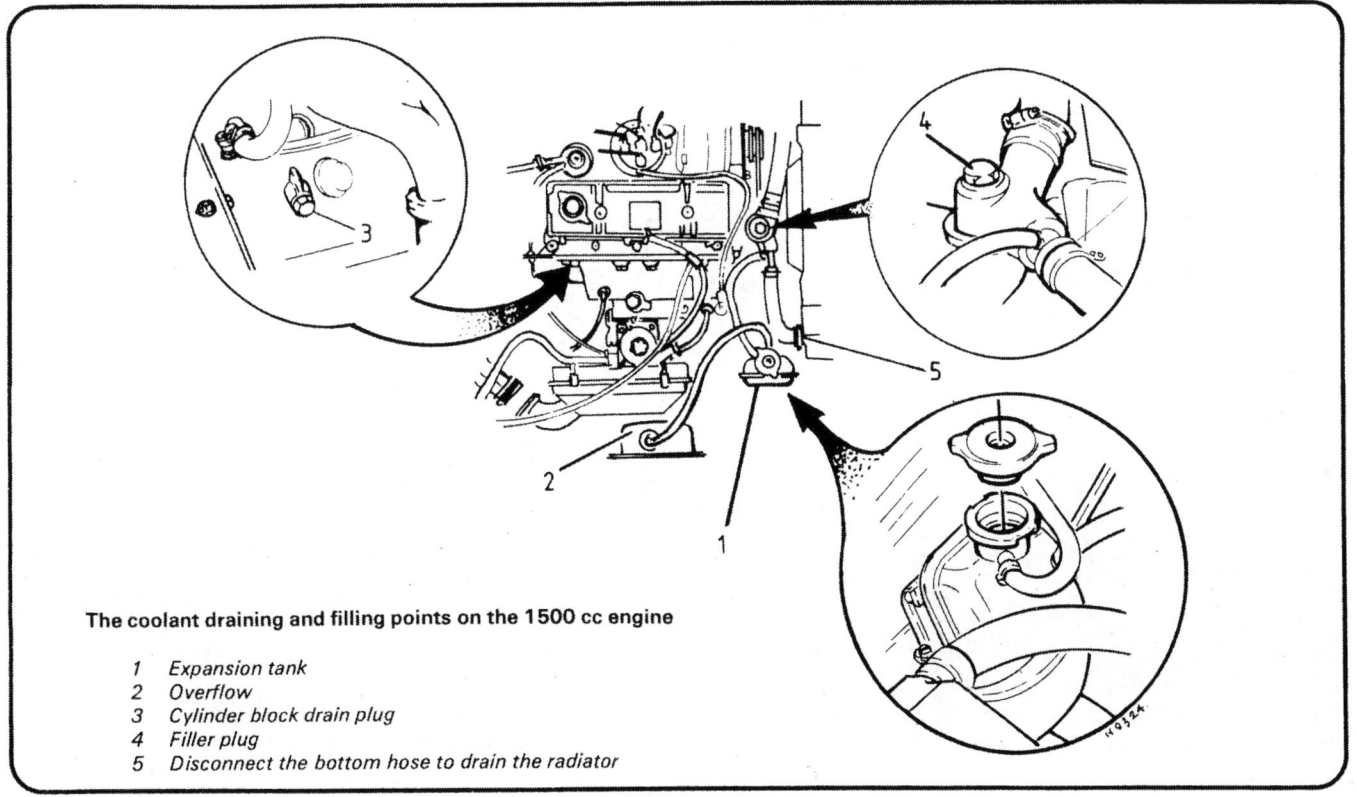

The coolant draining and filling points on the 1500 cc engine

    1   Expansion tank
    2   Overflow
    3   Cylinder block drain plug
    4   Filler plug
    5   Disconnect the bottom hose to drain the radiator

Topping up the coolant

Topping up the engine oil

Topping up the battery electrolyte

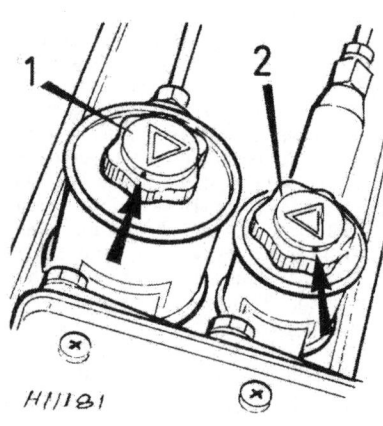

The brake (1) and clutch (2) hydraulic reservoir filler caps. Keep the breather hole (arrowed) clear

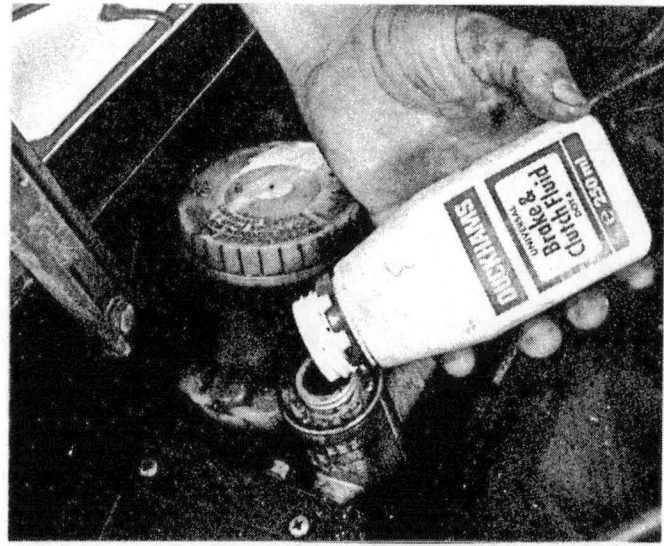

Topping up clutch hydraulic fluid

Use an accurate gauge to check tyre pressures

Every 3000 miles (5000 km) or three months, whichever comes first

(In addition to the work details in the previous schedule)

Clean and oil the air cleaners (wire gauze elements on Sprite Mk I only)
Top up carburettor dashpots and lubricate the throttle linkage
Check the drivebelt(s) for correct tension and adjust if necessary
Inspect the steering rack for oil or grease leaks
Inspect the shock absorbers for oil leaks
Using a grease gun, lubricate the steering balljoints, the front suspension and swivel joints, the propeller shaft and the handbrake cable and compensator, as applicable
Check and, if necessary, adjust the drum brakes linings
Inspect the brake hoses and pipelines for leaks and condition
Inspect the coolant system for leaks
Inspect the clutch hydraulic system for leaks
Inspect the fuel tank, pipelines, pump, and carburettors for fuel leaks
Check the operation of the windscreen wiper, and if necessary renew the blades
Check the operation of the windscreen washer
Inspect the seat belts for condition and security
Using engine oil or light lubricating oil lubricate all hinges, catches and pivots including pedal bearings

Topping up a carburettor dashpot

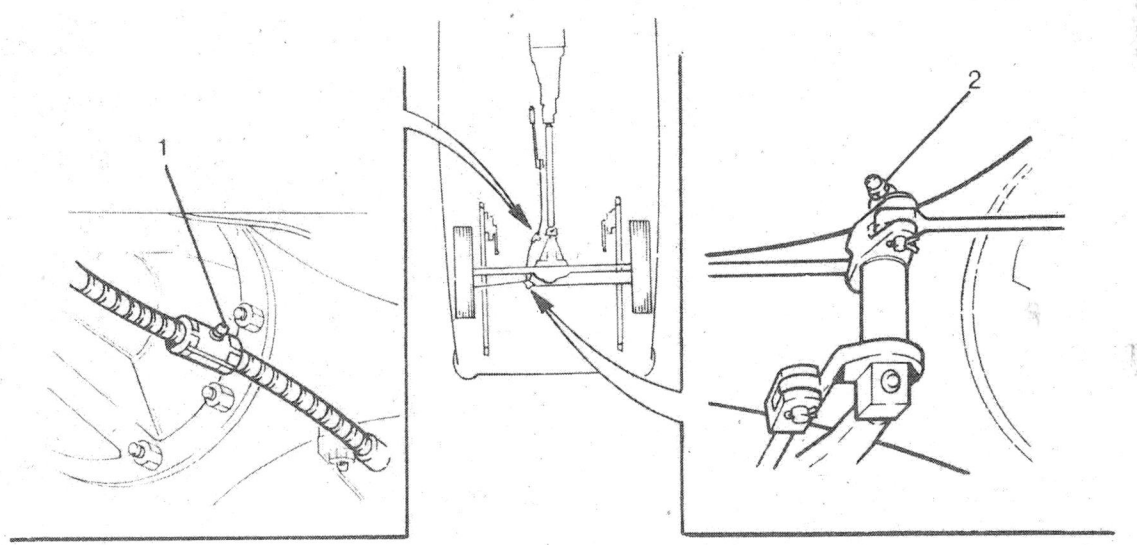

The handbrake cable (1) and compensator (2) grease nipples

Every 6000 miles (10 000 km) or six months, whichever comes first

(In addition to the work detailed in the previous schedules)

Drain the engine oil, preferably when hot, renew the oil filter and replenish with fresh engine oil
Inspect the exhaust system for condition and leaks
Inspect the disc brake pads for wear and the disc for condition
Check and if necessary adjust the handbrake
Clean and grease the battery connections using petroleum jelly.
Have the front wheel alignment and the headlight alignment checked by your BL agent
Check and if necessary top up the gearbox oil level
Check and if necessary top up the rear axle oil level
Check the contact breaker points gap, adjust if necessary, and lubricate the distributor
Clean and adjust the spark plugs
Where applicable, lubricate the dynamo rear bearing
Check and if necessary adjust the idle setting of the carburettor(s)

Lubricating the dynamo rear bearing

Every 12 000 miles (20 000 km) or twelve months, whichever comes first

(In addition to the work detailed in the previous schedules)
Renew the air cleaner elements (except Sprite Mk I)
Renew the spark plugs
Renew the contact breaker points and check the ignition timing. Clean the distributor cap
On early models, lubricate the coolant pump
Clean the fuel pump filter (mechanical pumps)
Clean the crankcase breather control valve and renew the oil filler/breather cap on models with closed crankcase ventilation system
Check the steering and suspension joints for wear
Lubricate oil charged steering racks (not those on 1500 cc models) with no more than 10 pump strokes of oil
Inspect and, if necessary, renew drum brake linings and clean out the brake drums
Check the tightness of the rear road spring bolts observing torque settings where specified
Lubricate the speedometer drive (all models) and the tachometer drive (early models only)
On models with a dynamo, check and if necessary clean the control box cut-out and regulator contacts

Every 24 000 miles (40 000 km) or two years, whichever comes first

(In addition to the work detailed in the previous schedules)
Drain, flush and refill the cooling system using fresh antifreeze mixture
Where fitted, check the air injection system hoses and pipes for condition and security
Where fitted, check the fuel evaporative loss system hoses, pipes, and restrictors for blockage, security and condition. Check the condition of the fuel filler cap seal, renewing it if necessary
Where fitted, check and if necessary adjust the deceleration bypass valve

Every 36 000 miles (60 000 km) or three years, whichever comes first

(In addition to the work detailed in the previous schedules)
Drain the brake system hydraulic fluid, renew all rubber components in the system and replenish with fresh hydraulic brake fluid
On 1500 cc models have the steering rack and pinion lubricated by your BL agent

Every 50 000 miles (80 000 km) or four years, whichever comes first

(In addition to the work detailed in the previous schedules)
Check and service the exhaust gas recirculation system, where applicable (see Chapter 3 for details)

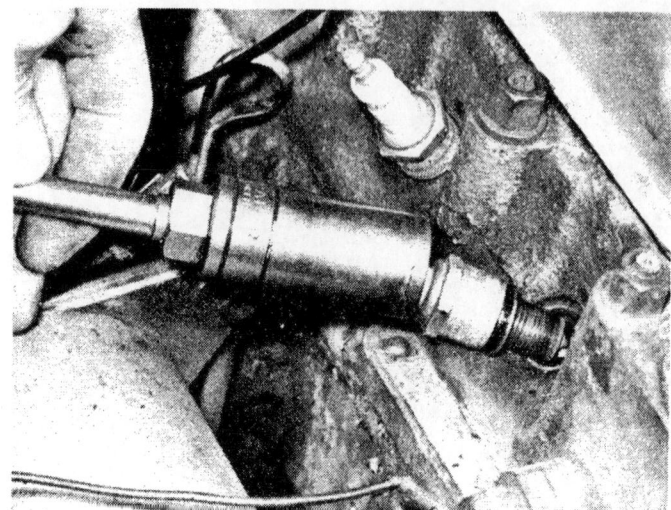

Removing a spark plug

Lubricating the early type steering rack with an oil gun (engine removed in this photo)

Renew the adsorption canisters in the fuel evaporative loss control system, where applicable (see Chapter 3 for details)
Renew the exhaust system catalytic converter, where applicable (see Chapter 3 for details)

Fault diagnosis

Introduction

The car owner who does his or her own maintenance according to the recommended schedules should not have to use this section of the manual very often. Modern component reliability is such that, provided those items subject to wear or deterioration are inspected or renewed at the specified intervals, sudden failure is comparatively rare. Faults do not usually just happen as a result of sudden failure, but develop over a period of time. Major mechanical failures in particular are usually preceded by characteristic symptoms over hundreds or even thousands of miles. Those components which do occasionally fail without warning are often small and easily carried in the car.

With any fault finding, the first step is to decide where to begin investigations. Sometimes this is obvious, but on other occasions a little detective work will be necessary. The owner who makes half a dozen haphazard adjustments or replacements may be successful in curing a fault (or its symptoms), but he will be none the wiser if the fault recurs and he may well have spent more time and money than was necessary. A calm and logical approach will be found to be more satisfactory in the long run. Always take into account any warning signs or abnormalities that may have been noticed in the period preceding the fault – power loss, high or low gauge readings, unusual noises or smells, etc – and remember that failure of components such as fuses or spark plugs may only be pointers to some underlying fault.

The pages which follow here are intended to help in cases of failure to start or breakdown on the road. There is also a Fault Diagnosis Section at the end of each Chapter which should be consulted if the preliminary checks prove unfruitful. Whatever the fault, certain basic principles apply. These are as follows:

Verify the fault. This is simply a matter of being sure that you know what the symptoms are before starting work. This is particularly important if you are investigating a fault for someone else who may not have described it very accurately.

Don't overlook the obvious. For example, if the car won't start, is there petrol in the tank? (Don't take anyone else's word on this particular point, and don't trust the fuel gauge either!) If an electrical fault is indicated, look for loose or broken wires before digging out the test gear.

Cure the disease, not the symptom. Substituting a flat battery with a fully charged one will get you off the hard shoulder, but if the underlying cause is not attended to, the new battery will go the same way. Similarly, changing oil-fouled spark plugs for a new set will get you moving again, but remember that the reason for the fouling (if it wasn't simply an incorrect grade of plug) will have to be established and corrected.

Don't take anything for granted. Particularly, don't forget that a 'new' component may itself be defective (especially if it's been rattling round in the boot for months), and don't leave components out of a fault diagnosis sequence just because they are new or recently fitted. When you do finally diagnose a difficult fault, you'll probably realise that all the evidence was there from the start.

Electrical faults

Electrical faults can be more puzzling than straightforward mechanical failures, but they are no less susceptible to logical analysis if the basic principles of operation are understood. Car electrical wiring exists in extremely unfavourable conditions – heat, vibration and chemical attack – and the first things to look for are loose or corroded connections and broken or chafed wires, especially where the wires pass through holes in the bodywork or are subject to vibration.

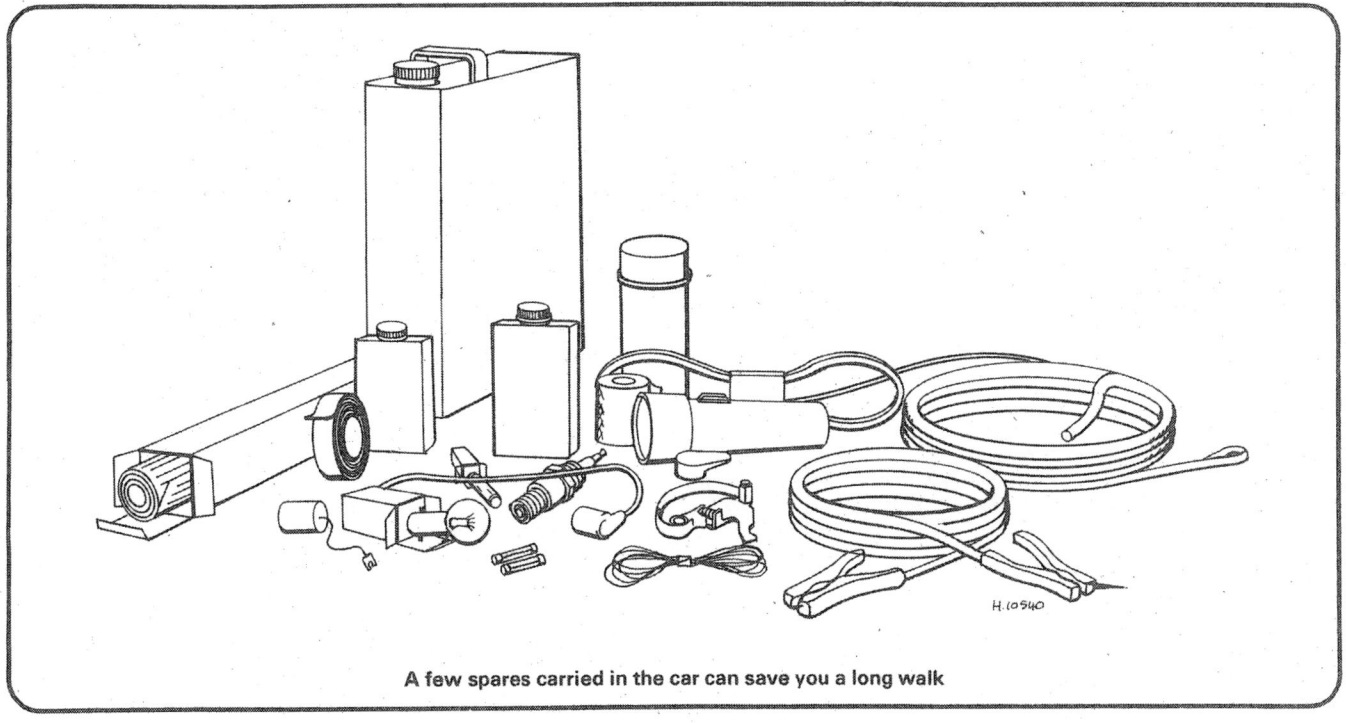

A few spares carried in the car can save you a long walk

All metal-bodied cars in current production have one pole of the battery 'earthed', ie connected to the car bodywork, and in nearly all modern cars it is the negative (–) terminal. The various electrical components' motors, bulb holders etc – are also connected to earth, either by means of a lead or directly by their mountings. Electric current flows through the component and then back to the battery via the car bodywork. If the component mounting is loose or corroded, or if a good path back to the battery is not available, the circuit will be incomplete and malfunction will result. The engine and/or gearbox are also earthed by means of flexible metal straps to the body or subframe; if these straps are loose or missing, starter motor, generator and ignition trouble may result.

Assuming the earth return to be satisfactory, electrical faults will be due either to component malfunction or to defects in the current supply. Individual components are dealt with in Chapter 10. If supply wires are broken or cracked internally this results in an open-circuit, and the easiest way to check for this is to bypass the suspect wire temporarily with a length of wire having a crocodile clip or suitable connector at each end. Alternatively, a 12V test lamp can be used to verify the presence of supply voltage at various points along the wire and the break can be thus isolated.

If a bare portion of a live wire touches the car bodywork or other earthed metal part, the electricity will take the low-resistance path thus formed back to the battery: this is known as a short-circuit. Hopefully a short-circuit will blow a fuse, but otherwise it may cause burning of the insulation (and possibly further short-circuits) or even a fire. This is why it is inadvisable to bypass persistently blowing fuses with silver foil or wire.

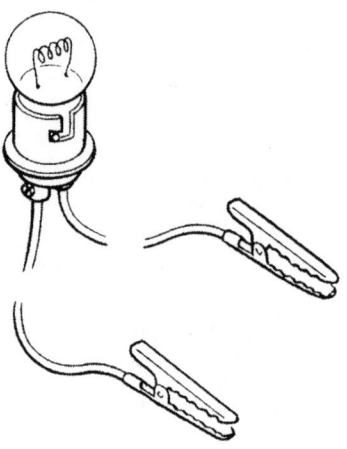

A simple test lamp is useful for tracing electrical faults

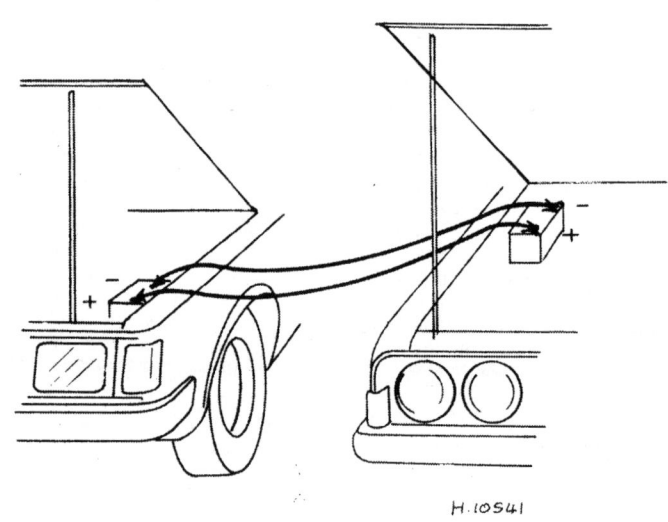

H.10541

Correct way to connect jump leads. Do not allow the car bodies to touch

Spares and tool kit

Most cars are only supplied with sufficient tools for wheel changing; the *Maintenance and minor repair* tool kit detailed in *Tools and working facilities,* with the addition of a hammer, is probably sufficient for those repairs that most motorists would consider attempting at the roadside. In addition a few items which can be fitted without too much trouble in the event of a breakdown should be carried. Experience and available space will modify the list below, but the following may save having to call on professional assistance:

Spark plugs, clean and correctly gapped
HT lead and plug cap – long enough to reach the plug furthest from the distributor
Distributor rotor, condenser and contact breaker points
Drivebelt(s) – emergency type may suffice
Spare fuses
Set of principal light bulbs
Tin of radiator sealer and hose bandage
Exhaust bandage
Roll of insulating tape
Length of soft iron wire
Length of electrical flex
Torch or inspection lamp (can double as test lamp)
Battery jump leads
Tow-rope
Ignition waterproofing aerosol
Litre of engine oil
Sealed can of hydraulic fluid
Emergency windscreen
Worm drive hose clips
Tube of filler paste

If spare fuel is carried, a can designed for the purpose should be used to minimise risks of leakage and collision damage. A first aid kit and a warning triangle, whilst not at present compulsory in the UK, are obviously sensible items to carry in addition to the above.

When touring abroad it may be advisable to carry additional spares which, even if you cannot fit them yourself, could save having to wait while parts are obtained. The items below may be worth considering:

Choke and throttle cables
Cylinder head gasket
Dynamo or alternator brushes
Tyre valve core

One of the motoring organisations will be able to advise on availability of fuel etc in foreign countries.

Engine will not start

Engine fails to turn when starter operated
Flat battery (recharge, use jump leads, or push start)
Battery terminals loose or corroded
Battery earth to body defective
Engine earth strap loose or broken
Starter motor (or solenoid) wiring loose or broken
Ignition/starter switch faulty
Major mechanical failure (seizure) or long disuse (piston rings rusted to bores)
Starter or solenoid internal fault (see Chapter 10)

Starter motor turns engine slowly
Partially discharged battery (recharge, use jump leads, or push start)
Battery terminals loose or corroded
Battery earth to body defective
Engine earth strap loose
Starter motor (or solenoid) wiring loose
Starter motor internal fault (see Chapter 10)

Starter motor spins without turning engine
Flat battery
Starter motor pinion sticking on sleeve
Flywheel gear teeth damaged or worn
Starter motor mounting bolts loose

Engine turns normally but fails to start
Damp or dirty HT leads and distributor cap (crank engine and check for spark)
Dirty or incorrectly gapped CB points
No fuel in tank (check for delivery at carburettor)
Excessive choke (hot engine) or insufficient choke (cold engine)
Fouled or incorrectly gapped spark plugs (remove, clean and regap)
Other ignition system fault (see Chapter 4)
Other fuel system fault (see Chapter 3)
Poor compression (see Chapter 1)
Major mechanical failure (eg camshaft drive)

Engine fires but will not run
Insufficient choke (cold engine)
Air leaks at carburettor or inlet manifold

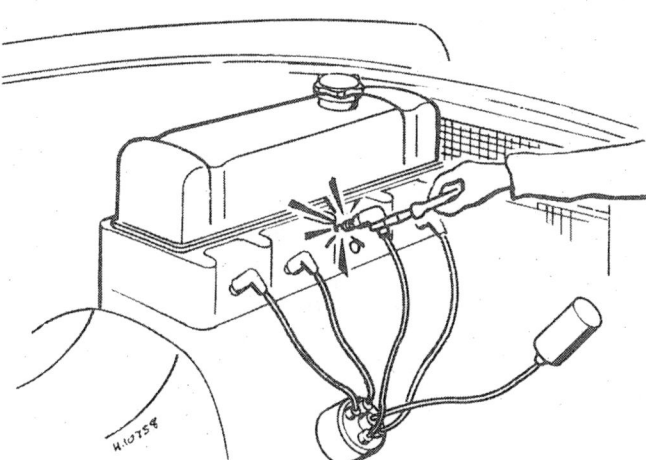

Crank the engine and check for a spark. Note the use of insulated pliers – dry cloth or a rubber glove will suffice

Fuel starvation (see Chapter 3)
Ballast resistor defective (where applicable), or other ignition fault (see Chapter 4)

Engine cuts out and will not restart

Engine cuts out suddenly – ignition fault
Loose or disconnected LT wires
Wet HT leads or distributor cap (after traversing water splash)
Coil or condenser failure (check for spark)
Other ignition fault (see Chapter 4)

Engine misfires before cutting out – fuel fault
Fuel tank empty
Fuel pump defective or filter blocked (check for delivery)
Fuel tank filler vent blocked (suction will be evident on releasing cap)
Carburettor needle valve sticking
Carburettor jets blocked (fuel contaminated)
Other fuel system fault (see Chapter 3)

Engine cuts out – other causes
Serious overheating
Major mechanical failure (eg camshaft drive)

Engine overheats

Ignition (no-charge) warning light illuminated
Slack or broken drivebelt – retension or renew (Chapter 2)

Ignition warning light not illuminated
Coolant loss due to internal or external leakage (see Chapter 2)
Thermostat defective
Low oil level
Brakes binding
Radiator clogged externally or internally
Engine waterways clogged
Ignition timing incorrect or automatic advance malfunctioning
Mixture too weak

Note: *Do not add cold water to an overheated engine or damage may result*

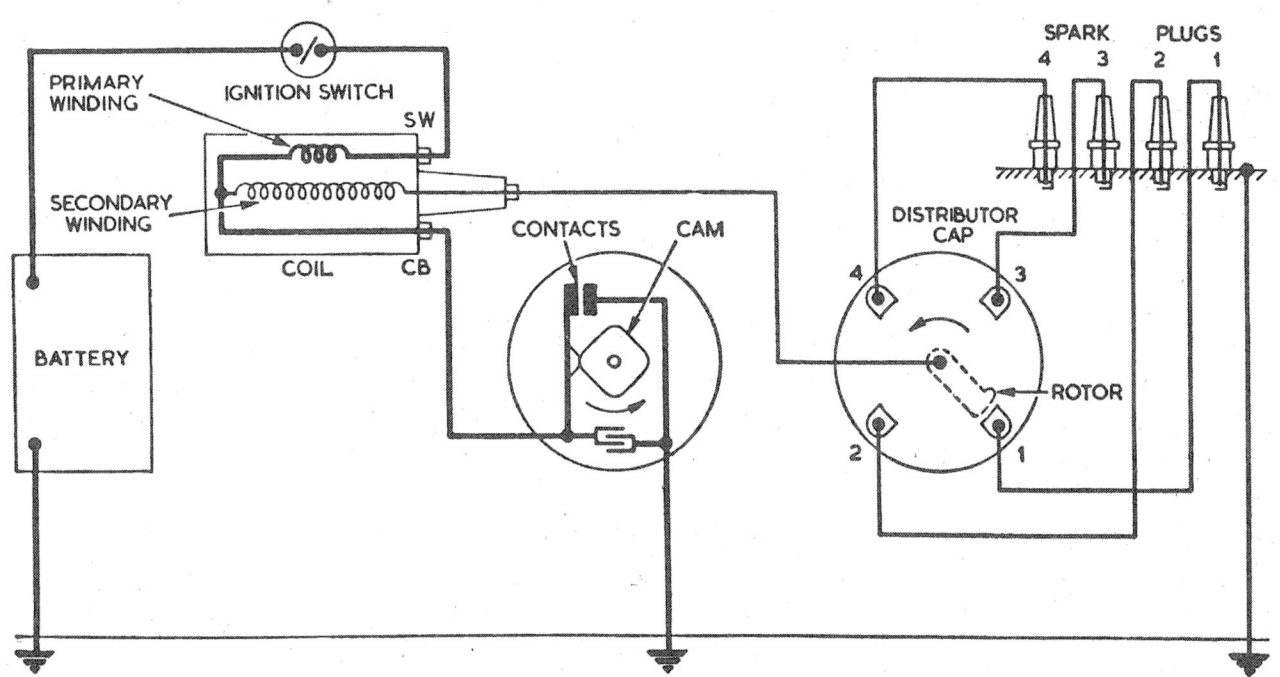

Ignition system schematic design. Some later models have a 6V coil and ballast resistor

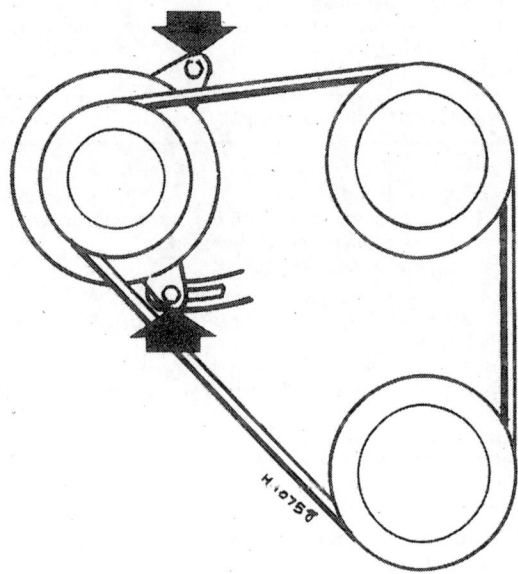

A slack drivebelt may cause overheating and battery charging problems. Slacken bolts (arrowed) to adjust – dynamo model shown

Low engine oil pressure

Gauge reads low or warning light illuminated with engine running
Oil level low or incorrect grade
Defective gauge or sender unit
Wire to sender unit earthed
Engine overheating
Oil filter clogged or bypass valve defective

Oil pressure relief valve defective
Oil pick-up strainer clogged
Oil pump worn or mountings loose
Worn main or big-end bearings

Note: *Low oil pressure in a high-mileage engine at tickover is not necessarily a cause for concern. Sudden pressure loss at speed is far more significant. In any event, check the gauge or warning light sender before condemning the engine.*

Engine noises

Pre-ignition (pinking) on acceleration
Incorrect grade of fuel
Ignition timing incorrect
Distributor faulty or worn
Worn or maladjusted carburettor
Excessive carbon build-up in engine

Whistling or wheezing noises
Leaking vacuum hose
Leaking carburettor or manifold gasket
Blowing head gasket

Tapping or rattling
Incorrect valve clearances
Worn valve gear
Worn timing chain
Broken piston ring (ticking noise)

Knocking or thumping
Unintentional mechanical contact (eg fan blades)
Worn fanbelt
Peripheral component fault (generator, water pump etc)
Worn big-end bearings (regular heavy knocking, perhaps less under load)
Worn main bearings (rumbling and knocking, perhaps worsening under load)
Piston slap (most noticeable when cold)

Chapter 1 Engine

Contents

PART A – 948, 1098 and 1275cc ENGINES

The engine originally fitted to the Austin Healey Sprite Mk I, the Mk II and MG Midget Mk I was 948 cc. From October 1962 the Sprite Mk II and Midget Mk I had the 1098 cc type 10CG engine. The Sprite Mk III and Midget Mk II had the type 10CC. For the Sprite Mk IV and Midget Mk III the engine size increased to 1275 cc.

948cc engines (type 9CG)

Engine (general)
Type .... 4-cylinder in-line ohv pushrod operated
Bore .... 2.478 in (62.94 mm)
Stroke .... 3.000 in (76.2 mm)
Capacity .... 57.87 cu in (948 cc)
Compression ratio:
    High .... 9 : 1
    Low .... 8.3 : 1
The 8.3 : 1 compression ratio was originally standard – later termed 'LOW' when 9 : 1 was standardised in 1961 – this was termed 'HIGH' as the 8.3 : 1 ratio was still available as an option for areas with low octane petrol only.
Capacity of combustion chamber (valves fitted) .... 24.5 cc
Oversize bore .... Max. 0.040 in (1 016 mm); 1st 0.010 in (0.254 mm)
Maximum torque (8.3 : 1 CR) .... 52 lbf ft (7.1 kgf m) at 3300 rpm
Maximum torque (9:1 CR) .... 52.8 lbf ft (7.2 kgf m) at 3000 rpm
Firing order 1-3-4-2
Location of No 1 cylinder .... Next to radiator

Camshaft and camshaft bearings
Inside bearing diameter reamed when fitted:
    Front bearing .... 1.667 to 1.6675 in (42.342 to 42.355 mm)
    Centre bearing .... 1.62425 to 1.62475 in (41.256 to 41.369 mm)
    Rear bearing .... 1.3745 to 1.3750 in (34.912 to 34.925 mm)
Endfloat .... 0.003 to 0.007 in (0.076 to 1.78 mm)
Journal diameters
    Front .... 1.6655 to 1.666 in (42.304 to 42.316 mm)
    Centre .... 1.62275 to 1.62325 in (41.218 to 41.231 mm)
    Rear .... 1.3725 to 1.3735 in (34.862 to 34.887 mm)
Clearance .... 0.001 to 0.002 in (0.025 to 0.051 mm)

Connecting rods and big-end bearings
Length between centres .... 5.75 in (14.605 cm)
Side clearance .... 0.008 to 0.012 in (0.203 to 0.305 mm)
Bearing internal diameter clearance .... 0.001 to 0.0025 in (0.025 to 0.063 mm)

Crankshaft and main bearings
Main journal diameter .... 1.7505 to 1.7510 in (44.46 to 44.47 mm)
Minimum main journal regrind diameter .... 1.7105 in (43.45 mm)
Crankpin journal diameter .... 1.6254 to 1.6259 in (41.28 to 41.30 mm)
Minimum crankpin regrind diameter .... 1.5854 in (40.27 mm)
Endfloat .... 0.002 to 0.003 in (0.051 to 0.076 mm)
Side thrust .... Taken by thrust washers located on either side of the centre main bearing
Undersizes available .... 0.010 in (0.254 mm); 0.020 in (0.508 mm); 0.030 in (0.762 mm); 0.040 in (1.02 mm)

Cylinder block
Type .... Cylinders cast integral with top half of crankcase
Water jackets .... Full length

Cylinder head
Type .... Cast iron with vertical valves. Siamesed inlet ports, 2 separate and 1 siamesed exhaust ports

Gudgeon pins
Type .... Semi-floating, held by clamp bolt
Fit to piston .... 0.0001 to 0.00035 in (0.0025 to 0.009 mm)
Fit in connecting rod .... 0.0001 to 0.0006 in (0.0025 to 0.015 mm)
Diameter (outer) .... 0.6244 to 0.6246 in (15.86 to 15.865 mm)

Lubrication system
Type .... Pressure fed main and big-end bearings, and camshaft. Reduced pressure to rocker shaft. Piston, pin and cylinder wall lubrication by splash
Oil filter .... Full-flow
Oil type/specification .... Multigrade engine oil, viscosity SAE 20W/50 (Duckhams Hypergrade)
Capacity of oil filter .... 1 Imp pint (1.2 US pints/0.57 litre)

Crankcase ventilation .... Directed flow via road draught tube on left-hand side of engine
Sump and filter capacity .... 6.5 Imp pints (7.8 US pints/3.7 litres)
Oil pump type .... Eccentric rotor or vane
Oil pump relief pressure .... 60 lbf/in^2 (4.2 kgf/cm^2)
Oil pressure:
    Normal .... 30 to 60 lbf/in^2 (2.1 to 4.2 kgf/cm^2)
    Idling (minimum) .... 10 to 25 lbf/in^2 (0.7 to 1.75 kgf/cm^2)
Relief valve spring:
    Free length .... 2.859 in (72.63 mm)

Pistons
Type .... Flat crown, anodised aluminium alloy, with 3 compression rings, 1 oil control ring

Clearance of piston
    Top of skirt .... 0.0036 to 0.0042 in (0.0914 to 0.1067 mm)
    Bottom of skirt .... 0.0016 to 0.0022 in (0.040 to 0.056 mm)
Piston oversizes available .... 0.010 in (0.254 mm); 0.020 in (0.508 mm); 0.030 in (0.762 mm); 0.040 in (1.02 mm)

Piston rings
Compression rings:
    Type:
        Top .... Plain
        2nd and 3rd .... Tapered
    Fitted gap .... 0.007 to 0.012 in (0.17 to 0.30 mm)
    Groove clearance .... 0.0015 to 0.0035 in (0.038 to 0.089 mm)
Oil control ring:
    Type .... Slotted scraper
    Fitted gap .... 0.007 to 0.012 in (0.17 to 0.30 mm)
    Groove clearance .... 0.0015 to 0.0035 in (0.038 to 0.089 mm)

Valves
Head diameter:
    Inlet .... 1.151 to 1.156 in (29.23 to 29.36mm)
    Exhaust .... 1.000 to 1.005 in (25.4 to 25.53 mm)
Valve lift .... 0.312 in (7.925 mm)
Seat angle .... Inlet and exhaust 45°
Valve clearance .... 0.012 in (0.305 mm) under normal conditions
0.015 in (0.38 mm) for competition work

Stem diameter:
    Inlet .... 0.2793 to 0.2798 in (7.094 to 7.107 mm)
    Exhaust .... 0.2788 to 0.2793 in (7.081 to 7.094 mm)
Valve stem-to-side clearance:
    Inlet .... 0.0015 to 0.0025 in (0.038 to 0.063 mm)
    Exhaust .... 0.002 to 0.003 in (0.051 to 0.076 mm)
Valve rocker bush bore (reamed) .... 0.5630 to 0.5635 in (14.30 to 14.31 mm)

Valve guides
Length .... 1.687 in (42.86 mm)
Outside diameter .... 0.4695 to 0.470 in (11.92 to 11.94 mm)
Inside diameter .... 0.2813 to 0.2818 in (7.145 to 7.177 mm)
Fitted height above head .... 19/32 in (15.1 mm)

Valve timing
Inlet valve:
    Opens .... 5° BTDC
    Closes .... 45° ABDC
Exhaust valve:
    Opens .... 51° BBDC
    Closes .... 21° ATDC
Valve timing marks .... Dimples on crankshaft and camshaft sprockets
Valve rocker clearance (timing only) .... 0.021 in (0.74 mm)

Valve springs
Type .... Double valve springs
No of coils .... Inner – 6½; Outer – 4½
Free length:
    Inner spring .... 1.672 in (42.47 mm)
    Outer spring .... 1.75 in (44.45 mm)

948 cc engines (type 9CC – Sprite Mk I)
The engine specification for the early Austin Healey Sprite Mk I is identical to the foregoing except for the differences detailed below:

Camshaft and camshaft bearings
Camshaft bearing clearance:
    Front .... 0.001 to 0.002 in (0.0254 to 0.0508 mm)
    Centre and rear .... 0.00125 to 0.00275 in (0.032 to 0.07 mm)

Pistons
Type .... Aluminium split skirt with 3 compression rings and 1 oil control ring
Clearance of piston:
    Bottom of skirt .... 0.001 to 0.0016 in (0.025 to 0.04 mm)

Valves
Head diameter:
    Inlet .... 1.094 in (27.8 mm)
    Exhaust .... 1.00 in (25.4 mm)
Valve lift .... 0.28 in (7.14 mm)

Valve timing
Inlet valve:
    Opens .... 5° BTDC
    Closes .... 45° ABDC
Exhaust valve:
    Opens .... 40° BBDC
    Closes .... 10° ATDC
Valve rocker clearance (timing only) .... 0.019 in (0.48 mm)

Valve springs
Type .... Single valve springs
Free length .... 1.75 in (44.44 mm)

1098 cc engines (type 10)
The type 10CG was fitted to MG Mk I and Sprite II. The type 10CC was fitted to MG Mk II and Sprite III. They differ from type 9CG as follows:

Engine (general)
Type .... 10CG and 10CC
Bore .... 2.543 in (64.58 mm)
Stroke .... 3.296 in (83.72 mm)
Capacity .... 67 cu in (1098 cc)
Compression ratio:
    High .... 8.9 : 1
    Low .... 8.1 : 1
Capacity of combustion chamber (valves fitted) ..... 28.2 cc
Oversize bore:
    1st .... 0.010 in (0.254 mm)
    Max .... 0.020 in (0.508 mm)
Maximum torque:
    Type 10CG 8.9 : 1 .... 62 lbf ft (8.6 kgf m) at 3250 rpm
    Type 10CG 8.1 : 1 .... 61 lbf ft (8.4 kgf m) at 3250 rpm
    Type 10CC 8.9 : 1 .... 65 lbf ft (8.9 kgf m) at 3500 rpm
    Type 10CC 8.1 : 1 .... 64 lbf ft (8.8 kgf m) at 3250 rpm

Pistons
Type .... Solid skirts
Bottom skirt clearance .... 0.0005 to 0.0011 in (0.013 to 0.028 mm)
Top skirt clearance .... 0.0021 to 0.0037 in (0.053 to 0.094 mm)
Oversizes .... 0.010 and 0.020 in (0.254 and 0.508 mm)

Piston rings
Compression rings:
    Type:
        Top compression .... Plain, internally chamfered chrome-faced
        Second and third compression .... Tapered
    Width:
        Top .... 0.062 to 0.625 in (1.575 to 1.587 mm)
        Second and third .... 0.0615 to 0.0625 in (1.558 to 1.587 mm)
    Thickness:
        All (except Duraflex 61) .... 0.106 to 0.112 in (2.69 to 2.84 mm)
        Clearance in groove .... 0.002 to 0.004 in (0.051 to 0.102 mm)

Oil control ring:
 Type:
  Early engines .... Slotted scraper
  Later engines .... Wellworthy-Duaflex 61
 Fitted gap:
  Rails .... 0.012 to 0.028 in (0.31 to 0.70 mm)
  Side spring .... 0.10 to 0.15 in (2.54 to 3.81 mm)

Gudgeon pin
Type .... Fully floating
Fit in piston .... Hand push

Crankshaft and main bearings
Main journal diameter:
 Type 10CC .... 2.0005 to 2.001 in (50.813 to 50.825 mm)
Main bearing:
 Length .... 1.063 in (27 mm)

1275 cc engines (type 12)
The engine specification and data is identical to the 1098 cc type 10 engine except for the differences listed below:

Engine
Bore .... 2.78 in (70.61 mm)
Stroke .... 3.2 in (81.28 mm)
Capacity .... 77.8 cu in (1275 cc)
Compression ratio:
 High .... 8.8 : 1
 Low .... 8.0 : 1
Maximum torque:
 High CR .... 72 lbf ft (9.936 kgf m) at 3000 rpm
 Low CR .... 64.5 lbf ft (8.901 kgf m) at 3000 rpm

Crankshaft and main bearings
Main journal diameter .... 2.0005 to 2.0010 in (50.813 to 50.825 mm)
Main bearing length .... 0.975 to 0.985 in (24.765 to 25.019 mm)
Crankpin journal diameter .... 1.6254 to 1.6259 in (41.28 to 41.29 mm)
Regrind; main and crankpin journals .... Maximum permissible, without heat treatment: 0.010 in (0.254 mm) below standard diameter
Main bearing diametrical clearance .... 0.0010 to 0.0027 in (0.0254 to 0.067 mm)

Connecting rods and big-end bearings
Length between centres .... 5.748 to 5.792 in (145.99 to 147.05 mm)
Big-end bearing length .... 0.840 to 0.850 in (21.336 to 21.590 mm)
Endfloat on crankpin .... 0.006 to 0.010 in (0.15 to 0.254 mm)
Big-end diametrical clearance .... 0.0010 to 0.0025 in (0.0254 to 0.063 mm)

Gudgeon pin
Type .... Interference
Fit in piston .... Hand push
Diameter (outer) .... 0.8123 to 0.8125 in (20.63 to 20.64 mm)
Fit to connecting rod .... 0.0008 to 0.0015 in (0.020 to 0.038 mm)

Pistons
Type .... Aluminium, solid skirt, dished crown
Clearances:
 Bottom of skirt .... 0.0015 to 0.0021 in (0.038 to 0.054 mm)
 Top of skirt .... 0.0029 to 0.0037 in (0.074 to 0.095 mm)

Piston rings
Compression rings:
 Type:
  Top .... Internally chamfered, chrome
  Second and third .... Tapered, cast iron
 Width of all compression rings .... 0.615 to 0.625 in (1.558 to 1.583 mm)
 Fitted gap:
  Top .... 0.011 to 0.016 in (0.279 to 0.406 mm)
  Second and third .... 0.008 to 0.013 in (0.203 to 0.330 mm)
 Ring-to-groove clearance:
  Top, second and third .... 0.0015 to 0.0035 in (0.038 to 0.088 mm)
Oil control ring:
 Type .... Duaflex 61
  Fitted gap (rails and sidespring) .... 0.012 to 0.028 in (0.305 to 0.70 mm)

Valves

Head diameter:
Inlet .... 1.307 to 1.312 in (33.198 to 33.21 mm)
Exhaust .... 1.1515 to 1.565 in (29.243 to 29.373 mm)
Stem diameter:
Inlet .... 0.2793 to 0.2798 in (7.094 to 7.107 mm)
Exhaust .... 0.2788 to 0.2793 in (7.081 to 7.094 mm)
Stem-to-guide clearance – inlet and exhaust .... 0.0015 to 0.0025 in (0.0381 to 0.0778 mm)
Valve-to-rocker clearance (cold) .... 0.012 in (0.30 mm)

Valve springs

Free length:
Inner spring .... 1.703 in (43.26 mm)
Outer spring .... 1.828 in (46.47 mm)
Valve lift – inlet and exhaust .... 0.318 in (8.076 mm)

Valve guides

Length:
Inlet .... 1.6875 in (42.87 mm)
Exhaust .... 1.6875 in (42.87 mm)
Fitted height above seat:
Inlet .... 0.540 in (13.72 mm)
Exhaust .... 0.540 in (13.72 mm)

Valve timing

Timing marks .... Dimples on timing gears
Rocker clearance: timing only .... 0.029 in (0.72 mm)
Inlet valve:
Opens .... 5° BTDC
Closes .... 45° ABDC
Exhaust valve:
Opens .... 51° BBDC
Closes .... 21° ATDC

Lubrication

System pressure:
Running .... 40 to 70 lbf/in^2 (2.81 to 4.92 kgf/cm^2)
Idling .... 20 lbf/in^2 (1.4 kgf/cm^2)
Oil pump .... Eccentric rotor; splined from camshaft
Oil filter .... Full-flow type, renewable element, differential pressure switch; later cars, disposable cartridge type
Oil pressure relief valve .... 50 lbf/in^2 (5.3 kgf/cm^2)
Relief valve spring:
Free length .... 2.86 in (72.64 mm)

Torque wrench settings

	lbf ft	kgf m
Cylinder head nuts:		
948 cc	40	5.5
1098 and 1275 cc:		
Plain studs	42	5.8
Studs stamped '22' or with drill point	50	6.9
Connecting rod nuts (1098 and 1275 cc):		
Plain nuts	40	5.5
Nyloc nuts	32 to 34	4.4 to 4.7
Connecting rod bolts (948 cc)	35	4.8
Crankshaft pulley bolt	70	9.6
Flywheel bolts	40	5.5
Main bearing bolts	60	8.7
Manifold nuts	15	2
Oil filter retaining nut	16	2.2
Oil pump retaining nuts/bolts (except 1098 cc)	12	1.6
Oil pump retaining nuts/bolts (1098 cc)	9	1.2
Oil pipe union adaptor (oil filter head)	19 to 21	2.6 to 2.9
Rocker cover retaining bolts	4	0.6
Rocker pedestal nuts	25	3.5
Sump retaining bolts	6	0.8
Tappet chest side covers (except deep pressed type)	2	0.3
Tappet chest side covers (deep pressed type)	5	0.7
Thermostat housing nuts	8	1.1
Timing cover $\frac{1}{4}$ in bolts	6	0.8
Timing cover $\frac{5}{16}$ in bolt	14	1.9
Water pump nuts	17	2.3
Distributor clamp:		
Fixed nut type	4	0.6
Fixed bolt type	3	0.4
Fan securing bolt (1275 cc)	8	1.1

PART B – 1500 cc ENGINE

Engine (general)

Type	PE94J
Number of cylinders	4
Bore	2.9 in (73.7 mm)
Stroke	3.44 in (87.5 mm)
Capacity	91 cu in (1493 cc)
Compression ratio:	
UK	9 : 1
USA and Canada	7.5 : 1
Firing order	1-3-4-2
Oversize bores	+0.020 in (+ 0.51 mm)
Valve operation	Overhead valves, pushrod and rocker operated

Crankshaft

Main journal diameter	2.3115 to 2.3120 in (58.713 to 58.725 mm)
Minimum main journal regrind diameter	2.2815 to 2.2820 in (57.935 to 57.948 mm)
Crankpin journal diameter	1.8750 to 1.8755 (47.625 to 47.638 mm)
Minimum crankpin journal regrind diameter	1.8450 to 1.8455 in (46.865 to 46.878 mm)
Crankshaft end thrust	Via rear main bearing thrust washer
Crankshaft endfloat	0.006 to 0.014 in (0.1524 to 0.3556 mm)

Main bearings

Number	3
Type	Thin wall
Length (front, centre and rear)	0.840 to 0.855 in (21.34 to 21.72 mm)
End thrust	Via rear main bearing thrust washers
Thrust washer oversize	0.005 in (0.13 mm)
Diametrical clearance	0.0005 to 0.002 in (0.013 to 0.050 mm)
Undersizes	0.010 to 0.020, 0.030 in (0.25, 0.51, 0.76 mm)

Connecting rods

Length between centres	5.748 to 5.752 in (145.90 to 146.10 mm)
Small-end bush diameter (reamed in position)	0.8126 to 0.8129 in (20.64 to 20.65 mm)

Big-end bearings

Length	0.672 to 0.692 in (17.20 to 19.58 mm)
Diametrical clearance	0.001 to 0.003 in (0.03 to 0.08 mm)
Undersizes	0.010, 0.020, 0.030 in (0.25, 0.51, 0.76 mm)

Gudgeon pin

Type	Fully floating
Connecting rod fit	Hand push
Outside diameter	0.8123 to 0.8125 in (20.63 to 20.64 mm)

Pistons

Type	Solid skirt, aluminium alloy
Bore size:	
'F' frade	2.8995 to 2.900 in (73.647 to 72.66 mm)
'G' grade	2.9001 to 2.9006 in (73.663 to 73.673 mm)
Bottom diameter of piston:	
'F' grade	2.8984 to 2.8989 in (73.619 to 73.632 mm)
'G' grade	2.8990 to 2.8995 in (73.635 to 73.647 mm)
Clearance of skirt in bore:	
Top	0.002 to 0.003 in (0.051 to 0.076 mm)
Bottom	0.0002 to 0.0016 in (0.005 to 0.041 mm)
Number of rings	2 compression and 1 oil control
Width of ring grooves:	
Top/second	0.064 to 0.065 in (1.625 to 1.650 mm)
Oil control	0.1578 to 0.1588 in (3.99 to 4.01 mm)
Gudgeon pin bore	0.8124 to 0.8126 in (20.63 to 20.64 mm)
Piston oversize	0.020 in (0.508 mm)

Piston rings

Compression:	
Type:	
Top	Plain type-chrome plated
Second	Tapered periphery
Width (top/second)	0.0615 to 0.0625 in (1.575 to 1.5787 mm)
Fitted gap (top/second)	0.012 to 0.022 in (0.305 to 0.559 mm)
Ring/groove clearance:	
Top and second	0.0015 to 0.0035 in (0.038 to 0.089 mm)

Oil control:
   Type .... Expander with two chrome-faced rings
   Fitted gap (chrome-faced rings) .... 0.015 to 0.055 in (0.38 to 1.40 mm)

Camshaft
Front and rear journal diameters .... 1.9659 to 1.9664 in (49.93 to 49.95 mm)
Centre journal diameter .... 1.9649 to 1.9654 in (49.90 to 49.92 mm)
Bore in block .... 1.9680 to 1.9695 in (49.980 to 50.025 mm)
Diametrical clearances:
   Front and rear .... 0.0016 to 0.0036 in (0.04 to 0.09 mm)
   Centre .... 0.0026 to 0.0046 in (0.07 to 0.12 mm)
End thrust .... At front end location plate
Endfloat .... 0.0045 to 0.085 in (0.120 to 0.216 mm)
Drive .... Chain and gear from crankshaft
Camshaft sprocket adjusting shims .... 0.004 and 0.006 in (0.102 and 0.152 mm)

Rocker gear
Rocker shaft outside diameter .... 0.5607 to 0.5612 in (14.27 to 14.35 mm)
Rocker arm bore diameter .... 0.563 to 0.564 in (14.30 to 14.33 mm)

Valves
Rocker arm-to-valve clearance (inlet and exhaust) .... 0.010 in (0.25 mm) cold
Seat angle (inlet and exhaust) .... 45.5°
Valve face angle (inlet and exhaust) .... 45°
Head diameter:
   Inlet .... 1.377 to 1.383 in (34.97 to 35.01 mm)
   Exhaust .... 1.168 to 1.172 in (29.66 to 29.76 mm)
Stem diameter:
   Inlet .... 0.3107 to 0.3113 in (7.89 to 7.91 mm)
   Exhaust .... 0.3100 to 0.3105 in (7.874 to 7.887 mm)
Stem guide clearance:
   Inlet .... 0.0007 to 0.0023 in (0.02 to 0.06 mm)
   Exhaust .... 0.0015 to 0.0030 in (0.04 to 0.07 mm)

Valve guides
Length (inlet and exhaust) .... 2.06 in (52.224 mm)
Fitted height .... 0.75 in (19.050 mm)
Diameter (inlet and exhaust):
   Outside .... 0.5015 to 0.502 in (12.73 to 12.75 mm)
   Inside .... 0.312 to 0.313 in (7.92 to 7.95 mm)

Valve springs – UK
Free length:
   Inner .... 1.14 in (30 mm)
   Outer .... 1.52 in (38.6 mm)

Valve springs – USA and Canada
Free length (inner and outer) .... 1.52 in (38.6 mm)

Valve timing
Timing mark .... Notch on crankshaft pulley – pointers on timing chest
Rocker arm/valve clearance – numbers 7 and 8 valves (for valve timing only) .... 0.050 in (1.27 mm)
Inlet valve opens .... 18° BTDC
Inlet valve closes .... 58° ABDC
Exhaust valve opens .... 58° BBDC
Exhaust valve closes .... 18° ATDC

Lubrication system
Type .... Wet sump pressure feed
Oil type/specification .... Multigrade engine oil, viscosity SAE 20W/50 (Duckhams Hypergrade)
System pressure (running) .... 40 to 60 lbf/sq in (2.81 to 4.2 kg f/sq cm)
Oil pump type .... Hobourn-Eaton eccentric lobe
Oil pump clearances:
   Inner rotor endfloat .... 0.0004 in (0.1 mm)
   Outer rotor endfloat .... 0.0004 in (0.1 mm)
   Rotor lobe clearance .... 0.010 in (0.25 mm)
   Outer rotor-to-body clearance .... 0.008 in (0.2 mm)
Oil filter type .... Full-flow, disposable cartridge
Bypass valve opens .... 8 to 12 lbf/in^2 (0.56 to 0.84 kgf/cm^2)
Oil pressure relief valve .... 53 lbf/in^2 (3.71 kgf/cm^2)
Relief valve spring:
   Free length .... 1:53 in (38.86 mm)

Flywheel
Run-out (maximum) .... 0.002 in (0.051 mm) measured at 3.0 in (76.2 mm) radius from axis
Concentricity .... 0.004 in (0.100 mm) maximum error

Distributor driveshaft
Endfloat .... 0.003 to 0.007 in (0.08 to 0.18 mm)

Torque wrench settings

	lbf ft	kgf m
Alternator to mounting bracket and front engine plate	22	3.0
Alternator to adjusting link	20	2.8
Clutch attachment to flywheel	22	3.0
Connecting rod bolt:		
Colour dyed	50	6.9
Phosphated	46	6.4
Chainwheel to camshaft	24	3.3
Crankshaft pulley nut	150	20.7
Cylinder block drain plug	35	4.8
Cylinder head to block	46	6.4
Distributor to pedestal	20	2.8
Fan attachment	9	1.2
Flywheel to crankshaft:		
Cadmium plated	40	5.5
Parkerised	45	6.2
Fuel pump to cylinder block	14	1.9
Gearbox and rear engine plate to block	14	1.9
Manifold inlet-to-exhaust	14	1.9
Manifold to head	25	3.5
Main bearing cap bolts	65	9.0
Oil sump drain plug	25	3.5
Oil sump to block	20	2.8
Oil pressure switch plug to cylinder head	14	1.9
Oil seal block attachment	14	1.9
Rocker cover to head	2	0.3
Rocker pedestal to cylinder head	32	4.4
Crankshaft rear seal housing	20	2.8
Rear engine mounting platform on frame	20	2.8
Sealing block to engine plate	20	2.8
Spark plug to head	20	2.8
Starter motor attachment	34	4.7
Timing cover to front engine plate:		
Small	10	1.4
Large	20	2.8
Water elbow to water pump	20	2.8
Water pump bearing housing to pump	14	1.9
Water pump to cylinder head	20	2.8

PART A – 948, 1098 and 1275cc ENGINES

Special note

Many of the characteristics of the 948, 1098 and 1275 cc engines are basically the same as that of the 1500 cc engine. Therefore to avoid duplication, where possible the dismantling, inspection and reassembly instructions for the various assemblies of ALL engines are included in 'Part A' of Chapter 1.

Those assemblies or procedures for the 1500 cc engine that differ considerably from the smaller engines have been included in 'Part B' of this Chapter.

All Sections in 'Part A' qualified by the words 'All models' apply to 948, 1098, 1275 and 1500 cc engines. Sections without this qualification apply to 948, 1098 and 1275 cc engine ONLY.

1   General description – 948, 1098 and 1275 cc engines

The engine has four cylinders and overhead valves. It is of 948 cc, 1098 cc or 1275 cc depending upon the car, mark and year. There are rubber mountings at the front of the engine and around the gearbox tail shaft.

Two valves per cylinder are mounted vertically in the cast iron cylinder head and run in pressed-in valve guides. They are operated by rocker arms and pushrods from the camshaft which is located at the base of the cylinder bores in the left-hand side of the engine.

The cylinder head has all five inlet and exhaust ports on the left-hand side. Cylinders 1 and 2 share a siamesed inlet port as do cylinders 3 and 4. Cylinders 1 and 4 have individual exhaust ports and cylinders 2 and 3 share a siamesed exhaust port.

The cylinder block and the upper half of the crankcase are cast together. The bottom half of the crankcase consists of a pressed steel sump.

The pistons are made from aluminium alloy with either split or solid skirts, depending on the model. Three compression rings and a slotted oil control ring are fitted to all types. The gudgeon pin was originally retained in the small-end of the connecting rod by a pinch bolt. Type 9CG and all type 10 (1098 cc) engines have fully floating pins retained by circlips. Type 12 have the gudgeon pin an interference fit in the connecting rod. Renewable big-end bearings are fitted.

At the front of the engine a single row (double row on 1275 cc engines) chain drives the camshaft via the camshaft and crankshaft sprockets. On early models the chain is tensioned by a ring tensioner, while later models make use of two rubber rings either side of the gearwheel teeth. The camshaft is supported in three bearings. On early 948 cc models, two were bored directly in the crankcase, with a renewable bearing at the sprocket end.

From the 9CG onwards, three steel-backed white metal camshaft bearings are fitted. These later engines also have no water passages between cylinders one and two, and three and four. The design of the coolant pump has changed several times. Bottom hose connections are not interchangeable. The oil filter and oil sump gauze strainer

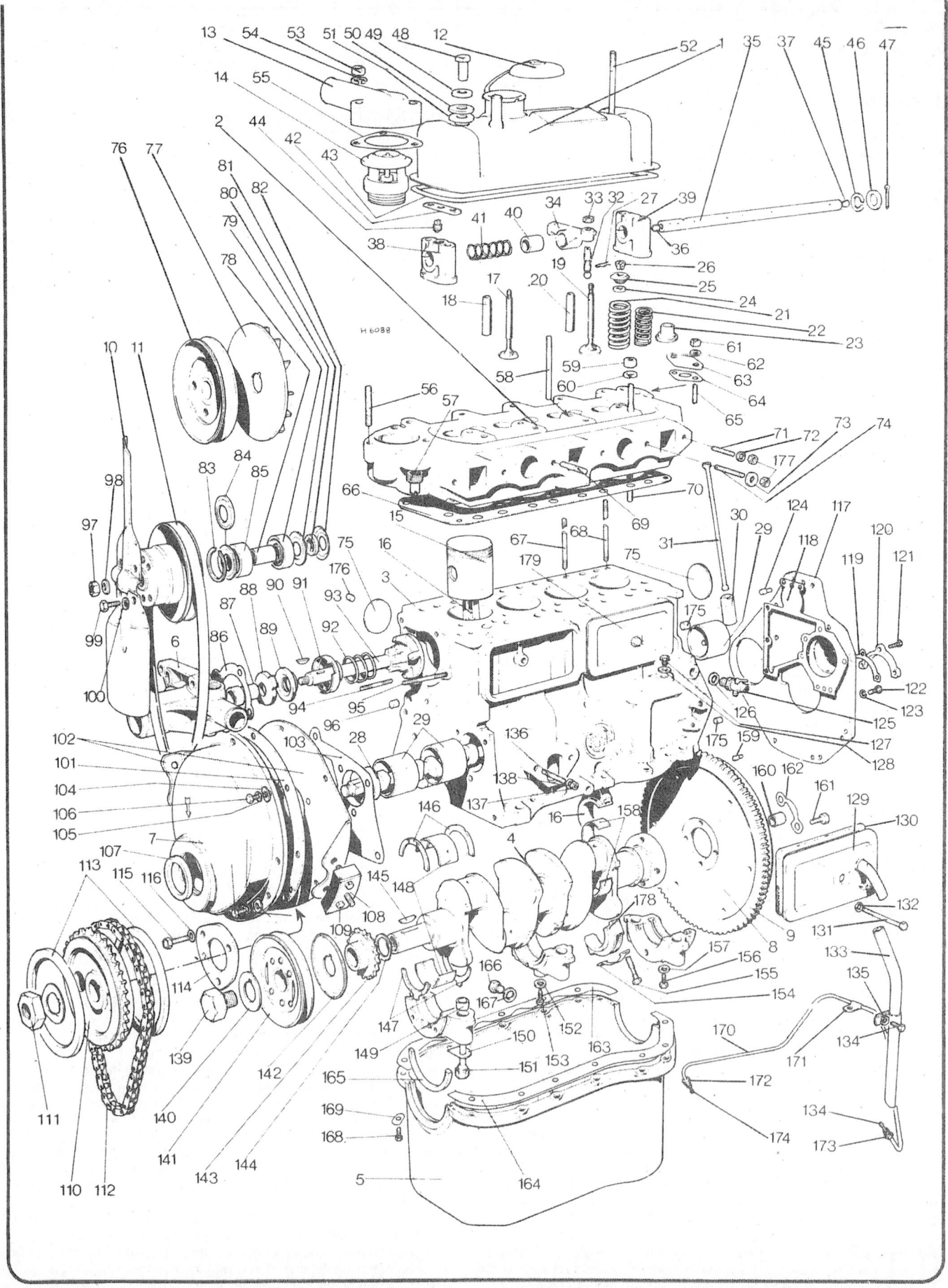

Fig. 1.1 Exploded view of a typical A-Series engine (Sec 1)

1 Rocker cover
2 Cylinder head
3 Cylinder block
4 Crankshaft
5 Sump
6 Water pump body
7 Timing cover
8 Flywheel
9 Starter ring
10 Fan blade
11 Fanbelt
12 Oil filler cap
13 Thermostat housing
14 Thermostat
15 Piston assembly
16 Connecting rod
17 Exhaust valve
18 Exhaust valve guide
19 Inlet valve
20 Inlet valve guide
21 Outer valve spring
22 Inner valve spring
23 Spring seating collar
24 Valve stem seal
25 Valve spring collet plate
26 Valve collet
27 Valve collet clip
28 Camshaft
29 Camshaft bearing liners
30 Tappet
31 Pushrod
32 Tappet adjusting screw
33 Locknut
34 Rocker (bushed)
35 Valve rocker shaft (plugged)
36 Rocker shaft plug (threaded)
37 Rocker shaft plug (plain)
38 Rocker shaft bracket (tapped)
39 Rocker shaft bracket (plain)
40 Rocker bush
41 Rocker spacing spring
42 Rocker shaft bracket plate
43 Gasket

44 Rocker shaft locating screw
45 Spring washer
46 Washer
47 Split pin
48 Nut
49 Cup washer
50 Distance piece
51 Cover bush
52 Rocker bracket stud (long)
53 Nut
54 Spring washer
55 Gasket
56 Stud
57 Bypass adaptor
58 Rocker bracket stud (short)
59 Cylinder head nut
60 Washer
61 Cover nut
62 Spring washer
63 Cover plate (heater take-off blank)
64 Cover plate joint gasket
65 Cover plate stud
66 Cylinder head gasket
67 Cylinder head stud (short)
68 Cylinder head stud (long)
69 Exhaust manifold stud (medium)
70 Cylinder head stud (long)
71 Exhaust manifold stud (short)
72 Small washer
73 Large clamping washer
74 Exhaust manifold stud (long)
75 Core plug
76 Dynamo pulley
77 Dynamo fan
78 Bearing distance piece
79 Bearing
80 Outer retainer for felt
81 Felt
82 Inner retainer for felt
83 Retainer circlip
84 Bearing grease retainer
85 Bearing
86 Water pump gasket
87 Distance piece
88 Seal

89 Seal rubber
90 Pulley key
91 Spring locating cup
92 Spring
93 Spindle with impeller
94 Water pump body stud (short)
95 Water pump body stud (long)
96 Oil gallery plug
97 Spindle nut
98 Spindle washer
99 Screw to pulley
100 Spring washer
101 Cover gasket
102 Front endplate
103 Endplate joint gasket
104 Plain washer
105 Spring washer
106 Screw
107 Seal
108 Rubber front mounting block
109 Attachment bolt
110 Camshaft sprocket
111 Sprocket nut
112 Camshaft drive chain
113 Tensioner rings
114 Locking plate
115 Screw
116 Shakeproof washer
117 Gearbox endplate
118 Gasket
119 Gasket
120 Rear cover
121 Cover screw
122 Screw
123 Spring washer
124 Dowel
125 Drain tap (water)
126 Tap washer
127 Oil priming plug
128 Copper washer
129 Block front side cover (with elbow)
130 Side cover gasket
131 Screw to block
132 Fibre washer
133 Fume vent pipe (with clip)

134 Clip screw
135 Spring washer
136 Stud
137 Nut
138 Washer
139 Pulley retaining bolt
140 Lockwasher
141 Crankshaft pulley
142 Oil thrower
143 Crankshaft sprocket
144 Adjusting shims
145 Crankshaft key
146 Upper thrust washers
147 Lower thrust washers
148 Main bearing
149 Main bearing cap dowel
150 Lockwasher
151 Bearing cap bolt
152 Shakeproof washer
153 Bearing cap screw
154 Lockwasher
155 Cap bolt
156 Bearing cap screw
157 Shakeproof washer
158 Big-end bearing
159 Dowel
160 First motion shaft bush
161 Flywheel-to-crankshaft bolt
162 Lockwasher
163 Sump right-hand gasket
164 Sump left-hand gasket
165 Main bearing cap seal
166 Sump drain plug
167 Drain plug washer
168 Screw
169 Washer
170 Vacuum pipe
171 Pipe clip
172 Pipe nut (distributor end)
173 Pipe nut (carburettor end)
174 Pipe olive
175 Oil gallery plug
176 Oil pressure relief passage plug
177 Stud nuts
178 Big-end cap
179 Block rear side cover

location and design have been changed and from the 12V engine onwards the filter is a thowaway type.

The forged steel crankshaft is supported by three renewable main bearings. Crankshaft endfloat is controlled by four semi-circular thrust washers, located on either side of the centre main bearing.

The centrifugal coolant pump and radiator cooling fan are driven together with the dynamo or alternator from the crankshaft pulley wheel by a rubber/fabric belt. The distributor is mounted towards the rear of the right-hand side of the cylinder block and advances and retards the ignition timing by mechanical and vacuum means. The distributor is driven at half crankshaft speed by a short shaft and skew gear from a skew gear on the camshaft. The oil pump is driven from the rear of the camshaft. The camshaft also drives the fuel pump on Sprite II and Midget I. Later models have SU electric pumps.

The 1275 cc engine introduced in 1966 differs from the two earlier types in the following details. It has a larger cylinder bore but a shorter stroke than the 1098 cc engines. It can be safely revved up to 6300 rpm compared with 6000 rpm of its predecessors. Other differences that affect work on the car, or make spare parts incompatible are:

(a) *The cylinder block is entirely different. There are no side covers forming a tappet chest*

(b) *The timing chain is 'Duplex' double links with two rows of teeth on the sprockets*

(c) *There is a damper on the front of the crankshaft to reduce torsional vibration*

(d) *The cylinder head is longer with the outlets to the radiator and heater at different angles. There are larger inlet and exhaust valves*

(e) *The coolant pump on later engines has a deeper impeller, and a larger inlet pipe. Radiator bottom hoses are not interchangeable*

(f) *There have been several changes of ignition distributor*

(g) *There are also variations to suit local regulations. This particularly applies to North America because of the USA's safety and emission regulations. It will help if the car numbering system is understood*

Car numbers

The car number has a series of prefixes of letters and numbers indicating, in code, the make, engine type, body type and so on as follows:

(a) *1st prefix: a letter to indicate name; G for MG, H for Healey and A for Austin*

(b) *2nd prefix: A for engine type*

(c) *3rd prefix: N for two-seater tourer*

(d) *4th prefix: a number indicating the series of model, eg, 9 meaning ninth series*

(e) *5th prefix: only used to indicate a variation from the standard right-hand drive, eg L for left-hand drive, or U for USA*

(f) *6th prefix: a letter indicating the model year on USA and Canadian models eg, A for 1970, to E for 1974 (on the Midget 1500 this continues F, 1975; G, 1976; H, 1977; J, 1978; L, 1979 and M, 1980)*

An example of the code, which need not contain all prefixes, is GAN6-27588 indicating that the vehicle is an MG with A series engine, two-seater tourer, 6th series and serial number 27588.

Engine numbers

Engine numbers have three main groups. The first group starts with a figure:

9 for 948 cc engines
10 for 1098 cc engines
12 for 1275 cc engines

These are followed by letters for the engine model. Thus the 12 CE engine followed the 12CC in the home market, and 12 CD and 12 CJ were for North America. The second group were originally the letters Da, meaning close ratio centre-change gearbox. This was changed to a serial number denoting the detailed specification of the power unit. The third group is the power unit serial number. In October 1972 the engines for the home market were type 12V/586F/H and for North America 12V/671Z/L. The H and L indicate high and low compression ratios.

2 Major operations possible with engine in place (all models)

1 Cylinder head removal and refitting.
2 Removal and refitting of the sump.
3 Removal and refitting of big-end bearings.
4 Removal and refitting of pistons and connecting rods.
5 Removal and refitting of the timing chain, sprockets and timing cover oil seal.
6 Removal and refitting of the camshaft (not 1275 cc).
7 Removal and refitting of the oil pump (1500 cc only).

3 Major operations requiring engine removal (all models)

1 Removal and refitting of the crankshaft.
2 Removal and refitting of the main bearings.
3 Removal and refitting of the flywheel.
4 Removal and refitting of the oil pump (all except 1500 cc).
5 Removal and refitting of camshaft (1275 cc only).

4 Engine – removal methods (all models)

There are two methods of removing the engine from the car. The engine can either be removed complete with gearbox, or by separating them it can be withdrawn as a single unit. Both methods are detailed in the following Sections.

5 Engine (without gearbox) – removal

Note: *On all models, the engine is lifted upwards, out of the engine compartment. Practical experience has proved that the engine can be removed easily and quickly by adhering to the following sequence of operations in the order given.*

1 Refer to Chapter 2 and drain the cooling system.
2 Disconnect the battery leads; for additional security from electrical shorts, it is best to remove the battery from the engine compartment.
3 With a suitable container in position unscrew the drain plug at the bottom right-hand corner of the sump and drain off the engine oil. When the oil is drained screw the plug back in tightly to ensure it is not mislaid.
4 Remove the bonnet as detailed below:
All models except the Sprite Mk I – Remove the set bolts and spring washers from each of the two bonnet hinges on the bonnet side of the hinge, and on later models unbolt the bonnet stay at one end. The bonnet can then be lifted away.
Austin Healey Sprite Mk I – The bonnet and wings lift off together as one unit. First, disconnect the wiring harness to the lights and direction indicators at the snap connectors. Remember to mark each side of each connection otherwise it is easy to reconnect them incorrectly and find that the headlamps flash when the flashing direction indicator switch is turned on, and so on. The wiring harness must also be disconnected from its securing clip located on the right-hand hinge. Remove the screw at the top of each of the two telescopic bonnet supports and, with the aid of a friend, lift the bonnet away. The bonnet is too heavy and cumbersome to be lifted away by one person only.
5 Unscrew the clip on the lower radiator hose at the radiator pipe outlet, and remove the hose from the pipe. Disconnect the expansion tank hose connection, if fitted. Unscrew the clip on the upper radiator hose at the thermostat housing outlet pipe and remove the hose from the pipe. Also disconnect the heater unit inlet and outlet hoses (on models fitted with heater units), by releasing the securing clips on the control valve and heater return pipe located on the inlet side of the water pump.
6 Remove the four bolts from the caged nuts (two on each side of the radiator) which secure the radiator to the body and, if fitted, the temperature gauge element (early models), then lift the radiator out. Close the drain tap if fitted. On later models, the radiator is removed in its cowling. To gain access to the screws take off the front grille. Disconnect the top, bottom and expansion hoses. Remove the two nuts and bolts securing the top of the cowl to the body. Slacken the two screws holding the bottom to the body. Take out the four screws at the sides, and remove the radiator.

7   Disconnect the throttle linkage and the choke control at the carburettor end.

8   Unscrew the exhaust pipe clamp bolts at the joint between the exhaust manifold and the exhaust pipe, and remove the exhaust pipe support from the bellhousing, if one is fitted, by releasing the appropriate bellhousing bolt. Pull the exhaust pipe away from the manifold.

9   Disconnect the low tension lead from the distributor, and the leads from the dynamo/alternator, the starter motor, and oil pressure warning bulb switch (where fitted).

10 On early Sprites and Midgets with cable driven tachometers, it is necessary to remove the reduction drive and cable from the rear of the dynamo. Alternatively, remove the cable by unscrewing the cable securing cap.

11 Unscrew the two bolts securing the starter motor in position and remove the motor. Remove the filter bowl (early models) but be prepared to catch spilt oil.

12 To gain better access to the right-hand engine mounting bracket it is helpful to remove the dynamo/alternator. Unscrew the securing bolts (two at the front and one at the rear) and lift off the fanbelt, and then the dynamo or alternator. If the coil is mounted on the dynamo (early models) it will also be necessary to remove the high tension lead to the distributor, and the low tension leads at the markings 'SW' (switch) and 'CB' (contact breaker). If the dynamo is not removed and the coil is mounted on it then it is only necessary to remove the low tension wire from the 'SW' terminal.

13 If a sling is to be placed round the engine then it is sound practice to remove the distributor cap and rotor arm. The cap is made from plastic and therefore fragile, and can be easily damaged while the engine is being lifted out. To remove the cap, first unscrew the high tension lead from the coil centre terminal. Pull the high tension leads away from the spark plugs, carefully marking which lead terminates at which plug. It may be possible to determine the correct lead order by the different length of each lead, with the longest lead to the plug furthest from the distributor, and the shortest to the closest. There is no need to mark the leads in this case.

14 On early models with a mechanical fuel pump unscrew the inlet fuel pipe at the fuel pump. On models with an SU electrical fuel pump, release the fuel inlet pipe at the carburettor end.

15 On models fitted with an oil pressure gauge, remove the pipe from its union at the rear left-hand side of the block by unscrewing the retaining nut.

16 Where fitted, disconnect the clutch lever return spring from the rear engine plate.

17 Take the weight of the engine on the lifting tackle. Either use slings round the front and rear, or connect them to the proper hooks which can be put under the rocker cover bolts. Position a jack or blocks under the gearbox to take its weight and remove the nuts and bolts securing the gearbox bellhousing to the engine rear plate. At the same time free the earth strap attached to the bottom right bellhousing bolt where this is fitted. Remove the two nuts securing the engine front plate to the engine mounting bracket on the right-hand side of the engine in the case of right-hand drive cars, and the left-hand side of the engine in the case of left-hand drive cars. Disconnect the complete engine mounting bracket from the body frame on the opposite side. For right-hand drive cars, this will be the left-hand side. If wished, for ease of manipulation, the complete engine mounting bracket can be removed from the two nuts and spring washers. Lift the engine

forwards and up out of the car, taking care to guide it clear of the surrounding body and fitments.

6   Engine (with gearbox) – removal

The procedure for removing the engine and gearbox together is the same as for removing the engine without the gearbox up to paragraph 16 in the preceding Section. There is one alteration, and this is that there is no necessity to remove the starter motor. The following sequence should now be applied to all models:

1   Drain the oil from the gearbox by removing the drain plug on the underside of the gearbox. It is essential that this operation is not skipped as failure to drain the gearbox will result in oil pouring out from the gearbox extension when the propeller shaft is removed and the gearbox is tilted for removal.

2   Unscrew the speedometer cable from the gearbox.

3   Disconnect the reversing light switch leads where a switch is fitted to the gearbox (1275 cc engines).

4   Remove the carpeting from around the gearbox tunnel and remove the gear lever cover by unscrewing the securing setscrews. Unscrew the bolts retaining the gear lever plate and the anti-rattle plunger (photo) and then lift out the gear lever (photo).

5   Release the gearbox mounting bracket from the bodyframe by removing the four set bolts and spring washers which retain it in place. To are located one on each side of the propeller shaft tunnel, and two underneath it.

6   While underneath the car, remove the two bolts and spring washers which secure the clutch operating cylinder to the bellhousing, or if difficulty is experienced here, release the hydraulic pipe at the operating cylinder end. Lose as little hydraulic fluid as possible by immediately plugging the open end of the pipe.

7   Also, while under the car, examine the accessibility of the propeller shaft at the gearbox end. If the propeller shaft tunnel is boxed in it will not be possible to slide the propeller shaft onto the gearbox drive shaft when the engine and gearbox is refitted in the car. In this case mark the flange of the propeller shaft to the rear axle flange to ensure assembly in the same relative position, remove the four nuts and bolts holding the flanges together, and remove the propeller shaft rearwards.

8   With lifting tackle connected to the lifting hooks or slung round the engine firmly and securely, raise the engine slightly and then pull forwards and up (photo). The engine and gearbox will then come out together with the gearbox mounting bracket still attached to the gearbox nosepiece.

7   Engine – general dismantling (all models)

1   It is best to mount the engine on a dismantling stand, but as this is frequently not available, then it is satisfactory to stand the engine on a strong bench so as to be at a comfortable working height. During the dismantling process the greatest care should be taken to keep the exposed parts free from dirt. As an aid to achieving this aim, it is a very sound scheme to thoroughly clean down the outside of the engine, removing all traces of oil and congealed dirt. A good proprietary grease solvent will make the job much easier, as, after the solvent has been

6.4a Removing the gear lever plate

6.4b Withdrawing the gear lever assembly

6.8 Lifting out the 1275 cc engine and gearbox

applied and allowed to stand for a time, a vigorous jet of water will wash off the solvent and all the grease and dirt. If the dirt is thick and deeply embedded, work the solvent into it with a wire brush.

2   Finally wipe down the exterior of the engine with a clean rag and only then, when it is finally quite free from dirt, should the dismantling process begin.

3   As the engine is stripped, clean each part in a bath of paraffin or petrol. Never immerse parts with oilways in paraffin, eg the crankshaft, but to clean wipe down carefully with a petrol dampened rag. Oilways can be cleaned out with pipe cleaners. If an air line is present all parts can be blown dry and the oilways blown through as an added precaution.

4   Re-use of old engine gaskets is a false economy and can give rise to oil and water leaks, if nothing worse. To avoid the possibility of trouble after the engine has been reassembled, always use new gaskets throughout. Do not throw the old gaskets away, as it sometimes happens that an immediate replacement cannot be found and the old gasket is then very useful as a template. Hang up the old gaskets as they are removed on a suitable hook or nail.

5   To strip the engine is is best to work from the top down. The sump provides a firm base on which the engine can be supported in an upright position. When the stage where the sump must be removed is reached the engine can be turned on its side and all other work carried out with it in this position.

6   Wherever possible, refit nuts, bolts and washers finger-tight from wherever they were removed. This helps avoid later loss and muddle. If they cannot be refitted then store them in such a fashion that it is clear from where they were removed.

7   If the engine was removed as an assembly complete with gearbox, separate them by removing the nuts and bolts joining the bellhousing to the engine and carefully lift the gearbox free. Do not allow the weight of gearbox to rest on the input shaft as it is being removed.

8   Engine ancillary components – removal

1   Engine dismantling begins with the removal of the following components:

> *Dynamo/alternator*
> *Distributor*
> *Thermostat*
> *Oil filter assembly and pipe*
> *Inlet manifold and carburettor/s*
> *Exhaust manifold*
> *Mechanical fuel pump (where fitted)*

It is possible to strip all these items with the engine in the car if it is merely the individual items that require attention, but always disconnect the battery connections first. Assuming the engine to be out of the car on the bench, starting on the right-hand side of the unit, follow this procedure. First slacken off the dynamo/alternator retaining bolts and remove the unit with its support brackets.

2   To remove the distributor, first disconnect the manifold vacuum advance/retard pipe. As an aid during reassembly, mark the distributor and block before removing it. First turn the crankshaft to align the distributor rotor on the approach to No 1 cylinder segment (make sure you turn in the correct direction of rotation, which is clockwise looking at the crankshaft pulley) and then continue turning until the mark on the pulley is aligned with the TDC timing mark. Carefully mark the distributor body and make an alignment mark on the crankcase. Another mark on the distributor adjacent to the rotor will tie the job up. Unscrew the bolt securing the clamp plate to the crankcase and remove the distributor complete with clamp plate.

3   Remove the thermostat cover by releasing the three nuts and spring washers which hold it in position, and then remove the gasket and thermostat unit.

4   Unscrew the bolts to the oil pipe leading from the filter to the block and remove the pipe. Mask over the hole left in the block with masking tape.

5   Remove the oil filter assembly by unscrewing the two retaining bolts which hold it to the block. The right-hand side of the engine is now stripped of all ancillary equipment.

6   Remove the inlet manifold complete with carburettor(s) if this item has not already been removed, by unscrewing the brass nuts and washers holding the manifolds to the cylinder head, and detaching the heat shield supports where applicable.

7   Remove the mechanical fuel pump, if fitted, by unscrewing the two retaining bolts which hold it to the block and release it from the petrol feed pipe to the carburettor.

8   The engine is now stripped of all ancillary components and is ready for major dismantling to begin.

9   Cylinder head – removal (engine on bench)

1   Release the clips on the small hose between the coolant pump and the cylinder head and remove the hose. In cases of extreme difficulty, and providing a replacement hose is available, cut the hose in half.

2   Unscrew the two rocker cover nuts and lift the rocker cover and gasket away.

3   Unscrew the rocker pedestal nuts (four) and the nine main cylinder head nuts half a turn at a time in the reverse order to that shown in Fig. 1.8. When all the nuts are slack they can be removed from their studs.

4   Remove the rocker assembly complete, and place it on one side.

5   Remove the pushrods, keeping them in the relative order in which they were removed. The easiest way to do this is to push them through a sheet of thick paper or thin card in the correct sequence, and noting which goes where by numbering.

6   The cylinder head can now be removed by lifting it upwards. If the head is jammed, try to rock it to break the seal. Under no circumstances try to prise it apart from the block with a screwdriver or cold chisel as damage may be done to the joint faces of the head or block. If the head will not readily free, turn the engine over by the flywheel, as the compression in the cylinders will often break the cylinder head joint. If this fails to work, strike the head sharply with a plastic headed hammer, or with a wooden hammer, or with a metal hammer with an interposed piece of wood to cushion the blows. Under no circumstances hit the head directly with a metal hammer as this may cause the iron casting to fracture. Several sharp taps with the hammer at the same time pulling upwards should free the head. Lift the head off and place it on one side.

10   Cylinder head – removal (engine in car)

When removing the cylinder head with the engine in the car, the following instructions apply in addition to those of Section 9. The various procedures in this Section must be carried out prior to those given in Section 9.

1   Disconnect the battery leads.

2   Drain the cooling system, referring to Chapter 2 for details, if required.

3   Loosen the clip at the thermostat housing end on the top coolant hose, and pull the hose from the thermostat housing pipe.

4   Remove the small coolant pump-to-cylinder head bypass hose.

5   Remove the heater/demister unit inlet hose by releasing the clip securing it to the cylinder head (on cars with heater/demister units).

6   If twin carburettors are fitted it is easier to leave them in position and release the accelerator and choke cables at the carburettor end.

7   The procedure is now the same as for removing the cylinder head when on the bench. One tip worth noting is that should the cylinder head refuse to free easily, the battery can be reconnected, and the engine turned over on the solenoid switch. However, remove the distributor cap first and, if an SU electrical pump is fitted, disconnect its supply lead.

11   Valves – removal

1   A conventional arrangement of double valve springs retained by split collets and a spring retainer is fitted to each valve. Early engines have a wire clip on the collets which should be removed before attempting to remove the valves. Compress each spring assembly in turn with a valve spring compressor until the two half collets can be removed. Then release the compressor and remove the spring retainer, the spring(s) and the valve.

2   If, when the valve spring compressor is screwed down, the valve spring retaining cap refuses to free and expose the split collet, do not continue to screw down on the compressor as there is a likelihood of damaging it. Gently tap the top of the tool directly over the cap with a light hammer. This will free the cap.

3   To avoid the compressor jumping off the valve spring retaining cap when it is tapped, hold the compressor firmly in position with one hand.

4   On 948 cc and 1098 cc engines slide the oil control rubber seal off of each valve stem before removing the valve.

5   On 1275 cc engines, later versions, only the inlet valves have seals and these fit over the top of the valve guide. In addition some versions do not have spring seats fitted.

6   It is essential that the valves are kept in their correct sequence unless they are so badly worn that they are to be renewed. If they are going to be kept and used again, place them in a sheet of card having eight holes numbered 1 to 8 corresponding with the relative positions the valves were in when fitted. Also keep the valve springs, washers, etc, in the correct order.

12 Rocker assembly – dismantling

1   To dismantle the rocker assembly, release the rocker shaft locating screw, remove the split pins, flat washers, and spring washers from each end of the shaft and slide from the shaft the pedestals, rocker arms, and rocker spacing springs.

2   Keep all component parts in their correct order of assembly and, where it is not obvious, identify which way round parts should be refitted.

3   Remove the screwed plug fitted to one end of the shaft for cleaning the oilway.

13 Timing cover, sprockets and chain – removal

The timing cover, sprockets, and chain can be removed with the engine in the car providing the radiator and fanbelt are removed. The procedure for removing the timing cover, sprockets and chain is otherwise the same irrespective of whether the engine is in the car or on the bench, and is as follows:

1   Bend back the locking tab of the crankshaft pulley locking washer under the crankshaft pulley retaining bolt, and with a large spanner remove the bolt and locking washer.

2   Placing two large screwdrivers behind the camshaft pulley wheel at 180° to each other, carefully lever the wheel off. It is preferable to use a proper pulley extractor if this is available, but large screwdrivers or tyre levers are quite suitable, providing care is taken not to damage the pulley flange.

3   Remove the Woodruff key from the crankshaft nose with a pair of pliers and keep it in a safe place until required for reassembly.

4   Unscrew the bolts holding the timing cover to the block. **Note:** *Four of the bolts are larger than the others, and each bolt makes use of a large flat washer as well as a spring washer.*

5   Remove the timing cover and gasket.

6   With the timing cover off, take off the oil thrower. **Note:** *The concave side faces forward and is marked with a letter F.*

7   Bend back the locking tab on the washer under the camshaft retaining nut and remove the nut and lockwasher. Note that the lockwasher is keyed to the sprocket.

8   To remove the camshaft and crankshaft sprockets complete with chain, ease each sprocket forward a little at a time levering behind each in turn with two large screwdrivers at 180° to each other. If the sprockets are locked solid then it will be necessary to use a proper sprocket and pulley extractor, and if one is available this should be used anyway in preference to screwdrivers. With both sprockets safely off, remove the Woodruff keys from the crankshaft and camshaft with a pair of pliers and place them in a jam jar for safe keeping. Note the number of very thin packing washers behind the crankshaft; tie them together after removal to prevent loss.

14 Camshaft and tappets – removal

1   The camshaft and tappets in the 948 cc and 1098 cc engines can be removed with the engine installed in the car or with the engine on the bench. If the engine is installed drain the cooling system and remove the radiator and fanbelt as described in Chapter 2. Remove the distributor as described in Section 8 of this Chapter and, with a bolt about 3.5 in (90 mm) long and with a $\frac{5}{16}$ in UNF thread screwed into the tapped end of the distributor driveshaft, withdraw the shaft from the crankcase. Remove the rocker assembly as described in Section 9 of this Chapter and then remove the pushrods. Undo the bolts securing the two tappet covers and remove the covers, taking note of the washers under the bolt heads. Lift out the tappets, keeping them in their correct sequence so that they can be refitted in their original locations.

2   If the engine is on the bench, carry out any work listed in paragraph 1 which has not already been done.

3   On an installed or removed engine, remove the three bolts and spring washers which hold the camshaft locating plate to the block. The bolts are normally covered by the camshaft sprocket.

4   Remove the plate. The camshaft can now be withdrawn. Take great care to remove the camshaft gently, and in particular ensure that the cam peaks do not damage the camshaft bearings as the shaft is pulled forward.

5   The 1275 cc engine camshaft cannot be removed with the engine in the car, as the tappets cannot be removed before the camshaft and they will therefore drop and lock the camshaft. It is necessary to remove the engine and invert it to prevent the tappets dropping before the camshaft can be withdrawn from the block.

6   After removing the camshaft, following the strip procedure for the smaller engines, the tappets in the 1275 cc engine can be removed by first removing the sump and lifting them out of their locations with a magnet. Alternatively they will slide out under their own weight if the engine is turned upright, but you will have to be careful to ensure that you can identify each tappet so that it can be refitted to its original position on reassembly. Of course, if it is intended to fit new tappets, this does not apply.

15 Sump and oil strainer – removal

1   The sump can be removed with the engine installed or removed. If installed, first drain the oil into a suitable container.

2   Remove the securing screws, shakeproof washers and special plain washers and remove the sump. If it appears to be stuck, a sharp blow with the palm of the hand on the side should free it, but if not insert a knife in the joint face.

3   Unscrew the oil suction pipe union from the crankcase and remove the two setscrews securing the strainer support bracket to the main bearing cap. Remove the strainer and bracket.

16 Pistons, connecting rods and big-end bearings – removal (all models)

1   The pistons, connecting rods and big-end bearings can be removed with the engine installed in the car or on the bench. If in the car, remove the cylinder head as described in Section 9 or, if on the bench, as described in Section 10. Remove the sump and oil strainer as described in the previous Section (all engines except 1500 cc) or remove the sump, oil pump and strainer as described in Section 80 (1500 cc engines).

2   Knock back the locking tabs on the big-end cap retaining bolts (except 1500 cc engines, to which no locktabs are fitted), undo and remove the bolts and locktabs.

3   Remove the big-end caps one at a time, taking care to keep them in the right order and the correct way round. Also ensure that the shell bearings are kept with their correct connecting rods and caps unless they are to be renewed, which is strongly recommended, regardless of their condition. Normally, the numbers 1 to 4 are stamped on adjacent sides of the big-end caps and connecting rods, indicating which cap fits on which rod and which way round the cap fits. If no numbers or lines can be found then, with a sharp screwdriver or file, scratch mating marks across the joint from the rod to the cap. One line for connecting rod No 1, two for connecting rod No 2 and so on. This will ensure there is no confusion later, as it is most important that the caps go back in the correct position on the connecting rods from which they were removed.

4   If the big-end caps are difficult to remove, they may be gently tapped with a soft hammer.

5   Push the connecting rod/piston assembly up the cylinder, taking care to ease the piston rings out at the top to avoid breakages, especially if a ridge exists due to wear. Make sure that you can reassemble all components in their original positions and, if necessary, mark components to prevent mistakes.

6   To remove the shell bearings, press the bearing opposite the groove in both the connecting rod and the connecting rod cap, and the bearings will slide out easily.

17 Gudgeon pins – removal (all models)

1   Three different types of gudgeon pin retention are employed depending on the age and type of engine.
2   To remove the gudgeon pin to free the piston from the connecting rod on early models, it is merely necessary to remove the small-end bolt and lockwasher. With the bolt removed, the gudgeon pin should push out through either side of the piston. If it shows reluctance to move, then on no account force it out, as this could damage the piston. Immerse the piston in a pan of boiling water for three minutes. On removal, the expansion of the aluminium should allow the gudgeon pin to slide out easily.
3   On later engines, fully-floating gudgeon pins are fitted, and these are retained in the pistons by circlips at each end of the pin. To extract the pin, remove the circlip at one end and push the pin out, immersing it in boiling water if it appears reluctant to move. Make sure the pins are kept with the same pistons for ease of refitting. Note that with this type of assembly the piston, the gudgeon pin, and the small-end bush are matched, and if it is intended to renew any single item they must all be changed for a matched set.
4   Certain late model engines use gudgeon pins which are an interference fit in the small-end of the connecting rod. The tightness of fit is their sole means of location. These pins must be pressed out and refitted using a special tool in order not to damage the connecting rods or pistons. This is therefore a job best left to your BL dealer or local engine specialist.
5   The 1500 engine has a floating gudgeon pin retained by circlips and, although matched sets are not used, the gudgeon pin bush in the connecting rod small-end must be pressed into place and reamed to size when being renewed. Again this will be a job for a BL dealer or specialist workshop, if it is necessary.

18 Pistons rings – removal (all models)

1   To remove the pistons rings, slide them carefully over the top of the piston, taking care not to scratch the surface of the piston which is made of aluminium alloy. Never slide them over the bottom of the piston skirt. It is very easy to break the cast iron rings if they are pulled off roughly, so this operation must be done with extreme care. It is helpful to make use of an old feeler gauge.
2   Lift one end of the piston ring to be removed out of its groove and insert the end of the feeler gauge under it.
3   Turn the feeler gauge slowly round the piston, and as the ring comes out of its groove apply slight upward pressure so that it rests on the ridge above. It can then be eased off the piston with the feeler gauge stopping it from slipping into any empty grooves.
4   If the rings are to be used again, usually a false economy unless they are nearly new, they must be kept in their respective order and with their respective pistons to ensure correct refitting.

19 Flywheel and engine endplate – removal (all models)

Having removed the clutch (see Chapter 5), the flywheel and engine endplate can be removed. It is only possible for this operation to be carried out with the engine out of the car.
1   Bend back the locking tabs (not fitted to certain 1500 cc engines), from the four bolts which hold the flywheel flange on the rear of the crankshaft.
2   Unscrew the bolts and remove them, complete with the two locking plates or the four washers.
3   Lift the flywheel away from the crankshaft flange. **Note:** *Some difficulty may be experienced in removing the bolts by the rotation of the crankshaft every time pressure is put on the spanner. The only answer is to lock the crankshaft in position while the bolts are removed. To lock the crankshaft a wooden wedge can be inserted between the crankshaft and the side of the block inside the crankcase.*
4   The engine endplate is held in position by a number of bolts and spring washers of varying sizes. Release the bolts, noting where different sizes fit and place them together to ensure none of them

become lost. Lift away the endplate from the block complete with the paper gasket.

20 Crankshaft and main bearings – removal

1   As the crankshaft can only be removed if the engine is not installed, carry out the work already described to remove the engine, and strip it down to the point reached in the previous Section.
2   Before removing the main bearing caps, check the crankshaft endfloat to see if new thrust washers will be needed on reassembly. To do this push the crankshaft hard in one direction along its fore and aft axis. Insert feeler gauges between the thrust washer and mating face of the crankshaft at the centre main bearing. Compare the clearance with that quoted in the Specifications to this Chapter.
3   Release the locking tabs from the six bolts which hold the three main bearing caps in place.
4   Unscrew the bolts and remove them together with the locking plates.
5   Remove the two bolts which hold the front main bearing cap against the engine front plate.
6   Remove the main bearing caps and the bottom half of each bearing shell, taking care to keep the bearing shells in the right caps.
7   When removing the centre bearing cap, retrieve the bottom semi-circular halves of the thrust washers, one half lying on either side of the main bearing. Lay them with the centre bearing along the correct side.
8   Slightly rotate the crankshaft to free the upper halves of the bearing shells and thrust washers, which should now be extracted and placed over the correct bearing cap.
9   Remove the crankshaft by lifting it away from the crankcase.

21 Lubrication system – general

For 1500 cc engines refer to Part B of this Chapter
1   A forced feed lubrication system is incorporated in these engines which circulates oil round the engine from a supply in the sump below the engine block. Engine oil level is indicated on a dipstick located on the right-hand side of the engine. It is marked to indicate the optimum level, which is the upper of the two marks; the lower mark indicates the minimum level to which the oil should be allowed to drop. Oil is replenished via the filler cap on the top of the rocker cover.
2   The oil pump is mounted at the end of the crankcase and is driven by the camshaft. Three different types of oil pump have been fitted at different times. These are the Burman rotary vane type, or the Hobourn Eaton, or the Concentric (Engineering) Ltd. concentric rotor type. All are of the non-draining variety to allow rapid pressure build-up when starting from cold.
3   Oil is drawn from the sump through a gauze screen strainer and is sucked up the pick-up pipe into the oil pump. From the pump it is forced under pressure along a gallery on the right-hand side of the engine, and through drillings to the big-end, main and camshaft bearings. A small hole in each connecting rod allows a jet of oil to lubricate the cylinder wall with each revolution.
4   From the camshaft front bearing, oil is fed through drilled passages in the cylinder block and head to the front rocker pedestal where it enters the hollow rocker shaft. Holes drilled in the shaft allow for the lubrication of the rocker arms, and the valve stems and pushrod ends. This oil is at a reduced pressure to the oil delivered to the crankshaft bearings. Oil from the front camshaft bearing also lubricates the timing gears and the timing chain. Oil returns to the sump by various passages, the tappets being lubricated by oil returning via the pushrod drillings in the block.
5   On all models a full-flow oil filter is fitted, and all oil passes through this filter before it reaches the main oil gallery. The oil is passed directly from the oil pump across the block to an external pipe on the right-hand side of the engine which feeds into the filter head.

22 Oil pressure relief valve – removal and refitting (all models)

1   A non-adjustable pressure relief valve is incorporated in the lubrication system to prevent excessive oil pressure being generated when, for example, the oil is cold.
2   On the 948, 1098 and 1275 cc engines, the relief valve is located

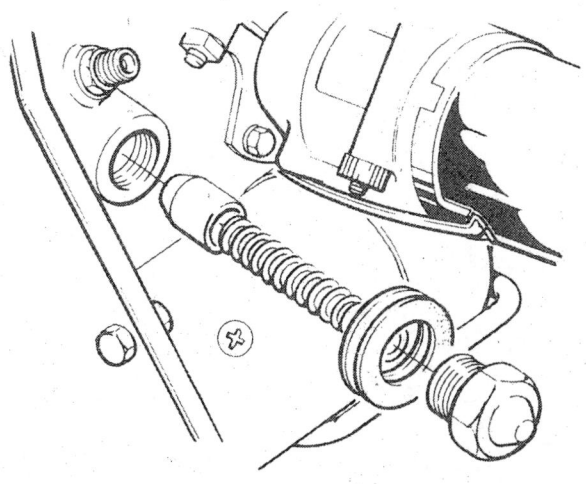

Fig. 1.2 The oil pressure relief valve (early engines) (Sec 22)

22.2 Removing the oil pressure relief valve (1500 cc engine)

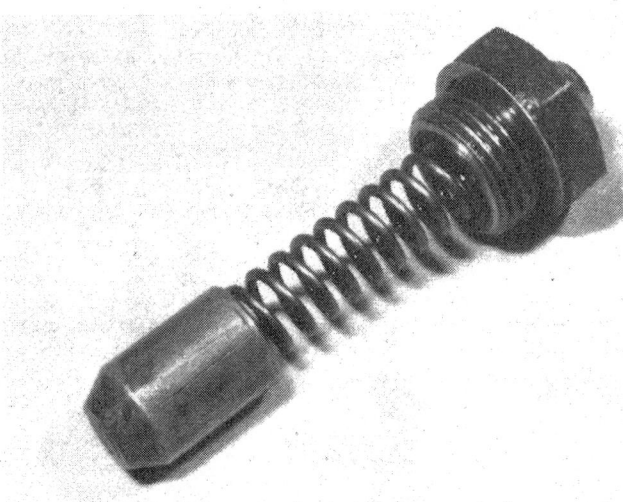

22.3 The relief valve removed (1275 cc engine)

on the right-hand side of the engine just below the oil pressure gauge union. On the 1500 cc engine the valve is located on the left-hand side of the engine just above the crankcase joint flange and in line with the distributor (photo).

3   To remove the assembly, undo the hexagon nut and withdraw the spring and cup shaped (all except 1500 cc) or plunger-shaped (1500 cc) valve (photo). Early engines had two fibre sealing washers but all later models have a copper sealing washer under the nut. The washer(s) should be discarded and renewed on reassembly.

4   When assembled the spring maintains a pressure on the valve which normally closes an oil return passage. If oil pressure exceeds that of the spring, the valve lifts to allow oil to return to the sump and thereby control the pressure in the system.

5   Wash the components in petrol and examine for scores and damage. Check the spring by measuring its length. If it is shorter than that quoted in the Specifications the spring must be renewed; also renew the valve if it is damaged in any way.

6   Refitting the valve is the reverse of the removal procedure. Lubricate the parts with clean engine oil and use a new copper sealing washer.

23 Oil filter – removal and refitting

1   The oil filter is located on the right-hand side of the engine towards the front. The early filter has a renewable element but the later type is a throwaway cartridge filter.

2   To remove and refit the early type of filter, first position a container under the filter case in which to catch spilled oil. Loosen the central securing bolt under the case and allow the oil to drain out. Then remove the bolt and the assembly from the engine.

3   Carefully separate the element from the case but take note of the sequence of assembly of the washers, pressure plate and spring on the retaining bolt so that they can be reassembled correctly. Discard the old element and wash the other parts in petrol, drying them with lint-free rag. Remove the old seal in the case-to-engine front and clean the mounting.

4   Fit the new seal, which is supplied with the new element, to the engine mounting making sure that it is properly seated all round its circumference. Fit the new element in the case, making sure that the components on the retaining bolt are in the correct sequence (Fig. 1.3). Hold the bolt hard against the case and fill the filter with clean engine oil. Offer up the assembly to the engine mounting and screw the bolt home, keeping the bolt head firmly in contact with the case to minimise oil loss. Before finally tightening the bolt rotate the casing slightly to and fro against the sealing ring to make sure that it is bedded down properly. Clean off all the spilt oil.

5   The later type of filter is in a cartridge which is screwed onto the mounting bracket and, although only hand tightened, it is often difficult to remove. To reach the filter turn the front wheels hard left and work through the triangular access hole as well as from underneath the filter.

6   If the cartridge resists removal by hand, use a strap or chain wrench. Alternatively the case can be 'stabbed' with a sharp tool which can then be used as a lever . Be prepared to catch spilt oil on removal. If such methods are unsuccessful the filter mounting bracket can be unbolted from the engine but this will involve removal of the dynamo or alternator and disconnection of the filter feed pipe (photo).

7   With the cartridge removed, clean the mounting face on the bracket. Smear the new seal with clean engine oil and carefully fit it in the cartridge groove. Make sure that it is bedded down properly all the way round and smear the engine bracket joint face with clean oil. Screw the new cartridge onto the threaded adaptor in the mounting bracket until the seal comes into contact with its mating face. Then give the cartridge a further third to half a turn by hand and no more. Clean off all the spilt oil.

8   On all models top up the engine oil and run the engine, checking for oil leaks around the filter. After stopping the engine allow the oil to settle and top it up again to the 'max' level on the dipstick.

24 Oil pump – removal and dismantling

1   The oil pump on these engines can only be removed with the engine out of the car and with the clutch, flywheel and engine rear

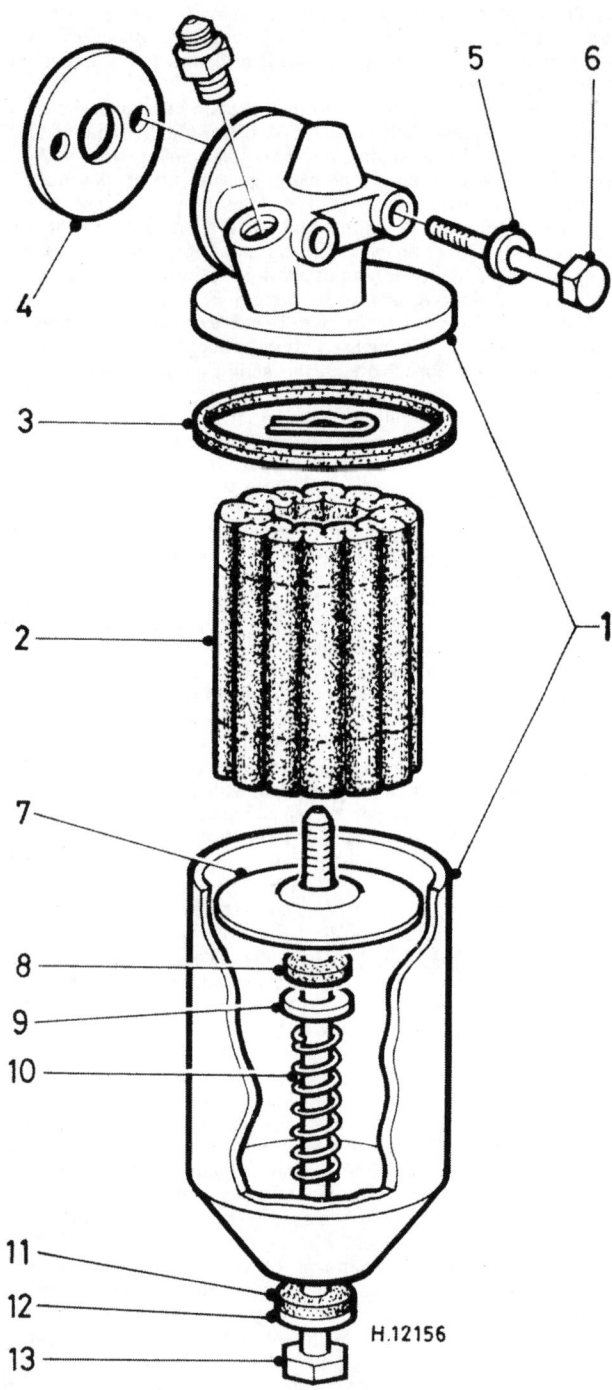

23.6 Refitting the oil filter bracket; note the new gasket

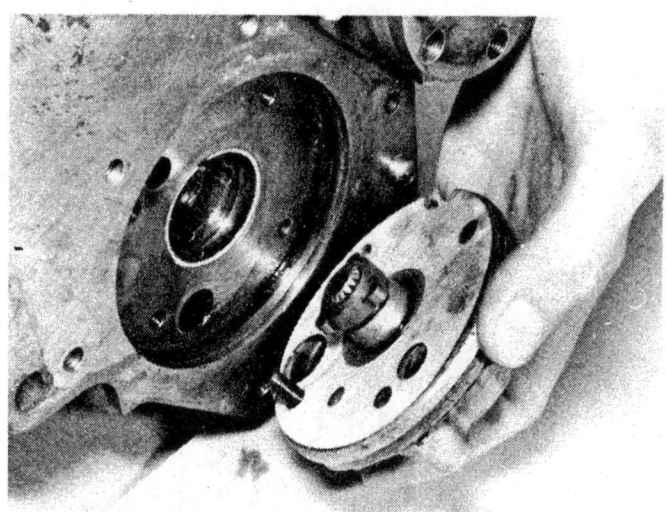

24.3 Removing the 'Concentric' type of oil pump

Fig. 1.3 Exploded view of the renewable element type oil filter, earlier cars (Sec 23)

1 Oil filter bowl and head	7 Pressure plate
2 Element	8 Felt or rubber washer
3 Sealing ring	9 Plain washer
4 Filter-to-cylinder block gasket	10 Spring
5 Spring washer	11 Rubber seal
6 Bolt	12 Body washer
	13 Bolt

plate removed. This should be done as already described in earlier Sections.

2   Bend back the lock washers if fitted, and remove the pump retaining screws. Remove the pump and note the position of the drive slot in order to assist refitting on the 948 and 1098 cc engines. On the

1275 cc engine the pump drive is transmitted from the camshaft by a separate coupling splined to the pump driveshaft. Note which way round this coupling is fitted, which is with the offset lugs against the pump on early couplings; later couplings have the lugs centralised.

3   Three types of pump have been used and dismantling, where possible, is as follows:

(a) *Concentric: This pump cannot be serviced and, if defective, must be changed for a new, or exchanged unit (photo)*

(b) *Hobourn-Eaton: Remove the cover securing screw and remove the cover from the pump body dowels. Remove the inner and outer rotors complete with driveshaft*

(c) *Burman: Unscrew and remove the two screws and spring washers securing the cover to the pump body. Remove the cover and withdraw the rotor and vane assembly. Prise off the retaining sleeve from the end of the rotor and remove the vanes, taking note of their assembly sequence for reference during reassembly*

25 Crankcase ventilation system – general

1   Later engines are fitted with a crankcase ventilation system to prevent the crankcase fumes, resulting from combustion gases leaking

past the piston rings, from being discharged into the atmosphere. Details of this system and its servicing are contained in Chapter 3.

26 Engine front mountings – removal and refitting

1 With time, the bonded rubber insulators, one on each of the front mountings, will perish causing undue vibration and noise from the engine. Severe juddering when reversing or when moving off from rest is also likely and is a further sign of worn mounting rubbers.
2 The front engine mounting rubbers can be changed with the engine in the vehicle.
3 Apply the handbrake firmly, jack up the front of the vehicle and support it adequately on stands.
4 Support the engine with suitable lifting equipment or take its weight on a jack under the front of the sump, but interpose a piece of wood to prevent damage.
5 Remove the securing nuts from both the right- and left-hand mounting rubbers and remove the mounting brackets-to-body securing screws. Undo the exhaust downpipe manifold clamp and remove the front downpipe from the support bracket.
6 Lift the engine carefully for about ¾ in (20 mm) and check that the cooling fan assembly will not foul the radiator fan cowling. Swing the engine gently over to the left-hand side as far as possible and remove the right-hand rubber mounting together with its body bracket. Then remove the left-hand rubber mounting and its body bracket.
7 When refitting new mountings, install the right-hand components first and get the left-hand components into position before refitting any setscrews or nuts. Tighten the fasteners and remove the lifting and/or jacking equipment. Refit the exhaust pipe clamp and support bracket.

27 Engine components – general examination and removal (all models)

With the engine stripped down and all parts thoroughly cleaned, it is now time to examine everything for wear. The items covered in the following Sections should be checked, and where necessary, renewed or renovated.

28 Crankshaft – examination and renovation (all models)

1 Examine the crankpin and main bearing journal surfaces for signs of scoring or scratches. Check the ovality of the crankpins at different positions with a micrometer.
2 If more than 0.001 in (0.025 mm) out of round, the crankshaft will have to be reground. It will also have to be reground if there are any scores or scratches present. Also check the main bearing journals in the same fashion.
3 On highly tuned engines the centre main bearing has been known to break up. This is not always immediately apparent, but slight vibration in an otherwise normally smooth engine and a very slight drop in oil pressure under normal conditions are clues. If the centre main bearing is suspected of failure it should be immediately investigated by dropping the sump and removing the centre main bearing cap. Failure to do this will result in a badly scored centre main journal.
4 If it is necessary to regrind the crankshaft, and fit new bearings, your local BL dealer or engine reconditioners will be able to advise on the amount of metal to grind off and the correct size shells required.
5 If it is necessary to grind below the permitted diameters to reface the journals, then a new crankshaft will have to be fitted.

29 Big-end and main bearing shells – examination and renovation (all models)

1 Big-end bearing failure is accompanied by a noisy knocking from the crankcase, and a slight drop in oil pressure. Main bearing failure is accompanied by vibration, which can be quite severe as the engine speed rises and falls, and a drop in oil pressure.
2 Bearings which have not broken up, but are badly worn will give rise to low oil pressure and some vibration. Inspect the big-ends, main bearings, and thrust washers for signs of general wear, scoring, pitting

and scratches. The bearings should be matt grey in colour. With lead-indium bearings, should a trace of copper colour be noticed, the bearings are badly worn as the lead bearing material has worn away to expose the indium underlay. Renew the bearings if they are in this condition or if there is any sign of scoring or pitting.
3 The bearing undersizes available are designed to correspond with the regrind sizes, eg -0.010 in (0.254 mm) bearings are correct for a crankshaft reground -0.010 in (0.254 mm) undersize. The bearings are in fact, slightly more than the stated undersize as running clearances have been allowed for during their manufacture.

30 Cylinder bores – examination and renovation (all models)

1 The cylinder bores must be examined for taper, ovality, scoring and scratches. Start by carefully examining the top of the cylinder bores. If they are at all worn a very slight ridge will be found on the thrust side. This marks the top of the piston ring travel. The owner will have a good indication of the bore wear prior to dismantling the engine, or removing the cylinder head. Excessive oil consumption accompanied by blue smoke from the exhaust is a sure sign of worn cylinder bores and piston rings.
2 Measure the bore diameter just under the ridge with a micrometer and compare it with the diameter at the bottom of the bore, which is not subject to wear. If the difference between the two measurements is more than 0.006 in (0.15 mm) then it will be necessary to fit special piston rings or to have the cylinders rebored and fit oversize pistons and rings. If a micrometer is not available, remove the rings from each piston in turn (do not mix the rings from piston to piston) and place each piston in its respective bore at about ¾ in (20 mm) below the top surface of the cylinder block. If a 0.010 in (0.254 mm) thick feeler gauge can be slid between the piston and the cylinder wall on the thrust side of the bore then remedial action must be taken. Oversize pistons are available which are 0.020 in (0.508 mm) larger than original but it might be possible to get other sizes if an old stock of spares which are no longer provisioned can be located. In severe cases dry liners can be fitted to a bored out block.
3 Oversize pistons and rings are accurately machined to just below these measurements so as to provide correct running clearances in cylinders bored out to the exact oversize dimensions.
4 If the bores are slightly worn, but not so bad as to justify a rebore, then special oil control rings and pistons can be fitted which will help restore compression and stop the engine burning oil. Different types are available and the manufacturer's instructions concerning their fitting must be closely followed.
5 If the block is to be sent away for reboring, it is essential to remove the cylinder head studs. If a stud remover is not available, then lock two nuts together on a stud (photo) and then wind the stud out by unscrewing the lower nut anti-clockwise.
6 If new pistons are being fitted and the bores have not been

30.5 Removing a stud by means of two nuts locked together

reground, it is essential to slightly roughen the hard glaze on the sides of the bores with fine emery paper so that the new piston rings will have a chance to bed in properly. Make sure that all abrasive dust is cleaned off after doing this.

31 Pistons and piston rings – examination and renovation (all models)

1 If the old pistons are to be refitted, carefully remove the piston rings and then thoroughly clean each piston. Take particular care to clean out the piston ring grooves. At the same time do not scratch the aluminium in any way. If new rings are to be fitted to the old pistons, or new piston assemblies are to be fitted to the original (non-rebored) cylinder bores, then the top ring must be stepped so as to clear the ridge left above the previous top ring. If a normal but oversize new ring is fitted, it will hit the ridge and break, because the new ring will not have worn in the same way as the old, which will have worn in unison with the ridge.

2 Before fitting the rings on the pistons, each should be inserted approximately 3 in (75 mm) down the cylinder bore and the gap measured with a feeler gauge (photo). This should be as specified at the front of this Chapter. It is essential that the gap is also measured at the bottom of the worn bore as, even if the gap is correct at the top, the ring could easily seize at the bottom due to the taper in the bore. If the ring gap is too small carefully reduce the ends of the ring with a fine, smooth file until the gap, when fitted, is correct. To keep the rings square in the bore for measurement, line each up in turn by inserting an old piston in the bore upside down, and use the piston to push the ring down about 3 in (75 mm). Remove the piston and measure the piston ring gap.

3 When fitting new pistons and rings to a rebored engine, the piston ring gap can be measured at the top of the bore as the bore will not now taper. It is not necessary to measure the side clearance in the piston ring grooves with the rings fitted, as the groove dimensions are accurately machined during manufacture.

4 When fitting new oil control rings to old pistons it may be necessary to have the grooves widened by machining to accept the new wider rings. In this case the maker's fitting instructions will indicate the necessary procedure.

5 Duaflex 61 oil control rings are fitted to some engines, and the following points should be noted in respect of these rings.

   (a) *The rails and side spring should be gapped to the specified size*
   (b) *The expander lugs must not be crossed, but should be butted and inserted in one of the holes in the scraper ring groove on the non-thrust side of the piston*
   (c) *Stagger the gaps of the twin rails and the side spring on the non-thrust side of the piston*
   (d) *Make sure that the ends of the rings are fully home in the groove when compressing the rings before fitting the pistons*
   (e) *Remove any cylinder bore glaze before fitting the pistons*

32 Camshaft and camshaft bearings – examination and renovation (all models)

1 Carefully examine the camshaft bearings for wear. Note that on early engines only the front camshaft bearing is renewable. If the bearings are obviously worn or pitted or the metal underlay is showing through, then they must be renewed. This is an operation for your local BL dealer or the local engineering works, as it demands the use of specialised equipment. The bearings are removed with a special drift after which new bearings are pressed in, care being taken to ensure the oil holes in the bearings line up with those in the block. With a special tool the bearings are then reamed in position.

2 The camshaft itself should show no sign of wear, but, if very slight scoring on the cams is noticed, the score marks can be removed by very gentle rubbing down with very fine emery cloth. The greatest care should be taken to keep the cam profiles smooth and all traces of abrasive must be thoroughly cleaned off on completion.

3 Deep scoring which has penetrated the surface hardening of the camshaft will necessitate renewal.

4 If a new camshaft is fitted, new tappets must be installed.

5 Examine the distributor drive skew gear for excessive wear, chipped teeth or other damage.

31.2 Measuring a piston ring gap with feeler gauges

6 Finally examine the inner face of the camshaft retaining plate for excessive wear, which will be self-evident. Renewal will be necessary if it exists but, if the wear is not excessive, make a note to check the camshaft endfloat on assembly. If that is excessive, a new retaining plate may restore it to within tolerance.

33 Valve guides – examination (all models)

1 Examine the valve guides internally for wear. If the valves are a very loose fit in the guides and there is the slightest suspicion of lateral rocking, then new guides will have to be fitted.

2 The work of renewing the valve guides should be undertaken by a BL dealer or specialist garage who will also recut the valve seats for you at the same time. This should be done, if it is necessary, before grinding in the valves as described in the next Section.

34 Valve and valve seats – examination and renovation (all models)

1 Examine the heads of the valves for pitting and burning, especially the heads of the exhaust valves. The valve seatings should be examined at the same time. If the pitting on valve and seat is very slight, the marks can be removed by grinding the seats and valves together with coarse, and then fine, valve grinding paste. Where bad pitting has occurred to the valve seats, it will be necessary to recut them and fit new valves. If the valve seats are so worn that they cannot be recut, then it will be necessary to fit new valve seat inserts. These latter two jobs must be entrusted to the local BL agent or engineering works. In practice it is very seldom that the seats are so badly worn that they require renewal. Normally, it is the valve that is too badly worn for refitting, and the owner can easily purchase a new set of valves and match them to the seats by valve grinding.

2 Valve grinding is carried out as follows: Smear a trace of coarse carborundum paste on the seat face and apply a suction grinder tool to the valve head (photo). With a semi-rotary motion, grind the valve head to its seat, lifting the valve occasionally to redistribute the grinding paste. When a dull matt even surface finish is produced on both the valve seat and the valve, then wipe off the paste and repeat the process with fine carborundum paste, lifting and turning the valve to redistribute the paste as before.

3 A light spring placed under the valve head will greatly ease this operation. When a smooth unbroken ring of light grey matt finish it produced, on both valve and valve seat faces, the grinding operation is complete.

4 Scrape away all carbon from the valve head and the valve stem. Carefully clean away every trace of grinding compound, taking great care to leave none in the ports or in the valve guides. Clean the valves

34.2 Grinding a valve and seat

37.1 A badly pitted tappet

and valve seats with a paraffin soaked rag then with a clean rag, and finally, if an air line is available, blow the valves, valve guides and valve ports clean.

35 Timing sprockets and chain – examination and renovation (all models)

1   Examine the teeth on the crankshaft sprocket and on the camshaft sprocket for wear. Each tooth forms an inverted 'V' with the sprocket wheel periphery and, if worn, the tension side of each tooth will be slightly concave in shape when compared with the other side of the tooth. If such wear is evident the two sprockets and chain should be renewed.
2   Examine the links of the chain for side slackness and renew the chain if any is noticeable when compared with a new chain. It is a sensible precaution to renew the chain if the engine is stripped down for a major overhaul, and has done more than 30 000 miles (48 000 km). The rollers on a very badly worn chain may be slightly grooved.

36 Rockers and rocker shaft – examination and renovation (all models)

1   If it hasn't already been done, remove the threaded plug with a screwdriver from the end of the rocker shaft and thoroughly clean out the shaft. As it acts as the oil passage for the valve gear, ensure that the oil holes in it are unobstructed and clean.
2   Check the shaft for straightness by rolling it on a flat surface such as a piece of plate glass. If it is out of true, a judicious attempt may be made to straighten it, but take care not to cause further damage such as dents, nicks or burrs. If unsuccessful, renew the shaft.
3   The surface of the shaft should be free from any worn ridges caused by the rocker arms. If any wear is present, renew the shaft. Wear is only likely to have occurred if the rocker shaft oil holes have become blocked, or if the engine has done a high mileage.
4   Check the rocker arms for wear of the rocker bushes, for wear at the rocker arm face which bears on the valve stem, and for wear of the adjusting ball-ended screws. Wear in the rocker arm bush can be checked by gripping the rocker arm tip and holding the rocker arm in place on the shaft, noting if there is any lateral rocker arm shake. If shake is present, and the arm is very loose on the shaft, remedial action must be taken.
5   Pressed steel valve rockers cannot be renovated by renewal of the rocker arm bush. It is necessary to fit new rocker arms.
6   Forged rocker arms which have worn bushes may be taken to your local BL agent or engineering works to have the old bushes pressed out and new bushes fitted.
7   Forged rockers and pressed steel rockers are interchangeable in sets of eight, but, where one or two pressed steel rockers only require

renewal, it is not advisable to replace them with the forged type.
8   Check the tip of the rocker arm where it bears on the valve head for cracking or serious wear on the case hardening. Check the lower half of the ball on the end of the rocker arm adjusting screw.
9   On high performance engines, wear on the ball and top of the pushrod is easily noted by the unworn 'pip' which fits in the small central oil hole on the ball. The larger this 'pip' the more wear has taken place to both the ball and the pushrod.
10   Check the pushrods for straightness by rolling them on a flat surface, and renew any that are bent.

37 Tappets (cam followers) – examination and renovation (all models)

1   Examine the surface of the tappets which bears on the cams on the camshaft. Any ridges, grooves, pitting or similar damage will necessitate renewal (photo).
2   Wash the tappets clean in paraffin and dry them with lint-free rag. Try each tappet in its relative location in the block and assess for wear by applying a side loading rocking action. If wear is evident they should be renewed.
3   Oversize tappets are available (not 1500 cc) and new tappets should be fitted by selective assembly so that they just fall into their guides under their own weight when lubricated with engine oil.

38 Flywheel starter ring – examination and renovation (all models)

1   The front edges of the gear teeth on the flywheel starter ring are prone to wear and damage from the starter pinion and when this wear becomes excessive the ring can be renewed independently of the flywheel.
2   The ring is cut off the flywheel, but first drill a $\frac{1}{4}$ in (6.35 mm) hole between any two teeth, taking care not to damage the flywheel. Hold the flywheel in a vice with packing to prevent marking it and put a piece of heavy material over the ring gear to restrain possible flying fragments. For the same reason wear protective glasses to shield the eyes. Use a cold chisel immediately over the drilled hole and strike it sharply to split the gear ring.
3   Check that the new rings and the mating surface on the flywheel are free from burrs and are both perfectly clean. The ring must be heated to expand it sufficiently to fit it to the flywheel, but it must not be overheated or its temper will be lost and its life drastically reduced. Some new rings have a strip of scarlet paint which will turn grey/brown when the correct temperature is reached. In the absence of this, and of suitable temperature measuring equipment, the ring should be polished with fine emery in three or four places around its periphery and heated until these spots show a coloured oxide film. The

colour will indicate the temperature and you should look for a light blue, indicating 300° to 400°C (572° to 752°F) for all engines except 1500 cc, and faint yellow indicating 200°C (392°F) for 1500 cc engines.

4   With the ring at this temperature, quickly fit it to the flywheel, making sure that the bevelled edges of the gear teeth face forwards (that is down as it is put on the flywheel). Tap the ring down to make sure that it is fitted fully into its register and then allow it to cool down naturally; don't quench it or force cool it. When the flywheel is assembled to the crankshaft it will be necessary to make a centring check to ensure that the ring gear is concentric with the centre of rotation.

39 Oil pump – examination and renovation

1   It is unlikely that the oil pump will be worn, but, if the engine is fully stripped down it is only sensible to check the pump for wear.
2   If it is the Burman pump, examine the inside of the pump body in which the vanes rotate, and the edges of the vanes for signs of scoring. If any is found, renew the complete pump unit.
3   If it is the Hobourn Eaton unit, check the rotor internally and the driveshaft lobes for any signs of excessive wear or scoring. In particular check the diametrical clearance between the pump body and the outer rotor. This should not exceed 0.010 in (0.25 mm).
4   Also check the clearance between the pump body jointing face and the face of the rotors by placing a straightedge across the rotor face. This clearance should not exceed 0.005 in (0.12 mm). Finally, check the clearance between the rotor lobes, which should not exceed 0.006 in (0.15 mm). Excessive wear beyond the figures quoted necessitates the renewal of the pump unit.

40 Cylinder head – decarbonisation (all models)

1   This can be carried out with the engine either in or out of the car. With the cylinder head off, carefully remove with a wire brush and blunt scraper all traces of carbon deposits from the combustion spaces and the ports. The valve head stems and valve guides should also be freed from any carbon deposits. Wash the combustion spaces and ports down with petrol and scrape the cylinder head surface free of any foreign matter with a blunt scraper.
2   Clean the pistons and top of the cylinder bores. If the pistons are still in the block then it is essential that great care is taken to ensure that no carbon gets into the cylinder bores as this could scratch the cylinder walls or cause damage to the pistons and rings. To ensure this does not happen, first turn the crankshaft so that two of the pistons are at the top of their bores. Stuff rag into the other two bores or seal them off with paper and masking tape. The waterways should also be covered with small pieces of masking tape to prevent particles of carbon entering the cooling system and damaging the water pump.
3   There are two schools of thought as to how much carbon should be removed from the piston crown. One opinion holds that a ring of carbon should be left around the edge of the piston and on the cylinder wall as an oil and compression seal. If your engine is fairly worn, having covered a high mileage, this would be the best course of action, for, if you do remove this seal, oil consumption will increase until it has reformed. To retain the carbon seal insert an old piston ring into the bore and press it onto the piston before decoking. The other approach is to clean out all carbon and combustion residue in the cylinders and on the pistons, and this should be your course of action if you are confident that the bores are not badly worn.
4   If all traces of carbon are to be removed, press a little grease into the gap between the cylinder walls and the two pistons which are to be worked on. With a blunt scraper, carefully scrape away the carbon from the piston crown, taking great care not to scratch the aluminium. Also scrape away the carbon from the surrounding lip of the cylinder wall. When all the carbon has been removed, scrape away the grease which will now be contaminated with carbon particles, taking care not to press any into the bores. To assist the prevention of carbon build-up, the piston crown can be polished with a metal polish. Remove the rags or masking tape from the other two cylinders and turn the crankshaft so that the two pistons which were at the bottom are now at the top. Place rag or masking tape in the cylinders which have been decarbonised and proceed as just described.

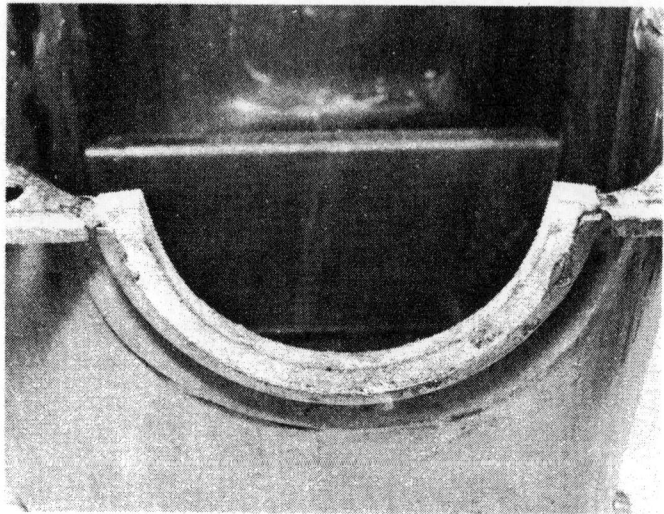

41.2 A new sump main bearing seal fitted

41 Sump – examination and renovation (all models)

1   Thoroughly wash out the sump with petrol and then inspect the flanges for signs of distortion; ensure that all traces of the old sealing gasket have been removed.
2   On 1275 cc engines and earlier models, renew the main bearing cap seals in the front and rear semi-circular housings. After removing the old seals, fit the new ones making sure that they bed well down in the housings and, if necessary, trim off any surplus protruding above the sump flange gasket level (photo).

42 Engine – general reassembly (all models)

To ensure maximum life with minimum trouble from a rebuilt engine, not only must everything be correctly assembled, but everything must be spotlessly clean, all the oilways must be clear, locking washers and spring washers must always be fitted where needed, and all bearing and other working surfaces must be thoroughly lubricated during assembly. Before assembly begins renew any bolts or studs the threads of which are in any way damaged, and wherever possible use new spring washers.

Apart from normal tools, a supply of non-fluffy clean rag, an oil can filled with clean engine oil (an empty washing-up liquid plastic bottle thoroughly cleaned out, will do), a supply of new spring washers, a set of new gaskets, and a torque wrench should be collected together.

43 Crankshaft – refitting

1   Ensure that the crankcase is thoroughly clean and that oilways are clear. A thin twist drill is useful for cleaning them out. If possible, blow them out with compressed air. Treat the crankshaft in the same fashion, and then inject engine oil into the crankshaft oilways.
2   If the original main bearing shells are being refitted (and it is false economy not to renew them unless the originals are virtually 'as new'), fit the three upper halves of the main bearing shells in their original locations in the crankcase after wiping the locations clean (photo).
3   If new bearing shells are being fitted, carefully clean off all traces of the protective grease with which they are coated before fitting them to the crankcase.
4   Note that on each half shell there is a locating tag which must be fitted to the recess in either the crankcase or bearing cap housings.
5   With the three upper bearing shells securely in place, wipe the lower bearing cap housings and fit the three lower shell bearings to their caps, ensuring that the right shell goes into the right cap if the old bearings are being refitted.
6   Wipe the recesses either side of the centre main bearing which locate the upper halves of the thrust washers, and fit the upper halves

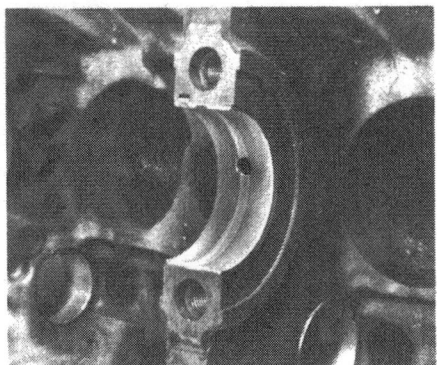

43.2 An upper half main bearing shell in position

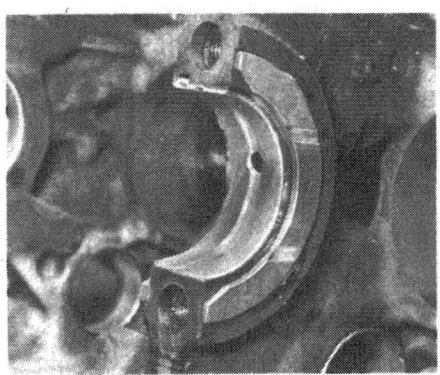

43.6 Note that the oil grooves in the upper half thrust washer face away from the bearing

43.7 The crankshaft installed in the upper half bearings

43.8 A half thrust washer fitted to the centre main bearing cap

43.11 Tightening the main bearing cap nuts with a torque wrench

43.13 Using feeler gauges to measure crankshaft endfloat

of the thrust washers (the halves without tabs) into the recesses; if necessary a touch of grease will hold them in position. Make sure that the oil grooves face away from the bearing.

7 Generously lubricate the crankshaft journals, and the upper main bearing shells, and carefully place the crankshaft in position (photo). Check that the half thrust washers have not been displaced.

8 Check that the six tubular locating dowels are fitted, either to the crankcase or to the main bearing caps. Fit the two half thrust washers to the centre main bearing cap, making sure that the oil grooves face away from the bearing and that the locating tab on each washer sits in the slot in the cap (photo).

9 Ensure that the mating surfaces on the caps and the crankcase are spotlessly clean, and apply a film of jointing compound to the rear bearing cap joint faces to act as an oil seal on assembly.

10 Fit the bearing caps after lubricating the main bearings and thrust washers. It is essential for each cap to be in its correct location and the right way round on assembly.

11 If applicable (early engines only) position the locking tabs on the three bearing caps. Refit the cap retaining nuts or bolts as applicable and run them down fingertight. Rotate the crankshaft a few turns and then tighten the nuts or bolts to the specified torque (photo).

12 Test the crankshaft for freedom of rotation. Should it be very stiff to turn or exhibit high spots, that is, intermittently free and stiff, then a most careful inspection must be made, preferably by a skilled mechanic, to trace the cause of the trouble. Fortunately it is very seldom that any trouble of this kind is experienced after taking care during the fitting of the bearings and crankshaft.

13 Using a screwdriver between one crankshaft web and a main bearing, carefully lever the crankshaft in one direction and check the amount of endfloat using feeler gauges (photo). This should be within the specified limits but if it is not, new or oversize thrust washers will need fitting.

14 When all is correct the tabs on the bearing cap lockwashers, where fitted, can be bent up.

44 Oil pump – reassembly and refitting

1 On early engines the oil pump must be fitted before the engine endplate, but on later engines which have an exposed pump this does not apply.

2 To reassemble the Hobourn Eaton pump, refit the outer rotor, inner rotor, and driveshaft into the pump body. Locate the cover on the dowels and secure with the retaining screw.

3 To reassemble the Burman pump, refit the vanes to the rotor and then refit the retaining sleeve. Fit the rotor and vane assembly to the pump body and then fit the cover and the two retaining bolts and washers.

4 Before refitting any pump, lubricate it well internally and check that rotation is free with no high spots. Use a new joint gasket and make sure that, when in position, it does not obstruct the inlet or outlet ports. Fit the retaining bolts and spring washers and tighten to the correct torque where specified.

5 On the 948 cc and 1098 cc engines the pump is driven by a slot and pin arrangement, but on the 1275 cc engine a three-lobed driving dog splined to the pump shaft is used. Early patterns of this driving dog have the lobes towards one face, and the dog must be fitted with the lobes adjacent to the pump (photo). Later dogs have the lobes centralised and they can be fitted either way round.

45 Camshaft and front endplate – refitting

1 On 1275 cc engines it is first necessary to insert the tappets into their respective bores in the cylinder block prior to refitting the camshaft. This is because they cannot be inserted from the top, and there is no tappet cover in the side of the engine. Lubricate them before fitting and make sure that, where original tappets are being refitted, they go back into their original locations (photo).

44.5 The oil pump drive is fitted with its lobes adjacent to the pump

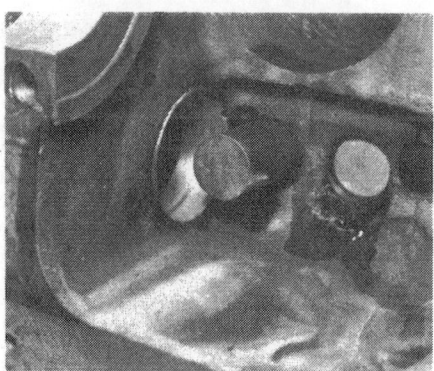

45.1 Inserting the tappets (1275 cc engine)

45.3 The camshaft being installed

45.5 The endplate gasket on the crankcase

45.6 The camshaft retaining plate being refitted

45.8 The two Allen screws being fitted in the endplate

2   Wipe the camshaft bearing journals clean and lubricate them generously with engine oil.
3   Carefully insert the camshaft into the crankcase, taking care not to damage the camshaft bearings with the sides of the lobes (photo).
4   With the camshaft inserted fully into the block, rotate it to ensure that the oil pump drive is engaged with the camshaft.
5   With the camshaft fully located, smear the endplate gasket with a sealing compound and place it in position on the crankcase (photo). Then locate the endplate, and retain it with bolts screwed in finger-tight.
6   The camshaft retaining plate can now be fitted and it is retained by three bolts (photo).
7   With the aid of a feeler gauge, check the camshaft endfloat and ensure that it is within the tolerances quoted in the Specifications. If not then a new endplate will have to be fitted.
8   Tighten all of the endplate retaining bolts, and the two lower Allen screws (photo).

---

46 Pistons and connecting rods – reassembly (all models)

1   If the original pistons, gudgeon pins and connecting rods are being refitted, it is important to mate the same components and fit them the same way round as they were originally installed. The procedure for reassembly will vary slightly with the type of assembly involved.

Split small-end with gudgeon pin secured by clamp bolt
2   When fitting new gudgeon pins, use the selective assembly procedure. Each pin should be a thumb-push fit for three quarters of its travel and be finally tapped home with a soft-faced hammer. For this technique all components should be at normal temperature.
3   Locate the connecting rod small-end in the piston, bearing in mind that the clamp bolt must be on the camshaft side of the engine and the 'FRONT' marking on the piston properly positioned to face the front of the engine.
4   Fit the gudgeon pin so that the bolt groove will align with the bolt hole in the small-end.

5   Fit a new spring washer under the clamp bolt head, fit the bolt and tighten it.

Interference fit gudgeon pin
6   As with the dismantling of this type of assembly, your BL garage should be allowed to reassemble the pistons to the connecting rods, as a special tool is necessary to insert the gudgeon pins.

Fully floating gudgeon pin
7   Fit a new gudgeon pin circlip at one end of the gudgeon pin hole in the piston and lubricate the pin bearing surface.
8   Position the connecting rod small-end in the piston. The piston is marked 'FRONT' or with a triangular arrow to point to the front of the engine, and the connecting rod big-end bearing cap must be on the camshaft side of the engine.
9   Slide the gudgeon pin through the bore in the piston and through the connecting rod small-end; this should be a hand push fit at normal room temperature.
10   Fit the second circlip to the piston; again, it should be a new one (photo).

---

47 Pistons rings – refitting (all models)

1   Check that the piston ring grooves and oilways are thoroughly clean and unblocked. Piston rings must always be fitted over the head of the piston and never from the bottom.
2   The easiest method to use when fitting rings is to wrap a 0.020 in (0.50 mm) feeler gauge round the top of the piston and place the rings one at a time, starting with the bottom oil control ring, over the feeler gauge.
3   The feeler gauge, complete with ring, can then be slid down the piston over the other piston ring grooves until the correct groove is reached. The piston ring is then slid gently off the feeler gauge into the groove (photo).
4   An alternative method is to fit the rings by holding them slightly open with the thumbs and both of your index fingers. This method

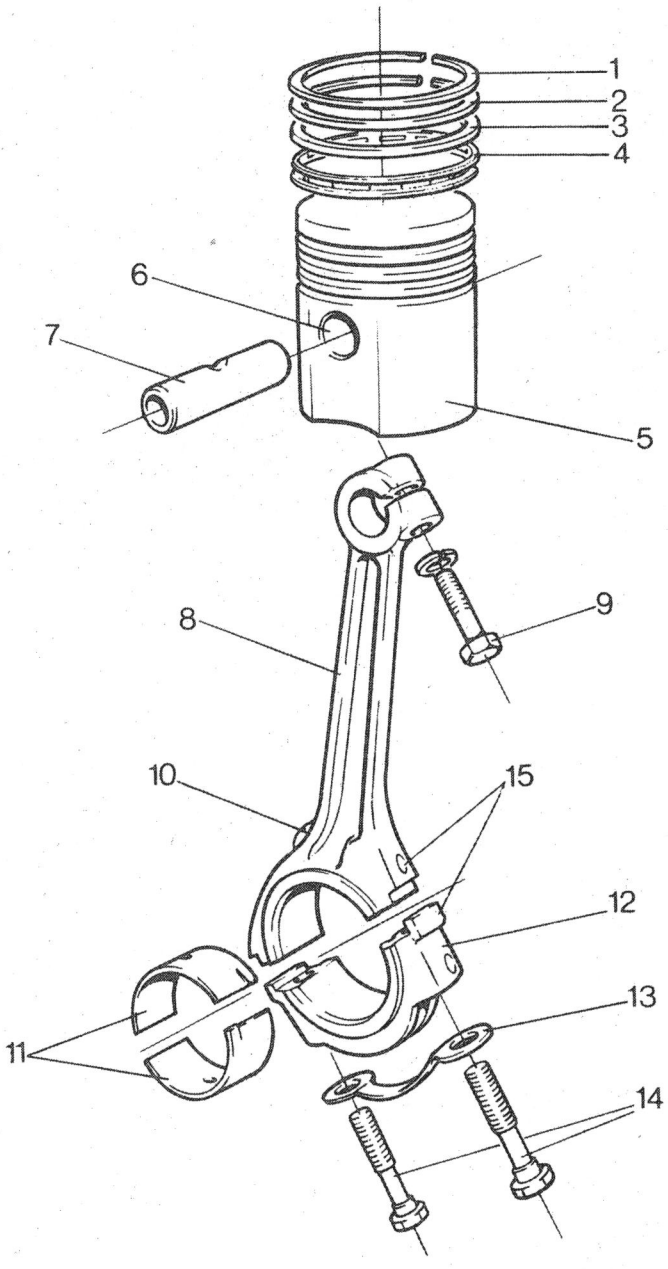

Fig. 1.4 Piston and connecting rod assembly – early models
(Sec 46)

1 Piston ring – parallel	9 Clamping bolt and washer
2 Piston ring – taper	10 Cylinder wall lubricating
3 Piston ring – taper	jet
4 Piston ring – scraper	11 Big-end bearings
5 Piston	12 Connecting rod cap
6 Gudgeon pin lubricating	13 Lockwasher
hole	14 Bolts
7 Gudgeon pin	15 Connecting rod and cap
8 Connecting rod	marking

requires a steady hand and great care as it is easy to open this ring too much and break it.

5   On 1500 cc engines the oil control ring expander, that is the middle of the three piece ring, should be fitted first followed by the bottom rail and then the top rail. Check that the ends of the expander are butted and not overlapped.

6   The stepped ring fitted in the second groove of these pistons should have the face marked 'TOP' towards the top of the piston.

7   On engines with tapered second and third compression rings, the

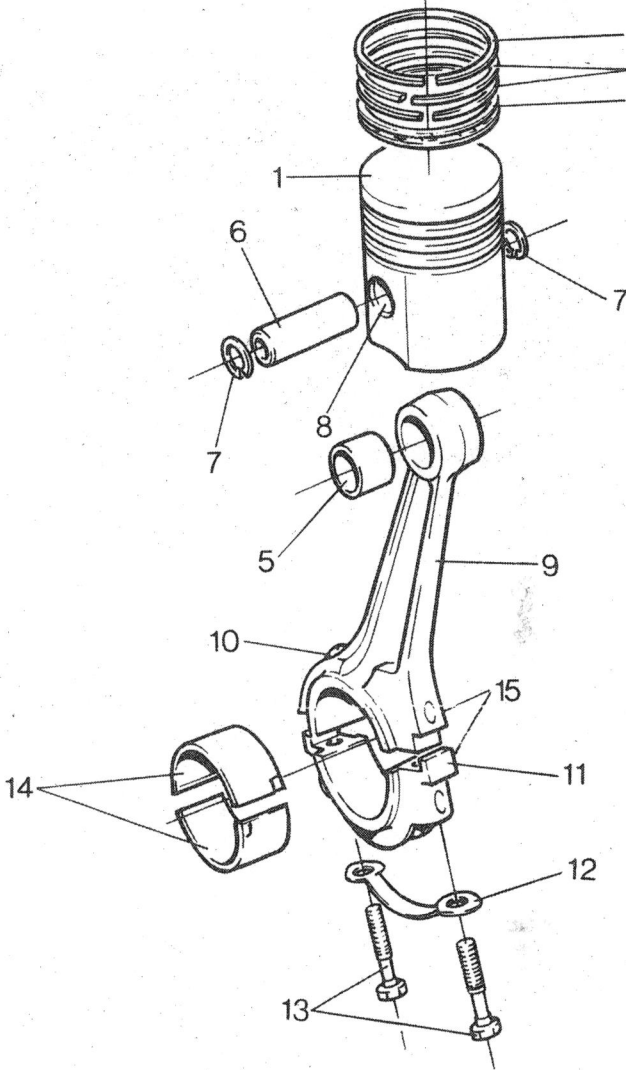

Fig. 1.5 Piston and connecting rod assembly – later models
(Sec 46)

1 Piston	9 Connecting rod
2 Piston ring – scraper	10 Cylinder wall lubricating
3 Piston rings – taper	jet
4 Piston ring – parallel	11 Connecting rod cap
5 Small-end bush	12 Lockwasher
6 Gudgeon pin	13 Bolts
7 Circlip	14 Big-end bearings
8 Gudgeon pin lubricating	15 Connecting rod and cap
hole	marking

top narrow side of the ring is marked with a 'T'. Always fit this side uppermost and carefully examine all rings for this mark before fitting.

8   On all pistons, arrange the rings so that the gaps are evenly disposed around the piston to reduce gas leakage.

48 Pistons and connecting rods – refitting (all models)

1   Before fitting each piston assembly, wipe the cylinder bore clean with non-fluffy rag and lubricate it with clean engine oil.

2   The piston assembly is fitted down into the cylinder and it is important to get the right assembly in each cylinder and facing the right way. To recapitulate, the 'FRONT' or triangular arrow mark on the piston must be towards the front of the engine; the number on each connecting rod will identify in which cylinder it fits; the rod number or the big-end bearing cap on later engines must be on the camshaft side of the engine; and finally, where the big-ends are offset on the

46.10 Fitting the second circlip to the piston assembly

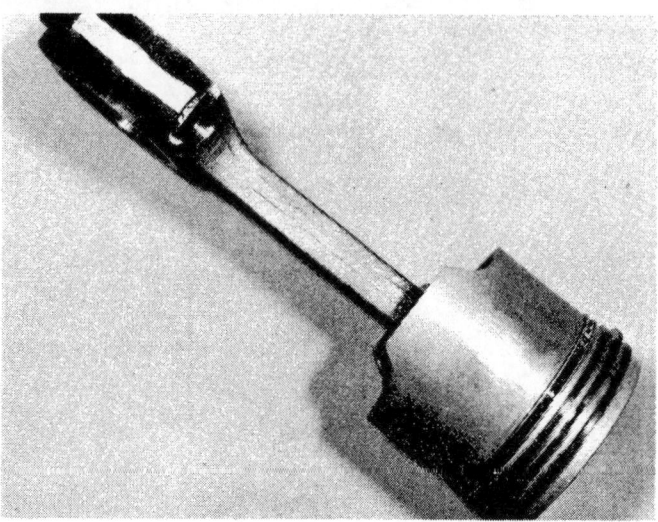

47.3 A piston assembly with all rings fitted

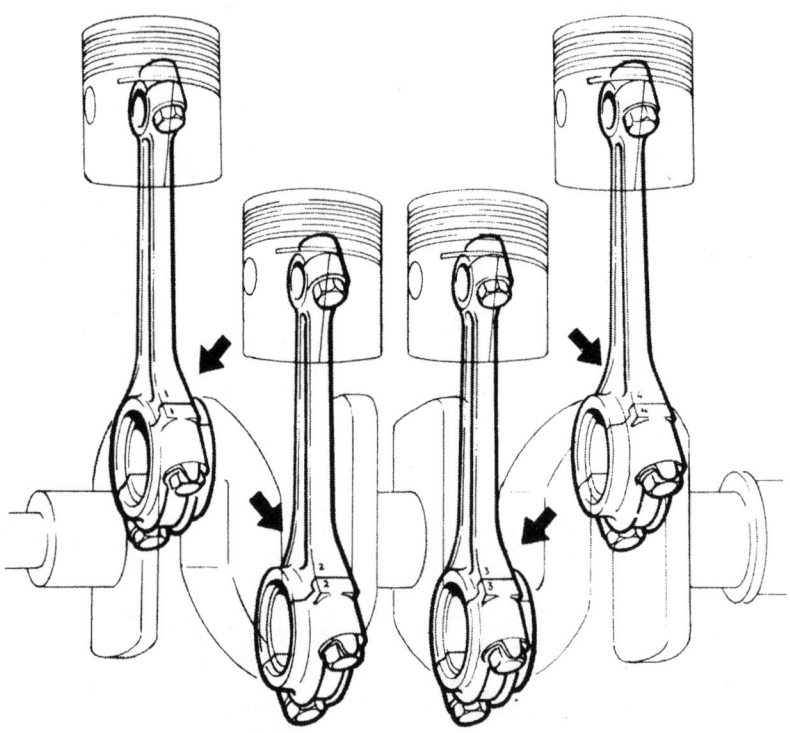

Fig. 1.6 The correct relationship of the offset big-end bearings (Sec 48)

connecting rods (later engines), numbers 1 and 3 are offset to the rear of the engine and 2 and 4 to the front, see Fig. 1.6.

3   To permit the pistons to enter the cylinder bores, the piston rings must be compressed in a ring compressor, although if one is not available, a suitably sized worm drive type hose clip can be used. First check that the ring gaps are equally distributed round the piston and then fit the compressor.

4   Enter the connecting rod carefully into the cylinder bore and, when the ring compressor contacts the cylinder head joint face, gently tap the piston head with the wooden shaft of a hammer until all rings have entered the cylinder (photo). Check that the big-end does not foul the crankshaft as it is entered.

49 Connecting rods to crankshaft – reassembly

1   Wipe the connecting rod big-end bearing shell location clean, and similarly wipe the bearing shell mating face clean. It is always best to fit new big-end bearing shells, regardless of condition, but if the originals are nearly new and it is intended to refit them, make sure that they all go back in their original locations.

2   Generously lubricate the crankpin journals with engine oil and turn the crankshaft so that the crankpin is in the best position for the connecting rod to be assembled to it.

3   Clean and assemble the bearing shell in the big-end bearing cap in a similar way to that in the connecting rod.

4   Generously lubricate the cap bearing shell and offer up the cap to the connecting rod. Fit the locking washer and bolts (early engines) or the bolts and nuts (1275 cc engines) and tighten them to their specified torque (photos). Bend up the locking tabs (where appropriate).

5   When all the connecting rods have been fitted, rotate the crankshaft and check that it is free without intermittent binding.

48.4 Entering the piston into the cylinder bore

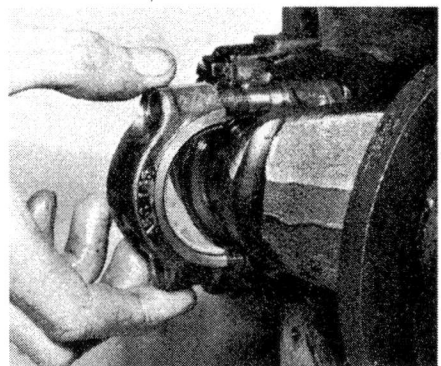

49.4a Fitting a big-end bearing cap ...

49.4b ... and tightening the retaining nuts to the correct torque

50.3 The gauze strainer in position

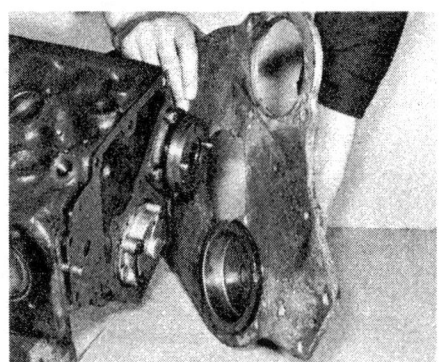

51.2 The rear endplate being fitted

51.5 The flywheel 1/4 mark for the TDC Nos 1 and 4 pistons

50 Gauze strainer and suction pipe – reassembly

1   The gauze strainer and suction pipe should be thoroughly cleaned in petrol, and then blown dry with a compressed air line.
2   Reassembly consists of refitting the gauze strainer to the strainer bracket with the two small bolts and star washers, and then refitting the bracket to the crankcase.
3   One leg rests on the centre main bearing cap, while the other rests on the rear main bearing cap. With spring washers under their heads, tighten down the two support bracket bolts (photo).
4   Reconnect the oil suction pipe to the threaded drilling in the crankcase.

51 Rear endplate and flywheel – refitting

1   Ensure that both the surface of the rear plate and rear cylinder block face are clean.
2   Locate the new gasket and refit the rear end plate (photo), securing with bolts and spring washers.
3   When refitting the flywheel it is important to ensure that it is placed in the correct relative position with the crankshaft.
4   To do this, turn the crankshaft until piston Nos 1 and 4 are at the top of their bores and lock the crankshaft in this position with a wedge of wood between the crankshaft and the crankcase.
5   Wipe the mating surfaces of the crankshaft flange and flywheel clean, and then fit the flywheel so that the marks '1/4' on the flywheel periphery are at the top (photo).
6   Screw in the four bolts and locking plates and tighten the bolts to retain the flywheel at this stage if you have renewed the starter ring. Using a dial test indicator (or clock gauge) mounted on the crankcase check that the flywheel starter ring eccentricity does not exceed 0.010 in (0.254 mm).
7   Tighten the bolts to the specified torque (photo) and bend up the locking tabs; then refit the clutch, referring to Chapter 5 for details.

52 Sump – refitting

1   Make sure that the joint faces on the sump and on the crankcase are clean, with all traces of the old gasket removed.
2   Position a new gasket on the sump flange and visually check that all is well in the crankcase; especially look for any tools, odd hose nuts, rag and so on.
3   Fit the sump into position and install the retaining bolts with a lockwasher under each head, and a special washer between each lockwasher and the sump flange (photo).
4   Progressively and evenly tighten the bolts to the specified torque.

53 Timing sprockets, chain and cover – refitting

1   Before starting the reassembly, check that the shim washers, which were between the crankshaft sprocket and the crankshaft flange before dismantling, are refitted to the crankshaft.
2   Refit the two Woodruff keys in their respective keyways on the crankshaft and on the camshaft, and make sure that they are seated properly. If necessary remove any nicks or burrs by rubbing them on a piece of fine grade emery laid on a flat surface, but don't overdo it or they will fit loosely in the keyways.
3   If new sprockets are being fitted, or if the crankshaft or the camshaft have been changed, the alignment of the sprockets must first be checked and, if necessary, corrected. Fit the sprockets into position on their shafts but without the timing chain; push them fully home and put a straight edge across their two faces. If one of the sprockets is out of line adjust their relative position by adding or removing shim washers behind the crankshaft sprocket (photo). When satisfactory remove the two sprockets.
4   Lay the two sprockets on a flat, clean surface and fit the timing chain, but arrange the position of the sprockets so that the timing marks lie opposite each other on a straight line through the sprocket centres; see Fig. 1.7.
5   Note the position of the keyways in the sprockets and turn the

51.7 Tightening the flywheel retaining bolts to the correct torque

52.3 Refitting the sump

53.3 The crankshaft sprocket adjusting shims (shown with endplate removed)

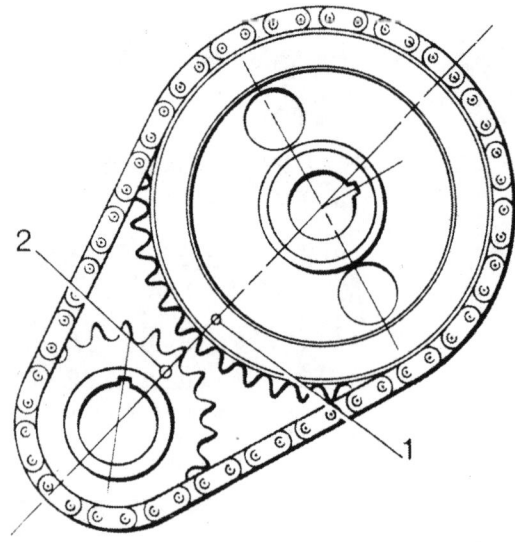

Fig. 1.7 The sprockets and chain assembled in the correct timing position (Sec 53)

1 and 2: Timing marks

camshaft and the crankshaft so that their keys lie in the same relative positions and with the crankshaft keyway at TDC (the camshaft keyway will be at approximately one o'clock viewed from the front). Fit the sprockets and chain assembly to the engine, adjusting the camshaft keyway position if necessary to get them to fit. Check that the timing marks are still in line on the straight line through the sprocket centres (photo).

6   Push the sprockets onto their shafts as far as they will go then fit the camshaft lock washer with its locating tab in the sprocket keyway.

Fit the retaining nut, tighten it securely and then bend up the locktab (photo).

7   Fit the oil thrower to the crankshaft with the concave face, marked 'F' on later engines, facing forward away from the engine (photo).

8   It is worth renewing the oil seal in the timing cover, so carefully knock the old one out using a suitable makeshift drift. Lubricate the new seal and fit it to the cover in the reverse fashion, taking care that the seal is the correct way round and that it is not damaged in the process (photo). Early engines have a felt seal and this should be lubricated thoroughly before fitting to the engine.

9   Check that the timing cover is clean and that all traces of the old gasket have been removed from the joint face. Fit a new gasket to the engine face, using a little grease, if necessary, to hold it in position. To prevent damage to the seal, prefit the crankshaft pulley. Check that the pulley is in good condition and clean, then copiously oil the bearing surface which runs in the seal. Carefully insert it into the seal from the front of the cover, turning it clockwise to help it go in.

10   Give a final check over to the sprockets and chain assembly to make sure that all is well and generously lubricate the chain and sprocket teeth. Push the pulley and cover onto the crankshaft, checking that the key enters the keyway in the pulley. Tap the pulley into position and then fit the cover retaining bolts using spring washers under the heads and the flat washers between the spring washers and cover flange. Tighten the bolts to their specified torques, noting the difference for smaller and larger bolts.

11   Fit the pulley retaining bolt lockwasher into position and then fit either the retaining bolt or the starter handle dog as appropriate. Tighten to the specified torque and bend up the lockwasher.

54 Valves and valve springs – reassembly

1   To gain access above and below the cylinder head, rest it on its side or, alternatively, with the head joint face down on a wooden bench so that it overhangs the bench. Before starting to fit the valves check that all components are thoroughly clean, including the cylinder head, especially if the valves have been ground in.

53.5 The timing sprockets and chain fitted to their shafts

53.6 Tightening the camshaft sprocket retaining nut to the correct torque

53.7 The oil thrower refitted to the crankshaft

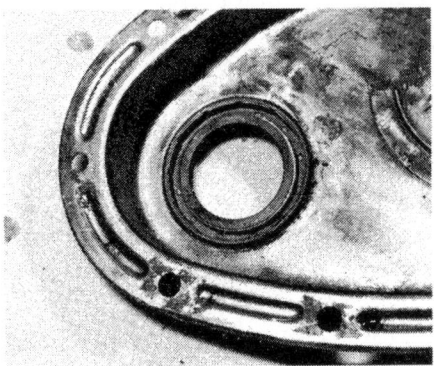

53.8 A new seal fitted to the timing cover (late model)

54.2a Fitting a valve spring seating collar ...

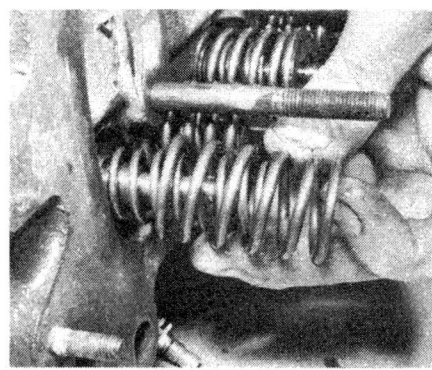

54.2b ... followed by the valve springs ...

54.2c ... and the spring collet plate

54.3 An inlet valve guide seal being fitted (1275 cc engine)

56.5 The cylinder head located on the block

2 Taking each valve in turn, first fit the valve spring seating collar (where applicable) over the top of the valve guide. Lubricate the valve stem and fit the valve to its original guide, if it has not been renewed. Fit the two springs and then fit a new seal to the valve stem, making sure that it sits at the bottom of the collet locating neck, not on the stem. Fit the spring collet plate and, using a spring compressor, compress the springs. Check that the stem seal is still correctly located and fit the two half collets. Release the compression load on the springs ensuring that the half collets sit correctly in the collet plate and on the valve stem. Remove the spring compressor and, on early engines, fit the wire collet clip (photos).

3 On 1275 cc engines a cup type oil seal is fitted to the top of each inlet valve guide. A new seal should be installed before fitting the two valve springs on these engines (photo). Later 1275 cc engines may not have spring seating collars fitted – in this case the valves sit directly on a machined surface on the cylinder head.

4 Repeat this procedure until all valves and springs are fitted, then, using a hammer, strike each valve stem just hard enough to move the valve in order to settle the springs and collets.

55 Rockers and rocker shaft – reassembly

1 Check that the threaded plug in the end of the rocker shaft is tight, and then fit that end of the shaft to the front pedestal bracket and secure it with the retaining grub screw.

2 Slide the springs, rocker arms, pedestal brackets and so on onto the shaft in the same sequence and the same way round that they were originally fitted. Finally fit the end washers and use new split pins to retain them.

56 Cylinder head – refitting

1 After checking that both the cylinder block and cylinder head mating faces are perfectly clean, generously lubricate each cylinder with engine oil.

2 Always use a new cylinder head gasket as the old gasket will be compressed and not capable of giving a good seal. It is also easier at this stage to refit the small hose from the water pump to the cylinder head.

3 Never smear grease on either side of the gasket as when the engine heats up the grease will melt and may allow a compression leak to develop. Never use gasket cement. If a new gasket is used and the head and block faces are true there should be no requirement for it.

4 The cylinder head gasket is marked 'FRONT' and 'TOP' and should be fitted in position according to the markings.

5 With the gasket in position carefully lower the cylinder head onto the cylinder block (photo).

6 With the head in position fit the cylinder head nuts and washers finger tight to the five cylinder head holding-down studs, which remain outside the rocker cover. It is not possible to fit the remaining nuts to the studs inside the rocker cover until the rocker assembly is in position.

7 Fit the pushrods as detailed in the next Section (photo).

8 The rocker shaft assembly can now be lowered over its eight locating studs. Take care that the rocker arms are the right way round. Lubricate the balljoints, and insert the rocker arm balljoints in the pushrod cups (photo). Note: Failure to place the balljoints in the cups can result in the balljoints seating on the edge of a pushrod, or outside it, when the head and rocker assembly is pulled down tight.

9 Fit the four rocker pedestal nuts and washers, and then the four cylinder head stud nuts and washers which also serve to hold down the rocker pedestals. Pull the nuts down evenly, but without tightening them right up.

10 When all is in position, the nine cylinder head nuts and the four rocker pedestal nuts can be tightened down in the order shown in Fig. 1.8. Turn the nuts a quarter of a turn a time and tighten the four rocker pedestal nuts and the nine cylinder head nuts to their separate, specified torques.

56.7 Fitting the pushrods

56.8 The rocker shaft assembly fitted to the cylinder head

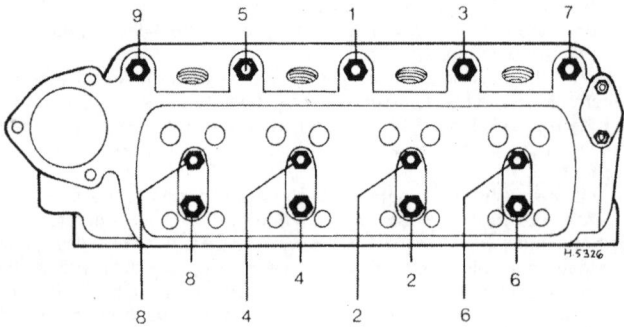

Fig. 1.8 Cylinder head nut tightening sequence (Sec 56)

57 Tappets (cam followers) and pushrods – refitting

1   If not already fitted, generously lubricate the tappets internally and externally and insert them in the bores from which they were removed through the tappet chest, (not 1275 cc engines).

2   With the cylinder head in position fit the pushrods in the same order in which they were removed. Ensure that they locate properly in the stems of the tappets, and lubricate the pushrod ends before fitment.

3   Examine the tappet cover gaskets and the rubber bushes fitted under the cover securing bolt heads. Renew those that are not in good condition, and refit the covers after lubricating the tappets. Tighten the bolts to the specified torque; this is important as overtightening can distort the covers and cause oil leaks.

4   On 1275 cc engines the tappets must be fitted from inside the cylinder block before fitting the camshaft (see Section 45), and there are no tappet covers as on the smaller capacity engines. Fit the pushrods after fitting the cylinder head, if this has been removed, as explained in paragraph 2 above.

58 Valve clearances – adjustment (all models)

1   The valve clearance adjustments should be made with the engine cold. The importance of correct rocker arm/valve stem clearances cannot be overstressed as they vitally affect the performance of the engine.

2   If the clearances are set too wide, the efficiency of the engine is reduced as the valves open late and close earlier than was intended. If, on the other hand, the clearances are set too close, there is a danger that the expansion on heating of the valve and pushrod will not allow the valve to close properly, which will cause burning of the valve head and seat and possible warping.

3   If the engine is in the car, to get at the rockers it is necessary to remove the two holding-down dome nuts from the rocker cover, and then to lift the rocker cover and gasket away.

4   It is important that the clearance is set when the tappet of the valve being adjusted is on the heel of the cam, (ie opposite the peak). This can be effected by carrying out the adjustments in the following order (which also avoids turning the crankshaft more than necessary). Valves are numbered 1 to 8 from the front of the engine.

Valve fully open	Check and adjust
Valve No 8	Valve No 1
Valve No 6	Valve No 3
Valve No 4	Valve No 5
Valve No 7	Valve No 2
Valve No 1	Valve No 8
Valve No 3	Valve No 6
Valve No 5	Valve No 4
Valve No 2	Valve No 7

5   The correct valve clearance is given in the Specifications at the beginning of this Chapter. It is achieved by slackening the hexagonal locknut with a spanner while holding the ball-pin against rotation with a screwdriver. Then, while pressing down with the screwdriver, insert a feeler gauge of the required thickness between the valve stem and thrust pad on the rocker arm. Adjust on the ball-pin until you can move the feeler gauge to and fro and feel a dragging resistance without nipping (photo). Then, still holding the ball-pin, tighten its locknut. Check the clearance again to make sure that it didn't alter when tightening the locknut. Repeat the procedure on all the other valves.

6   If the engine is installed, check that the rocker cover gasket and the rubber bushes under the dome nuts are in good condition, renewing them if necessary, and then refit the cover and gasket and secure with the dome nuts and washers.

59 Distributor drive and distributor – refitting

1   It is important to fit the distributor drive correctly, otherwise the ignition timing will be set totally wrong. It is easy to set the driveshaft in apparently the right position, but in fact exactly 180° out, by not working on the correct cylinder – which must not only be at TDC, but also on the end of the compression and start of the power stroke with both valves closed. The distributor driveshaft should therefore not be fitted until the cylinder head and rocker assembly are fitted, and the timing chain and sprockets assembled so that the valve operations can be seen.

58.5 Adjusting a valve clearance

2   Rotate the crankshaft so that No 1 piston is at TDC at the start of the power stroke. This is when the inlet valve on No 4 cylinder is just opening and the exhaust valve just closing.
3   Screw a $\frac{5}{16}$ in UNF bolt about $3\frac{1}{2}$ in (90 mm) long into the threaded hole in the top of the distributor driveshaft. Insert the end of the driveshaft into its location, but before engaging the skew gears turn the shaft so that the offset drive slot for the distributor dog is aligned horizontally, leaving the larger of the two segments (one on each side of the slot) at the top. Push the shaft home to engage the skew gears; as this happens, the shaft will turn slightly anti-clockwise so that the right-hand end of the drive slot is at about two o'clock (photos). Make another attempt if this position is not achieved. Remove the bolt from the driveshaft when satisfactory.
4   Refit the distributor housing and secure it with the special bolt and washer (photo). Check that the head of the bolt does not protrude above the face of the housing when it has been tightened.
5   Refit the distributor and the two securing bolts and washers which hold the clamp plate to the distributor housing. In doing this, align the marks which were made during dismantling. If the clamp bolt on the clamp plate was not disturbed the ignition timing should be as originally set. However, if the clamp bolt has been loosened, or if alignment marks were not made on dismantling it will be necessary to retime the ignition as explained in Chapter 4.

60 Final assembly – general

1   If they have not already been refitted, fit the two covers to the tappet locations (see Section 57) and fit the rocker cover (see Section 58).
2   As a basic rule, all ancillary components and fittings should be reassembled in the engine before installation, if only because access in almost every instance is easier. This means that the manifolds (with new gaskets), the carburettors (again with new gaskets), the dynamo or alternator as applicable, the thermostat and housing (see Chapter 2), the oil filter element or cartridge as applicable, and the mechanical fuel pump, if appropriate, should all be fitted while the engine is on the bench.
3   If the engine and gearbox were removed as an assembly, refit the gearbox to the engine following the reverse of the procedure for removal. Remember not to allow the weight of the gearbox to rest on the input shaft or the clutch driven plate as it is being assembled.

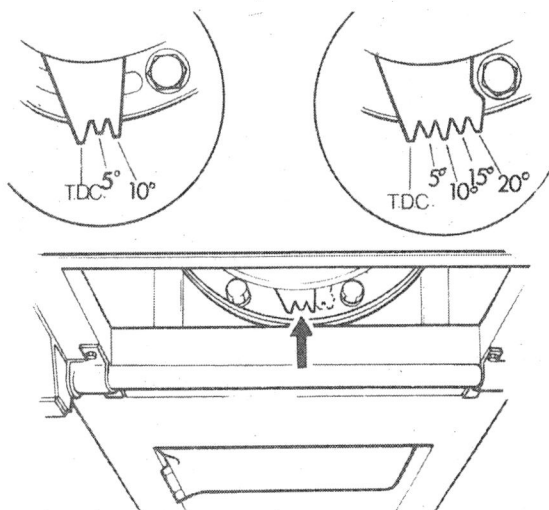

Fig. 1.9 The timing pointer on the timing case cover; later models have more notches. Note that the degrees indicated are BTDC (Sec 59)

61 Engine (without gearbox) – refitting

1   Although the engine can be installed unaided, using a suitable hoist, it is much easier if an assistant is available. This will allow one to control the lowering of the engine while the other guides it into position and ensures that nothing gets caught up. Engine refitting is basically the reverse of the removal procedure, but several aspects need special attention as explained in the following sequence.
2   Connect the lifting tackle to the lifting hooks, or place suitable slings round the front and rear of the engine.

59.3a Use a bolt to insert the distributor driveshaft

59.3b. The distributor driveshaft when No 1 piston is at TDC commencing the power stroke

59.4 The distributor housing being refitted

3   Raise the engine, and if using a fixed hoist, roll the car under it and lower the engine into the engine compartment.

4   When the engine is nearly at rest on the engine mountings, position the car so that the main driveshaft from the gearbox can be cleanly entered in the spigot in the centre of the clutch plate. Do not yet release the engine slings or tighten down the engine mounting bolts.

5   Refit the nuts, bolts, and spring washers which hold the engine endplate to the gearbox bellhousing and remember to refit the earth strap to the bottom right bellhousing bolt on cars where the earth strap is fitted in this position. It is sometimes taken from the gearbox mounting bolt.

6   Do not yet insert the bellhousing bolt which also serves as the attachment point for the exhaust pipe bracket.

7   While under the car securing the bottom bellhousing bolts, refit the starter motor with the two bolts and lockwashers.

8   To line up the mounting bracket holes, it may be necessary to move the engine about slightly, and this will be found much easier to do while the slings are still in position and taking most of the strain. Refit the nuts, bolts, and spring washers to the engine mounting brackets and tighten them finger tight.

9   Lower the engine so that its weight rests on the mountings, tighten the nuts and bolts down securely, and remove the slings or lifting tackle.

10   Refit the exhaust manifold downpipe to the exhaust pipe, refit the clamp, and secure the joint with the two clamp bolts.

11   Refit the exhaust pipe support bracket to its attachment point on the appropriate bellhousing nut and bolt.

12   Reconnect the fuel inlet pipe to the mechanical fuel pump on early models using this type of pump. With models using an SU electrical fuel pump, connect the inlet pipe from the pump to the carburettor(s).

13   Refit the distributor cap and reconnect the high tension leads to the appropriate spark plugs.

14   Reconnect the high tension lead from the centre of the distributor cap to the coil, and the low tension lead from the relevant terminal on the coil to the terminal on the side of the distributor.

15   Reconnect the leads to the dynamo or alternator. The different sized terminals should ensure that no mistake can be made. Also reconnect the starter motor cable to the starter motor.

16   Refit the tachometer drive where applicable.

17   Reconnect the accelerator and choke cables and refit the air cleaner(s) on the carburettor(s).

18   Reconnect the oil pressure sender unit, or the oil pressure gauge pipe line, to the threaded take-off point at the right-hand side of the engine.

19   If the small bypass hose between the cylinder head and the water pump was not refitted when the head was refitted, then this must be done now. This can sometimes be a difficult operation, but should be carried out fairly easily if the small jubilee clips are slipped over each end of the tube, which is then squeezed in a vice, and is quickly fitted before the hose has time to expand to its normal length again.

20   Refit the radiator, heater, and radiator hoses. Always use new hoses if the old hoses show signs of internal or external cracking or other deterioration.

21   Reconnect the water temperature gauge sender unit to the tapped holes at the front right-hand side of the cylinder head or into the thermostat housing on some models.

22   Refit the bonnet (easier with two people) and reconnect the lights, where applicable.

23   Reconnect the battery. Check that the drain taps are closed and refill the cooling system. Replenish the engine with the correct quantity and grade of oil.

24   Refer to Section 63 and run the engine.

62 Engine (with gearbox) – refitting

1   The procedure for refitting the engine and gearbox together as a unit is similar to that for refitting the engine by itself; except that it is easier to fit the starter motor before the power unit is lowered into the engine compartment, and of course all the bellhousing bolts (except the one for the earth lead and the one for the exhaust pipe bracket) will be already tightened into place. Generally, the work is a reversal of the removal sequence, but as an aid to rapid refitting, the following points should be noted.

2   On cars with an enclosed propeller shaft tunnel, the propeller shaft must be mounted on the gearbox mainshaft splines before the rear end of the gearbox enters the transmission tunnel.

3   On cars without an enclosed propeller shaft tunnel, where the shaft can be slid over the gearbox output splines whilst still bolted to the rear axle pinion flange, it is helpful to roll the car forward an inch or two to allow the splines to mate easily.

4   For all models the following applies:

   (a) *With the gearbox mounting bracket in position in the body-frame, refit the four set bolts and spring washers which hold it in place. Do this while the engine is still supported in the slings and before the engine support mounting brackets are tightened down*

   (b) *Rescrew the speedometer cable to the side of the gearbox*

   (c) *Refit the clutch operating cylinder to the bellhousing with the two set bolts and spring washers and bleed the system as detailed in Chapter 5. Reconnect the reversing light switch leads, where fitted*

   (d) *Refit the gear lever, anti-rattle plunger, gearbox retaining plate, and the gear lever cover. Refit the carpeting around the transmission tunnel*

   (e) *Refill the gearbox with the correct grade of oil*

   (f) *Complete the installation as described in the previous Section*

63 Engine – initial start-up after overhaul or repair (all models)

1   Make sure that the battery is fully charged and that all lubricants, coolant and fuel are replenished.

2   If the fuel system has been dismantled, it will require several revolutions of the engine on the starter motor for the mechanical type of fuel pump to fill the system and carburettor(s).

3   If the engine does not fire after repeated attempts check the following points:

   (a) *Ignition and battery leads are securely and correctly connected. Check the spark plug HT lead sequence in particular*

   (b) *The choke is correctly connected and operating*

   (c) *The distributor has been correctly installed and not fitted 180 degrees out*

   (d) *Work systematically through the faults Section at the end of this Chapter*

4   As soon as the engine fires and runs, keep it going at a fast tickover only (no faster) and bring it up to normal working temperature.

5   As the engine warms up there will be odd smells and some smoke from parts getting hot and burning off oil deposits. Look for water or oil leaks, which will be obvious is serious, and listen for abnormal noises. Check also the clamp connection of the exhaust pipe to the manifold, as this sometimes doesn't settle into a gas-tight position until warmth and vibration has acted on it, and it is almost certain that it will need further tightening. This should be done, of course, with the engine stopped.

6   When normal running temperature has been reached, adjust the carburettor slow running and mixture settings as described in Chapter 3.

7   Stop the engine, and after a few minutes recheck it for oil or water leaks. When the engine has cooled, recheck the valve clearances and generally check over the accessible nuts and bolts, hose clips etc for tightness, using the specified torque wrench settings where applicable. Check the oil and coolant levels.

8   Road test the car to check that the timing is correct and gives the necessary power and smooth running, but don't race the engine. If new bearings and/or pistons have been fitted it should be treated as a new engine and progressively run in.

64 Fault diagnosis – engine (all models)

Symptom	Reason(s)
Engine fails to turn over when starter is operated	
No current at starter motor	Flat or defective battery
	Loose battery leads
	Defective starter solenoid or switch, or broken wiring
	Engine earth strap disconnected
Current at starter motor	Jammed starter motor drive pinion
	Defective starter motor
Engine turns but will not start	
No spark at spark plug	Ignition damp or wet
	Ignition leads to spark plugs loose
	Shorted or disconnected low tension leads
	Dirty, incorrectly set, or pitted contact breaker points
	Faulty condenser
	Defective ignition switch
	Ignition leads connected wrong way round
	Faulty coil
	Contact breaker point spring earthed or broken
No fuel at carburettor float chamber or at jets	No petrol in petrol tank
	Vapour lock in fuel line (in hot conditions or at high altitude)
	Blocked float chamber needle valve
	Fuel pump filter blocked
	Choked or blocked carburettor jets
	Faulty fuel pump
Excess of petrol in cylinder or carburettor flooding	Too much choke allowing too rich a mixture to wet plugs
	Float damaged or leaking or needle not seating
	Float lever incorrectly adjusted
Engine stalls and will not start	
No spark at spark plug	Loose connections or breaks in low or high tension circuits
	Contact breaker points require cleaning and resetting
	Defective condenser
	Damp ignition leads and distributor cap
No fuel at jets	No petrol in petrol tank
	Petrol tank breather choked
	Sudden obstruction in carburettor(s)
	Water in fuel system
Engine misfires or idles unevenly	
Intermittent sparking at spark plug	Ignition leads loose
	Battery leads loose on terminals
	Battery earth strap loose on body attachment point
	Engine earth lead loose
	Low tension leads to SW and CB terminals on coil loose
	Low tension lead from CB terminal side to distributor loose
	Dirty, or incorrectly gapped plugs
	Dirty, incorrectly set, or pitted contact breaker points
	Tracking across inside of distributor cover
	Ignition too retarded
	Faulty coil
Fuel shortage at engine	Mixture too weak
	Air leak in carburettor(s)
	Air leak at inlet manifold to cylinder head or inlet manifold to carburettor
Mechanical wear	Incorrect valve clearances
	Burnt out exhaust valves
	Sticking or leaking valves
	Weak or broken valve springs
	Worn valve guides or stems
	Worn pistons and piston rings

Symptom	Reason(s)
Lack of power and poor compression	
Fuel/air mixture leaking from cylinder	Burnt out exhaust valves
	Sticking or leaking valves
	Worn valve guides and stems
	Weak or broken valve springs
	Blown cylinder head gasket
	Worn pistons and piston rings
	Worn or scored cylinder bores
Incorrect adjustments	Ignition timing wrongly set. Too advanced or retarded
	Contact breaker points incorrectly gapped
	Incorrect valve clearances
	Incorrectly set spark plugs
	Carburation too rich or weak
Carburation and ignition faults	Dirty contact breaker points
	Fuel filters blocked causing top end fuel starvation
	Distributor automatic balance weights or vacuum advance and retard mechanisms not functioning correctly
	Faulty fuel pump giving top end fuel starvation
Excessive oil consumption	
Oil being burnt by engine	Badly worn, perished or missing valve stem oil seals
	Excessively worn valve stems and valve guides
	Worn piston rings
	Worn pistons and cylinder bores
	Excessive piston ring gap allowing blow-by
	Piston oil return holes choked
Oil being lost due to leaks	Leaking oil filter gasket
	Leaking rocker cover gasket
	Leaking tappet chest gasket
	Leaking timing case gasket
	Leaking sump gasket
	Loose sump plug

PART B – 1500 cc ENGINE

Special note

The Sections in this 'Part B' of Chapter 1 apply to the 1500 cc engine only. They cover the dismantling, inspection, rebuilding and refitting or renewal of those engine components that differ entirely from those of the smaller engine types.

As mentioned in 'Part A' of this Chapter, we have not included procedures in 'Part B' that are identical to those procedures described in 'Part A' (eg rocker arm/valve clearance adjustment). Therefore, if a particular Section you may require is not listed in the contents of 'Part B', refer to the contents of 'Part A' and look for the Section required, which will be marked 'All models'.

65 General description – 1500 cc engine

The engine is a four-cylinder, overhead valve type. It is supported on rubber mountings to reduce noise and vibration.

Two valves per cylinder are mounted vertically in the cast iron cylinder head and run in pressed-in valve guides. They are operated by rocker arms, pushrods and tappets from the camshaft, which is located at the base of the cylinder bores in the left-hand side of the engine. The correct valve stem-to-rocker arm pad clearance can be obtained by adjusting the screws in the ends of the rocker arms.

The cylinder block and the upper half of the crankcase are cast together. The bottom half of the crankcase consists of a pressed steel sump.

The pistons are made from aluminium alloy with split or solid skirts. Two compression rings and a slotted oil control ring are fitted. The gudgeon pin is retained in the small-end of the connecting rod by

circlips or by interference fit. Renewable shell type big-end bearings are fitted.

At the front of the engine, a single chain drives the camshaft via the camsnaft and crankshaft chain wheels, which are closed in a pressed steel cover. The chain is tensioned automatically by a spring blade, which presses against the non-driving side of the chain, so reducing any lash or rattle.

The camshaft is supported by four bearings bored directly into the cylinder block, except on certain later engines which are fitted with renewable bearings. Endfloat is controlled by a forked retaining plate positioned on the front endplate.

The statically and dynamically balanced forged steel crankshaft is supported by three renewable thinwall shell main bearings, which are in turn supported by substantial webs which form part of the crankcase. Crankshaft endfloat is controlled by semi-circular thrust washers located on each side of the rear main bearing.

The centrifugal water pump and radiator cooling fan are driven, together with an alternator from the crankshaft pulley wheel by a rubber/fabric belt. On cars fitted with exhaust emission control, a double pulley wheel is fitted which also drives the system's air pump by another belt.

The distributor is mounted in the middle of the left-hand side of the cylinder block and advances and retards the ignition timing by mechanical and vacuum means. The distributor is driven at half crankshaft speed by a short shaft and skew gear from a skew gear on the camshaft located between the second and third journals.

The oil pump is located in the crankcase and is driven by a short shaft from the skew gear on the camshaft.

Attached to the end of the crankshaft by four bolts and two dowels is the flywheel, to which is bolted the clutch. Attached to the engine endplate is the gearbox bellhousing.

66 Engine (without gearbox) – removal

1 Remove the bonnet.
2 Disconnect the battery leads from the terminals.
3 Unscrew the heater air intake hose retaining clip and remove the hose.
4 Refer to Chapter 2 and drain the cooling system, then remove the radiator.
5 Undo the four cooling fan bolts and remove the fan.
6 Drain the engine oil.
7 Refer to Chapter 3 and remove the carburettor(s) and air cleaner assembly. After disconnecting the accelerator and choke cables, move them to one side out of the way.
8 Now disconnect the exhaust manifold-to-downpipe clamp bolts.
9 On USA models, the running-on control valve vacuum pipe is next disconnected from the inlet manifold.
10 The heater hose can be disconnected from the water return pipe and the heater control valve hose from the the inlet manifold.
11 From the thermostat housing, remove the water temperature gauge capillary tube, or disconnect the electrical lead from the coolant temperature transmitter, as appropriate.
12 On cars with emission control, disconnect the air supply hose from the check valve and undo the clips supporting the air injection pipe. Unscrew the check valve from the air injection pipe, taking care not to twist the pipe. Disconnect the four unions connecting the pipe to the cylinder head (later systems) or the single union connecting the pipe to the exhaust manifold (earlier systems) and remove the air injection pipe.
13 Disconnect the alternator leads plug from the alternator.
14 Remove the distributor cap and disconnect the HT leads from the spark plugs and coil. Remove the assembly, and then the rotor arm. Disconnect the LT lead from the distributor.
15 On cars with emission control remove the air pump, referring to Chapter 3 if necessary.
16 Disconnect the oil pressure gauge pipe from its engine union or, alternatively, disconnect the lead from the oil pressure transmitter switch.
17 Undo the bolt securing the earth strap to the engine and move the strap out of the way.
18 Remove the supply lead from the starter motor and remove the starter by undoing the two retaining nuts and bolts to release the starter, adaptor plate and shim.
19 Disconnect the fuel feed pipe at the connection adjacent to the bellhousing/engine flange joint.
20 Disconnect the heater hose connection from the heater unit and the inlet manifold T-pipe connection at the rear of the manifold.
21 Remove the nuts, bolts and washers securing the clutch bellhousing to the engine and, on USA models, move the restraint cable out of the way.
22 Position a jack under the gearbox to take its weight and fit slings or suitable lifting tackle to the engine.
23 Take the weight of the engine and undo the engine mountings. Make a thorough, progressive check around the engine that all connections with the rest of the car have been undone and carefully lift the engine. It will be necessary to move the engine forward to withdraw the gearbox input shaft from the clutch, and care must be taken to avoid placing load on the shaft as this is done.
24 Remove the engine from the car.

67 Engine (with gearbox) – removal

1 To remove the engine and gearbox as a complete assembly proceed as described in the previous Section as far as paragraph 18. Although the starter supply lead must be disconnected it is not necessary to remove the starter, although it may be found more convenient to do so at this stage.
2 Remove the three nuts and bolts which secure the front exhaust pipe to the rear pipe and retrieve the olive from the joint.
3 Instead of disconnecting the fuel pipe near the bellhousing, paragraph 19 in the previous Section, disconnect it at the joint in the gearbox tunnel. Whilst in this area, disconnect the reversing light switch leads by separating the connector in the gearbox tunnel and pulling the lead clear of the brake pipe.
4 From underneath the car, undo the front propeller shaft universal joint connecting flange bolts to the gearbox, through the underbody central panel aperture. Mark the flanges to ensure correct mating alignment on reassembly. To enable the shaft to rotate, so that the opposing bolts can be undone, jack up the car at the rear, place chocks under the front wheels and place the gear selector in neutral. Release the handbrake and the propeller shaft may now be rotated by hand from underneath.
5 Withdraw the clutch slave cylinder from the clutch housing by removing the clamp bolt and nut.
6 Withdraw the speedometer drive by unscrewing the retaining clamp bolt and washer. Remove the clamp and disconnect the cable. Withdraw the speedometer drivegear unit from the rear extension housing (photo).
7 On USA models, detach the gearbox restraining cable from the gearbox.
8 Unscrew and remove the gear lever knob.
9 Remove the lever tunnel carpet and unscrew the gear lever gaiter retaining screws. Lift clear the gaiter complete with retaining cover and anti-rattle cap (photo). With the gearchange in neutral, press down the lever and twist it and then lift it clear, collecting the spring and plunger (photo).
10 From underneath, unscrew the two bolts and washers securing the rear gearbox mounting bracket to the floor panel.
11 Next remove the two securing bolts from the rear mounting bracket to the gearbox tunnel.
12 Place the engine lifting slings securely in position to take the weight of the engine unit. The engine will have to be tilted to approximately 70° when lifted, and the slings should therefore be located accordingly with a shorter sling to the front.
13 With the slings in position, lift to take up any slack and then remove the right- and left-hand engine mounting bolts (two each side) and the two nuts on USA models.
14 Check that all of the engine and gearbox attachments to the body and surrounding components are disconnected and carefully lift the engine. An assistant will be needed to lift the gearbox rear coupling over the gearbox tunnel crossmember.
15 With the engine and gearbox lifted clear push the car rearwards and lower the engine/gearbox unit.

67.6 The speedometer drive cable and retaining clamp

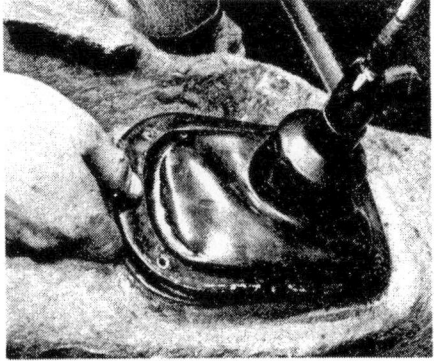
67.9a Removing the gear lever gaiter and retaining cover

67.9b Removing the gear lever assembly

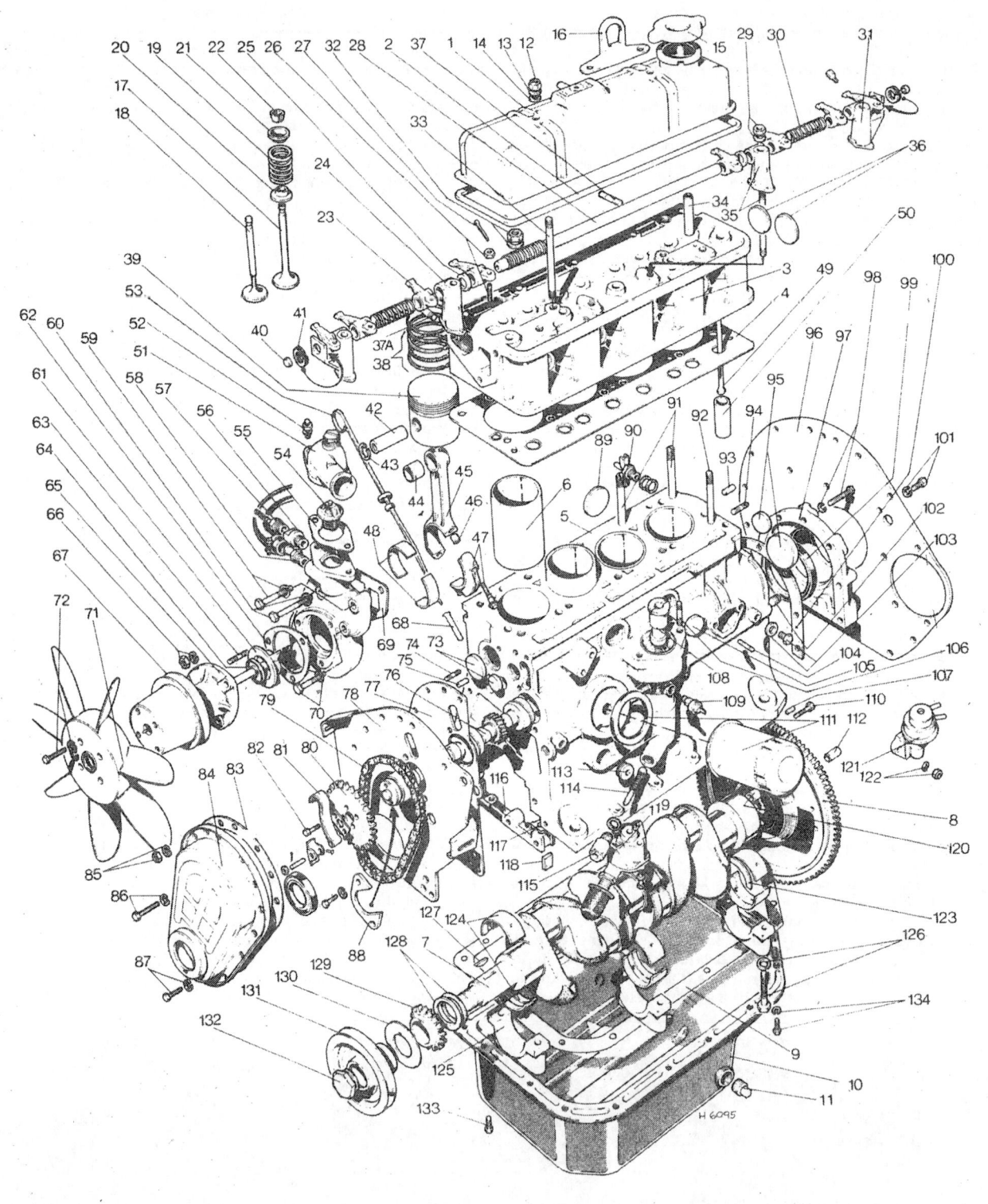

H 6095

Fig. 1.10 Exploded view of a typical 1500 cc engine (Sec 65)

1 Rocker cover
2 Gasket
3 Cylinder head
4 Cylinder head gasket
5 Cylinder block
6 Cylinder liner
7 Crankshaft
8 Starting ring and flywheel
9 Sump gasket
10 Sump
11 Sump drain plug
12 Self-locking nut
13 Washer
14 Fibre washer
15 Oil filler cap
16 Lifting bracket
17 Exhaust valve
18 Inlet valve
19 Valve spring
20 Valve spring seating collar
21 Valve spring collet plate
22 Valve collet
23 Rocker
24 Rocker shaft bracket
25 Spacer
26 Tappet adjusting screw and locknut
27 Split pin
28 Rocker shaft
29 Nut and washer
30 Rocker spacing spring
31 Rocker shaft bracket
32 Head securing nut and washer
33 Rocker cover securing stud
34 Valve guide
35 Rocker shaft bracket and stud
36 Core plugs

37 Inlet manifold stud
37a Exhaust manifold stud
38 Piston rings
39 Piston
40 Plug
41 Spring washer
42 Gudgeon pin
43 Circlip
44 Small-end bush
45 Connecting rod
46 Sleeve
47 Big-end cap and bolts
48 Big-end bearing shells
49 Pushrod
50 Tappet
51 Water pump elbow
52 Elbow securing stud, nut and lockwasher
53 Dipstick
54 Thermostat
55 Gasket
56 Adaptor for temperature sensor
57 Temperature sensor unit
58 Hose adaptor
59 Water pump securing bolt (medium) and washer
60 Water pump securing bolt (long) and washer
61 Spindle and impeller
62 Spindle housing gasket
63 Spindle housing plug
64 Seal
65 Spindle and bearing housing
66 Spindle housing nut and lockwasher
67 Fan pulley and hub
68 Dipstick guide
69 Water pump housing gasket

70 Water pump securing bolt (short) and washer
71 Fan
72 Fan securing bolt and lockwasher
73 Core plugs
74 Stud
75 Dowel
76 Camshaft
77 Gasket
78 Front endplate
79 Timing chain
80 Camshaft sprocket
81 Chain tensioner
82 Sprocket bolt
83 Timing cover gasket
84 Timing cover
85 Timing cover securing nut and lockwasher
86 Timing cover securing bolt and lockwasher (long)
87 Timing cover securing bolt and lockwasher (short)
88 Camshaft locating plate
89 Core plug
90 Drain tap (washer)
91 Head securing studs (grooved)
92 Head securing stud (standard)
93 Dowel
94 Stud
95 Core plugs
96 Rear endplate
97 Rear oil seal housing
98 Seal housing bolt and lockwasher
99 Rear oil seal
100 Oil seal housing gasket
101 Bolt and lockwasher

102 Oil gallery plug
103 Drain plug and washer
104 Securing stud for fuel pump
105 Core plug
106 Securing stud for distributor housing
107 Dowel
108 Distributor driveshaft
109 Oil pressure sensing unit
110 Flywheel bolt
111 Oil filter and seal
112 Sleeve
113 Plug
114 Oil pressure relief valve
115 Relief valve nut
116 Sealing block
117 Gasket
118 Seal
119 Oil pump
120 First motion shaft bush
121 Fuel pump
122 Fuel pump securing nut and lockwasher
123 Rear main bearing thrust washer
124 Main bearing shells
125 Main bearing cap
126 Bearing cap bolt and lockwasher
127 Crankshaft key
128 Adjusting shims
129 Crankshaft sprocket
130 Oil thrower
131 Crankshaft pulley
132 Pulley retaining bolt
133 Sump securing bolt
134 Securing bolt and lockwasher

68 Ancillary engine components – removal

1   Before basic engine dismantling, the following ancillary items must be removed:

  (a) *Alternator*
  (b) *Distributor*
  (c) *Thermostat housing and water pump*
  (d) *Oil filter if it is not already removed with the air pump (USA models)*
  (e) *Inlet and exhaust manifolds, and carburettor(s)*
  (f) *Fuel pump*
  (g) *Starter motor, if not already removed*

2   Remove the alternator from its bracket complete with spacer.
3   Rotate the crankshaft to align the timing notches on the crankshaft pulley to the 10° BTDC mark on the timing indicator or 2° ATDC for California models only. Check that the distributor rotor arm is in the firing position for number 1 spark plug, and lightly mark the distributor body opposite the rotor arm pointer. Undo the two flange nuts and spring washers and remove the distributor. Note and retain the shims between the housing and the block. Do not loosen the square nut on the clamp on the base of the distributor or the timing will be lost. Remove the spark plugs.
4   The distributor/oil pump driveshaft can also be withdrawn from the block at this stage.
5   Unscrew and remove the oil filter.
6   Undo the water pump retaining nuts and lightly tap it away from the block at the front, complete with thermostat.
7   If they have not already been removed, disconnect the inlet and exhaust manifolds together with the carburettor(s) from the cylinder head. Note the bridging 'plate washers' between the two manifolds on the top row of the studs. The inner nuts are best removed with a thin ring spanner.
8   Remove the two manifolds together. If stiff, lightly tap the manifolds with a piece of wood.
9   Remove the fuel pump from the block by unscrewing the two retaining nuts and washers.
10 Remove the starter motor, if applicable, by unscrewing the two retaining nuts and washers, and withdrawing the motor complete with shims and adaptor plate.

69 Cylinder head (engine in car) – removal

1   Due to the various different arrangements of emission control systems that have been introduced, and the changes that have occurred over the years, it is not possible to provide a straightforward removal procedure to suit all installations. However, by using the broad outline of the basic work involved which follows as a guide, it should be possible, by modifying it to suit your own particular car's arrangement, to remove the cylinder head with the engine in the car with few problems.
2   Disconnect the battery connections.
3   Drain the cooling system as described in Chapter 2.
4   Disconnect and remove the carburettor(s).
5   Remove the temperature transmitter from the thermostat housing.
6   Remove the fanguard and slacken the alternator adjusting link bolt.
7   Remove the three bolts securing the thermostat housing/water pump to the cylinder head.
8   Disconnect and remove the coolant and air hoses impeding access to, or connected to, the cylinder head and the manifolds. These, of course, vary with installations.
9   Disconnect the exhaust pipe from the exhaust manifold.
10 Disconnect the HT leads from the spark plugs and remove the leads together with the distributor cap.
11 Remove the rocker cover fasteners and remove the rocker cover.
12 Undo the four nuts securing the rocker shaft assembly to the cylinder head and remove the assembly.
13 Remove the pushrods, identifying them so that they can be refitted in their original locations.
14 Remove the ten cylinder head nuts following the reverse sequence to that shown in Fig. 1.14. Slacken the nuts in sequence progressively before removing them.

15 Remove the engine lifting bracket and then remove the cylinder head from the engine.

70 Cylinder head (engine on bench) – removal

The sequence for removing the cylinder head with the engine removed from the car is basically the same as for the later operations of its removal in the car. Therefore refer to Section 69 and follow the instructions given in paragraphs 11 to 15.

71 Engine and gearbox – separation

1   With the engine and gearbox removed from the car, disconnect the starter motor unit (if this has not already been done) by unscrewing the two retaining nuts and washers.
2   Withdraw the starter motor from the clutch housing complete with shim and adaptor plate.
3   Undo the respective gearbox to engine retaining bolts around the clutch housing and withdraw the engine from the gearbox. Do not let the gearbox hang on the first motion shaft unsupported, or damage may occur.

72 Crankshaft and main bearings – removal

1   With the engine removed from the car remove the water pump, the timing cover, chain and sprockets, the sump, the oil pump, the clutch and the flywheel, referring if necessary to the appropriate Sections elsewhere for details.
2   Remove the seven securing screws and remove the engine rear adaptor plate from the cylinder block.
3   Remove the two bolts securing the camshaft locating plate and remove the plate.
4   Remove the three bolts securing the front mounting plate to the block and remove the mounting plate.
5   Remove the crankshaft Woodruff key and any shims that may have been fitted behind the crankshaft sprocket wheel.
6   Remove the two screws retaining the front sealing block which is located across the No 1 main bearing cap, and remove the sealing block and its gaskets.
7   Undo the seven bolts securing the crankshaft rear oil seal housing to the block, and remove the housing with the rear oil seal in it.
8   Note the identification marks on the big-end and main bearing caps for reference during reassembly.
9   Remove the big-end bearing cap bolts from each connecting rod and remove the caps and half bearing shells.
10 Undo and remove the main bearing cap bolts. Remove the caps and half bearing shells. Remove the two semi-circular thrust washers from the rear main bearing and make sure that, when they need to be refitted, you will be able to fit each in the correct location.
11 Carefully lift out the crankshaft and retrieve the upper half bearing shells from the main bearings and the connecting rod big-ends. In each case identify them so that, if you do not intend to renew them, they can all be refitted in their original positions.

73 Rocker shaft assembly – dismantling

1   With the rocker shaft assembly removed from the cylinder head, take out the split pin from the front end of the shaft and carefully slide off the rockers, pedestals, springs and spacers noting the sequence of components for use on reassembly.
2   Remove the screw in the rear pedestal to release the shaft from the pedestal and slide the pedestal off together with the washer and rocker.

74 Timing cover, sprockets and chain – removal

1   If the engine is installed in the car, some removal or repositioning of components will be necessary before the crankshaft pulley can be removed, more especially in the case of USA models. For this reason separate procedures are provided up to the removal of the pulley.

UK models

2   Refer to Chapter 2 and drain the cooling system, remove the radiator and the fan. Slacken the alternator mounting bolts and remove the fanbelt.

3   Undo and remove the pinch bolt and nut from the bottom of the steering column. Remove the two bolts and washers in each clamp securing the steering rack to its mounting brackets. Then remove the three bolts and washers which secure each mounting bracket to the chassis crossmember.

4   Remove the mounting brackets, but look out for packing washers fitted under the bracket at the pinion end of the rack. Keep these washers carefully so that they can be refitted on reassembly.

5   Disconnect the steering column from the rack pinion shaft and carefully ease the rack forwards and downwards to provide access to the crankshaft pulley nut.

6   Lock the crankshaft by engaging top gear and applying the handbrake fully. Undo the pulley retaining nut and remove the pulley from the crankshaft.

USA and Canada models

7   Refer to Chapter 2 and drain the cooling system, remove the radiator and the fan.

8   With a suitable receptacle to catch oil spillage, remove the oil filter by unscrewing it from its mounting. Disconnect the hose from the air pump, and remove the pump and its drivebelt.

9   Slacken the alternator mounting bolts and remove the fanbelt.

10 Refer to Chapter 3 and remove the carburettor.

11 Remove the pre-heater duct after pressing in its retaining clips.

12 Remove the six nuts retaining the catalytic converter to the exhaust manifold.

13 Support the engine on a jack with a piece of wood interposed to protect the sump.

14 Remove the nuts, bolts and washers securing both engine front mountings to the mounting plate.

15 Carefully lift the engine assembly sufficient for removal of the crankshaft pulley.

16 Undo the pulley nut; as this will be tight, lock the crankshaft by engaging top gear and fully applying the handbrake. Remove the pulley from the crankshaft.

Engine on the bench

17 With the engine on the bench the only likely difficulty will be to restrain the crankshaft whilst undoing the pulley retaining nut. If the starter is removed, a large screwdriver or other suitably strong item can be inserted to jam the flywheel starter ring teeth. Alternatively, if the sump is going to be removed, do this now and interpose a block of wood between a crankshaft throw and the inner wall of the crankcase to prevent rotation. Undo the nut and remove the pulley.

All models, installed or on the bench

18 If difficulty is experienced in removing the crankshaft pulley, use two large levers to ease it off, or use a universal puller.

19 On UK models, remove the eleven setscrews and the one nut together with their washers (or on USA and Canada models, remove the eight setscrews, the one bolt, the three nuts together with their washers) and spacer securing the timing cover to the block and, on USA and Canada models, the air pump adjusting links.

20 Where fitted, remove the bottom air pump bolt and the spacer.

21 Remove the timing cover together with its gasket. It's worth checking the timing chain at this stage to see it if will need renewing on reassembly. Lay a straight edge along the slack leg of the chain run and measure the extent of chain slack from the straight edge. If it is more than 0.4 in (10 mm) the chain should be renewed.

22 Turn the crankshaft to align the timing marks, referring to Fig. 1.12. To turn the crankshaft, chock the front wheels and jack one of the rear wheels clear of the ground; check that the jack supporting the engine (USA and Canada cars procedure only) is stable. Release the handbrake and select top gear. By rotating the rear wheel in the forward roll direction, the engine can be turned in the normal direction of rotation. The marks on the two sprockets should be adjacent to each other on a straight line joining the two sprocket centres.

23 Remove the oil thrower from the crankshaft and bend back the locktabs on the camshaft sprocket bolts. Note that an alignment mark on the camshaft sprocket is adjacent to the one on the camshaft which can be seen through one of the holes in the camshaft sprocket – if there are no alignment mark(s), make one. Undo and remove the two camshaft sprocket retaining bolts.

76.2 Removing the distributor and pedestal

24 From this stage on, take care not to move the camshaft or crankshaft. Ease the two sprocket wheels off their shafts complete with timing chain; if necessary, use two suitable levers to do this, working on alternate sprockets until the assembly is free. Retrieve the crankshaft drive key to prevent its loss, and remove the shim washers from behind the crankshaft sprocket if any are fitted.

75 Timing chain tensioner – removal, inspection and refitting

1   The spring blade timing chain tensioner is located in the timing cover and should be renewed at the same time as the timing chain. Wear can be clearly seen as two grooves on the face of the tensioner where it presses against the chain.

2   To remove the tensioner, bend it back and then pull out from its securing pin.

3   On refitting, fit the open end of the tensioner over the pin and press the blade into place with the aid of a screwdriver until it snaps into its location.

76 Distributor driveshaft – removal

1   To remove the distributor driveshaft with the sump still in position, first undo the two nuts which hold the distributor pedestal in place.

2   Lift off the distributor and distributor pedestal (photo), and then with a pair of long-nosed pliers, lift out the driveshaft. As the shaft is removed, turn it slightly to allow the shaft skew gear to disengage from the camshaft skew gear.

77 Camshaft – removal

1   The camshaft can be removed with the engine installed in the car, but only at the expense of extensive dismantling. This work has already been described elsewhere in this Chapter and consists, in brief, of the following. Drain the cooling system, remove the radiator, and water pump housing. Remove the timing cover, sprockets and chain. Remove the cylinder head and gasket. Remove the fuel pump.

2   Where the engine has been removed from the car it should also be dismantled down to the same state; then proceed as follows.

3   Remove the distributor drive as described in the previous Section. Then withdraw the tappets from their locations in the cylinder block, but make sure that each is identified so that they can all be refitted in their original positions on reassembly.

4   Next check the camshaft endfloat before removing it. To do this, move the camshaft fully forward against the locating plate and measure the gap between the back of the camshaft drive flange and the front of the locating plate using feeler gauges. Compare the endfloat with that listed in the Specifications to this Chapter; if it is excessive, the locating plate will need renewing.

5   Undo and remove the two bolts securing the camshaft locating plate and remove the plate. Withdraw the camshaft, but be careful that the sharp edges of the cam lobes do not damage the bearings.

78 Lubrication and crankcase ventilation systems – description

1   A forced feed system of lubrication is fitted, with oil circulated round the engine from the sump below the block. The level of engine oil in the sump is indicated on the dipstick, which is fitted on the right-hand side of the engine. It is marked to indicate the optimum level, which is the maximum mark.
2   The level of the oil in the sump, ideally, should not be above or below this line. Oil is replenished via the filler cap on the rocker cover.
3   The eccentric rotor-type oil pump is bolted in the left-hand side of the crankcase, and is driven by a short shaft from the skew gear on the camshaft which also drives the distributor shaft.
4   The pump is the non-draining variety to allow rapid pressure building-up when starting from cold.
5   Oil is drawn into the pump from the sump via the pick-up pipe. From the oil pump the lubricant passes through a non-adjustable relief valve to the full-flow filter. Filtered oil enters the main gallery which runs the length of the engine on the left-hand side. Drillings from the main gallery carry the oil to the crankshaft and camshaft journals.
6   The crankshaft is drilled so that oil under pressure reaches the crankpins from the crankshaft journals. The cylinder bores, pistons and gudgeon pins are all lubricated by splash and oil mist.
7   Oil is fed to the valve gear via the hollow rocker shaft at a reduced pressure by means of a scroll and two flats on the camshaft rear journal.
8   Drillings and grooves in the camshaft front journal lubricate the camshaft thrust plate, and the timing chain and gearwheels. Oil returns to the sump by gravity, the pushrods and cam followers being lubricated by oil returning via the pushrod drillings in the block.
9   The standard crankcase ventilation system is the closed type where air enters the oil filler cap on the rocker cover. This air and internal fumes from the engine are drawn through an oil separator/flame trap in the top of the rocker cover, then through hoses to the carburettors where the gas mixes with the induction charge to be burnt in the engine.
10   On USA and Canada cars fitted with emission control, the system is similar to the closed ventilation system, but more efficient and complex. The tube from the rocker cover is interconnected between the carburettor and the primary charcoal absorption canister. The engine normally draws air from the breather hole in the oil filler cap in the rocker cover. However, systems that have a carburettor fuel evaporative loss control have a sealed oil filler cap, and instead draw air through the two charcoal absorption canisters. The airflow from the canisters goes to the rocker cover and the feed pipe incorporates a restricter connection to the carburettor.

79 Oil filter – removal and refitting

1   Located on the left-hand side of the engine, the oil filter is of the disposable cartridge type.

2   To remove the filter on USA and Canada cars, first disconnect the air pump hose. On all cars place a container underneath and unscrew the cartridge and discard it. If the cartridge will not unscrew by hand, a chain or strap wrench will be needed.
3   Prior to fitting the new cartridge, wipe the jointing surfaces clean and smear the new seal with clean engine oil.
4   Fit the seal to the cartridge groove, screw the adaptor into the block, and hand-tighten the cartridge (photo). Reconnect the air pump hose, where applicable.
5   With the engine refilled with oil, start it and check the cartridge joint to the cylinder block for any signs of leakage.
6   If there are signs of a leak, stop the engine, remove the cartridge and check the seal for correct seating.
7   On completion allow the oil to settle for a few minutes, then check the level and top up if necessary.

80 Oil pump – removal and dismantling

1   To remove the oil pump, it is necessary to drain the engine oil and remove the sump and gasket.
2   Loosen the oil strainer locknut and then unscrew the strainer from the oil pump cover.
3   Now unscrew the three oil pump retaining bolts and washers, and remove the pump unit.
4   To dismantle, remove the cover plate and withdraw the inner rotor shaft assembly. Then remove the outer rotor.

81 Crankshaft – refitting

1   Ensure that the crankcase is thoroughly clean and that all oilways are clear. A thin twist drill or a pipe cleaner is useful for cleaning them out. If possible, blow them out with compressed air. Treat the crankshaft in the same fashion, and then inject engine oil into the crankshaft oilways. Commence work on rebuilding the engine by refitting the crankshaft and main bearings.
2   If the original main bearing shells are being refitted (and it is false economy not to renew them unless the originals are virtually as new), fit the three upper halves of the main bearing shells in their original positions in the crankcase after wiping their locations clean (photo).
3   If new bearing shells are being fitted, carefully clean off all traces of the protective grease with which they are coated before fitting them to the crankcase.
4   Note that on each half shell there is a locating tag which must be fitted to the recess in either the crankcase or bearing cap housing location.
5   With the three upper bearing shells securely in place, wipe the lower bearing cap housings and fit the three lower shell bearings to their caps ensuring that the right shell goes into the right cap if the old bearings are being refitted.
6   Wipe the recesses either side of the rear main bearing which locate the thrust washers.
7   Generously lubricate the crankshaft journals and the upper and lower main bearing shells, and carefully lower the crankshaft into place (photo).
8   Fit the upper halves of the thrust washers into their grooves on

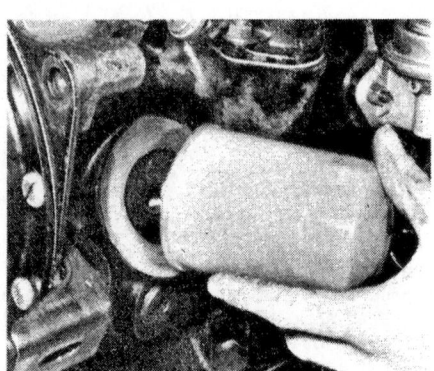

79.4 Fitting a new oil filter cartridge

81.2 Fitting a new main bearing shell to the crankcase; note the half thrust washer in position

81.7 The crankshaft being installed

each side of the rear main bearing, rotating the crankshaft in the direction towards the main bearing tabs (so that the main bearing shells do not slide out). At the same time feed the thrust washers into their locations with their oil grooves outwards away from the bearing.

9   Fit the main bearing caps in position ensuring that they locate properly (photo). The mating surfaces must be spotlessly clean or the caps will not seat correctly. As the bearing caps were assembled to the cylinder block and then line bored during manufacture, it is essential that they are returned to the same positions from which they were removed.

10 Refit the main bearing cap bolts and washers and tighten the bolts to their specified torque (photo).

11 Test the crankshaft for freedom of rotation. Should it be very stiff to turn or exhibit high spots, that is, intermittently free and stiff, then a most careful inspection must be made, preferably by a skilled mechanic, to trace the cause of the trouble. Fortunately it is very seldom that any trouble of this kind is experienced after taking care during the fitting of the bearings and crankshaft.

12 Move the crankshaft hard in one direction along its length and, using feeler gauges, measure the amount of endfloat (photo). This should be within the specified limits but, if it is not, new or oversize thrust washers will need to be fitted.

13 Next fit the sealing block and gaskets over the front main bearing cap. Smear the ends of the block with jointing compound and fit the gaskets and the block in place. Fit the securing screws but do not tighten fully. Fit new wedge seals at each end and line up the front face of the block with the front of the cylinder block (photo).

14 Do not fully tighten the securing screws until the front plate is in position (see Section 83). This prevents any distortion between the sealing block and plate.

15 When the plate is fitted, fully tighten the screws and cut the wedge seals flush with the crankcase flange.

82 Connecting rods to crankshaft – reassembly

1   Wipe the connecting rod half of the big-end bearing cap and the underside of the shell bearing clean, and fit the shell bearing in position with its locating tongue engaged with the corresponding rod.

2   If the old bearings are nearly new and are being refitted, then ensure that they are refitted in their respective locations on the correct rods.

3   Generously lubricate the crankpin journals with engine oil, and turn the crankshaft so that the crankpin is in the most advantageous position for the connecting rod to be drawn onto it.

4   Wipe the connecting rod bearing cap and back of the shell bearing clean and fit the shell bearing in position, ensuring that the locating tongue at the back of the bearing engages with the locating groove in the connecting rod cap (photo).

5   Generously lubricate the shell bearing and offer up the connecting rod bearing cap to the connecting rod.

6   The makers recommend that new bolts are fitted to the connecting rod big-ends on reassembly; tighten them to their specified torque noting that this varies with the type of bolt used.

7   When all the connecting rods have been fitted, rotate the crankshaft to check that everything is free, and that there are no high spots causing binding.

83 Camshaft and front endplate – refitting

1   Fit a new gasket in place over the front of the cylinder block. Lightly smear it with a gasket cement to locate it.

2   Now locate the front endplate into position over the location dowel and stud in the front of the cylinder block (photo). Loosely refit the respective screws and nuts into position.

3   Tighten the two lower screws first (photo) and then tighten the crankshaft sealing block retaining screws. Now tighten the three bolts in the front of the plate.

4   Wipe the camshaft bearing journals clean and lubricate them generously with engine oil.

5   If a new camshaft is being fitted, use a centre punch to mark it in exactly the same position as the mark on the front of the drive flange on the old camshaft.

81.9 Fitting a main bearing cap and ...

81.10 ... tightening the cap bolts to the correct torque

81.12 Measuring crankshaft endfloat

81.13 The crankcase sealing block fitted over the front main bearing cap

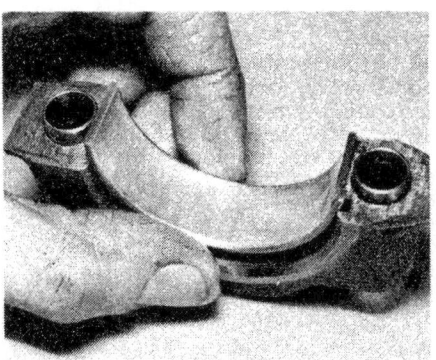

82.4 Fitting a bearing shell to a connecting rod big-end cap

83.2 The front endplate being fitted ...

83.3 ... and the two lower screws being tightened first

83.6 The camshaft being installed ...

83.7 ... and its locating plate being fitted

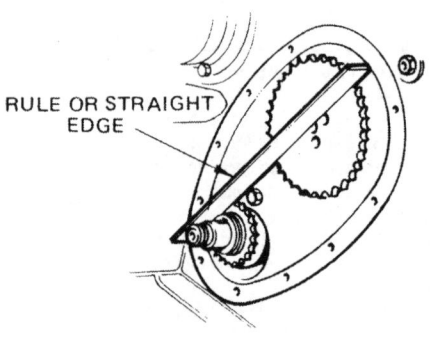

Fig. 1.11 Method of checking sprocket tooth alignment (Sec 84)

84.2a Fitting the shim washers to the crankshaft and ...

84.2b ... fitting the crankshaft key

6   Gently insert the camshaft into the crankcase (photo) taking care not to damage the camshaft bearings with the cams.
7   Refit the camshaft locating plate and tighten down the two retaining bolts and washers (photo).
8   With a feeler gauge, check that the camshaft endfloat is within the specified tolerance. If it is not, renew the camshaft locating plate.

84 Timing sprockets, chain, chain tensioner, and cover – refitting

1   Check that the shim washers, if any, are refitted to the crankshaft. Leave the crankshaft key out of its key slot for the moment.
2   Fit the two sprockets into position on their shafts but without the timing chain; push them fully home and put a straight edge across their two faces. If one of the sprockets is out of line adjust their relative position by adding or removing shim washers behind the crankshaft sprocket. When satisfactory remove the two sprockets and fit the crankshaft key (photos).
3   Lay the sprockets on a clean surface so that the two timing marks are adjacent to each other. Slip the timing chain over them and pull the sprockets back into mesh with the chain so that the timing marks, although further apart, are still adjacent to each other.
4   With the timing marks adjacent to each other, hold the sprockets above the crankshaft and camshaft. Turn the camshaft and crankshaft so that the Woodruff key will enter the slot in the crankshaft sprocket, and the camshaft sprocket is in the correct position relative to the camshaft. This will be indicated by being able to see the alignment mark on the camshaft driving flange, through the hole in the camshaft sprocket, nearest to the alignment mark near the bolt holes – see Fig. 1.12. Some models do not have these alignment marks, so use the marks made at dismantling. If new components are being used, position the camshaft so that, when standing at the front of the car and looking backwards, the larger groove in the flange is to the left. This groove should be visible through the sprocket hole (see photo 84.6).
5   Fit the timing chain and sprockets assembly onto the camshaft and crankshaft, keeping the timing marks adjacent to each other (photo). Fit a new double tab washer in place on the camshaft sprocket, then fit and tighten the two retaining bolts to their specified

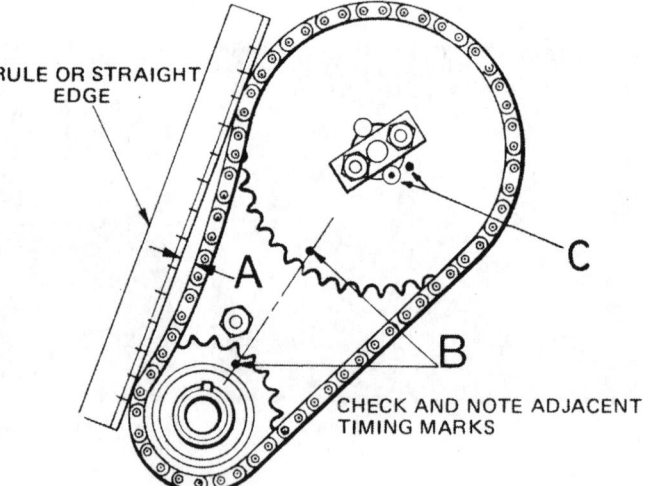

Fig. 1.12 Checking chain wear and aligning timing sprockets (Sec 84)

A   Measure maximum deflection to assess chain wear
B   Timing marks aligned and on straight line between sprocket centres
C   Sprocket-to-camshaft alignment marks

torque.
6   Lever up the tabs on the lockwasher to lock the bolts (photo).
7   The oil seal in the front cover should be renewed before refitting the cover. Press or lever the old seal out, taking care to avoid damaging the cover.
8   Lubricate the new seal with engine oil and carefully press or tap it into position in the cover, ensuring that the seal lip will face in towards the crankshaft sprocket on assembly (photo).
9   Fit the oil deflector onto the crankshaft (photo). Make sure that the dished periphery is towards the cover when it is fitted. Generously

84.5 The timing sprockets and chain fitted to their shafts

84.6 Bending up the lockwasher tabs

84.8 A new seal fitted to the timing cover

84.9 The oil deflector being fitted to the crankshaft

84.10 With a new gasket fitted to the block, refit the timing cover

84.13 Refitting the crankshaft pulley

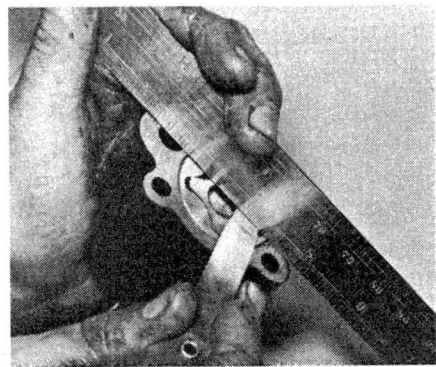

85.2 Measuring the oil pump rotor endfloat ...

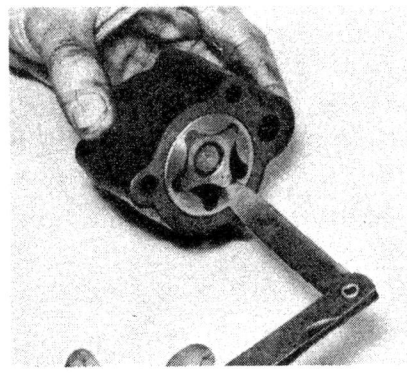

85.3 ... and the lobe clearance

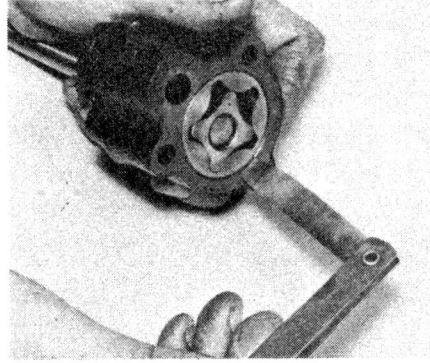

85.4 Measuring the outer rotor-to-body clearance

lubricate the chain and sprockets with engine oil and visually check that all is ready for fitting the cover.

10 Fit a new gasket to the endplate, making sure that it is properly located on the dowels (photo).

11 It may be possible to fit the cover by holding it at an angle, so that the chain tensioner can be first located, then swinging the cover into its correct position. Alternatively, use a bent piece of stiff wire to hold the tensioner away from the chain while the cover is being put on and, just before pushing the cover home, carefully remove the wire, making sure that the gasket is not damaged in the process.

12 Refit the setscrews, nut(s) and bolt (where appropriate) with their washers and spacer to their original positions and tighten them progressively and evenly to their specified torque.

13 Check that the crankshaft pulley is clean and undamaged and oil the seal housing surface. Carefully insert the pulley into the seal, aligning the keyway with the key, and push it fully home (photo). Fit the retaining nut.

14 Tighten the retaining nut to its specified torque. To hold the crankshaft whilst this is done, insert a clean piece of wood between the crankshaft and crankcase if the engine is on the bench or, if

installed, make sure that both rear wheels are on the ground, that the handbrake is fully on, and that top gear is selected.

85 Oil pump – examination and renovation

1 Thoroughly clean and dry all the component parts before checking the rotor endfloat and lobe clearances in the following manner.

2 Fit the rotors into the pump body, but make sure that the chamfered edge on the outer rotor is at the driving end of the body of the pump. Lay a straight edge across the pump body face and measure the clearance between the rotors and the straight edge using feeler gauges (photo).

3 Next measure the clearance between the crest of the inner rotor lobes and the outer rotor at the points midway between each of the five extremities of the internal space (photo).

4 Finally slide a feeler gauge between the outer rotor and the pump body to measure the diametrical clearance (photo).

5 Compare the measured clearances with those quoted in the

Specifications; if any are excessive a new pump should be fitted. It would also be worth fitting a new pump even if the clearances are just on the permitted limit, where the engine is undergoing major overhaul or you have had problems with oil pressure.

6 Examine all components for scoring or other signs of damage and check the cover plate for distortion. Examine the pump driveshaft bearing surface and the related pump body bearing surface for signs of excessive wear or scoring. Renew the pump where necessary or where any doubt exists.

86 Oil pump – refitting

1 Fit the pump assembly to the crankcase, and check that the driveshaft engages with the drivegear if this has not been removed.
2 Prime the pump with engine oil to reduce any possibility of oil starvation when the engine starts.
3 Refit the cover and strainer to the pump and tighten down the three securing bolts and washers (photo).

87 Crankshaft rear oil seal, rear endplate, and flywheel – refitting

1 If it has not already been done, remove the old seal from the crankshaft rear oil seal housing and clean the housing. Lightly grease the outside of a new seal and carefully press or tap it into the housing with the lip facing in towards the crankshaft bearings.
2 Check that all traces of the old gasket have been removed from the crankcase joint face and apply a film of fresh jointing compound. Then position a new gasket on the joint face.
3 Lubricate the seal bearing surface on the crankshaft with oil and carefully fit the seal and its housing on to the crankshaft and bed the housing onto the new gasket (photo).
4 Fit the seven retaining bolts and washers, but make sure that the top bolt has a plain copper washer under its head (photo). Turn the crankshaft over several times to centralise the seal, then progressively and evenly tighten the bolts to their specified torque.

5 No gasket is fitted between the rear endplate and the block. Check that the plate and its mounting face are clean and position the plate on its locating dowels in the block. Fit and tighten the seven retaining bolts and washers (photo).
6 Clean the end of the crankshaft on which the flywheel mounts, and make sure that the spigot bush is correctly positioned in its location in the end of the shaft. Clean the mating face of the flywheel and fit it to the crankshaft locating it on its dowel.
7 Fit the four retaining bolts and tighten them to their specified torque (photo).
8 If the starter ring gear has been renewed, a concentricity check should be made using a dial test indicator gauge (clock gauge). Mount the gauge on the rear endplate and measure the concentricity on the gear teeth crests. This should not exceed that quoted in the Specifications. After this, check the run-out of the flywheel by mounting the gauge to register at a point 3.0 in (76.2 mm) from the flywheel axis and rotate the crankshaft. Run-out, or wobble on the flywheel face, should not exceed that quoted in the Specifications.
9 Refer to Chapter 5 and refit the clutch assembly.

88 Sump – refitting

1 After the sump has been thoroughly cleaned, scrape all traces of the old sump gasket from the sump and crankcase flanges, fit a new a gasket in place, and then refit the sump (photo).
2 Insert and tighten down the sump bolts and washers. The four longer bolts fit to the rear sump strengthening plates (photo).

89 Valves and valve springs – reassembly

1 To gain access above and below the cylinder head, rest it on its side or, alternatively, with the head joint face down on a wooden bench so that it overhangs the bench. Before starting to fit the valves, check that all components are thoroughly clean, including the cylinder head, especially if the valves have been ground in.

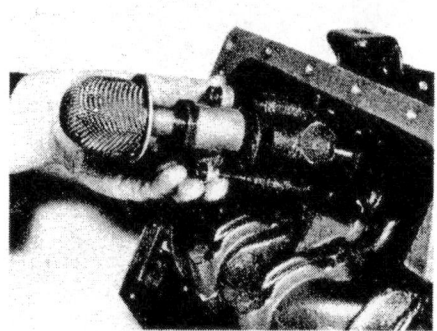
86.3 Refitting the oil pump cover and strainer

87.3 After refitting the crankshaft rear seal housing ...

87.4 ... make sure that a copper plain washer is fitted under the top retaining bolt

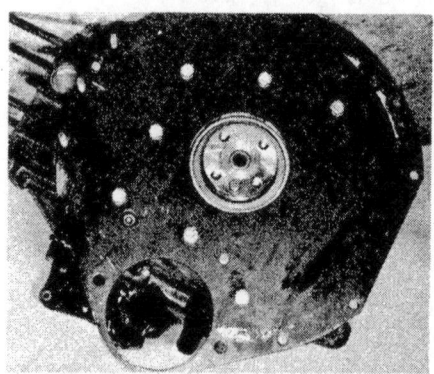
87.5 The rear endplate fitted to the block

87.7 Tightening the flywheel retaining bolts to the correct torque

88.1 The sump being refitted

88.2 Fit the longer bolts in the sump rear reinforcing plates

89.2a Fitting the valve springs ...

89.2b ... and using a spring compressor in order to fit the valve stem collets

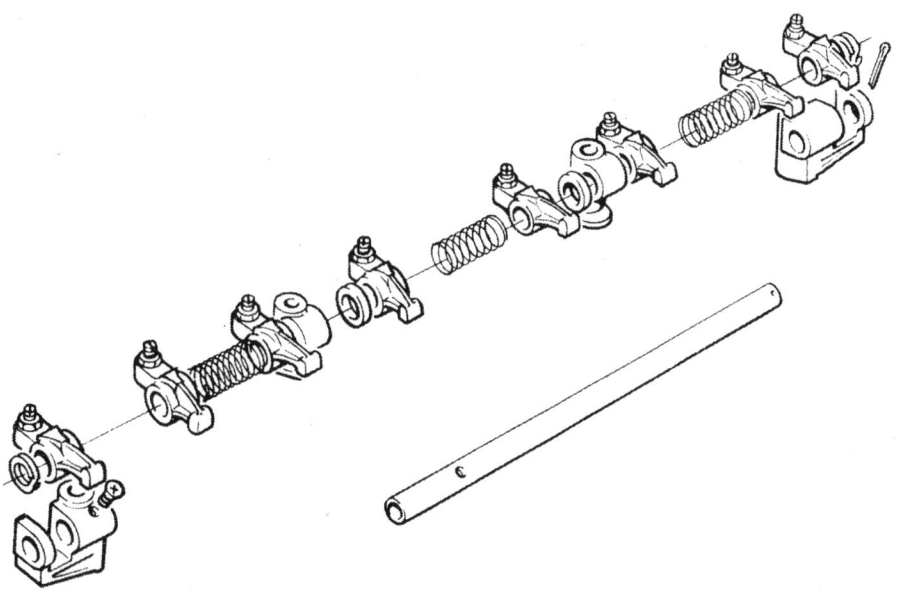
Fig. 1.13 The component parts of the rocker shaft assembly (Sec 90)

2   Taking each valve in turn, first fit the valve spring seating collar over the top of the valve guide. Lubricate the valve stem and fit the valve to its original guide if it has not been renewed. Fit the two springs (photo) with the close coils adjacent to the cylinder head and then fit the spring collet plate. With the base of a valve spring compressor on the valve head, compress the springs and fit the two half collets (photo). Slowly release the spring compressor and check that the half collets sit correctly in the collet plate and on the valve stem. Remove the spring compressor.

3   Repeat this procedure until all valves and springs are fitted. Then, using a hammer, strike each valve stem just hard enough to move the valve in order to settle the springs and collets.

90 Rocker shaft assembly – reassembling

1   Lubricate and fit the No 8 rocker into position in the rear pedestal complete with its spring washer, and insert the shaft through the pedestal and rocker bores.

2   Apply a suitable thread-locking compound to the threads of the pedestal/shaft locating screw and fit the screw to the pedestal, making sure that it correctly engages with the shaft. Tighten the screw.

3   Now, in their original sequence and positions, slide the individual springs, rockers, pedestals, and washers onto the rocker shaft, lubricating with engine oil as the assembly is built-up. Finally fit a new split pin to secure the assembly on the shaft.

91 Cylinder head, tappets and rocker assembly – refitting

1   The tappets must be fitted before the cylinder head gasket. Generously lubricate each tappet and its bore location in the cylinder block. Fit each tappet to the block in its original position where the tappets have not been renewed (photo).

2   Thoroughly clean the cylinder block top face and check that the cylinder head joint face is also perfectly clean. Generously lubricate each cylinder with clean engine oil.

3   Fit a new cylinder head gasket to the block, easing it carefully over the studs to avoid damage. Make sure that the 'TOP' marked face is uppermost and don't use any jointing compound (photo).

4   Lower the cylinder head into place, keeping it parallel with the block to avoid binding on the studs (photo).

5   With the head in position refit the lifting bracket and, on UK models only, the fuel pipe bracket to the right-hand rear studs. Fit the ten cylinder head nuts and washers and run them down fingertight.

6   Following the sequence shown in Fig. 1.14 tighten down the nuts a part of a turn at a time to the torque wrench setting quoted in the Specifications.

7   Insert the pushrods in the same positions from which they were removed, checking that the ball ends enter the tappets (photo).

8   Refit the rocker assembly to the cylinder head, checking that each rocker balljoint sits properly in the cup on its associated pushrod (photo).

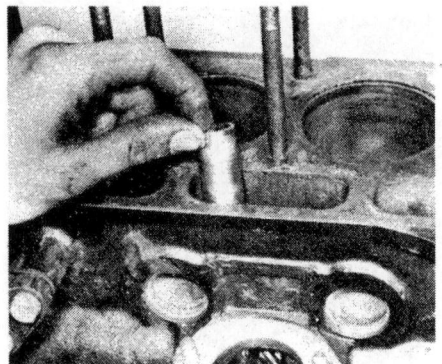

91.1 Installing a tappet

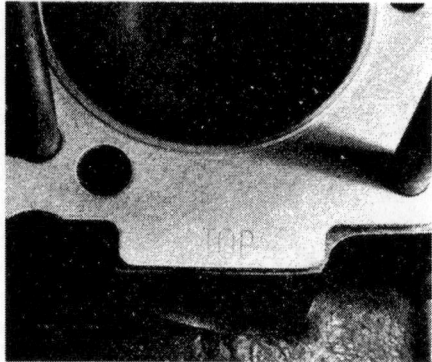

91.3 Fit the cylinder head gasket with 'TOP' mark uppermost

91.4 Lowering the cylinder head into position

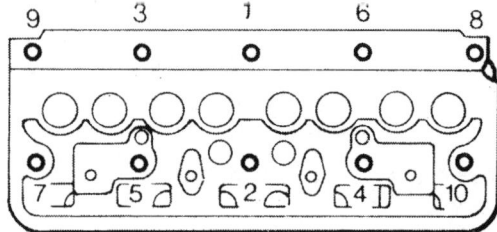

Fig. 1.14 Cylinder head nut tightening sequence (Sec 91)

9   Fit the four pedestal retaining nuts and washers, then progressively and evenly tighten them down to their specified torque wrench setting.
10 Set the valve clearances as described in Section 58.

92 Distributor driveshaft and distributor – refitting

1   It is important to fit the distributor drive correctly, otherwise the ignition timing will be totally wrong. It is easy to set the driveshaft in apparently the right position but in fact exactly 180° out, by not working on the correct cylinder, which must not only be at TDC but also at the end of compression and the start of the power stroke with both valves closed. The distributor driveshaft should therefore not be fitted until the cylinder head and rocker assembly are fitted and the timing chain and sprockets assembled so that the valve operations can be observed. Alternatively, if the timing cover has not be fitted, the distributor driveshaft can be refitted when the timing marks on the sprockets are adjacent to each other on a straight line through the sprocket centres.
2   Rotate the crankshaft so that No 1 piston is at TDC at the start of the power stroke (photo). This is when the inlet valve on No 4 cylinder is just opening and the exhaust valve just closing, or when the sprocket timing marks are aligned.

3   Before fitting the driveshaft in its timed position, its endfloat when installed must be checked. This endfloat is controlled by selecting an appropriate thickness gasket which fits between the flange on the distributor pedestal and the cylinder block mounting face. To determine the thickness of gasket required you will need a washer of known thickness which will fit on the driveshaft below the skew gear, and a set of feeler gauges. The washer should be 0.5 in (12.7 mm) diameter. The procedure is as follows.
4   Remove the distributor pedestal/cylinder block gasket if fitted, put the washer on the lower end of the shaft assembly and fit the shaft, making sure that its drive mates with the oil pump spindle. If necessary turn the oil pump with a screwdriver and try the driveshaft in several positions to determine which is correct.
5   Fit the distributor pedestal, without gasket of course, and holding it down on the driveshaft gear, measure the gap between its flange and the block with feeler gauges (see Fig. 1.15) (photo).
6   Calculate the thickness of the gasket required. Three situations can arise; (i) the gap size equals the thickness of the washer; (ii) the gap is smaller than the washer; or (iii) the gap is larger than the washer. Proceed as follows.
7   *Gap equals washer:* In this case the gasket must equal the amount of endfloat needed.
8   *Gap smaller than washer:* In this case, without the washer there would be some endfloat, and this will equal the washer thickness minus the gap size. The gasket must therefore be thick enough to increase this difference to the required endfloat.
9   *Gap larger than washer:* In this case, if the washer was removed there would be an end load on the driveshaft by an amount equal to gap size minus washer thickness. Therefore the gasket must be equal to this amount plus the amount of endfloat required.
10 Remove the distributor pedestal, the driveshaft and the washer used for endfloat measurements and, with No 1 piston still at TDC at the end of the compression stroke, refit the driveshaft. This must be done so that, in addition to engaging the oil pump drive spindle, the offset slot in the top of the driveshaft is in the position shown in Fig. 1.16 when fully engaged with the camshaft skew gear. As the driveshaft turns every time it is fitted or removed, in order to arrive at

91.7 Inserting a pushrod

91.8 Refitting the rocker shaft assembly

92.2 The crankshaft pulley notch aligned with the TDC mark

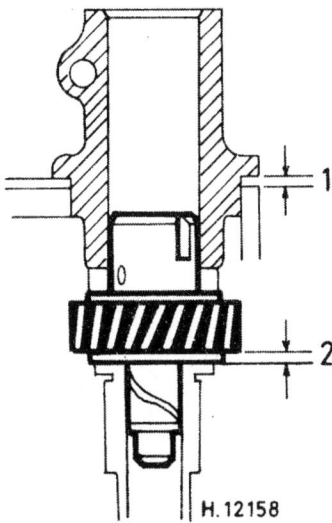

Fig. 1.15 Checking the distributor driveshaft endfloat (Sec 92)

1 Measure gap with feeler gauges
2 Washer of known thickness

92.5 Measuring the gap between the distributor pedestal flange and the block using feeler gauges

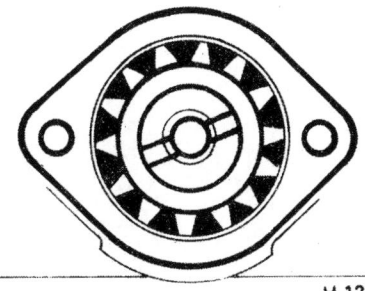

Fig. 1.16 The position of the distributor drive slot with No 1 piston at TDC commencing power stroke (Sec 92)

the correct final position, several attempts at pre-positioning the shaft before fitting it may be necessary on a trial-and-error basis. On completion check that the oil pump spindle is engaged with the driveshaft.

11 Fit the gasket of the required thickness to achieve the specified driveshaft endfloat and then fit the distributor pedestal and its two nuts and washers. On USA and Canada models, two spacers are fitted to the pedestal studs together with a diverter bracket on a cylinder block stud.

12 Lubricate the distributor driveshaft with clean engine oil and then fit the distributor to the pedestal, aligning the drive with the driveshaft and securing the clamp plate with the nut, bolt and washer. In doing this, align the marks which were made during dismantling. If the clamp bolt was not disturbed the ignition timing should be as originally set. However, if the clamp bolt has been loosened, or if alignment marks were not made on dismantling, it will be necessary to re-time the ignition as explained in Chapter 4.

93 Final assembly – general

1 Fit a new gasket to the rocker cover and carefully fit the cover in place.

2 Refit the washers over the retaining studs and ensure that the sealing washer is located under the flat steel washer. Refit the rocker cover nuts or screws as appropriate.

3 Fit the spark plugs and then refit any other ancillary components to the engine in the reverse order of removal.

4 As a basic rule, all ancillary components and fittings should be reassembled to the engine before installation, if only because access in almost every instance is easier. This means that the manifolds (using new gaskets), the carburettor(s) (again with new gaskets), the alternator, the thermostat and water pump housing, the air pump (USA and Canada models), the oil filter cartridge, and the fuel pump (using a new gasket) should all be fitted while the engine is still on the bench.

5 If the engine and gearbox were removed as an assembly, refit the gearbox to the engine following the reverse of the procedure for removal. Make sure that the weight of the gearbox is not allowed to rest on the input shaft or the clutch driven plate during reassembly.

94 Engine (without gearbox) – refitting

1 Although the engine can be refitted by one man with a suitable winch, it is advisable to have an assistant at hand for certain operations. These are principally to help guide the engine into position and ensure that it does not foul anything.

2 Generally speaking, engine refitting is a direct reversal of the removal sequence, but several items should be mentioned and these are as follows.

3 Ensure that all loose leads, cables etc are tucked out of the way.

4 Ensure that the engine lifting sling is correctly located around the engine and that the lifting equipment is in good condition.

5 Carefully lower the engine into the car and locate to the gearbox and front engine mountings with the respective bolts.

6 Then reconnect the following components:

(a) Oil pressure switch
(b) Wiring to coil, distributor and alternator
(c) Carburettor fittings
(d) Fuel pipe to pump
(e) Air cleaner/s
(f) Exhaust manifold to downpipe
(g) Earth strap and starter motor cables
(h) Radiator, hoses and associate fittings
(i) Heater hoses
(j) Water temperature capillary tube and sender unit or the electrical leads as appropriate
(k) Vacuum advance retard
(l) Battery

7 On USA models the emission control components will also have to be reconnected. If necessary refer to Chapter 3 for details.

8 Finally check that the cooling system hoses are correctly fitted and refill the cooling system (see Chapter 2).

9 Refill the engine with the correct grade and quantity of oil. The car is now ready to start.

95 Engine (with gearbox) – refitting

1 The instructions for refitting the engine with gearbox into the car, are basically the same as in the previous Section but with the following additional items.

2 When the engine and gearbox have been lowered into position, reconnect the gearbox mounting brackets.

3 Reconnect the propeller shaft to gearbox driveshaft flange ensuring that the mating marks align.

4 Relocate the clutch slave cylinder.

5 Reconnect the speedometer cable.

6 Reconnect the reversing light switch cable, and on top of the gearbox, refit the fuel line pipe clip to the top cover bolt.

7 Reinsert the gearchange remote control and lever, then refill the gearbox with the correct grade and quantity of oil to the level plug. This will have to be filled from underneath the car on the right-hand side of the gearbox.

8 Refit the carpets and gearchange gaiter.

Chapter 2 Cooling system

Contents

Specifications

System type .... Thermo-syphon, pump assisted, pressurised and fan cooled

Coolant capacity

	Imp pints	US pints	Litres
948 cc (without heater)	10	12	5.7
1098 cc (without heater)	10	12	5.7
1275 cc (with heater)	6	7	3.4
1500 cc (with heater), except US models	7.5	9	4.3
1500 cc (with heater), US models	9.5	11.4	5.4
Heater, all models	0.5	0.6	0.25

Thermostat opening temperature

948 cc models	65° to 70°C (149° to 158°F)
1098 and 1275 cc models:	
Standard	82°C (180°F)
Hot climates	74°C (165°F)
Cold climates	88°C (190°F)
1500 cc models:	
Standard	82°C (180°F)
Cold climates	88°C (190°F)

Filler cap pressure

948, 1098 and early 1275 cc models	7 lbf/in^2 (0.49 kgf/cm^2)
Later 1275 cc, and 1500 cc models	15 lbf/in^2 (1.05 kgf/cm^2)

Fan drivebelt tension .... 0.5 in (13 mm) deflection in middle of longest belt run

Water pump

Type	Centrifugal impeller
Lubricant type	General purpose grease (Duckhams LB 10)

Antifreeze type .... Ethylene glycol base to specification BS 3151, BS 3152 or BS 6580
(Duckhams Universal Antifreeze and Summer Coolant)

Torque wrench settings
948, 1098 and 1275 cc engines

	lbf ft	kgf m
Coolant pump bolts	17	2.3
Coolant outlet elbow bolts	8	1.1
Fan securing bolts	8.3	1.15

1500 cc engine

Alternator mounting	22	3.0
Alternator adjusting link	20	2.8
Cylinder block drain plug	35	4.8
Fan securing bolts	9	1.2
Coolant outlet elbow bolts	20	2.8
Coolant pump bearing housing-to-pump bolts	14	1.9
Coolant pump-to-cylinder head bolts	20	2.8

1   General description

The cooling system is of the pump assisted, thermal syphon type and is pressurised by means of a pressure valve in the filler cap. The main components in the system include a radiator, an impeller type coolant pump, a heat sensitive wax thermostat, a cooling fan and connecting hoses.

The operation of the system is as follows. Cold coolant is drawn from the bottom of the radiator by the pump, which then feeds it into the coolant passages of the cylinder block and the cylinder head. Heat from the combustion chambers and cylinders is absorbed by the coolant, which is then directed to the top of the radiator. Air passing through the radiator, due to the cooling fan and to the movement of the car, extracts heat from the coolant as it passes through the matrix to the radiator outlet, where the cycle is repeated as a continuing process.

In order to accelerate warming up on starting a cold engine, a thermostat is fitted to the cylinder head outlet in the feed to the radiator. When the coolant is cold the thermostat, which is simply a heat-sensitive valve, is closed and the coolant is prevented from flowing to the radiator. As the coolant temperature increases the thermostat opens to allow normal circulation through the radiator.

On cars which are fitted with an interior heater, hot coolant is tapped from the system and directed to a small heater matrix before returning to the system. An electric fan assists in blowing air through the matrix, where it is heated before passing into the car to warm the interior. A manually operated valve is fitted to control the coolant supply to the heater.

The coolant system is pressurised in order to prevent the coolant boiling, and also to reduce the amount of coolant necessary to cool the engine. Later models are fitted with an expansion tank which collects excess coolant as it expands on heating. As the system cools after stopping the engine, the excess coolant is returned to the main system. This facility greatly reduces the amount of topping up that would otherwise be necessary.

2   Cooling system – draining

All models, except 1500 and later 1275

1   With the car on level ground drain the system as follows: If the engine is cold remove the filler cap from the radiator by turning the cap anti-clockwise. If the engine is hot having just been run, then turn the filler cap very slightly until the pressure in the system has had time to disperse. Use a rag over the cap to protect your hand from escaping steam. If, with the engine very hot, the cap is released suddenly, the drop in pressure can result in the coolant boiling. With the pressure released the cap can be removed.

2   If antifreeze is in the system, drain it into a clean bucket or bowl for re-use.

3   Open the two drain taps. When viewed from the front, the radiator drain tap is on the bottom right-hand side of the radiator, and the

engine drain tap is halfway down the rear right-hand side of the cylinder block. A short length of rubber tubing over the radiator drain tap nozzle will assist draining the coolant into a container without splashing.

4   When the coolant has finished running, probe the drain tap orifices with a short piece of wire to displodge any particles of rust or sediment which may be blocking the taps and preventing all the coolant draining out.

5   If required, drain the heater unit by means of the drain tap.

1500 models and later 1275 models

6   Follow the instructions given in paragraphs 1, 2, 4 and 5 above but note that the filler cap is located in the expansion tank (photo).

7   In addition the filler plug must also be removed from the outlet elbow in the top of the thermostat housing (photo), or radiator, depending on model.

8   Slacken the bottom hose retaining clip, and with a suitable container placed underneath, disconnect the hose to drain.

9   To drain the cylinder block, remove the drain plug located at the rear of the block on the right of the exhaust manifold.

3   Cooling system – flushing

1   With time the cooling system will gradually lose its efficiency as the radiator and cylinder block become choked with rust scales, deposits from the water, and other sediment. To clean the system out, remove the filler cap, the drain tap and the cylinder block tap (where fitted) and leave a hose pipe running in the filler cap orifice for five to ten minutes to flush with clean water.

2   In very bad cases the radiator should be reverse flushed. This can be done with the radiator in position. The cylinder block tap is closed and a hose placed over the open radiator drain tap. Water, under pressure, is then forced up through the radiator and out of the header tank filler orifice.

3   On later models not having a radiator drain tap, water should be allowed to flow through the system until it is flowing clean from the drain points. If you can make an adaptor to fit your garden hose to the radiator bottom connection, then you can reverse flush the radiator in this way.

4   To reverse flush a badly choked radiator, it should be removed from the car and flushed by inserting the water hose into the bottom hose orifice. With the radiator inverted, allow the water to flow through the core until it flows cleanly from the top hose connection. Then refit the radiator in the car.

5   The hose is then removed and placed in the filler orifice and the radiator flushed out in the usual fashion.

4   Cooling system – refilling

1   Check the condition and security of all cooling system hoses and connections and, on earlier models, ensure that the drain taps are firmly closed. On later models reconnect the bottom hose connection to the radiator and refit the cylinder block drain plug.

2.6 The expansion tank filler cap (1500 cc model shown)

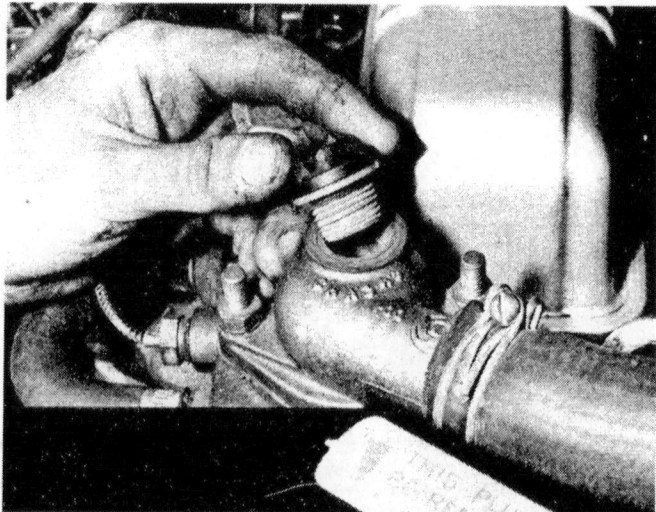

2.7 The main coolant filler plug on the 1500 cc engine

2   Fill the system slowly to ensure that no air locks develop. If a heater unit is fitted, check that the valve to the heater unit is open, otherwise an air lock may form in the heater. The best type of water to use in the cooling system is rain water to prevent scale build-up, so use this whenever possible.

Models without an expansion tank
3   Fill the system through the radiator filler cap. Do not fill the system higher than within 1/2 in (12 mm) of the filler orifice.

Models with an expansion tank
UK models
4   Release the clip securing the hose to the expansion tank and disconnect the hose. Support the hose with its free end higher than the radiator.
UK and US models
5   Fill the system through the thermostat housing until the coolant reaches the bottom of the threads in the filler neck. Refit the plug.
6   Pour coolant into the expansion tank until it is half full. Overfilling will merely result in wastage, which is especially to be avoided when anti-freeze is in use.
7   On UK models, reconnect the hose to the expansion tank.

All models
8   Only use antifreeze mixture with a glycerine or ethylene base and with an anti-corrosion inhibitor.
9   Refit the radiator or expansion tank filler cap and turn firmly clockwise to lock into position.
10 Start the engine and let it idle until the coolant is just warm; check for leaks whilst doing so. Then accelerate the engine several times to a fast speed to help move any air locks and then switch the engine off.
11 Allow the system to cool, or open the filler cap cautiously, covering it with a thick cloth and waiting at the first stop on the cap for the pressure to dissipate. On early models, top up the radiator as described in paragraph 3. On models with an expansion tank, check that the coolant level is about halfway up the tank.

5   Radiator – removal, inspection and cleaning

1   Drain the cooling system as described in Section 2.
2   Remove the radiator as described in Chapter 1, Section 5, paragraphs 5 and 6.
3   The radiator matrix, the hot and cold radiator tanks (that is, top and bottom on early models, or left and right on the later cross-flow type radiators) and the hose connectors should be thoroughly examined for signs of damage, deterioration or leakage. Very often a leak will be apparent by the deposit of rusty sediment in its vicinity.
4   After locating any leaks the radiator should be flushed clean as described in Section 3 of this Chapter and the matrix and exterior cleaned of dirt and dead flies with a strong jet of water.
5   Radiator repairs are best left to a specialist organisation as, without the appropriate equipment, it is quite easy to turn a small repair into a big one. Some small leaks can be rectified by using a proprietary sealing compound, but read the directions for use and the limitations on usage before committing yourself to this expediency. If the drain tap (where fitted) is leaking, this may be due to a defective

sealing washer behind the tap. In this case renew the washer, but if this is not the cause a new tap will be required.
6   Renew the radiator rubber strips if they are badly worn or perished.

6   Radiator – refitting

1   Where appropriate, refit the fan guard and radiator cowl to the radiator. If the bottom hose has been removed, reconnect it to the coolant pump, but do not fully tighten the clip at this stage.
2   Relocate the radiator into poisition (photo), and reconnect the top and bottom hoses, and expansion tank hose where applicable, complete with clips, the bottom hose passing under the rack and pinion steering gear to the radiator.
3   Relocate the radiator securing bolts and tighten (photo).
4   Now tighten the hose clips and refit the water temperature gauge element into the radiator (on early models).
5   Refill the system and start the engine to pressurise the system and check for leaks, as described in Section 4.

7   Expansion tank – removal and refitting

1   With the engine cold, remove the filler cap by turning it anti-clockwise. If the engine is hot, either wait for it to cool, or turn the cap very slowly and just enough so that the pressure in the system has had time to disperse. Then remove, using a rag over your hand to protect it from escaping steam.
2   Disconnect the expansion tank-to-radiator hose from the tank, and keep its end up to reduce coolant loss.
3   To remove the tank, unscrew its retaining screws.
4   To refit the expansion tank to the car, then refill with coolant to approximately the half-full mark. Reconnect the hose from the radiator. If a lot of coolant has been lost, it will be necessary to top up the radiator (Section 4). Refit the cap.

8   Thermostat – removal, resting and refitting

1   To remove the thermostat, partially drain the cooling system (4 Imp pints/2.5 litres/5 US pints is enough), loosen the upper radiator hose at the thermostat elbow end (photo) and pull it off the elbow.
2   On early models, unscrew the three set bolts and spring washers from the thermostat housing. On later models, the thermostat housing elbow is removed by unscrewing the three retaining nuts from the studs (photo), followed by the spring washers, and carburettor vacuum pipe retaining clip (where applicable). On 1500 cc models, the thermostat is located on top of the water pump over two studs. Unscrew the retaining nuts to remove the thermostat and its housing.
3   Remove the housing or housing elbow and gasket, and take out the thermostat.
4   Test the thermostat for correct functioning by immersing it in a saucepan of cold water together with a thermometer. Heat the water and note when the thermostat begins to open. Compare this with the figures given in the Specifications. It is advantageous in winter to fit a thermostat that does not open until 88°C (190°F), and will obviate

6.2 Refit the radiator taking care not to damage the matrix on surrounding projections

6.3 The radiator mounting bolts are located through the body aperture, and are reached using a socket and extension through the front grille aperture

8.1 The radiator top hose (1275 cc engine)

8.2 The thermostat housing with nuts and washers removed (1275 cc engine)

8.5 Use a new gasket when refitting the thermostat housing

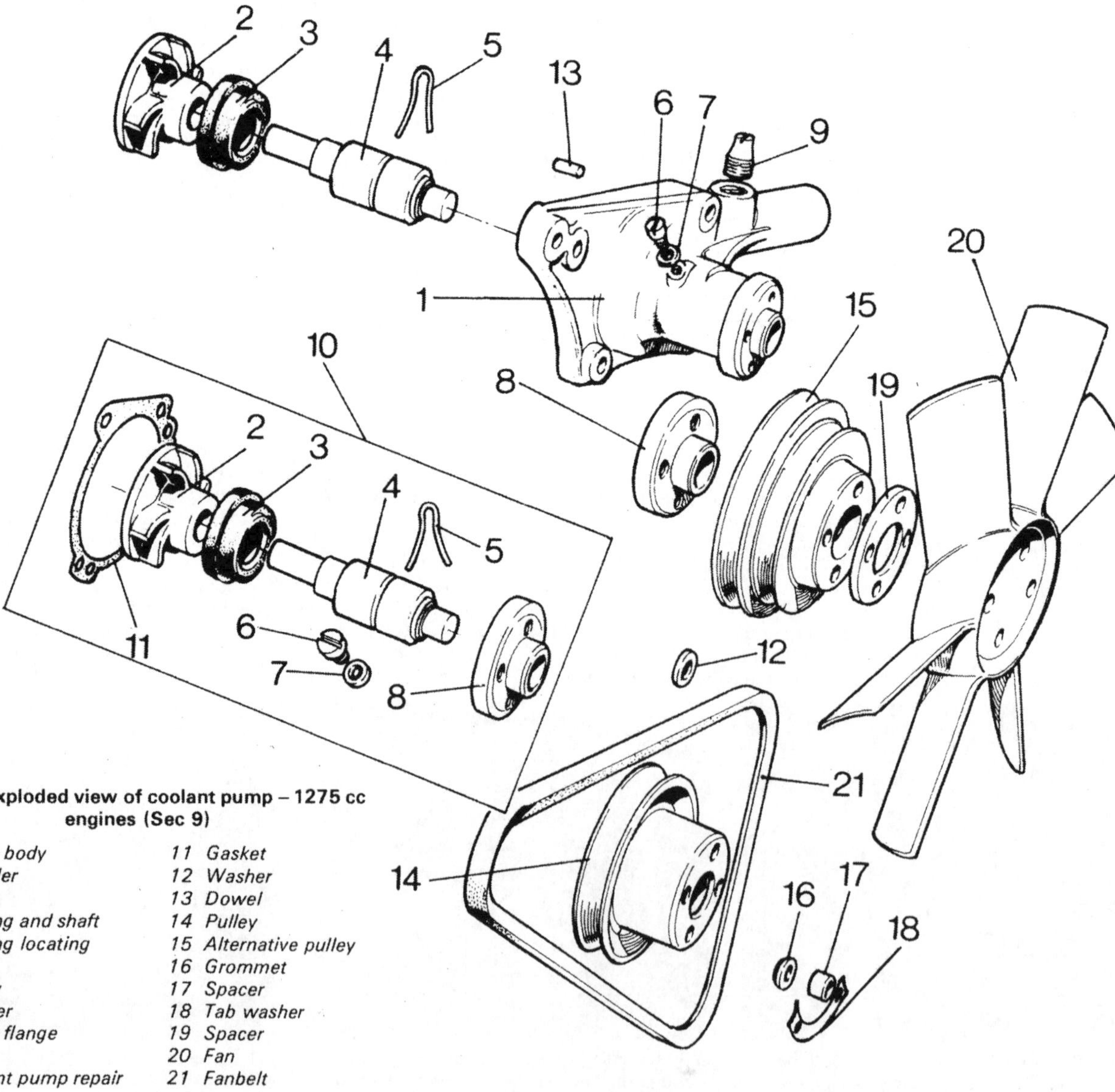

Fig. 2.1 Exploded view of coolant pump – 1275 cc engines (Sec 9)

1	Pump body	11	Gasket
2	Impeller	12	Washer
3	Seal	13	Dowel
4	Bearing and shaft	14	Pulley
5	Bearing locating clip	15	Alternative pulley
6	Screw	16	Grommet
7	Washer	17	Spacer
8	Pulley flange	18	Tab washer
9	Plug	19	Spacer
10	Coolant pump repair kit	20	Fan
		21	Fanbelt

9.2 Removing the fan and pulley (1275 cc engine)

9.4 Removing the coolant pump; note the locating dowels in the cylinder block (1275 cc engine)

any need to fit a radiator blind. Discard the thermostat if it opens too early. Continue heating the water until the thermostat is fully open. Then let it cool down naturally. If the thermostat will not open fully in boiling water, or does not close down as the water cools, then it must be exchanged for a new one. If the thermostat is stuck open when cold this will be apparent when removing it from the housing and it must be renewed.

5   Refitting the thermostat is a reversal of the removal procedure. Remember to use a new gasket between the thermostat housing elbow and the thermostat (photo). Renew the thermostat elbow if it is badly corroded.

9   Coolant pump (general) – removal, overhaul and refitting

Note: *For 1300 cc engines, refer to Section 10.*

1   Drain the cooling system as described in Section 2 and then remove the radiator as described in Section 5.

2   Remove the drivebelt from the fan pulley as described in Section 13 and, if it makes the job easier at this stage, remove the fan (photo).

3   On US models, after removing the air pump drivebelt, withdraw the adjusting link bolt and hinge the pump unit upwards to its limit without stretching the hoses, then tighten a securing bolt to hold it in that position.

4   Disconnect the associated coolant hoses, remove the four bolts retaining the pump to the block and remove the pump (photo).

5   To dismantle the pump, first remove the fan (if this has not already been done) and then, using a puller, carefully remove the pulley flange from the pump shaft. Withdraw the bearing locating clip and tap the shaft rearwards to remove it, complete with the bearing assembly, from the pump case. Again, use a puller to remove the impeller from the shaft and then remove the seal, which should be discarded. Some pumps have a spring-loaded seal housing; note the sequence of assembly for use later.

6   Check for wear; if any exists new parts must be fitted. Check that the pulley flange interference fit with the shaft has not been lost; renew the flange if it has.

7   Reassembly is basically the reverse of the dismantling sequence. The pulley flange must be pressed on so that its hub face is flush with the end of the shaft. Refer to Fig. 2.2 and note the particular clearances, etc that are necessary for your type of pump. Use a general purpose grease to lubricate the bearing, but don't feed it under pressure as the seal efficiency can be reduced. Lubricate the seal with engine oil immediately before assembly.

8   Refitting is basically a reverse of the removal procedure. Use a new gasket when refitting the pump to the block and make sure that the bypass hose is correctly fitted (photo).

9   Refit and tension the fanbelt, and the air pump drivebelt on US models, referring to Section 13 for details. Refill the system as

described in Section 4. On completion run the engine and check for leaks.

10   Coolant pump (1500 cc engine) – removal and refitting

Note: *For engines other than 1500 cc, refer to Section 9.*

1   The pump can be removed with or without the thermostat housing. In either care first drain the cooling system as described in Section 2. and then remove the radiator as described in Section 5. Remove the drivebelt from the fan pulley as described in Section 13. Disconnect the battery earth lead.

2   To remove the pump complete with thermostat housing, unscrew and disconnect the temperature gauge element from its aperture adjacent to the induction manifold hose connection or, on later models, disconnect the electrical connection to the temperature sender unit located in the same position.

3   Unscrew the hose clip and disconnect the induction manifold hose from its adaptor in the thermostat housing. If required the adapter can also be unscrewed to remove it at this stage.

4   Disconnect the return coolant pipe union at the rear of the pump housing.

5   Disconnect and remove the thermostat and its elbow cover as described in Section 8; or if preferred, these can be left fitted, but the distributor vacuum pipe must be disconnected from its clip on the housing.

6   Remove the three bolts securing the assembly to the cylinder head and note the positions of the different bolt lengths. Remove the assembly from the cylinder head (photo). The hose and pipe connections may be unscrewed to remove them if required.

7   To remove the pump without the thermostat housing, carry out the work listed in paragraph 1, except that it is not necessary to disconnect the battery earth lead. Then remove the three nuts and washers securing the pump to the thermostat housing and remove the pump.

8   To remove the fan from the pump assembly, it is only necessary to remove the four securing bolts and washers or, on USA and Canadian models, the four bolts, washers and nuts. Retrieve the balance weight, if fitted, and note its position for reassembly.

9   USA and Canadian models have a clutch coupling between the fan and the pulley shaft. If it is intended to remove the coupling, first remove the fan as described in the previous Section. Using a universal puller, withdraw the coupling from the pulley shaft and retrieve the tolerance ring fitted between the coupling and the shaft.

10 To refit the coupling, first fit the tolerance ring to the pump pulley shaft and, holding the tolerance ring it its locating groove on the shaft, press the fan coupling on. This can be done in a large vice, but if one is not available, the coupling can be carefully drifted into position by supporting the pump shaft and using a piece of wood between the coupling and the hammer.

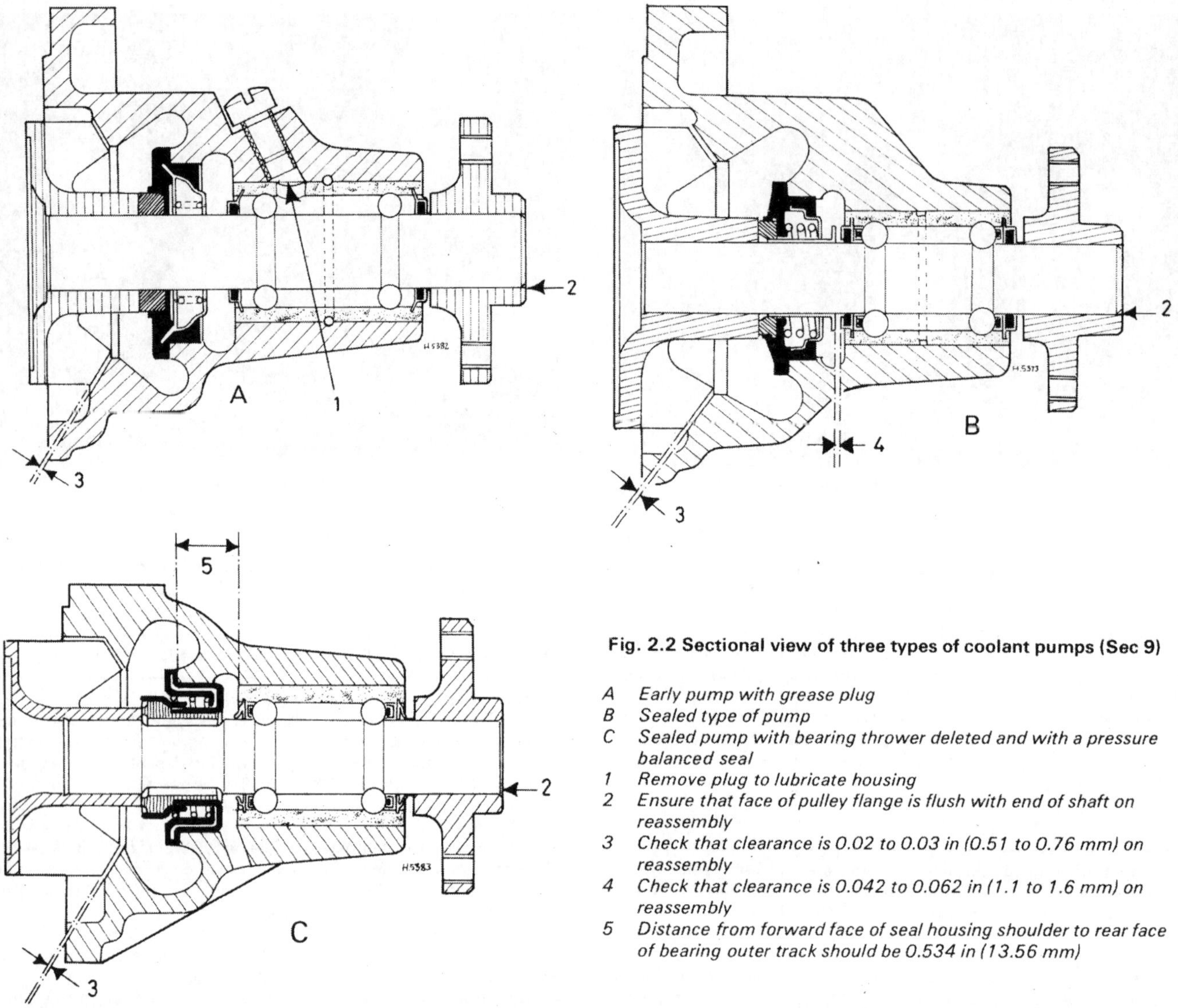

Fig. 2.2 Sectional view of three types of coolant pumps (Sec 9)

A   Early pump with grease plug
B   Sealed type of pump
C   Sealed pump with bearing thrower deleted and with a pressure
    balanced seal
1   Remove plug to lubricate housing
2   Ensure that face of pulley flange is flush with end of shaft on
    reassembly
3   Check that clearance is 0.02 to 0.03 in (0.51 to 0.76 mm) on
    reassembly
4   Check that clearance is 0.042 to 0.062 in (1.1 to 1.6 mm) on
    reassembly
5   Distance from forward face of seal housing shoulder to rear face
    of bearing outer track should be 0.534 in (13.56 mm)

9.8 Check that the bypass hose is correctly fitted

10.6 Removing the pump and thermostat housing assembly (1500 cc engine)

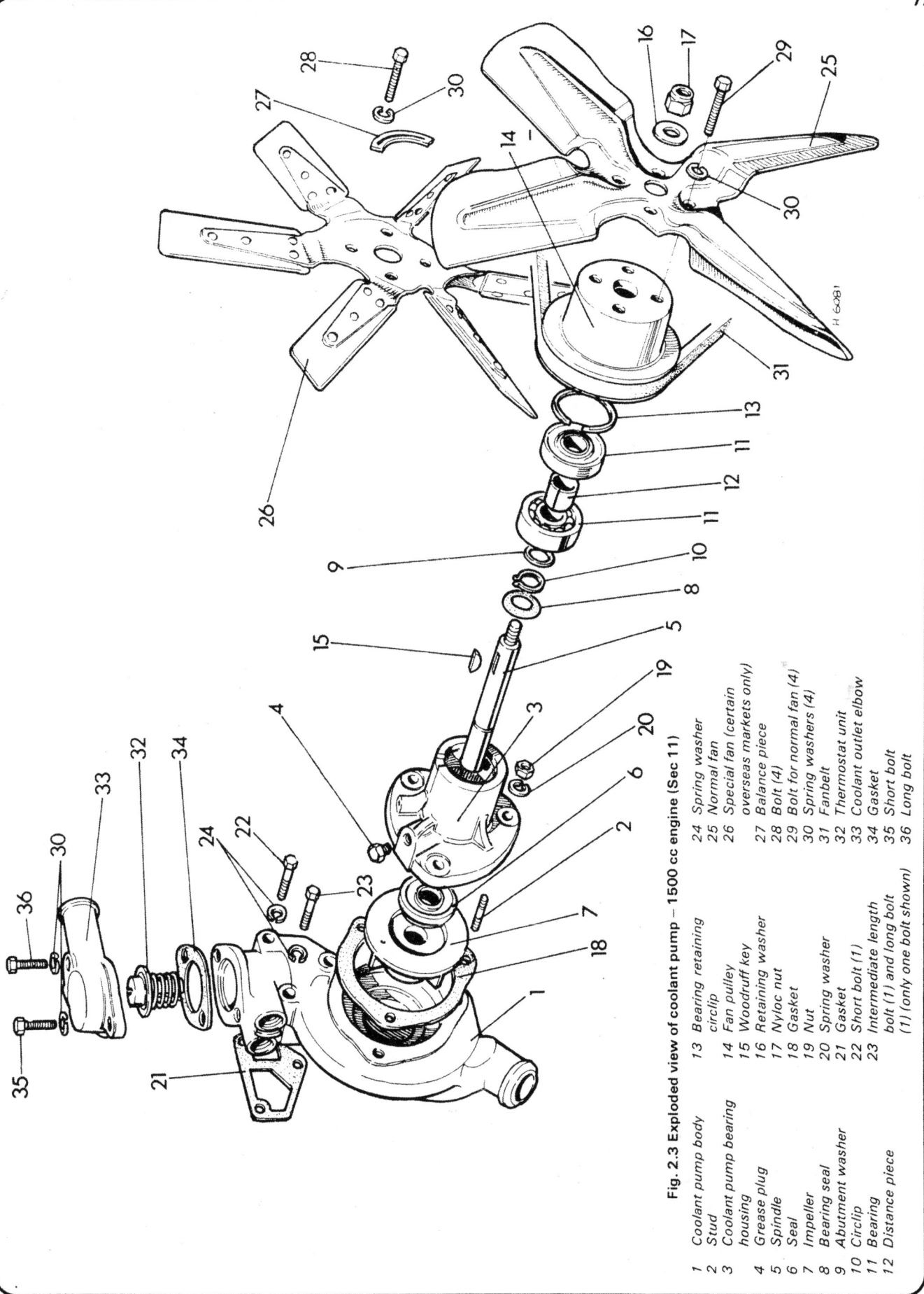

Fig. 2.3 Exploded view of coolant pump – 1500 cc engine (Sec 11)

1 Coolant pump body
2 Stud
3 Coolant pump bearing housing
4 Grease plug
5 Spindle
6 Seal
7 Impeller
8 Bearing seal
9 Abutment washer
10 Circlip
11 Bearing
12 Distance piece
13 Bearing retaining circlip
14 Fan pulley
15 Woodruff key
16 Retaining washer
17 Nyloc nut
18 Gasket
19 Nut
20 Spring washer
21 Gasket
22 Short bolt (1)
23 Intermediate length bolt (1) and long bolt (1) (only one bolt shown)
24 Spring washer
25 Normal fan
26 Special fan (certain overseas markets only)
27 Balance piece
28 Bolt (4)
29 Bolt for normal fan (4)
30 Spring washers (4)
31 Fanbelt
32 Thermostat unit
33 Coolant outlet elbow
34 Gasket
35 Short bolt
36 Long bolt

11 Before refitting a coolant pump, ensure that all mating faces are cleaned free of all traces of old gasket, sealing compound and any corrosion that may be present. Refitting is the reverse of the removal procedure, but the following additional points need attention.

(a) Always use new gaskets in joints that were broken during dismantling
(b) Tighten the nuts, bolts, etc listed under 'Torque wrench settings' in the Specifications section of this Chapter to their correct torque load
(c) Refill the cooling system as described in Section 4 of this Chapter
(d) Adjust the fanbelt tension as described in Section 13 of this Chapter
(e) Run the engine and check for leaks

11 Coolant pump (grease plug type) – dismantling, repair and reassembly

1 It is possible to repair the early type of coolant pump (grease plug type) providing that spares can be obtained. If not the pump will have to be renewed when defective or worn out, as is the case with the later types of pumps. With spares available, first remove the fan and, if fitted, the fan coupling as described in the previous Section.
2 Undo and remove the nut and washer which hold the fan pulley in place and, with the aid of an extractor, pull off the pulley wheel and prise out the Woodruff key.
3 Undo the three nuts and spring washers which hold the bearing housing to the pump body and pull out the bearing housing.
4 With the aid of a vice and an extractor pull the impeller off the spindle. Remove the sealing gland from the back of the impeller.
5 Remove the bearing retaining circlip from the bore of the housing and pull out the spindle complete with bearings. The bearings distance piece, circlip, washer and bearing seal can now all be removed.
6 If the pump is badly worn, the bearings will require renewal and the gland face on the housing recut. (This is a job for a BL garage or your local engineerig works). A new sealing gland and bearing seal, together with a new gasket must also be obtained.
7 Reassembly of the water pump is a reversal of the above sequence (photo). The following additional points should be noted.
8 Position the bearings so that their unshielded sides are adjacent to the distance piece and the grease seal faces outwards. Pack the bearings and area round the distance piece with grease.
9 The shaft and bearings are fitted to the housing with the aid of a drift made from a piece of tubing.
10 Press the impeller onto the spindle until a 0.030 in (0.76 mm) clearance, measured with a feeler gauge, exists between the flat face of the spindle and the housing. The impeller should then be soldered to the shaft to prevent water seepage down the spindle.

11 When fitting the pulley wheel, fan and balance weight, note if a small alignment hole has been drilled in these units. If so, line the components up with the aid of a $\frac{1}{16}$ in (1.5 mm) drill or similar while the securing bolts are being done up.
12 Regrease the water pump on completion of the assembling operations.

12 Temperature gauge – general

1 The temperature gauge assembly fitted to early models consists of a dial-type gauge, a wire coil protected pipe filled with mercury, and a temperature sensitive bulb.
2 The gauge is mounted on the instrument panel, to which it is secured by a bridge piece and knurled nut behind the gauge. To remove the gauge from the panel, undo the nut, remove the bridge piece and lift the gauge out of the instrument panel. The temperature sensitive bulb is located in the radiator header tank, the cylinder head or the thermostat housing depending on model (photo). No attempt should be made to separate the gauge or the bulb from the interconnecting pipe, and if the gauge ceases to function it is necessary to renew the complete assembly. In this case, consideration should be given to installing the later type of electrical gauge system.
3 Later models are fitted with an electrical temperature gauge consisting of a dial-type gauge, a temperature sensor and inteconnecting wires. The gauge is similar in appearance and is mounted in the same way as the earlier model. Removal follows a similar procedure, except that the gauge can be removed independently by disconnecting the electrical leads on the back. An illuminating bulb in the back of the case will also need removing. On USA and Canadian models, the centre console will first need moving. To do this, remove the gearbox tunnel carpeting, then remove the screws securing the centre console and move it back and aside towards the steering column. To remove the temperature sensor, or transmitter, hold the adaptor in the thermostat housing (1500 models) with a suitable spanner and unscrew the unit. If a replacement is fitted quickly, little coolant will be lost and it will be unnecessary to drain the system, although it should be topped up afterwards.

13 Drivebelt(s) – removal, refitting and adjustment

1 To remove the fanbelt, loosen the dynamo or alternator adjusting link bolt and the hinge bolts. Swing the unit in towards the engine to slacken the fanbelt, which can then be lifted out of the pulleys and over the fan for removal. USA and Canadian models will first require removal of the emission control air pump drivebelt. This is done in a similar fashion by slackening the securing bolt above the pump, and then slackening the two adjusting link bolts beneath the pump,

11.7 Refitting the pump to the thermostat housing using a new gasket

12.2 The temperature sensitive bulb of the coolant temperature gauge being removed (1275 cc engine)

swinging the pump in towards the engine and lifting the belt off the pulleys.

2 Refit the fanbelt, and the air pump drivebelt where applicable, by the reverse procedure, but don't fully tighten the mounting bolts and nuts.

3 Adjust the fanbelt tension so that there is 0.5 in (13 mm) of lateral movement at the middle of the longest run of the belt (between dynamo/alternator and crankshaft) when deflected by moderate hand pressure. This is achieved by swinging the dynamo/alternator out to tighten the belt to the required tension, and then tightening the mounting and adjusting bolts to their specified torque wrench settings. If required you can use a length of wood as a lever, but make sure that any load on the alternator is only applied at the pulley end where the case is stronger. USA and Canadian models will require the emission control air pump drivebelt tensioned in a similar fashion to the same tension by swinging the air pump out and tightening its bolts.

4 Following renewal of the fanbelt or the air pump drivebelt, or following readjustment of the belt tension, the tension should be rechecked after the car has been used for two or three hundred miles and, where necessary, readjusted to the correct tension. New belts in particular tend to stretch a little after initial use and this must be corrected.

14 Antifreeze – general

1 The cooling system should always be filled with antifreeze mixture of suitable strength. Apart from protecting the engine from frost damage in winter, it will also reduce the risk of corrosion all the year round due to the inhibitors that good quality antifreeze fluids contain.

2 However, the mixture should be renewed every two years because, in performing their function, the inhibitors slowly decay and their efficiency diminishes. Furthermore, a periodic flushing of the system is beneficial in eliminating sediment which tends to accumulate with time.

3 After draining and flushing the system, systematically check all hose clips in the system for tightness, and all hoses for condition. Renew any defective clips or hoses. The mixture can be made up in a separate, clean container, but the easiest way is to put the required amount of antifreeze fluid in the system, top up with clean water (preferably rain water if your local tap water is hard) and then run the engine to mix the fluid and water. Later models which have a separate expansion tank should have a 0.25 pint (0.15 litre, 0.3 US pint) of neat antifreeze fluid added to the expansion tank. Refer to Section 4 for the filling procedure.

4 The following table gives a guide to the amount of protection provided by different strengths of antifreeze mixture. The capacity of your system is indicated in the Specifications to this Chapter.

Antifreeze fluid %	Protection to
50	-37°C (-34°F)
40	-25°C (-13°F)
30	-16°C (+3°F)
25	-13°C (+9°F)
20	-9°C (+15°F)
15	-7°C (+20°F)
10	-4°C (+25°F)

5 Remember that any topping up of the mixture in the system should be done using a mixture made up in similar proportions to the original to maintain the correct concentration; don't use just water, which will dilute the mixture!

15 Fault diagnosis – cooling system

Symptom	Reason(s)
Overheating (heat generated in cylinder not being successfully disposed of by radiator)	Insufficient coolant in cooling system Fanbelt slipping (accompanied by a shrieking noise on rapid acceleration) Radiator core blocked or radiator grille restricted Bottom coolant hose collapsed, impeding flow Thermostat not opening properly Ignition advance and retard incorrectly set (accompanied by loss of power, and perhaps misfiring) Carburettor(s) incorrectly adjusted (mixture too weak) Exhaust system partially blocked Oil level in sump too low Blown cylinder head gasket (coolant/steam being forced down the radiator overflow pipe under pressure) Engine not yet run-in Brakes binding
Underheating (too much heat being dispersed by radiator)	Thermostat jammed open Incorrect grade of thermostat fitted allowing premature opening of valve Thermostat missing
Loss of coolant (leaks in system)	Loose clips on coolant hoses Top, bottom, or by-pass coolant hose perished and leaking Radiator core leaking Thermostat gasket leaking Radiator pressure cap spring worn or seal ineffective Blown cylinder head gasket (pressure in system forcing coolant/steam down overflow pipe) Cylinder wall or head cracked

Chapter 3 Fuel, exhaust and emission control systems

Contents

Specifications

Air cleaner type
Sprite Mk I .... Twin 'pancake' wire gauze elements
All other models .... Paper element(s)

Fuel pump type
Sprite Mk I & Mk II, Midget Mk I .... AC Y-type, mechanical
Sprite Mk III & Mk IV, Midget Mk II & Mk III (except 1500) ..... SU AUF 200, 206 or 216, electrical
Midget Mk III (1500) .... AC Delco RA1, mechanical

Fuel tank capacity
Sprite Mk I, Mk II, Mk III & Mk IV, Midget Mk I, Mk II &
Mk III (up to engine no. G-AN5-105501) .... 6.0 UK gal (7.2 US gal/27.3 litres)
Midget Mk III (1500, USA) .... 7.7 US gal (29 litres)
All other models .... 7.0 UK gal (8.6 US gal/32 litres)

Fuel octane requirement (min)
Sprite Mk I 90
Catalytic converter models (USA) .... Unleaded fuel
All other models 97

Exhaust gas CO content
Sprite Mk IV, Midget Mk III (USA, up to 1972) .... 2.5% max
Midget Mk III (USA, 1972) .... 3% max
Midget Mk III (USA, 1973 and 1974) .... 2.5% max
Midget Mk III (USA, 1975 to 1977) .... 0.5 to 2%
Midget Mk III (USA & Canada, 1978 to 1980, except 1978
California) .... 3 to 7% (5% nominal)
Midget Mk III (California, 1978) .... 0.5 to 6% (3% nominal)
All other models .... Not specified

Carburettor(s)

Type
Sprite Mk I	Twin SU HS1
Sprite Mk II, Midget Mk I	Twin SU HS2
Sprite Mk III, Midget Mk II	Twin SU HS2
Sprite Mk IV, Midget Mk III (except 1500)	Twin SU HS2
Midget Mk III (1500, except USA)	Twin SU HS4
Midget Mk III (1500 USA, up to 1978)	Single Zenith-Stromberg 150 CD4
Midget Mk III (1500 USA and Canada, 1978 to 1980)	Single Zenith-Stromberg 150 CD4T

Needle(s)
Sprite Mk I	GG (Standard), MOW (Weak), EB (Rich)
Sprite Mk II, Midget Mk I (948 cc)	V3 (Standard), GX (Weak), V2 (Rich)
Sprite Mk II, Midget Mk I (1098 cc)	GY (Standard), GG (Weak), M (Rich)
Sprite Mk III, Midget Mk II	AN (Standard), GG (Weak), H6 (Rich)
Sprite Mk IV, Midget Mk III (up to 1971, except USA)	AN (Standard), GG (Weak), H6 (Rich)
Midget Mk III (1971 and 1972, except USA)	AAT
Sprite Mk IV, Midget Mk III (up to 1972, USA)	AN (fixed needle), AAC spring-loaded needle
Midget Mk III (1973 and 1974, except USA)	AAC
Midget Mk III (1972, USA)	AAT
Midget Mk III (1973 and 1974, USA)	ABC
Midget Mk III (1975 to 1980, except USA)	ABT
Midget Mk III (1975 to 1978, USA)	44A
Midget Mk III (1978 to 1980, USA and Canada, except California)	45Q (D9 choke needle)
Midget Mk III (1978, California)	45K (D9 choke needle)
Midget Mk III (1979 on, California)	45R (D9 choke needle)

Piston spring colour
Sprite Mk I	Natural
All other models	Blue
Dashpot oil type/specification	Multigrade engine oil, viscosity SAE 20W/50 (Duckhams Hypergrade)

Idle speed (hot)
Sprite Mk I, Mk II & Mk III, Midget Mk I & Mk II (except USA)	550 rpm approx
Sprite Mk IV, Midget Mk III (up to 1974, USA)	1000 rpm
Sprite Mk IV, Midget Mk III (except 1500)	700 rpm (approx)
Midget Mk III (1500, except USA)	650 to 680 rpm
Midget Mk III (1500 USA and Canada)	800 ± 100 rpm

Fast idle speed or setting (where specified)
Sprite Mk IV, Midget Mk III (up to 1974, USA)	1100 to 1200 rpm
Midget Mk III (1500, except USA)	1100 to 1300 rpm
Midget Mk III (1975 to 1978, USA)	1800 rpm (set with hot engine)
Midget Mk III (1978 on, USA and Canada)	0.035 in (0.9 mm)

Torque wrench settings
	lbf ft	kgf m
Fuel tank drain plug	9.0	1.25
Mechanical fuel pump to block	14.0	1.9

1 General description

Basically, the fuel system comprises a rear mounted fuel tank, a mechanically or electrically operated fuel pump (according to year and model) and twin SU carburettors on standard models.

On the 1500 cc engines version for the USA, a single Zenith-Stromberg carburettor is fitted which incorporates the necessary emission control modifications to comply with the strict emission regulations. Similarly, the 1275 cc engined with twin SU carburettors that are export models for the USA have the required emission control fitments incorporated.

2 Air cleaners – removal, servicing the refitting

1 The carburettors fitted to early models of the Austin Healey Sprite are of the H1 type and are fitted with expanded gauze air filters.
2 Every 3000 miles (5000 km) the cleaners should be removed by first disconnecting the breather pipe from the front unit, and then by releasing the two bolts which hold them to the carburettor flanges. The units should be washed in clean petrol.
3 When the gauze is dry, oil it with engine oil, wiping any surplus away. Remount the cleaners on the carburettor flanges, renewing the air cleaner/carburettor gaskets as necessary. Reconnect the breather pipe to the elbow on the rocker cover.
4 On later models, release the breather pipe (where applicable), unscrew the centre securing nut and washer on the tie bracket, release

the bolts which hold the two cleaners to the carburettor flanges and lift the air cleaners away (photo). The paper element should be changed at intervals of 12 000 miles (20 000 km), and more frequently in very hot and dusty conditions.

2.4 The air cleaner elements and containers removed – 1275 cc model

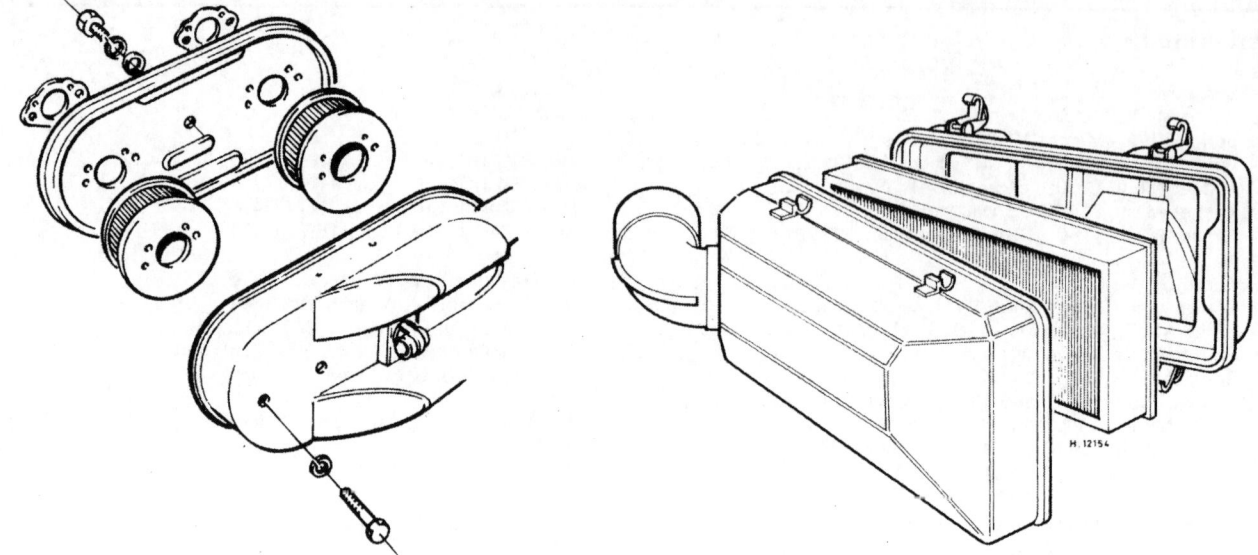

Fig. 3.1 Exploded view of air cleaners – 1500 cc engine with twin SU carburettors (Sec 2)

Fig. 3.2 Exploded view of air cleaner – 1500 cc engined USA and Canada models (Sec 2)

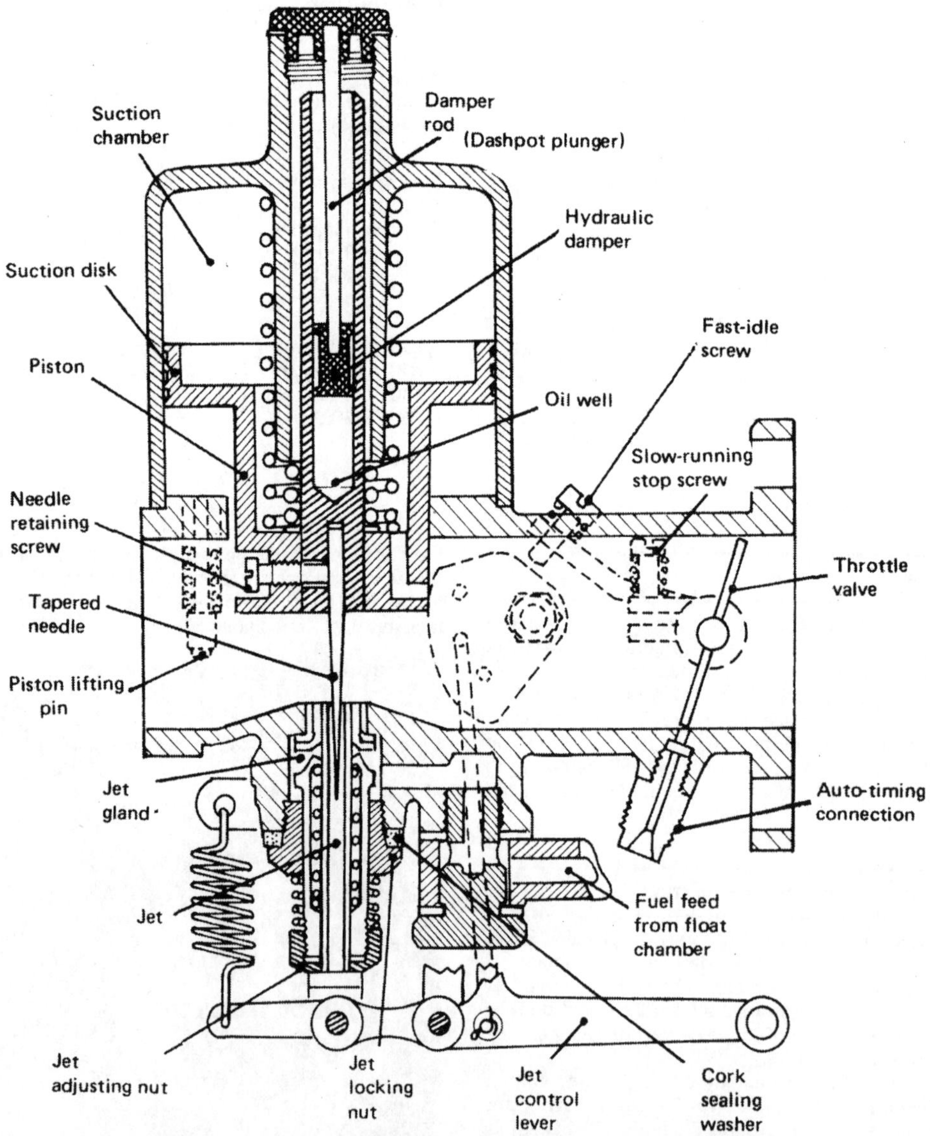

Suction chamber

Damper rod (Dashpot plunger)

Hydraulic damper

Suction disk

Fast-idle screw

Piston

Oil well

Slow-running stop screw

Needle retaining screw

Throttle valve

Tapered needle

Piston lifting pin

Jet gland

Auto-timing connection

Jet

Fuel feed from float chamber

Jet adjusting nut

Jet locking nut

Jet control lever

Cork sealing washer

Fig. 3.3 Cross-sectional view of H type SU carburettor (Sec 3)

5 The 1500 cc engine air cleaner as fitted to the Twin SU carburettors, comprises a single canister containing two paper elements. Remove the cleaners as follows: disconnect the fuel pipe from its retaining clip. Remove the air cleaner unit from the carburettors by unscrewing the four retaining bolts and lift it clear. Unscrew the central securing bolt to 'split' the container and withdraw the elements. Refit in the reverse order, but clean out the canister before inserting the new elements.

6 On USA and Canada models fitted with the Zenith-Stromberg carburettor, the air cleaner is removed by first removing the hot air pipe from the temperature control valve. Then release the two clips on top of the cleaner case and move the cover to one side to withdraw the element. Clean the case and cover internally before fitting a new element, and reassemble in the reverse order.

7 To check the operation of the air temperature control valve fitted to the USA and Canada models, with the engine and air cleaner cold, check that the valve plate is against the cold air intake, that it, in the hot air supply position. Start the engine and run it to reach its normal running temperature. Check that the valve plate moves towards the hot air hose, that it, in the cold air supply position. Switch off the engine. Renew the assembly if it fails to function correctly.

3 Carburettors – description

1 On all earlier model Austin Healey Sprites and MG Midgets, twin SU type H1/H2 carburettors were fitted, whilst the later 'chrome-bumpered' models have twin SU HS2 types.

2 The later 1500cc UK models have twin SU type HS4 carburettors and these have been adapted to comply with the exhaust emission control regulations now enforced in some countries.

3 On the 1500 cc engined MG Midget USA model, a single Zenith-Stromberg 150 CD4T, or 150 CD4 model carburettor is fitted. The 150 CD4T is fitted to those models having a catalytic convertor and incorporates an automatic choke. The 150 CD4 model has a manually operated choke. Otherwise they are basically the same type of carburettor.

4 These carburettors have a variable choke and the main jet contains a tapered needle connected to a piston (SU) or diaphragm (Zenith-Stromberg) sensitive to the venturi depression surrounding the jet. As engine speed increases, the piston or diaphragm lifts the needle out of the jet to supply more fuel to the engine. Mixture strength is adjusted by turning the main jet in or out on its screw thread. A conventional float chamber and needle valve are fitted to maintain a constant fuel supply to the jet.

4 Carburettors – removal and refitting

UK models except 1500 cc

1 Release the clip which secures the breather hose to the rocker cover, and pull the hose from the rocker cover pipe (early models). On later models the breather hose is attached to the timing cover, and may be disconnected at either end.

2 Unscrew the union which holds the vacuum advance pipe to the carburettor body, or pull the pipe off, depending on the model.

3 Remove the air cleaner complete by releasing the securing bolts and lockwashers from the carburettor flange.

4 Unscrew the union or clip securing the fuel inlet pipe to the float chamber and pull away the pipe.

5 Remove the choke and accelerator cables or accelerator interconnection rod, from the carburettor linkages (photo).

6 Unclip the three throttle return springs from the carburettor linkages (photo).

7 Remove the two nuts and lockwashers which hold the carburettor to the inlet manifold. The bottom nut is sometimes difficult to unscrew, but merely requires patience. Lift the carburettor away from the inlet manifold together with the inlet manifold gasket. If twin carburettors are being removed, then the procedure is exactly the same as above, but both carburettors will have to be lifted off together as they are joined by a common spindle.

8 To refit the carburettors reverse the above procedure using new gaskets where required. Do not omit to fit the spring washers.

1500 cc models except USA and Canada

9 Disconnect the fuel feed pipe and the distributor vacuum pipe from the rear carburettor. Disconnect the engine breather pipe and adaptor from each carburettor.

10 Undo the clamp bolt and release the choke control cable from the rear carburettor; retrieve the trunnion and bolt.

11 Release the clip and disconnect the throttle control linkage from the interconnecting rod arm. Unhook the three springs from the throttle linkage (photo).

12 Undo and remove the four bolts and washers retaining the carburettors to the inlet manifold and remove the carburettors and air cleaner assembly, retrieving the heat shield and gaskets.

13 Disconnect the fuel hoses from each carburettor and remove the fuel pipe from its clip on the air cleaner.

14 Undo and remove the four bolts and washers securing the air cleaner to the carburettors and remove the air cleaner and gaskets.

15 Separate the carburettors, retrieving the interconnection rods.

16 Refitting is the reverse of the removal procedure, but when fitting the assembly to the inlet manifold start the two top bolts first and make sure that the gaskets are properly located before tightening the four bolts.

1500 cc USA and Canada models

17 The procedure varies depending on whether or not an automatic choke is fitted, but start off by removing the air cleaner element as explained in Section 2, then remove the two retaining bolts to release the air cleaner cover, gasket and, if fitted, the heat shield.

18 Remove the evaporative loss control-purge pipe and the EGR valve flame trap pipe. On manual choke carburettors remove the EGR air bleed pipe from the choke valve.

19 On California models remove the anti-run-on valve pipe and, where appropriate, disconnect the distributor flame trap from the vacuum pipe and remove the pipe from the carburettor.

20 Disconnect the evaporative loss control canister vapour pipe from the carburettor and, just below, squeeze the clip on the fuel supply pipe and remove the pipe.

21 On manual choke carburettors, loosen the clamp screw and remove the choke control cable. On auto-choke models, slacken the clips and reconnect the two coolant hoses from the auto-choke unit.

4.5 The carburettor interconnecting linkage on 1275 cc models

4.6 The throttle return springs – 1275 cc models

4.11 The throttle return springs – 1500 cc models

22 On manual choke models, remove the split pin from the throttle link spring retaining rod, remove the spring and rod to release the throttle link, and then remove the throttle outer cable from its bracket.

23 On auto-choke models, remove the two screws and washers retaining the throttle cable bracket to the inlet manifold. Undo the cable locknut and remove the cable and spring from the bracket. Remove the split pin and washers to disconnect the cable and return spring rod from the throttle lever on the carburettor.

24 Undo and remove the two nuts retaining the carburettor to the inlet manifold, then remove the carburettor and its insulating block.

25 Refitting is the reverse of the removal procedure. Adjust the throttle cable nuts to remove excess slack in the cable. On manual choke models adjust the valve as follows:

(a) *Pull the choke knob and check that the lever on the carburettor butts against the stop. Adjust the cable as necessary*

(b) *Push the cable knob in and check that the lever on the carburettor moves the EGR valve fully home*

26 On auto choke models check and adjust the auto-choke as described in Section 16.

5 SU carburettors – dismantling

1 Before starting to dismantle the carburettor, thoroughly clean it externally to prevent contaminating the internal parts. Unscrew the piston damper on top of the chamber and remove it from the piston assembly. Retrieve the washer under the damper nut.

2 Using a sharp tool, scratch alignment marks on the suction chamber and the carburettor body so that they can be reassembled in their original relative position. Undo and remove the suction chamber retaining screws and carefully lift the suction chamber off, leaving the piston assembly in place.

3 Lift the spring from the piston, noting which way round it is fitted, and then carefully lift the piston straight up, avoiding any side load on the needle underneath it. Invert the piston to drain out the oil from the damper bore. Do not remove the metering needle unless you have a good reason to; the assembly can be safely stored by placing it on a narrow necked jar with the needle inside to protect it.

4 If you do have to remove the metering needle, unscrew the guide locking screw in the side of the piston check and carefully withdraw the needle, avoiding bending it. Remove the spring from the needle where fitted.

5 If a piston lifting-pin is fitted, push the pin up to expose its circlip. Remove the circlip and withdraw the pin and spring downwards.

6 Where a link is fitted to move the jet, support the plastic base of the jet and remove the link screw. Undo the fuel pipe sleeve nut from the float chamber, noting the assembly sequence of gland, washer and ferrule, then remove the jet assembly.

7 Remove the jet adjusting nut and its spring, then undo and remove the jet locking nut and the jet bearing. Leave the lever assembly in place unless it is essential to renew parts.

8 Undo and remove the float chamber retaining bolt to release the float chamber from the body of the carburettor.

9 Scratch alignment marks on the float chamber cover and chamber body, then remove the securing screws. Remove the cover and float, and retrieve the joint gasket. The float can be removed by sliding out the pivot pin. Remove the float needle from its seat and, if required, unscrew the seat from the cover.

10 It should not be necessary to remove the throttle disc or its spindle, but if you intend to do so first make a light alignment mark on the throttle disc (but not near the limit valve) and the carburettor body so that they can be reassembled correctly.

11 Reassembly is the reverse of the dismantling sequence and, provided that due note was taken of the order in which related parts were fitted, there should be few problems. The following points will need attention:

(a) *When refitting the throttle disc to the spindle, if it was removed, position the disc in the spindle and open and close the throttle to centralise the disc in the carburettor bore. Fit new screws, but only tighten them after checking that the disc closes fully. After tightening the screws open the split ends just sufficient to prevent them turning*

(b) *Only use fuel to clean the piston and suction chamber and dry*

with lint-free cloth. Don't use abrasives and don't lubricate them on assembly

(c) *Test the operation of the piston as described in Section 10, paragraph 4*

(d) *Refit and centre the jet as described in Section 9*

(e) *Use a new joint washer when refitting the float chamber cover, and check the float level as described in Section 8*

(f) *When assembling the jet adjustment nut, run it as far as it will go, then back it off two complete turns in order to provide an initial adjustment. Final adjustment must be done after refitting the carburettors with the engine still running as described in Section 11 or Section 12*

6 SU carburettors – examination and renovation

1 Following extensive use, some parts of the carburettor will show signs of wear and these must be examined closely when dismantled as follows.

2 The carburettor needle: if this has been incorrectly assembled at some time so that it is not centrally located in the jet orifice, then the metering needle will have a tiny ridge worn on it. If a ridge can be seen then the needle must be renewed. SU carburettor needles are made to very fine tolerances and should a ridge be apparent no attempt should be made to rub the needle down with fine emery paper. If it is wished to clean the needle it can be polished by rubbing it with a piece of rough cloth damped with fuel; don't forget that removal of metal from the needle will affect your fuel consumption adversely. Check that the needle is the correct one by referring to the code stamped on its shank. Any ridging or marks on the needle could be an indication that it is not perfectly straight so, with it mounted in the piston, roll the piston on a flat surface and check that the needle does not appear to wobble at its tip. If it is bent fit a new one.

3 The carburettor jet: if the needle is worn, it is likely that the rim of the jet will be damaged where the needle has been striking it. It should be renewed as otherwise fuel consumption will suffer. The jet can also be badly worn or ridged on the outside from where it has been sliding up and down between the jet bearings every time the choke has been pulled out. Removal and renewal is the only answer here as well.

4 Check the edges of the throttle and the choke tube for wear. Renew if worn.

5 The washers fitted to the base of the jet, to the float chamber and to the petrol inlet union may all leak after a time and can cause fuel wastage. It is best to renew them automatically when the carburettor is stripped down.

6 After high mileages the float chamber needle and seat are likely to be ridged. They are not expensive to renew and should be renewed as a set. They should never be renewed separately.

7 Check the throttle spindle fit in the body for excessive play, and if necessary renew. Also check the carburettor linkage for excessive play, again renewing parts where necessary.

7 SU carburettors float chamber – dismantling, examination and reassembly

1 To dismantle the float chamber, first disconnect the inlet pipe from the fuel pump at the top of the float chamber cover. Scratch the alignment marks on the cover and the body to permit correct reassembly.

2 On early cars a fuel filter was fitted in the inlet union. This consisted of a spring-loaded thimble of fine gauze. On removal of the securing screw and the fuel pipe banjo, the backing spring will force the filter half out of its housing in the float chamber cover, making removal for cleaning simple. If the gauze does not come forward in this fashion, lever round its rim with a small screwdriver to free it. Clean the gauze in petrol with a toothbrush. Never try to clean the gauze with a piece of rag.

3 On the H1/H2 carburettor unscrew the nut in the middle of the float chamber cover and lift away the cover. Note that there is a fibre float chamber body.

4 On the HS2 and HS4 carburettors the cover is held in position by three setscrews.

5 If it is not wished to remove the float chamber completely and the carburettor is still attached to the engine, carefully insert a thin piece of bent wire under the float and lift the float out (early models). On

later models the float is attached to the cover by its pivot and will come out as the cover is removed.

6   To remove the float chamber from the carburettor body on H1/H2 instruments, release the hexagon-headed retaining bolt at the base of the carburettor that passes through the float chamber extension casting. On the HS2 and HS4 units, release the bolt which runs horizontally through the carburettor. Make a careful note of the rubber grommets and washers, and on reassembly ensure that they are refitted in the correct order.

7   With the float chamber removed, it is a simple matter to turn it upside down to drop the float out, early models. On later models, remove the float from the cover by sliding the pivot pin out, serrated end first. Check that the float is not cracked or leaking. If it is it must be repaired or renewed.

8   The float chamber cover contains the needle valve assembly which regulates the amount of fuel which is fed into the float chamber.

9   On early models, one end of the float lever rests on top of the float, rising and falling with it, while the other end pivots on a hinge pin which is held by two lugs. On the float cover side of the float lever is a needle which rises and falls in its seating according to the movement of the lever. With the cover in place the hinge pin is held in position by the walls of the float chamber. With the cover removed the pin is easily pushed out, so freeing the float lever and the needles.

10   Examine the top of the needle and the needle seating for wear. Wear is present when there is a discernable ridge in the chamfer of the needle. If this is evident, then the needle and seating must be renewed. This is a simple operation and the hexagon head of the needle housing is easily screwed out. Never renew either the needle or the seating without renewing the other part, as otherwise it will not be possible to get a fuel tight joint.

8   SU carburettors float chamber – float level adjustment

1   It is essential that the float level in the float chamber is always correct, otherwise excessive fuel consumption may occur. On reassembly of the float chamber check the float level before refitting the float chamber cover, in the following manner:

2   Invert the float chamber so that the needle valve is closed. On early cars with H1 carburettors it should be possible to just slide a 7/16 in (11 mm) bar between the lip of the float chamber cover. On later models with H2 carburettors, a 5/16 in (8 mm) bar should be used.

3   If the bar lifts the lever or if the lever stands proud of the bar, then it is necessary to bend the lever at the point between the shank and the curved portion shown in Fig. 3.4 until the clearance is correct. Never bend the float portion of the lever.

4   On later cars with a conical float use a 1/8 in (3.2 mm) bar and place it parallel to the float lever hinge pin and in the centre of the float chamber cover. Reset the angle of the float by bending the lever as necessary (Fig. 3.5).

9   SU carburettors (except HS4 models) – jet centring

1   When the suction piston is lifted and then released it should fall freely, landing with a soft, metallic click. It should do this with the jet head in its upper or lower position with no difference in sound. This indicates that the jet is correctly centred, but if there is a difference in sound or no sound at all with the nut in one position, then the jet must be correctly centred. The procedure is as follows.

2   Disconnect the link between the jet lever and the jet head, then remove the union securing the fuel feed to the float chamber and withdraw the pipe and jet together. Unscrew the jet adjusting nut and remove the spring. Refit the adjusting nut, run it right up to its uppermost position, then refit the jet and feed pipe. Slacken the nut slightly so that the jet bearing can just be turned with the fingers.

3   Remove the damper nut and damper from the top of the suction chamber and gently press the piston fully down. Tighten the jet locking nut, keeping the jet head in its correct angular position.

4   Lift the piston and release it, checking that it falls freely and evenly, landing with a soft metallic click. Lower the jet and repeat the piston lifting and falling procedure to compare the sound of it landing. The click should be identical with the jet raised or lowered. If not, the whole centring procedure must be carried out again until the correct result is achieved.

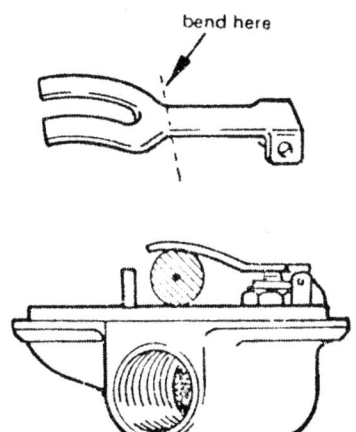

Fig. 3.4 Checking and adjusting the float level on H1 or H2 carburettors (Sec 8)

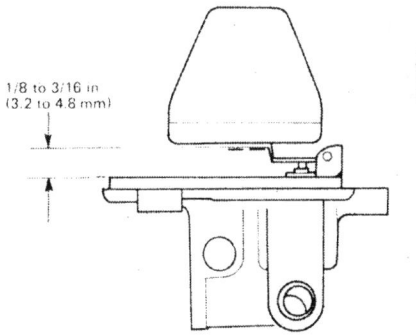

Fig. 3.5 Checking and adjusting the float level on HS2 or HS4 carburettors (Sec 8)

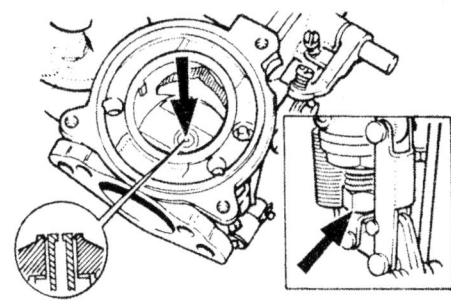

Fig. 3.6 Centralising the jet on H1 or H2 carburettors (Sec 9)

5   When all is correct remove the adjusting nut, refit the lock spring, the adjusting nut and jet, and the jet head lever link. Finally, adjust the carburettor mixture as described in Section 11 or 12.

6   Later models of the carburettor have a spring mounted needle and jet centring is not necessary.

10   SU carburettors piston and suction chamber – removal, cleaning and refitting

1   A fault peculiar to this type of carburettor arises when the piston sticks or rubs on the inside of the suction chamber. When new there is a fine clearance between the piston and wall of the suction chamber, but extensive use results in wear and this, as well as contamination such as dirt or grit, can cause the piston to contact the chamber wall. Piston sticking will result in incorrect mixture strength causing erratic and uneven running, overheating or high fuel consumption. To rectify this fault proceed as follows.

2   Scratch alignment marks on the suction chamber and the

carburettor body, Thoroughly clean the outside of the carburettor and then remove the damper rod from the top of the suction chamber. Undo and remove the suction chamber securing screws and carefully lift the chamber up vertically to remove it, revealing the piston and spring. Remove the spring and carefully lift the piston vertically, avoiding bending or side loads on the needle underneath it. Empty the oil out of the piston and support the piston on a narrow necked jar to protect the needle.

3   Clean off fuel deposits and stains using only petrol or methylated spirit and a piece of rough cloth – on no account use any abrasive, and this includes metal polish. Dry the parts after cleaning with lint-free rag.

4   A reasonably accurate test for wear on the piston or suction chamber can be made as follows. Lightly oil the piston rod in which the damper fits (but don't oil the piston periphery) and its bore in the suction chamber and reassemble the piston without its spring. Fit the damper and, using modelling clay, block off the suction transfer holes in the bottom of the piston. Hold the unit upside down and push the piston fully in. Then turn the assembly the right way up and, while preventing the piston from dropping out, time how long it takes the piston to move fully down. The correct time is five to seven seconds and if the piston travel time is outside this tolerance recheck for cleanliness and/or mechanical damage. Renew the assembly if it cannot be brought within the permitted time tolerance.

5   Reassembly follows the reverse of the dismantling procedure. Top up the damper with multigrade engine oil to a level of 0.5 in (13 mm) above the top of the hollow piston rod and refit the damper, not forgetting its sealing washer.

11 SU carburettors (H1 and H2) – adjustments and turning

1   Adjustments on SU carburettors are limited to setting the mixture strength and the idling speed. It is important that the spark plugs are in good condition, the contact breaker points are correctly adjusted, the valves and the springs are in good condition and the valve clearances correctly adjusted before making any adjustment on the carburettors. In addition the engine must be run until it has reached its normal running temperature. Remove the air intake cleaner before starting the adjustments.

2   Disconnect the carburettor throttle interconnection by slackenig the actuating arms. Unscrew each of the throttle adjusting screws to fully close the throttle then screw down each idling adjustment screw one full turn to open the throttle.

3   Remove the suction chambers and carefully lift out the pistons, identifying them so that they can be refitted to their correct carburettor, and disconnect the choke control cable. Turn the jet adjusting nuts so that each jet is flush with the bridge in the induction passage, or as near as possible, with both jets in the same relative positions. Refit the pistons and suction chambers and check that the pistons fall freely after being lifted. Turn down each jet adjusting nut two full turns (12 flats).

4   Restart the engine and adjust the idling speed by turning each throttle adjusting screw the same amount. Use a piece of tubing placed close to the carburettor intake and compare the hiss by listening to each carburettor in turn. Adjust the throttle adjusting screws to get the hiss similar in both intakes and the idling speed as specified. This procedure synchronises the throttles (Fig. 3.8). An easier (and for most people more accurate) method is to employ the use of a carburettor balancing device. These can be easily obtained at most good auto-accessory shops. The balancer should be used by following the manufacturer's instructions.

5   Once this has been achieved adjust the mixture strength by screwing each jet adjusting nut up or down by the same amount until the fastest idling speed is obtained with the engine running smoothly. Whilst making this adjustment, keep the jets pressed upwards to ensure that they are in contact with the adjusting nuts.

6   As the mixture is adjusted, it is likely that the idling speed will increase. If so, reduce the speed by adjusting the two throttle adjusting screws, each by the same amount.

7   Check the mixture strength by lifting the piston of the front carburettor by about 1/32 in (1 mm) and listen to the engine speed; this will indicate one of the following:

(a) *If the speed increases, then the front carburettor mixture strength is too rich*
(b) *If the speed immediately drops, then the mixture strength is too weak*
(c) *If the speed momentarily increases slightly, then stabilises, the mixture strength is correct*

8   Repeat the procedure on the rear carburettor and, after adjustment, recheck the front carburettor. Both carburettors are inter-dependant and the checking, adjusting and rechecking must be repeated until the mixture is correct on both carburettors and the idling speed is correct.

9   Once the mixture appears to be correct listen to the noise of the exhaust; it should be a regular, even note. If it is irregular with a splashy type of beat and no visible colour then the mixture is too weak. If there is a regular or rythmical type of beat together with traces of black smoke, the mixture is too rich.

10 Set the throttle linkage clearance by putting a 0.012 in (0.3 mm) feeler gauge between the throttle shaft stop at the top and the carburettor heat shield (Fig. 3.9). Move the throttle shaft lever down until the lever pin just rests on the lower arm of the fork in the carburettor throttle lever and then tighten the throttle shaft lever clamp bolt. Repeat the procedure on the other carburettor and then remove the feeler gauge. Operate the throttle and check that a clearance exists in both throttle pin/fork connections.

11 Reconnect the choke cable, making sure that the jet heads return against the lower face of the jet adjusting nuts when the choke knob is pushed fully home. Pull the choke knob out until the linkage is just about to move the carburettor jets (at least 0.25 in or 6 mm) and adjust the fast idle screws an equal amount to produce an engine speed of about 1000 rpm with the engine hot.

12 Refit the air intake cleaner.

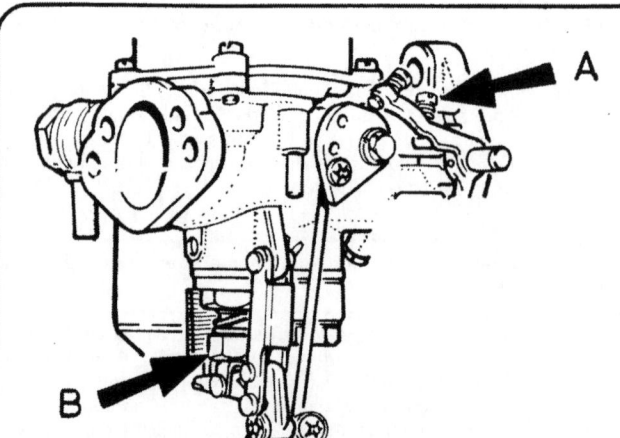

Fig. 3.7 The H1 or H2 carburettor throttle idle adjusting screw (A) and the mixture adjuster (B) (Sec 11)

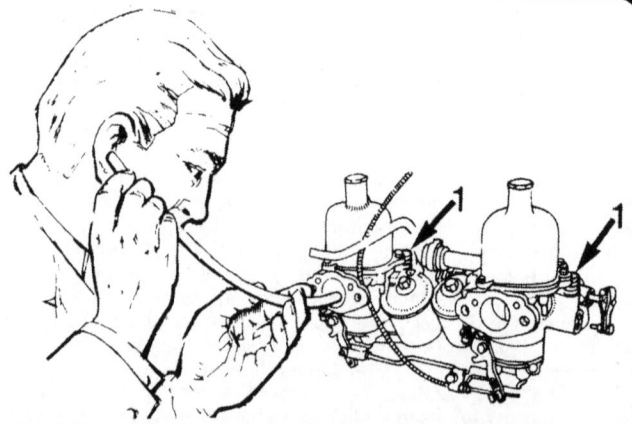

Fig. 3.8 Tuning twin carburettors by listening to the intake hiss using a length of tubing. Note the throttle idle adjustment screw (1) (Sec 11)

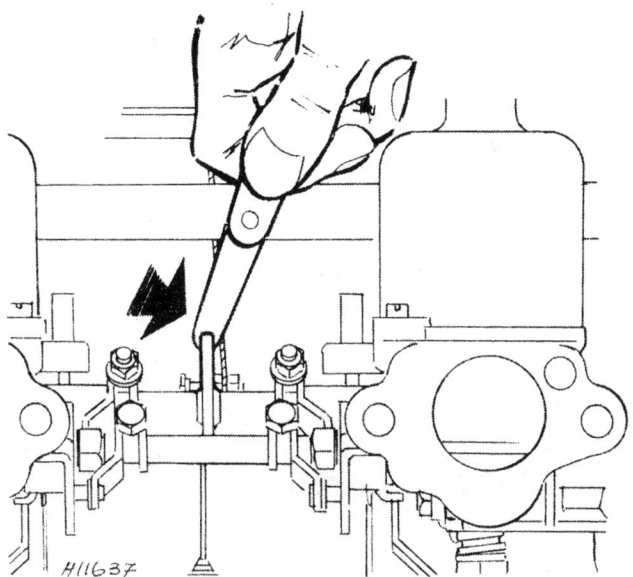

Fig. 3.9 Setting the throttle linkage clearance using a feeler gauge (Sec 11)

12.3 Removing the piston damper cap and oil dashpot plunger

12 SU carburettors (HS2 and HS4) – adjustments and tuning

1   Before any adjustments are made to the carburettors, it is essential that the ignition timing and all other engine adjustments are known to be as specified.
2   For vehicles used in countries with emission control regulations, it is advisable to tune the engine using an exhaust gas analyser (CO meter) or alternatively have it checked as soon as possible by your local BL dealer, who has the necessary equipment for the task.
3   Commence by removing the air cleaner(s). Remove each piston damper cap (photo) and top up the oil level if required with the specified engine oil to $\frac{1}{2}$ in (13 mm) over the top of the hollow piston rod.
4   Check that the throttle connections are working correctly, and that the mixture control (choke) returns fully with a small amount (about $\frac{1}{16}$ in 1.5 mm) of free play at the control knob end. There should be a small clearance between the fast idle screws and cams.
5   Lift and lower each piston in turn through the air intake aperture to ensure that they both move smoothly.
6   Run the engine at fast idle speed to its normal working temperature, then throttle up for about 30 seconds and then down to clear the inlet manifold of any excess fuel. Repeat this procedure every three minutes if the job is not completed within that time.
7   Now allow the engine to idle, and check the tachometer to see if the engine idles at the specified speed.
8   Should the idle speed be incorrect, stop the engine and loosen the throttle interconnection clamp bolts, and the cold start connection clamp bolts.
9   Restart the engine and listen to the 'hiss' in each carburettor intake in turn. To equalise the hiss, adjust the throttle screw of each carburettor. When this is achieved, the idle speed can be adjusted. Alternatively, use a carburettor balancing device in accordance with the manufacturer's instructions.
10   If the correct idle speed has been reached but the engine seems 'lumpy' or erratic, then the mixture jets will have to be adjusted.
11   Stop the engine and screw the jet adjustment nuts of each carburettor upwards so that the jets are level with the bridge of the carburettors, or as near as possible. Check that both of the jets are at the same level and then unscrew each adjustment downwards by two complete turns, (12 flats).
12   Now with the engine running at idle speed, simultaneously turn the two adjustment nuts one flat at a time, either down to enrichen the mixture or up to weaken it, until you get the fastest engine speed indicated on the tachometer with the engine running smoothly. Turn each nut up to the point where the speed just starts to drop to achieve correct idling.
13   With the engine running smoothly, readjust, if necessary, the idle screws (equally) to obtain the correct engine speed.

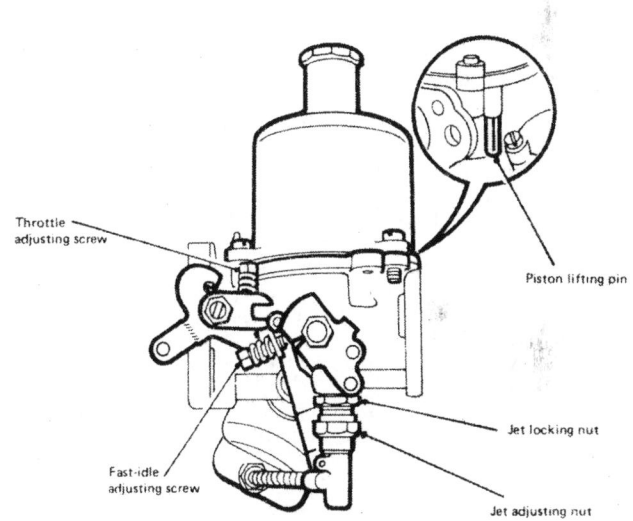

Fig. 3.10 The adjustments on the HS2 or HS4 carburettors (Sec 12)

Throttle adjusting screw

Piston lifting pin

Fast-idle adjusting screw

Jet locking nut

Jet adjusting nut

14   On engines with emission control equipment, the exhaust gas (CO) reading should be checked with an analyser, and the jet adjustment nuts turned by a maximum of half a turn to comply with the specified figure. If a half turn does not achieve the required figure, the carburettor must be removed and overhauled.
15   Reset the throttle connecting clamp lever so that the lever pins touch the lower arms of the forks.
16   Fit a 0.050 in (1.27 mm) feeler gauge between the throttle control bracket and shaft top, then tighten the interconnecting clamp bolts, and remove the feeler gauge. There should be about 1/32 in (1 mm) endfloat on the connection rod. The clearance between each lever pin and fork bottom on each carburettor should now be 0.012 in (0.3 mm) (photos).
17   Restart the engine and run at 1500 rpm. Now check that the throttle linkage connection is correct by ensuring that the carburettors are equally balanced. See paragraph 7 and 8 in the previous Section.
18   The cold start interconnections are set with the fast idle cams of each carburettor against their stops. Both cams should now start to move together. There should be 1/16 in (1.5 mm) free play before the choke cable operates the cams.
19   Pull the mixture control (choke) so that the linkage is about to operate the jet and then turn the fast idle screws to reach the correct fast idle speed, whilst listening to ensure a balanced adjustment is made.
20   The air cleaner(s) can now be refitted.

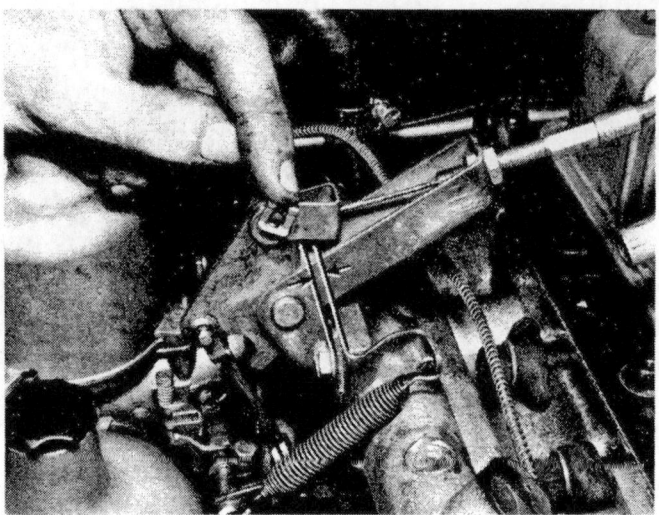

12.16a The throttle control bracket clearance – 1500 cc models

12.16b The clearance between the throttle fork and lever pin

13 Emission control carburettors (SU) – general

1   Some of the later SU carburettors incorporate refinements designed to meet some of the existing emission control regulations.

2   The throttle butterfly disc carries a small spring-loaded valve which opens when the throttle is closed and the engine is overrunning. This maintains a suitable mixture flow to reduce undesirable combustion products under these conditions.

3   The carburettor needle is mounted in a spring-loaded mounting in the piston, biased to one side so that it always rubs on the side of the jet. The normal type, which is meant to be set central, actually will always vary slightly from true and give uncontrolled variations of mixture. By using this biased needle, the effect on the mixture will be a known constant.

4   Spring-loaded needles are supplied complete with shouldered spring seats. No attempt should be made to alter the position of the spring seat or to convert a fixed type needle to spring-loaded application. The raised pip form in the needle guide ensures that the needle is correctly centralised. This pip should not be removed or repositioned. The needle with its spring and in its guide should be assembled into the piston so that the lower edge is exactly flush with the face of the piston. The needle must be at the correct axis in the piston. Some guides have a line etched on their face. This must be between the two piston transfer holes. Alternative needle guides have a flat machined on them which must be positioned so that the locking screw tightens down onto it. If the guide is incorrectly positioned the locking screw will stick out from the piston. Guide locking screws for spring-loaded needles are shorter than those for normal fixed needles.

5   The jet adjusting nut has an 'adjustment restrictor' (Fig. 3.11). This limits the amount of adjustment on the nut unless the tag on the restrictor is unsealed and bent up. Provided that the needle is in the correct position the range of movements should be sufficient to obtain the correct mixture. If it is not, then a full carburettor tuning service will be needed, which involves undoing the tag. Before doing this beware of local regulations that might be broken by the undoing of seals. Also, unless the person making the adjustment has the necessary skill and test equipment, such as an exhaust gas analyser, the engine emissions might be outside the allowed amount. The adjustment restrictor can be disengaged from the jet adjusting nut be bending up its tag. When the jet adjustment is correct the restrictor should be engaged as follows:

(a)   *Holding the jet adjusting nut to prevent it turning, the adjustment restrictor is moved until the vertical tag contacts the carburettor body on the left-hand side when viewed from the air cleaner flange*

(b)   *The tag is then bent down onto the flat of the jet adjusting nut*

(c)   *The restrictor will now follow the movements of the jet adjusting nut. It will allow weakening of the mixture but not enrichment*

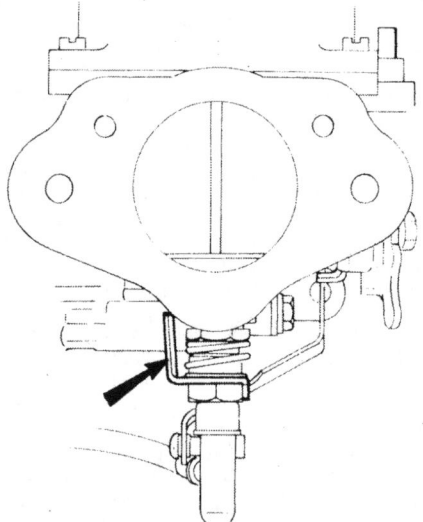

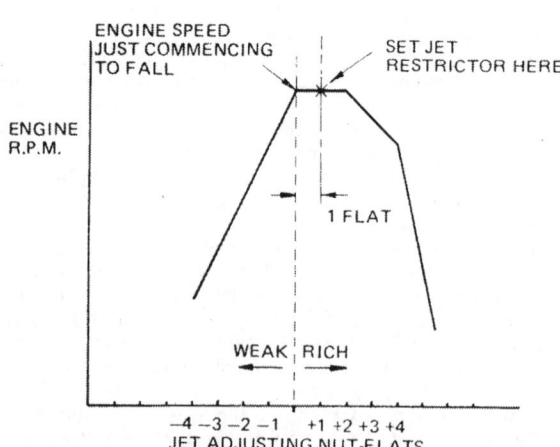

Fig. 3.11 Jet adjustment restrictor on SU emission control carburettors (top) and point of adjustment (bottom) (Sec 13)

14 Zenith-Stromberg 150 CD4 and 150 CD4T carburettors – dismantling, inspection and reassembly

Note: *Before dismantling, check the availability of spare parts. If the needle is to be adjusted, special tool No 'S353' will be required.*

1   With the carburettor removed from the car, clean off the exterior.

2   Remove the damper cap by unscrewing, then carefully lift the piston whilst simultaneously withdrawing the retaining cap from the air valve unit.

3   From the float chamber, pull out the bottom plug, and drain the oil and fuel from the carburettor.

4   Now unscrew the screws retaining the float chamber to one body and remove it complete with gasket.

5   Prise the spindle from the clip at opposing ends of the float assembly and remove it. Note that the float supporting plate is located towards the outside of the float.

6   Unscrew the needle valve and washer.

7   Remove the top cover by unscrewing the four retaining screws. Lift off the cover complete with spring and the air valve unit. Note the diaphragm outer tag position in the carburettor body.

8   The diaphragm can now be carefully removed after unscrewing the four securing screws, and lifting off the retaining ring. Note the diaphragm inner tag position in the air valve assembly.

9   At this stage the special tool No S353 is needed. Loosen the needle retaining grub screw in the side of the air valve and insert the special tool into the air valve stem. Engage the needle mounting and unscrew it two or three turns. Remove the grub screw and carefully pull the needle and mounting out of the air valve. Remove the special tool but don't remove the needle adjuster from the air valve.

10   For automatic choke carburettors carry on at paragraph 14. On manual choke units remove the starter box retaining screws and withdraw the starter box.

11   Remove the EGR air bleed valve and bracket.

12   Dismantle the starter box assembly by unscrewing the nut and lockwasher from the spindle, remove the choke cable lever and the fast idle cam, and then withdraw the starter disc and spindle.

13   Remove the C-clip and spring from the starter disc spindle.

14   On all models remove the idle air regulator cover, if fitted, then remove the idle air regulator and its gasket after removing the two securing screws.

15   Withdraw the deceleration bypass valve unit and gasket by removing its three retaining screws. To dismantle this unit, release the basepate from the valve housing by unscrewing the retaining screws and then disconnect the spring, valve and gaskets from the body of the deceleration valve. To release the adjustment screw, remove the star washer. Now remove the adjustment screw O-ring and unscrew the locknut.

16   For auto-choke carburettors carry on at paragraph 19. On manual choke carburettors unscrew the idle adjustment screw and spring.

17   Withdraw the split pin and clevis pin with washers from the throttle spindle lever and disconnect it.

18   The throttle lever retaining nut can now be removed from the spindle to disconnect the lever with retainer and spring.

19   On auto-choke models, undo and remove the nut securing the linkage rod lever, remove the washer and lever with its brush and spring, and then remove the stop lever and spring.

20   After removing the three securing screws and spring washers remove the auto-choke unit and its gasket from the carburettor body.

21   Dismantle the auto-choke unit by first removing the water jacket after removing its securing bolt and washer. Remove the water jacket sealing ring. Then undo and remove the three screws to release the heat mass and its insulator. Finally remove the vacuum kick piston cover and gasket after removing the three retaining screws.

22   On all models, with the carburettor fully dismantled the various internal parts can be cleaned using clean fuel and allowed to drain dry – don't use rag. After cleaning, lay all components out on a flat, clean surface ready for examination.

23   Inspect all parts for wear or damage. In particular, closely examine the float needle and seat, the air valve, and its diaphragm, all of which, unless they are in near perfect condition, should be renewed. If the following parts are damaged the complete carburettor should be renewed:

(a)   *Manual choke models: starter box, idle and air regulator or deceleration bypass valve*

(b)   *Auto-choke models: auto-choke idle and air regulator or deceleration by pass valve*

24   Before reassembly, obtain a repair kit for the carburettor, which contains the relevant seals and gaskets which must be renewed.

25   Reassemble the components of the carburettor in the reverse order of dismantling paying particular attention to the following:

(a)   *Ensure that all components are spotlessly clean. Do not overtighten retaining screws and use only hand-pressure to fit the components*

(b)   *When fitting the deceleration bypass valve between the baseplate gaskets, ensure that the spring register is towards the valve body*

(c)   *(Not auto-choke models) When refitting the disc unit to the starter body, ensure that the lug detent ball is located in the disc slot and the largest of the series of holes*

(d)   *(Not auto-choke models) When refitting the cam and choke cable levers, ensure that the cam lever is located with the detent ball*

(e)   *When using special tool 'S353' to engage the needle valve threads with those of the adjusting valve screw, turn the tool clockwise until the needle housing slot is in line with the grub screw. Then tighten the grub screw. The grub screw does not tighten onto the needle housing – it only locates into the slot, which ensures that during adjustment, the needle remains in its operating position*

(f)   *When fitting the diaphragm it locates to the inner tag in the recess of the air valve*

(g)   *The air valve is fitted so that the outer tag of the diaphragm is located in the recesses of the carburettor body*

(h)   *The top cover is located in position with the bulge of the housing neck to the air intake. Tighten the top cover retaining screws evenly*

(i)   *When the float assembly has been refitted, the float height is checked by measuring between the carburettor gasket face and the high point of the floats. It is essential that the float height is equal and set to 0.625 in to 0.672 in (16 mm to 17 mm). If adjustment is required bend the tab accordingly, but the tab must seat on the needle valve at right-angles (Fig. 3.12).*

(j)   *(Auto-choke models only) Check and adjust the auto-choke as described in Section 16*

(k)   *When the carburettor is refitted to the car, the damper dashpot is lubricated with clean engine oil. Use the damper as a dipstick; when the threaded plug is 0.25 in (6 mm) above the dashpot, resistance should be felt. Then lift the piston and press the damper securing cap into the air valve taking great care. Screw the damper cap into the cover*

(l)   *The carburettor is now ready for tuning – see the next Section*

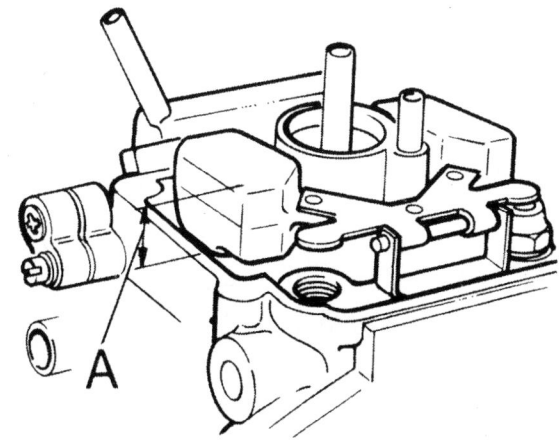

Fig. 3.12 Checking the float level (A) on Zenith-Stromberg 150 CD4 and 150 CD4T carburettors – see text (Sec 14)

Fig. 3.13 Exploded view of Zenith-Stromberg 150 CD4 carburettor. Top left: auto-choke components on the 150 CD4T carburettor (Sec 14)

1 Damper cap
2 Bottom plug
3 Float chamber and gasket
4 Float
5 Needle valve and washer
6 Top cover
7 Spring
8 Air valve unit
9 Retaining ring and diaphragm
10 Grub screw
11 Piston
12 Starter box unit
13 Choke cable lever
13a Choke operated EGR control valve
14 Starter disc and spindle
15 Air regulator and gasket
16 Deceleration bypass valve unit and gasket
17 Idle adjustment screw and spring
18 Throttle lever clevis pin and split pin
19 Throttle lever and spring unit
20 Special tool No S353
21 Nut, washer and linkage rod lever
22 Auto-choke operating lever, bush and spring
23 Stop lever and spring
24 Auto-choke and gasket
25 Water jacket and sealing ring
26 Heat mass and insulator
27 Vacuum kick piston cover

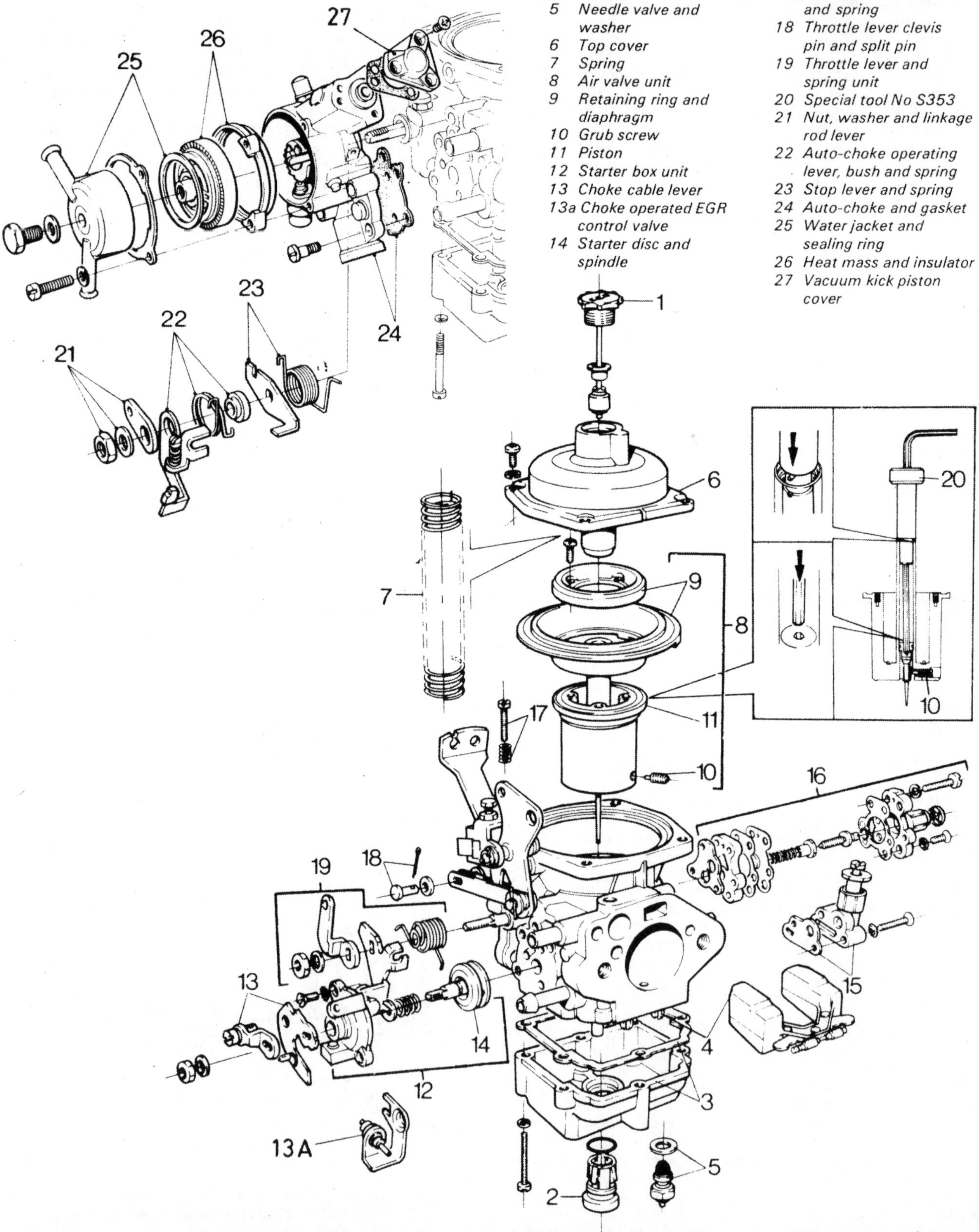

15 Zenith-Stromberg 150 CD4 and 150 CD4T carburettors – checks and adjustments

1   Tuning of the carburettor is limited to topping up the damper, setting the idle speed and the mixture strength at idle, and adjusting the deceleration bypass valve. Success will depend on the engine having correct ignition timing, spark plug gaps accurately set and correct valve clearances. In addition the following seals must all be in good condition: oil filler cap to rocker cover, rocker cover to cylinder head, oil dipstick to cylinder block, carburettor to inlet manifold, exhaust manifold to cylinder head, and all inlet manifold tappings. Adjustments should only be attempted using an accurate tachometer and an exhaust gas (CO) analyser, and you will also require the use of special tool No S353 if adjusting the mixture strength. CO percentage cannot be achieved on the fine idle CO screw. Without these it would be better to let your BL agent make the adjustments as he will have the necessary equipment.
2   Tuning must be carried out as soon as the engine reaches its normal running temperature and if it cannot be completed within three minutes, the engine speed should be increased to about 2000 rpm for 30 seconds to clear the inlet manifold. This procedure should be repeated at three-minute intervals until the job is finished.

Idle speed check and adjustment

3   With the tachometer connected in accordance with the maker's instructions, start the engine and warm it up to its normal temperature. On manual choke models check that there is a small clearance between the fast idle screw and the cam. Check the idle speed and if necessary adjust the idle speed screw to achieve the specified rpm (Fig. 3.14).

Mixture strength CO percentage at idle

4   Check and, if necessary, adjust the idle speed as previously explained.
5   Disconnect the air pump outlet hose at the pump end and plug the hose; make sure that the pump outlet remains clear or the pump could be damaged with the engine running if it is blocked. Recheck the idle speed after doing this.
6   Following the maker's instructions, check the percentage CO at idle speed using the exhaust gas analyser. Compare the indicated and permitted values, and if necessary adjust the fine idle CO screw clockwise to enrich or anti-clockwise to weaken. If you can adjust the indicated value to within the permitted limit proceed to paragraph 12, ignoring the intervening paragraphs. If the permitted value cannot be achieved proceed as follows.
7   Stop the engine and remove the air cleaner. Lift the piston using a finger, and at the same time unscrew and raise the damper. Carefully ease the retaining cup from the hollow piston rod to permit removal of the damper assembly from the piston. Refer to Section 17 for more detail.
8   Carefully insert the special tool S353 into the dashpot, engaging the outer part of the tool in the air valve and the inner part of the hexagon in the plug of the needle adjuster. Check that the tool is properly engaged and hold the outer part firmly whilst using it to avoid tearing the diaphragm.
9   Start the engine and, holding the outer part of the tool firmly, turn the inner part clockwise to enrich, or anti-clockwise to weaken the mixture as required.
10   Stop the engine and remove the tool. Hold the piston up and top up the hollow rod with engine oil to a level of $\frac{1}{4}$ in (6 mm) below the top of the hollow piston rod. Don't use a heavy bodied oil in the damper. Lower the piston and check that the oil level is still correct. If so raise the piston again and carefully press the retainer cup into the hollow piston rod, then screw the damper cap into the top of the carburettor.
11   Refit the air cleaner and start the engine. Recheck the idle speed and recheck the percentage CO at idle; if necessary adjust on the fine idle CO screw to achieve the permitted value.
12   Stop the engine, remove the plug from the air pump hose and reconnect the hose securely to the pump.

Fast idle speed checking and adjusting

13   For auto-choke carry on at paragraph 15. On manual choke check that the mixture control cam lever contacts its stop and then pull the choke control knob about $\frac{1}{4}$ in (6 mm) to engage the fast idle cam in

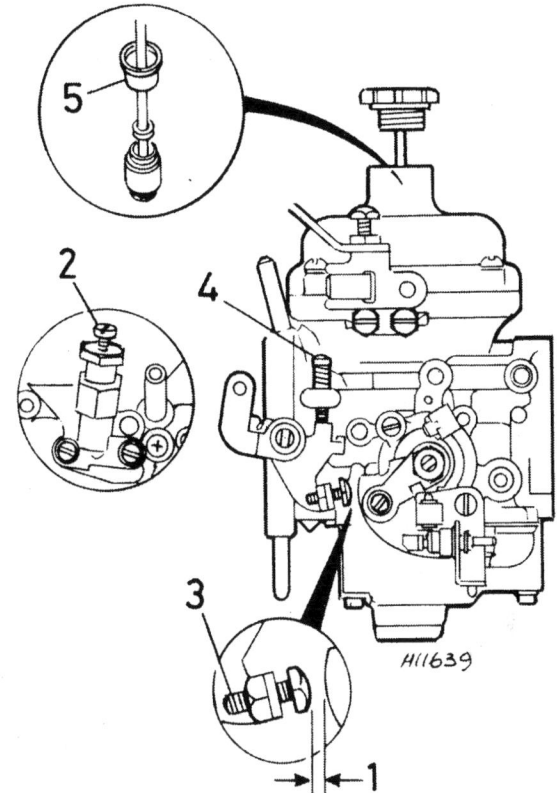

Fig. 3.14 Adjusting the Zenith-Stromberg 150 CD4 carburettor (Sec 15)

1 *Check for this clearance before adjusting idle speed*	3 *Fast idle screw*
	4 *Idle speed screw*
2 *Fast idle CO screw*	5 *Damper retaining cup*

the ball locator. Check that the ball and cam are correctly engaged.
14   Start the engine and check the idle speed. Slacken the locknut, if necessary, to adjust the fast idle screw to produce the correct engine speed. Tighten the locknut, push the choke knob fully in and stop the engine.

Deceleration bypass valve checking and adjustment

15   On all models start the engine and, if necessary, run until it has reached its normal working temperature, then continue running at a fast idle for a further five minutes.
16   With the engine still running, disconnect the vacuum pipe at the distributor end and, while noting the engine speed, place a finger over the end of the pipe to block it.
17   If you should notice the engine speed rise to about 1300 rpm, but if it rises sharply to 2000 to 2500 rpm then the deceleration bypass valve will need adjusting.
18   Plug the end of the vacuum pipe and carefully unscrew the adjusting screw (Fig. 3.15) until the engine speed drops to 1300 rpm. 'Blip' the throttle to momentarily increase the speed and check that it drops again to 1300 rpm. If necessary readjust on the screw. When correct, give the screw half a turn anti-clockwise to seat the valve correctly. Unplug the vacuum pipe, reconnect it to the distributor and stop the engine.

16 Zenith-Stromberg 150 CD4T carburettor auto-choke – checking and adjusting

1   First remove the carburettor as described in Section 4 and if necessary clean it externally to prevent internal contamination.
2   Move the throttle to the open position and hold it there with a suitable wedge.
3   Remove the auto-choke coolant jacket and sealing ring after

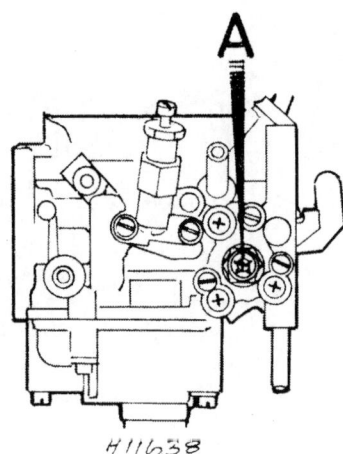

Fig. 3.15 The deceleration bypass valve adjusting screw (A) on the Zenith-Stromberg 150 CD4 carburettor (Sec 15)

removing the retaining bolt and washer. Then remove the three screws and washers which hold the heat mass in place and remove the heat mass and its insulator.

4   Rotate the operating arm and make the following checks (Fig. 3.16):

(a) Check the vacuum kick piston and rod for full and free-movement

(b) Check that the fast idle cam and thermostat lever are free on the pivot

(c) Move the cam from the lever and check that it returns to the lever under spring pressure. Rotate the lever, checking that the cam remains on the lever

Remove the throttle wedge after making these checks.

5   Refer to Fig. 3.16 and adjust the idle screw to set the gap 'A' between the throttle levers and choke to $\frac{3}{32}$ in (2.4 mm).

6   Loosen the throttle stop screw locknut and adjust the screw to produce a clearance 'B' between the end of the fast idle pin and the cam of 0.035 in (0.9 mm), then tighten the locknut.

7   Refit the heat mass, its insulator and the coolant jacket with its sealing ring. Make sure that the moving end of the temperature coil registers properly on the operating arm, and if necessary use a new sealing ring under the coolant jacket. Do not tighten the three screws in the clamp plate or the coolant jacket centre bolt just yet.

8   Align the index marks on the heat mass with the datum mark on the auto-choke body, and then tighten the three screws.

9   Turn the coolant jacket to correctly align the hose connections, and then tighten the centre bolt.

10 Refit the carburettor as described in Section 14 and tune it as described in Section 15.

17 Carburettor damper (all models) – topping up

1   It is important not to use a heavy bodied oil in the carburettor damper, as the functioning of the carburettor will be adversely affected. Use a fresh sample of the recommended engine oil.

SU carburettors

2   Unscrew the cap on top of the suction chamber and, on later models, withdraw the damper with the cap. Check the oil level, and if necessary top up to $\frac{1}{2}$ in (13 mm) from the top on early models, or $\frac{1}{2}$ in (13 mm) above the top of the hollow piston rod on later models.

3   Push the damper back into position, if fitted, and tighten the blanking cap.

Zenith-Stromberg carburettors

4   Unscrew the damper cap and lift the damper to the limit of its travel. Carefully refit the damper; if the oil level is correct, a resistance

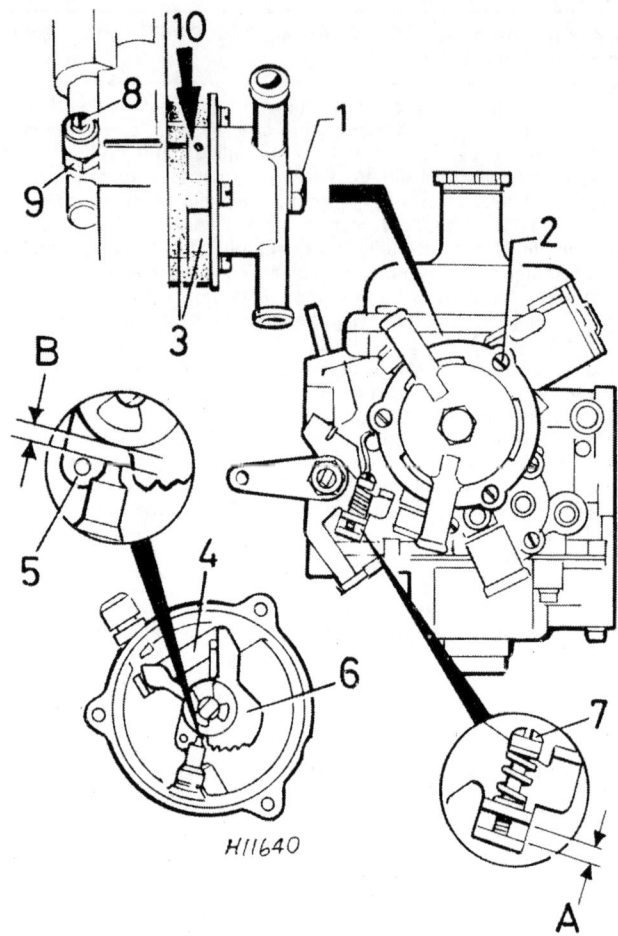

Fig. 3.16 Checking and adjusting the auto-choke (Sec 16)

1   Auto-choke water jacket retaining bolt
2   Heat mass retaining screw
3   Heat mass and insulator
4   Check vacuum kick piston and rod
5   Check fast idle cam and thermostat lever
6   Move cam and check return
7   Idle speed screw
8   Throttle stop screw
9   Locknut
10 Align heat mass index with datum
A and B – see text

will be felt when there is a gap of about $\frac{1}{4}$ in (6 m) between the bottom of the cap and the top of the suction chamber. If the level is correct refit the damper cap but, if topping up is needed, proceed as follows.

5   Remove the air cleaner and, with the damper cap still unscrewed, carefully lift the piston with a finger and ease the retaining cup out of the hollow piston rod to release the damper (Fig. 3.17).

6   With the piston raised, top up the oil level until it is $\frac{1}{4}$ in (6 mm) below the top of the hollow piston rod. Lower the piston and check that the oil level is still correct. Raise the piston again, refit the damper retaining cup, lower the piston and refit the damper cap to the top of the carburettor. Finally, refit the air cleaner.

18 Exhaust pipe and silencers – removal and refitting

1   The exhaust system on the earliest models consists of a straight-through pipe with silencer. The later standard consists of a two-piece system with a downpipe connected to the manifold, (which on USA and Canada models incorporates a catalytic converter for emission control) and a separate tailpipe incorporating two silencer boxes. The tailpipe is suspended from the bodywork on brackets with built-in resilient rubber mountings.

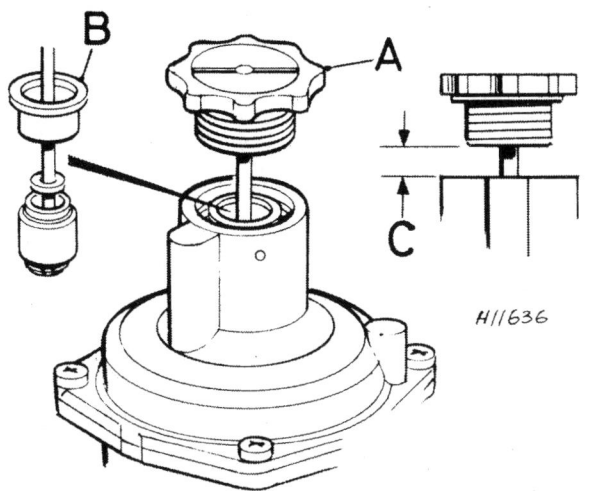

Fig. 3.17 Topping up the damper on the Zenith-Stromberg carburettors (Sec 17)

A Damper cap
B Damper retaining cup
C Height of cap when oil level is correct

Front pipe removal and refitting

2   For models employing a catalytic converter refer to Section 40. On other models jack up the front of the car and support it on stands. Apply the handbrake fully. Refer to Section 2 and remove the air cleaner. Disconnect the throttle return spring (where applicable) attached to the bracket on the exhaust by unhooking it from the throttle mechanism lever.

3   Two types of manifold/front pipe connection have been used. With the first type, a simple butt-type joint is used, the front pipe being held on its angled flange to the manifold by two semi-circular clamp halves by two bolts with nuts. To disconnect this type, slacken and remove the two nuts, then remove the two clamp halves and bolts, being careful not to loose the special 'washers'. The front pipe may now be disconnected from the manifold. With the second type, undo and remove the three nuts and bolts securing the pipe to the manifold and retrieve the washers and the throttle spring bracket. Disconnect the front pipe from the manifold and remove the gasket.

4   Undo and remove the three nuts, bolts and washers securing the front and tailpipes. Remove the front pipe and retrieve the joint olive between the two pipes. On earlier types it will be necessary to remove the exhaust clamp securing the front pipe to the silencer section. In some cases it may be necessary to first remove the tailpipe/silencer assembly as detailed below.

5   Refitting the front pipe is the reverse of removal, but use a new joint gasket between the pipe and manifold (where applicable). Get all the bolts, washers and nuts into position, not forgetting the throttle spring bracket (where applicable), before tightening any, and then tighten the pipe-to-manifold bolts or clamp before the front-to-tailpipe bolts or clamp. If necessary fit new gaskets to the air cleaner on refitting it.

Tailpipe and silencers removal and refitting

6   Jack up the rear of the car and support it on stands. Chock the front wheels in front and behind.

7   Undo and remove the three nuts, bolts and washers connecting the front pipe to the tailpipe, or remove the clamp. Separate the joint and retrieve the joint olive from between the pipes, where applicable.

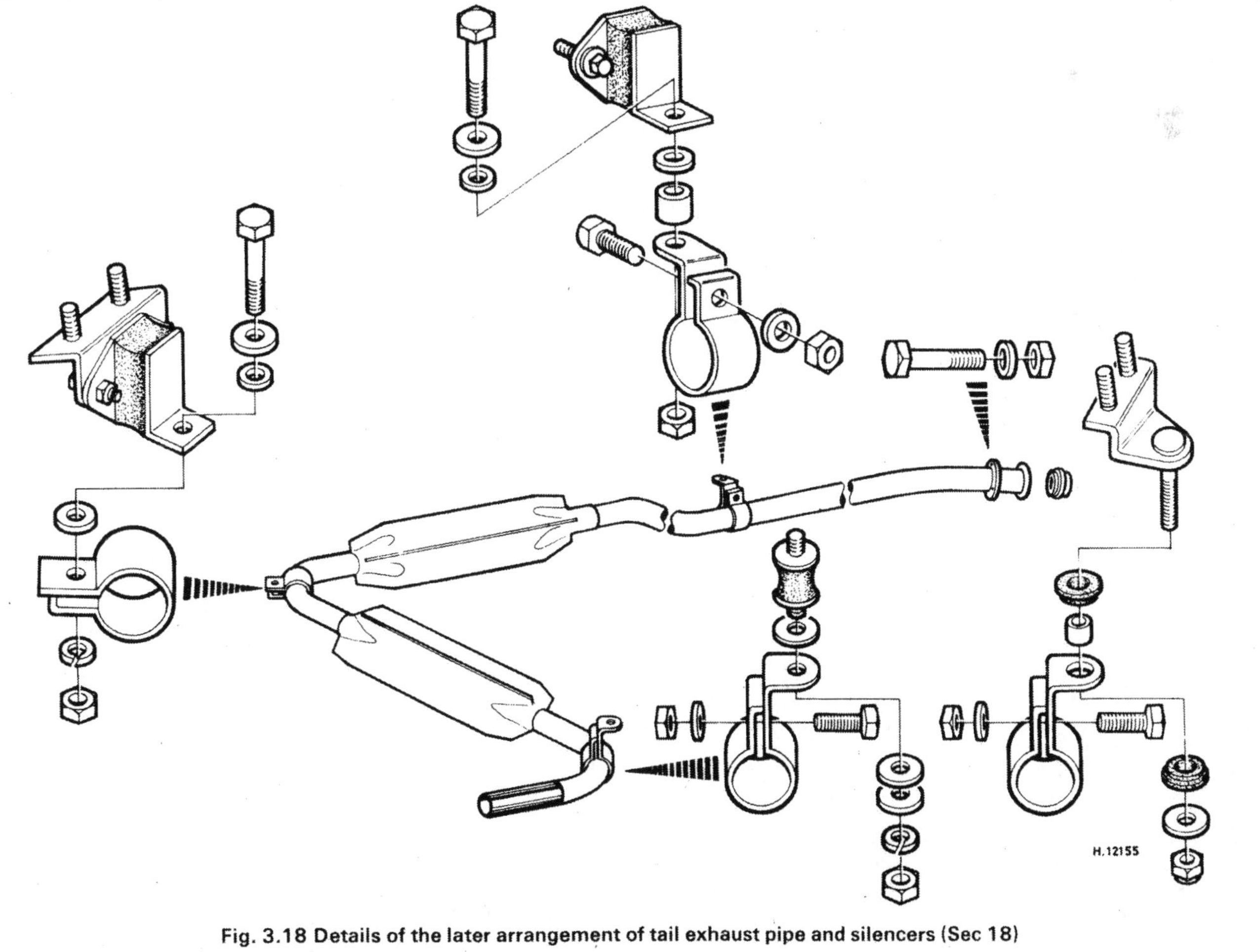

Fig. 3.18 Details of the later arrangement of tail exhaust pipe and silencers (Sec 18)

8   The tail-pipe is suspended on these mountings. Remove the nuts, bolts and washers from the middle mounting, then undo the front mounting, but leave the pipe loosely suspended. Undo and remove the rear mounting bolts, nuts and washers, lower the pipe to the ground, disconnect the front mounting and remove the pipe from the car.

9   Before refitting the tailpipe, examine all fasteners, brackets, washers, etc, and renew those that are corroded or deteriorated. Get the pipe into position with all fasteners, mountings and brackets loosely assembled and then start tightening everything working back from the front to the rear.

10   After the initial engine run, which should be sufficient to warm the system up to its normal temperature, check all fasteners for tightness.

19 AC fuel pump – description

The mechanically operated AC fuel pump is actuated through a spring-loaded rocker arm. One arm of the rocker bears against an eccentric on the camshaft and the other arm operates a diaphragm pullrod.

As the engine camshaft rotates, the eccentric moves the pivoted rocker arm outwards, which in turn pulls the diaghragm pullrod and the diaphragm down against the pressure of the diaphragm spring. This creates sufficient vacuum in the pump chamber to draw in fuel from the tank through the sediment chamber, fuel filter gauze, and non-return inlet valve.

The rocker arm is held in constant contact with the eccentric by an anti-rattle spring, and as the engine camshaft continues to rotate, the eccentric allows the rocker arm to move inwards. The diaphragm spring is thus free to push the diaphragm upwards, forcing the fuel in the pump chamber out to the carburettor through the non-return outlet valve.

When the float chamber in the carburettor is full the float chamber needle valve will close so preventing further flow from the fuel pump. The pressure in the delivery line will hold the diaphragm downwards against the pressure of the diaphragm spring, and it will remain in this position until the needle valve in the float chamber opens to admit more petrol.

20 AC fuel pump – removal and refitting

1   Disconnect the battery earth lead.

2   On USA and Canada models remove the screw and nut from the car heater intake hose bracket and remove the hose.

3   Remove the fuel inlet and outlet pipes by unscrewing the union nuts, or on later models, compress the clips, or unscrew the clips (photo).

4   Unscrew the two set bolts and spring washer which hold the pump to the crankcase.

5   Lift the pump together with the gasket away from the crankcase.

6   Refitting of the pump is a reversal of the above procedure. Remember to use a new crankcase-to-fuel pump gasket to ensure no oil leaks, ensure that both faces of the flange are perfectly clean, and check that the rocker arm lies on top of the camshaft eccentric and not underneath it (photo).

21 AC fuel pump – testing

1   Assuming that the fuel lines and unions are in good condition and that there are no leaks anywhere, check the performance of the fuel pump in the following manner.

2   Disconnect the fuel pipe at the carburettor inlet union, and the high tension lead to the coil, and with a suitable container or a large rag in position to catch the ejected fuel, turn the engine over on the starter motor solenoid.

3   A good spurt of petrol should emerge from the end of the pipe every second revolution.

22 AC fuel pump – dismantling and maintenance

1   Unscrew the securing bolt from the centre of the cover and lift the cover away. Note the fibre washer under the head of the bolt (photo).

2   Remove the cork sealing washer and the fine mesh filter gauze.

3   Routine maintenance consists of carefully washing the filter gauze in petrol, and cleaning all traces of sediment from the chamber. To reassemble the pump, reverse the above procedure.

4   Some pumps cannot be dismantled any further and, in the event of a defect, must be renewed as a complete unit. Other pumps have five screws securing the two body halves together and if the condition of the diaphragm is suspect or for any reason it is wished to dismantle the pump fully, proceed as follows. Mark the upper and lower flanges of the pump that are adjacent to each other. Unscrew the five screws and spring washers which hold the two halves of the pump body together. Separate the two halves with great care, ensuring that the diaphragm does not stick to either of the two flanges.

5   Unscrew the three screws which retain the valve plate and remove the plate and gasket together with the inlet and outlet valves. (Some later pumps have a simplified valve plate arrangement which is released by one screw).

6   Rotate the diaphragm a quarter of a turn (in either direction) to release the pullrod from the operating lever, and lift away the diaphragm and pullrod (which is securely fixed to the diaphragm and cannot be removed from it). Remove the diaphragm spring and the metal fibre washer underneath it.

7   If it is necessary to dismantle the rocker arm assembly, remove the retaining circlips and washer from the rocker arm pivot rod and slide out the rod, which will then free the rocker arm, operating rod, and anti-rattle spring.

23 AC fuel pump – examination and reassembly

Note: *This Section applies to only those pumps which can be dismantled; see previous Section.*

1   Check the condition of the cork cover sealing washer. If it is hardened or broken it must be renewed. The diaphragm should be checked similarly and renewed if faulty. Clean the pump thoroughly and agitate the valves in clean fuel to clean them out. This will also improve the contact between the valve seat and the valve. It is unlikely that the pump body will be damaged, but check for fractures and cracks. Renew the cover if distorted by over-tightening.

2   To reassemble the pump proceed as follows: Refit the rocker arm assembly comprising the operating link, rocker arm, anti-rattle spring and washer in their relative positions in the pump body. Align the holes in the operating link, rocker arm, and washers with the holes in the body and insert the pivot pin.

3   Refit the circlips to the grooves in each end of the pivot pin.

4   Earlier pumps use valves which have to be built up, while later versions use ready assembled valves which are merely dropped into place in the inlet and outlet ports. Ensure that the correct valve is dropped into each port.

5   Reassemble the earlier type of valve as follows: position the delivery valve in place on its spring. Place the inlet valve in position in the pump body and then fit the spring. Place the small four-legged inlet valve spring retainer over the spring with the legs positioned towards the spring.

6   Place the valve retaining gasket in position, refit the plate, and tighten down the three securing screws, (or single screw in the case of later models). Check that the valves are working properly with a suitable piece of wire.

7   Position the fibre and steel washers in that order in the base of the pump and place the diaphragm spring over them.

8   Refit the diaphragm and pullrod assembly with the pullrod downwards and the small tab on the diaphragm adjacent to the centre of the flange and rocker arm.

9   With the body of the pump held so that the rocker arm is facing away from you, press down the diaphragm, turning it a quarter of a turn to the left at the same time. This engages the slot on the pullrod with the operating lever. The small tab on the diaphragm should now be at an angle of 90° to the rocker arm and the diaphragm should be firmly located.

10   Move the rocker arm until the diaphragm is level with the body flanges and hold the arm in this position. Reassemble the two halves of the pump, ensuring that the previously made marks on the flanges are adjacent to each other.

11   Insert the five screws and lockwashers and tighten them down finger tight.

12   Move the rocker arm up and down several times to centralise the

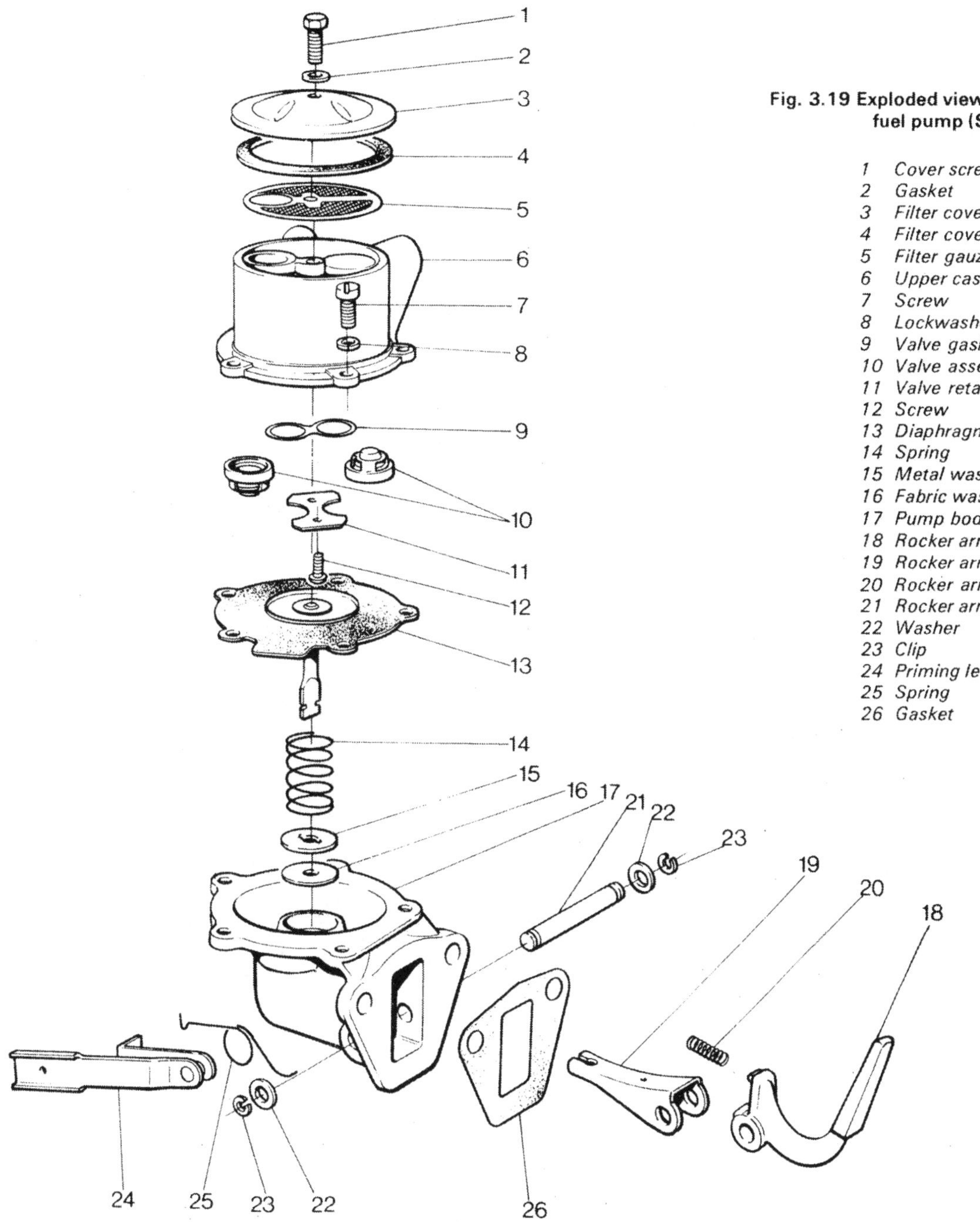

Fig. 3.19 Exploded view of the AC 'Y' type fuel pump (Sec 19)

1   Cover screw
2   Gasket
3   Filter cover
4   Filter cover gasket
5   Filter gauze
6   Upper casting
7   Screw
8   Lockwasher
9   Valve gasket
10 Valve assembly
11 Valve retainer
12 Screw
13 Diaphragm
14 Spring
15 Metal washer
16 Fabric washer
17 Pump body
18 Rocker arm
19 Rocker arm link
20 Rocker arm spring
21 Rocker arm pin
22 Washer
23 Clip
24 Priming lever
25 Spring
26 Gasket

20.3 The AC mechanical fuel pump on the 1500 cc engine

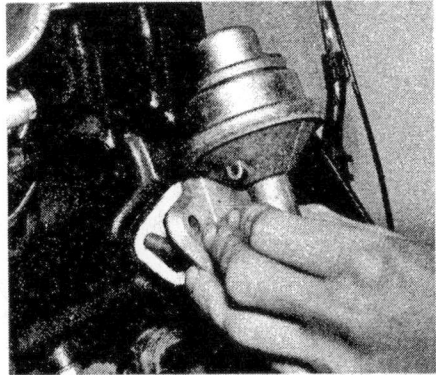

20.6 Refitting the AC fuel pump – note the new gasket in position

22.1 The AC fuel pump cover and filter removed, showing top cover (1), cover sealing gasket (2), cover retaining screw (3), filter (4) and retaining screw sealing gasket (5)

diaphragm, and then with the arm held down, tighten the screws securely in a diagonal sequence.
13 Refit the gauze filter in position. Fit the cork cover sealing washer, fit the cover, and insert the bolt with the fibre washer under its head. Do not overtighten the bolt but ensure that it is tight enough to prevent all leaks.

24 SU fuel pump – description

Three types of SU fuel pumps have been fitted over the years. As the pumps are so similar, it is quite possible that a non-standard one has been fitted on an exchange basis, and for this reason the differences between the pumps will be listed in the text as they occur, so that if a later type of pump has been fitted it will create no difficulty. The following can apply equally to all three types of pump except where otherwise stated.

The SU 12-volt electric fuel pump consists of a long outer body casing housing the diaphragm, armature and solenoid assembly, with at one end the contact breaker assembly protected by a bakelite cover, and at the other end a short casting containing the inlet and outlet ports, filter, valves, and pumping chamber. The joint between the bakelite cover and the body casing is protected with a rubber sheath.

The pump operates in the following manner. When the ignition is switched on current travels from the terminal on the outside of the bakelite cover through the coil located round the solenoid core, which becomes energised and, acting like a magnet, draws the armature towards it. The current then passes through the points to earth. When the armature is drawn forward it brings the diaphragm with it against the pressure of the diaphragm spring. This creates sufficient vacuum in the pump chamber to draw in fuel from the tank through the fuel filter and non-return inlet valve. As the armature nears the end of its travel a 'throwover' mechanism operates which separates the points, so breaking the circuit. The diaphragm return spring then pushes the diaphragm and armature forwards into the pumping chamber, so forcing the fuel in the chamber out to the carburettor through the non-return outlet valve. When the armature is nearly fully forward the throw-over mechanism again functions, this time closing the points and re-energising the solenoid, so repeating the cycle.

25 SU fuel pump – removal and refitting

1 Disconnect the battery.
2 Disconnect the earth and the supply wires from their terminals on the pump body, and clean off all external dirt from the pump.
3 Remove the fuel inlet and outlet pipes by undoing the union nuts or the clip screws. Remove the vent pipe connector where fitted, at this stage.
4 Unscrew the two bolts and spring washers which hold the pump in position (photo) and remove the pump.

25.4 The SU fuel pump and retaining bracket. Due to the exposed position regular servicing is recommended

5 Refitting of the pump is a reversal of the above procedure. Two particular points to watch are that:

  (a) *The fuel inlet and outlet pipes are connected up the right way round*
  (b) *A good electrical earth connection is made*

26 SU fuel pump – dismantling

1 The filter and inlet and outlet arrangements differ between the three pumps, and for this reason it is necessary to deal with them individually at this stage:

  (a) *Type 'SP': Remove the inlet nozzle by unscrewing it, and take out the filter from the inlet port. Note the fibre washer under the nozzle head. The outlet nozzle is pressed into the end casting and cannot be removed*
  (b) *Type 'AUF': Release the inlet and outlet nozzles, valves, sealing washers, and filter by unscrewing the two screws from the spring clamp plate which hold them all in place*
  (c) *Type 'L': Unscrew the hexagon-headed plug from the underside of the fuel pump and remove the sealing washers and inlet and outlet valves. If it is wished to dismantle the valve cage, remove the circlip from the cage, so freeing the valve*

2 Mark the flanges adjacent to each other, and separate the housing, holding the armature and solenoid assembly, from the pumping chamber casting by unscrewing the six screws holding both halves of the pump together. Take great care not to tear or damage the diaphragm as it may stick to either of the flanges as they are separated. On the 'SP' pump, remove the pan-headed screw which holds the valve retainer in place to the floor of the pumping chamber, and remove the retainer and the inlet and outlet valves which have already been removed on the 'AUF' and 'L' pumps.
3 The armature spindle which is attached to the armature head and diaphragm is unscrewed anti-clockwise from the trunnion at the contact breaker end of the pump body. Lift out the armature, spindle, and diaphragm. Remove the impact washer from the under the head of the armature, (this washer quietens the noise of the armature head hitting the solenoid core), and the diaphragm return spring.
4 Slide off the protective sheath and unscrew the terminal nut, connector (where fitted), and the washer from the terminal screw, then remove the bakelite contact breaker cover.
5 Unscrew the screws which hold the contact spring blade in position and remove it with the blade and screw washer.
6 Remove the cover retaining nut on the terminal screw, and cut through the lead washer under the nut on the terminal screw with a pocket knife.
7 Remove the two bakelite pedestal retaining screws complete with spring washers which hold the pedestal to the solenoid housing, then remove the braided copper earth lead, and the coil lead from the terminal screw.
8 Remove the pin on which the rockers pivot by pushing it out sideways, and remove the rocker assembly. The pump is now fully dismantled. It is not possible to remove the solenoid core and coil, and the rocker assembly must not be broken down, as it is only supplied on exchange as a complete assembly.

27 SU fuel pump – inspection and servicing

1 Although not given in the official manufacturer's servicing charts, it is a sound scheme to service the SU fuel pump every 12 000 miles (20 000 km) to minimise the possibility of failure.
2 Remove the filter as has already been detailed and thoroughly clean it in petrol. At the same time clean the points by gently drawing a piece of thin card between them. Do this very carefully so as not to disturb the tension of the spring blade. If the points are burnt or pitted, they must be renewed and a new blade and rocker assembly fitted.
3 If the filter is coated with a gum-like substance very like varnish, serious trouble can develop in the future unless all traces of this gum (formed by deposits from the fuel) are removed.
4 To do this boil all steel and brass parts in a 20% solution of caustic soda, then dip them in nitric acid and clean them in boiling water. Alloy parts can be cleaned with a clean rag after they have been left to soak for a few hours in methylated spirit.

5   With the pump stripped down, wash and clean all the parts thoroughly in paraffin and renew any that are worn, damaged, fractured, or cracked. Pay particular attention to the gaskets and diaphragm.

28 SU fuel pump – reassembly

1   Fit the rocker assembly to the bakelite pedestal and insert the rocker pivot pin. The pin is case hardened and wire or any other substitute should never be used if the pin is lost.
2   Place the spring washer, wiring tag from the short lead from the coil, a new lead washer, and the nut on the terminal screw, and tighten the nut down.
3   Attach the copper earth wire from the outer rocker immediately under the head of the nearest pedestal screw, and fit the pedestal to the solenoid housing with the two pedestal securing screws and lockwashers. It is unusual to fit an earth wire immediately under the screw head, but this is because in practice the spring washer had been found to be a not particularly good conductor.
4   Fit the lockwasher under the head of the spring blade control securing screw, then the last lead from the coil, and then the spring blade so that there is nothing between it and the bakelite pedestal. It is important that this order of assembly is adhered to. Lightly tighten the screw.
5   The static position of the pump when it is not in use is with the contact points making firm contact and this forces the spring blade to be bent slightly back. Move the outer rocker arm up and down and position the spring blade so that the contact on the rocker or blade wipes over the centre-line of the other point. Note that with the 'L' type of pump only one set of points is fitted. When open the blade should rest against the small ledge on the bakelite pedestal just below the points. (This also applies to the 'AUF' and 'SP' pumps). The points should come into contact with each other when the rocker is halfway forward. To check that this is correct press the middle of the blade gently so that it rests against the ridge with the points just having come into contact. It should now be possible to slide a 0.030 in (0.76 mm) feeler gauge between the rocker rollers and the solenoid housing. If the clearance is not correct bend the tip of the blade very carefully until it is (Fig. 3.20). On the 'AUF' and 'SP' pumps with the outer rocker against the coil housing and the spring blade contact resting against the pedestal, the gap between the points should be 0.030 in (0.76 mm).
6   Tighten down the blade retaining screw, and check that with 'AUF' and 'SP' models a considerable gap exists between the underside of the spring blade and the pedestal ledge, with the rocker contact bearing against the blade contact and the rocker fully forward in the normal static position. With the rocker arm down, ensure that the underside of the blade rests on the ledge of the pedestal. If not, remove the blade and very slightly bend it until it does.
7   Place the impact washer on the underside of the armature head, fit the diaphragm return spring with the wider portion of the coil against the solenoid body, place the brass rollers in position under the diaphragm and insert the armature spindle through the centre of the

solenoid core, then screw the spindle into the rocker trunnion.
8   It will be appreciated that the amount the spindle is screwed into the rocker trunnion will vitally affect the functioning of the pump. To set the diaphragm correctly, turn the steel blade to one side, and screw the armature spindle into the trunnion (Fig. 3.21) until, if the spindle was screwed in a further sixth of a turn, the throw-over rocker would not operate the points-closed to points-open position. Now screw out the armature spindle four holes ($\frac{2}{3}$ of a turn) to ensure that wear in the points will not cause the pump to stop working. Turn the blade back to its normal position.
9   Reassembly of the valves, filters, and nozzles into the pumping chamber is a reversal of the dismantling process. Use new washers and gaskets throughout.
10   With the pumping chamber reassembled, refit it carefully on the solenoid housing, ensuring that the previously made mating marks on the flanges line up with each other. Screw the six screws in lightly on the 'L' model, and firmly on the 'AUF' and 'SP' models.
11   For the best results on the 'L' type pump, it is necessary to have the diaphragm in the fully forward position, ie at the end of the induction stroke when the fuel chamber would be full of fuel. To achieve this, connect up the pump to the battery; with a matchstick behind the rollers to hold the points closed, electrical current will hold the armature against the return spring in the fully forward position. Tighten down the six screws, and remove the matchstick.
12   Fit the bakelite cover and refit the shakeproof washer, Lucar connector, cover nut, and terminal knob to the terminal screw in the case of 'SP' and 'AUF' models, and the terminal nut to the terminal screw in the case of the 'L' type model. Then refit the terminal lead and cover nut, so locking the lead between the cover nut and the terminal nut. Assembly of all three types is now complete.

29 Fuel tank – removal and refitting

1   Disconnect the battery earth lead. Jack the rear of the car and support it on stands. Chock the front wheels fore and aft securely.
2   Remove the filler cap and empty the tank. On early models a drain plug is provided; this should be removed, the contents drained into a suitable container, and the plug and washer securely refitted. Later models have no drain plug, but the fuel can be siphoned into a container using a length of tubing.
3   Loosen the spare wheel retainer and move the wheel away from the tank filler hose.
4   Undo the hose clip(s) and separate the filler hose from the tank filler neck.
5   On USA and Canadian models, disconnect the evaporative loss control separation tank flexible pipe from its connection on the tank near the filler neck.
6   Undo the electrical connection from the fuel gauge sender unit and remove the wiring harness from its securing clips on the tank flange.
7   Undo the fuel feed pipe from the tank. Support the tank on suitable blocks and undo and remove the six securing nuts and washers, noting the location of the wiring clip.

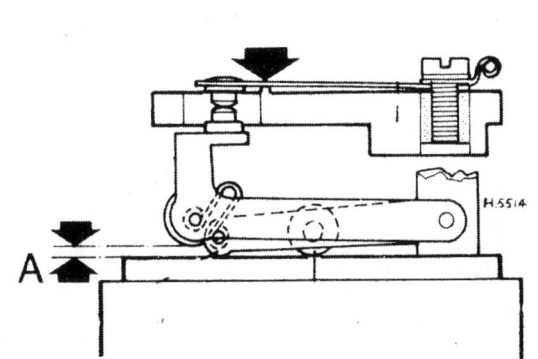

Fig. 3.20 The contact gap 'A' on the early type of rocker assembly in the SU fuel pump – see text (Sec 28)

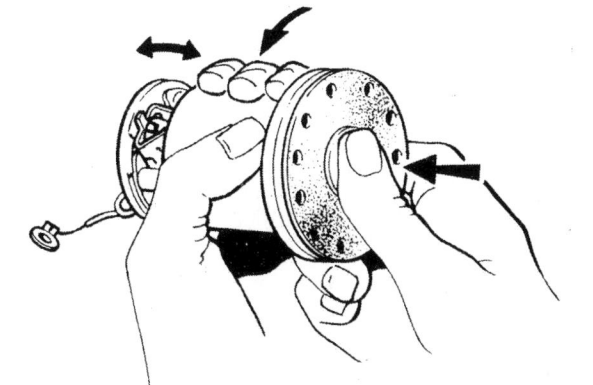

Fig. 3.21 Unscrewing the diaphragm of the SU fuel pump so that the rocker just throws over (Sec 28)

8   Remove the tank from the car, retrieving the packing for use on reassembly.

9   Refitting the tank is essentially the reverse of the removal procedure. Make sure that the sealing ring around the filler neck (not on early models) makes an efficient seal with the car body and check for fuel leaks after the initial replenishment.

30 Fuel tank gauge sender unit – removal and refitting

1   Remove the tank as described in the previous Section.

2   On early models, undo and remove the six screws holding the fuel gauge sender unit in the tank. On later models the unit is retained by a large ring nut and to undo this a special spanner is required. If possible try to hire or borrow this tool, No 18G 1001, but in its absence you may be fortunate in removing the nut by judiciously turning it with a makeshift system of levers. When extracting the sender unit from the tank be extra careful not to damage the float or bend the float arm. Remove and discard the old gasket.

3   Refitting the sender unit is the reverse of the removal procedure. Use a new gasket and smear it with jointing compound on assembly.

31 Fuel tank – cleaning

1   With time it is likely that sediment will collect in the bottom of the fuel tank. Condensation, resulting in rust and other impurities, will usually be found in the fuel tank of any car more than three or four years old.

2   When the tank is removed, it should be vigorously flushed out and turned upside down, and if facilities are available, steam cleaned.

32 Throttle cable – removal and refitting

1   On early models slacken the throttle cable clamp fixture at the carburettor end and withdraw the inner cable from the clamp. Disconnect the inner cable from the operating arm at the foot pedal end and remove the throttle cable from the car.

2   Refitting a cable is the reverse of removal. Adjust the cable by pulling sufficient through the clamp to remove all slack and to seat the throttles on the throttle stop, then tighten the clamp bolt.

3   On later models slacken the throttle cable adjuster locknut at the carburettor end of the control and slip the adjuster and cable out of the mounting bracket.

4   On USA and Canada models, undo and remove the two screws securing the throttle cable bracket to the manifold, and then release the bracket from the return spring rod and retrieve the spring. Remove the split pin and washers from the cable retaining pin and remove the pin to release the cable end fitting. Slip the cable end fitting out of the foot pedal lever and remove the cable from the car.

5   On UK models, after releasing the cable adjuster, remove the clip from the end of the cable retaining pin, then remove the pin and washer to release the cable. Slip the cable end fitting out of the foot pedal lever and remove the cable from the car.

6   Refitting a cable, on either USA and Canada or UK models, is the reverse of the removal procedure. Adjust the cable adjuster to remove all slack and to seat the throttle(s) on the throttle stop(s), and then tighten the adjuster locknut.

33 Choke (mixture control) cable – removal and refitting

1   Loosen the clamp bolt securing the choke control inner cable at the carburettor end, pull the inner cable free and remove the outer cable from its mounting bracket.

2   Undo any straps or clips securing the control cable assembly in the engine compartment. Then loosen the assembly securing nut behind the facia to free the control knob and its mounting.

3   Pull the cable assembly out of the facia, retrieving the retaining nut and washer as they are freed.

4   Refitting a choke control cable assembly is the reverse of the removal procedure. Adjust the position of the inner cable at the carburettor end so that the control knob must be pulled $\frac{1}{16}$ in (2 mm) before the carburettor lever starts to move. This ensures that the choke will fully close when the knob is pushed home.

34 Crankcase ventilation system – description and servicing

1   All engines except very early models have a closed ventilation system for removing fumes from the crankcase and directing them to the combustion chambers where they are burnt. On earlier systems the fumes are drawn through an oil separator on the timing cover and piped to a breather control valve on the induction manifold. Later systems pipe the fumes direct to the carburettor chamber between the piston and throttle butterfly valve (photo). The breather control valve on the early systems prevented imbalance of the air/fuel mixture supplied to the engine, but the later systems avoid the need for this valve.

2   Airflow through the crankcase enters at the oil filler cap on early systems, but where a fuel evaporative loss control system is incorporated the airflow is drawn through a canister purge pipeline and a sealed oil filler cap is used. Restrictors in the system ensure that a depression exists in the crankcase at all times.

3   As the installations vary, their servicing will differ accordingly depending on the components that are fitted. These may include an oil filler cap incorporating an air filter, a breather control valve, connecting hoses and restrictors.

4   *Oil filler cap and filter:* no servicing is possible on this assembly, which must be renewed when defective or on a routine basis as indicated in Routine Maintenance Section at the beginning of this manual. Make sure that the correct type of assembly is fitted on removal and use a new seal.

5   *Breather control valve:* where fitted, this can be recognised as a flat-topped assembly mounted on the inlet manifold, and it needs cleaning and examining periodically as indicated in the Routine Maintenance Section. Undo the hose clips and remove the valve from the engine. Remove the top spring clip and take off the cover plate, the diaphragm, the metering valve and the spring behind it. Clean all the metal parts in petrol. If the deposits are difficult to remove, don't use abrasives of any kind but immerse the parts in boiling water and let them soak before having another go at cleaning them with petrol. Examine the parts for wear and damage, and if this is evident fit a complete new valve assembly. Otherwise reassemble the parts, making sure that the metering needle is in the guides and that the diaphragm is correctly seated. Refit the valve to the engine and test it as described in the next paragraph.

6   To test the breather control valve, start the engine and, when it has warmed to normal running temperature, run it at idling speed. Listen to the engine speed and remove the oil filler cap to allow an unrestricted airflow into the engine. The engine speed should increase slightly if the valve is satisfactory, and you may get signs of weak mixture such as intermittent firing. Refit the filler cap and switch the engine off.

7   *Hoses and restrictors:* examine the hoses for deterioration, renewing where necessary, and ensure that they are clean internally and unblocked. Wash the restrictors in paraffin to clean them, where fitted, and on completion ensure that all hose clips are tight.

34.1 The crankcase ventilation system pipe connections at the carburettors on the later 1275 cc models

35 Exhaust emission control – general

Cars for the USA and Canadian market are equipped with an exhaust emission control system designed to meet the requirements of the anti-pollution regulations. Due to progressive improvements there are some detailed variations between models, but the main features are as follows:

An air injection system uses a rotary vane type pump, belt driven by a twin pulley on the crankshaft, to supply air to the exhaust

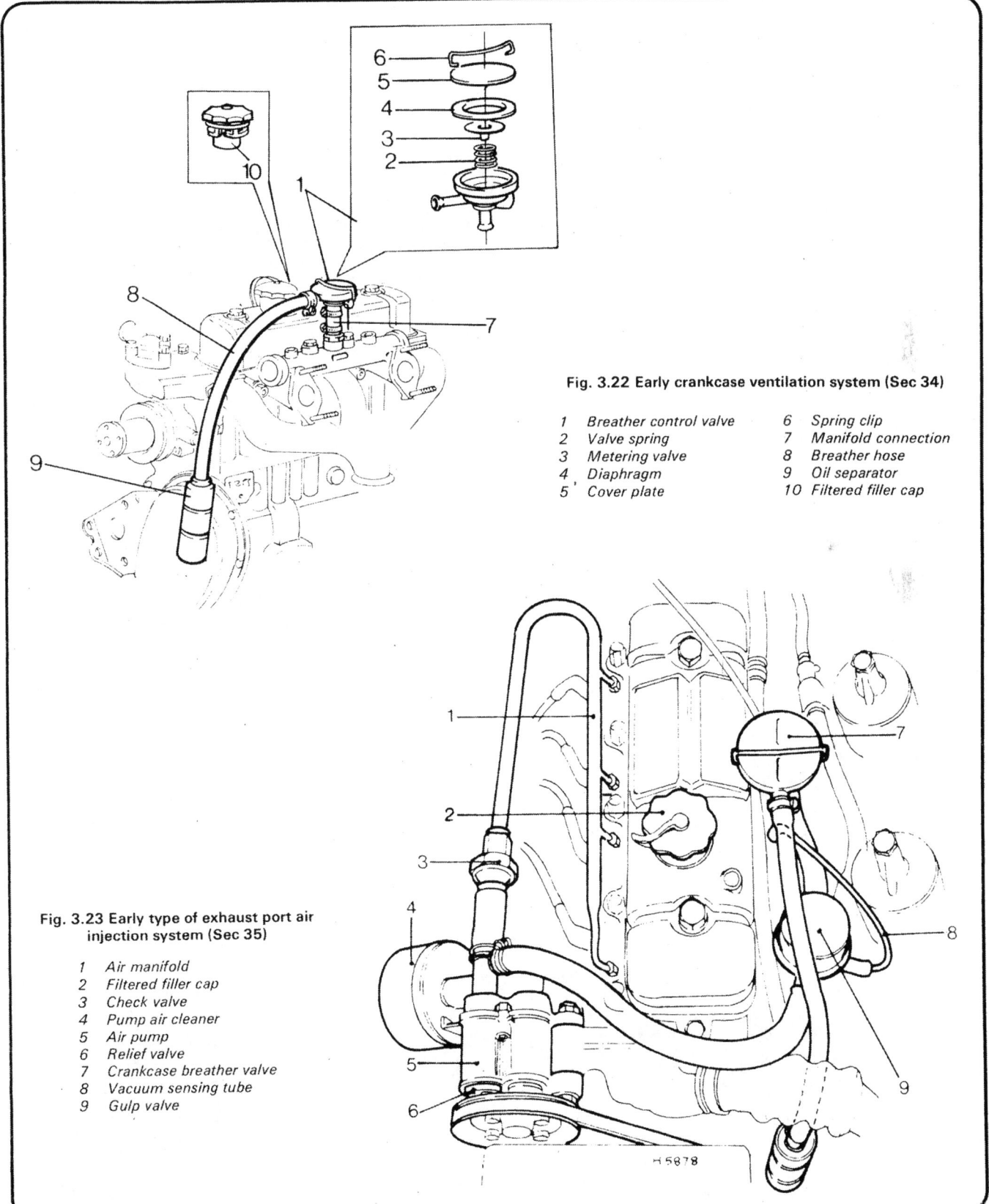

Fig. 3.22 Early crankcase ventilation system (Sec 34)

1	Breather control valve	6	Spring clip
2	Valve spring	7	Manifold connection
3	Metering valve	8	Breather hose
4	Diaphragm	9	Oil separator
5	Cover plate	10	Filtered filler cap

Fig. 3.23 Early type of exhaust port air injection system (Sec 35)

1 Air manifold
2 Filtered filler cap
3 Check valve
4 Pump air cleaner
5 Air pump
6 Relief valve
7 Crankcase breather valve
8 Vacuum sensing tube
9 Gulp valve

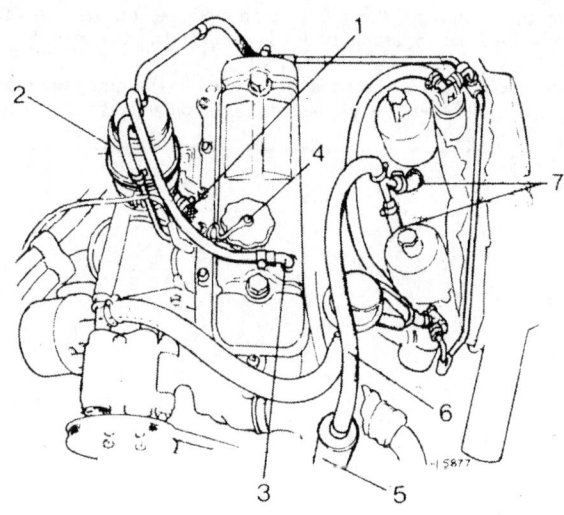

Fig. 3.24 Early type of emission control combining air injection and fuel evaporative loss control (Sec 35)

1 Ventilation air intake	4 Sealed oil filler cap
2 Adsorption canister	5 Oil separator
3 Restricted connection to	6 Breather hose
rocker cover	7 Connections to carburettors

manifold. This air converts the undesirable hydrocarbon and carbon monoxide constituents of the exhaust gas into relatively harmless water and carbon dioxide, thereby reducing air pollution.

A controlled amount of exhaust gas is recirculated back to the inlet manifold to reduce combustion chamber temperatures.

A carburettor having a special exhaust emission control specification is fitted and tuned to give the best engine performance consistent with maximum emission control.

A running-on control valve is fitted to Californian models to prevent prolonged running-on when the engine is switched off.

Servicing details of the principal components, except the carburettor (see Sections 14 to 16 inclusive), are given in the following Sections.

36 Air pump – removal, refitting and testing

1   Undo the air vent hose bracket and remove the hose. Then position a container under the oil filter to collect spilt oil and remove the oil filter from its adaptor.

2   Undo the hose clip and remove the outlet hose from the air pump. Loosen the pump mounting and adjusting link bolts, swing the pump in towards the engine and slip the drivebelt off the pump pulley.

3   Remove the nuts and bolts retaining the pump to the engine, noting their individual positions and those of the spacer and washers, then remove the pump from the engine.

4   Refitting an air pump is the reverse of the removal procedure. Before tightening the mounting bolts and nuts, tension the drivebelt as described in Chapter 2. Refit the oil filter as described in Chapter 1.

5   A defective air pump will probably make a lot of noise when

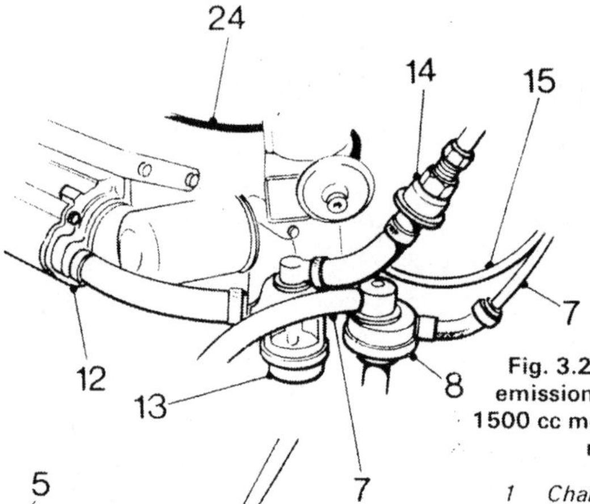

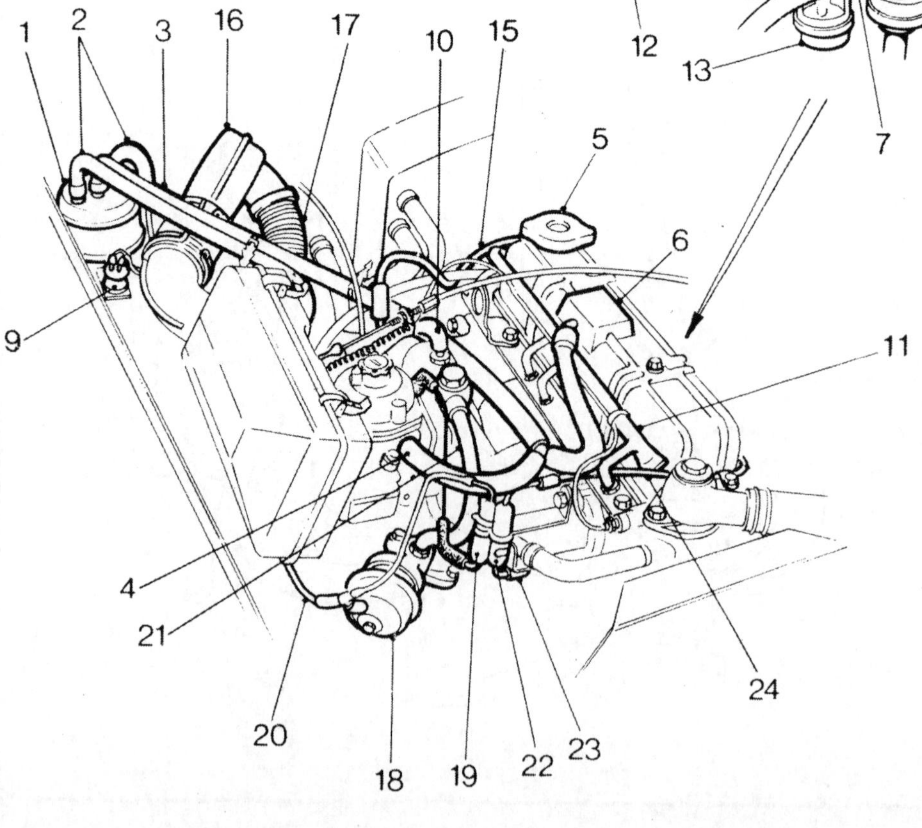

Fig. 3.25 Early arrangement of emission control components on 1500 cc models for USA and Canada market (Sec 35)

1   Charcoal adsorption canister
2   Vapour lines
3   Purge line
4   Restricted connection
5   Sealed oil filler cap
6   Oil separator/flame trap
7   Fuel pipe
8   Fuel pump
9   Running-on control valve
10 Running-on control pipe
11 Air manifold
12 Air pump
13 Diverter valve
14 Check valve
15 Diverter valve pipe
16 Air temperatire control
    valve
17 Hot air hose
18 EGR valve
19 EGR valve flame trap
20 EGR valve line to carburettor
    choke cam
21 EGR valve pipe
22 Distributor flame trap
23 Distributor flame trap line to
    carburettor
24 Flame trap line to distributor
    vacuum unit

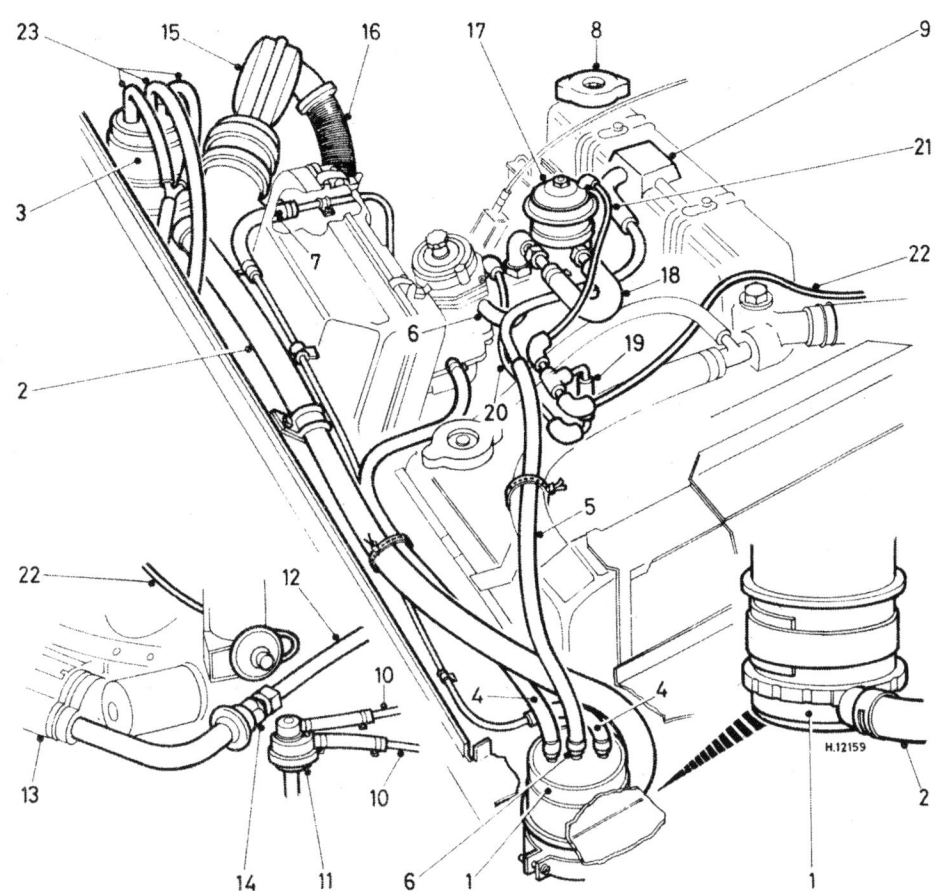

Fig. 3.26 Later arrangement of emission control components (Canada, and USA except California) (Sec 35)

1   Primary adsorption canister
2   Interconnecting pipe
3   Secondary adsorption canister
4   Vapour lines
5   Purge lines
6   Restricted connection
7   Restrictor
8   Sealed oil filler cap
9   Oil separator/flame trap
10 Fuel pipe
11 Fuel pump
12 Air injection pipe
13 Air pump
14 Check valve
15 Air temperature control valve
16 Hot air hose
17 Exhaust gas recirculation valve
18 EGR valve pipe
19 Flame trap
20 Flame trap line to carburettor
21 Flame trap line to EGR valve
22 Flame trap line to distributor vacuum unit
23 Vent pipes

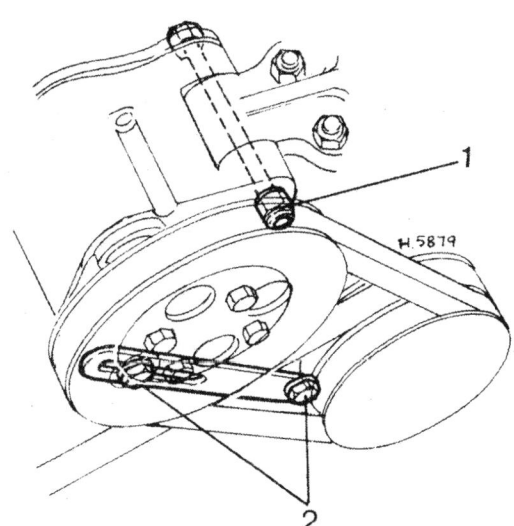

Fig. 3.27 The air pump and mountings on 1275 cc engines (Sec 36)

1   Mounting bolt and nut   2   Adjustment link bolts

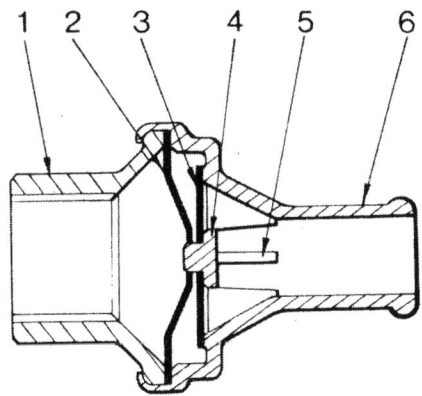

Fig. 3.28 Sectional view of the check valve (Sec 37)

1   Air manifold connection   4   Valve pilot
2   Diaphragm   5   Guide
3   Valve   6   Air supply from pump

running, but to test it you will require a tachometer and a pressure gauge indicating through 0 to 10 lbf/in² (0 to 69 bar) which can be connected to the diverter valve hose. If you haven't got these items your BL agent will test the pump for you.

6   If you have the equipment, connect the tachometer up following the maker's instructions, and connect the pressure gauge to the diverter valve hose after disconnecting the hose from the valve. Run the engine at 850 rpm and check that the gauge reading is not less than 1 to 1.5 lbf/in² (0.069 to 1.035 bar). If this pressure is not achieved the pump should be renewed.

37 Check valve – testing

1   A check valve is fitted in the emission control air pump delivery line to prevent possible blow-back from high pressure exhaust gases. It can be checked as follows.

2   Undo the hose clip and remove the air hose from the check valve. Hold the air manifold connecting union to prevent it turning and undo the check valve from the manifold.

3   Test the valve by blowing through it orally in each direction. *On no account should you use a pressure supply for this test.* Air should only pass through the valve when blown at the air supply hose connection. If air passes when blown at the manifold connection renew the valve.

4   Refitting the valve is the reverse of the removal procedure.

38 Air injection pipe or manifold – removal and refitting

1   On early systems the emission control air is delivered by a manifold of four branches connected to the cylinder head. On later systems the air is fed to the exhaust manifold through a single pipe union and, on the latest system fitted to Californian models, the air is once more fed to the cylinder head by a manifold of four branch pipes.

2   Removal and refitting the air supply pipe is a straightforward procedure of disconnection and reassembly. On the system having a single connection to the exhaust manifold, it will be necessary to remove the air intake before removing the air supply pipe. Details are given in Section 2 of this Chapter. If you experience difficulty in undoing the air pipe connection(s) from the cylinder head or exhaust manifold, use penetrating oil and allow it to soak in to the connections before making another attempt to undo them.

39 Gulp valve – removal and refitting

1   A gulp valve is fitted, to Californian models only, in the supply between the air pump and the inlet manifold. Its purpose is to lean off the rich fuel/air mixture present in the manifold immediately after closing the throttle following running at full throttle, that is on engine overrun. The valve is located on a cylinder head bracket adjacent to the oil filler cap.

2   To remove the valve, disconnect the hoses from the valve, then undo and remove the three screws securing the valve to the bracket. Refitting is the reverse of removal, but make sure that the hoses are secure and air-tight.

40 Catalytic converter – removal and refitting

1   A catalytic converter is fitted in the exhaust system of certain models to further reduce the emission of hydrocarbons and carbon monoxide. The converter must be renewed periodically as indicated in the Routine Maintenance Section and certain precautions are essential to avoid damage and malfunction as follows:

   (a)   Avoid shock impacts on the converter case as the internal material can be damaged
   (b)   It is imperative that only unleaded fuel is used or the emission control efficiency will be impaired
   (c)   As the catalytic converter gets very hot in use, make sure that it is allowed to cool before touching it
   (d)   Engine misfiring can damage the catalytic element and the cause must be identified and rectified immediately this occurs

2   To remove the catalytic converter, jack up the front of the car and support on stands. Apply the handbrake firmly. Allow the system to cool if necessary. Undo the two nuts securing the support bracket at the bottom of the converter pipe and remove the bracket. Undo the three nuts and bolts securing the converter pipe to the exhaust pipe and retrieve the olive from the joint after separating the pipes.

3   Refer to Chapter 4 and remove the carburettor, swinging it out of the way. Undo the two screws securing the air cleaner casing and heat shield to the carburettor. Press in the pre-heater duct retaining clips and remove the duct. Undo the two nuts on each of the three studs securing the converter to the manifold, and remove the converter together with the flange gasket.

4   Refitting a converter is the reverse of the removal procedure. Take care to handle the new one cautiously and use new gaskets at the exhaust flange joint and at the carburettor flange joint. Check the tightness of all the fasteners after the first engine run. On Californian models where a service interval counter is fitted, reset the counters to zero using a key in the button.

41 Exhaust gas recirculation (EGR) – general and servicing

1   The EGR valve is located on the exhaust manifold and its operation is controlled by the amount of inlet manifold depression measured at the throttle edge. At idle or full throttle the valve is closed and there is no exhaust gas recirculation, but at part load conditions a controlled amount of exhaust gas is delivered to the inlet manifold. A

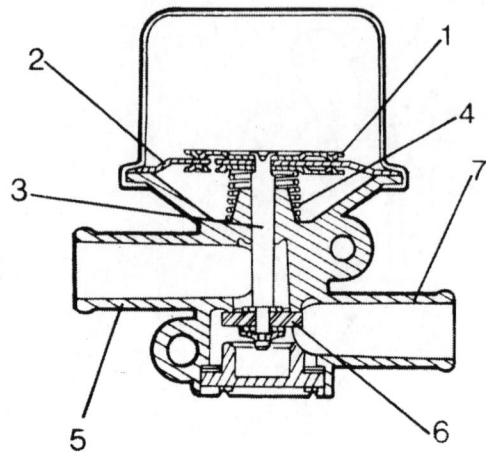

Fig. 3.29 Sectional view of the gulp valve (Sec 39)

1   Metering balance orifice
2   Diaphragm
3   Valve spindle
4   Return spring
5   Inlet manifold connection
6   Valve
7   Air pump connection

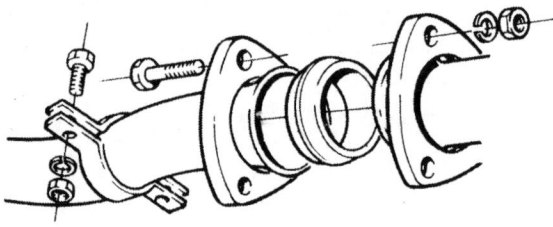

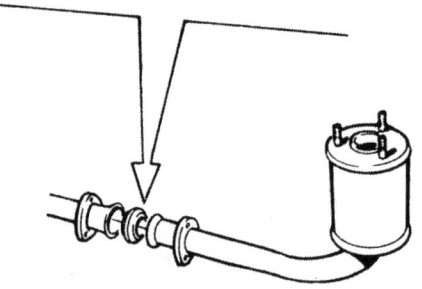

Fig. 3.30 Assembly details of the catalytic converter and exhaust downpipe (Sec 40)

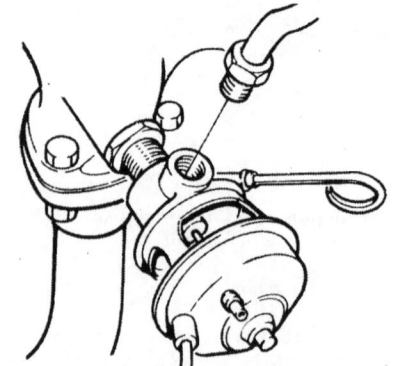

Fig. 3.31 Removing the exhaust gas recirculation valve (Sec 41)

valve on the carburettor (manual choke) isolates the system when the choke is operated.

2   To remove and clean the EGR valve first disconnect the vacuum control pipe from the top of the valve, then undo the banjo bolt retaining the metal pipe to the inlet manifold.

3   Loosen the nut retaining the metal pipe to the EGR valve. Loosen the locknut and turn the EGR valve anti-clockwise to remove it from the exhaust manifold.

4   Clean the joint faces of the EGR valve with a wire brush. The valve and seat are best cleaned using a spark plug cleaning machine. The valve opening is inserted into the machine, the diaphragm carefully and evenly raised, and the valve blasted for a short burst of about 30 seconds. Repeat if required to remove all the carbon deposits. The steel pipe can be cleaned out using a flexible wire brush. All parts, when cleaned, should be blown clear with compressed air to remove any traces of carbon grit.

5   Pipes or fittings showing signs of damage or deterioration must be renewed.

6   Refit in the reverse order and check that all connections are good. Ensure that the EGR valve is operating correctly by starting the engine and running up to its normal operating temperature. Then, with the choke fully off, open and close the throttle a few times to see if the EGR valve is operating with the corresponding change in engine speed. If the valve does not operate, have it checked by your local BL agent and renew it if necessary.

7   The EGR valve service warning indicator will have to be reset and this will be best done by your local BL agent who has the necessary key.

42 Running-on control valve (Californian models only) – general, removal and refitting

1   The running-on control valve is an electrically operated valve which is closed when the engine is running. On turning off the ignition the valve opens and admits air into the inlet manifold to prevent run-on. The valve is connected into the fuel evaporative loss control system which is dealt with in Section 43.

2   To remove the valve, first disconnect the battery earth lead then disconnect the electrical leads from the valve which is located adjacent to the forward absorption canister (early systems) or rear canister (later systems).

3   Release the hose clips and disconnect the three hoses from the valve. Turn the valve through 45° to align the square base with the cut-out in the mounting and lift the valve out of the mounting.

4   Refitting the valve is the reverse of the removal procedure.

43 Fuel evaporative loss control system – general

This system is designed to prevent fuel fumes from the fuel tank and carburettor vents being emitted to the atmosphere. When the engine is not running the fumes are conducted to two absorption canisters containing charcoal which store the fuel vapour until the engine is next started. Then, when the engine is running, air is drawn through the canisters, which give up the fuel vapour. This is then drawn via the crankcase emission control system to the combustion chambers where it is burnt.

The fuel and oil filler caps in this system are of the non-ventilated type and the efficiency of the system depends on it being completely sealed. Provisions are made to prevent overfilling the fuel tank, thus ensuring that adequate fuel expansion space exists, and liquid fuel is prevented from being drawn into the canisters.

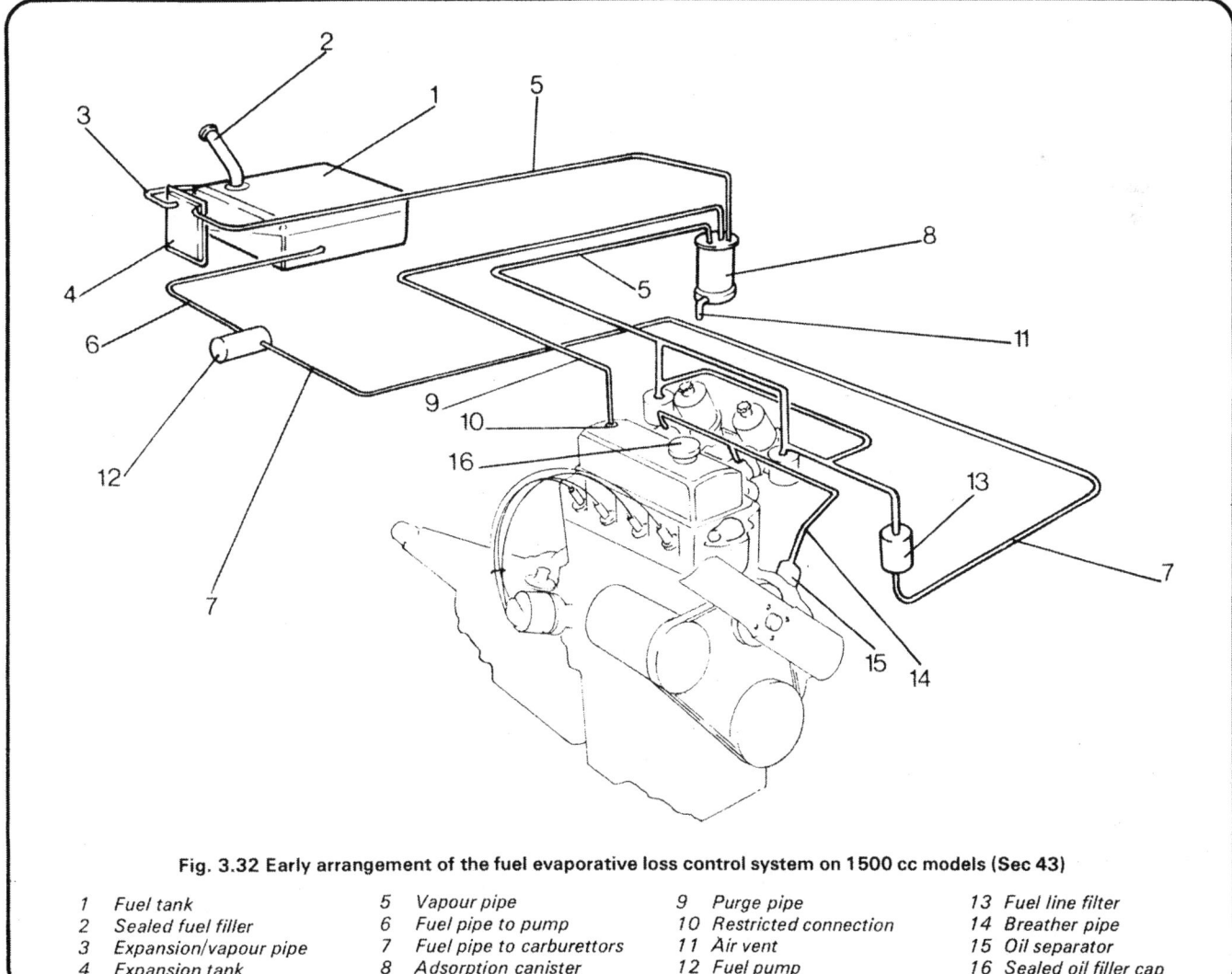

Fig. 3.32 Early arrangement of the fuel evaporative loss control system on 1500 cc models (Sec 43)

1 Fuel tank	5 Vapour pipe	9 Purge pipe	13 Fuel line filter
2 Sealed fuel filler	6 Fuel pipe to pump	10 Restricted connection	14 Breather pipe
3 Expansion/vapour pipe	7 Fuel pipe to carburettors	11 Air vent	15 Oil separator
4 Expansion tank	8 Adsorption canister	12 Fuel pump	16 Sealed oil filler cap

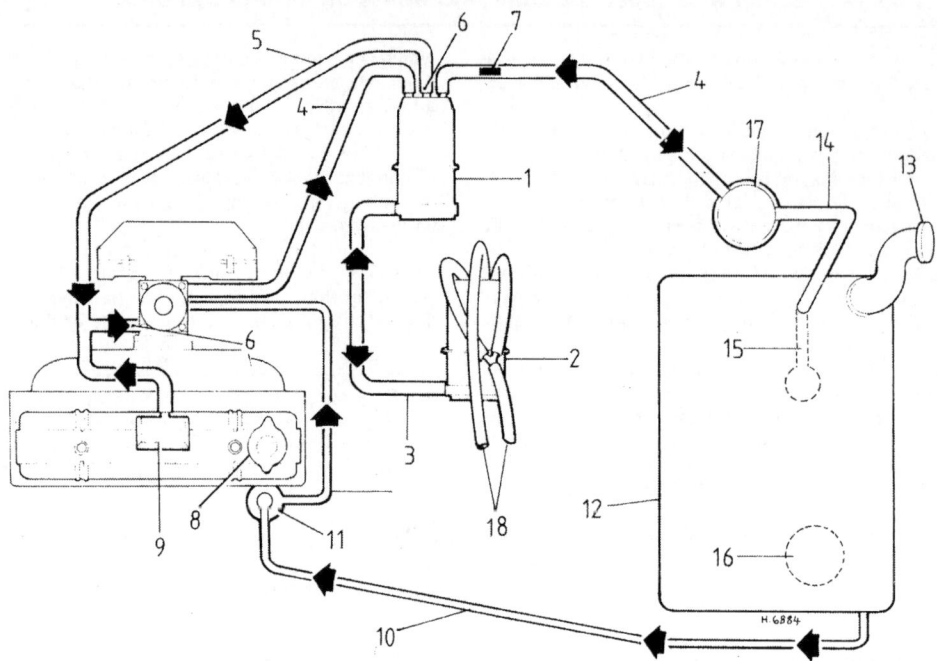

Fig. 3.33 Later arrangement of the fuel evaporative loss control system (USA and Canada models except California) (Sec 43)

1   Primary adsorption canister
2   Secondary adsorption canister
3   Canister inter-connecting pipe
4   Vapour lines
5   Purge line
6   Restricted connection
7   Restrictor
8   Sealed oil filler cap
9   Oil separator flame trap
10 Fuel pipe
11 Fuel pump
12 Fuel tank
13 Sealed fuel filler cap
14 Vapour line
15 Vapour tube
16 Capacity limiting tank
17 Separation tank
18 Vent pipes

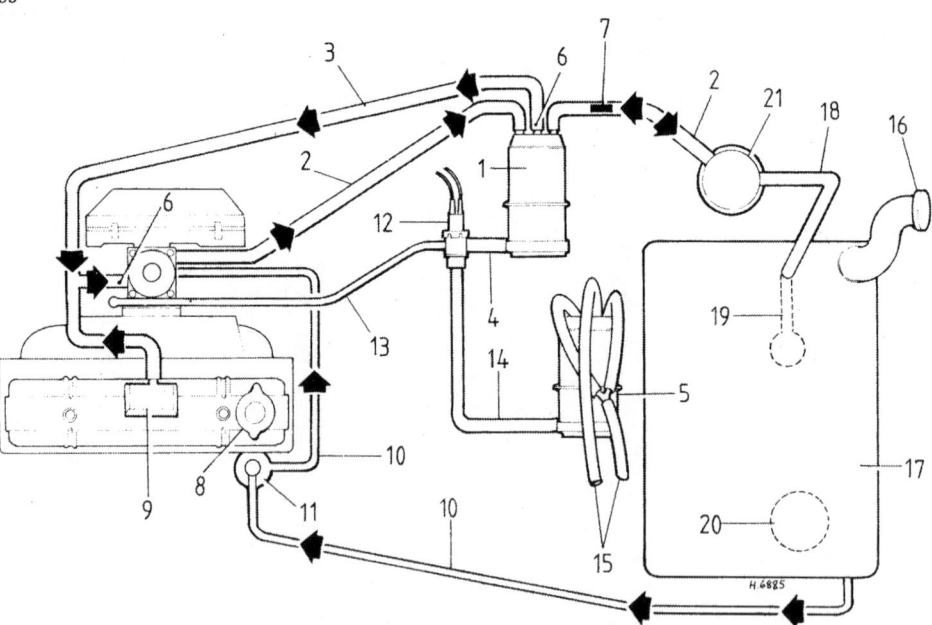

Fig. 3.34 Later arrangement of the fuel evaporative loss control system (California models) (Sec 43)

1   Primary charcoal adsorption canister
2   Vapour lines
3   Purge line
4   Connecting pipe
5   Secondary charcoal adsorption canister
6   Restricted connection
7   Restrictor
8   Oil filler sealed cap
9   Oil separator/flame trap
10 Fuel pipe
11 Fuel pump
12 Running-on control valve
13 Sensing pipe
14 Running-on control hose
15 Air vents
16 Fuel filler sealed cap
17 Fuel tank
18 Vapour line
19 Vapour tube
20 Capacity limiting tank
21 Separation tank

In time the ability of the charcoal in the canisters to absorb and release fuel vapour deteriorates. For this reason the canisters must be renewed periodically as indicated in the Routine Maintenance Section at the beginning of this Manual.

44 Fuel evaporative loss control system – leak testing

1 The system should be tested for leaks whenever a fault is suspected or whenever components, other than the absorption canisters, have been removed and refitted. A pressure gauge reading 0 to 10 lbf/in^2 (0.69 bar) will be required, together with a low pressure air supply such as a foot pump. If these are not available your BL agent will be able to test the system for you.
2 California models with the anti-running-on valve fitted can be given a quick preliminary check for leaks by running the engine, and then temporarily blocking the air vent pipe of the running-on valve. If the system is air tight the engine will stop almost immediately, but if it continues to run an air leak is indicated.
3 To leak test the system, first ensure that there is at least a gallon of fuel in the tank and run the engine for a minute or so to prime the fuel system, then stop the engine. Using suitable pieces of hose connect your pressure gauge in to the fuel tank ventilation pipe after disconnecting the vapour hose. Make sure that the oil and fuel filler caps are on tight, then carefully pressurise the system to 1 lbf/in^2 (0.069 bar) is registered on the pressure gauge. Be very careful not to exceed this pressure at any time.
4 Check that the pressure does not fall below 0.5 lbf/in^2 (0.035 bar) within 10 seconds. If the pressure is not maintained, check for leaks, especially at the filler cap seals. With pressure in the system check for fuel leaks.
5 When satisfactory, remove the fuel tank filler cap and check that the gauge reading falls to zero. Remove the pressure gauge and reconnect the fuel tank ventilation pipe vapour hose, making sure that the clip is tight.

45 Fuel evaporative loss control system – absorption canister renewal

1 Although differences exist in the system layouts of different models, depending on the date of the model or the area for which it was designed, renewing the absorption canister is basically the same procedure.
2 Take careful note of the individual hose connections to each canister and, to avoid later mistakes, mark them so that they can be refitted to their correct connections.
3 Undo the hose clips and remove the hoses from the canister (work on one canister at a time to avoid mixing components). Undo the securing bracket nut and bolt and remove the canister from the bracket.
4 The purge pipe connection (the central one of the three connections) on the primary canister (that is the forward canister on USA and Canada models or the rear canister on California models) has a restrictor in it. This must be extracted and refitted to the new canister.
5 Refit the new canister and its hoses following the reverse procedure to that for removal. Make sure that the hoses are fitted to their correct connections and that the clips are tight. On California models take care not to disturb the running-on control valve, or its connection, adjacent to the secondary (forward) canister.
6 Repeat the procedure on the other canister on those systems with two canisters.

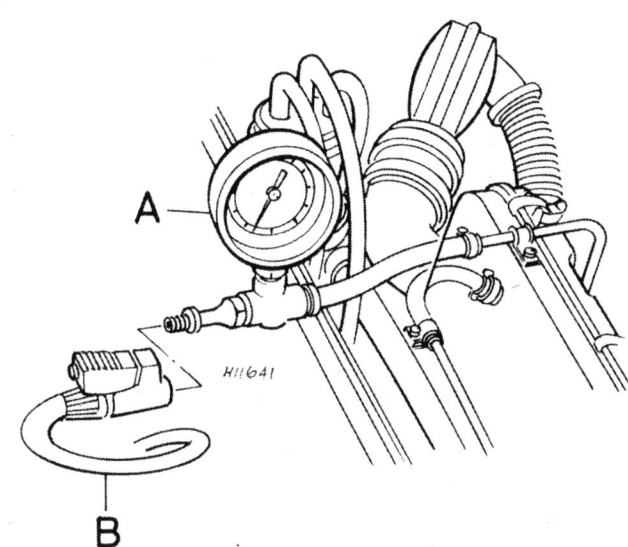

Fig. 3.35 Leak testing the fuel evaporative loss control system (not California models) (Sec 44)

A   Pressure gauge connected into the fuel tank ventilation pipe
B   Low pressure air supply (foot pump)

46 Fuel evaporative loss control system – restrictor cleaning

1 Periodically, as indicated in the Routine Maintenance Section at the beginning of this Manual, the restrictors in this system must be checked for blockage and, if necessary, cleaned. Depending on the individual system, up to three restrictors may be fitted, and although they are positioned in the same places in the system, their precise location on the car may vary with different models.
2 The restrictors are located as follows:

(a)   Primary absorption canister restrictor: the front canister on USA and Canada models excepting California, or the rear canister on California models has a restrictor in the top centre hose connection

(b)   Carburettor restrictor: this is located in the purge line at its connection to the carburettor

(c)   Vapour line restrictor (later systems only): this is located in the fuel vapour line to the primary absorption canister. It can be found in the short length of hose just behind the carburettor air cleaner case

3 Working on one restrictor at a time to avoid mixing components, disconnect the appropriate hose connection and extract the restrictor. Clean off any dirt or deposit and, if necessary clear the bore with a piece of wire. Refit the restrictor and reconnect the hose connection. Repeat on the remaining restrictors.
4 On completion leak test the system as described in Section 44.

See overleaf for 'Fault diagnosis – fuel, exhaust and emission control systems'.

47 Fault diagnosis – fuel, exhaust and emission control systems

Unsatisfactory engine performance and excessive fuel consumption are not necessarily the fault of the fuel system or carburettor(s). In fact they are frequently due to ignition or mechanical faults. Before acting on the fuel system, make sure that the ignition system is performing correctly and that the valve clearances, contact breaker gap, and spark plug gaps are all correctly adjusted. Even though a defect exists in the fuel system, it will be difficult to trace unless the rest of the engine and ignition system are working properly, and the following table assumes that this is the case.

Symptom	Reason(s)
Smell of petrol when engine is stopped	Leaking fuel lines or unions Leaking fuel tank
Smell of petrol when engine is idling	Leaking fuel line unions between pump and carburettor(s) Overflow of fuel from carburettor float chamber due to wrong level setting or ineffective needle valve or punctured float
Excessive fuel consumption for reasons not covered by leaks or float chamber faults	Worn needle Sticking needle
Difficult starting, uneven running, lack of power, cutting out	One or more blockages in fuel lines, carburettor(s) etc Float chamber fuel level too low or needle sticking Fuel pump not delivering sufficient fuel Inlet manifold gaskets leaking, or manifold fractured
Low CO content of exhaust gases (weak or lean mixture)	Incorrect fuel level in carburettor(s) Incorrectly adjusted carburettor(s)
High CO content of exhaust gases (rich mixture)	Incorrectly adjusted carburettor(s) Choke sticking Adsorption canister(s) blocked Incorrect fuel level in carburettor(s) Air injection system faulty
Noisy air injection pump	Belt tension incorrect Relief valve faulty Check valve faulty Split or leaking hoses
Rough idling	Faulty or dirty EGR valve Disconnected or leaking vacuum hose
Fuel gauge gives no reading	Fuel tank empty Tank sender unit-to-gauge cable earthed or loose Gauge case not earthed Gauge unit defective No power supply
Fuel gauge continually reads full	Tank sender unit-to-gauge cable broken or disconnected

Chapter 4 Ignition system

Contents

Specifications

System type
All models except USA 1500 .... Battery, coil and mechanical contact breaker
USA 1500 .... Electronic

Firing order
All models .... 1, 3, 4, 2 (No 1 cylinder nearest radiator)

Spark plugs
Type
    948 cc and 1098 cc engines .... Champion N5
    1275 cc engines .... Champion N9Y
    1500 engines (1975 to 1978, except USA) .... Champion N9Y
    All other engines .... Champion N12Y
Electrode gap .... 0.025 in (0.64 mm)

Ignition coil
Type
    948 cc and 1098 cc engines .... Lucas LA12
    1275 cc engines .... Lucas 11C12 or HA12
    All other engines .... Lucas 15C6
Primary resistance at 20°C (68°F)
    LA12 coil .... 3.2 to 3.4 ohms
    11C12 and HA12 coils .... 3.0 to 3.4 ohms
    15C6 coil .... 1.30 to 1.45 ohms
Ballast resistor (15C6 coil) .... 1.30 to 1.50 ohms

Distributor
Type
    Sprite Mk I .... Lucas DM2PH4
    Sprite Mk II, Midget Mk I (948 cc) .... Lucas DM2P4
    Sprite Mk II, Midget Mk I (1098 cc) and
    Sprite Mk III, Midget Mk II (1098 cc) .... Lucas 25D4
    Sprite Mk IV, Midget Mk III (1275 cc) .... Lucas 23D4* or 25D4
    Midget Mk III (1500, except USA) .... Lucas 45D4
    Midget Mk III (1500 USA and Canada) .... Lucas 45DE4 (electronic)
    The 23D4 distributor has no vacuum advance unit
Contact breaker points gap .... 0.014 to 0.016 in (0.35 to 0.40 mm)
Pick-up air gap (45DE4) .... 0.014 to 0.016 in (0.35 to 0.40 mm)
Rotation (at rotor) .... Anti-clockwise
Condenser capacity (except 45DE4) .... 0.18 to 0.25 μF
Drive resistor (45DE4) .... 9.5 ohms $\pm$ 5%
Dwell angle
    DM2PH4, DM2P4, 23D4 and 25D4 distributors .... 60 $\pm$ 3°
    45D4 distributors .... 51 $\pm$ 5°

Ignition timing (static)

Sprite Mk I	5° BTDC
Sprite Mk II, Midget Mk I (948 cc)	4° BTDC (HC), 1° BTDC (LC)
Sprite Mk II, Midget Mk I (1098 cc) and Sprite Mk III,	
Midget Mk II (1098 cc)	5° BTDC
Sprite Mk IV, Midget Mk III (1275 cc, except USA)	7° BTDC
Sprite Mk IV, Midget Mk III (USA, up to 1972)	4° BTDC
Midget Mk III (USA, 1972 to 1974)	TDC
Midget Mk III (1500, except USA and Canada)	10° BTDC
Midget Mk III (1500, California)	2° ATDC**
Midget Mk III (1500, USA and Canada, except California)	10° BTDC**

*** These figures are given for distributor refitting purposes only*

Ignition timing (dynamic, vacuum line disconnected)

Sprite Mk I	Not specified
Sprite Mk II, Midget Mk I (948 cc)	6° BTDC at 600 rpm
Sprite Mk II, Midget Mk I (1098 cc) & Sprite Mk III,	
Midget Mk II (1098 cc)	8° BTDC at 600 rpm
Sprite Mk IV, Midget Mk III (1275 cc, 23D4 distributor)	22° BTDC at 1200 rpm
Sprite Mk IV, Midget Mk III (1275 cc, except USA)	13° BTDC at 1000 rpm
Sprite Mk IV, Midget Mk III (1275 cc, up to 1972, USA)	10° BTDC at 1000 rpm
Midget Mk III (1275 cc, 1972 to 1974, USA)	9° BTDC at 1500 rpm
Midget Mk III (1500, except USA)	10° BTDC at 680 rpm
Midget Mk III (1500, 1975 to 1978, USA)	2° ATDC at 800 rpm
Midget Mk III (1500, 1978 on, USA and Canada)	10° BTDC at 800 rpm
Midget Mk III (1500, 1978 on, California)	2° ATDC at 800 rpm

Torque wrench settings

	lbf ft	kgf m
Spark plugs	20	2.8
Distributor to pedestal (1500)	20	2.8

1 General description

In order that the engine can run correctly, it is necessary for an electrical spark to ignite the fuel/air mixture in the combustion chamber at exactly the right moment in relation to engine speed and load. The ignition system is based on feeding low tension voltage from the battery to the coil, where it is converted to high tension voltage. The high tension voltage is powerful enough to jump the spark plug gap in the cylinders many times a second under high compression pressures, providing that the system is in good condition and that all adjustments are correct.

The ignition system is divided into two circuits. The low tension circuit and the high tension circuit. The low tension (sometimes known as the primary) circuit consists of the battery, lead to the control box (where fitted), lead to the ignition switch, lead from the ignition switch to the low tension or primary coil windings, and the lead from the low tension coil windings to the contact breaker points and condenser (in the conventional distributor) or to the pick-up unit (in the electronic ignition distributor). The high tension circuit consists of the high tension or secondary coil windings, the heavy ignition lead from the centre of the coil to the centre of the distributor cap, the rotor arm, and the spark plug leads and spark plugs.

The system functions in the following manner. In distributors fitted with a conventional contact breaker, low tension voltage is changed in the coil to high tension voltage by the opening of the contact breaker points in the low tension circuit. In distributors fitted with an electronic breakerless circuit, an engine driven trigger passing a pick-up causes the electronic circuit to control the coil, which, as in the contact breaker driven system, transfers low tension voltage into high tension voltage pulses. The high tension voltage is then fed via the carbon brush in the centre of the distributor cap to the rotor arm of the distributor. The rotor arm revolves inside the distributor cap, and each times it comes in line with one of the four metal segments in the cap, which are connected to the spark plug leads, the opening and closing of the contact breaker points, or the operation of the electronic trigger, causes the high tension voltage to build up, jump the gap from the rotor arm to the appropriate metal segment and so via the spark plug lead to the spark plug, where it finally jumps the spark plug gap before going to earth.

The ignition is advanced and retarded automatically, to ensure the spark occurs at just the right instant for the particular load at the prevailing engine speed. The ignition advance is controlled both mechanically and by a vacuum operated system. The mechanical governor mechanism comprises two weights, which move out from the distributor shaft, as the engine speed rises, due to centrifugal force. As they move outwards they rotate the cam relative to the distributor shaft, and so advance the spark. The weights are held in position by two light springs, and it is the tension of these springs which is largely responsible for correct spark advancement. The vacuum control consists of a diaphragm, one side of which is connected via a small bore tube to the carburettor, and the other side to the contact breaker plate. Depression in the inlet manifold and carburettor, which varies with engine speed and throttle opening, causes the diaphragm to move, so moving the contact breaker plate, and advancing or retarding the spark. A fine degree of control is achieved by a spring in the vacuum assembly.

Later models incorporate a ballast resistor in the ignition circuit. This takes the form of a wire integral with the wiring harness. Used in conjunction with a six volt coil, this gives improved starting, especially in cold conditions.

2 Contact breaker points – adjustment

1   To adjust the contact breaker points to the correct gap, first pull off the two clips securing the distributor cap to the distributor body, and lift away the cap. Clean the cap inside and out with a dry cloth. It is unlikely that the four segments will be badly burned or scored, but if they are the cap will have to be renewed.

2   Push in the carbon brush located in the top of the cap once or twice, to make sure that it moves freely.

3   Gently prise the contact breaker points open to examine the condition of their faces. If they are rough, pitted, or dirty, it will be necessary to remove them for resurfacing, or for replacement points to be fitted.

4   Assuming the points are satisfactory, or that they have been cleaned and renewed, measure the gap between the points by turning the engine over until the contact breaker arm is on the peak of one of the four cam lobes. A feeler gauge of the specified size should now just fit between the points (photo).

5   If the gap varies from this amount, slacken the contact plate securing screw, and adjust the contact gap by inserting a screwdriver in the notched hole at the end of the plate. Turning clockwise to decrease and anti-clockwise to increase the gap. Tighten the securing screw and check the gap again.

6   Refit the rotor arm and distributor cap, and clip the spring blade retainers into position.

7   A more accurate method of checking the points adjustment is with the use of a dwell meter. Where the dwell angle of a particular

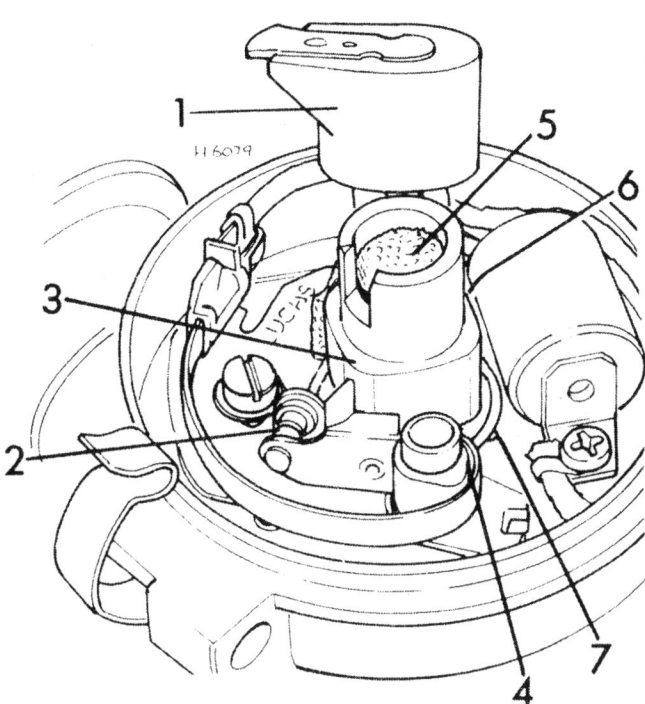

Fig. 4.1 View of distributor with cap removed – Lucas 45D4
(Sec 2)

1	Rotor arm	4	Pivot post
2	Contact breaker	5	Felt lubrication pad
	points	6	Oiling hole in baseplate
3	Cam	7	Oiling hole in baseplate

distributor is known (see Specifications) and a dwell meter is available or can be borrowed, and provided the points are in good condition, the results tend to be more accurate than using feeler gauges.

8   The dwell angle is the number of degrees of distributor cam rotation in which the contact breaker points remain closed. If the contact breaker gap is small the points will open sooner and close later than intended, thus resulting in a large dwell angle, and vice versa. A dwell meter accurately measures this angle so that the points can be adjusted, without using feeler gauges, to achieve the recommended setting.

9   A variety of dwell meters is available and each must be connected into the ignition circuit according to the maker's instructions. If necessary the meter should also be set to zero following the maker's directions. When this has been done the engine is turned over on the starter by switching on the ignition (or in some cases, the engine allowed to idle) and the dwell angle read off the dwell meter. Where the indicated angle is incorrect, adjust by increasing the contact breaker gap to reduce the dwell angle or by reducing the gap to increase the angle. Always recheck the dwell angle after adjusting the contact breaker points.

---

3   Contact breaker points – removal and refitting

1   If the contact breaker points are burned, pitted or badly worn, they must be removed and either renewed, or their faces must be filed smooth.

2   To remove the points on early models, unscrew the terminal nut and remove it together with the steel washer under its head. Remove the flanged nylon bush and then the condenser lead and the low tension lead from the terminal pin. Lift off the contact breaker arm and then remove the large fibre washer from the terminal pin. The adjustable contact breaker plate is removed by unscrewing the one hold-down screw and removing it, complete with spring and flat washer. On later models, unscrew the retaining screw and remove complete with spring and flat washer. Raise the contact points and press the spring to release the terminal plate.

2.4 Adjusting the contact breaker points gap

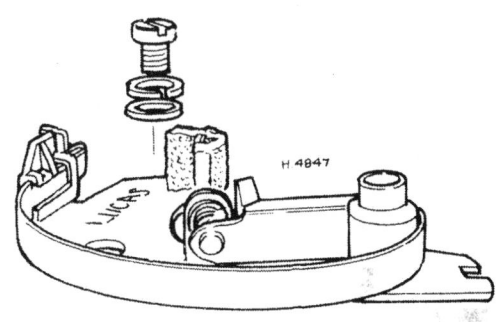

Fig. 4.2 Contact breaker points set (Sec 3)

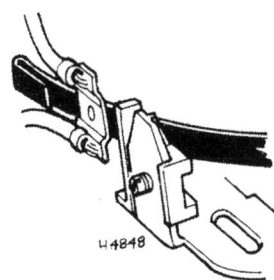

Fig. 4.3 Low tension cable and contact breaker points spring
attachment to the terminal plate (Sec 3)

3   To reface the points, rub their faces on a fine carborundum stone, or on fine emery paper. It is important that the faces are rubbed flat and parallel to each other so that there will be complete face-to-face contact when the points are closed. One of the points will be pitted and the other will have deposits on it.

4   It is necessary to completely remove the built-up deposits, but not necessary to rub the pitted point right down to the stage where all the pitting has disappeared, though obviously if this is done it will prolong the time before the operation of refacing the points has to be repeated.

5   Before refitting new or refaced points, clean the contacts with methylated spirit or petrol and lightly smear the pivot post with grease.

6   To refit the points, first position the adjustable contact breaker plate, and secure it with its screw spring and flat washer. On the early models, fit the fibre washer to the terminal pin, and fit the contact breaker arm over it. Insert the flanged nylon bush with the condenser lead immediately under its head, and the low tension lead under that,

over the terminal pin. Fit the steel washer and screw on the securing nut. On later models, check that the contact breaker spring is correctly located on the insulator.

7   The points are now reassembled and the gap should be set as detailed in Section 2.

8   If new points have been fitted their gap should be re-checked after 500 miles (800 km). On bedding-in the gap may have closed fractionally.

4   Condenser – removal, testing and refitting

1   The purpose of the condenser (sometimes known as a capacitor) is to ensure that when the contact breaker points open, there is no sparking across them which would 'waste' voltage, and cause severe pitting.

2   The condenser is fitted in parallel with the contact breaker points, and if it develops a short circuit, will cause ignition failure, as the points will be prevented from interrupting the low tension circuit.

3   If the engine becomes very difficult to start or begins to miss after several miles running and the breaker points show signs of excessive burning, then the condition of the condenser must be suspect. A further test can be made by separating the points by hand with the ignition switched on. If this is accompanied by a strong flash it is indicative that the condenser has failed. Without special test equipment the only sure way to diagnose condenser trouble is to replace a suspected unit with a new one and note if there is any improvement.

4   To remove the condenser from the distributor, remove the distributor cap and the rotor arm. On the earlier models, unscrew the contact breaker arm terminal nut, and remove the nut, washer and flanged nylon bush and release the condenser lead from the bush. Unscrew the condenser retaining screw from the breaker plate and remove the condenser. On later models, simply unscrew the retaining screw, and lift the condenser clear.

5   Refitting is the reversal of the above procedure, but ensure that the condenser lead connections are clean.

5   Distributor – removal and refitting

1   Remove the distributor cap and leads, and on later models, disconnect the intake air hose from the heater and place out of the way.

2   Disconnect the low tension lead from the distributor. (On US models with electronic ignition there are three low tension leads).

3   Unscrew the union holding the vacuum tube to the distributor vacuum housing, or pull the tube off, depending on model (not 23D4 distributor).

4   Turn the crankshaft in the normal direction of rotation until the notch on the pulley is aligned with the appropriate static timing mark (see Specifications) and the distributor rotor is opposite the segment feeding No 1 spark plug. The engine can be turned by engaging top gear and, with the ignition turned off, pushing the car forward. If this is not possible, chock the front wheels, jack up one of the rear wheels and, with top gear engaged and the ignition switched off, turn the wheel in the forwards direction until the correct timing position is achieved. Slacken the clamp pinch bolt and remove the distributor (photo).

5   Refitting is a reversal of the above procedure, providing that the engine has not been turned in the meantime. If the engine has been turned, it will be necessary to retime the ignition – see Section 10.

6   Distributor (conventional ignition system) – dismantling

1   Various kinds of distributors have been fitted to the Sprite and Midget over the years. Some models had no vacuum unit to advance or retard the ignition according to manifold depression. Another variation concerned the method of timing adjustment; some models had a vernier knob on the vacuum unit for fine adjustment and some models did not. In following the procedure given below for dismantling the distributor, ignore those aspects which do not relate to the type on which you are working.

2   Before overhauling a worn distributor, consideration should be given to obtaining a factory reconditioned unit. If it is decided to dismantle the original unit, first check the availability of spare parts.

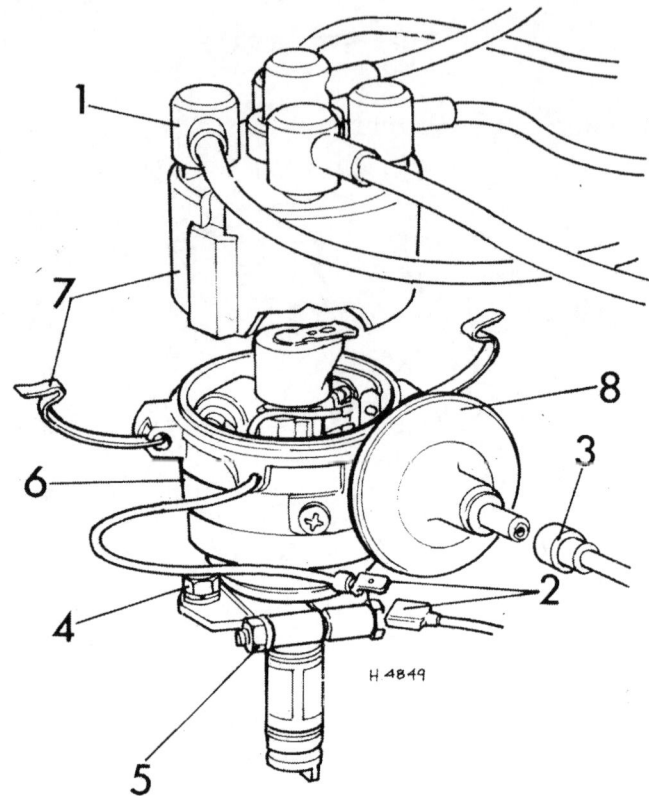

Fig. 4.4 Distributor external components – Lucas 45D4 (Sec 5)

1 HT lead	5 Pinch bolt
2 LT lead	6 Distributor body
3 Vacuum pipe	7 Cap and clip
4 Clamp plate screw	8 Vacuum capsule

5.4 Removing the distributor

For later US models fitted with electronic ignition see Section 7.

3   Remove the distributor as described in the previous Section.

4   The distributor should be dismantled on a clean work area and the respective components laid out in order.

5   Remove the rotor arm and points, as described in this Chapter.

6   Remove the condenser, and on later models, the cam oiler pad.

7   Unhook the vacuum unit spring from its mounting pin on the

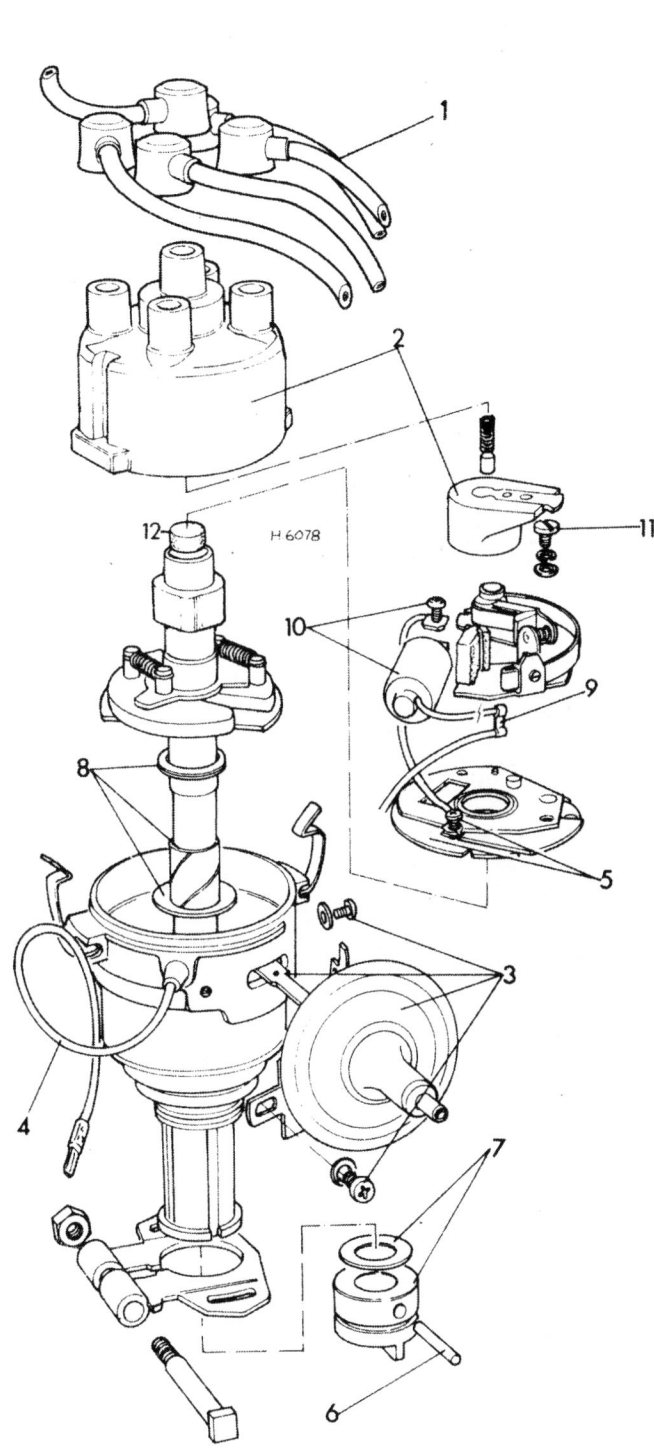

Fig. 4.5 Exploded view of the Lucas 45D4 distributor (Sec 6)

1 HT leads	8 Shaft assembly with
2 Cap and rotor arm	spacer and steel washer
3 Vacuum unit	9 Terminal plate
4 LT lead	10 Condenser
5 Baseplate assembly	11 Contact set screw
6 Drive dog-to-shaft pin	12 Lubrication pad
7 Drive dog and thrust	
washer	

Fig. 4.6 Assembled relationship of drive dog to rotor arm (Sec 6)

moving contact breaker plate. Remove the contact breaker plate.

8   Unscrew the two screws and lockwashers which hold the contact breaker baseplate in position and remove the earth lead from the relevant screw. Remember to refit this lead on reassembly. Lift out the contact breaker baseplate.

9   Note the position of the slot in the rotor arm drive in relation to the offset drive dog (Fig. 4.6) at the opposite end of the distributor. It is essential that this is reassembled correctly as otherwise the timing will be 180° out.

10 Unscrew the cam spindle retaining screw, which is located in the centre of the rotor arm drive, and remove the cam spindle.

11 Lift out the centrifugal weights together with their springs.

12 To remove the vacuum unit on early models, spring off the small circlip which secures the advance adjustment nut, which should then be unscrewed. With the micrometer adjusting nut removed, release the spring and the micrometer adjusting nut lock spring clip. This is the clip that is responsible for the 'clicks' when the micrometer adjuster is turned. It is small and easily lost, as is the circlip, so put them in a safe place. Do not forget to refit the lock spring clip on reassembly. To remove the vacuum unit on later models, disconnect the connecting tube and unscrew the vacuum unit retaining screws from the distributor body. Lift the operating arm from the movable plate and remove the complete unit.

13 It is only necessary to remove the distributor driveshaft or spindle if it is thought to be excessively worn. With a thin punch drive out the retaining pin from the driving tongue collar on the bottom end of the distributor driveshaft. The shaft can then be removed. The distributor is now completely dismantled.

7   Distributor (electronic ignition system) – dismantling, overhaul and reassembly

1   Refer to Fig. 4.7. Remove the distributor as described in Section 5 with the crankshaft turned to the 10° BTDC mark and with the rotor arm adjacent to No 1 segment.

2   Remove the distributor cap, rotor arm and anti-flash shield.

3   Withdraw the felt pad from the spindle recess, and then disconnect the pick-up unit by unscrewing the retaining screws with spring and plain washers.

4   Unscrew the amplifier module retaining screws and unclip the vacuum retard link from the location pin on the moving plate. Disconnect the amplifier connecting wire grommet from the distributor body and remove the amplifier unit complete.

5   To remove the vacuum retard unit from the amplifier, the retaining pin must be driven out.

6   Unclip the circlip and remove it with the washer from the timing rotor. Withdraw the rotor complete with rubber O-ring.

7   To remove the baseplate from the distributor body, unscrew the securing screws.

8   If the driving dog is badly worn, remove it by driving out its

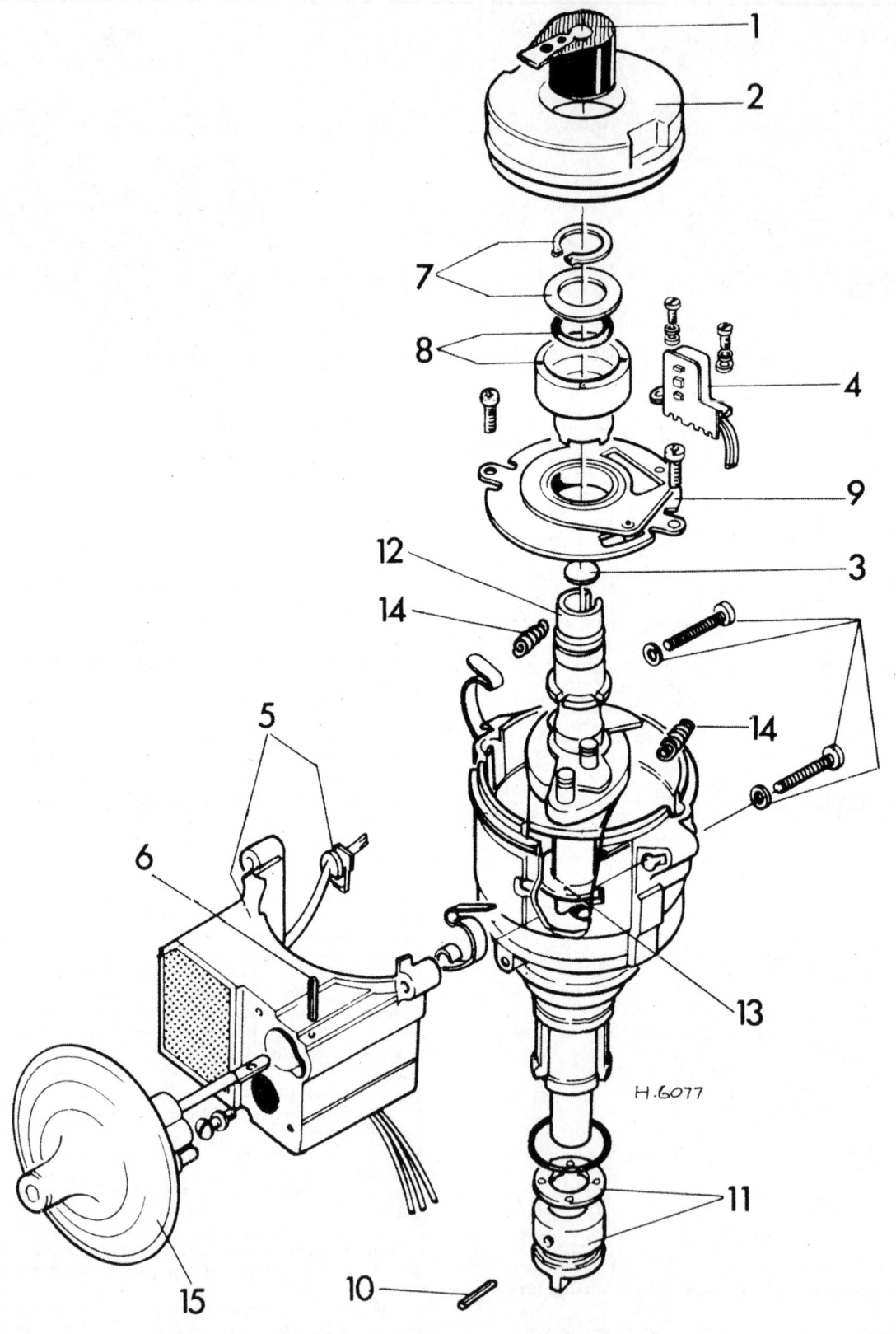

H.6077

Fig. 4.7 Exploded view of the Lucas 45DE4 electronic ignition distributor (Sec 7)

1	Rotor arm	5	Amplifier module	9	Baseplate	13	Shim
2	Anti-flash shield	6	Roll pin	10	Roll pin	14	Return springs
3	Felt pad	7	Circlip and washer	11	Drive dog and thrust washer	15	Vacuum retard unit
4	Pick-up unit	8	Timing rotor and O-ring	12	Spindle		

location pin from the distributor drive spindle, and remove with thrust washers.

9   The spindle can now be withdrawn from the distributor body and the centrifugal weights and their springs removed.

10 Inspect and renew any suspect or worn parts, as described in Section 8 of this Chapter.

11 Reassemble in the reverse order, but note the following:

   (a) *The timing rotor must be fitted with its large locating lug in its respective slot*

   (b) *The amplifier module and wiring grommet must be correctly located before tightening the three retaining screws*

12 The pick-up air gap is adjusted as follows:

   (a) *With the battery disconnected, and the distributor cap, anti-flash shield and rotor arm removed, use feeler gauges to measure the air gap between the timing rotor and the pick-up unit after making sure that the ignition circuit is not switched on. The gap should be 0.014 to 0.016 in (0.35 to 0.40 mm)*

   (b) *Adjust by slackening the two pick-up locking screws, and then move the pick-up to suit. Retighten the screws to lock the pick-up with the correct gap setting*

   (c) *Re-check the gap after the pick-up screws have been tightened to ensure that the correct gap has been retained*

   (d) *Lubricate with light oil all mechanical moving parts, especially those shown in Fig. 4.8*

Special note: *Do not insert the feeler gauge into the gap with the ignition circuit switched on!*

8   Distributor (conventional ignition system) – inspection and repair

1   Check the contact breaker points as already detailed. Check the distributor cap for signs of tracking, indicated by a thin black line between the segments. Renew the cap if any signs of tracking are found.

2   If the metal portion of the rotor arm is badly burned or loose, renew the arm. If slightly burnt clean the arm with a fine file.

3   Check that the carbon brush moves freely in the centre of the distributor cap.

4   Examine the fit of the breaker plate on the bearing plate, and also check the breaker arm pivot for looseness or wear and renew as necessary.

5   Examine the balance weights and pivot pins for wear, and renew the weights or cam assembly if a degree of wear is found.

6   Examine the length of the balance weight springs and compare them with new springs. If they have stretched, they must be renewed.

7   Examine the shaft and the fit of the cam assembly on the shaft. If the clearance is excessive, compare the items with new units, and renew either, or both, if they show excessive wear. If the shaft is a loose fit in the distributor bushes and can be seen to be worn, it will be necessary to fit a new shaft and bushes. The old bushes in the early distributor, or the single bush in later ones, are simply pressed out. **Note:** *Before inserting new bushes they should be stood in engine oil for 24 hours.*

9   Distributor (conventional ignition system) – reassembly

1   Reassembly is the reverse of the dismantling procedure, but note the additional points covered below.

2   Lubricate the contact points pivot post with grease, but be very sparing with it as excessive lubrication can lead to ignition failure. Similarly oil the balance weights, distributor shaft and bearing(s) with engine oil, but do not overdo it.

3   On reassembling the cam driving pins with the centrifugal weights, check that they are in the correct position so that, when viewed from above, the rotor is at the twelve o'clock position with the small offset on the driving dog to the left – see Fig. 4.6. Check the action of the weights over their full range of movement and ensure that there is no binding.

4   On the Lucas type 45D4 distributors fit a new thrust washer if a new spindle is fitted and, on assembly, tap the drive end with a hammer to flatten the washer pips and thereby provide the correct endfloat.

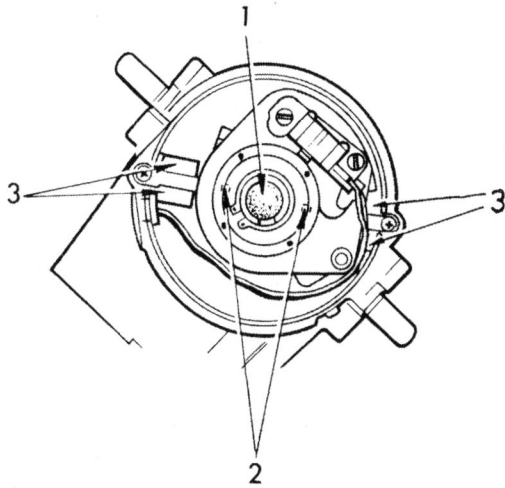

Fig. 4.8 Lubrication points on the electronic ignition distributor – Lucas 45DE4 (Sec 7)

   1   Felt washer
   2   Pick-up plate centre bearing lubrication
   3   Central timing control lubrication holes

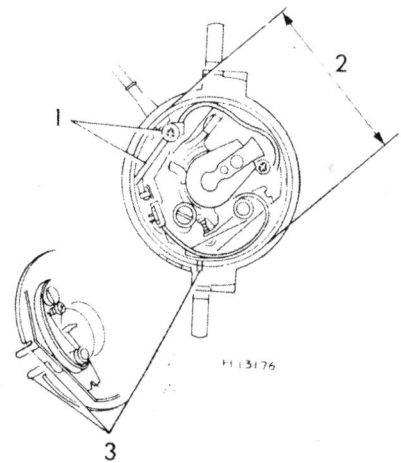

Fig. 4.9 Assembling the single-screw type baseplate to the Lucas 45D4 distributor (Sec 9)

   1   Positioning the earth lead
   2   Measure the distributor cap locating spigot
   3   Position the two downward pointing prongs

5   Where the contact breaker baseplate is secured by a single screw, position the assembly so that the two downward-pointing prongs will straddle the screw hole below the cap clip. Press the baseplate into the body until it engages with the undercut. Take an accurate measurement across the spigot on which the distributor cap locates, at right angles to the slot in the baseplate. Position the earth lead, then fit and tighten the baseplate securing screw. Take another measurement across the cap locating spigot. If the measurement has not increased by at least 0.006 in (0.15 mm) the baseplate assembly must be renewed. If satisfactory, check that the two downward-pointing prongs of the baseplate still straddle the screw hole and refit the vacuum unit, making sure that the operating arm is engaged with the moving plate pin (Fig. 4.9).

6   Where applicable, set the micrometer adjusting nut to the middle position on the scale.

7   Finally, set the contact breaker gap to the correct clearance, wipe off all surplus lubricant, and fit a new O-ring to the distributor body extension.

10 Ignition timing – adjustment

1   It is necessary to check, and perhaps adjust, the ignition timing whenever the contact breaker points gap has been altered, or when the distributor-to-clamp plate alignment has been disturbed. Check the contact breaker points gap before checking the timing. If contact breaker ignition is fitted, the timing may be checked statically (with the engine stopped) or dynamically (with the engine running). If electronic ignition is fitted, only dynamic timing is possible. Dynamic timing is quicker and more accurate.

2   The timing is checked at the exact moment of opening of the points with regard to the position of the dimple in the crankshaft pulley in relation to the pointers on the timing gear cover case. On all except 1500 models, the longest pointer indicates TDC and each of the two shorter pointers indicate 5° BTDC and 10° BTDC, respectively. A more complex timing mark is used on later cars. It is still below and behind the crankshaft pulley. It has more marks to facilitate stroboscopic checking of the ignition timing. Some later models may have a timing scale mounted on the timing cover, on which each tooth corresponds to 4° BTDC. The long tooth at the right-hand end corresponds to TDC. See Fig. 4.12 for clarification. On 1500 models, the timing marks are different. The crankshaft pulley notch is aligned with the appropriate mark on the scale mounted on the timing cover over the top of the pulley. The scale is divided up into 4° divisions, these being subdivided into 2° increments. Upon inspection it will be seen that the scale is comprehensively marked and is self-explanatory.

3   Check the Specifications for the correct position of the crankshaft pulley wheel when the points should be just beginning to open. This is shown as 'static' or 'dynamic', depending on the timing method used.

Static timing
Initial setting

4   If timing has been lost completely (eg during engine rebuild), commence by turning the crankshaft in the normal direction of rotation until No 1 piston is rising on the compression stroke. This can be ascertained by removing No 1 spark plug and feeling the compression being developed in the cylinder, or by removing the rocker cover and noting when both valves on No 4 are open and both valves on No 1 are closed. Continue to rotate the crankshaft until the notch in the crankshaft pulley is in line with the correct timing pointer (see Specifications). If the distributor has been removed, refit it now, turning the distributor shaft so that the rotor arm points to No 1 segment in the distributor cap. Set the vernier adjuster (if fitted) to the middle of its travel and slacken the clamp plate pinch-bolt. Now proceed as described below.

Checking and adjusting

5   With the timing marks aligned as described in paragraph 4, the contact breaker points should be just separating. (The marks will be aligned when either No 1 or No 4 cylinder is commencing the firing stroke, but as long as the distributor is fitted correctly it does not matter which cylinder is firing). To check when the points are separating, connect a 12V test lamp between the coil LT connection to the distributor and earth (any bare metal part of the car). With the ignition on, when the points are open, the lamp will light. Remove the distributor cap so that the engine cannot fire.

6   Rotate the crankshaft in the normal direction of rotation until the timing marks are again approaching correct alignment and observe when the test lamp lights. (It will come on and go out again during rotation for the firing stroke of No 2 or No 3 cylinder – ignore this).

7   If the lamp lights before the marks are aligned, the ignition timing is advanced. With the marks correctly aligned, slacken the distributor clamp plate pinch-bolt and slowly turn the distributor body anticlockwise until the test lamp goes out, then turn it clockwise until the lamp just comes on again. Tighten the pinch-bolt.

8   If the lamp does not light until after the timing marks are aligned, ignition timing is retarded. With the marks correctly aligned, slacken the clamp plate pinch-bolt and slowly turn the distributor body clockwise until the lamp just comes on. Tighten the pinch-bolt.

9   Turn the crankshaft through a complete revolution until the timing marks are again aligned and check that the test lamp lights at the right moment. Small errors can be corrected by rotating the vernier adjuster (if fitted) in the direction arrowed (on the distributor) A to advance or R to retard.

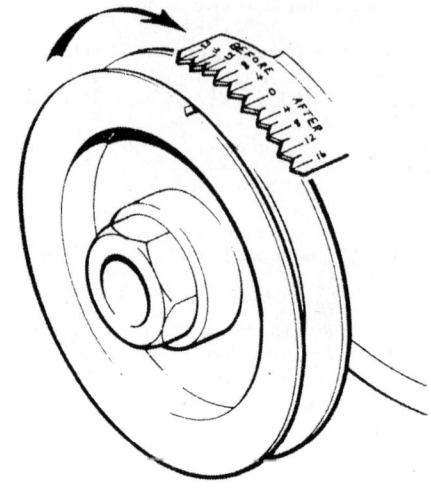

Fig. 4.10 The 1500 cc engine timing marks (Sec 10)

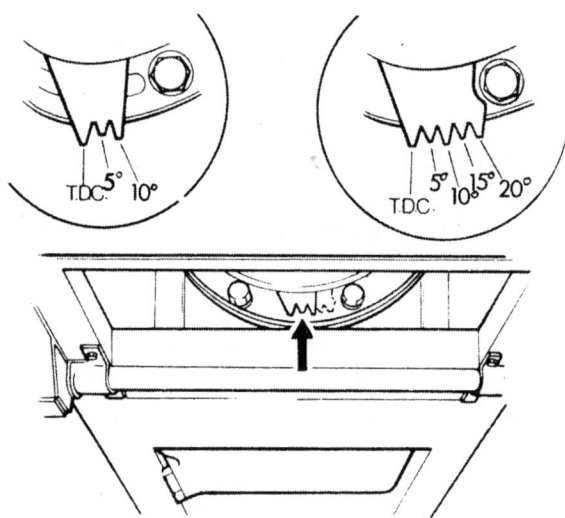

Fig. 4.11 Timing marks used in all models except 1500; scale shows number of degrees BTDC (Sec 10)

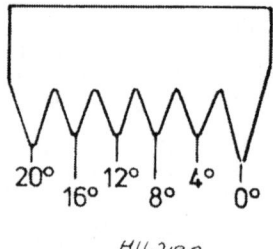

H16280

Fig. 4.12 Timing scale used on later A-series engine (Sec 10)

10 Switch off the ignition, remove the test lamp and refit the distributor cap. Static timing is now complete.

Dynamic timing

11 Connect a stroboscopic timing light to No 1 spark plug lead in accordance with the manufacturer's instructions. Mark the notch on the crankshaft pulley and the correct dynamic timing mark (see Specifications) with quick-drying white paint – typist's correcting fluid is ideal. Disconnect the distributor vacuum pipe (if fitted) and plug it.

12 Start the engine and adjust the tickover to that specified. Shine

the timing light onto the timing marks, when they will appear stationary and, if the timing is correct, in alignment.

13 If the marks are not in alignment, slacken the distributor clamp plate pinch-bolt and rotate the distributor body clockwise to advance the ignition (pulley mark will drift anti-clockwise) or anti-clockwise to retard (pulley mark will drift clockwise). Small adjustments may be made on the vernier adjuster (if fitted). Tighen the pinch-bolt when adjustment is correct.

14 Increase the engine speed and check that the pulley mark drifts anti-clockwise as the centrifugal advance mechanism comes into operation. Reconnect the distributor vacuum pipe (if fitted) and look for a small further advance from the vacuum advance unit.

15 If the pulley mark appears blurred or jerks about, this may be due to a worn distributor or to general wear in the timing gear. If the automatic advance mechanisms are jerky or inoperative, they should be investigated.

16 Stop the engine, disconnect the timing light and remake the original connections.

17 Small readjustments under running conditions can be beneficial. Start the engine, allow to warm up to normal temperature, accelerate in top gear from 30 to 50 mph and listen for heavy pinking. If this occurs, retard the ignition slightly until just the faintest trace of pinking can be heard under these conditions.

18 The fullest advantage of any change of fuel will only be attained by readjustment of the ignition settings. Vary the setting on the vernier adjuster (where fitted) by one or two divisions until the best all-round result is achieved.

11 Automatic advance – testing

1 Ignition advance to suit engine speed is given by centrifugal action on spring-loaded bobweights under the contact breaker plate. These can be checked when the contact breaker plate is removed to change the points, and the confirmed by turning the spindle forwards.

2 Advance to suit light load is given by the suction device connected to the manifold. Garages check this by electronic testers. The fact that it is working can be simply checked by disconnecting the vacuum advance pipe at its carburettor connection and sucking by mouth on the end. The contact breaker plate should be observed to move a small amount. Provided it moves, the connections must be airtight and the diaphragm functioning, and it is a safe assumption that the actual advance given is correct.

12 Spark plugs, HT leads and coil

1 The correct functioning of the spark plugs is vital for the correct running and efficiency of the engine.

2 Depending on the model, at intervals of approximately 12 000 miles (20 000 km), or every 12 months if sooner, the plugs should be renewed. The condition of the spark plugs will also tell much about the overall condition of the engine.

3 If the insulator nose of the spark plug is clean and white, with no deposits, this is indicative of a weak mixture, or too hot a plug (a hot plug transfers heat away from the electrodes slowly – a cold plug transfers it away quickly). If the tip and insulator nose is covered with hard black deposits, then this is indicative that the mixture is too rich. Should the plug be black and oily, then it is likely that the engine is fairly worn, as well as the mixture being too rich.

4 If the insulator nose is covered with light tan to greyish brown deposits, then the mixture is correct and it is likely that the engine is in good condition.

5 If there are any traces of long brown tapering stains on the outside of the white portion of the plug, then the plug will have to be renewed, as this shows that there is a faulty joint between the plug body and the insulator, and compression is being allowed to leak away.

6 Plugs are best cleaned by a sandblasting machine, to free them of carbon deposits. Your local garage will probably possess such a machine. The spark plugs can also be tested under compression to measure their efficiency.

7 The spark plug type and gap are most important. The correct type of plug is detailed in the Specifications Section at the beginning of this Chapter. If the plug gap is too small or large, the spark produced will be of impaired efficiency.

8 To set the gap, measure with a feeler gauge the existing gap, and

then carefully bend open, or close, the outer electrode to suit until the desired gap is achieved. A feeler gauge of the specified size should be a fine interference fit between the outer and central electrode.

9 When refitting plugs, new washers should be fitted, and the plugs tightened to the specified torque wrench setting.

10 Ignition HT leads require little attention, but they should be kept clean and dry. Their connections to the plugs and distributor cap and coil must be in good order.

11 If refitting the plug leads at any time, fit them one at a time, to ensure they are refitted correctly in the right firing order.

12 The later type ignition high tension leads are graphite impregnated cord. These give suppression of radio interference to domestic VHF or UHF receivers. Connectors for metal core cable are unsuitable. Special tangs are needed in the ends to make a suitable contact, and the cables are a push fit into the end connectors.

13 Difficult starting is usually caused by dirt on the leads allowing the high tension current to leak away, particularly in damp weather. But after long mileage the graphited cord in the leads deteriorates. Renewal should help, either with similar material, or the more expensive metal cored cable with suppressors in the end fittings.

14 The coil is normally an extremely reliable component, but if failure has been diagnosed (see Section 13), the only course of action is renewal. Early coils will be marked 'SW' and 'CB', these terminals being connected to the ignition switch and distributor/contact breaker points respectively. Later coils are marked '+' and '−'. On cars wired with a positive earth system, the '−' terminal is connected to the ignition switch, and the '+' terminal to the distributor/contact breaker points. On later cars with a negative earth system, these connections are reversed, ie '+' to ignition switch, '−' to distributor/contact breaker points.

13 Fault diagnosis – ignition system

There are two main symptoms indicating ignition faults. Either the engine will not start or fire, or the engine is difficult to start and misfires. If it is a regular misfire, so that the engine is only running on two or three cylinders, the fault is almost sure to be in the secondary, or high tension, circuit. If the misfiring is intermittent, the fault could be in either the high or low tension circuits. If the car stops suddenly, or will not start at all, it is likely that the fault is in the low tension circuit. Loss of power and overheating, apart from faulty carburation settings, are normally due to faults in the distributor or incorrect ignition timing.

Engine will not start

If the engine fails to start, it is likely that the fault is in the low tension circuit. It will be known whether there is a good charge in the battery by the way the starter motor spins over. If the battery is evidently in good condition, then check the distributor.

Remove the distributor cap and rotor arm; and check that the contact points are not burnt, pitted or dirty. If the points are badly pitted, or burnt or dirty, clean or renew and reset them.

If the engine still refuses to fire check the low tension circuit further. Check the condition of the condenser. Switch on the ignition and turn the crankshaft until the contact breaker points have fully opened. With either a voltmeter, or bulb and length of wire, connect the contact breaker plate terminal to earth on the engine. If the bulb lights, the low tension circuit is in order, and the fault is in the contact breaker points. If the points have been cleaned and reset, and the bulb still lights, then the fault is in the high tension circuit.

If the bulb fails to light, connect it between the ignition coil 'switch' terminal and earth. If it lights, it points to a damaged wire or loose connection in the cable from the coil 'contact breaker' terminal to the terminal on the contact breaker plate.

If the bulb fails to light, connect it between the ignition coil 'switch' terminal and earth. If the bulb lights it indicates a fault in the primary winding of the coil, and it will be necessary to fit a replacement unit.

Should the bulb not light at this stage, then check the cable to the 'switch' side of the coil for faults or a loose connection. Connect the bulb from the negative terminal of the battery to the 'switch' terminal of the coil. If the bulb lights, then the fault is somewhere in the switch, or wiring and control box. Check further as follows:

(a)   Check the cable feeding current to the ignition switch. If the bulb fails to light, then this indicates that the cable is damaged, or one of the connections loose, or that there is a fault in the switch

(b)   Connect the bulb between the ignition switch 'feed' cable terminal and earth. If the bulb fails to light, this indicates a fault in the switch or in the wiring leading to the switch

(c)   Connect the bulb to the other ignition switch terminal and then to earth. If the bulb fails to light, this indicates a fault or loose connection in the wiring leading to the switch

(d)   Connect the bulb between the lighting and ignition terminal in the control box, and then to earth. If the bulb fails to light, this indicates a faulty control box (where applicable)

(e)   Connect the bulb from the fuse unit terminal to earth. If the bulb fails to light this indicates a fault or loose connection in the wire 'feeding' starter solenoid

(f)   Connect the bulb from the input terminal of the solenoid switch to earth. If the bulb fails to light then there is a fault in the cable from the battery to the solenoid switch, or the earth lead of the battery is not properly earthed, and the whole circuit is dead

If the fault is not in the low tension circuit, check the high tension circuit. Disconnect each plug lead in turn at the spark plug end, and hold the end of the cable about $\frac{3}{16}$ in (5 mm) away from the cylinder block. Spin the engine on the starter motor. Sparking between the end of the cable and the block should be fairly strong with a regular blue spark. (Hold the lead with rubber to avoid electric shocks). Should there be no spark at the end of the plug leads, disconnect the coil-to-distributor lead at the distributor cap, and hold the end of the lead about $\frac{1}{4}$ in (6 mm) from the block. Spin the engine as before, when a rapid succession of blue sparks between the end of the lead and the block indicate that the coil is in order, and that either the distributor cap is cracked, or the carbon brush is stuck or worn, or the rotor arm is faulty.

Check the cap for cracks and tracking, and the rotor arm for cracks or looseness of the metal portion and renew as necessary. If there are no sparks from the end of the lead from the coil, then check the connections of the lead to the coil and distributor head. If they are good, and the low tension side is without fault, then it will be necessary to fit a replacement coil.

Engine misfires

If the engine misfires regularly, run it at a fast idling speed, and short out each of the plugs in turn by placing a short screwdriver across from the plug terminal to the cylinder. Ensure that the screwdriver has an insulated handle, and hold it only by the handle. Alternatively pull off each plug lead from the plug one at a time in turn, refitting the lead before moving to the next one. No difference in engine running will be noticed when the plug on the defective cylinder is short circuited or its lead is removed, but the misfiring and rough running will worsen when the other plugs are isolated. Remove the plug lead from the end of the defective plug and hold it about $\frac{3}{16}$ in (5 mm) away from the block. Restart the engine. If the sparking is fairly strong and regular, the fault must lie in the spark plug. The plug may be loose, the insulation may be cracked, or the points may have burnt away giving too wide a gap for the spark to jump. Worse still, one of the points may have broken off. Either renew the plug, or clean, gap, and test it.

If there is no spark at the end of the plug lead, or if it is weak and intermittent, check the ignition lead from the distributor to the plug. If the insulation is cracked or perished, renew the lead. Check the connections at the distributor cap.

If there is still no spark, examine the distributor cap carefully for tracking. This can be recognised by a very thin black line running between two or more electrodes, or between an electrode and some other part of the distributor. These lines are paths which now conduct electricity across the cap, thus letting it run to earth. The only answer is a new distributor cap.

Apart from the ignition timing being incorrect, other causes of misfiring have already been dealt with in the sub-Section dealing with the failure of the engine to start. To recap, these are that:

(a)   The coil may be faulty giving an intermittent misfire

(b)   There may be a damaged wire or loose connection in the low tension circuit

(c)   The condenser may be short circuiting

(d)   There may be a mechanical fault in the distributor (broken driving spindle or contact breaker spring)

If the ignition timing is too far retarded, it should be noted that the engine will tend to overheat, and there will be a quite noticeable drop in power. If the engine is overheating and the power is down, and the ignition timing is correct, then the carburation should be checked, as it is likely that this is where the fault lies. See Chapter 3 for further details on this.

Chapter 5 Clutch

Contents

Specifications

Clutch type

948 cc and 1098 cc models	Single dry plate with coil springs
1275 cc and 1500 cc models	Single dry plate with diaphragm spring

Diameter

948 cc models	6.25 in (16.0 cm)
1098 cc models	7.25 in (18.4 cm)
1275 cc models	6.5 in (16.5 cm)
1500 cc models	7.25 in (18.4 cm)

Release bearing
Type:

948, 1098 and 1275 cc models	Graphite pad
1500 cc models	Ball bearing

Clutch fluid type/specification

Hydraulic fluid to SAE J1703 or FMVSS 116 DOT 3 (Duckhams Universal Brake and Clutch Fluid)

---

1 General description

The clutch assembly of earlier models comprises a steel cover which is bolted and dowelled to the rear face of the flywheel, and contains the pressure plate, pressure plate springs, release levers, and clutch disc or driven plate. The pressure plate, pressure spring, and release levers are all attached to the clutch assembly cover. The clutch disc is free to slide along the splined first motion shaft and is held in position between the flywheel and the pressure plate by the pressure of the pressure plate springs. Friction lining material is riveted to the clutch disc and it has a spring cushioned hub to absorb transmission shocks and to help ensure a smooth take-up of drive.

The clutch is actuated hydraulically. The pendant clutch pedal, is connected to the clutch master cylinder and hydraulic fluid reservoir by a short pushrod. The master cylinder and hydraulic reservoir are mounted on the engine side of the bulkhead in front of the driver. A common reservoir serves both the clutch and brake master cylinders on early models, but individual reservoirs are fitted for the systems on later cars.

All Sprite Mk IV and Midget Mk III models are fitted with a Borg and Beck diaphragm spring clutch which is removed from the car in the same way as the early type of clutch. The clutch driven plate can be renewed in the normal way, but it is not possible to service the pressure plate or the diaphragm spring and these must be renewed as a unit. Very little maintenance is required apart from periodical checking of the hydraulic fluid in the master cylinder, and topping up to the correct level if required. If there is a constant need to top up the reservoir, the system should be thoroughly checked for signs of leakage.

Cleanliness is of the utmost importance during any jobs undertaken on the hydraulic fluid. Before checking the level of fluid in the master cylinder reservoir, carefully clean the cap and body of the reservoir with a clean rag to ensure that no dirt enters the system when the cap is removed. Do not overfill and ensure that no fluid is dropped onto the car bodywork or your hands; it is quite toxic and removes paint very effectively!

---

2 Hydraulic system – bleeding

1 Gather together a clean jam jar, a 9 in (230 mm) length of rubber tubing which fits tightly over the bleed nipple in the slave cylinder, and a tin of hydraulic brake fluid. An assistant will also be required.
2 Check that the master cylinder is full, and if not, fill it, and cover the bottom inch (25 mm) of the jar with hydraulic fluid.
3 Remove the rubber dust cap from the bleed nipple on the slave cylinder, and with a suitable spanner open the bleed nipple one turn.
4 Place one end of the tube securely over the nipple and insert the other end in the jam jar so that the tube orifice is below the level of the fluid.
5 The assistant should now depress the clutch pedal and hold it down at the end of the stroke. Close the bleed nipple and allow the foot pedal to return to its normal position.
6 Continue this sequence of operations until clear hydraulic fluid with no traces of air bubbles emerges from the end of the tubing.

Check frequently to ensure that the fluid level in the reservoir doesn't drop too far, thus letting air get into the system.

7   When no more air bubbles appear, close the bleed nipple when the foot pedal is depressed.

8   Refit the rubber dust cap to the bleed nipple. Top up the reservoir until the level is up to the bottom of the filler neck and, before refitting the filler cap, check that its breather hole is clear. Discard the fluid bled from the system as it is unfit for use in any hydraulic system.

3   Slave cylinder – removal and refitting

1   Wipe around the filler cap on the hydraulic reservoir and remove the cap. Place a piece of thin plastic sheet over the filler orifice and refit the cap. This will reduce the loss of hydraulic fluid when the pipeline is undone.

2   Wipe around the pipe union on the slave cylinder and disconnect the pipeline from the cylinder. On some models a rigid pipe is fitted, but on others a flexible pipe is used. Take care not to twist the pipeline when undoing the union and position a container to catch spilt fluid, although this should not amount to much.

3   *On models except 1500 cc*, remove the split pin from the pin joining the slave cylinder pushrod to the clutch release arm and remove the pin and washers. Undo and remove the two bolts securing the slave cylinder to the clutch housing and remove the slave cylinder (photo).

4   *On 1500 cc models*, undo and remove the clamp bolt, nut and washer securing the slave cylinder in its mounting, and then slide the slave cylinder from the housing (photo).

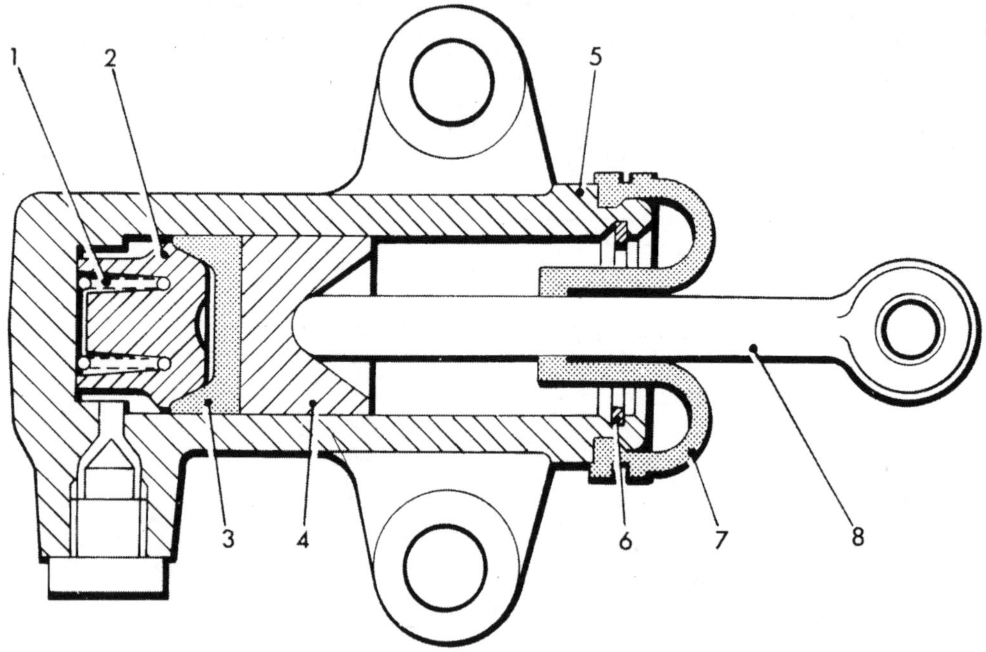

Fig. 5.1 Cross-sectional view of the early pattern clutch slave cylinder (Sec 3)

1 Spring	3 Cup	5 Body	7 Rubber boot
2 Cup filler	4 Piston	6 Circlip	8 Pushrod

3.3 The early pattern clutch slave cylinder

3.4 Removing the later pattern clutch slave cylinder from the clutch housing mounting – 1500 cc models

5   Refitting is the reverse of the removal procedure, but the following points should be noted:

(a)   *On 1500 cc models, centralise the pushrod in the cylinder housing before fitting the slave cylinder and align the groove on the slave cylinder with the bolt hole before attempting to fit the bolt*

(b)   *After reconnecting the hydraulic pipeline on all models, top up the reservoir with fresh fluid and bleed the system as described in the previous Section*

4   Slave cylinder – dismantling, examination and reassembly

1   Clean the outside of the slave cylinder before dismantling and work in a clean area to minimise contamination.

2   Pull off the rubber boot and, on all models except 1500 cc, remove the pushrod and the circlip in the open end of the cylinder.

3   With a finger over the open end, shake the cylinder hard to remove the internal components. Carefully note the order in which they fit and which way round they are fitted. If the piston, seal etc prove stubborn, use a foot pump connected to the hydraulic hose connection and, with a cloth pad over the open end of the cylinder, cautiously blow the components out. Take care to prevent them shooting out and getting lost or damaged.

4   Wash all internal parts, except rubber items, in either clean brake fluid or methylated spirit then dry them with non-fluffy rag.

5   Inspect the bore of the cylinder and the piston for wear and scores. Don't try to remove them if any are visible, as it is much better to fit a new assembly. It is false economy to re-use the rubber seal and boot; new ones, as supplied in the repair kit, should be used on reassembly.

6   Soak the rubber seal in fluid before assembly, and thoroughly lubricate the internal components and the cylinder bore with clean fluid during assembly. Ensure that each part is assembled in its correct sequence and the right way round, as noted during dismantling. Make sure that the circlip (not 1500 cc models) is properly bedded in.

7   Wipe the assembly dry and apply a little grease to the pushrod bearing area on the piston. Apply a smear of rubber grease (or disc brake grease) to the seating area of the rubber boot before fitting it.

5   Master cylinder – removal, inspection and reassembly (Sprite Mk III, Midget II and earlier models)

1   The master cylinders for the clutch and brake are both housed in the base of a common hydraulic fluid reservoir, so it is necessary either to free both pedals from the master cylinder pushrods prior to dismantling the clutch master cylinder or, if desired, the pedal may be withdrawn with the master cylinder, in which case ignore paragraph 2 for the moment.

2   Remove the circlips from the end of the clevis pin and remove the pins to free the pedals from the master cylinder pushrods.

3   Remove the two union nuts from the ends of the hydraulic pipes where they enter the cylinder, and gently pull the pipes clear. Cover the pipe ends and their unions to prevent dirt ingress.

4   Unscrew the bolts holding the master cylinder in position and remove the assembly. If the pedals are being removed as well, guide them through the bulkhead complete with the master cylinder. They can then be removed as described in paragraph 2.

5   Unscrew the filler cap and drain the hydraulic fluid into a glass jar or similar. Check that the vent hole in the cap is clear.

6   Unscrew the fixing screws and shakeproof washers which hold the boot fixing plate against the cylinder barrel and tank.

7   Remove the fixing plate, pushrod and rubber boot.

8   Remove the secondary cup, piston, piston washer, main cup,

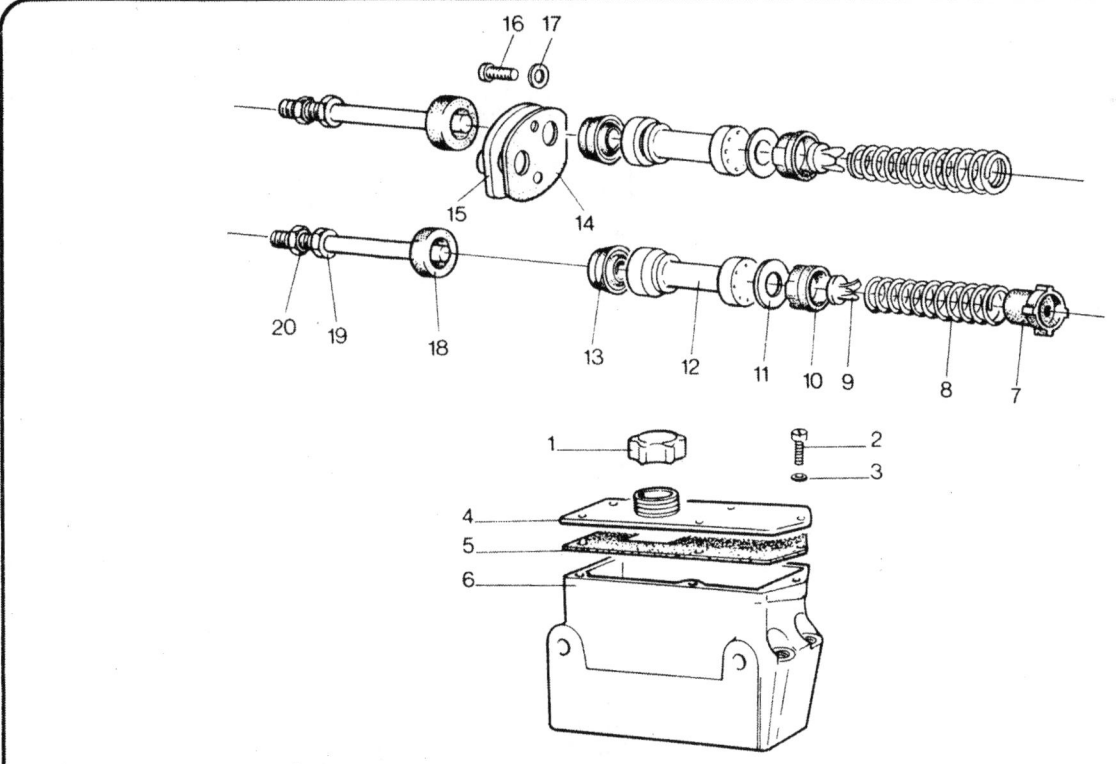

Fig. 5.2 Exploded view of the early pattern combined reservoir with clutch and brake master cylinders (Sec 5)

1 Filler cap	6 Cylinder barrel and	10 Main cup	15 Boot fixing plate
2 Fixing screw	reservoir	11 Piston washer	16 Fixing screw
3 Shakeproof washer	7 Valve (brake bore only)	12 Piston	17 Shakeproof washer
4 Reservoir cover	8 Return spring	13 Secondary cup	18 Boot
5 Reservoir cover gasket	9 Spring retainer	14 Gasket	19 Pushrod
			20 Pushrod adjuster

spring retainer, and the return spring from the cylinder barrel.

9 Clean all the components thoroughly with hydraulic fluid or alcohol and then dry them off, using non-fluffy rag.

10 Discard the rubber components, as it is far better to fit new items on reassembly. Carefully examine the cylinder bore and piston for wear and heavy scoring. It is not possible to rectify these faults satisfactorily and new items should be fitted where defective.

11 Reassembly is a straight reversal of the dismantling procedure but note the following points:

(a) As components are returned to the cylinder barrel, lubricate them with the correct grade of hydraulic fluid

(b) Reset the effective length of the pushrod by the pushrod adjuster nut (if this nut has been disturbed) so that there is $\frac{1}{32}$ in (0.8 mm) of free play between the pushrod and the piston, which corresponds to $\frac{5}{32}$ in (4 mm) free play at the clutch pedal. It is essential that this play is present

(c) On completion of reassembly, top up the reservoir tank with the correct grade of hydraulic fluid and bleed the system

(d) Remember that it will be necessary to bleed the brake system as well as the clutch system

6 Master cylinder – removal and refitting (Sprite Mk IV, Midget Mk III and Midget 1500)

1 On these later models a completely separate master cylinder is fitted for the clutch system (photo).

2 First remove the pedal box cover located behind the master cylinder. On 1500 cc models the coil is located on the cover and USA models will need the leads disconnecting first. Undo the four screws retaining the cover and remove the cover together (on 1500 cc models) with the coil (photo).

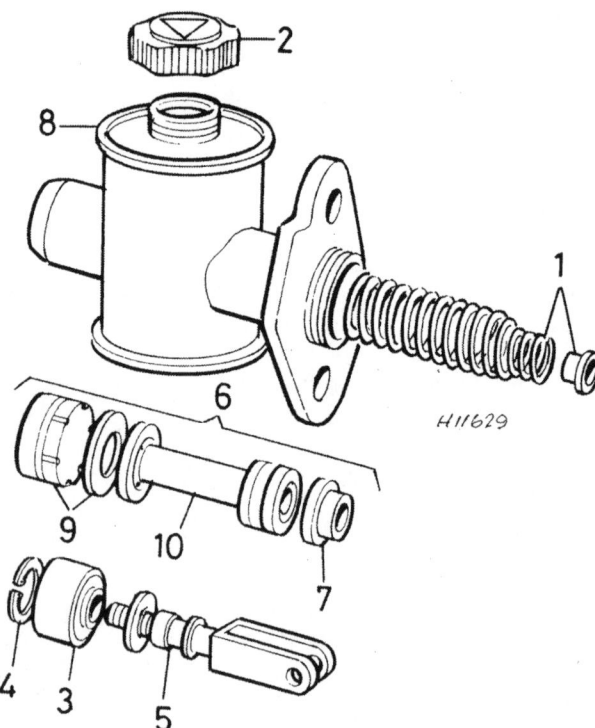

Fig. 5.3 Exploded view of the later pattern clutch master cylinder (Sec 7)

1 Spring and spring retainer	*6 Piston assembly*
2 Reservoir filler cap	*7 Secondary cup seal*
3 Dust excluding boot	*8 Body*
4 Circlip	*9 Main cup seal and washer*
5 Pushrod	*10 Piston*

3 Remove the split pin and washer from the clevis pin connecting the pushrod to the pedal, and remove the clevis pin.

4 Position a container to catch spilt hydraulic fluid and disconnect the pipe union from the master cylinder. Cover the open end of the pipe to prevent dirt ingress.

5 Remove the two bolts, nuts and washers securing the master cylinder to the pedal box and remove the master cylinder from the car. Take care to prevent hydraulic fluid dripping on the car paintwork.

6 Refitting is the reverse of the removal procedure. On completion, bleed the hydraulic system as described in Section 2.

7 Master cylinder – dismantling, examination and reassembly (Sprite Mk IV, Midget Mk III and Midget 1500)

1 Remove the filler cap, empty out the fluid and clean the outside of the unit. Discard the fluid removed from the reservoir, as it is unfit for further use in a hydraulic system.

2 Prise the rubber boot off the cylinder body and slide it along the pushrod.

3 With a pair of circlip pliers remove the circlip which holds the pushrod in place and withdraw the pushrod complete with the rubber boot and dished washer.

4 Slide the piston complete with the secondary cup from the bore of

6.1 The individual clutch and brake master cylinders – 1500 cc model shown

6.2 The pedal cover removed, revealing the brake (left) and clutch pedal connections to their master cylinders

the cylinder. Then withdraw the piston washer, the main cup, the spring retainer, and the spring.

5   The secondary cup can now be removed from the piston by easing it over the end of the piston using the fingers only. Note that it is correctly fitted when the lip of the cup faces towards the piston head.

6   Clean all parts thoroughly using the recommended hydraulic fluid, then dry them off with a non-fluffy rag.

7   Closely examine the bore of the cylinder for wear and scores or grooves. If these are apparent, renew the complete assembly as it is not possible to repair this type of fault. Renew all the rubber items in the unit; a kit of parts is available which includes everything necessary to overhaul the master cylinder.

8   Before starting reassembly immerse all the internal parts in clean hydraulic fluid and assemble them whilst wet.

9   Refit the secondary cup seal to the piston with its lip facing towards the piston head. Fit the retainer into the small end of the spring and insert the spring into the body, larger end first.

10   Fit the main cup seal with its flat end facing towards the open end of the body. Refit the piston washer and carefully insert the piston into the bore with the small end of the piston towards the piston washer. Make sure that the lip of the seal is not damaged or does not roll over as it enters the bore.

11   Lightly grease the ball end of the pushrod and refit the pushrod assembly. Slide down the plain washer and secure in place with the circlip, making sure that it is bedded in properly.

12   Smear the seating areas of the rubber boot with rubber grease, or disc brake grease, and refit it to the cylinder body. Wipe the assembly clean ready for refitting.

8   Clutch (all models) – removal

1   To inspect or renew the clutch unit, it is necessary to remove the engine from the car, as described in Chapter 1. Alternatively the engine and gearbox can be removed as a unit if preferred. It is not possible to

withdraw the gearbox from the engine in the car in order to repair the clutch.

2   Assuming the engine is removed from the gearbox, note the relative markings of the flywheel and clutch cover, and then undo the cover retaining bolts in diagonal sequence half a turn at a time to prevent distortion of the cover flange.

3   Having removed the bolts and spring washers, or Allen screws, lift the clutch cover assembly off the two locating dowels (photo). The clutch disc is now free to be removed, as it is not attached to anything.

8.3 Removing the diaphragm spring type clutch unit from the flywheel – note the location dowels

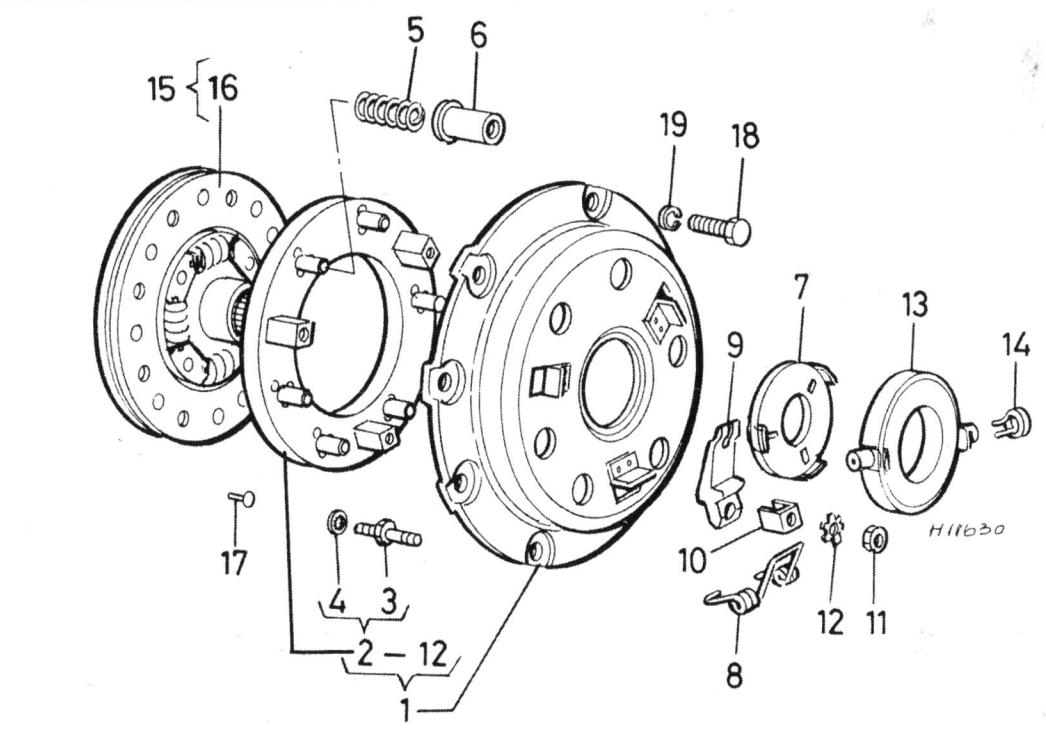

Fig. 5.4 Exploded view of the clutch unit fitted to 948 cc models (Sec 8)

1 Cover assembly	6 Spring cup	11 Nut	15 Driven plate
2 Pressure plate	7 Thrust plate	12 Tab washer	16 Lining
3 Stud	8 Retainer	13 Release bearing and	17 Rivet
4 Washer	9 Release lever	cup assembly	18 Screw
5 Thrust spring	10 Bearing plate	14 Bearing retainer	19 Washer

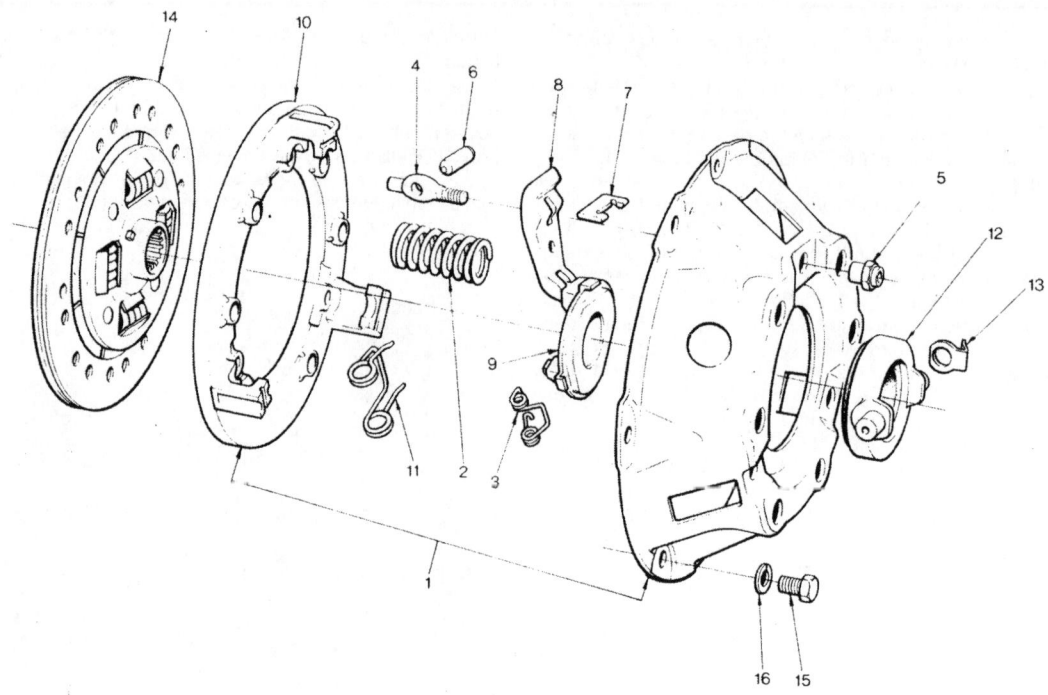

Fig. 5.5 Exploded view of the clutch unit fitted to 1098 cc models (Sec 8)

1	Clutch assembly	5	Eyebolt nut	9	Bearing thrust plate	13	Retainer
2	Thrust spring	6	Release lever pin	10	Pressure plate	14	Driven plate assembly
3	Release lever retainer	7	Strut	11	Anti-rattle spring	15	Clutch-to-flywheel screw
4	Eyebolt	8	Release lever	12	Release bearing	16	Spring washer

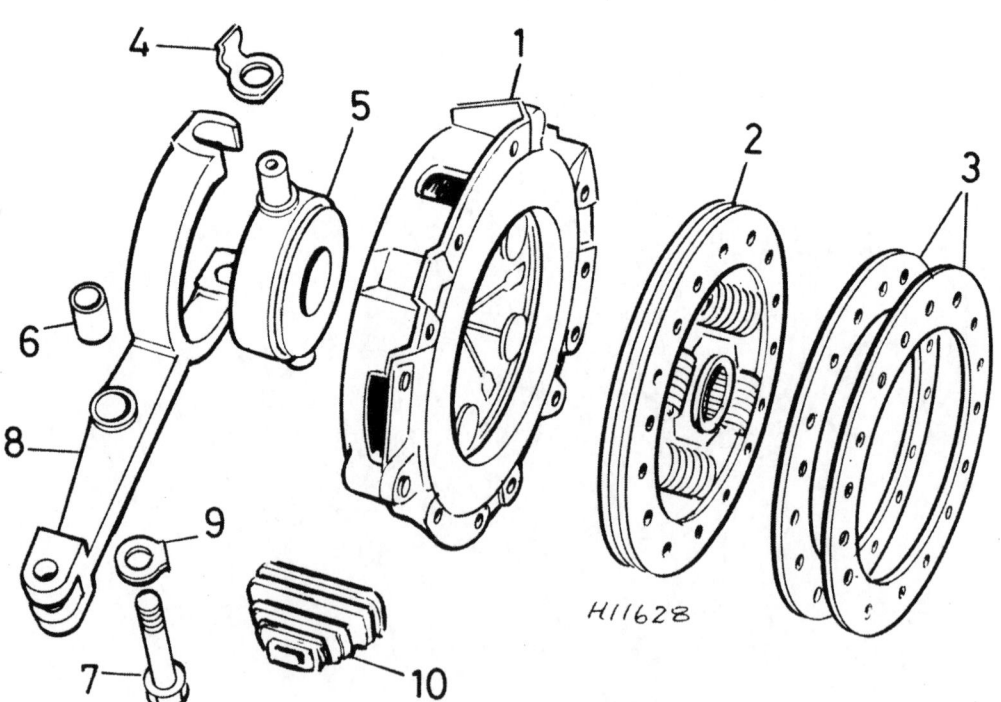

H11628

Fig. 5.6 Exploded view of the clutch unit fitted to 1275 cc models (Sec 8)

1	Clutch assembly	4	Retainer	7	Release lever pin	9	Tab washer
2	Driven plate	5	Release bearing	8	Release lever	10	Dust cover
3	Clutch linings	6	Bush				

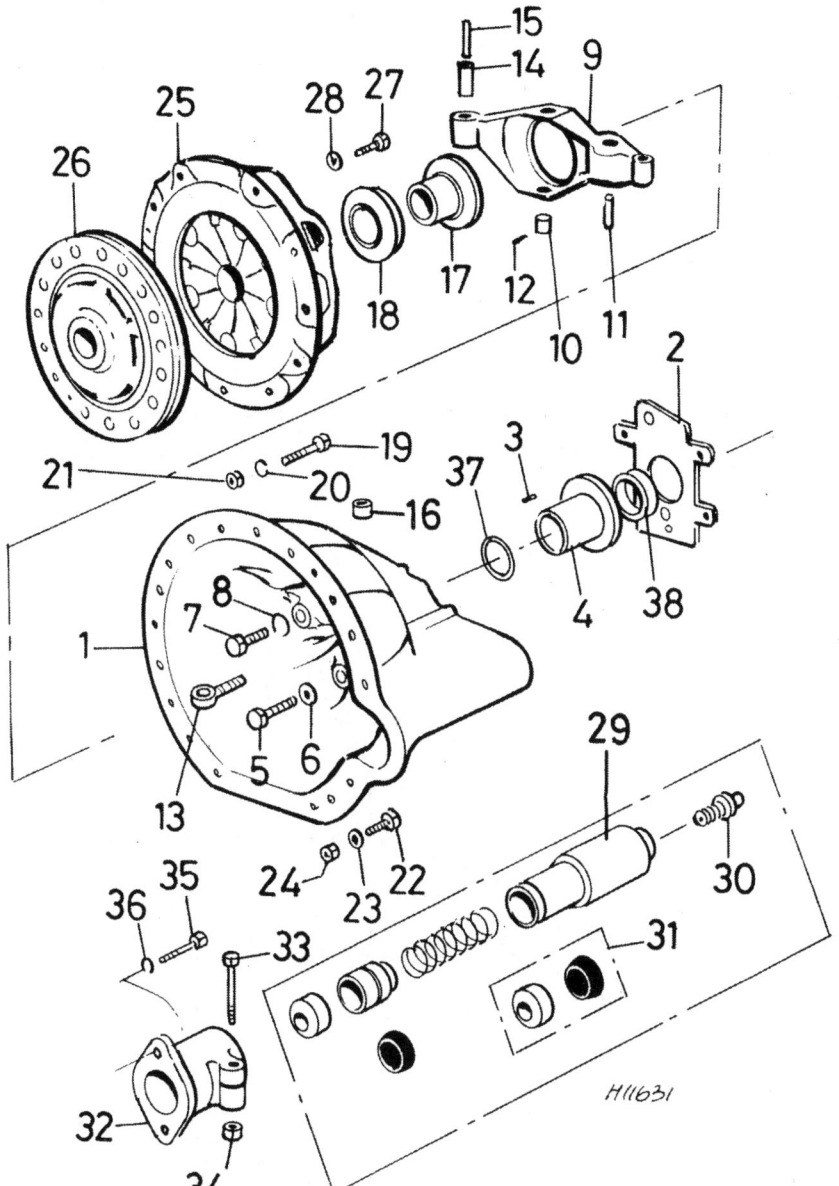

Fig. 5.7 Exploded view of the clutch unit fitted to 1500 models (Sec 8)

1	Clutch housing
2	Gasket
3	Dowel
4	Front cover
5	Bolt
6	Copper washer
7	Bolt
8	Spring washer
9	Operating lever
10	Thrust plug
11	Pin
12	Dowel
13	Pushrod
14	Tolerance ring
15	Pin
16	Bush
17	Sleeve
18	Release bearing
19	Bolt
20	Spring washer
21	Nut
22	Dowel bolt
23	Washer
24	Nut
25	Clutch cover
26	Driven plate
27	Bolt
28	Washer
29	Clutch operating cylinder
30	Bleed screw
31	Repair kit
32	Boss
33	Bolt
34	Nut
35	Screw
36	Spring washer
37	O-ring
38	Oil seal

H11631

9 Clutch (early spring type) – dismantling

1 Refer to Fig. 5.4. If a new clutch disc is being fitted it is a false economy not to renew the release bearing at the same time. This will preclude having to renew it at a later date when wear on the clutch linings is still very small. It should be noted here that it is preferable to purchase an exchange clutch cover assembly unit, which has been built up by the manufacturers and properly balanced, rather than to dismantle and build up your existing clutch cover assembly. A special tool is necessary to ensure that the job is done properly. Assuming that it is possible to borrow from your local BL agent clutch assembly tool 18G99A, proceed as follows.

2 Mark the clutch cover, release levers, and pressure plate lugs so that they can be refitted in the same relative positions. Unhook the springs from the release bearing thrust plate and remove the plate and spring.

3 Place the three correctly sized spacing washers provided with the clutch assembly tool on the tool baseplate in the positions indicated by the chart (found inside the lid of the assembly tool container).

4 Place the clutch face down on the three spacing washers so that the washers are as close as possible to the release levers, with the six holes in the cover flange in line with the six holes in the baseplate.

5 Insert the six bolts provided with the assembly tool through the six holes in the cover flange, and tighten the cover down diagonally onto the baseplate.

6 With a suitable punch, tap back the three tab washers and then remove the three adjusting nuts and bearing plates from the pressure plate bolts on early models, or just unscrew the three adjusting nuts on later models.

7 Unscrew the six bolts holding the clutch cover to the baseplate, in diagonal sequence a turn at a time, so as to release the cover evenly. Lift the cover off, and extract the six pressure springs and the spring retaining cups.

10 Clutch (early spring type) – examination

1 Examine the clutch disc friction linings for wear and loose rivets and the disc for rim distortion, cracks, broken hub springs, and worn splines. It is always best to renew the clutch driven plate as an assembly to preclude further trouble, but, if it is wished to merely renew the linings, the rivets should be drilled out and not knocked out with a punch. The manufacturers do not advise that only the linings are renewed and experience dictates that it is far more satisfactory to

renew the driven plate complete than to try and economise by only fitting new friction linings.

2   Check the machine faces of the flywheel and the pressure plate. If either are badly grooved they should be machined until smooth, or renewed. If the pressure plate is cracked or split it must be renewed, as it should if the areas on the other side of the plate in contact with the three release lever tips are grooved.

3   Check the release bearing thrust plate for cracks and renew it if any are found.

4   Examine the tips of the release levers which bear against the thrust plate, and renew the levers if more than a small flat has been worn on them.

5   Renew any clutch pressure springs that are broken or shorter than standard.

6   Examine the depressions in the release levers which fit over the knife edge fulcrums and renew the levers if the metal appears badly worn.

7   Examine the clutch release bearing in the gearbox bellhousing; if it is worn to within $\frac{1}{16}$ in (1.5 mm) of the rim of the metal cup, or if it is cracked or pitted, it must be removed and renewed

8   Removal of the clutch release bearing is easily accomplished by pulling off the two retaining springs.

9   Also check the clutch withdrawal lever for slackness. If this is evident, withdraw the lever and renew the bush.

11 Clutch (early spring type) – reassembly

1   During clutch reassembly ensure that the marked components are placed in their correct relative positions.

2   Place the three spacing washers on the clutch assembly tool base in the same position as for dismantling the clutch.

3   Place the clutch pressure plate face down on the three spacing washers.

4   Position the three release levers on the knife edge fulcrums (or release lever floating pins in the later clutches) and ensure that the anti-rattle springs are in place over the inner end of the levers.

5   Position the pressure springs on the pressure plate bosses.

6   Fit the flanged cups to the clutch cover and fit the cover over the pressure plate in the same relative position as it was originally.

7   Insert the six assembly tool bolts through the six holes in the clutch cover flange and tighten the cover down diagonally, a turn at a time.

8   Refit the three bearing plates, tag washer, and adjusting nuts over the pressure plate studs in the early units, and just screw the adjusting nuts into the eyebolts in the later models.

9   To correctly adjust the clutch release levers use the clutch assembly tool as detailed below:

   (a) *Screw the actuator into the baseplate and settle the clutch mechanism by pumping the actuator handle up and down a dozen times. Unscrew the actuator*

   (b) *Screw the tool pillar into the baseplate and slide the correctly sized distance piece (as indicated in the shaft in the tool's box) recessed side downwards, over the pillar, and turn the release lever adjusting nuts, until the height fingers, when rotated and held firmly down, just contact the highest part of the clutch release lever tips*

   (c) *Remove the pillar, refit the actuator, and settle the clutch mechanism as in (a)*

   (d) *Refit the pillar and height finger and recheck the clutch release lever clearance, and adjust if not correct*

10 With the centre pillar removed, lock the adjusting nuts found on early clutches by bending up the tab washers.

11 Refit the release bearing thrust plate and fit the retaining springs over the thrust plate hooks.

12 Unscrew the six bolts holding the clutch cover to the baseplate, in diagonal sequence, a turn at a time and assembly is now complete.

12 Clutch (diaphragm type) – inspection

1   Clean and inspect the clutch driven plate and pressure plate unit. If badly worn or damaged, renew both units on an exchange basis. It is not practical or economical to rebuild them yourself.

2   If the driven plate is being renewed, also renew the release bearing at the same time to avoid later dismantling.

3   Renew the driven plate if the linings are worn down to, or almost to, the rivets. If the linings are oil stained on dismantling, not only should the driven plate be renewed but the source of the oil leak should be investigated, and rectified. The gearbox front oil seal or crankshaft rear oil seal will almost certainly be the culprit, and should be renewed at this stage also.

4   Examine the splines in the driven plate hub (if it is not being renewed) for wear, and check that the hub is not loose. Renew the driven plate if defective.

13 Clutch (all models) – refitting

1   It is important that no oil or grease gets on the clutch disc friction linings, or the pressure plate and flywheel faces. It is advisable to refit the clutch with clean hands and to wipe down the pressure plate and flywheel faces with a clean dry rag before assembly begins.

2   Position the clutch friction disc against the flywheel with the side marked 'flywheel' towards the flywheel. If fitted the other way round the clutch will not operate.

3   Refit the clutch cover assembly loosely on the two dowels, with mating marks in alignment. Refit the six bolts and spring washers and tighten them finger-tight so that the clutch disc is gripped but can still be moved.

4 . The clutch disc must now be centralised so that when the engine and gearbox are mated, the gearbox input shaft splines will pass through the splines in the centre of the driven plate hub. Centralisation can be carried out quite easily by inserting an old first motion shaft, a round bar or long screwdriver through the hole in the centre of the clutch, so that the end of the bar rests in the small hole in the end of the crankshaft containing the input shaft bearing bush. Using the input shaft bearing bush as a fulcrum, moving the bar sideways or up and down will move the clutch disc in whichever direction is necessary to achieve centralisation. Centralisation is easily judged by removing the bar and viewing the driven plate hub in relation to the hole in the release bearing. When the hub appears exactly in the centre of the release bearing hole all is correct. Take care not to damage the input shaft bearing bush.

5   Tighten the clutch bolts in a diagonal sequence to ensure that the cover plate is pulled down evenly and without distortion of the flange. Mate the engine and gearbox, and check that the clutch is operating properly.

14 Clutch release bearing and lever – removal and refitting

Note: *To renew the release bearing or lever on all models, it is necessary to remove the engine from the gearbox. Then proceed as follows:*

1   On early models, prise off the two retaining springs from the clutch release bearing and remove it from the clutch lever.

2   On later models with the diaphragm clutch, simply twist the bearing spring retainers and remove the bearing.

3   On Midget 1500 models, the release bearing operating lever must be removed before the bearing can be disconnected. The operating lever is hinged and retained on the opposite side of the slave cylinder by means of a pin. This is an interference fit in two bushes which in turn are located in the bellhousing.

4   To remove the lever, drive the pin out of the clutch housing with a fine punch and hammer (photo).

5   With the operating lever free, the two Mills pins (photo) must be pressed out of the operating lever, so that the bearing sleeve plugs (photo) can be unscrewed.

6   With the bearing removed from the lever, the bearing sleeve can be pressed from within the bearing. It may be necessary to use a special service tool for this operation, and it should therefore either be taken to your local BL agent to do, or if they are willing, borrow or hire the tool from them (No 18G1270). It is also preferable to use this tool during the reassembly of the bearing and sleeve.

7   Refitting of the three types is the reversal of removal, but ensure that the retaining springs are correctly located. On the third type the bearing and sleeve should be greased prior to assembly. On this type, never hit or press the bearing face when fitting to the sleeve.

14.4 Driving out release lever pin from the clutch housing

15.2 The clutch and brake pedals on the 1275 cc model

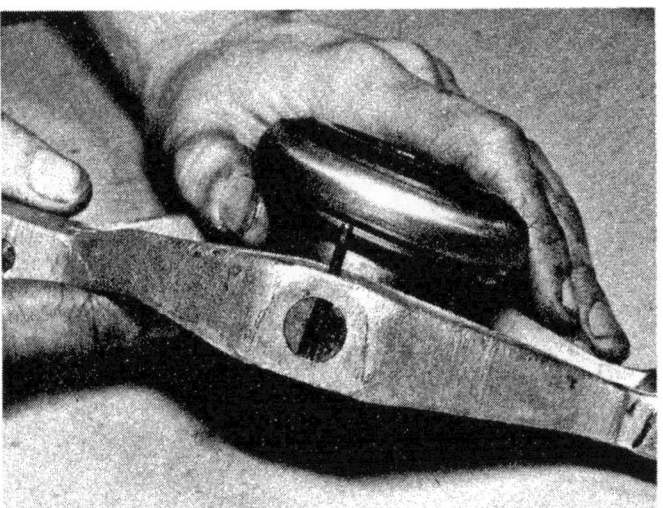

14.5a The release lever and bearing showing a Mills pin partly removed

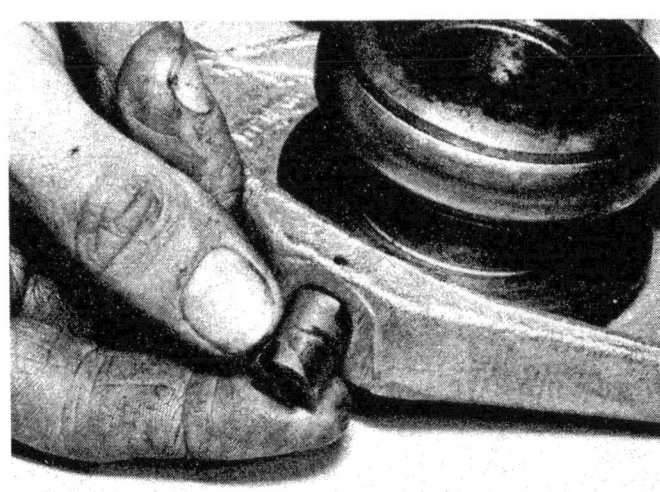

14.5b Removing the bearing sleeve plugs

15 Clutch pedal (Sprite Mk IV, Midget Mk III and earlier models) – removal and refitting

1   Open the bonnet and remove the spring clips and clevis pins from the cylinder pushrods to free the clutch and brake pedal levers.

2   From underneath the facia release the return springs, unscrew the nut and spring washer retaining the fulcrum pin (photo) and withdraw the pin together with the distance piece between the pedals, then remove the pedals.

3   The clutch and brake pedals can be removed complete with the master cylinders and fluid reservoir if required. If a heater is fitted, remove the screws which hold the heater motor bracket in position, and release the two electrical leads to the motor. Lift the motor unit away.

4   Unscrew the two union nuts from the ends of the hydraulic pipes where they enter the master cylinder mounting plate to the bulkhead.

5   Lift the complete assembly up and out of the car, manipulating the pedals through the aperture in the bulkhead.

6   Refit in the reverse order. The clutch and brake hydraulic systems will both require bleeding on completion.

16 Clutch pedal (Midget 1500) – removal and refitting

1   First disconnect and remove the return springs from both the clutch and brake pedals.

2   Disconnect the battery and, on USA models, disconnect the leads from the coil and ballast resistor.

3   Undo the four securing screws and remove the cover plate from the pedal box including, on USA models, the coil. Disconnect the wiring from the stop light switch, and on USA models, where fitted, disconnect the drive cable from the service interval counter.

4   Jack up the front of the car and drive the front of the car onto ramps or over a pit. If jacked up on ramps, chock the rear wheels, and when jacked up support the car on blocks or axle stands.

5   Empty the clutch and brake hydraulic reservoirs by attaching a piece of tube to the bleed screw on the clutch slave cylinder, opening the bleed screw and, by pumping the foot pedal, transferring the fluid into a container. Repeat the procedure, which is similar to that described for bleeding the system in Section 2, on the brake system using a bleed screw on the front brakes. Discard the fluid as it is unfit for re-use.

6   Disconnect the fluid pipes from the clutch master cylinder and the brake master cylinder, and cover the ends of the pipes and the cylinder unions to prevent dirt ingress.

7   Remove the split pin and washer from the clutch pedal clevis pin, then remove the clevis pin.

8   Note the position of the bolts securing the oil pressure pipe clips and remove the bolts and screws retaining the pedal box to the

structure. Lift the box as far as possible and support it in this position.
9   Undo and remove the nut and spring washer from the pedal pivot bolt and remove the bolt far enough to clear and release the clutch pedal. Remove the pedal and its spacer washer.
10 Refitting is a staightforward reversal of the removal procedure, but both the clutch and brake hydraulic systems will need topping up and bleeding on completion.

17 Fault diagnosis – clutch

There are four main faults to which the clutch and release mechanism are prone. They may occur by themselves, or in conjunction with any of the other faults. Thet are clutch squeal, slip, spin, or judder. All of these faults are covered in the following Sections.

18 Clutch – squeal

1   If, on taking up the drive or when changing gear, the clutch squeals, this is indicative of a badly worn clutch release bearing.
2   As well as regular wear due to normal use, wear of the clutch release bearing is much accentuated if the clutch is 'slipped', or held down for long periods in gears, with the engine running. To minimise wear of this component the car should always be taken out of gear at traffic lights and for similar hold-ups.
3   The clutch release bearing is not an expensive item but is difficult to get at, requiring engine removal as for the clutch assembly.

19 Clutch – slip

1   Clutch slip is a self-evident condition which occurs when the clutch friction plate is badly worn, oil or grease have got onto the flywheel or pressure plate faces, or the pressure plate itself is faulty.
2   The reason for clutch slip is that, due to one of the faults above, there is either insufficient pressure from the pressure plate, or insufficient friction from the friction plate to ensure positive drive.
3   If small amounts of oil get onto the clutch, they will probably be burnt off due to the heat generated on clutch engagement and, in the process, gradually darken the friction plate linings. Excessive oil will result in a glazed carbon deposit which can cause quite bad slip, or fierceness, spin and judder.
4   If clutch slip is suspected and confirmation of this condition is required, a number of tests can be made.
5   With the engine in second or third gear and pulling lightly, sudden depression of the accelerator pedal may cause the engine speed to increase without any increase in road speed. Easing off on the accelerator will then result in a definite drop in engine speed without the car slowing.
6   In extreme cases of clutch slip the engine will race under normal acceleration conditions. The cure is to renew the clutch driven (friction) plate and trace and rectify any oil leak.

20 Clutch – spin

1   Clutch spin is a condition which occurs when there is a leak (possibly internal) in the clutch hydraulic actuating mechanism, when there is an obstruction in the clutch (either in the first motion shaft or in the operating lever itself), or where oil may have partially burnt on the friction linings and left a resinous deposit, which is causing the clutch friction plate to stick to the pressure plate or flywheel.
2   The reason for clutch spin is that due to any, or a combination, of the faults just listed the clutch pressure plate is not completely releasing the driven (friction) plate even with the clutch pedal fully depressed.
3   If clutch spin is suspected, it can be confirmed by experiencing great difficulty in engaging first gear from rest, difficulty in changing gear, and by very sudden take up of the clutch drive at the fully depressed end of the clutch pedal travel as the pedal is released.
4   Check the clutch master cylinder, the slave cylinder and the connecting hydraulic pipe for external fluid leaks. Fluid in one of the rubber dust covers (or boots) fitted over the end of either the master or slave cylinder is a sure sign of a leaking piston seal. Bleed the hydraulic system, as air in the system could cause spin.
5   If these points are checked and found to be in order, then the fault lies internally in the clutch, which would have to be removed for examination.

21 Clutch – judder

1   This is a self-evident condition which occurs when the gearbox or engine mountings are loose, worn or too flexible, when there is oil on the face of the clutch friction plate, or when the clutch pressure plate has been incorrectly adjusted.
2   The reason for clutch judder is that, due to one or more of the faults just listed, the clutch pressure plate and friction plate are not engaging or freeing smoothly, with the result that they are snatching.
3   Clutch judder is normally most evident when the clutch pedal is released in first or reverse gear and the whole car shudders as it moves forwards or backwards.

Chapter 6 Gearbox

Contents

Specifications

PART A – 948, 1098 and 1275 cc MODELS

Austin Healey Sprite Mk 1 – 948 cc

Type .... Helical, constant mesh; synchromesh on second, third and top gears

Lubrication

Oil type/specification .... Multigrade engine oil, viscosity SAE 20W/50 (Duckhams
Hypergrade)
Oil capacity .... 2.25 Imp pts (2.7 US pts) (1.3 litres)

Gear ratios

First .... 3.627 : 1
Second .... 2.374 : 1
Third .... 1.412 : 1
Top .... 1.0 : 1
Reverse 4.664 1

Overall ratios

First .... 15.32 : 1
Second .... 10.02 : 1
Third .... 5.96 : 1
Top .... 4.22 : 1
Reverse .... 19.68 : 1

Austin Healey Sprite Mk II and MG Midget Mk 1 – 948 cc

Type .... Helical, constant mesh; synchromesh on second, third and top gears

Lubrication

Oil type/specification .... Multigrade engine oil, viscosity SAE 20W/50 (Duckhams
Hypergrade)
Oil capacity .... 2.25 Imp pts (2.7 US pts) (1.3 litres)

Gear ratios

First .... 3.200 : 1
Second .... 1.916 : 1
Third .... 1.357 : 1
Top .... 1.0 : 1
Reverse .... 4.114 : 1

Overall ratios

First .... 13.504 : 1
Second .... 8.085 : 1
Third .... 5.726 : 1
Top .... 4.22 : 1
Reverse .... 17.361 : 1

Speedometer gear ratio 5/13

Austin Healey Sprite Mk II and III and MG Midget Mk 1 and II – 1098 cc

The gearbox of 1098 cc models is identical to the above with the following exceptions:

Gear ratios
Reverse .... 4.120 : 1

Overall ratios
Reverse .... 17.32 : 1

Austin Healey Sprite Mk IV and MG Midget Mk III – 1275 cc

Type .... Helical, constant mesh; synchromesh on second, third and top

Lubrication
Oil type/specification .... Multigrade engine oil, viscosity SAE 20W/50 (Duckhams Hypergrade)
Oil capacity .... 2.25 Imp pts (2.7 US pts) (1.3 litres)

Gear ratios
Top .... 1 : 1
Third .... 1.357 : 1
Second .... 1.916 : 1
First .... 3.200 : 1
Reverse .... 4.114 : 1

Overall ratios
Top .... 3.9 : 1
Third .... 5.292 : 1
Second .... 7.472 : 1
First .... 12.480 : 1
Reverse .... 16.044 : 1

Speedometer gear ratio 5/13

PART B – 1500 cc MODELS

Type .... Four-speed; synchromesh on all forward gears

Gear ratios
Top .... 1 : 1
Third .... 1.433 : 1
Second .... 2.119 : 1
First .... 3.4118 : 1
Reverse .... 3.7529 : 1

Overall ratios (early models)
Top .... 3.909 : 1
Third .... 5.602 : 1
Second .... 8.255 : 1
First .... 13.337 : 1
Reverse .... 14.670 : 1

Overall ratios (later models)
Top .... 3.7 : 1
Third .... 5.302 : 1
Second .... 7.814 : 1
First .... 12.624 : 1
Reverse .... 13.886 : 1

Roadspeed per 1000 rpm (top gear)
Early models .... 16.4 mph (26.24 kph)
Later models .... 17.3 mph (27.7 kph)

Lubrication
Oil type/specification:
    Top-up only .... Hypoid gear oil, viscosity SAE 90EP (Duckhams Hypoid 90S)
    Refill .... Hypoid gear oil, viscosity SAE 80EP (Duckhams Hypoid 80)
Oil capacity .... 1.5 Imp pts (1.75 US pts) (0.85 litre)

2nd and 3rd gear endfloat on bushes .... 0.002 to 0.006 in (0.050 to 0.152 mm)

Endfloat of 2nd and 3rd gear bushes on mainshaft .... 0.004 to 0.006 in (0.101 to 0.152 mm)

Washer sizes available (2nd and 3rd gear bush endfloat)
Colour code:

Plain	0.152 to 0.154 in (3.860 to 3.911 mm)
Green	0.156 to 0.158 in (3.962 to 4.013 mm)
Blue	0.161 to 0.163 in (4.089 to 4.140 mm)
Orange	0.165 to 0.167 in (4.191 to 4.241 mm)
Yellow	0.169 to 0.171 in (4.293 to 4.343 mm)

Laygear needle roller retaining rings
Fitted depth:

Inner	0.840 to 0.850 in (21.336 to 21.590 mm)
Outer	0.010 to 0.015 in (0.254 to 0.381 mm)

Centre bearing selective washer-to-circlip endfloat .....   0.000 to 0.002 in (0.000 to 0.050 mm)

Washer sizes available (centre bearing)
Colour code:

Plain	0.119 to 0.121 in (3.022 to 3.073 mm)
Green	0.122 to 0.124 in (3.123 to 3.173 mm)
Blue	0.125 to 0.127 in (3.198 to 3.248 mm)
Orange	0.128 to 0.130 in (3.273 to 3.323 mm)

Reverse idler gear bush – fitted depth ....   Flush to 0.010 in (0.254 mm) below gear face

Torque wrench settings

	lbf ft	kgf m
Flywheel housing retaining bolts	28 to 30	3.9 to 4.1
Rear extension to gearbox bolts	18 to 20	2.4 to 2.7
Drive flange nut	90 to 100	12.4 to 13.8

PART A – 948, 1098 and 1275 cc MODELS

1 General description

The gearbox fitted to all models contains four forward gears and reverse. Synchromesh is fitted to second, third and top gears. Early gearboxes have cone synchronisers, plain bearings, and a side cover which is held in place by setbolts. Later gearboxes make use of baulk ring synchromesh, needle roller bearings, and a side cover held in place by nuts and studs. Otherwise the gearboxes are virtually identical.

2 Gearbox – removal

1 The gearbox can be removed in unit with the engine through the engine compartment, as described in detail in Chapter 1.
2 If wished, the gearbox can be separated from the engine at the clutch bellhousing, and removed through the engine compartment after the removal of the engine. These are the only two ways in which the gearbox can be removed.
3 The car must first be positioned high enough to enable it to be worked on in reasonable comfort and safety from underneath. If a ramp or pit is not available then jack up the front of the car as high as possible.
4 Support the front of the car on stands or blocks – remember that it is extremely dangerous to work under a car raised only on jacks. Apply the handbrake, and as an additional precaution chock the rear wheels.
5 If it is intended to remove the engine and gearbox separately, first remove the engine as described in Chapter 1.
6 Drain the gearbox and then place a jack under it to support it.
7 From inside the car, unscrew the self-tapping screws retaining the gear lever cover and lift the cover clear.
8 From the side of the gear lever turret, disconnect the anti-rattle plunger spring, then remove the gear lever cover setscrews and the gear lever.
9 Roll back the central tunnel carpet and remove the gearbox rear mounting setscrews.
10 From underneath the car, disconnect the speedometer drive cable from the rear extension.
11 Disconnect the clutch slave cylinder.
12 Mark the flanges of the propeller shaft to the rear axle pinion shaft flange to ensure correct alignment during reassembly, and remove the securing bolts and nuts.

13 Slightly push the shaft forward to separate the two flanges and then lower or raise it and pull it rearwards to disengage the gearbox mainshaft splines.
14 Disconnect the remaining gearbox mounting setscrews and then manoeuvre the gearbox clear of the car.

3 Gearbox – dismantling

Note: *Having removed the gearbox unit from the car, it is first advisable to clean off the dirt from the outside prior to dismantling. This can be achieved by brushing with a suitable grease solvent and then, after a short period (to let the solvent soak into the congealed oil or dirt), hosing off with a jet of water. Finally wipe off the gearbox with a clean dry cloth.*

1 Remove the remote control housing, gasket, and rear extension to the gearbox, by unscrewing the eight nuts and spring washers holding the remote control housing in place, and the nine nuts and spring washers holding the rear extension to the gearbox. To remove the rear extension, pull it back a little and then turn it anti-clockwise to enable the control lever to slide out from the fork rod end (photo).
2 The side cover on early models is held in place by eight setbolts and spring washers. On later models the side cover is held in place by studs, nuts and spring washers. Remove the setbolts or nuts and take off the side cover and gasket. Turn the gearbox on its side and shake it, to free the two springs and plungers from their separate holes in the front edge of the gearbox side cover flange.
3 Working from inside the bellhousing, prise off the two retaining springs from the clutch release bearing and remove the bearing.
4 Knock back the locking tab on the clutch release arm bolt and remove the nut, spring washer and tab. Unscrew the bolt from its housing and withdraw the clutch release arm.
5 Unscrew the seven nuts and spring washers inside the bellhousing and pull off the front cover and front cover joint gasket. Remove the bearing packing washer.
6 On the forward portion of the side cover of the gearbox casing are two plugs. Unscrew the lower of these together with its fibre washer. Tilt the gearbox and shake out the reverse plunger and spring. Unscrew the upper plug and washer.
7 Place the gears in neutral by lining up the slots in the selector rods.
8 Turn the gearbox onto its side so that the open side cover faces upward.

9 Working through the drain plug hole (photo), unscrew the reverse fork locating nut, the reverse fork locating bolt, and remove together with the lockwasher.

10 Working through the hole in the side of the gearbox casing, unscrew the locating bolts, locknuts, and lockwashers from the first and second speed fork, and the third and fourth speed fork.

11 Pull out from the rear of the gearbox the third and fourth speed selector rod, first and second speed selector rod and reverse selector rod, in this order. As the rods are withdrawn the interlock balls, and the interlock plunger, should emerge from their holes in the front and rear of the gearbox side cover flange. If necessary shake the casing to free them. The rods may be drifted out gently if they prove difficult to remove.

12 Measure the endfloat of the laygear with a feeler gauge. If the endfloat exceeds 0.003 in (0.076 mm) for Sprite Mk II and III and Midgets Mk I and II, or 0.005 in (0.12 mm) for Sprite Mk IV and Midgets Mk III, then new thrust washers must be refitted on reassembly. If the reading is in excess of that given, write it down so that the correctly sized washers can be obtained at a later stage.

13 With a suitable metal rod, drift the layshaft forward out into the bellhousing. The laygear cluster and the two thrust washers will drop to the bottom of the gearbox casing as the drift used to push out the layshaft is withdrawn.

14 The mainshaft is removed from the rear of the gearbox casing with the large ball bearing and the bearing housing complete as one assembly. Freeing the bearing housing from the gearbox casing is

sometimes difficult. Try gently tapping the bearing housing at alternate, diagonally opposite, points from inside the casing. Alternatively, unscrew the mainshaft nut, and remove the distance piece and speedometer gear drive. Refit the nut and tap vigorously against its underside. The housing will gradually emerge from the gearbox casing; as soon as it is sufficiently far out, place a puller or levers under the lip of the bearing housing to accelerate the complete removal of the third motion shaft assembly from the gearbox. Take great care not to damage the bearing housing or the gearbox casing during this operation.

15 Insert a metal rod through the large hole in the gearbox casing left by the mainshaft bearing housing, and locate the end of the rod in the hole in the end of the first motion shaft. Tap the first motion shaft complete with bearing into the bellhousing. Lift out the laygear (photo).

16 Unscrew the reverse shaft setbolt and the spring washer and remove.

17 With a screwdriver, working from the rear of the gearbox casing, turn the slotted end of the reverse shaft and at the same time push it forwards into the gearbox.

18 As the shaft emerges the gear and bush will fall away freely and can be lifted out.

19 The gearbox is now completely stripped. The component parts should now be examined for wear as detailed later, and the layshaft, first motion shaft, and mainshaft broken down further as detailed in Section 5.

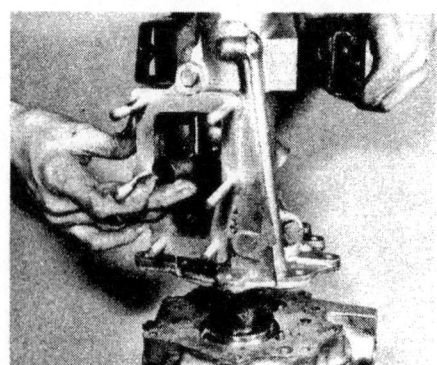

3.1 Removing the rear extension

3.9 Undoing the reverse fork locking nut using a socket and extension through the drain plug hole

3.15 Removing the layshaft gears

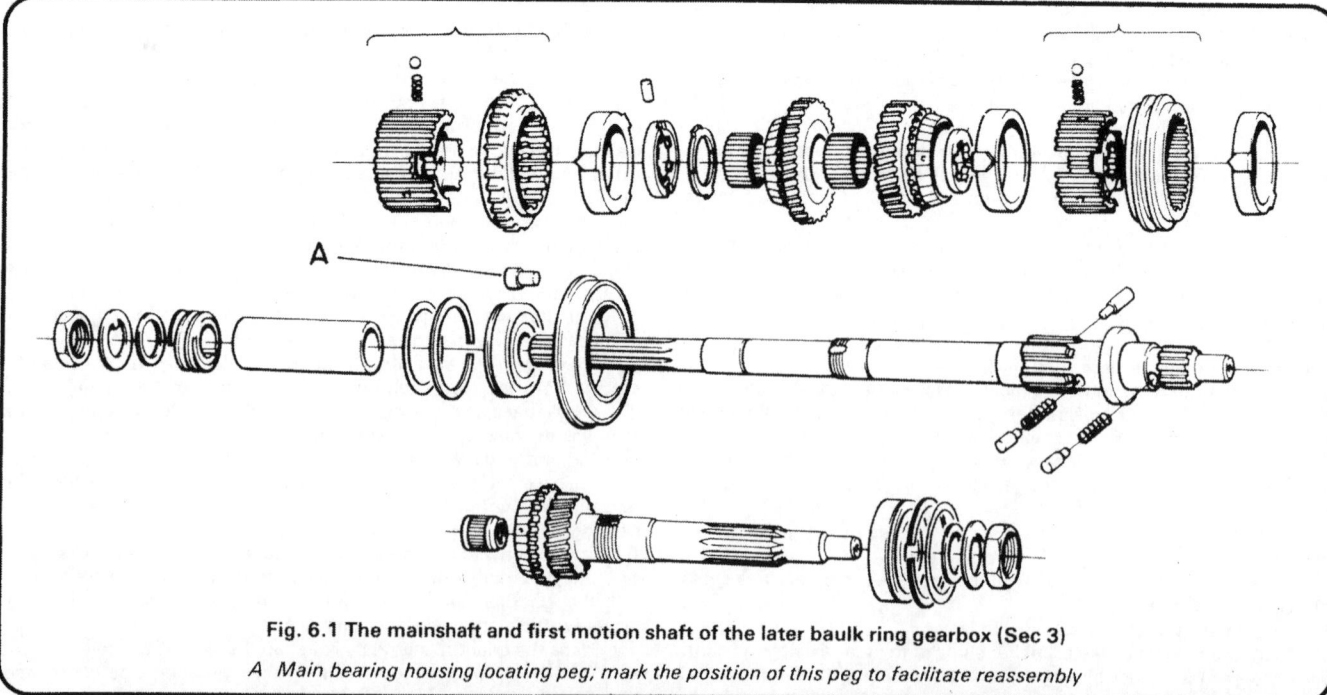

Fig. 6.1 The mainshaft and first motion shaft of the later baulk ring gearbox (Sec 3)

A Main bearing housing locating peg; mark the position of this peg to facilitate reassembly

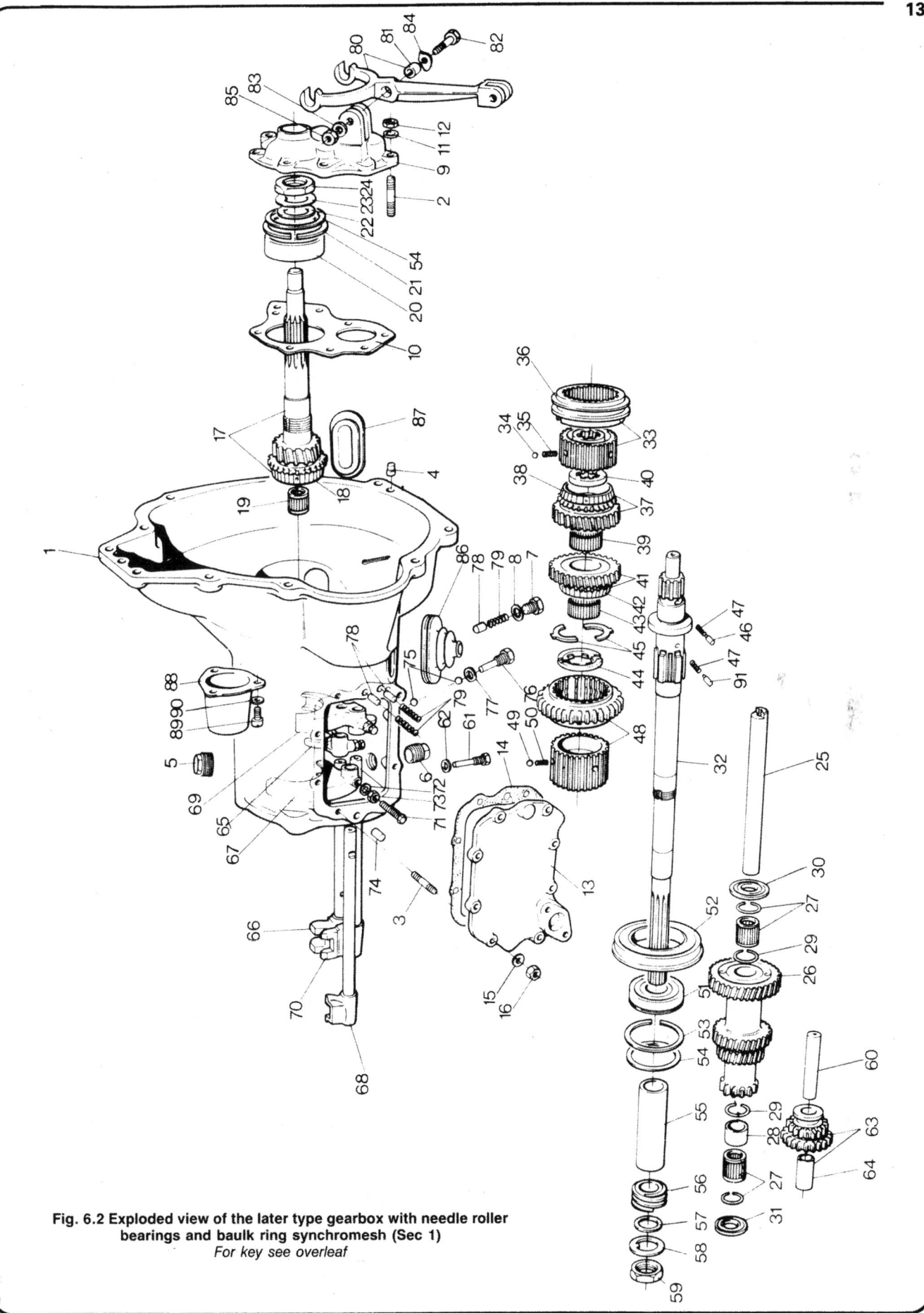

Fig. 6.2 Exploded view of the later type gearbox with needle roller bearings and baulk ring synchromesh (Sec 1)
For key see overleaf

Fig. 6.2 Exploded view of the later type gearbox with needle roller bearings and baulk ring synchromesh (Sec 1)

1 Gearbox bellhousing/casing
2 Stud
3 Stud
4 Dowel
5 Filler plug
6 Drain plug
7 Reverse plunger spring plug
8 Washer
9 Front cover
10 Front cover gasket
11 Spring washer
12 Nut
13 Side cover
14 Gasket
15 Spring washer
16 Nut
17 First motion shaft with cone
18 Synchronising cone
19 Needle roller bearing
20 First motion shaft journal
   ball bearing
21 Spring ring
22 Washer
23 Lockwasher
24 Nut
25 Layshaft
26 Laygear
27 Needle roller bearing
   with spring ring
28 Distance piece
29 Spring ring
30 Thrust washer (front)
31 Thrust washer (rear)
32 Third motion shaft/mainshaft
33 Third and fourth speed
   synchroniser
34 Ball
35 Spring
36 Sleeve
37 Third speed gear with cone
38 Synchronising cone
39 Needle roller
40 Third speed gear locking
   collar
41 Second speed gear with cone
42 Synchronising cone
43 Needle roller
44 Splined locking washer
45 Split washer
46 Peg for locking collar
47 Springs for pegs
48 First speed gear assembly
49 Ball
50 Spring for ball
51 Third motion shaft journal
   ball bearing
52 Bearing housing
53 Spring ring
54 Bearing packing washer
55 Third motion shaft distance
   piece
56 Speedometer gear
57 Plain washer
58 Locking washer
59 Third motion shaft nut
60 Reverse gear shaft
61 Locking screw
62 Spring washer
63 Reverse gearwheel and bush
64 Bush
65 Reverse fork
66 Reverse fork rod
67 First and second speed
   fork
68 First and second speed
   fork rod
69 Third and fourth speed
   fork
70 Third and fourth speed
   fork rod
71 Fork locating bolt
72 Shakeproof washer
73 Nut
74 Interlock plunger
75 Interlock ball
76 Plug
77 Washer
78 Plunger for fork rod
79 Spring
80 Clutch withdrawal lever
   with bush
81 Bush
82 Bolt
83 Spring washer
84 Locking washer
85 Nut
86 Dust cover
87 Dust cover for bell housing
88 Starter pinion cover
89 Screw
90 Washer
91 Spring-loaded plunger

4 Remote control assembly and gearbox rear cover – dismantling and reassembly

1　Unscrew the speedometer pinion sleeve and remove together with the pinion and washers.

2　To free the control lever from the control shaft, unscrew the control shaft locating screw, and to assist removal of the control shaft, which is a push fit in the rear cover, screw the locating screw into the tapped hole at the front end of the shaft, extract the shaft, and lift out the lever.

3　Turn the remote control housing upside-down and remove the four bolts and spring washers which hold the bottom cover and gasket in place under the gear lever.

4　If the gear lever has not already been removed, unscrew the three setbolts and spring washers from the gearbox seat cover and remove the anti-rattle spring cap, its washer, spring, and plunger and the lever locating peg, before lifting the gear lever and seat cover off. If the plunger and spring are not removed before the gear lever is lifted off, then should they fall into the remote control housing they should be retrieved and placed with their cap until reassembly.

5　Unscrew the reverse plunger cap and remove the reverse plunger spring and ball.

6　Remove the rubber ring, thrust button and thrust button spring from the rear selector lever, and place with the lever after they have been removed, for ease of reassembly.

7　To remove the front and rear selector levers, extract the two welch plugs from either end of the remote control housing, unscrew the setbolt and spring washer from each lever and drift out the remote control shaft.

8　To remove the split tapered bush from the selector lever, release the circlip holding the halves together.

9　Reassembly is a reversal of the dismantling procedure.

5 Gearbox components – examination and renovation

1　Carefully examine all the component parts starting with the synchronising cones or baulk rings. The cones are copper in colour and are shrunk onto the sides of the second, third, and fourth speed gears. If the ridges are badly worn, or if the cones are loose on their gears, or if the cones are cracked or broken, they must be renewed. It is normal practice to purchase new gears and synchronising cones complete.

2　If engineering facilities are available, it is possble to shrink on new cones to existing gearwheels, and then machine the cones to the correct dimensions. This is highly skilled work, it is most unlikely that the private owner or the majority of garages have the necessary equipment, and the saving is not sufficient to make it worthwhile. It is altogether better to purchase either a complete reconditioned mainshaft or new gears and synchronising units and fit them to the mainshaft yourself.

3　Examine the gearwheels for excessive wear (photo) and chipping of the teeth and renew them as necessary.

4　If the laygear endfloat is above the permitted tolerance (see paragraph 12 of Section 3), the thrust washers must be renewed. The smaller thrust washer fitted at the rear end is available from your local BL agent in varying thicknesses to compensate for laygear wear.

5　The correct reassembled endfloat tolerances are as follows:

Sprite Mk I, II and III – 0.001 to 0.003 in (0.025 to 0.076 mm)
Midget Mk I and II　 – 0.001 to 0.003 in (0.025 to 0.076 mm)
Sprite Mk IV　　　 – 0.003 to 0.005 in (0.076 to 0.127 mm)
Midget Mk III　　　 – 0.003 to 0.005 in (0.076 to 0.127 mm)

To achieve these tolerances, rear thrust washers are available in thicknesses from 0.123 in to 0.131 in (3.124 mm to 3.327 mm).

6　A needle roller bearing is fitted internally to each end of the laygear (photo). To examine them, prise out the retaining clips from each end, and with a finger pull out the outer race, needle rollers, and inner race. At the end of the laygear with the smaller gear, extract the distance piece and the inner spring rings from both ends. Renew the roller bearings and races, if worn.

7　It is helpful to refit the roller bearings round a dummy shaft inside the laygear. Dealing first with the smaller end of the laygear, place it upright with the smaller end at the top and fit the inner spring ring, the distance piece, and slide the new roller bearing, which comes in a

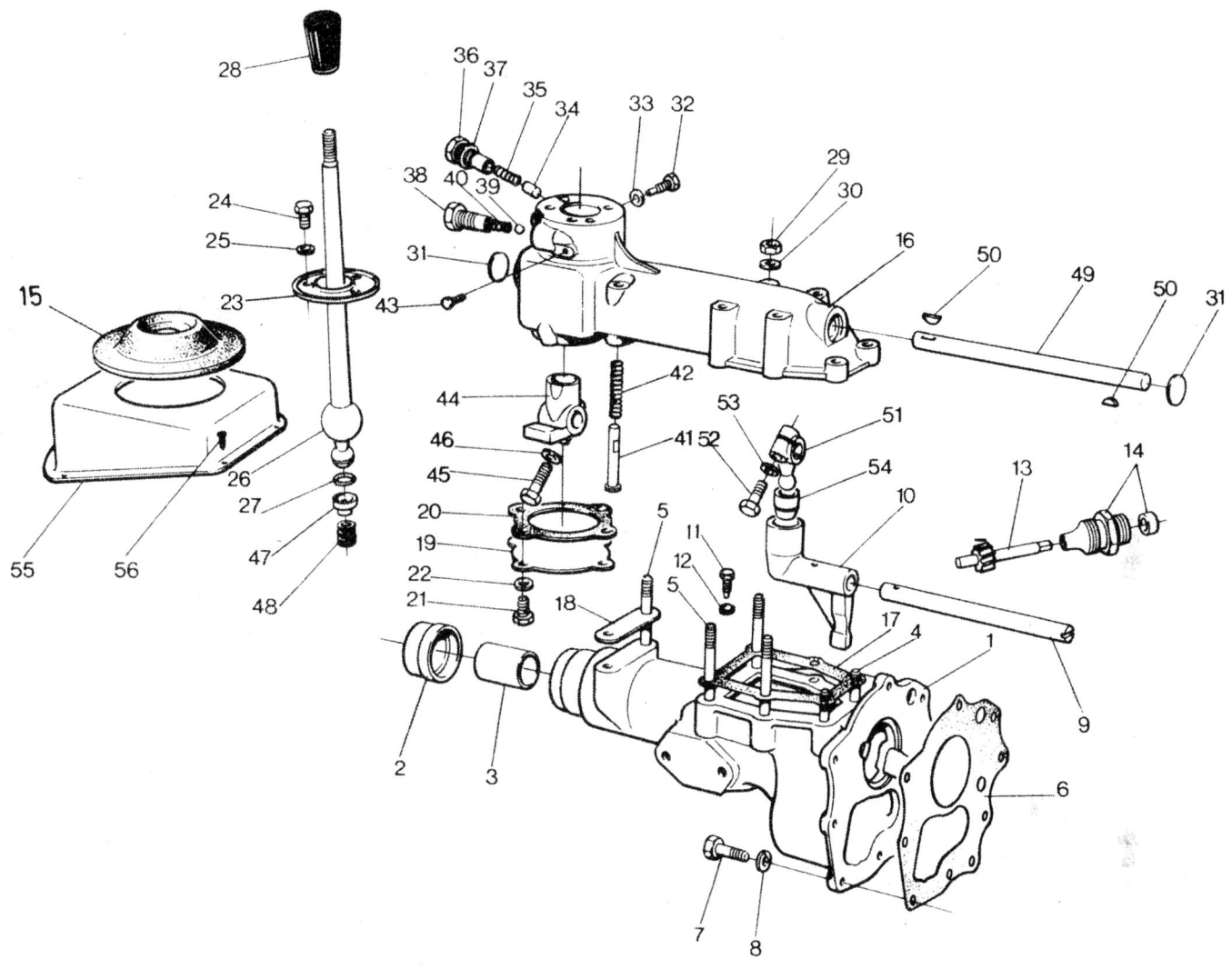

Fig. 6.3 Exploded view of the remote control assembly and gearbox rear cover (Sec 4)

1 Rear extension	15 Grommet	30 Spring washer	43 Reverse selector plunger
2 Oil seal	16 Remote control casing	31 Welch plug	locating pin
3 Sliding joint bush	17 Extension front joint gasket	32 Lever locating peg	44 Rear selector lever
4 Short stud	18 Extension rear joint gasket	33 Spring washer	45 Bolt
5 Long stud	19 Lever tower bottom cover	34 Control shaft damper	46 Spring washer
6 Joint gasket	20 Joint gasket	plunger	47 Thrust button
7 Screw	21 Bolt	35 Spring	48 Spring
8 Spring washer	22 Spring washer	36 Spring retaining cap	49 Remote control shaft
9 Control shaft	23 Lever seat cover	37 Washer	50 Key
10 Control lever	24 Bolt	38 Reverse selector detent	51 Front selector lever
11 Control lever locating peg	25 Spring washer	plug	52 Bolt
12 Spring washer	26 Gear lever	39 Ball	53 Spring washer
13 Speedometer pinion	27 Rubber ring	40 Spring	54 Front selector lever bush
14 Speedometer pinion oil seal	28 Knob	41 Reverse selector plunger	55 Remote control cover
assembly	29 Nut	42 Spring	56 Screw

cage, into position, ensuring that the ends of the needle rollers enter into the retaining nicks in the bearing end races. Slip the spring retaining ring into the groove. Repeat this procedure for the larger end of the laygear, turning the laygear round, and omitting, of course, the distance piece.

8   Examine the condition of the main ball bearings, one on the first motion shaft, and the other on the third motion shaft. If there is looseness between the inner and outer races, the bearings must be pulled off and renewed.

9   On the first motion shaft it is necessary to remove the retaining nut and lockwasher before the bearing is pulled (photo). Note the

position of the spring ring. On refitting a new bearing to the first motion shaft, position the tap on the lockwasher in the shaft keyway so that it faces towards the nut.

10 On the mainshaft, place the shaft in a vice with padded jaws, release the mainshaft nut, locking washer, speedometer gear, and distance piece, if this has not already been done, and then pull the bearing housing and bearing off the shaft. The bearing can then be drifted away from its housing.

11 Examine the first motion shaft spigot bush, which should have a clearance of 0.002 to 0.003 in (0.050 to 0.076 mm) with the mainshaft. If the clearance is excessive, either the bush or the

5.3 Wear marks on the layshaft gear teeth

5.6 Laygears and shaft with bearings fitted

5.9 Removing the first motion shaft bearing retaining nut and tab washer

mainshaft, depending if either, or both, are worn, must be renewed.
12 On later gearboxes a needle roller bearing instead of a bush is fitted and must also be examined and renewed as necessary.
13 If it is wished to renew the synchronisers, or to examine the second and third gear brushes or needle roller bearings, the mainshaft must be dismantled as detailed in the next Section.

6 Gearbox (early models) cone synchromesh gear bushes — dismantling and reassembly

1 Slide the sleeve together with the third and fourth gear synchroniser off the front end of the mainshaft.
2 To separate the third and fourth speed synchroniser and the sleeve, wrap a piece of cloth round the synchroniser and press out the sleeve. The cloth will retain the three balls and springs which hold the sleeve to the synchroniser. If a piece of cloth is not wrapped round the synchroniser the balls will fly out and probably become lost.
3 With an electrical screwdriver or piece of thin rod, press down the spring-loaded plunger through the semi-circular hole at the front of the synchroniser cone, and turn the splined locking washer so that a spline holds the plunger down and the ring is so positioned that it can slide forwards off the end of the mainshaft.
4 Remove the now exposed plunger and spring and slide off the third speed gear and the needle roller bearing on later gearboxes.
5 Slide off the bush interlocking ring and second speed gear. Examine the condition of the second speed gear bush and, if worn, chisel it off, and sweat on a new bush.
6 Finally, pull off the splined rear thrust washer, the first speed gearwheel, and the second gear synchroniser. The first speed gearwheel is separated from the second gear synchroniser in the same way as described in paragraph 3.
7 Reassembly is a direct reversal of the dismantling instruction.

7 Gearbox (later models) baulk ring synchromesh, needle roller bearings — dismantling

1 In addition to the differences already listed at the beginning of the Chapter, the mainshaft is of a quite different design to that used in the early gearboxes. This means that the second and first speed gears have to be taken off the opposite end of the shaft to the third speed gear.
2 Repeat the dismantling process as for early gearboxes down to paragraph 4 of Section 6. Then proceed as follows:
3 With the mainshaft nut, locking washer, speedometer drivegear, distance piece, and bearing already removed, pull off the first speed gear and second speed synchroniser assembly. Separate the synchroniser from the hub as described in the previous Section.
4 With an electrical screwdriver or piece of thin rod, press down the spring-loaded plunger and turn the splined locking washer so that one of the splines holds the plunger down, and the ring is so positioned that it can slide rearwards off the end of the mainshaft.
5 Remove the split washer and slide the second speed gear off the end of the third motion shaft complete with needle roller bearing. Examine the needle roller bearing for wear and renew as necessary.
6 Reassembly is detailed in Section 8.

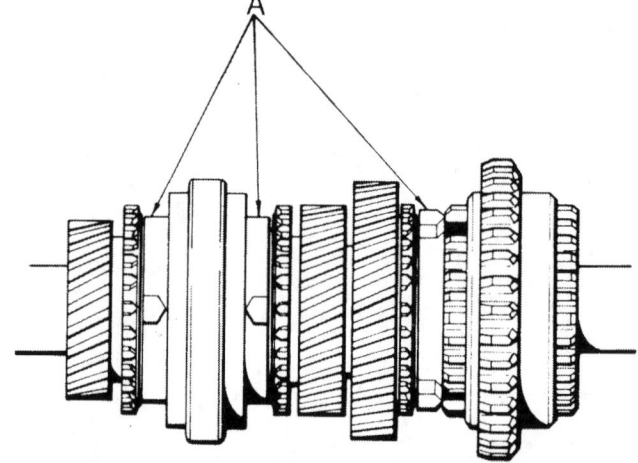

Fig. 6.4 The baulk ring synchronisers (A), used instead of cone synchronisers, are fitted to the later gearbox (Sec 7)

8 Mainshaft — reassembly

1 Fit the second gear to the shaft. Lubricate and insert the needle rollers and locate the gear to the shaft flange (photo).
2 Position the shaft in a soft-jawed vice and insert the half thrust washers into the second gear recess (photo).
3 Fit the locking ring and locate its slots with the thrust washer tabs (photo). Having aligned the lock ring and thrust washers, press in the peg in the shaft with a small screwdriver or similar (photo) to locate the lock ring.
4 Inert the shaft in a vice and insert the spring and peg into position (photo).
5 Smear the shaft with general purpose grease, locate the third gear onto the shaft and insert the needle roller bearings.
6 Slide the third gear locking collar over the splines, depress the peg and rotate the collar to enable the peg to lock it in position (photo).
7 Refit the third/fourth speed synchro-hub , with the boss facing out (photo).
8 Now reassemble the first/second gear synchro-hub. On later cars note the following.

   (a) Fit the springs and balls to the synchro-hub (photo).
   (b) Insert the plunger into the hub (photo). It must be in line with the cutaway tooth in the gear unit, and the hub cone end and the tapered side of the gearteeth must be on opposite sides of the assembly (See Fig. 6.5). Second gear cannot be engaged if this procedure is not followed correctly.

9 Fit the first gear and synchro-hub onto the shaft.
10 Now fit the rear bearing and housing to the shaft (photo).
11 Locate the distance collar onto the shaft, and butt against the

8.1 Second gear on shaft showing needle roller bearings

8.2 Second gear half washers being positioned (note lock ring peg)

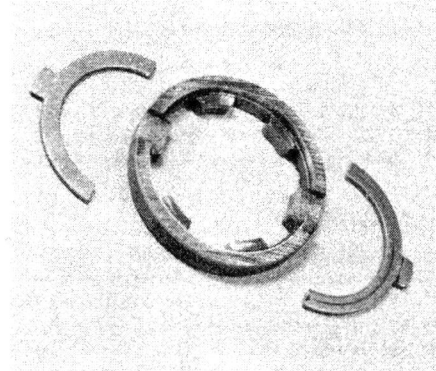

8.3a Half washers and lock ring showing tabs and slots

8.3b Pressing the lock ring peg down

8.4 Spring and peg location

8.6 Third gear locking ring in position – note peg

8.7 Third/fourth speed synchro-hub in position

8.8a A ball spring in position in a synchro-hub

8.8b The plunger in the hub

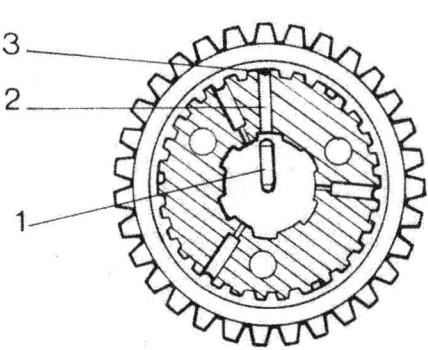

Fig. 6.5 Assembly details of the later gearbox synchronisers: Plunger (1), Hub (2), Cutaway in outer gear (3) (Sec 8)

8.10 Rear bearing and housing – note the cutaway section on the housing

8.12 The speedometer worm gear in position with the shim, washer and nut being fitted

bearing. Then refit the speedometer drivegear, using a suitable pipe drift and butt the drivegear against the distance collar.

12 Fit the shim, tab washer and retaining nut (photo). Tighten the nut and bend over the tab washer to lock.

13 The mainshaft is now fully assembled (photo).

9 Gearbox – reassembly and refitting

1 Position the reverse gear in the gearbox and slide the reverse gear shaft into position (photo). Turn the shaft, by means of a screwdriver in the rear slot, until the holes in the shaft and the casing coincide. Insert and tighten down the locking screw and spring washer.

2 Turn the gearbox on end, and place the laygear in position, remembering the thrust washers at each end (photo). Place a long rod or tommy bar through the laygear and the holes in either end of the gearbox casing so that on turning the gearbox back, the laygear and thrust washers will not drop to the bottom of the casing.

3 Insert the first motion shaft from the rear (photo), and locate the bearing into its aperture in the front of the gearbox. Press or drift it into position, ensuring that it enters and aligns in the aperture correctly or it will damage the aluminium casing.

4 With the bearing fully into position, refit the locating C-clip to the protruding bearing outer race (photo).

5 From inside the gearbox, insert the needle roller bearing into the spigot bore (photo). Lubricate it with general purpose grease.

6 The mainshaft can now be refitted through the rear of the gearbox (photo). Locate it at the front into the first motion shaft spigot bearing. Note that the cutaway portion of the mainshaft rear flange locates over the reverse idler.

7 Tap the flange home with a soft-faced hammer or drift, and ensure that the location holes end up at the rear.

8 With the two shafts interconnected, check that the first motion shaft is fully located in the clutch housing. If the bearing and retaining clip are not flush to the housing, lightly tap the shaft inwards so that the clip is against the housing.

9 Lubricate the clip shaft and carefully insert it into the gearbox through the front face. Support the laygear and take care not to damage the needle roller bearings when drifting the shaft into position. Keep the ends of the shaft and rod in contact until the layshaft is fully in position to prevent the thrust washers slipping out (photo).

10 Align the layshaft so that the front cutaway section is in line with the two studs (photo).

11 Position the reverse fork so that its tapped hole is in line with the gearbox drain hole.

12 Refit the first and second speed fork so that it fits over the first speed gearwheel.

13 Refit the third and fourth speed fork so that it fits over the third and fourth speed coupling sleeve.

14 Place the gearbox on its side so that the hole in the side cover of the casing faces upwards. Insert the reverse fork rod through the lowest hole in the rear of the casing, through the reverse fork, and through the hole in the third and fourth speed fork (photo).

15 Line up the hole in the rod with the hole in the reverse fork and insert and tighten down the locking screw, lockwasher, and locking nut.

16 Insert the double-ended interlock plunger into the hole in the middle of the casing side cover rear face (photo).

17 Insert the first and second speed rod through the top selector rod hole in the rear of the gearbox, through the hole in the first and second speed fork and then into the hole in the front of the gearbox casing.

18 Lock the fork to the fork rod with the fork locating screw, shakeproof washer, and locknut (photo).

19 Insert the third and fourth speed fork rod through the middle selector rod hole in the rear of the gearbox casing, and then through the hole in the third and fourth speed fork, so that the rod just enters in to the hole in the front gearbox casing (photo).

20 With the underside of the gearbox casing facing towards you, and the side cover hole upwards, insert a ball into the hole in the bottom right-hand corner of the side flange. Make sure that the ball is firmly against the third and fourth speed rod, and that it is centralised in the slot in the rod by pressing the ball down firmly with a suitable rod.

21 Turn the gearbox upside-down, with the drain plug uppermost,

8.13 The assembled mainshaft

9.1 Reverse gear in position on its shaft

9.2 The laygear front thrust washer positioned in the gearbox

9.3 Inserting the first motion shaft

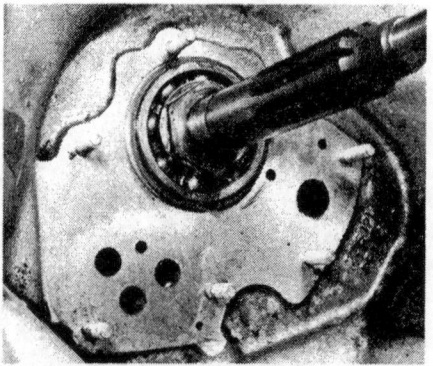

9.4 The first motion shaft bearing location with C-clip fitted

9.5 Inserting the needle roller bearing

9.6 Inserting the mainshaft unit

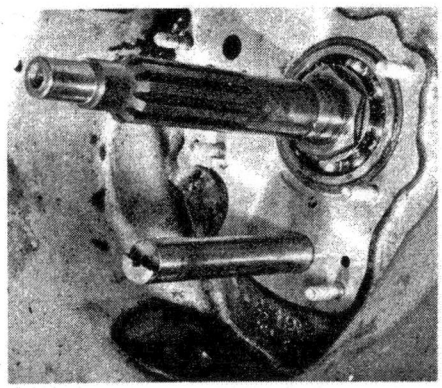

9.9 Inserting the laygear shaft

9.10 The correct fitted position of the layshaft

9.14 Reverse gear selector fork and shaft in position

9.16 The double-ended interlock plunger in position

9.18 The first/second speed rod located and locked in position

9.19 The third/fourth speed selector fork and rod in position

9.24 Fitting the reverse plunger and spring

9.25 Plunger and spring in side cover face holes

9.27 Front cover and shims

9.28 The gearbox rear joint face before fitting the rear extension; note the flange locating dowel, the shim and the joint gasket

9.29 Joint gasket located on the rear extension before fitting the remote control unit

9.30 The nylon bush positioned on the selector lever

9.33 Refitting the speedometer pinion unit

9.34 The clutch release fork assembled

and drop the other ball into the hole level with the drain plug and ensure that it rests between the first and second, and third and fourth speed rods. Insert a rod into the hole and press the ball down firmly to centralise the slot in the rod.

22 Push the third and fourth speed rod fully in and lock the fork to the fork rod with the fork locating screw, shakeproof washer, and locknut. **Note:** *All the rods should be pushed in by hand pressure only. If a rod will not fully enter the casing, centralise the ball in the selector rod slot by pushing firmly on the ball with a suitable rod down the ball's hole. With the ball no longer standing proud of its hole is will be found that the rod can be pushed in easily.*

23 Insert the long-shanked aluminium plug and fibre washer into the upper hole in line with the drain plug.

24 Insert the reverse plunger with its rounded end first into the bottom hole on the underside of the casing. Follow it with the spring, and the plug bolt with a fibre washer under its head (photo).

25 Insert the remaining plungers into the two adjacent holes in the front end of the side cover flange, with their rounded ends first, and place a spring in each hole (photo).

26 Fit the side cover and paper gasket in position over the studs and tighten down the nuts and spring washers diagonally. (Early models make use of spring washers and setbolts).

27 From inside the bellhousing, place the paper front cover gasket in position. With the packing shim (photo) held in the front cover bearing recess with a smear of grease, offer up the cover to the gearbox casing and tighten down the nuts and spring washers.

28 At the rear of the gearbox, lightly tap into position the bearing flange location peg (on late models only). Then position the paper gasket, place a 0.006 in (0.15 mm) shim in the rear cover bearing recess (photo), and refit the rear extension. Tighten down the nine long setbolts and spring washers diagonally. Note that although a 0.006 in (0.15 mm) packing shim is usually correct for both the front and rear cover bearing recesses, if confirmation is required on this point, proceed as follows:

(a) Measure how much the bearing outer race stands proud of the casing, and how deep the bearing recess is in the cover

(b) Fit the covers without the packing shims, but with the paper gaskets, and tighten down normally

(c) Remove the covers and measure the thickness of the paper gasket

(d) Add together the depth of the bearing recess in the cover and the thickness of the paper gasket. From this total subtract the amount by which the bearing outer race stands proud of the casing. This figure is the correct one to use for the shim thickness.

29 If the remote control casing has been removed, this can now be refitted by first placing the gasket over the studs of the rear extension after smearing the gasket on both sides lightly with a sealing solution (photo).

30 Place the nylon bush over the selection lever and smear it with grease (photo).

31 Place the gasket over the two studs of the extension rear joint, and then locate the remote control casing over the rear extension studs and carefully tap it down into position. Ensure that the nylon bush locates round the control lever ball end.

32 Fit the nuts and spring washers onto their studs, and if a reversing light is fitted, relocate the wire and clips to the rear and front extension studs, on the appropriate side. Check the movement of the gear lever and the gear selection.

33 Refit the speedometer pinion unit (photo).

34 In the clutch housing, refit the clutch withdrawal lever and release bearing into position (photo). Locate the rubber gaiter into the clutch housing, and refit the clutch withdrawal lever assembly. Ensure that the tab washer, under the head of the withdrawal lever to the front cover fork bolt, is folded over both the fork and bolt head when the bolt is tightened.

35 Check the movement of the lever to ensure it is free.

36 The gearbox is now ready for refitting to the car.

37 Refitting is the reversal of the removal procedure in Chapter 1. When the gearbox is fully located in the car, check that the drain plug is in place and tight, and then top up the gearbox with the recommended lubricant.

10 Fault diagnosis – gearbox

Symptom	Reason(s)
Weak or ineffective synchromesh (general wear)	Synchronising cones worn, split or damaged Synchromesh dogs worn or damaged
Jumps out of gear (general wear or damage)	Broken gearchange fork rod spring Gearbox coupling dogs badly worn Selector fork rod groove badly worn
Excessive noise (lack of maintenance)	Incorrect grade of oil in gearbox or oil level too low Bush or needle roller bearings worn or damaged Gear teeth excessively worn or damaged Laygear thrust washers worn allowing excessive endplay
Excessive difficulty in engaging gear (clutch not fully disengaging)	Clutch malfunction

PART B – 1500 cc MODELS

11 General description

The manual gearbox contains four forward gears and one reverse gear. Synchromesh is fitted to all forward gears. The gear lever is mounted on the extension housing and operates the selector mechanism in the gearbox by a long shaft. When the gear lever is moved sideways the shaft is rotated so that the pins in the gearbox end of the shaft locate in the appropriate selector fork. Forward or rearward movement of the gear lever moves the selector fork, which in turn moves the synchromesh unit outer sleeve until the gear is firmly engaged. When reverse gear is selected, a pin on the selector shaft engages with a lever, and this in turn moves the reverse idler gear into mesh with the laygear reverse gear and mainshaft. The direction of rotation of the mainshaft is thereby reversed.

The gearbox input shaft is splined and it is onto these splines that the clutch driven plate is located. The gearbox end of the input shaft is in constant mesh with the laygear cluster, and the gears formed on the laygear are in constant mesh with the gears on the mainshaft, with the exception of the reverse gear. The gears on the mainshaft are able to rotate freely, which means that when the neutral position is selected the mainshaft does not rotate.

When the gear lever moves the synchromesh unit outer sleeve via the selector fork, the synchromesh cup first moves and friction caused by the conical surfaces meeting takes up initial rotational movement until the mainshaft and gear are both rotating at the same speed. This condition achieved, the sleeve is able to slide over the dog teeth of the selected gear, thereby giving a firm drive. The synchromesh unit hub is splined to the mainshaft and, because the outer sleeve is splined to the inner hub, engine torque is passed to the mainshaft and propeller shaft.

12 Gearbox – removal and refitting

1   The gearbox can be removed from the car in one of two ways. The first is to remove the engine and then the gearbox separately. The second is to remove the engine and gearbox as a unit from the car.

2   To remove the engine and gearbox as a unit, refer to Chapter 1, Part B, Section 67, paragraphs 1 to 15.

3   To remove the engine and gearbox separately, first remove the engine as described in Section 67, of Chapter 1, Part B. Then refer to Section 67 of Chapter 1, Part B, and follow the instructions given in paragraphs 2 to 9, then proceed as follows.

4   Place a jack under the gearbox to support it.

5   From underneath unscrew the two bolts and washers securing the gearbox rear mounting bracket to the floor panel.

6   Unscrew the gearbox rear mounting bracket to the gearbox tunnel retaining bolts.

7   The gearbox should now be free to be withdrawn from the car. Manoeuvre the gearbox forward and get an assistant to lift the gearbox rear coupling over the gearbox tunnel crossmember. Remove the gearbox to the workbench.

8   Refitting is a reversal of the removal sequence.

13 Gearbox – dismantling

1   Prior to commencing work, clean the exterior of the gearbox using paraffin or a suitable grease solvent. After the solvent has been applied and allowed to stand for a time, a vigorous jet of water will wash off the solvent together with the oil and dirt. Finally wipe down the exterior of the unit with a dry non-fluffy rag.

2   Undo and remove the five bolts securing the clutch housing to the gearbox casing. Note that the lowermost bolt has a plain copper washer as opposed to the spring washers of the other bolts.

3   Withdraw the clutch housing. Recover, if possible, the paper gasket from the front face of the gearbox casing, and then withdraw the three laygear preload springs from their respective apertures in the gearbox front face, and store in a safe place.

4   Unscrew the top cover retaining bolts and remove the cover together with its gasket. Lift out the interlock spool plate, noting which way up it is fitted.

5   Withdraw the oil seal carrier from the clutch housing and ease off

the rubber O-ring. If signs of oil leaks from the front of the gearbox to clutch housing are present, the oil seal should be removed using a screwdriver, and a new one obtained for refitting. Note that the seal lip faces outwards.

6   Undo and remove the one bolt and spring washer securing the reverse lift plate to the rear extension. Lift away the lift plate.

7   Using a screwdriver carefully remove the rear extension end cover.

8   With a self-gripping wrench hold the drive flange, and using a socket wrench undo and remove the locking nut and plain washer.

9   Tap the drive flange from the end of the mainshaft.

10   Lift out the speedometer drive pinion and housing assembly from the rear extension.

11   Make a special note of the location of the selector shaft pegs and interlock spool so that there will be no mistakes on reassembly.

12   Using a suitable diameter parallel pin punch, carefully remove the roll pin from the bellhousing end of the selector shaft.

13   Undo and remove the eight bolts and spring washers securing the rear extension to the gearbox casing.

14   Draw the rear extension rearwards whilst at the same time feeding the interlock spool from the selector shaft.

15   With the rear extension and selector shaft away from the gearbox casing, lift out the interlock spool.

16   Recover the paper gasket from the rear face of the gearbox casing.

17   If oil was leaking from the end of the rear extension or the bearing requires renewal, the oil seal must be removed and discarded. Ease it out with a screwdriver noting which way round the lip is fitted.

18   To remove the bearing, obtain a long metal drift and tap it out working from the inside of the rear extension. Note which way round the bearing is fitted as indicated by the lettering.

19   Slide the thrust washer from over the end of the mainshaft.

20   Make a special note of the location of the speedometer drivegear on the mainshaft, if necessary by taking a measurement.

21   To remove the speedometer drive from the mainshaft, place an open-jawed spanner of suitable size to take the mainshaft firmly in a vice with jaws protruding. With the aid of an assistant, support the gearbox and position it with the mainshaft into the jaws of the spanner so that the speedo gear is butting against the spanner jaws. Temporarily replace the nut on the end of the mainshaft, and with a hammer or mallet, strike the shaft nut (photo), to remove the speedometer gear from the shaft. Do not strike the gear – it can easily break or distort.

22   Using a suitable diameter drift, tap out the selector fork shaft toward the front of the gearbox casing.

23   Note the location of the two forward gear selector forks and lift these from the synchromesh sleeves.

24   Using a suitable diameter drift, tap out the layshaft, working from the front of the gearbox casing. This is because there is a layshaft restraining pin at the rear to stop it rotating.

25   Invert the gearbox and this will allow the laygear cluster to drop into the bottom of the casing.

26   Using a small drift placed on the bearing outer track, tap out the

13.21 Removing the speedometer drivegear

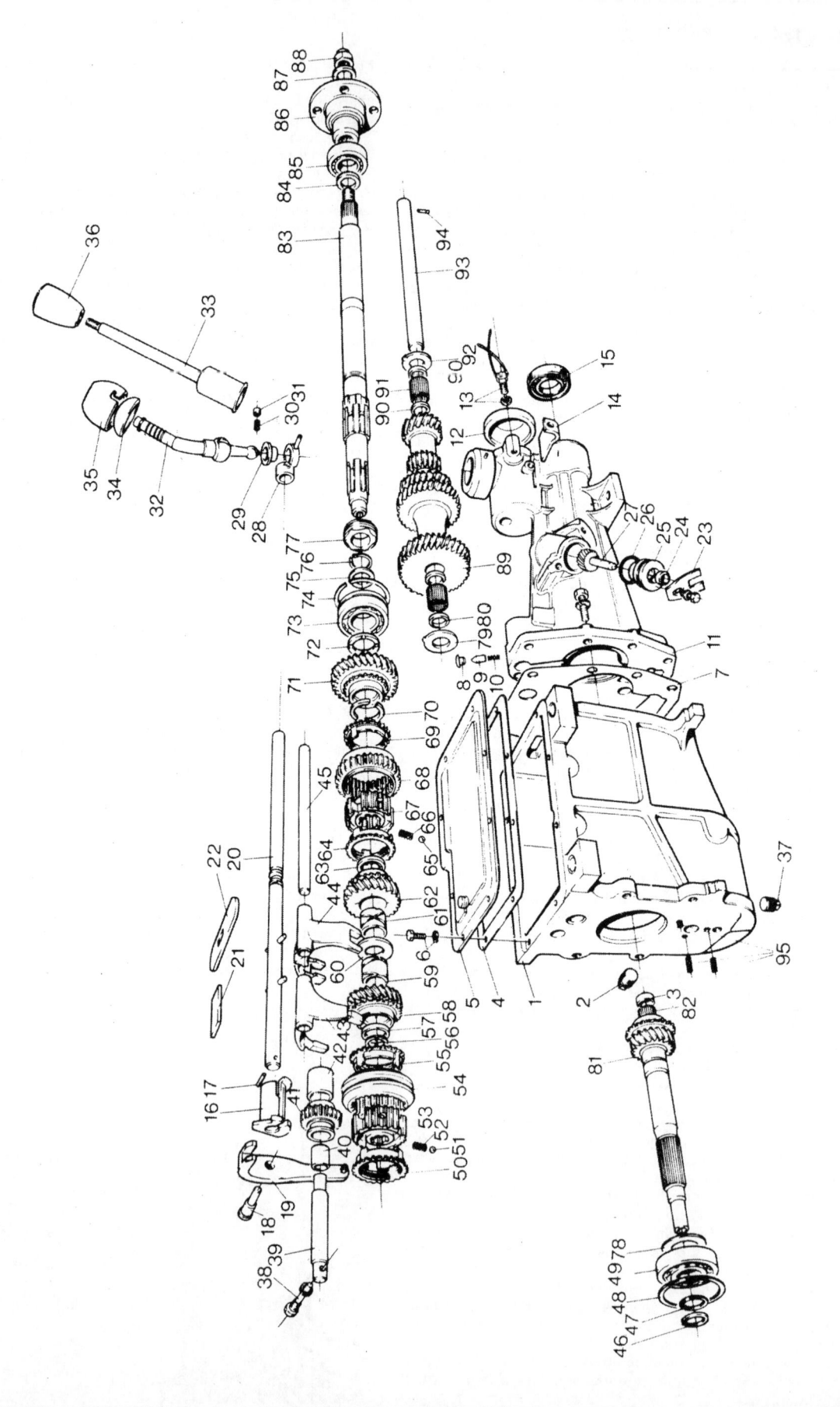

Fig. 6.6 Exploded view of the 1500 cc engine gearbox (Sec 11)

1 Gearbox case
2 Oil filler/level plug
3 Spacer
4 Joint gasket
5 Top cover
6 Bolt and washer
7 Joint gasket
8 Plug
9 Detent plunger
10 Detent spring
11 Rear extension
12 End cover
13 Reversing light switch
14 Reversing lift plate
15 Oil seal
16 Interlock spool
17 Selector shaft roll pin
18 Reverse operating lever pin
19 Reverse operating lever
20 Gear selector shaft
21 Magnet

22 Interlock spool plate
23 Retaining clip
24 Seal
25 Housing
26 O-ring
27 Speedometer pinion
28 Gear lever yoke
29 Seat
30 Spring
31 Anti-rattle plunger
32 Lower gearchange lever
33 Upper gearchange lever
34 Dust cover washer
35 Dust cover
36 Knob
37 Drain plug
38 Reverse idler spindle locating screw
39 Reverse idler spindle
40 Reverse idler gear bush
41 Reverse idler gear

42 Reverse idler distance piece
43 3rd and 4th speed selector forks
44 1st and 2nd speed selector forks
45 Selector fork shaft
46 Circlip
47 Backing washer
48 Snap-ring
49 Ball bearing
50 Synchromesh cup
51 Ball
52 Spring
53 3rd and 4th speed synchromesh hub
54 3rd and 4th speed operating sleeve
55 Synchromesh cup
56 Mainshaft circlip
57 3rd speed gear thrust washer

58 3rd speed gear
59 Gear bush
60 Selective washer
61 Gear bush
62 2nd speed gear
63 Thrust washer
64 Synchromesh cup
65 Ball
66 Spring
67 1st and 2nd speed operating sleeve
68 Mainshaft reverse gear
69 Synchromesh cup
70 Split collar
71 1st speed gear
72 Thrust washer
73 Mainshaft centre bearing
74 Snap-ring
75 Selective washer
76 Circlip
77 Speedometer wheel

78 Oil flinger
79 Front thrust washer
80 Bearing outer retaining ring
81 1st motion shaft
82 Needle roller bearing
83 Mainshaft
84 Washer
85 Ball bearing
86 Drive flange
87 Washer
88 Self-locking nut
89 Laygear gear cluster
90 Bearing inner retaining ring
91 Needle rollers
92 Rear thrust washer
93 Layshaft
94 Layshaft dowel
95 Laygear preload springs

gearbox input shaft. If necessary recover the caged needle roller bearing from the end of the mainshaft.

27 The mainshaft may now be drifted rearwards slightly, sufficiently to move the bearing and locating circlip. Using a screwdriver between the circlip and gearbox casing, ease the bearing out of its bore and from its locating shoulder on the mainshaft. Lift away the bearing from the end of the mainshaft.

28 The complete mainshaft may now be removed through the top of the gearbox main casing.

29 Unscrew the dowel bolt that locks the reverse idler shaft to the gearbox casing and remove the bolt and spring washer.

30 Using a small drift, tap the reverse idler shaft rearwards, noting the hole in the shaft into which the dowel bolt locates.

31 Note which way round the reverse idler is fitted and lift it from the casing.

32 Lift out the laygear cluster, noting which way round it is fitted.

33 Recover the two thrust washers, noting that the tags locate in the grooves in the gearbox casing.

14 Gearbox components – examination and renovation

1 The gearbox has been stripped, presumably because of wear or malfunction, or possibly excessive noise, ineffective synchromesh, or failure to stay in a selected gear. The cause of most gearbox ailments is failure of the ball bearings on the input or mainshaft and wear on the synchro-rings, both the bore surfaces and dogs. The nose of the mainshaft which runs in the needle roller bearing in the input shaft is also subject to wear. This can prove very expensive as the mainshaft would need renewal and this represents about 20% of the total cost of a new gearbox.

2 Examine the teeth of all gears for signs of uneven or excessive wear and, of course, chipping. If a gear on the mainshaft requires renewal check that the corresponding laygear is not equally damaged. If it is the whole laygear may need renewing as well.

3 All gears should be a good running fit on the shaft with no signs of rocking. The hubs should not be a sloppy fit on the splines.

4 Selector forks should be examined for signs of wear or ridging on the faces which are in contact with the operating sleeve.

5 Check for wear on the selector rod and interlock spool.

6 The ball bearings may not be obviously worn, but if one has gone to the trouble of dismantling the gearbox it would be shortsighted not to renew them. The same applies to the four synchroniser rings, although for these the mainshaft has to be completely dismantled for the new ones to be fitted.

7 The input shaft bearing retainer is fitted with an oil seal and this should be renewed if there are any signs that oil has leaked past it into the clutch housing or, of course, if it is obviously damaged. The rear extension has an oil seal at the rear as well as a ball bearing race. If either have worn or oil has leaked past the seal, the parts should be renewed.

8 Before finally deciding to dismantle the mainshaft and renew parts, it is advisable to make enquiries regarding the availability of parts and their costs. If may still be worth considering an exchange gearbox even at this stage. You should reassemble it before exchange.

15 Input shaft – dismantling and reassembly

1 Place the input shaft in a vice with protected or soft jaws and with its splined end upwards. With a pair of circlip pliers, remove the circlip which retains the ball bearing in place. Lift away the backing washer.

2 With the bearing resting on the top of the open jaws of the vice and splined end upwards, tap the shaft through the bearing with a soft-faced hammer. Note that the offset circlip groove in the outer track of the bearing is towards the splined end of the input shaft.

3 Lift away the oil flinger.

4 Remove the oil caged needle roller bearing from the centre of the rear of the input shaft if it is still in place.

5 Remove the circlip from the old bearing outer track and transfer it to the new bearing.

6 To reassemble, refit the oil flinger and, with the aid of a block of wood and vice tap the bearing into place. Make sure it is the right way round.

7 Finally, refit the backing washer and bearing retaining circlip.

16 Mainshaft – dismantling and reassembly

1 The component parts of the mainshaft are shown in Fig. 6.6.

2 Lift the 3rd and 4th gear synchromesh hub and operating sleeve assembly from the end of the mainshaft.

3 Remove the 3rd gear synchromesh cup.

4 Using a small screwdriver, ease the 3rd gear retaining circlip from its groove in the mainshaft. Lift away the circlip.

5 Lift away the 3rd gear thrust washer.

6 Slide the 3rd gear and bush from the mainshaft, followed by the thrust washer. Note that this is a selective thrust washer.

7 Slide the 2nd gear and bush from the mainshaft followed by the grooved washer. Note which way round it is fitted.

8 Detach the 2nd gear synchromesh cup from inside the 2nd and 1st gear synchromesh hub and lift away.

9 Slide the 2nd and 1st gear synchromesh hub and reverse gear sleeve assembly from the mainshaft. Recover the 1st synchromesh cup.

10 Using a small electrician's screwdriver, lift out the two split collars from their groove in the mainshaft.

11 Slide the 1st gear from the mainshaft together with the thrust washer.

12 The mainshaft is now completely dismantled.

13 Before reassembling, measure the endfloat on the 2nd and 3rd gears on their respective bushes. To do this, place a gear face down on a flat surface (a piece of plate glass will do) with its bush fitted. Lay a straight edge across the bush and measure the difference in axial lengths between the straight edge and the adjacent face of the gear using feeler gauges. The difference, ie endfloat, should be within the limits quoted in the Specifications. Obtain a new bush if necessary to achieve the correct endfloat.

14 Temporarily refit the 2nd gear washer, oil grooved face away from

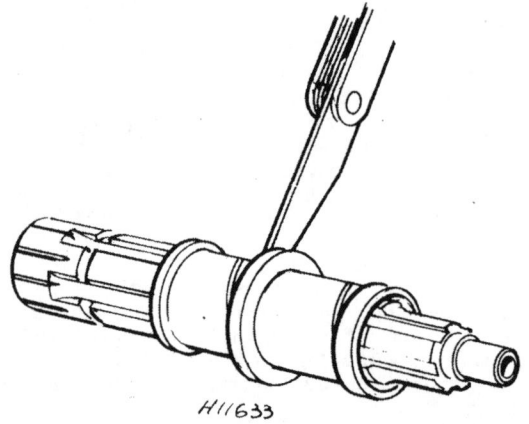

Fig. 6.7 Measuring the mainshaft endfloat with the 2nd and 3rd gear bushes and associated components temporarily assembled (Sec 16)

the mainshaft shoulder to the mainshaft. Assemble to the mainshaft the 3rd gear bush, selective washer, 2nd gear bush, 3rd gear thrust washer with its oil grooved face to the bush, and fit the 3rd gear mainshaft circlip. Measure the endfloat of the bushes on the mainshaft using feeler gauges; this should be within the limits quoted in the specifications. Obtain a new selective washer to ensure the correct endfloat if necessary. Remove the parts from the mainshaft and restore the bushes to their respective gears – don't mix them.

15 To reassemble, slide the 1st gear onto the mainshaft (photo).

16 Fit the two halves of the split collar into the groove in the mainshaft and push the 1st gear hard up against the collar (photo).

17 Fit the synchromesh cup onto the cone of the 1st gear.

18 Slide the 1st and 2nd gear synchromesh hub and reverse gear sleeve on the mainshaft and engage it with the synchromesh cup (photo).

19 Fit the 2nd gear washer onto the end of the mainshaft splines so that the oil grooved face is towards the front of the mainshaft (photo).

20 Fit the 2nd gear synchromesh cup to the synchromesh hub.

21 Slide the 2nd gear bush onto the mainshaft (photo).

22 Fit the 2nd gear onto the bush on the mainshaft and engage the taper with the internal taper of the synchromesh cup (photo).

23 Fit the 2nd and 3rd gear selective washer (photo).

24 Slide the 3rd gear bush onto the mainshaft (photo).

25 Fit the 3rd gear onto the bush on the mainshaft, the cone facing the front of the mainshaft (photo).

26 Slide the 3rd gear thrust washer onto the mainshaft splines (photo), with the grooved side facing forwards.

27 Fit the 3rd gear synchromesh cup onto the cone of the 3rd gear.

28 Ease the 3rd gear retaining circlip into its groove in the mainshaft. Make quite sure it is fully seated (photo).

29 Finally slide the 3rd and 4th gear synchromesh hub and operating sleeve assembly onto the shaft and engage it with the synchromesh cup (photo).

30 If the assembled mainshaft is not being inserted directly into the gearbox, it is a good idea to hold the gears on the shaft by temporarily retaining them with a worm-drive clip.

17 Gearbox – reassembly

1 Position the laygear needle roller bearing inner retainers into the laygear bore. Use a depth gauge to check that their fitted depths are as quoted in the Specifications. Apply general purpose grease to the ends of the laygear and refit the needle rollers. Retain in position with the outer retainers (photo).

2 Make up a piece of tube the same diameter as the layshaft, and the length of the laygear plus thrust washers, and slide the tube into the laygear. This will retain the needle rollers in position. Apply grease to the thrust washers and fit to the ends of the laygear. The tags must face outwards.

3 Carefully lower the laygear into the bottom of the gearbox casing (photo).

4 Fit the brush to the reverse idler gear and check that the bush is the same axial length as the gear or up to 0.010 in (0.254 mm) shorter, ie below the gear face. Then fit the reverse gear operating

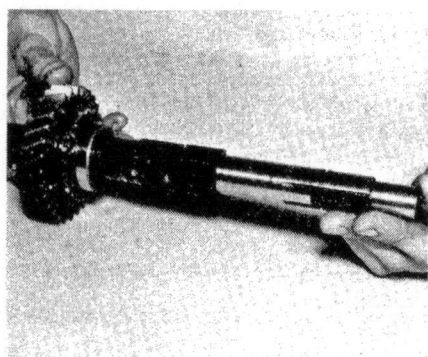

16.15 Refitting the 1st gear to the mainshaft

16.16 Fitting the split collar to the shaft groove

16.18 Fitting the 1st/2nd synchro-hub and reverse gear

16.19 Fitting the 2nd gear washer – note oil groove in face

16.21 Fitting the 2nd gear bush to the mainshaft ...

16.22 ... and sliding the 2nd gear onto the bush

16.23 Fit the selective washer between the 2nd and 3rd gears

16.24 Fitting the 3rd gear bush ...

16.25 ... followed by the 3rd gear onto the bush

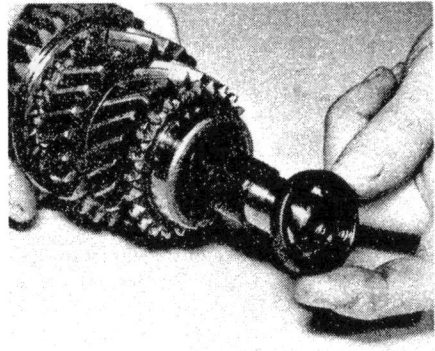

16.26 Fit the 3rd gear thrust washer with its grooved face towards the forward end of the shaft

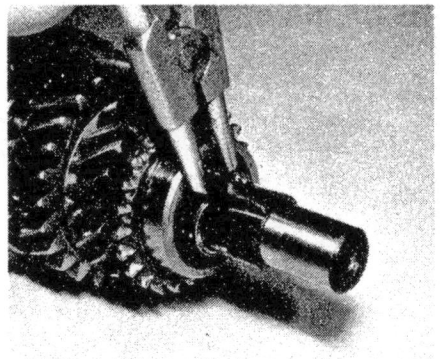

16.28 Fitting the 3rd gear retaining circlip

16.29 The 3rd/4th synchro-hub being fitted

lever to the operating lever pivot. Hold the reverse idler in its approximate fitted position and slide in the idler shaft, drilled end first (photo).

5 Carefully line up the drilled hole in the idler shaft and gearbox casing and refit the dowel bolt and spring washer (photo).

6 The assembled mainshaft may now be fitted into the gearbox casing (photos), and the worm-drive clip removed if refitted.

7 Ease the mainshaft bearing up the mainshaft, circlip offset on the outer track towards the rear (photo).

8 Place a metal lever in the position shown (photo) so supporting the mainshaft spigot.

9 Using a suitable tube, carefully drift the mainshaft bearing into position in the rear casing (photo).

10 Fit the 4th gear synchromesh cup onto the end of the input shaft.

11 Insert the spacer and needle roller bearing into the end of the input shaft. Lubricate with general purpose grease, prior to assembly (photo).

12 Fit the input shaft to the front of the gearbox casing, taking care to engage the synchromesh cup with the synchromesh hub (photo).

13 Tap the input bearing until the circlip is hard up against the front gearbox casing. Check that the mainshaft bearing outer track circlip is hard up against the rear casing. Refit the washer and circlip. Use feeler gauges to measure the gap between the washer and the circlip and, if necessary, change the washer for one that gives the correct clearance; see Specifications.

14 Invert the gearbox. Fit the pin into the drilled hole in the layshaft and carefully insert the layshaft from the rear of the main casing. This will push out the previously inserted tube. The pin must be to the rear of the main casing (photo).

15 Line up the layshaft pin with the groove in the rear extension, and push the layshaft fully home.

16 Fit the 3rd and 4th gear selector fork to the synchromesh sleeve.

17 Fit the 1st and 2nd gear selector fork to the synchromesh sleeve (photo).

18 Slide the selector fork shaft from the front through the two selector forks and into the rear of the main casing (photo).

19 Fit a new gasket to the rear face of the main casing and retain in position with a little grease.

17.1 Refitting the laygear needle rollers

17.3 The laygear lowered into the gearbox

17.4 Fitting the reverse idler gear shaft

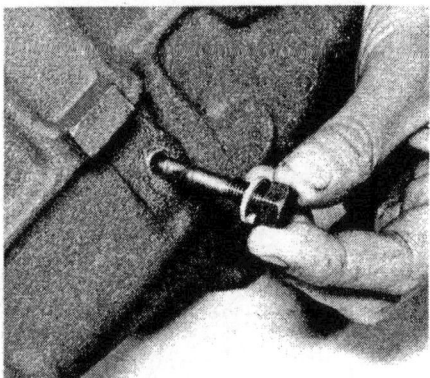
17.5 Fitting the dowel bolt to retain the reverse idler shaft

17.6a Refitting the mainshaft

17.6b If fitted, remove the worm drive clip (arrowed) when the mainshaft is in the gearbox

17.7 Refitting the mainshaft bearing – note the position of the offset circlip in the outer race

17.8 Use a metal bar to support the mainshaft

17.9 Tap the bearing into position using a tubular drift

17.11 Inserting the spacer and bearing into the input shaft

17.12 Fitting the input shaft

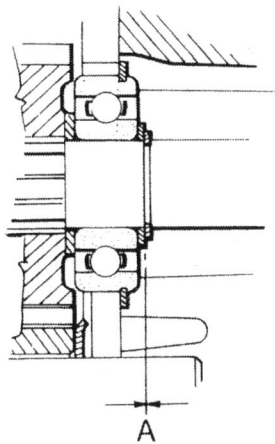

Fig. 6.8 Measure the centre bearing endfloat at A (Sec 17)

20 Place the speedometer drivegear onto the mainshaft, and using a tube, drive the gear into its previously noted position (photo).

21 Slide the washer up the mainshaft to the shoulder (photo).

22 Place the rear extension bearing into its bore, letters facing outwards.

23 Tap the bearing into position using a suitable diameter socket.

24 Fit a new rear extension oil seal after lubricating it with gearbox oil and tap into position with the previously used socket. The lip must face inwards (photo).

25 Place the interlock spool on the selector forks with the flanges correctly engaged.

26 Offer the gearbox rear extension to the rear of the main casing, at the same time feeding the selector shaft through the interlock spool. It will be necessary to rotate the selector shaft to obtain correct engagement (photos).

27 Secure the rear extension with the eight bolts and spring washers.

28 Refit the roll pin into the end of the selector shaft, ensuring that the ends are equidistant from the shaft (photo).

29 Insert the speedometer driven gear and housing into the rear extension (photo).

30 Fit the drive flange onto the mainshaft splines (photo).

31 Hold the drive flange and tighten the retaining nut and washer fully.

32 Refit the reverse lift plate to the rear extension and secure with the bolt and spring washer.

33 Refit the rear extension and end cover and tap into position with the end of the lip flush with the end of the casting.

34 Refit the interlock spool plate in the same position as was noted before removal (photo).

35 Fit a new gasket to the gearbox casing and refit the top cover (photo).

36 Secure the top cover with the nine bolts and spring washers, which should be progressively tightened in a diagonal manner.

37 Re-insert the three laygear preload springs into their respective holes in the front gearbox face (photo).

38 Fit a new gearbox casing front face gasket and retain in position with a little grease.

39 Move the gearbox to the end of the bench and offer up the clutch housing (photo).

40 Refit the five bolts securing the clutch housing to the main casing. Note four bolts have spring washers and the fifth (lowermost) has a copper washer (photo).

41 Slide the clutch release bearing assembly onto its guide, at the same time engaging the release lever.

42 If the gearbox was removed in unit with the engine it may now be reattached. Secure in position with the retaining nuts, bolts and spring washers.

43 Refill the gearbox with lubricant to the specified grade.

17.14 The layshaft (with roll pin) fitted

17.17 The selector forks fitted to their synchro-hubs

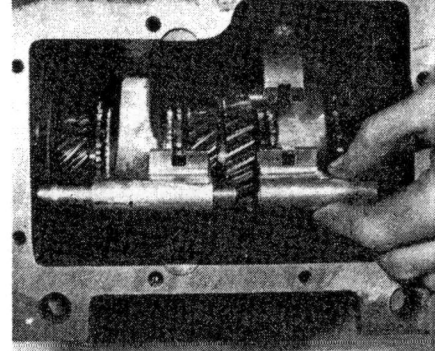

17.18 Fitting the selector fork shaft

17.20 Using a tubular drift to fit the speedometer gear to its marked position (at pen tip)

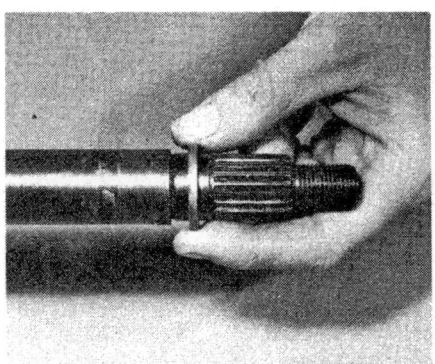

17.21 The mainshaft washer being fitted

17.24 The oil seal fitted to the rear extension

17.26a The rear extension being mated with the gearbox

17.26b Guiding the selector shaft through the interlock spool

17.28 The roll pin refitted to the front end of the selector shaft

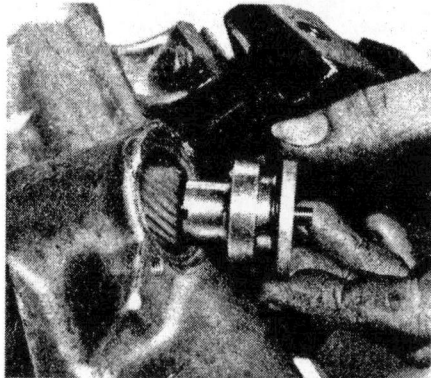

17.29 Refitting the speedometer driven gear

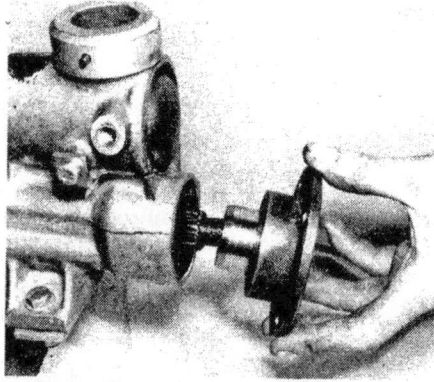

17.30 Refitting the drive flange to the mainshaft

17.34 The interlock spool plate refitted

17.35 The top cover being refitted – note the new gasket

17.37 The laygear preload springs being refitted

17.39 Refitting the clutch housing

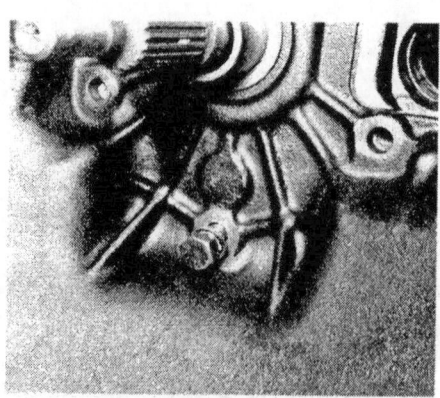

17.40 The bottom bolt has a copper sealing washer

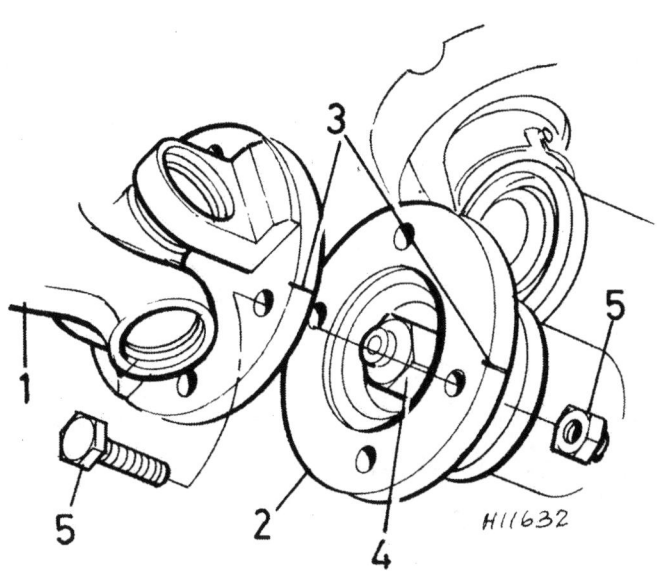

Fig. 6.9 Removing the gearbox drive flange to renew the oil seal
(Sec 18)

1   Propeller shaft
2   Gearbox drive flange
3   Alignment marks
4   Flange retaining nut
5   Propeller shaft-to-gearbox
*   securing nut and bolt*

18   Gearbox extension rear oil seal – removal and refitting

1   Oil leaking from the gearbox extension rear oil seal indicates that
the seal is defective and renewal is necessary. This is a relatively
simple job and can be done without removing the gearbox or
extension.
2   Apply the handbrake and jack up the front of the car. Support it
firmly on axle stands or blocks.
3   Clean off the dirt and oil residues from the vicinity of the rear oil
seal. With a file or similar tool, mark the propeller shaft and gearbox
drive flanges so that they can be reassembled in the same relative
position.
4   Remove the four locknuts from the flange bolts to release the
propeller shaft flange from the gearbox flange and tie the shaft up out
of the way to one side.
5   Restrain the gearbox drive flange with a lever on bolts inserted in
the flange, or with a special spanner if available. Undo and remove the
flange retaining nut and washer.
6   Withdraw the drive flange from the gearbox shaft, using a
universal puller if it is tight.
7   Prise the old seal out of the extension. It doesn't matter if it gets
damaged, but take care not to damage the extension, the shaft or the
bearing inside the extension.
8   Wipe the seal location in the extension clean. Dip the new seal in
gearbox oil and fit it to the extension. Make sure that the seal lip faces
inwards and tap it carefully home until it is flush with the extension.
9   Reassembly is the reverse of the removal procedure, but ensure
that the flange retaining nut is tightened to the specified torque and
that the flanges are correctly aligned.

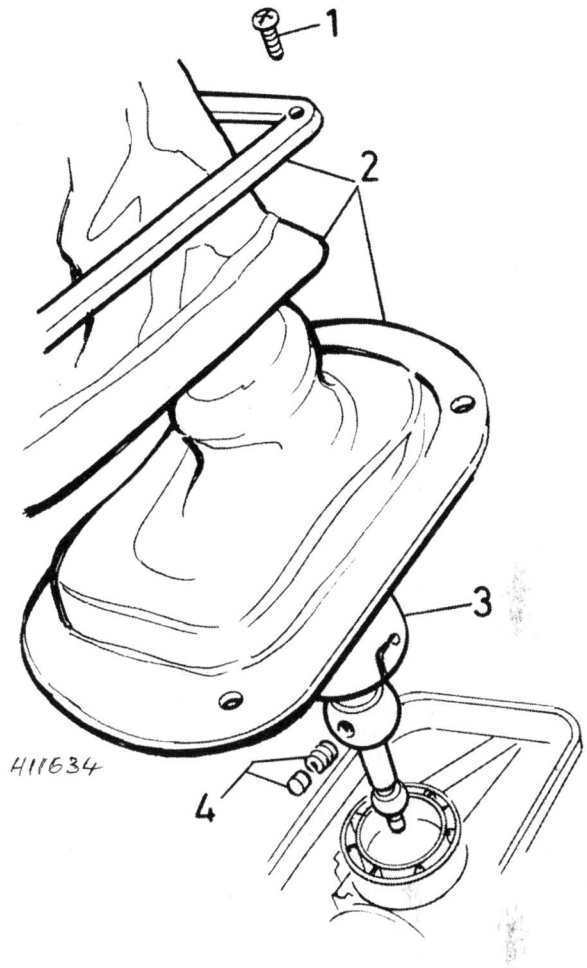

Fig. 6.10 Removing the gear lever (Sec 19)

1   Gaiter retaining plate securing screw
2   Retaining plate, gaiter and draught excluder
3   Lever retaining cover
4   Anti-rattle plunger and spring

19   Gear lever – removal and reassembly

1   To remove the gear lever, first remove the carpet surrounding the
gear lever gaiter and unscrew and remove the lever knob.
2   Undo and remove the screws securing the gaiter retaining plate,
then slide off the retaining plate, the gaiter and the draught excluder
over the gear lever.
3   Move the gear lever to the neutral position, press and turn the
lever retaining cover anti-clockwise and lift the assembly from the
gearbox. As you do this retrieve the plunger and spring located in the
back of the lever ball mounting.
4   Reassembly is the reverse of the removal procedure; lubricate the
spherical bearing surfaces on the gear lever stub with Duckhams
Laminoid 'O' grease or its equivalent.

Chapter 7 Propeller shaft

Contents

Specifications

Lubrication

Universal joints on early models only, and sliding joints of 1500 models only .... General purpose grease (Duckhams LB 10)

1 General description

Drive is transmitted from the gearbox to the rear axle by means of a finely balanced tubular propeller shaft. Fitted at each end of the shaft is a universal joint which allows for vertical movement of the rear axle. Fore-and-aft movement of the rear axle is absorbed by a sliding spline, which on early models was in the connection with the gearbox mainshaft. On this assembly lubrication was provided by internal holes supplying oil from the gearbox. Later models have the sliding spline incorporated in the propeller shaft, just behind the front drive coupling, and on these models lubrication is achieved by periodically hand-pumping oil or grease (depending on year) through a nipple on the sliding yoke. On some early models grease nipples were also provided on the front and rear coupling spiders through which grease could be pumped to lubricate the coupling needle roller bearings. These bearings on later models are pre-packed with lubricant and require no maintenance after installation.

2 Propeller shaft – removal and refitting

1   Jack up the rear of the car, or position the rear of the car over a pit or on a ramp.
2   If the rear of the car is jacked up, supplement the jack with support blocks so that danger is minimised should the jack collapse.
3   If the rear wheels are off the ground place the car in gear and put the handbrake on to ensure that the propeller shaft does not turn when an attempt is made to loosen the four nuts securing the propeller shaft to the differential drive flange.
4   Unscrew and remove the four self-locking nuts, bolts and securing washers which hold the flange on the propeller shaft to the differential drive flange.
5   The propeller shaft is carefully balanced to fine limits and it is important that it is refitted in exactly the same position it was in prior to its removal. Clean off the flange peripheral faces and inspect to see if there are any relative markings across the two flanges. If not, scratch a mark on the propeller shaft and differential drive flanges to ensure accurate mating when the time comes for reassembly.
6   Slightly push the shaft forward to separate the two flanges, and then lower the end of the shaft and pull it rearwards to disengage the gearbox mainshaft splines (photo), (early models).
7   If the front universal joint is to be removed (later models), the disconnecting sequences are the same as given in the preceding paragraphs (photo). Remove the complete shaft unit before dismantling.
8   Place a large can or tray under the rear of the gearbox extension to catch any oil which is likely to leak through the spline lubricating holes when the propeller shaft is removed (early models).
9   Refitting of the propeller shaft is a reversal of the removal procedure. Ensure that the mating marks scratched on the propeller shaft and differential drive flanges line up, and on later models, that the sliding spline joint is fitted to the gearbox, not the differential.

3 Universal joints – inspection

1   Wear in the needle roller bearings is characterised by vibration in the transmission, 'clonks' on taking up the drive, and in extreme cases of lack of lubrication, metallic squeaking, and ultimately grating and shrieking sounds as the bearings break up.
2   It is easy to check if the needle roller bearings are worn with the

2.6 The propeller shaft repositioned rearwards

2.7 The front universal joint drive flange disconnected from the gearbox drive flange

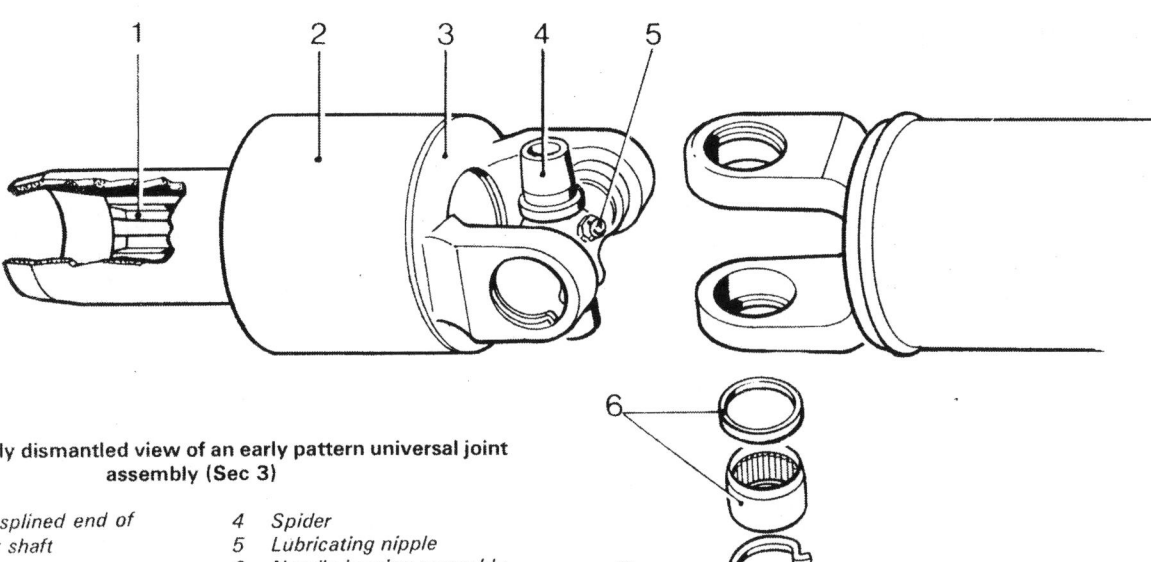

Fig. 7.1 Partly dismantled view of an early pattern universal joint assembly (Sec 3)

1 Internal splined end of	*4 Spider*
propeller shaft	*5 Lubricating nipple*
2 Dust cover	*6 Needle bearing assembly*
3 Front half coupling	*7 Clip*

propeller shaft in position, by trying to turn the shaft with one hand, the other hand holding the rear axle flange when the rear universal joint is being checked, and the front half coupling when the front universal joint is being checked. Any movement between the propeller shaft and the front and the rear half couplings is indicative of considerable wear. If worn, the old bearings and spiders will have to be discarded and a repair kit, comprising new universal joint spiders, bearings, oil seals, and retainers purchased. Check also by trying to lift the shaft and noticing any movement in the joints.

3   Examine the propeller shaft splines for wear. If worn, it will be necessary to purchase a new front half coupling, or if the yokes are badly worn, an exchange propeller shaft. It is not possible to fit oversize bearings and journals to the trunnion bearing holes.

---

4   Universal joints – dismantling and reassembly

Note: *To overhaul the universal joints, it is necessary to remove them complete with the propeller shaft from the car as described in Section 2. Then proceed as follows:*

1   Clean away all trace of dirt and grease from the circlips located on the ends of the spiders, and remove the clips by pressing their open ends together with a pair of pliers and levering them out with a screwdriver. If they are difficult to remove, tap the bearing face resting on top of the spider with a mallet, which will ease the pressure on the circlip.

2   Mark the flange and coupling yokes in relation to the propeller shaft yokes for correct mating on reassembly.

3   Hold the propeller shaft in one hand and remove the bearing cups and needle rollers by tapping the yoke at each bearing with a copper or hide-faced hammer. As soon as the bearings start to emerge, they can be drawn out by hand or a pair of pliers. If difficulty is experienced, mount the shaft in a vice, and, using a large spanner socket, drift the mating yoke off the spider to expose a bearing cup (photo). The cup can then be removed with a self-gripping wrench (photo).

4   When one pair of bearings has been removed, turn the spider so that it can be rolled out of the yoke (photo). Where a grease nipple is fitted, some leverage may be necessary to get the spider free.

5   Repeat the procedure on the other two bearings, then thoroughly clean the yokes and their bearing journals.

6   The repair kit contains all the new parts required to refurbish one universal joint (photo).

7   Fit new oil seals and retainers to each of the four arms of the spider and locate it in one half of the universal joint (photo). Assemble the needle rollers in one bearing cup using some grease to retain the rollers. After filling the bearing cup to a depth of $\frac{1}{8}$ in (3 mm) with grease, and filling the reservoir holes in the spider journals with grease, press the cup into its journal, and at the same time on to the spider

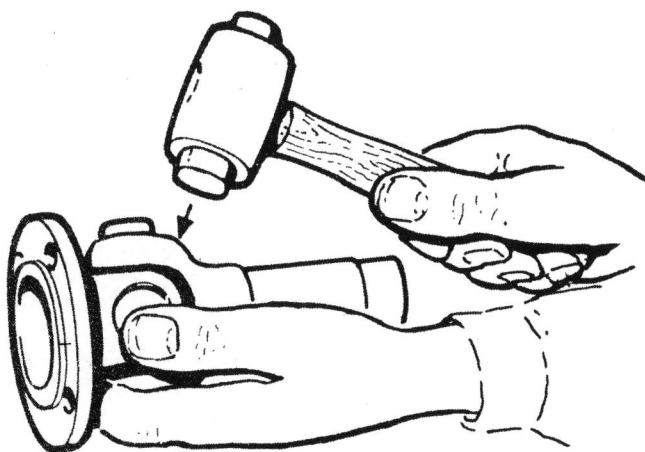

Fig. 7.2 Tap the yoke to eject a bearing cup (Sec 4)

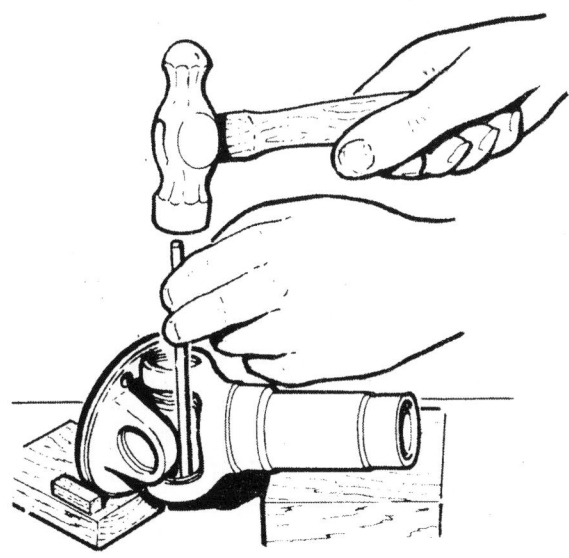

Fig. 7.3 An alternative method of removing the bearing cups (Sec 4)

4.3a Using a large spanner socket to drift a yoke free

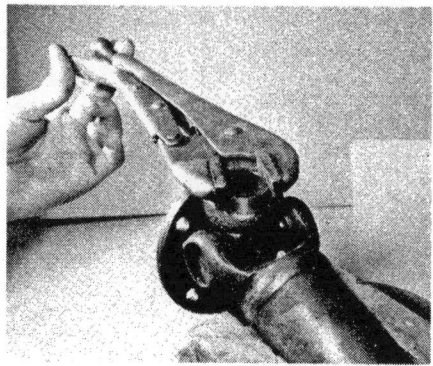

4.3b Removing a bearing cup

4.4 Disconnecting one half of the coupling

4.6 A universal coupling repair kit

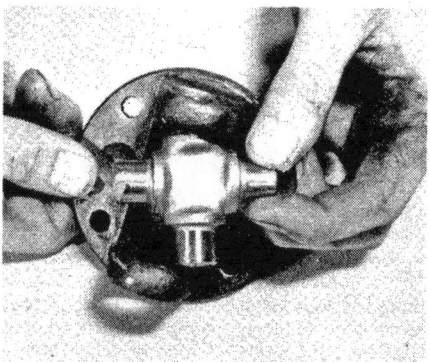

4.7a Locating the spider in a yoke

4.7b Fitting a bearing cup ...

4.7c ... and fitting the retaining C-clips

4.8a Assembling the universal joint

4.8b Pressing in a bearing cup

arm, using a suitably sized spanner socket in a vice (photo). When in position repeat the procedure for the directly opposed bearing and then fit the retaining circlips (photo).

8   Locate the spider in the mating half of the coupling, making sure that the assembly marks are aligned, and fit the bearings and circlips

as already described (photos). Where a grease nipple is fitted, lubricate the spider and wipe off surplus grease.

9   Check the joint for full, free movement with no binding or tight spots. Repeat the whole procedure on the propeller shaft's other universal joint.

5   Fault diagnosis – propeller shaft

Symptom	Reason(s)
'Clunk' on taking up drive	Wear in propeller shaft universal joints and splines Wear in differential Wear in the hub splines on wire wheel models
Vibration at all speeds	Propeller shaft out of balance or bent Universal joints worn

Chapter 8 Rear axle

Contents

Specifications

Type .... Three-quarter-floating

Ratio
Early models .... 4.22 : 1
Later models (from car Nos GAN4 77591 and HAN9 66226)
and 1500 cc models .... 3.909 : 1

Lubrication
Oil type/specification .... Hypoid gear oil, viscosity SAE 90EP (Duckhams Hypoid 90S)
Oil capacity .... 1¾ Imp pts (2.1 US pts) (1 litre)

Crownwheel
Maximum permissible run-out .... 0.002 in (0.05 mm)
Backlash to pinion .... Etched in rear face of crownwheel

Torque wrench settings

	lbf ft	kgf m
Differential/gear carrier retaining cap nuts	65	8.99
Pinion drive flange retaining nut	140	19.4

1 General description and maintenance

The rear axle is of the three-quarter-floating type, and is held in place by semi-elliptic springs (except in the case of the early Sprite which was fitted with quarter-elliptic springs and upper suspension rods which acted as radius arms). The semi-elliptic springs provide the necessary lateral and longitudinal location of the axle. The rear axle incorporates a hypoid crownwheel and pinion, and a two pinion differential. All repairs can be carried out to the component parts of the rear axle without removing the axle casing from the car.

The crownwheel and pinion together with the differential gears are mounted in the differential carrier unit which is bolted to the front face of the banjo-type axle casing.

The halfshafts are easily withdrawn and are splined at their inner ends to fit into the splines in the differential wheels. The inner wheel bearing races are mounted on the outer ends of the axle casing and are secured by nuts and lockwashers. The rear wheel bearing outer races are located in the hubs.

Very little routine maintenance is required, apart from periodical checks of the differential casing oil level (photo), and occasionally draining and refilling with new oil as prescribed in the maintenance section at the beginning of the book.

Occasionally check the wheels and hubs for signs of oil leakage through the respective axle end housings. If oil is present, inspect and renew the hub seals as soon as possible. Also check the differential carrier nose-piece for signs of leakage from the differential casing through the pinion shaft oil seal. Renew the seal, as described in this Chapter, if it is suspected of being faulty.

Do not overfill the axle with oil. Only use the recommended type and grade of oil.

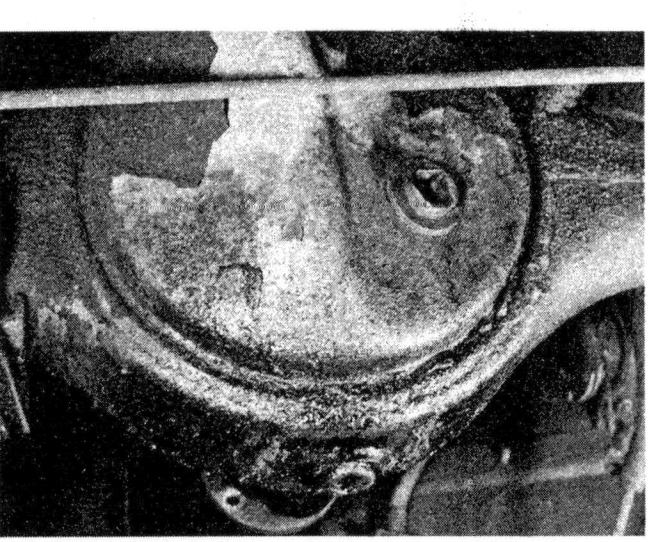

1.4 The rear axle housing showing oil level and drain plugs – 1275 cc model

2 Rear axle – removal and refitting

1 Remove the rear wheel hub caps and loosen the wheel nuts, or in the case of cars with wire wheels, slacken the single hub nut on each rear wheel.

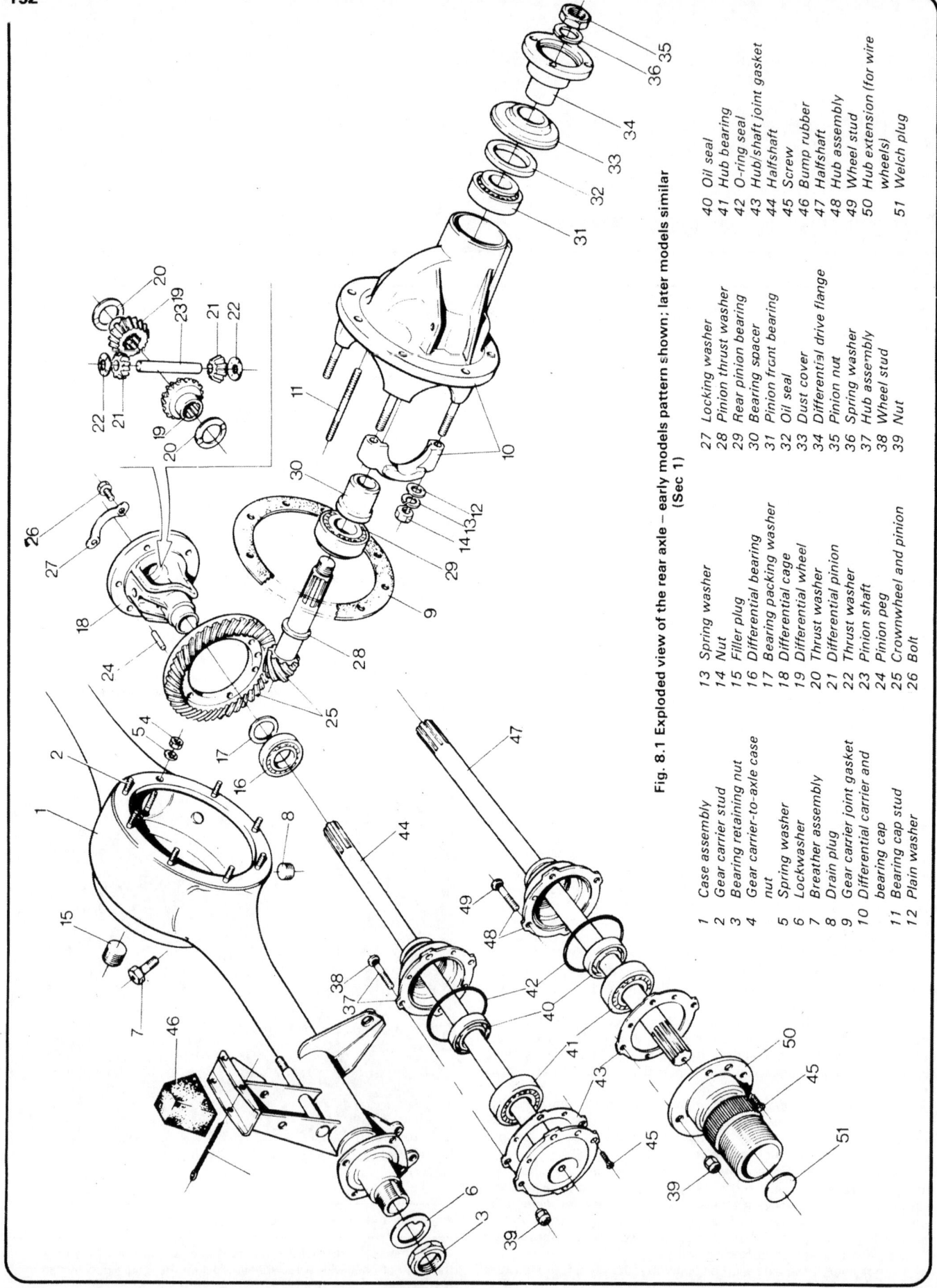

Fig. 8.1 Exploded view of the rear axle – early models pattern shown; later models similar
(Sec 1)

1	Case assembly	13	Spring washer	27	Locking washer	40	Oil seal
2	Gear carrier stud	14	Nut	28	Pinion thrust washer	41	Hub bearing
3	Bearing retaining nut	15	Filler plug	29	Rear pinion bearing	42	O-ring seal
4	Gear carrier-to-axle case	16	Differential bearing	30	Bearing spacer	43	Hub/shaft joint gasket
	nut	17	Bearing packing washer	31	Pinion front bearing	44	Halfshaft
5	Spring washer	18	Differential cage	32	Oil seal	45	Screw
6	Lockwasher	19	Differential wheel	33	Dust cover	46	Bump rubber
7	Breather assembly	20	Thrust washer	34	Differential drive flange	47	Halfshaft
8	Drain plug	21	Differential pinion	35	Pinion nut	48	Hub assembly
9	Gear carrier joint gasket	22	Thrust washer	36	Spring washer	49	Wheel stud
10	Differential carrier and	23	Pinion shaft	37	Hub assembly	50	Hub extension (for wire
	bearing cap	24	Pinion peg	38	Wheel stud		wheels)
11	Bearing cap stud	25	Crownwheel and pinion	39	Nut	51	Welch plug
12	Plain washer	26	Bolt				

2 Raise and support the rear of the car body and the differential casing with stands or blocks. The body is best supported just forward of the front hangers of the rear springs. Chock the front wheels to prevent car movement.

3 Remove both rear wheels and place the wheel nuts in the hub caps for safe-keeping.

4 If the exhaust pipe runs under the rear axle, remove the exhaust pipe and silencer by releasing the appropriate securing nuts and bolts.

5 If check straps are fitted, remove them by unscrewing the nuts and bolts which retain the straps to the body.

6 Free the dampers at their attachment point to the rear axle casing.

7 Disconnect the handbrake cable at the compensating lever or the rear brake cylinders, depending on model.

8 Clean around the brake hydraulic reservoir filler cap, remove the cap and cover the filler orifice with a piece of thin plastic sheet, then refit the cap. This will minimise fluid loss when the brake line is disconnected. Undo the brake pipe union at the point just forward of the differential housing and cover both pipe open ends to prevent dirt ingress. Disconnect the flexible hose on the rear axle from its bracket on the car bodywork.

9 Undo the nuts and remove them together with the spring washers from the propeller shaft flange bolts. Remove the bolts after having marked the propeller shaft and differential drive flanges to ensure refitting in the same relative positions.

10 Check that the jack is under the differential casing and taking the weight of the rear axle, and then unscrew the nuts from under the spring retaining plate. These nuts screw onto the ends of inverted U-bolts which retain the axle to the spring. Tap out the U-bolts and remove the pad which rests between the spring and the axle bracket. (In the case of early models of the Sprite with quarter-elliptic rear springs, unscrew the nuts from the bolts which hold each of the two radius rods to the brackets on the rear axle, withdraw the bolts, and then unscrew and extract the shackle pins).

11 Lower the jack so that the axle rests on the springs. Now, with the aid of an assistant, withdraw the axle unit over the left-hand spring, and remove to the work area.

12 Refit the axle in the reverse sequence, but note the following:

(a) *Do not overtighten the U-bolt nuts. Do not fully tighten the nuts until the car is fully reassembled and off the jacks*

(b) *If the rear spring mounting rubbers are worn or perished, they should also be renewed at this time*

(c) *Bleed the brake system and re-check the handbrake adjustment before use*

3 Halfshaft, hub and bearing – removal and refitting

1 If a halfshaft is being removed, it is advisable to drain the rear axle oil before commencing to strip the halfshaft, as this will prevent oil spilling onto the brake linings on removal of the shaft.

2 Follow the instructions given in paragraphs 1, 2 and 3 of Section 2.

3 Release the handbrake and slacken the brake adjusters right off.

4 Unscrew the two countersunk brake drum retaining screws and pull off the brake drum. If necessary tap the brake drums off with a wooden or hide hammer. On cars fitted with wire wheels, it is necessary to bend back the tab washers and unscrew the four nuts from their studs which serve instead of retaining screws.

5 Unscrew the single shaft flange locating screw and pull the halfshaft by its flange out from the axle casing. On cars fitted with wire wheels it is necessary to unscrew the screws holding the hub extension flanges to the hub and pull off the hub extension before the halfshaft can be withdrawn.

6 To remove the hub, knock back the tab of the locking washer and unscrew the hub retaining nut. Note that the left-hand side nut has a left-hand thread and must be turned clockwise to undo it. The right-hand nut has a normal right-hand thread.

7 Remove the lockwasher from the axle casing end by lifting the washer so that its key is freed from the locating groove.

8 With a hub puller, pull off the hub complete with bearing and oil seal. The bearing and oil seal can now be removed from the hub if required by pressing out.

9 Refitting is a reversal of the above procedure, but the following points should be noted:

(a) *If fitting a new oil seal, carefully drift it into position before the bearing and ensure that it is placed with the lip facing outwards towards the wheel. Lubricate the seal with oil*

(b) *Before fitting the rear bearings, lubricate them with lithium based grease*

(c) *Always renew the gasket between the hub assembly and the halfshaft flange, and if making one up ensure that it is cut from paper at least 0.008 in (0.2 mm) thick. Renew the O-ring seal*

(d) *Remember to knock back the locking tab of the locking washer*

(e) *Check and if necessary readjust the brakes*

(f) *Check and if necessary top up the rear axle oil level*

4 Pinion oil seal – removal and refitting

1 If oil is leaking from the front of the differential nose piece it will be necessary to renew the pinion oil seal. If a pit is not available, jack up and chock up the rear of the car. It is much easier to do this job over a pit, or with the car on a ramp.

2 Drain the oil from the differential housing.

3 Mark the propeller shaft and pinion drive flanges to ensure their refitting in the same relative positions.

4 Unscrew the nuts from the four bolts holding the flanges together, remove the bolts and separate the flanges.

5 If the oil seal is being renewed with the differential nose piece in position, drain the oil and check that the handbrake is firmly on to prevent the pinion flange moving.

6 Unscrew the nut in the centre of the pinion drive flange. Although it is very tight it can be removed fairly easily with a long extension arm fitted to the appropriate socket spanner. If necessary restrain the flange by using a lever and bolts in the flange holes. Remove the nut and spring washer.

7 Pull off the splined drive flange, which may be a little stubborn, in which case it should be tapped with a hide mallet from the rear. Alternatively use a universal puller to remove the drive flange. Then remove the pressed steel end cover, and prise out the oil seal with a screwdriver, taking care not to damage the lip of its seating.

8 Refitting is a reversal of the above procedure, but note the following additional points:

(a) *Lubricate the new seal with oil before fitting, and install it with the lip facing in towards the bearing, until it is flush with the end of the casing*

(b) *Tighten the drive flange retaining nut to its specified torque, but take care not to exceed that figure as it could affect the preload on the pinion gear*

(c) *Check and, if necessary, top up the rear axle oil level*

5 Differential unit – removal and refitting

Note: *If for any reason the differential unit has to be renewed, it is now normal practice to renew the crownwheel and pinion assembly as a complete unit. If only one gear is damaged or badly worn, it will be pointless to renew this alone, as meshing a new gear with a used one is not just bad engineering practice, but it will almost certainly mean a considerable increase in noise from the axle when under load. In addition special tools and knowledge are required to dismantle and reassemble the differential unit so that the critical gear mesh is achieved. Therefore, if you have a noisy or damaged differential unit, remove it as follows and replace it with a new or exchange factory built unit.*

1 First drain the axle and remove the halfshafts as described in Section 3.

2 Mark the propeller shaft and pinion flanges to ensure their refitting in the same relative position.

3 Unscrew the nuts from the four bolts holding the flanges together, remove the bolts and separate the flanges, lowering the propeller shaft out of the way.

4 Remove the ring of nuts and spring washers which join the differential carrier/cover to the axle casing, and pull the carrier/cover complete with differential assembly out of the casing.

5   Carefully clean the inside of the axle casing, fit a new gasket to the casing joint, and then fit the exchange or rebuilt differential assembly. Refitting is a reversal of the removal procedure.

6   Refill the differential with the correct grade of oil and run the axle in slowly for the first 500 miles (800 km), and then change the oil when it is hot.

6   Fault diagnosis – rear axle

Symptom	Reason(s)
Noise on drive, coasting or overrun	Shortage of oil
	Incorrect grade of oil
	Incorrect crownwheel-to-pinion mesh
	Worn pinion bearings
	Worn side bearings
	Loose bearing cap bolts
Noise on turn	Differential side gears worn, damaged or tight
Knock on taking up drive or during gearchange	Excessive crownwheel-to-pinion backlash
	Worn gears
	Worn halfshaft splines
	Pinion bearing pre-load too low
	Loose drive coupling nut
	Loose securing nuts or bolts within unit
	Loose roadwheel nuts or elongated stud holes
Oil leakage	Defective gaskets or oil seals
	Clogged breather
	Oil level too high

Chapter 9 Braking system

Contents

Specifications

System type
Sprite Mk I & Mk II, Midget Mk I (948 cc) .... Hydraulically operated drum brakes, front and rear. Mechanically operated handbrake to rear wheels

All other models .... Hydraulically operated front disc and rear drum brakes. Mechanically operated handbrake to rear wheels

Brake drums
Nominal diameter .... 7 in (17.78 cm)

Brake discs
Nominal diameter .... 8.25 in (209.5 mm)
Thickness .... 0.300 to 0.305 in (7.62 to 7.75 mm)
Minimum regrind thickness .... 0.290 in (7.37 mm)
Maximum run-out .... 0.006 in (0.152 mm)

Brake pads
Minimum thickness .... $\frac{1}{16}$ in (1.59 mm)

Handbrake cable and compensator lubricant type ...... General purpose grease (Duckhams LB 10)

Brake fluid type .... Hydraulic fluid to SAE J1703 or FMVSS 116 DOT 3 (Duckhams Universal Brake and Clutch Fluid)

Torque wrench settings

	lbf ft	kgf m
Brake disc to hub	43	5.9
Brake caliper to stub axle	48	6.7
Brake pressure failure warning valve and plug	16.6	2.3

1 General description

Most Sprite Mk I and II, and Midget Mk I models are fitted with drum brakes on front and rear wheels. Later Sprite Mk II and Midget Mk I models and all later models (including the 1500 cc series) are fitted with disc brakes on the front wheels with drum brakes on the rear. In all cases they are operated by hydraulic pressure generated in the master cylinder when the brake pedal is depressed. This pressure is transmitted to each wheel cylinder by a system of metal pipes and flexible hoses.

Early models have the master cylinder mounted in a common reservoir with the clutch hydraulic master cylinder, but later models have entirely separate systems including reservoirs. On the USA 1500 cc models and late UK models, the brake system is split to serve two

separate halves of the system so that, in the event of a failure on one half, the other half of the system is retained.

The early front drum brakes are of the twin leading shoe type with a separate wheel cylinder for each shoe. All rear brakes have one leading and one trailing shoe, both operated by a single wheel cylinder. The front disc brakes have a single caliper working on the disc. The caliper carries two pistons operating a pair of pads which, when the brakes are operated, bear on the disc. Although the disc brakes are self-adjusting, all drum brakes need periodic adjustment to compensate for wear.

A handbrake operating on the rear wheels is fitted to all models. It consists of a handlever, flexible cable, compensator and rods connected to levers which operate the rear brake shoes. Provided that the shoes are kept in adjustment, little attention apart from lubrication is needed.

Caution: *All work undertaken on the braking system must be to the highest standard. It is vitally important to maintain the integrity of the system. You must always use the right fasteners with correct locking devices where appropriate. Adjustments must be within specifications where these apply, and spare parts must be new or in faultless condition. Absolute cleanliness when assembling hydraulic components is essential. New seals and fresh hydraulic fluid must be used and any fluid drained, bled or removed from the system should be discarded. Your life, and that of others, could depend on these points, and if you are in any doubt at all concerning what to do or how to do it, you should get professional advice or have the job done by a skilled mechanic.*

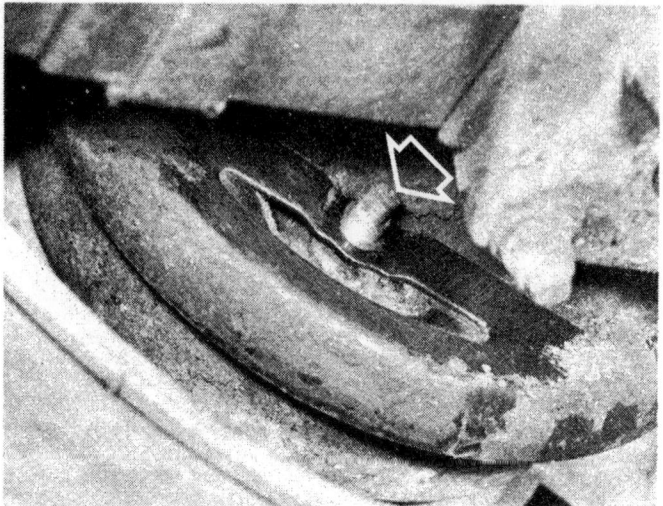

2.2 A rear brake adjuster (arrowed)

2 Drum brakes – adjustment

1   Brake adjustment must be carried out on the drum brakes at the specified intervals or whenever pedal travel is excessive. Adjustment compensates for brake lining wear by moving the shoes closer to the drums.

2   On early models, access to the adjusters involves removing the hub cap and a rubber dust cover, and then rotating the wheel to align the access hole with the adjuster. There are two adjusters on front drum brakes, but only one on each rear brake. On later models the adjusters are easier to get at, as they protrude from the brake backplate (photo) and can be recognised by having a spanner square instead of a hexagon. Despite the differences in adjusters, the procedure is basically the same for all models.

3   Jack up the wheel to be adjusted and, where it is necessary to get under the car, support the car on stands or blocks – *don't work under the car if it is lifted on the wheel-changing jack.* Clean off the dirt from the exposed type of adjuster or, on the other type, remove the hub cap and dust plug and turn the wheel to align the access holes.

4   Using a brake adjuster spanner or a screwdriver as appropriate, turn the adjuster in a clockwise direction so that, when the wheel is spun, the shoe comes into contact with the drum and stops the wheel turning. Then carefully back off the adjuster until the wheel is just free to spin without the lining rubbing – a light rubbing noise can be ignored if the wheel spins freely. On front brakes repeat the procedure on the other adjuster on the brake assembly.

5   Lower the wheel to the ground, where applicable refit the dust plug and hub cap, then repeat the adjustment on the remaining wheels or wheel. When adjusting rear brakes the handbrake must be released, of course, so make sure that the front wheels are chocked before getting under the car.

Fig. 9.1 Adjusting one of the two adjusters on the early front drum brake (Sec 2)

3 Handbrake – adjustment

1   If the handbrake appears ineffective, or if it is necessary to lift the handlever to the limit of its travel to apply the brake, readjustment is necessary. However, it is essential that the brake shoes are first properly adjusted as described in the previous Section before any attempt is made to adjust the handbrake.

2   Jack up the rear of the car and support it on stands or blocks, then chock the front wheels to prevent car movement.

3   Adjust the brake shoes as outlined in the previous Section, then apply the handbrake lever as far as the third notch on the ratchet.

4   Check the braking effect on the rear wheels by attempting to rotate them. They should be held or tending to bind. If this is not the case, adjust the handbrake cable adjuster located at the end of the flexible sheath (photo). Loosen the locknut and turn the adjustment nut to achieve the correct effect, which is when the wheels can just be rotated with both wheels offering equal braking resistance, then tighten the locknut.

5   Release the handbrake lever and check that both rear wheels can be rotated freely. If necessary repeat the adjustments.

6   Lower the car to the ground.

4 Brake hydraulic system – bleeding

1   If any of the hydraulic components in the braking system have been removed or disconnected, or if the fluid level in the master cylinder has been allowed to fall appreciably, it is inevitable that air will have been introduced into the system. The removal of all this air from

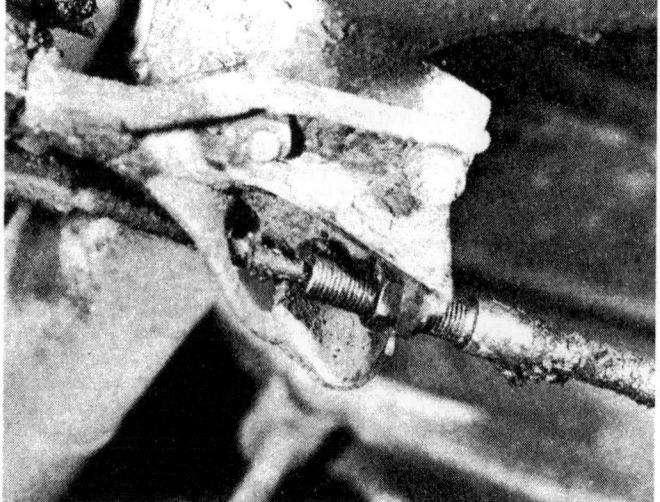

3.4 The handbrake cable adjuster at the rear axle

the hydraulic system is essential if the brakes are to function correctly, and the process of removing it is known as bleeding.

2   There are a number of one-man, do-it-yourself brake bleeding kits currently available from motor accessory shops. It is recommended that one of these kits should be used wherever possible, as they greatly simplify the bleeding operation and also reduce the risk of expelled air and fluid being drawn back into the system.

3   If you can't get hold of one of these kits, then it will be necessary to gather together a clean jar and a suitable length of clear plastic tubing which is a tight fit over the bleed screw, and also engage the help of an assistant.

4   Before starting to bleed the system, check that all the rigid pipes and flexible hoses are in good condition and that all hydraulic unions are tight. Take great care not to allow hydraulic fluid to come into contact with the car's paintwork, otherwise the finish will be seriously damaged. Wash off any spilled fluid immediately with cold water.

5   If hydraulic fluid has been lost from the master cylinder reservoir due to a leak in the system, ensure that the cause is traced and rectified before proceeding further or a serious malfunction of the braking system may occur.

6   To bleed the system, clean around the bleed screw at the wheel cylinder to be bled (photo) and then refer to paragraph 10 for the sequence. If the hydraulic system has only been partially disconnected and suitable precautions were taken to prevent further loss of fluid, such as covering the filler cap orifice with a piece of polythene or temporarily fitting a dummy filler cap with a sealed breather hole, then it should only be necessary to bleed that part of the system concerned. However, if the entire system is to be bled, follow the full sequence recommended in paragraph 10.

7   Before bleeding the system, top up the master cylinder reservoir. Periodically check the fluid level during the bleeding operation and top up as required.

8   If a one-man bleeding kit is being used, connect the outlet tube to the bleed screw and open the screw half a turn. If possible, position the unit so that it can be seen from the driver's position, then depress the brake pedal to the floor and slowly release it. The one-way valve in the kit will prevent expelled air or fluid from returning to the system at the end of each stroke. Repeat this operation until clean hydraulic fluid, free from air bubbles, can be seen coming through the tube. Then tighten the bleed screw, remove the outlet tube and, if appropriate, repeat the process on the rest of the system.

9   If a one-man brake bleeding kit is not available, connect one end of the plastic tubing to the bleed screw and immerse the other end in the jar containing sufficient clean hydraulic fluid to keep the end of the tube submerged. Open the bleed screw half a turn and get your assistant to depress the brake pedal slowly to the floor. Tighten the bleed screw at the bottom of the stroke and slowly release the pedal. In this way, expelled air and fluid are not drawn back into the system. Repeat the operation until clean, air-free fluid can be seen coming through the tube. Finally tighten the bleed screw (with the pedal depressed of course), remove the tube, release the pedal, and if

appropriate, repeat the procedure on the rest of the system. Don't forget to periodically check and, if necessary, replenish the reservoir.

10   The sequence for bleeding a complete system varies with the type of system concerned.

Single line system
Start on one of the rear brakes and, once this is done, move to the other rear brake. Then bleed the front left-hand brake followed by the front right-hand brake.

Dual circuit system
With a dual brake circuit, a different sequence of bleeding is necessary. Attach bleeder tubes to the front right-hand and the rear right-hand brake bleed screws. Operate the foot pedal using light strokes, and don't push the pedal through its entire stroke. If the brake pressure failure warning light glows (the ignition must be switched on to register this) continue with the bleeding until the right-hand system is free of air. Repeat the procedure on the front left-hand and rear left-hand brakes. If the warning light glows, complete the bleeding procedure and then, with a bleed tube attached to the bleed screw on the rear left-hand brake, open the screw half a turn, slowly depress the pedal and immediately the light goes out release the pedal and tighten the bleed screw. If the light does not go out, transfer the bleed tube and jar to the front right-hand brake bleed screw. Open the screw half a turn, slowly depress the pedal, and immediately the light goes out release the pedal and tighten the bleed screw. With the light out the shuttle valve piston in the brake pressure differential warning actuator valve will have been centralised.

11   On completion of the brake system bleeding, check the reservoir fluid level, and top up if required, then refit the cap after checking that the breather hole is clear. Check the feel of the brake pedal, which should be firm and free from any sponginess; this would indicate that air is still present in the system. Hold the pedal hard down for several seconds to pressurise the system, then check for any signs of leaks.

12   Discard the fluid which was expelled from the system during the bleeding procedure as it is likely to be contaminated with air, dirt or moisture, making it unfit for further use.

5   Drum brakes – removal, inspection and refitting

Note: *After high mileages it will be necessary to fit replacement brake shoes with new linings. Refitting new brake linings to old shoes is not always satisfactory, but if the services of a local garage or workshop with brake lining equipment are available, then there is no reason why your own shoes should not be successfully relined.*

1   Where applicable, remove the wheel hub cap, loosen the wheel nuts and jack the car up, supporting it on stands or blocks. If the front wheels are being worked on, apply the handbrake, or if the rear wheels, chock the front wheels securely. Remove the roadwheel, undo the drum retaining screws and remove the drum (photo). If difficulty is

4.6 A front disc brake bleed nipple

5.1 A rear brake with drum removed to inspect the brake linings and wheel cylinder

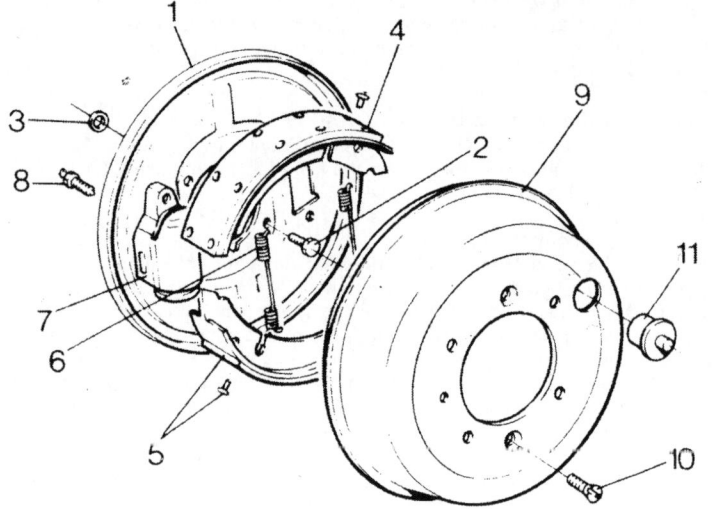

Fig. 9.2 Exploded view of the early front drum brake (Sec 5)

1	Backplate
2	Setscrew
3	Shakeproof washer
4	Brake shoe assembly
5	Lining and rivets
6	Pull-off spring
7	Wheel cylinder
8	Bleed nipple
9	Brake drum
10	Setscrew
11	Plug

3   Detach the shoes and return springs by pulling one end of each shoe away from the slot in the closed end of one of the brake cylinders, or in the case of rear wheel brakes, pull the ends of both shoes out of the pivot post. To enable this to be done on the rear brakes of early models, it will first be necessary to depress each of the shoe steady springs, then turn it to release it from the backplate. Allow the return spring to pull the free end of the brake shoe down the side of the brake cylinder, and then slide the adjuster and mask outwards off the piston head where applicable. Repeat this process at the other brake shoe and then lift both brake shoes away. It may be useful to make a pictorial note of where all the components are fitted before dismantling.

4   Clean the backplate and drum free from all traces of dust, preferably using methylated spirit and a stiff brush. *Do not* use compressed air as it will only disperse the dust into the air. Brake dust contains asbestos; it is a danger to health and must not be inhaled. Brake dust in the drums can cause brake judder or squeal if present in sufficient quantity.

5   Examine the friction surface on the inside of the drum. Normally this should be completely smooth and bright but, after some use, scores and shallow grooves will be apparent. If these are only slight they are not serious, but heavy scoring means that the drum must be reconditioned or renewed. A suitably equipped workshop can skim out the drums, but it is a precision job requiring special care to keep the lining track concentric with the axle axis.

6   Check that the pistons are free in their cylinders and that the rubber dust covers are undamaged. Any signs of hydraulic leak will necessitate prompt rectification (see Section 6). If the shoes have to be removed, temporarily tie the pistons into their cylinders and make sure that the brake pedal is not depressed at anytime when the brake drums are removed.

7   Reassembly is the reverse of the removal procedure, but several points should be noted.

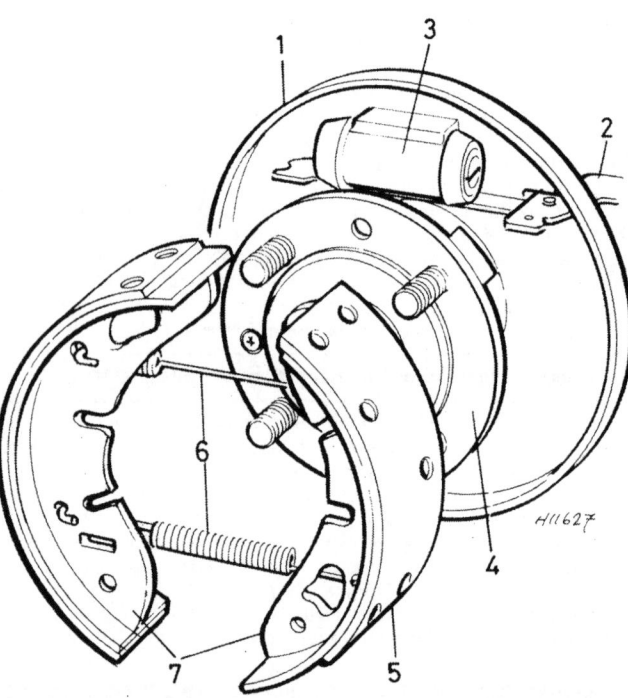

H11627

Fig. 9.3 Exploded view of the rear brake (late model) (Sec 5)

1	Backplate	5	Shoe lining
2	Handbrake lever	6	Return springs
3	Wheel cylinder	7	Brake shoes
4	Hub		

(a)   Lightly lubricate all sliding or moving metallic faces or pivots with a trace of brake grease or a good quality high melting point grease. Be careful not to use excessive grease or to contaminate the brake linings or their tracks in the drums

(b)   Unscrew the brake adjusters after renewing linings, if they were not unscrewed on dismantling

(c)   Make sure that the return springs are in their correct holes and that they are on the correct side of the brake shoe webs (photo). Renew any corroded or weak springs

(d)   After refitting the drums, operate the foot pedal several times (but first check that all drums really are fitted) to centralise the shoes, and then adjust the brakes as described in Section 2

(e)   Refit the roadwheels and lower the car to the ground. Carry out a brake test, but exercise caution until you have established their effect. Remember that relined brakes will take some time to bed in, say 500 miles (800 km), before they reach full efficiency, and then they will need readjusting to take up the bedding-in clearance

experienced turn the brake adjusters back to retract the linings and, using a soft-faced hammer, carefully tap the drum off.

2   The early car front drum brake has two wheel cylinders; all rear brakes have only one. Examine the brake shoe linings. They should be renewed if they are so worn that the rivet heads are almost flush with the surface of the lining. If the linings are contaminated with lubricant or brake fluid, don't try to clean them; they must be renewed irrespective of the amount of wear, and the cause of contamination attended to. Brake shoes must always be renewed in axle sets, that is all four shoes on the rear wheel brakes for example, and they should always be of the same grade of lining material. Be careful when buying new linings, as there are sub-standard products on the market. To be safe you should deal with reputable firms, such as your BL agent. Serious consequences can result from out-of-balance braking due to mixing of linings or defective lining material.

5.7 The rear brake shoes seated in the adjuster; note location of bottom return spring

6 Wheel cylinders (drum brakes) — removal, overhaul and refitting

1   Any malfunctioning of the wheel cylinders or any sign of fluid leaks will require prompt rectification. Even if no fault is evident, it is recommended that all rubber seals, as well as the flexible hoses and hydraulic fluid, should be renewed periodically (see Routine Maintenance Section at the beginning of this manual). For such work the wheel cylinders should be removed from the brake assemblies.

2   Remove the brake drums and brake shoes as described in the previous Section. To avoid mixing parts of different brake assemblies, it's best to work on one at a time, but if this is not preferred, make arrangements to keep the parts of each assembly segregated when dismantled.

3   To minimise the loss of hydraulic fluid, remove the reservoir filler cap and place a piece of plastic film over the filler neck before refitting the cap. Alternatively, if you can get hold of a spare cap, seal off the breather hole in the cap and fit this instead of the original. It is most important that a cap with a sealed breather is *not* fitted for normal use.

4   *Front brake wheel cylinders:* Disconnect the bridging pipe between the two cylinders complete with banjo adaptors. Undo the cylinder fastening bolts and remove the cylinders from the backplate.

5   *Rear brake wheel cylinders:* Undo and remove the bolt attaching the banjo adaptor to the cylinder (early models), or disconnect the pipe union at the back of the cylinder (later models). On early models, swing the handbrake lever to clear the shoulder from the backplate and slide the cylinder forward. Pivot the cylinder to withdraw its rear end, slide the cylinder back and remove it from the backplate. On later models, remove the bleed screw and the circlip and washer (or C-clip) securing the cylinder to the backplate, then remove the cylinder from the backplate.

6   On all cylinders, remove the rubber dust seal(s) and extract the piston(s). If difficulty is experienced, wrap the cylinder in a piece of rag leaving the hydraulic connection exposed, and to that apply low pressure air from, say, a foot pump. The rag is to prevent the piston(s) and old seal(s) from flying out and getting damaged. Carefully note the sequence of assembly.

7   Discard all the rubber components as they will need renewing. Wash all the metal parts in methylated spirit or fresh brake fluid and dry with non-fluffy rag.

8   Inspect the cylinder bore closely. If it is ridged, scored or damaged, the whole cylinder assembly must be renewed as it is pointless, as well as dangerous, attempting to service a unit with an unsatisfactory bore. Examine all parts for corrosion or damage, again renewing where these exist. Keep everything meticulously clean and covered until ready for reassembly.

9   Before assembly, immerse all parts including the new seals (but not the dust covers) in fresh hydraulic fluid and assemble them whilst still wet. Fit each new seal, manipulating it with the fingers only, into the cylinder with its flat face towards its piston or, on later rear brake cylinder assemblies, fit the new seals to the pistons with the flat surface of the seal towards the slotted end of the piston. Wipe the exterior of the cylinder assembly dry before fitting the dust cover(s), and in the case of early models the Micram adjuster and mask. Turn the piston(s) to align the slot ready to accept the brake shoe where appropriate.

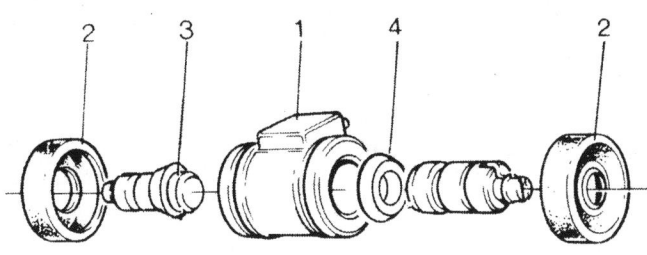

Fig. 9.4 Exploded view of a rear wheel cylinder (Sec 6)

1	Cylinder body	3	Piston
2	Rubber boot	4	Seal

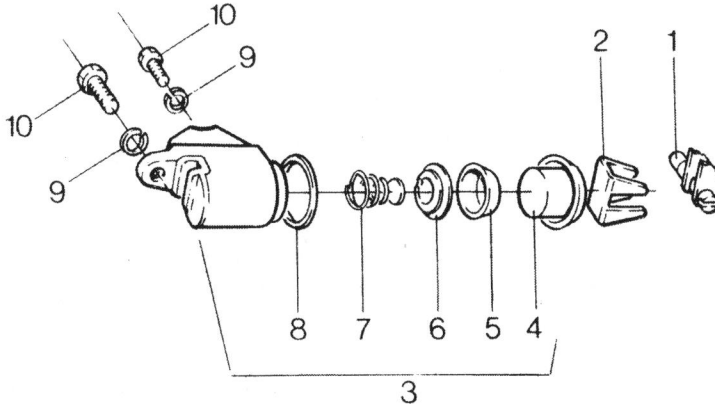

Fig. 9.5 Exploded view of the early front drum brake wheel cylinder (Sec 6)

1	Micram adjuster	4	Piston and dust cover	7	Spring	9	Spring washer
2	Mask	5	Cup	8	Sealing ring	10	Screw
3	Wheel cylinder unit	6	Cup filler				

10 Refitting the wheel cylinders is the reverse of the removal procedure. On completion of reassembly, adjust the brakes as described in Section 2; remove the plastic from the filler orifice, or remove the dummy filler cap as appropriate, and bleed the hydraulic system as described in Section 4. Finally road test the brakes.

7 Disc brake pads – removal, inspection and refitting

1 To check the thickness of pad material on the front disc brakes it is only necessary to examine them from the front of the car looking into the aperture in the caliper on each brake. When the lining material has worn down to $\frac{1}{16}$ in (1.6 mm) thickness, or if it is likely to have done before the next check is due, the pads must be renewed. Pads must be renewed as an axle set, and if only one pad is defective all four must be changed.

2 Apply the handbrake, jack up the front of the vehicle, support it securely on stands or blocks, and remove the roadwheels.
3 Turn one wheel outwards to improve access to the caliper, but avoid forceful movement of the steering when jacked clear of the ground as internal damage in the steering mechanism can result.
4 Press down on the pad retaining spring (photo) and extract the split pins. The retaining spring may now be removed.
5 With a slight rotational movement, remove the friction pads (photo) from the caliper unit complete with the anti-squeal shims. Use a pair of long nosed pliers if necessary.
6 Carefully clean the recesses in the caliper in which the friction pad assemblies lie, and the exposed face of each piston, from all traces of dirt and rust. Inspect the brake disc. If badly scored or worn it will have to be renewed before refitting the pads.
7 In order to accommodate the increased thickness of new pads, the caliper pistons should be depressed evenly and equally into their

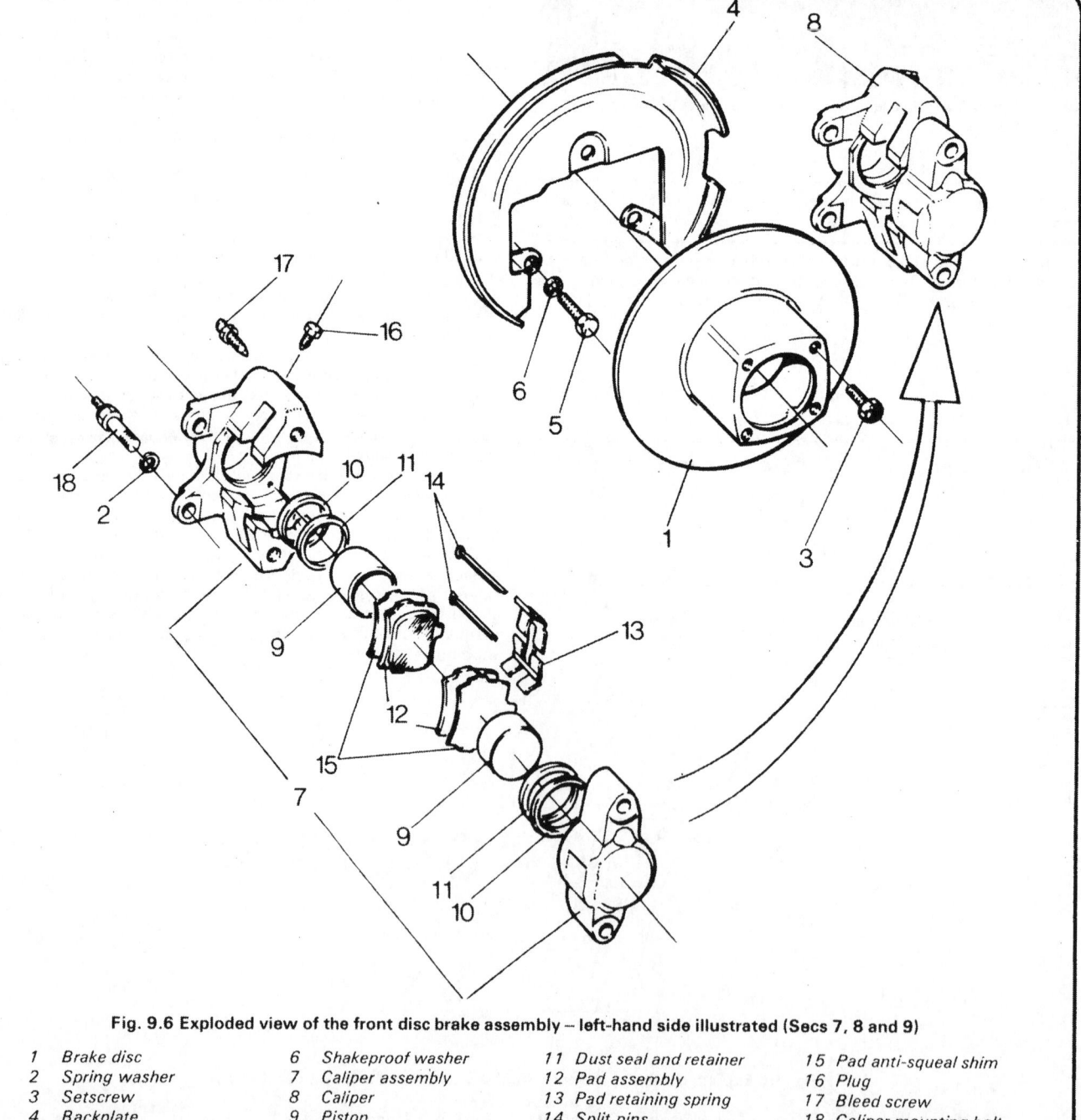

Fig. 9.6 Exploded view of the front disc brake assembly – left-hand side illustrated (Secs 7, 8 and 9)

1 Brake disc	6 Shakeproof washer	11 Dust seal and retainer	15 Pad anti-squeal shim
2 Spring washer	7 Caliper assembly	12 Pad assembly	16 Plug
3 Setscrew	8 Caliper	13 Pad retaining spring	17 Bleed screw
4 Backplate	9 Piston	14 Split pins	18 Caliper mounting bolt
5 Setscrew	10 Inner seal		

7.4 Pressing down the disc pad retaining spring ...

7.5 ... and removing a disc brake pad

cylinders using a short piece of wood. As the pistons are depressed the hydraulic fluid level will rise in the master cylinder. It is therefore necesssary to place a piece of rag around the base of the master cylinder filler neck so that any displacement of fluid is not spilt onto paintwork on the surrounding components.

8   Alternatively fit a bleed tube to the caliper bleed nipple and submerge its open end into a clean jar containing a little hydraulic fluid. Release the bleed nipple a turn and as the pistons are depressed, the displaced fluid will be expelled into the jar. Retighten the bleed nipple on completion.

9   After checking that the relieved face of each piston is facing downwards, fit the new friction pads into the calipers and position the anti-squeal shims between the friction pad and the piston.

10 Check that the new friction pad assemblies move freely in the caliper recesses and remove any high spots on the edge of the pressure plate by careful filing.

11 Check that the retaining spring clips show no sign of damage or loss of tension and then, if sound, refit them, press them down and fit the two split pins, opening their ends to lock them.

12 Repeat the procedure on the other front brake and then refit the roadwheels. Lower the car to the ground and operate the brake foot pedal to adjust the positions of the pistons. Top up the hydraulic reservoir as required and discard any fluid which was removed from the system when repositioning the pistons.

8 Disc brake caliper units – removal, overhaul and refitting

Special note: *Each caliper unit is built up from two halves, but on no account should you separate these two halves.*

1   Prepare the car as described in paragraphs 2 and 3 of the previous Section, then remove the brake pads as described. Remove the hydraulic reservoir filler cap, cover the orifice with a piece of plastic film and refit the cap or, alternatively, if you can get hold of a spare cap, seal off its breather hole and temporarily fit it to the reservoir. The aim is to seal the reservoir and minimise the loss of brake fluid when the system is disconnected.

2   Undo and remove the banjo bolt and two sealing washers connecting the brake fluid flexible hose to the back of the caliper unit. Cover the open end of the hose to prevent dirt ingress.

3   After bending back the lockwasher tabs, undo and remove the caliper retaining bolts and the hose support bracket. Remove the caliper unit from the axle.

4   Thoroughly clean the outside of the caliper using only methylated spirit or brake fluid, as other cleaning fluids could damage the internal seal between the two caliper halves.

5   Using a piece of scrap sheet metal make up a simple U-bracket which will fit onto the caliper to restrain one piston from moving. This need not be elaborate but must be strong enough for the job. With the

temporary restrainer in place to hold the piston in the mounting side of the caliper, eject the other piston using a low pressure air supply applied at the fluid inlet port. If difficulty is experienced, temporarily reconnect the caliper to its flexible hose on the car, supporting the caliper to avoid damaging the hose, and gently depress the foot pedal to eject the piston. Note which way round it is fitted so that you can reassemble it correctly.

6   Taking care to avoid damage to the caliper bore or seal groove, remove the dust seal retainer from the mouth of the caliper bore and remove the dust seal. Similarly, carefully remove the fluid seal from its groove.

7   Remove the piston restrainer from the mounting-half piston, temporarily refit the outer-half piston, without seals, into the bore and fit the restrainer to hold it in place. Then remove the mounting-half piston following the same procedure as that for the outer-half piston. Remove the dust seal retainer, the dust seal and the fluid seal following the earlier procedure, and then remove the temporary restrainer and the outer-half piston. Finally remove the bleed screw.

8   Clean all parts in methylated spirit or fresh brake fluid, and dry with non-fluffy rag.

9   Examine all components for signs of wear, damage or corrosion. In particular look for scores, grooves or ridges on the cylindrical walls of the pistons, especially over the area on which the seals bear. Don't attempt to rectify such damage; the only satisfactory, and safe, remedy is renewal of the unit. Discard all rubber seals after removal.

10 It is most important to start reassembly with everything meticulously clean, and during reassembly every care must be taken to prevent any contamination of the unit.

11 Lubricate the pistons and new seals in fresh brake fluid and assemble these parts whilst still wet with fluid as follows.

12 Taking each cylinder in turn, carefully fit a new fluid seal into its groove, making sure that it is bedded in properly and is not damaged. Lubricate the piston with brake fluid and press it into the cylinder, aligning the undercut in the same position as it was originally. Press the piston in squarely until about $\frac{1}{4}$ in (6 mm) protrudes from the cylinder.

13 Assemble a new dust seal into its retainer and then fit it to the raised portion of the piston, pressing the piston and seal home.

14 When the assembly is complete on one cylinder, reassemble the piston and seals on the other and wipe the caliper assembly clean and dry ready for installation. Refit the bleed screw.

15 Refit the caliper to the disc and axle following the reverse procedure to removal. Then refit the brake pads and bleed the system as previously described. Carry out a road test on completion.

9 Front brake discs – inspection, removal and refitting

1   Ineffective front brake action or excessive wear of the disc pads

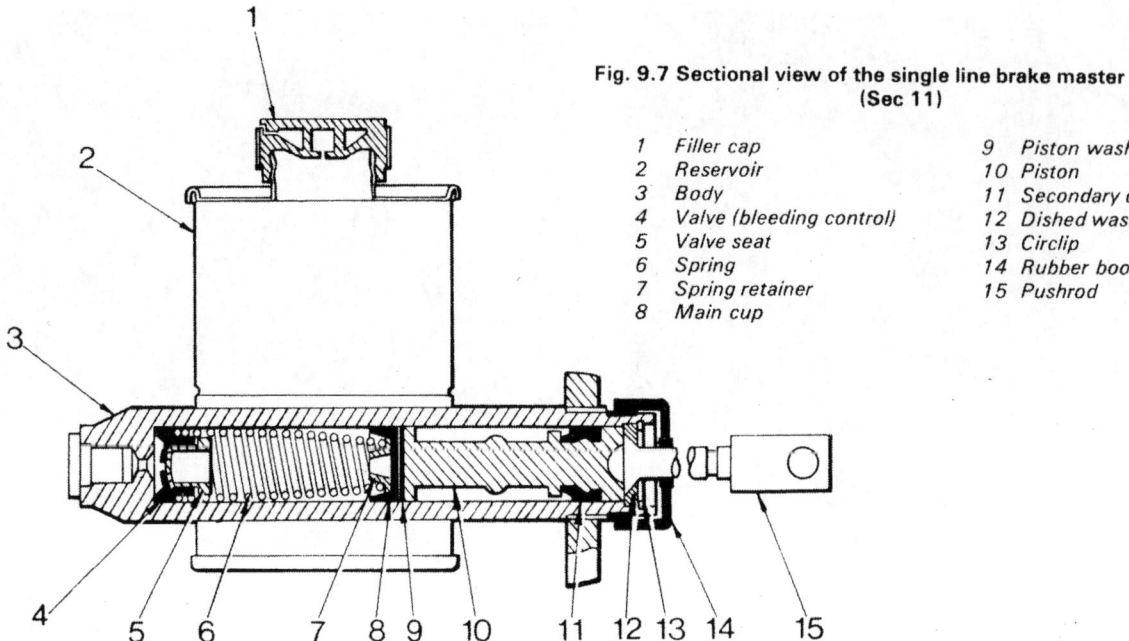

Fig. 9.7 Sectional view of the single line brake master cylinder
(Sec 11)

1	Filler cap	9	Piston washer
2	Reservoir	10	Piston
3	Body	11	Secondary cup
4	Valve (bleeding control)	12	Dished washer
5	Valve seat	13	Circlip
6	Spring	14	Rubber boot
7	Spring retainer	15	Pushrod
8	Main cup		

might be due to defective discs, and these should be checked when front brake faults arise or when the disc pads are removed.

2   With the disc pads removed (see Section 7), spin the hub slowly and examine both sides of the disc for scores, grooves or cracks.

3   Mount a dial test indicator (clock gauge) with its stud pressing at right angles to the disc face near the disc periphery and turn the hub to check run-out. If this exceeds the figure given in the Specifications the disc is unfit for further use. It might be possible for a suitably equipped engineering workshop to salvage a disc which is only slightly out-of-true but excessive run-out, heavy scores, and grooves or cracks will require disc renewal.

4   To remove a disc, first remove the brake caliper as described in Section 8, then remove the hub as described in Chapter 11.

5   Separate the disc from the hub by undoing and removing the four retaining bolts and lockwashers.

6   Reassembly and refitting are the reverse of the removal and dismantling sequences.

10 Master cylinder (early models) – removal, overhaul and refitting

On the earlier models the removal and overhaul of the brake master cylinder is identical to that of the clutch master cylinder, as detailed in Chapter 5.

On dismantling of this type it will be found that the brake master cylinder has a valve situated behind the return spring, as shown in Fig. 5.3, item 7. This valve is not fitted to the clutch master cylinder.

11 Master cylinder (later single line models) – removal, overhaul and refitting

Note: *The procedure described below applies to the most commonly found master cylinder. Two slightly different units will be encountered on some models, one of these having a remote fluid reservoir. The procedures applicable to these units basically follow that given below; any differences should be noted by reference to Figs. 9.8 and 9.9.*

1   On these models, the master cylinder is a completely separate unit from the clutch master cylinder. Removal is carried out as follows.

2   Lift the bonnet and remove the lid of the pedal box.

3   Drain out the hydraulic fluid from the master cylinder by attaching a bleed tube to a loosened bleed nipple of one of the front brakes, and by pumping the pedal extract the fluid from the cylinder into a jar. Discard the old fluid.

4   Disconnect the hydraulic pipe from its union to the master cylinder. Then from inside the pedal box, withdraw the split pin from

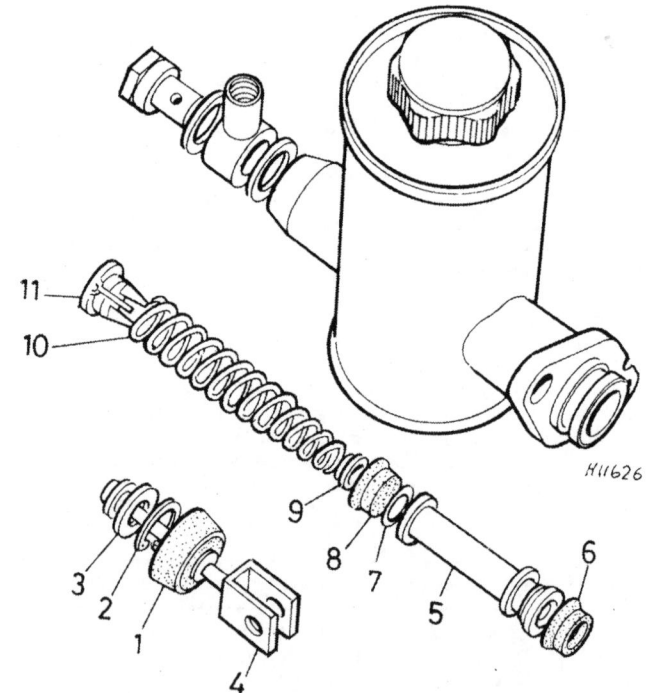

H11626

Fig. 9.8 Alternative type of single line master cylinder with integral reservoir (Sec 11)

1	Rubber boot	7	Washer
2	Circlip	8	Main cup seal
3	Dished washer	9	Spring retainer
4	Pushrod	10	Spring
5	Piston	11	Valve
6	Secondary cup seal		

the clevis pin retaining the master cylinder pushrod to the brake pedal, and remove the clevis pin.

5   Now remove the two bolts retaining the master cylinder to the pedal box, and lift the cylinder clear, taking care not to spill any remaining fluid onto the car paintwork.

6   Remove the filler cap and empty out the remaining hydraulic fluid.

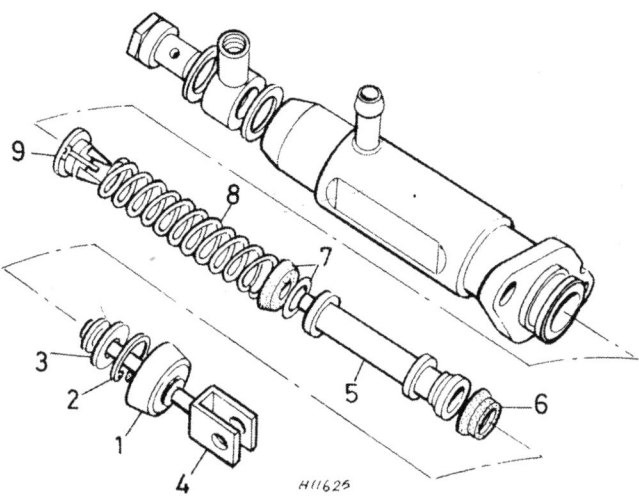

Clean off the outside of the assembly before starting to dismantle it.

7   Prise the rubber boot from its location on the body of the master cylinder and slide it down the pushrod.

8   With a pair of pliers, remove the circlip which holds the pushrod in place and withdraw the pushrod complete with the rubber boot and dished washer.

9   Slide the piston complete with the secondary cup from the bore of the cylinder. Then withdaw the piston washer, the main cup, the spring retainer, spring and valve.

10 The secondary cup can now be removed from the piston by easing it over the end of the piston using the fingers only. Note that it is correctly fitted when the lip of the cup faces towards the piston head.

11 Clean all parts thoroughly using the recommended hydraulic fluid or methylated spirit, then dry them off with a non-fluffy rag.

12 Discard all the rubber components and fit new items instead. Carefully examine all metal parts for signs of wear, damage or corrosion. In particular examine the bore of the master cylinder for scores, grooves or ridges and if any are obvious, renew the complete assembly, as there is no effective remedy for this type of defect.

13 Lubricate all parts in clean hydraulic fluid and reassemble them whilst wet in the reverse order to the dismantling procedure. On completion wipe the assembly dry.

14 Refitting is the reverse of the removal procedure. If the pushrod adjusting nuts were disturbed during the dismantling/reassembly process, or if they are incorrectly set, readjust them to give $\frac{5}{32}$ in (4 mm) clearance at the foot pedal before the pushrod begins to move. If the pedal is depressed by hand it will be quite obvious when the clearance is taken up due to the increased resistance offered by the pushrod.

15 After refitting, refill the reservoir with fresh brake fluid and bleed the system as described in Section 4.

Fig. 9.9 Alternative type of single line master cylinder with remote reservoir (Sec 11)

1	Rubber boot	6	Secondary cup seal
2	Circlip	7	Main cup seal and washer
3	Dished washer	8	Spring
4	Pushrod	9	Valve
5	Piston		

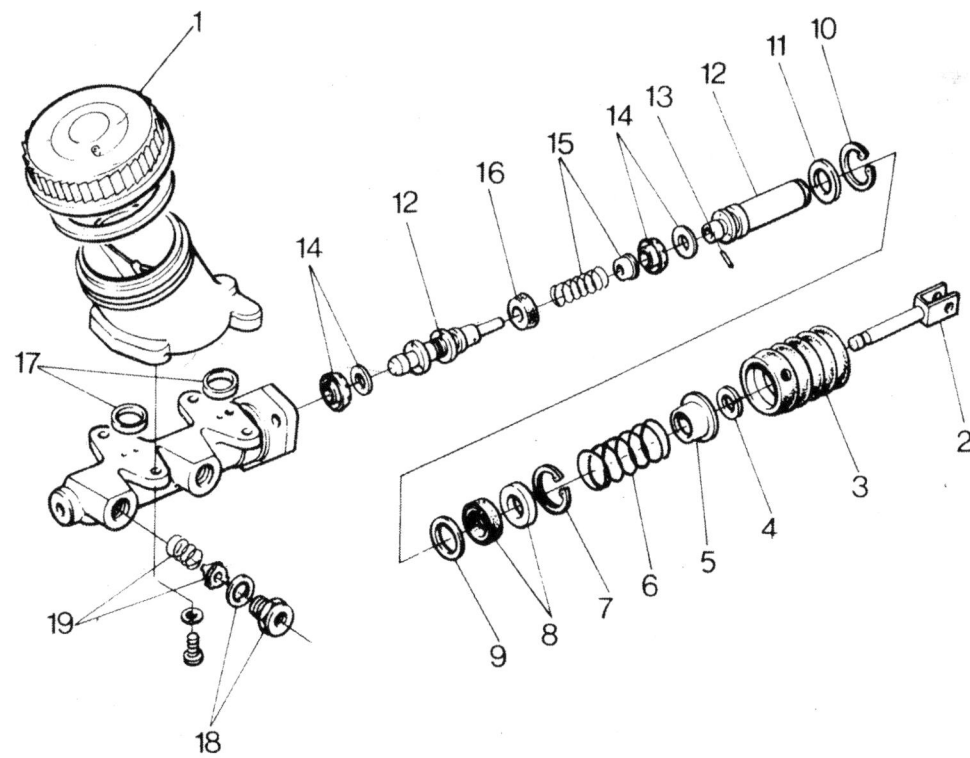

Fig. 9.10 Exploded view of the dual line brake master cylinder (Sec 12)

1	Filler cap	7	Circlip	12	Primary and secondary piston	16	Cup seal
2	Pushrod	8	Nylon guide bearing and seal	13	Roll pin	17	Sealing ring
3	Rubber boot	9	Plain washer	14	Cup seal and washer	18	Adaptor and copper washer
4	Spirolox ring	10	Inner circlip	15	Spring and retainer	19	Spring and trap valve
5	Retainer	11	Stop washer				
6	Spring						

12 Master cylinder (later dual circuit models) – removal, overhaul and refitting

1 Working with the bonnet lifted, disconnect the earth strap to the battery and then disconnect the coil and resistor leads. Unscrew the four pedal cover retaining screws and lift the cover away together with the coil.

2 Inside the pedal box, remove the split pin in the clevis pin securing the pushrod to the brake foot pedal and remove the clevis pin and washer.

3 Disconnect the pipe unions from the master cylinder, taking precautions to retain spilt fluid, then cover the open pipe line ends and the open apertures on the master cylinder to prevent dirt ingress.

4 Remove the nuts, bolts and washers securing the master cylinder to the pedal box and remove the unit from the car. Thoroughly clean the outside of it to prevent contamination during dismantling.

5 Drain the remaining fluid from the reservoir and refit the cap. Prise the rubber boot from the body of the master cylinder and remove it, together with the pushrod.

6 Place the tandem master cylinder, with the mouth of the bore uppermost, in a soft-jawed vice.

7 Compress the return spring and remove the Spirolox ring from its groove in the primary piston. Take extreme care not to distort the coils of the spring or damage the bore of the cylinder. Remove the retainer and spring.

8 Using a pair of long-nosed circlip pliers, remove the piston seal retaining circlip.

9 Gently move the piston up and down in the cylinder bore to free the nylon guide bearing and the cap seal. Remove the plain washer.

10 Once again using the long-nosed circlip pliers, remove the inner circlip.

11 Withdraw the primary and secondary piston assembly from the bore together with the stop washer. Remove the stop washer.

12 Compress the spring that separates the two pistons and take out the pin which retains the piston link.

13 Make a careful note of the position of the rubber cups by their moulded shape and then remove the cups and washers from the pistons.

14 Remove the four screws and lockwashers which secure the plastic reservoir to the master cylinder body and lift off the reservoir. Remove the two reservoir sealing rings.

15 Clean all the components thoroughly with hydraulic fluid or methylated spirit and dry them with a clean non-fluffy rag.

16 Match the new rubber seals, etc, in the repair kit with the original items so that you know what fits where and which way round it fits. Then discard all the old rubber items. Carefully examine all metal parts for signs of wear, damage or corrosion. In partiucular examine the bore of the master cylinder for scores, grooves or ridges, and if any are obvious renew the complete assembly as there is no effective remedy for this type of defect.

17 Before starting to reassemble, dip all the internal components in fresh brake fluid and assemble them wet. Remember that it is of the utmost importance to keep everything perfectly clean. Reassembly is the reverse of the dismantling sequence but note the following points:

(a) *Fit the piston washers and seals in the same positions noted during dismantling and make sure that each is properly bedded into its groove or location*

(b) *If necessary fit a new roll pin to the secondary piston retaining link*

(c) *Take every precaution to avoid damaging the cylinder bore and the seal lips during assembly*

18 When reassembled, wipe the unit clean and dry, then refit it to the car, reversing the removal sequence. Fill the reservoir with fresh brake fluid and bleed the system following the procedure described in Section 4 for dual circuit models.

13 Brake pressure failure warning switch – removal, inspection and refitting

1 The brake pressure failure warning switch is fitted between the two systems of those cars with dual circuit brakes, and is designed to illuminate a warning light if the pressure in one circuit fails. A shuttle valve in the switch is affected by the pressure in both circuits when operating normally, but if the pressure in one system fails the pressure in the other moves the shuttle valve to operate an electrical switch in the warning light circuit. Note that one circuit is inadequate for normal use, and driving with caution should be limited to getting the car to a convenient repair location, where the cause of the failure can be identified and rectified.

2 Following repair of the fault, the system will need bleeding and this should follow the procedure contained in Section 4, which also includes resetting of the warning switch, or pressure differential warning actuator as BL terms it. If it becomes necessary to renew the switch or remove it for investigation proceed as follows.

3 Thoroughly clean the switch, which is located at the ends of the pipes coming from the master cylinder, and clean the pipes and their unions. Remove the brake fluid reservoir filler cap and cover the filler neck with a piece of thin plastic film, then refit the filler, or alternatively if you can get a spare filler cap, seal off its breather hole and fit it instead of the normal cap. Don't on any account use such a cap for any purpose except servicing the system – a clear breather hole in the filler is essential for correct brake system functioning.

4 Disconnect the battery earth lead and then disconnect the electrical leads from the switch. Undo the unions of the five pipes and seal the ends of the pipes to prevent dirt ingress. Note which pipe connects to which union so that there can be no mistake when reconnecting them. Undo and remove the valve retaining bolt and

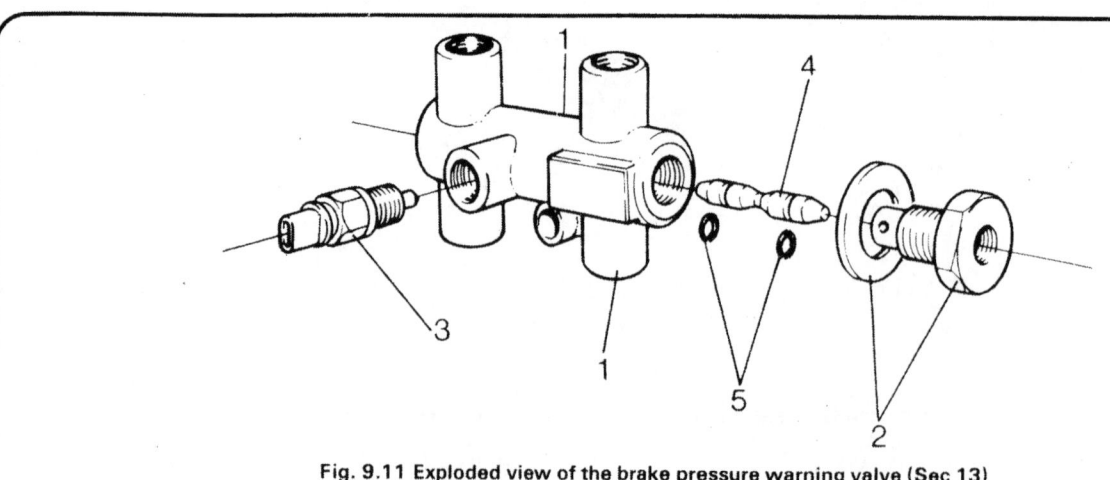

Fig. 9.11 Exploded view of the brake pressure warning valve (Sec 13)

1	*Valve body*	3 *Switch*
2	*End plug and copper*	4 *Shuttle valve piston*
	washer	5 *Piston seals*

remove the valve from the car, taking care that brake fluid does not drip onto the paintwork.

5   To dismantle, start by unscrewing the endplug and copper washer. The endplug also serves as the left-hand front brake pipe connection.

6   Next unscrew the nylon switch from the side of the pressure valve body.

7   Invert the pressure valve body and withdraw the shuttle valve from the bore.

8   Clean and inspect all the parts. In particular, look for signs of scoring within the bore of the valve body, and renew if these are found.

9   The seals of the shuttle valve and the copper washer of the endplug must be renewed.

10 Check the switch by reconnecting the wires and, with the ignition switched on, depress the switch plunger and check that the light is functioning. If it is not, then check the wiring and bulb of the warning light; if in order then the switch must be faulty and must be renewed.

11 Before reassembly, smear the bore and shuttle valve with clean hydraulic fluid, and refit the respective parts in the reverse order of removal. Ensure that the seals of the shuttle valve are fitted with the lips facing outwards and that they remain in their respective grooves during entry into the bore.

12 Refit the endplug and tighten to the specified torque, then fit the switch.

13 Wipe the assembly clean and dry, and refit it to the car. Reconnect following the removal procedure in reverse, taking care to refit each pipe to its correct connection and avoid getting dirt into the system.

14 Bleed the system following the procedure contained in Section 4, ensuring that the shuttle valve is centralised in the process.

14 Brake lines (flexible and rigid) – inspection, removal and refitting

Flexible hoses

1   Inspect the condition of the flexible hydraulic hoses leading from the chassis mounted metal pipes. If any are swollen, damaged, cut, or chafed, they must be renewed.

2   Unscrew the metal pipe union nut from its connection to the hose, and then holding the hexagon on the hose with a spanner, unscrew the attachment nut and washer. The chassis end of the hose can now be pulled from the chassis mounting bracket.

3   Disconnect the flexible hydraulic hose at the other end by unscrewing it from the brake cylinder or connector. Note when releasing the hose from a backplate, the chassis end must always be free first.

4   Refitting is a reversal of removal. The flexible hoses may be twisted no more than a quarter of a turn in either direction if it is necessary to provide a 'set', to ensure that they do not rub or chafe against any adjacent component. Check that they have adequate clearance when the car is on or off the jacks and when steering is fully applied in either direction.

5   Bleed the system on completion.

Rigid pipes

6   At regular intervals wipe the metal brake pipes clean and examine them for rust or damage caused by flying stones.

7   Examine the retaining clips and ensure that they retain the pipes securely without letting them rattle or vibrate.

8   Check that the pipes are not chafing against any adjacent components or part of the vehicle, and bend away to clear if they are, checking the extent of wear on the pipe. Renew the pipe if in any doubt.

9   Although pipes are plated when new, any section of pipe, particularly those more exposed to the elements, will become rusty with time. Brake pipes are available to the correct length and profile, ready fitted with unions from your BL agent. In addition they can be made to pattern by many motor factors and accessory shops. When installing the new pipes, the old pipes may be used as a guide to achieve the correct profile. Never overbend a pipe – it will crease and fracture.

10 On completion the hydraulic system will have to be bled.

15 Handbrake lever – removal, dismantling and refitting

1   If your car has a handbrake warning light fitted, first disconnect the battery earth cable. To improve access to the handbrake lever remove the front left-hand seat.

2   Unscrew the handbrake-to-mounting plate screws, and, if fitted, remove the wires from the handbrake warning switch.

3   Fold back the central tunnel floor covering and unscrew the setscrews retaining the mounting plate to the tunnel.

4   Twist the mounting plate through 180° and lift the handbrake lever from the tunnel.

5   Withdraw the split pin and remove the clevis pin and washer.

6   The handbrake lever and mounting plate may now be removed. If fitted, the handbrake warning switch can be removed by unscrewing the locknut from its retaining bracket.

7   The handbrake may now be dismantled for cleaning and inspection by unscrewing the cable lever retaining nut and washer, followed by the ratchet plate and spring washer.

8   Remove the split pin to withdraw the catch rod from the pawl. The pawl and flat washers can be released from its pivot by withdrawing its retaining split pin.

9   The catch rod may be withdrawn from the handbrake lever and the Mills pin retaining the press button can be drifted out if required; the catch rod spring and washer can then be removed from the handbrake lever.

10 Clean and renew parts as required, and prior to reassembly grease the pivot points. Always use new split pins and Mills pins.

11 Reassemble in the reverse order. When refitting the handbrake warning switch move the lever to the 'brake off' position, reconnect the battery earth lead and slacken the switch locknut. Turn the ignition on and adjust the switch so that the warning light is just extinguished. Tighten the locknut, apply the brake and check that the light comes on, then turn the ignition off.

12 Finally check that the handbrake operates the rear wheel brakes correctly, and if necessary adjust as explained in Section 3.

16 Handbrake cable – removal and refitting

1   Chock the front wheels securely, jack up the rear of the car and support it on stands or blocks.

2   Remove the handbrake lever, as described in Section 15.

3   Withdraw the split pin from the compensating lever clevis pin and remove the pin.

4   The cable adjustment nut must now be unscrewed and slid along the cable. Remove the threaded sleeve from the bracket and withdraw the cable from the compensator.

5   The cable front bracket nut can now be unscrewed and slid along the cable. Then remove the cable from the bracket and withdraw the cable.

6   Refit in the reverse order using new split pins; when fitting the cable rear fork ensure that its relieved faced is towards the compensator.

7   When refitting the handbrake lever, grease all of the pivot points and check the warning light switch adjustment (if fitted). Lubricate the nipple (photo) in the cable. Finally, check the handbrake adjustment, as described in Section 3.

17 Handbrake compensator lever (earlier models) – removal and refitting

1   On earlier models the handbrake cable operates a compensator mounted on the rear axle which equalises the handbrake application on the two rear brakes (photo). To remove and refit the compensator lever proceed as follows.

2   Chock the front wheels securely front and rear and jack the rear of the car up, supporting it firmly on stands or blocks. Release the handbrake. Clean off all loose dirt from the compensator.

3   Remove the split pin from the clevis pin which connects the handbrake cable to the compensating lever, and remove the clevis pin and washer.

4   Undo the rear nut on the cable adjuster and run it off the threads of the adjuster. Pull the cable forwards and slide it out of the mounting bracket.

5   Disconnect the two brake rods from the compensator by removing the split pins, two clevis pins and their felt pads.

6   Undo and remove the two nuts and bolts securing the com-

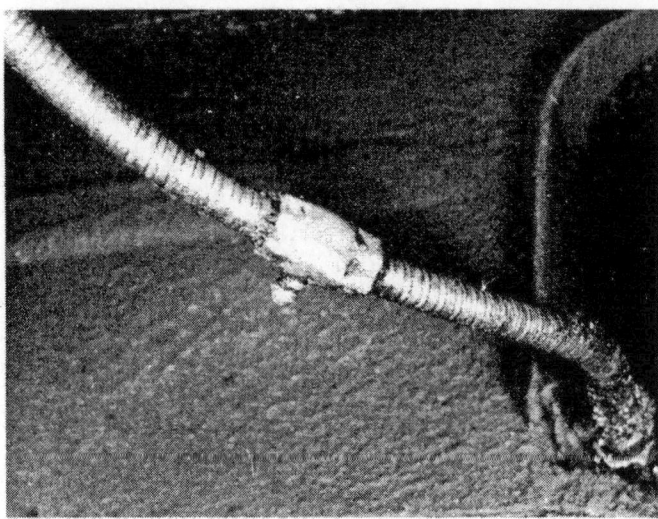

16.7 The handbrake cable grease nipple

17.1 The handbrake compensator unit located at the rear axle (earlier models)

pensator support bracket to the rear axle and remove the compensator and its bracket.

7 Unscrew the compensator balance lever and its carrier from the support bracket, and then unscrew the carrier from the balance lever, retrieving the felt washer from under the lever. Finally unscrew the grease nipple from the top of the balance lever.

8 Thoroughly clean all the components and inspect for wear and corrosion. Renew where necessary. Soak the felt pads in oil before reassembly.

9 Reassembly is basically the reverse of the dismantling sequence. When screwing the carrier into the balance lever, first fit the felt washer, screw the carrier home and then back it off a full turn, aligning its threaded hole (which fits onto the support bracket) in the same plane as the two arms to which the brake rods connect. Grease the assembly on completion and check that the compensator swivels freely before connecting the brake rods.

10 After reconnecting the handbrake cable, readjust the handbrake as described in Section 3.

---

18 Brake pedal – removal, refitting and adjustment

---

1 The brake pedal is removed in the same manner as the clutch pedal, described in Chapter 5.

2 On later models, the correct free movement of the brake pedal is $\frac{1}{8}$ in (3 mm), 'A' in Fig. 9.12.

3 If adjustment is required, loosen the stoplight switch locking nut and rotate the switch in the desired direction – clockwise to decrease, or anti-clockwise to increase, the free play. When correct adjustment is achieved, retighten the stoplight switch locknut.

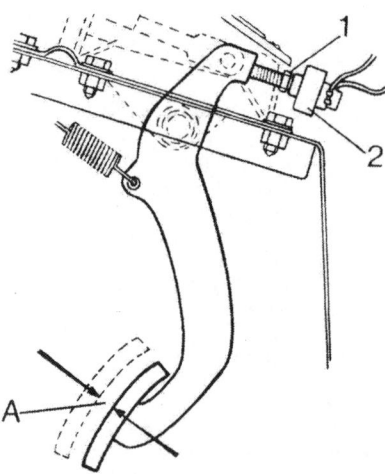

Fig. 9.12 Adjusting the brake pedal free play – later models (Sec 18)

1 *Switch locknut*	$A = \frac{1}{8}$ *in (3.2 mm)*
2 *Stoplight switch*	

19 Fault diagnosis – braking system

Symptom	Reason(s)
Pedal travels almost to floor before brakes operate	Brake fluid level too low Wheel cylinder or caliper leaking Master cylinder leaking (bubbles in master cylinder fluid) Brake flexible hose leaking Brake line fractured Brake system unions loose Linings 75% worn Drum brakes badly out of adjustment
Brake pedal feels springy	New linings not yet bedded-in Brake drums or discs badly worn or cracked Master cylinder securing nuts loose
Brake pedal feels spongy or soggy	Wheel cylinder or caliper leaking Master cylinder leaking (bubbles in master cylinder reservoir) Brake pipe line or flexible hose leaking Unions in brake system loose and leaking
Brakes uneven and pulling to one side	Linings and brake drums or discs contaminated with oil, grease, or hydraulic fluid Tyre pressures unequal Brake shoes or pads fitted incorrectly Different type of linings fitted at each wheel Anchorages for front or rear suspension loose Brake drums or discs badly worn, cracked or distorted
Brakes tend to bind, drag or lock-on	Brake shoes adjusted too tightly Handbrake cable over-tightened Master cylinder pushrod out of adjustment giving too little brake pedal free movement (early models only) Reservoir vent hole in cap blocked with dirt Master cylinder bypass port restricted Brakes seized in 'on' position Wheel cylinder seized in 'on' position Drum brake shoe pull-off springs broken, stretched or loose Drum brake shoe pull-off springs fitted wrong way round, omitted, or wrong type used

Chapter 10 Electrical system

Contents

Specifications

Sprite Mk I, II and III, MG Midget Mk I and II – 948 and 1098 cc

	Sprite Mk I	Sprite Mk II and III and Midget Mk I and II
Polarity	Positive earth	Positive earth
Battery		
Type:		
Home	Lucas BT7A	Lucas N9
Export	Lucas BTZ7A	Lucas NZ9
Voltage and capacity at 20 hour rate	12 volts, 43 amp hr	12 volts, 43 amp hr
Dynamo		
Type	Lucas C39 PV2	Lucas C40-1
Cut-in speed	1060 to 1200 rpm	1200 to 1400 rpm
Maximum output	13.5 volts, 19 amps	13.5 volts, 22 amps
Field resistance	6.1 ohms	6.0 ohms
Control box		
Type	Lucas RB106/1 or 106/2	Lucas RB106/2
Cut-in voltage	12.7 to 13.3 volts	12.7 to 13.3 volts
Drop-off voltage	8.5 to 11 volts	8.5 to 11 volts
Reverse current	3 to 5 amps	3 to 5 amps

Starter motor
Type .... Lucas M35 G/1 Four-brush   Lucas M35 G/1 Four-brush

Windscreen wiper motor
Type ....   Lucas DR2   Lucas DR3A
Normal running current ....   2.3 to 3.1 amps   2.3 to 3.1 amps
Armature resistance ....   0.34 to 0.41 ohms   0.28 to 0.35 ohms
Field resistance ....   12.8 to 14 ohms   8 to 9.5 ohms

Fuse unit
Type (2 live, 2 spare fuses) ....   Lucas SF6   Lucas 4FJ
Fuses ....   50 amp (AUX) and 35 amp   2 by 35 amps (AUX, IGN)

Bulbs
	Watts	**Watts**
Headlamps	50/40	60/45
Sidelamps	6	6
Tail/stoplamps	21/6	21/6
Front and rear flasher	21	21
Panel lamps	2.2	2.2
Courtesy lamp	6	6
Number plate lamp	6	6
Ignition warning lamp, oil pressure warning lamp, headlamp main beam warning lamp, direction indicator warning lamp	2.2	2.2

Sprite Mk IV and MG Midget Mk III – 1275 and 1500 cc
Polarity ....   Positive earth early cars; negative earth from Sprite Mk IV
HAN9-72041, and Midget Mk III GAN4-60460

Battery
Make/type ....   Lucas A9/AZ9 A11/AZ11
Capacity at 20 hr rate ....   A9/AZ9: 40 amp hr; A11/AZ11: 50 amp hr

Dynamo
Type ....   Lucas C40

Regulator
Make/type ....   Lucas RB106 and RB340
Brush spring tension ....   28 ozf (0.8 kgf)
Cut-in voltage ....   12.7 to 13.3 volts
Drop-off voltage ....   9.5 to 11.0 volts

Alternator (from Midget Mk III, car number GAN5-105501, and all 1500 models)
Type ....   Lucas 16 ACR
New brush length ....   0.5 in (12.6 mm)
Minimum brush length ....   0.2 in (0.5 mm) protruding from brush box
Output at 14 volts ....   34 amps @ 6000 alternator rpm
Current flow at 12 volts ....   3 amps

Starter
Make/type ....   Lucas M34J, M35G or M35J
Brush spring tension ....   28 ozf (0.8 kgf)
Minimum brush length .... $\frac{3}{8}$ in (9.5 mm)
Minimum commutator thickness ....   0.08 in (2.05 mm)
Lock torque ....   7 lbf ft (0.97 kgf m) at 250 to 375 amps
Light running current ....   65 amps at 8000 to 10 000 rpm
Maximum armature endfloat ....   0.010 in (0.25 mm)
Torque at 1000 rpm ....   4.4 lbf ft (0.61 kgf m) at 260 to 275 amps

Windscreen wiper motor
Type ....   Lucas 14W
Reversing current with rack disconnected ....   1.5 amp
Wiper speed ....   46 to 52 rpm (low); 60 to 70 rpm (high)
Armature endfloat ....   0.004 to 0.008 in (0.102 to 0.2 mm)
Minimum brush length .... $\frac{3}{16}$ in (4.7 mm)

Fusebox
Make/type ....   Lucas 7FJ
Fuse value ....   17 amp continuous (35 amp blow)

Bulbs
	Watts
Sidelight (with flasher)	5/21
Stop/tail lamp	5/21
Reversing lamp	18

Bulbs

	Watts
Number plate lamp	6
Direction indicator lamp	21
Front and rear side marker lamp	5
Ignition warning lamp	2
Main beam warning lamp	2
Direction indicator warning lamp	2
Brake warning lamp	1.5
EGR valve warning lamp	2
Catalyst warning lamp	2
Panel lamp	2.2
Cigar lighter illumination lamp	2.2
Luggage compartment lamp	6
Courtesy lamp	6
Seatbelt warning lamp	2
Switch illumination lamp	2
Heater rotary control illumination lamp	2
Headlamp sealed beam units:	
UK	50/40
USA	60/50

Torque wrench settings

	lbf ft	kgf m
Alternator pulley nut	25	3.5
Starter motor retaining nuts	34	4.7
Windscreen wiper motor (14W) yoke bolts	1.7	0.24
Steering column upper fixing bolts	12 to 17	1.7 to 2.3
Steering column pinch bolt	9 to 12	1.3 to 1.7

1 General description

All models are fitted with a 12 volt electrical system and, although very early models have a positive earth supply, since car numbers GAN4-60460 and HAN9-72041 a conventional negative earth system has been incorporated.

The electrical system consists of a 12 volt battery, an electrical generator, a starter motor and a wide range of electrical components varying with specific models.

The battery supplies a steady source of current for the starting, ignition, lighting and other electrical circuits and provides a reserve of electricity when the current consumed by the electrical system exceeds that produced by the generator.

The generator on early models was a two-brush dynamo working in conjunction with a voltage regulator and cut-out to control output. On later models an alternator is fitted and this has an integral control circuit. The generator, irrespective of type, is driven by the cooling fan drivebelt and its mounting is designed to provide adjustment for the belt tension. Certain precautions are essential where an alternator is fitted and reference should be made to Section 14.

When fitting electrical accessories to cars with a negative earth system it is important, if they contain silicon diodes or transistors, that they are connected correctly, otherwise serious damage may be caused to the accessory concerned. Equipment such as radios, tape recorders, electronic clocks, tachometers and so on must be checked for correct polarity.

It is important that the battery earth lead is always disconnected if the battery is to be boost charged or if any body repairs are to be done using electric arc welding equipment. Serious damage can be caused to delicate instruments, especially those containing semiconductors. Note that, on cars with an alternator fitted, the battery should never be disconnected while the engine is running.

2 Battery – removal and refitting

1   The earthed battery terminal should always be removed first. Therefore on the later negative earth cars remove the negative lead before the positive, and refit the negative lead last. Disconnect the leads from the battery terminals posts by slackening the clamp retaining nuts and bolts, or by unscrewing the terminal cap retaining screws if these are fitted, and then removing the leads from the terminal posts.
2   Remove the battery clamp holding the battery and then carefully lift the battery out of its location. Keep the battery level to avoid spilling electrolyte.
3   Refitting a battery is the reverse of the removal procedure. Before refitting the battery leads make sure that they, and the battery terminal posts, are clean and smear them with petroleum jelly to prevent corrosion. Don't use ordinary car grease, which is unsuitable. Ensure that the terminal attachments are tight on assembly.

3 Battery – maintenance and inspection

1   Normal weekly battery maintenance consists of checking the electrolyte level of each cell to ensure that the separators are covered by $\frac{1}{4}$ in (6.5 mm) of electrolyte. If the level has fallen, top up the battery with distilled water only. Do not overfill. If the battery is overfilled or any electrolyte spilled, immediately wipe away the excess as electrolyte attacks and corrodes most metal it comes into contact with very rapidly.
2   There is a wide range of batteries suitable for these cars, but if your battery is of the Lucas Pacemaker design, a special topping up procedure is necessary as follows.
3   The electrolyte levels are visible through the translucent battery case or they may be checked by fully raising the vent cover and tilting it to one side. The level in each cell must be kept such that the separator plates are just covered. To avoid flooding, the battery must not be topped up within half an hour of it having been charged from any source other than the car's own generator.
4   To top up the levels in each cell, raise the vent cover and pour distilled water into the trough until all the rectangular filling tubes are full and the bottom of the trough is just covered. Wipe the cover seating grooves dry and press the cover firmly into position. The correct quantity of distilled water will automatically be distributed to each cell.
5   The vent cover must be kept closed at all times, except when being topped up, to avoid the possibility of flooding.
6   Another type of battery has a removable, one-piece filler cover which should be removed, and the separator plates examined to see that they are covered with electrolyte. To top up this type of battery, proceed as follows.
7   Make sure that all the filling valves are raised.
8   Pour distilled water into the filling trough until all the valves and the connecting trough are full.
9   Press the cover firmly into position – the electrolyte level should not be above the high marks, if these exist on the walls of the battery case.
10 As well as keeping the terminals clean and covered with petroleum jelly, the top of the battery, and especially the top of the cells, should be kept clean and dry. This helps prevent corrosion and ensures that the battery does not become partially discharged by leakage through dampness and dirt.
11 Once every three months remove the battery and inspect the

battery securing bolts, the battery clamp plate, tray, and battery leads for corrosion (white fluffy deposits on the metal which are brittle to touch). If any corrosion is found, clean off the deposits with ammonia, and paint over the clean metal with an anti-rust/anti-acid paint. At the same time inspect the battery case for cracks. If a crack is found, clean and plug it with one of the proprietary compounds marketed for this purpose. If leakage through the crack has been excessive then it will be necessary to refill the appropriate cell with fresh electrolyte as detailed later. Cracks are frequently caused to the top of the battery case by pouring in distilled water in the middle of winter *after* instead of *before* a run. This gives the water no chance to mix with the electrolyte and so the former freezes and splits the battery case.

12 If topping up the battery becomes excessive and the case has been inspected for cracks that could cause leakage, but none are found, the battery is being over-charged and the voltage regulator (on early models with a dynamo circuit) or the alternator (on later models) will have to be tested by a specialist or a dealer.

13 With the battery on the bench at the three monthly interval check, measure its specific gravity with a hydrometer to determine its state of charge and condition of the electrolyte. There should be very little variation between the different cells and if a variation in excess of 0.025 is present it will be due to either:

(a) *Loss of electrolyte from the battery at some time caused by spillage or a leak resulting in a drop in the specific gravity of the electrolyte, when the deficiency was replaced with distilled water instead of fresh electrolyte, or*

(b) *An internal short circuit caused by buckling of the plates or a similar malady pointing to the likelihood of total battery failure in the near future*

14 The specific gravity of the electrolyte for fully charged and fully discharged conditions at the electrolyte temperature indicated, is listed below.

Fully discharged	Electrolyte temperature	Fully charged
1.098	38°C (100°F)	1.268
1.102	32°C (90°F)	1.272
1.106	27°C (80°F)	1.276
1.110	21°C (70°F)	1.280
1.114	16°C (60°F)	1.284
1.118	10°C (50°F)	1.288
1.122	4°C (40°F)	1.292
1.126	-1.5°C (30°F)	1.296

Note that distilled water may not be easy to get, but it is quite in order to use purified water obtainable from chemists, or the special de-ionised water made for batteries which is obtainable at accessory shops. On no account should you use tap water, which can rapidly shorten the life of a battery.

4 Battery – electrolyte replenishment

1 If the battery is in a fully charged state and one of the cells maintains a specific gravity reading which is 0.025 or more lower than the others, and a check of each cell has been made with a voltage meter to check for short circuits (a four to seven second test should give a steady reading of between 1.2 and 1.8 volts), then it is likely that electrolyte has been lost from the cell with the low reading at some time.

2 Top up the cell with a solution of 1 part sulphuric acid to 2.5 parts of distilled or purified water. If the cell is already fully topped up, draw some electrolyte out of it with a pipette.

3 When mixing the sulphuric acid and water *never add water to sulphuric acid* – always pour the acid slowly onto the water in a glass container. *If water is added to sulphuric acid it will explode.* Continue to top up the cell with the freshly made electrolyte and then recharge the battery and check the hydrometer readings.

5 Battery – charging

1 In winter time when heavy demand is placed upon the battery, such as when starting from cold, and much electrical equipment is continually in use, it is a good idea to occasionally have the battery fully charged from an external source at the rate of 3.5 to 4 amps.

2 Continue to charge the battery at this rate until no further rise in specific gravity is noted over a four hour period. Alternatively, a trickle charger charging at a rate of 1.5 amps, can be safely used overnight.

3 Specially rapid 'boost' charges which are claimed to restore the power of the battery in 1 to 2 hours are most dangerous, unless they are thermostatically controlled, as they can cause serious damage to the battery plates through overheating. While charging the battery, note that the temperature of the electrolyte should never exceed 100°F (37.8°C).

6 Generator drivebelt – tension adjustment

1 The drivebelt (fanbelt) should be tight enough to ensure no slip between the belt and the generator pulley. If a shrieking noise comes from the engine when the unit is accelerated rapidly, then it is likely that it is the fanbelt slipping. On the other hand, the belt must not be too taut or the bearings will wear rapidly and cause generator failure or bearing seizure. Ideally $\frac{1}{2}$ in (12 mm) of total free movement should be available on the belt midway along its longest leg between pulleys.

2 The procedure for adjusting the belt tension is contained in Chapter 2.

7 Dynamo – routine maintenance

1 Routine maintenance on the dynamo fitted to early cars is limited to lubrication at appropriate intervals – see the Routine Maintenance Section at the start of this manual.

2 Lubrication of early model Lucas C39PV2 dynamos consists of unscrewing the lubricator cap from the end bracket, removing the spring felt pad from the cap, half-filling the cap with high melting point grease, refitting the spring and felt pad in the cap, and screwing home the cap to the dynamo.

3 Lubrication on the C40-1 dynamo consists of inserting three drops of engine oil in the small oil hole in the centre of the commutator end bracket. This lubricates the rear bearing. The front bearing is pre-packed with grease and requires no attention.

8 Dynamo – testing in position

1 If, when the engine running, no charge comes from the dynamo, or the charge is very low, first check that the fanbelt is in place and is not slipping.

2 Then check that the leads from the control box to the dynamo are firmly attached and that one has not come loose from its terminal. The lead from the 'D' terminal on the dynamo should be connected to the 'D' terminal on the control box, and similarly the 'F' terminals on the dynamo and control box should also be connected together.

3 Disconnect the leads from terminals 'D' and 'F' on the dynamo and then join the terminals together with a short length of wire. Attach to the centre of this length of wire the negative clip of a 0 to 20 volts

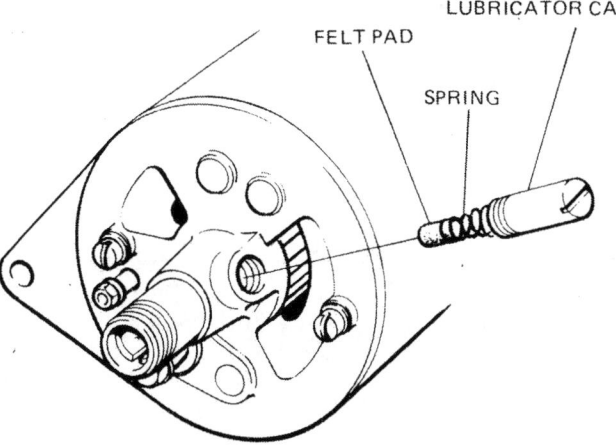

Fig. 10.1 Early type dynamo showing rear bearing with lubricator cap (Sec 7)

voltmeter and run the other clip to earth. Start the engine and allow it to idle at approximately 750 rpm. At this speed the dynamo should give a reading of about 15 volts on the voltmeter. There is no point in raising the engine speed above a fast idle as the reading will then be inaccurate.

4   If no reading is recorded, then check the brushes and brush connections. If a very low reading of approximately 1 volt is observed then the field winding may be suspect. On early dynamos it was possible to remove the dynamo cover band and check the dynamo and brushes in position. With the Lucas C40-1 windowless yoke dynamo, fitted to later models, the dynamo has to be removed and dismantled before the brushes and commutator can be attended to.

5   If the voltmeter shows a good reading, then with the temporary link still in position connect both leads from the control box to 'D' and 'F' on the dynamo ('D' to 'D' and 'F' to 'F'). Release the lead from the 'D' terminal at the control box end and clip one lead from the voltmeter to the end of the cable, and the other lead to a good earth. With the engine running at the same speed as previously, an identical voltage to that recorded at the dynamo should be noted on the voltmeter. If no voltage is recorded then there is a break in the wire. If the voltage is the same as recorded at the dynamo then check the 'F' lead in similar fashion. If both readings are the same as at the dynamo then it will be necessary to test the control box.

9 Dynamo – removal and refitting

1   Slacken the two dynamo retaining bolts, and the nut on the sliding link, and move the dynamo in towards the engine so that the fanbelt can be removed.

2   Disconnect the two leads from the dynamo terminals. **Note**: *If the*

9.4 The dynamo installed, awaiting the drivebelt; note slotted adjusting link

ignition coil is mounted on top of the dynamo, remove the high tension wire from the centre of the coil by unscrewing the knurled nut, and unscrew the nuts holding the two low tension wires in place.

3   Remove the nut from the sliding link bolt, and remove the two upper bolts. The dynamo is then free to be lifted away from the engine.

4   Refitting is a reversal of the above procedure. Do not finally tighten the retaining bolts and the nut on the sliding link (photo) until the fanbelt has been tensioned correctly (see Chapter 2).

5   If it is wished to fit a replacement dynamo, check the identification marks which will be found on the yoke, and quote these to your local BL or Lucas agent prior to handing the dynamo in, to ensure that the correct replacement is obtained.

10 Dynamo – dismantling and reassembly

1   Remove the dynamo pulley after unscrewing the nut and lock-washer which retains it to the armature shaft. (It is not necessary to do this if only the brushes and commutator are to be examined).

2   From the commutator end bracket remove the nuts, spring, and flat washers from the field terminal post.

3   Unscrew the two through-bolts and remove them together with their spring washers.

4   Take off the commutator end bracket, and remove the driving end bracket complete with the armature.

5   Lift the brush springs and draw the brushes out of the brush holders. Unscrew the screws and lockwashers holding the brush leads to the commutator end bracket.

6   The bearing needs not be removed, or the armature shaft separated from the drive end bracket unless the bearings or the armature are to be renewed. If it is wished to remove the armature shaft from the drive end bracket and bearing then the bearing retaining plate must be supported securely, and with the Woodruff key removed, the shaft pressed out of the end bracket.

7   When a new armature is fitted or the old one refitted, it is most important that the inner journal of the ball bearing is supported by a steel tube of suitable diameter so that no undue strain is placed on the bearing as the armature shaft is pressed home.

8   Reassembly is a straight reversal of the above procedure. A point worth noting is that when fitting the commutator end plate with brushes attached, it is far easier to slip the brushes over the commutator if the brushes are raised in their holders and held in this position by the pressure of the springs resting against their flanks rather than on their heads. Readjust the springs to their proper position after installation is completed.

11 Dynamo – inspection and repair

1   Check the brushes for wear. Any brush on early C39 type dynamos less than $\frac{11}{32}$ in (8.7 mm) long or $\frac{9}{32}$ in (7 mm) long on the C40 unit, must be renewed.

2   Check that the brushes move freely and easily in their holders by removing the retaining springs and then pulling gently on the wire brush leads. If either of the brushes tend to stick in its holder, clean the brush with a petrol moistened rag, and if still stiff, lightly polish the sides of the brush with a very fine file until it moves quite freely and easily in its holder.

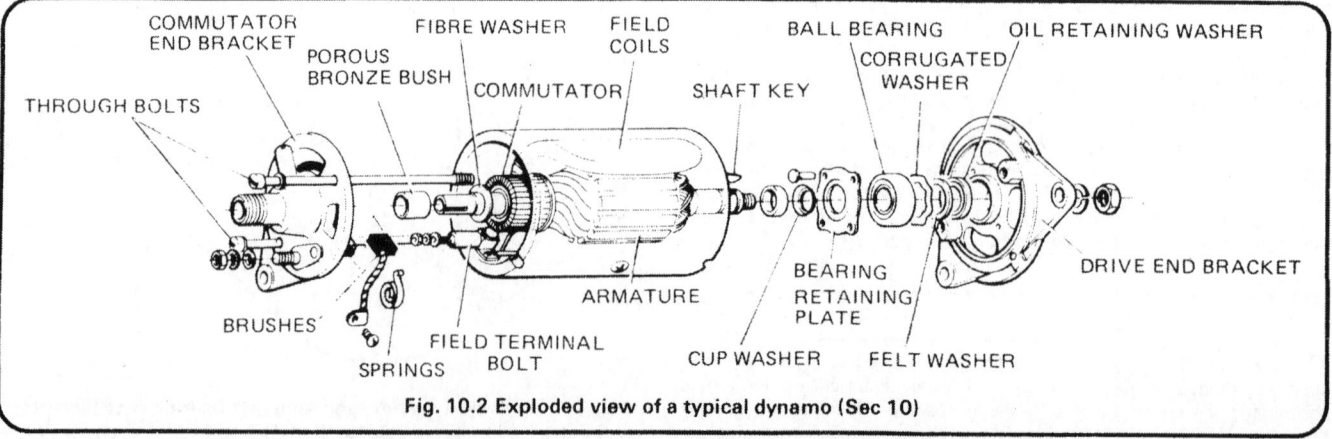

Fig. 10.2 Exploded view of a typical dynamo (Sec 10)

3   If the brushes are only slightly worn and are to be used again, then ensure that they are placed in the same holders from which they were removed.

4   Check the tension of the brush springs with a spring balance. The torsion of the springs when new was 20 to 25 oz (567 to 709 g) on the C39 dynamo and the springs should be renewed if the tension falls below 15 oz (425 g). On the C40 unit the tension, new, was 30 oz (850 g) and renewal is necessary when it falls to 13 oz (369 g) or below.

5   Check the condition of the commutator. If the surface is dirty or blackened, clean it with a petrol dampened rag. If the commutator is in good condition, the surface will be smooth and quite free from pits or burnt areas, and the insulated segments clearly defined.

6   If, after the commutator has been cleaned, pits and burnt spots are still present, then wrap a strip of glasspaper, not emery cloth, round the commutator and rotate the armature to clean the segments.

7   In extreme cases of wear the commutator can be mounted in a lathe and, with the lathe turning at high speed, a very fine cut may be taken off the commutator. Then polish the commutator with glasspaper. If the commutator has worn so that the insulators between the segments are level with the top of the segments, then undercut the insulators to a depth of $\frac{1}{32}$ in (0.8 mm). The best tool to use for this purpose is half a hacksaw blade ground to the thickness of the insulators, and with the handle end of the blade covered in insulating tape to make it comfortable to hold.

8   Check the armature for open or short circuited windings. It is a good indication of an open circuit armature when the commutator segments are burnt. If the armature has short circuited, the commutator segments will be very badly burnt, and the overheated armature windings badly discoloured. If open or short circuits are suspected then test by substituting the suspect armature for a new one.

9   Check the resistance of the field coils. To do this, connect an ohmmeter between the field terminal and the yoke and note the reading on the ohmmeter, which should be about 6 ohms. If the ohmmeter reading is infinity, this indicates an open circuit in the field winding. If the ohmmeter reading is below 5 ohms this indicates that one of the field coils is faulty and must be renewed.

10   Field coil renewal involves the use of a wheel operated screwdriver, a soldering iron, caulking and riveting and this operation is considered to be beyond the scope of most owners. Therefore, if the field coils are at fault, either purchase a rebuilt dynamo, or take the casing to a reputable electrical engineering works for new field coils to be fitted.

12 Dynamo bearings – inspection, removal and refitting

1   With the dynamo partially stripped down, check the condition of the bearings. They must be renewed when wear has reached such a state that they allow visible side movement of the armature shaft. A bush bearing is fitted to the commutator end bracket and a ball bearing to the drive end bracket. To renew the bush bearing proceed as follows:

2   With a suitable extractor pull out the old bush from the commutator end bracket. Alternatively, screw a suitable tap into the bush and pull out the bush together with the tap. **Note:** *When fitting the new bush bearing, as it is of the porous bronze type, it is essential that it is allowed to stand in engine oil for at least 24 hours before fitment.*

3   Carefully fit the new bush into the endplate, pressing it in until the end of the bearing is flush with the inner side of the endplate. If available, press the bush in with a smooth shouldered mandrel the same diameter as the armature shaft. To renew the ball bearing fitted to the drive end bracket, remove the armature from the end bracket as detailed in Section 10, and then proceed as follows.

4   Drill out the rivets which hold the bearing retainer plate to the end bracket and lift off the plate.

5   Press out the bearing from the end bracket and remove the corrugated washer, felt washer, and oil retaining washer from the bearing housing.

6   Thoroughly clean the bearing housing, and the new bearing, and pack with high melting-point grease.

7   Place the oil retaining washer, felt washer, and corrugated washer, in that order, in the end bracket bearing housing, and then press in the new bearing.

8   Refit the plate and fit new rivets, opening out the rivet ends to hold the plate securely in position. (**Note:** *On the C40 dynamo the rivets are fitted from the outer face of the end bracket*).

13 Alternator – general description

The Lucas 16 ACR series alternator is a standard fitment on all later models. The main advantage of the alternator lies in its ability to provide a high charge at slow engine revolutions. Driving slowly in heavy traffic with a dynamo usually means no charge is reaching the battery. In similar conditions even with the wipers, heater, lights and perhaps radio switched on, an alternator will ensure a charge reaches the battery.

An important feature of the alternator is a built-in output control regulator, based on 'thick film' hybrid integrated micro-circuit technique, which results in this alternator being a self-contained generating and control unit.

The system provides for direct connection of a charge light, and eliminates the need for a field switching relay and warning light control unit, necessary with former systems.

The alternator is of the rotating field ventilated design and comprises principally, a laminated stator on which is wound a star connected three-phase output winding, a twelve pole rotor carrying the field windings (each end of the rotor shaft runs in ball race bearings which are lubricated for life), natural finish aluminium die cast end brackets incorporating the mounting lugs, a rectifier pack for converting the AC output of the machine to DC for battery charging, and an output control regulator.

The rotor is belt driven from the engine through a pulley keyed to the rotor shaft. A pressed steel fan adjacent to the pulley draws cooling air through the machine. This fan forms an integral part of the alternator specification. It has been designed to provide adequate air flow with a minimum of noise, and to withstand the high stresses associated with maximum speed. Rotation is clockwise viewed on the drive end. Maximum continuous rotor speed is 12 500 rpm.

Rectification of alternator output is achieved by six silicon diodes housed in a rectifier pack and connected as a three-phase full-wave bridge. The rectifier pack is attached to the outer face of the slip ring end bracket and also contains three field diodes. At normal operating speeds, rectified current from the stator output windings flows through these diodes to provide self-excitation of the rotor field, via brushes bearing on face type slip rings.

The slip rings are carried on a small diameter moulded drum attached to the rotor shaft outboard of the rotor, and the outer ring has a mean diameter of $\frac{3}{4}$ inch (19.1 mm). By keeping the mean diameter of the slip rings to a minimum, relative speeds between brushes and rings, and hence wear, are also minimal. The slip rings are connected to the rotor field windings by wires carried in grooves in the rotor shaft.

The brush gear is housed in a moulding screwed to the outside of the slip ring end bracket. This moulding thus encloses the slip ring and brush gear assembly, and, together with the shielded bearing, protects the assembly against the entry of dust and moisture.

The regulator is set during manufacture and requires no further attention. Briefly the 'thick film' regulator comprises resistors and conductors screen printed onto a 1 inch square alumina substrate. Mounted on the substrate are Lucas semi-conductors consisting of three transistors, a voltage reference diode and a field recirculation diode, and also two capacitors. The internal connections between these components and the substrate are made by Lucas patented connectors. The whole assembly is $\frac{1}{16}$ inch (1.5 mm) thick, and is housed in a recess in an aluminium heat sink, which is attached to the slip ring end bracket. Complete hermetic sealing is achieved by a silicone rubber encapsulant to provide environmental protection.

Electrical connections to external circuits are brought out to Lucas connector blades, these being grouped to accept a moulded connector socket which ensures correct connections.

14 Alternator – special precautions

1   Take extreme care when making circuit connections to a vehicle fitted with an alternator and observe the following. When making connections to the alternator from a battery always match correct polarity. Before using electric-arc welding equipment to repair any part of the vehicle, disconnect the connector from the alternator and

disconnect the positive battery terminal. Never start the car with a battery charger connected. Always disconnect both battery leads before using a main charger.

2   When connecting another battery to boost your own to start the car, if you've got a flat battery, observe the following precautions:

(a)   Check that the booster battery is 12V and that the connecting cables are capable of carrying the high starting current

(b)   Connect the cables to the booster battery first, ensuring red positive (+ve) to positive and green negative (-ve) to negative

(c)   Once started, reduce engine speed to below 1000 rpm before disconnecting the booster battery and never disconnect your own car's battery while the engine is running.

15 Alternator – routine maintenance

1   In service, a minimum amount of maintenance is required, the only items subject to wear being the brushes and bearings.
2   The brushes should be examined after 60 000 miles (100 000 km) and renewed if necessary; refer to Section 17.
3   The bearings are pre-packed with grease for life and should not require any further attention.

16 Alternator – removal and refitting

1   To remove the alternator, first disconnect the battery and then release the spring clip and remove the multi-connector plug from the alternator end cover (photo).
2   On models with an emission control air pump, remove the nut and bolt securing the top end of the alternator fan guard and which is located in the adjusting link, and then remove the fan guard bottom securing nut and washer to permit removal of the fan guard. On other models remove the adjusting link nut and bolt.
3   On all models slacken the pivot bolt and nut below the alternator, swing the alternator in towards the engine and remove the drivebelt from the alternator pulley.
4   Where an air pump is fitted, slacken the bolt securing the pump mounting bracket to the engine front mounting plate, and also slacken the bolt securing the pump to the pump mounting bracket. Remove the bolt securing the alternatior to the pump mounting bracket and remove the alternator from the car.
5   On other models remove the pivot bolt and spacer (photo) and remove the alternator from the car.
6   If another alternator is going to be fitted, the pulley and fan will have to be transferred from the old alternator. Hold the pulley in a soft-jawed vice and remove the pulley retaining nut. Withdraw the fan, pulley and key from the alternator rotor shaft.
7   Before fitting a replacement alternator fit the key, fan and pulley followed by the retaining nut and tighten the nut to its specified torque.
8   Refitting an alternator is the reverse of the removal procedure. Before tightening the attachment bolts and nuts, refer to Chapter 2 for the procedure for adjusting the drivebelt tension (photo).

17 Alternator – overhaul

1   Due to the need for special testing equipment, and the possibility of damage being caused to the alternator diodes if incorrect testing methods are adopted, it is recommended that overhaul be limited to the renewal of the brushes if they have worn below their specified limit. Where other faults occur, an exchange unit should be obtained.
2   With the alternator removed from the car, withdraw the end cover (two screws).
3   Record the wiring colours and sequence to the rectifier spade terminals and disconnect the lead.
4   Remove the screw which retains the surge protection diode to the end bracket.
5   Remove the brush box (two screws) and the regulator (one screw) from the end bracket. On later models the regulator is integral with the brush gear.
6   If the slip rings are burned or discoloured, polish them with very fine grade glasspaper (not emery).
7   Remove the brushes, noting the leaf spring which is fitted at the side of the inner brush.

16.1 Removing the multi-connector plug from the alternator

16.5 Removing the alternator and retrieving the pivot bolt spacer

16.8 Check the drivebelt tension in the middle of its longest run between pulleys

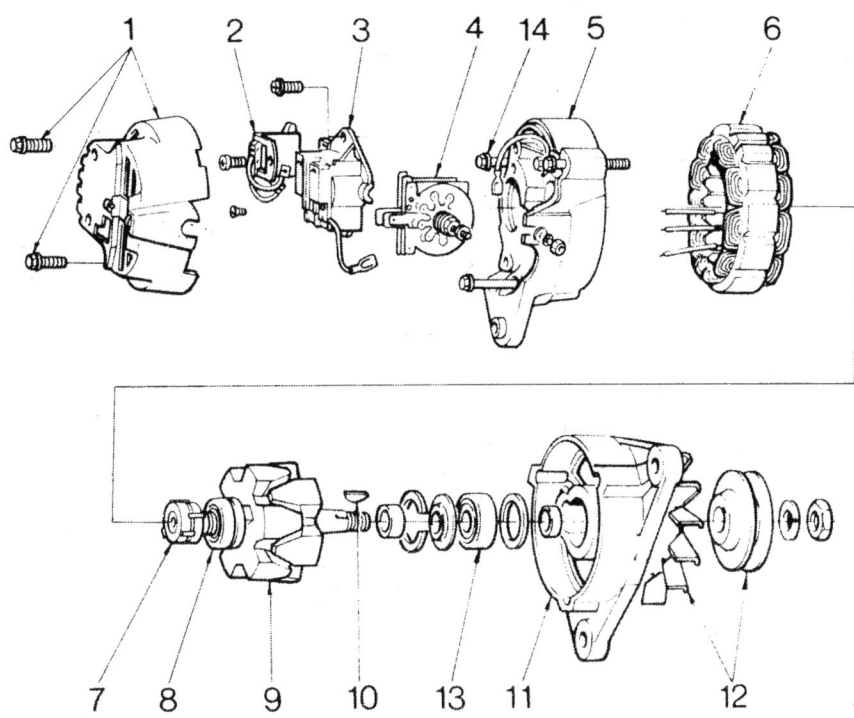

Fig. 10.3 Exploded view of the alternator (Sec 17)

1 Moulded cover and screws
2 Regulator
3 Brush box
4 Rectifier
5 Slip ring end bracket
6 Stator
7 Slip ring
8 Slip ring end bearing
9 Rotor
10 Key
11 Drive end bracket
12 Fan and pulley
13 Drive end bearing
14 Through-bolt

8   Reassembly is a reversal of dismantling, but make quite sure that the internal terminal connections are correctly made to the regulator.

18 Starter motor – general description

On early models, the starter motor is mounted on the right-hand lower side of the engine endplate (on later models it is on the left), and is held in position by two bolts which also clamp the bellhousing flange. The motor is of the four field coil, four pole piece type, and utilises four spring-loaded commutator brushes. Two of these brushes are earthed, and the other two are insulated and attached to the field coil ends.

Later starter motors, type M35J, have a different brush layout and shape. On this type the fitting of new brushes requires their tags to be soldered to the field winding leads and the endplate post.

19 Starter motor – testing on engine

1   If the starter motor fails to operate then check the condition of the battery by turning on the headlamps. If they glow brightly for several seconds and then gradually dim, the battery is in an unchanged condition.
2   If the headlamps glow brightly and it is obvious that the battery is in good condition, then check the tightness of the battery wiring connections (and in particular the earth lead from the battery terminal to its connection on the bodyframe). Check the tightness of the connections at the relay switch and at the starter motor. Check the wiring with a voltmeter for breaks or shorts.
3   If the wiring is in order, then check the starter motor switch. If it is working the starter motor will be heard to 'click' as it tries to rotate. Alternatively, check it with a voltmeter.
4   If the battery is fully charged, the wiring in order, and the switch working and the starter motor fails to operate, then it will have to be removed from the car for examination. Before this is done, however, ensure that the starter pinion has not jammed in mesh with the flywheel. Check by turning the square end of armature shaft with a

spanner. This will free the pinion if it is stuck in engagement with the flywheel teeth.

20 Starter motor – removal and refitting

1   Disconnect the battery earth lead and apply the handbrake.
2   Depending on your model, some equipment may need removing to improve access to the starter motor. For example, you may need to remove the air vent hose, and also the fuel pump if you have an engine driven pump (see Chapter 3 for details).
3   When you can get to the starter, undo and remove the nut and washer securing the electrical cable to the starter motor and move the cable out of the way.
4   Remove the two nuts and washers retaining the starter motor to the engine and withdraw the motor from the bolts (photo). Retrieve the shim and adaptor noting the sequence in which they are fitted.
5   Refitting a starter motor is the reverse of the removal procedure, but make sure that, when the motor is being fitted, the terminal for the electrical cable is uppermost. Tighten the retaining nuts to their specified torque and finally, refit any components you had to remove.

21 Starter motor – dismantling, inspection and reassembly

1   Before commencing overhaul of a defective starter motor, make sure that spare parts are available and enquire as to their price. The time and cost of reconditioning an old motor may compare unfavourably with the cost of an exchange starter motor, especially if this has a guarantee.
2   Clean off all external dirt from the motor before taking it to a clean work area. The following procedures relate to the Lucas M35J inertia type of starter motor, which is fitted to the vast majority of these models now on the road. However, if you do happen to have the earlier motor, you should have little problem adapting the procedures to your motor, as they are similar in many respects.
3   Undo the two screws in the drive end bracket, remove the screws

20.4 Removing the starter motor

and spring washers, and then withdraw the drive end bracket together with the armature and drive. Take the thrust washer off the armature shaft at its commutator end and put it in a safe place.

4　Undo and remove the four screws in the commutator end bracket and remove the bracket from the yoke (the main body part). As you do this, extract the two field brushes (which are connected to the field winding in the yoke) from the brush holder so that you can then separate the end bracket from the yoke.

5　To dismantle the Bendix drive assembly on the armature shaft, a special spring compressor tool is necessary and, unless you hire or borrow the tool, it should be safer not to attempt dismantling it yourself, but to take the shaft to a garage or workshop with a press to have the job done. If you have the tool, fit it to the spring so that you can get the circlip on the end of the shaft when the spring is compressed. With the spring compressed, remove the circlip and release the spring compression. Slide the components off the shaft taking careful note of their assembly sequence and orientation. Note that early starter motors have a split-pinned nut on the end of the shaft in place of the circlip. With the drive assembly removed, the drive end bracket can be slid off the shaft.

6　First check the armature shaft for straightness. A rough method is to roll the armature on a smooth flat surface and look for wobble at the drive end of the shaft. If doubt exists, mount the armature in two V-supports bearing on the bearing surfaces and spin the shaft. If the shaft is bent it will have to be renewed; as it is expensive, it is worth considering renewing the whole starter.

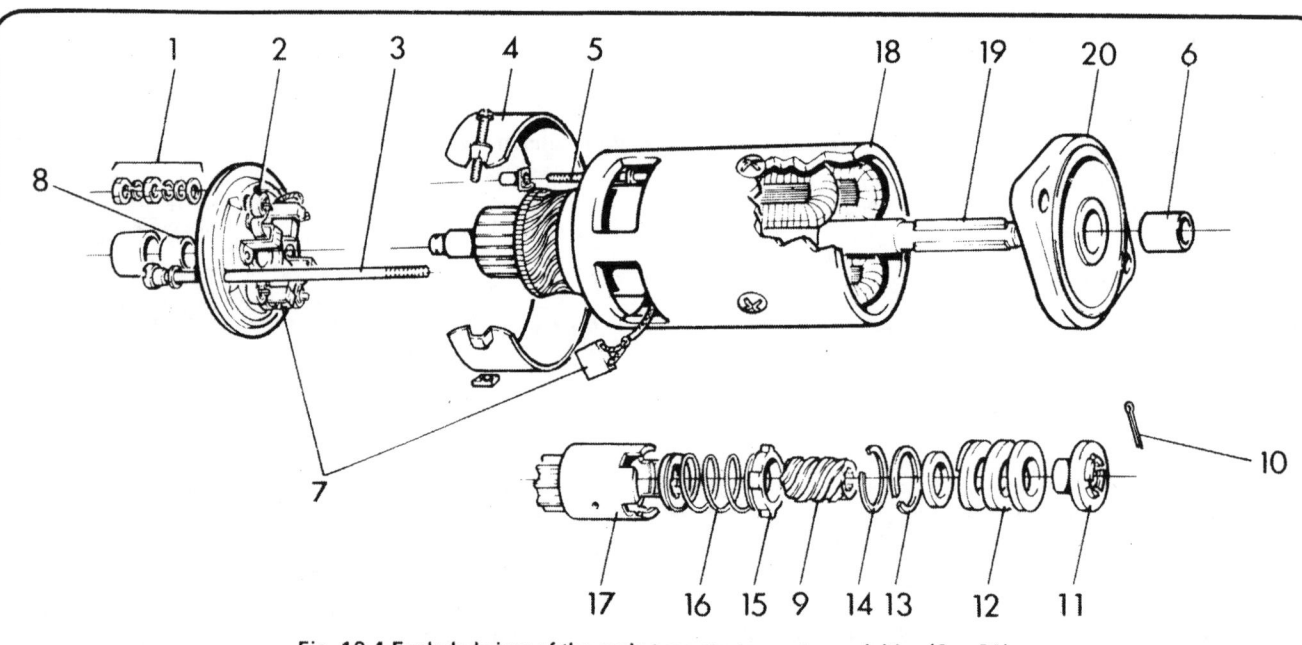

Fig. 10.4 Exploded view of the early type starter motor and drive (Sec 21)

1	Terminal nuts and washers	6	Bearing bush	11	Shaft nut	16 Restraining spring
2	Brush spring	7	Brushes	12	Main spring	17 Pinion and barrel
3	Through-bolt	8	Bearing bush	13	Retaining ring	18 Yoke
4	Band cover	9	Sleeve	14	Washer	19 Armature shaft
5	Terminal post	10	Split pin	15	Control nut	20 Driving end bracket

Fig. 10.5 Exploded view of the later type starter motor (M35J) and drive (Sec 21)

7 Next check the brush gear. To check the brush spring tension, use a new brush fitted into each holder in turn and, with an accurate spring balance, load the brush until it protrudes approximately $\frac{1}{16}$ in (1.6 mm) from the holder. Make a note of the spring balance reading which should be as given in the Specifications. Repeat on all four springs. Weak springs should be renewed.

8 Inspect the brushes for wear. If they are longer than their specified minimum length, check their fit in the holders. Brushes shorter than the minimum permissible length must be renewed and the new brushes must be tested in their holders. If there is a tendency to stick, lightly polish the brush sides with a very fine file until the brushes move freely in their holders.

9 If you have to renew the field winding brushes, cut the flexible tail at about $\frac{1}{4}$ in (6 mm) from the field winding connector and solder the tail of the new brush to the remaining stub and insulate the joint. To renew the end bracket brushes cut the flexibles from the terminal post and make a groove in the top of the terminal post deep enough to accommodate the new flexibles. Solder the short and the long flexibles into the groove.

10 Clean the commutator brush surface with a petrol-moistened cloth, if necessary first carefully cleaning off any small burnt spots with fine glasspaper — don't use emery cloth. If the commutator is badly worn or burnt, it might be possible to skim it to clean it up. This involves mounting the armature in a lathe and taking a fine cut off the commutator at high speed. It is important to remove only the absolute minimum amount of metal, and when finished the thickness of remaining copper must be not less than quoted in the Specifications. After skimming, polish the surface with fine glasspaper and wipe clean with a petrol-moistened cloth. Do *not* undercut the insulation between the copper segments.

11 Check the condition of the armature brushes. If there is sufficient wear to permit visible sideways movements of the armature shaft, they should be renewed.

12 To remove the commutator end bracket bush, screw a $\frac{1}{2}$ in (12 mm) tap part way into the bush and withdraw the bush from the bracket. The drive end bracket bush can be removed by supporting the bracket and pressing the brush out, if necessary in a soft-jawed vice.

13 Before fitting new bushes they must be soaked in clean engine oil for 24 hours. A mandrel should be turned to the same diameter as the armature shaft, having a shoulder and polished finish, and should be used to press the bushes into position. There is no need to ream the bushes after fitment.

14 Electrical insulation tests require a 110 volt ac supply and a 15 watt test lamp. If these are available you can made the following tests:

(a) *Armature insulation: Test between a commutator segment and the shaft, repeating on all segments. If the lamp lights at any time, defective insulation exists and the armature will need renewing*

(b) *Brush gear insulation: Test between each brush spring in turn and the commutator end bracket, and then between the bracket and the terminal post*

(c) *Field winding insulation: Remove the rivet securing the field winding connection to the yoke. Make sure that the connection is clear of the yoke and test between each brush in turn and the yoke. Refit the field winding-to-yoke rivet after the test*

15 Electrical continuity tests on the field windings can be made using a 12 volt battery and a 12 watt test lamp as follows. Test between each field brush in turn and the yoke. Where a failure exists (light does not come on), examine as far as possible for a break in the circuit, but if it cannot be traced, renewal or repair by a specialist is necessary. Make sure the your test equipment works properly if you do suspect a failure in the field windings.

16 Examine all mechanical parts for signs of wear and damage, especially the Bendix drive components. Wash these parts in paraffin and dry them with fluff-free cloth.

17 Reassembly of the starter motor is basically the reverse of the dismantling sequence. Do not lubricate the drive components as this can, after some use, cause the pinion to stick. Check that the armature shaft rotates freely on completion.

22 Control box (RB106 and RB340) – general description

The control box comprises the voltage regulator and the cut-out; later models also have a current regulator.

The voltage regulator controls the output from the dynamo depending on the state of the battery and the demands of the electrical equipment, and ensures that the battery is not overcharged.

The cut-out is really an automatic switch and connects the dynamo to the battery when the dynamo is turning fast enough to produce a charge. Similarly, it disconnects the battery from the dynamo when the engine is idling or stationary so that the battery does not discharge through the dynamo.

Ordinary screw-type terminals are used in early Lucas control boxes, but later modified RB106/2 types make use of Lucar connectors.

The control box used with the Lucas C40 dynamo is the type RB340 (photo). Instead of the single regulating armature that controls both voltage and current as on the former type RB106, there are separate armatures, and these with the cut-out make three armatures in the control box.

23 Control box (RB106 and RB340) – cut-out and regulator contacts maintenance

Every 12 000 miles (20 000 km) check the cut-out and regulator contacts. If they are dirty or rough or burnt, place a piece of fine glasspaper (**do not use emery paper or carborundum paper**) between the cut-out contacts, close them manually and draw the glasspaper through several times.

Clean the regulator contacts in exactly the same way, but use emery or carborundum paper *and not glasspaper*. Carefully clean both sets of contacts to remove all traces of dust, with a rag moistened in methylated spirit.

24 Control box (RB106) – adjustments

Regulator adjustment

1 The regulator requires very little attention normally, but if the battery doesn't keep its charge, or if the dynamo output does not fall when the battery is fully charged, the setting should be checked and, if necessary, adjusted. Before doing this make sure that the rest of the circuit is in good condition and this includes the battery, the dynamo, the drivebelt and its tension, and the condition of the electrical wires including correct connections.

2 Check the regulator setting by removing and joining together the cables from the control box terminals 'A1' and 'A'. Then connect the negative lead of a 20-volt voltmeter to the 'D' terminal on the dynamo and the positive lead to a good earth. Start the engine and increase its

22.5 The RB340 control box

speed until the voltmeter needle flicks and then steadies. This should occur at about 2000 rpm. If the voltage at which the needle steadies is outside the limits listed below, then remove the control box cover and turn the adjusting screw (item 1, Fig. 10.6), clockwise a quarter of a turn at a time to raise the setting, and a similar amount anti-clockwise to lower it.

Air Temperature	Type RB106/1 Open circuit voltage	Type RB106/2 Open circuit voltage
10°C or 50°F	16.1 to 16.7	16.1 to 16.7
20°C or 68°F	15.8 to 16.4	16.0 to 16.6
30°C or 86°F	15.6 to 16.2	15.9 to 16.5
40°C or 104°F	15.3 to 15.9	15.8 to 16.4

3 It is essential that the adjustments be completed within 30 seconds of starting the engine as otherwise the heat from the shunt coil will affect the readings.

Cut-out adjustment

4 Check the voltage required to operate the cut-out by connecting a voltmeter between the control box terminals 'D' and 'E'. Remove the control box cover, start the engine and gradually increase its speed until the cut-outs close. This should occur when the reading is between 12.7 and 13.3 volts. If the reading is outside these limits turn the cut-out adjusting screw (item 2, Fig. 10.6) a fraction at a time clockwise to raise the voltage, and anti-clockwise to lower it. To adjust the drop-off voltage bend the fixed contact blade carefully. The adjustment to the cut-out should be completed within 30 seconds of starting the engine as otherwise heat build-up from the shunt coil will affect the readings.

5 If the cut-out fails to work, clean the contacts, and if there is still no response renew the cut-out and regulator unit.

25 Control box (RB340) – adjustments

1 The control box is located on the right-hand side of the engine bulkhead, or on the adjacent wing valance, depending on model, and it consists of three units: a voltage regulator, a separate current regulator and a cut-out relay. Adjustment is achieved by turning a cam on each of the units, and although the special tool provided for this purpose is best, they can be turned by carefully using long-nosed pliers. The two regulators are adjusted separately, voltage being adjusted first. For this the dynamo is disconnected so that there is no current flow, and for current adjustments the voltage regulator is made ineffective by clamping its points or wedging them closed and the dynamo loaded by switching on all the lights and other electrical circuits. Again, as with the early control box, it is important that the rest of generating and battery circuit is in good condition before attempting to adjust the control box.

2 The cover to the control box containing the regulators and cut-out is held on by plastic rivets. The voltage and cut-out checks described in the following paragraphs can be done without removing this cover; it needs to be taken off to check the current control, or to make any adjustments. To remove it:

(a) *The rivets holding the cover are spread by plastic rod inserts. Push these on through the rivets with a nail, being careful not to catch them as they fall out behind*

(b) *Carefully pull the cover towards you, not letting one end come before the other. The cover should come off bringing the rivets with it*

3 Before making any adjustments mark the position of the cams. It is suggested that with an old battery, or a car used for 'stop-start' journeys, the voltage regulator should be set near the top end of the specified voltage range given below; whilst with a new battery, and in summer, the low end of the range should be advantageous. Adjustment is made as follows (see Fig. 10.7).

4 *Voltage regulator:* This is the end armature, above the terminal 'E' (earth). Pull the wires off the terminals marked 'B' to disconnect the dynamo, but to let the car be run off the battery, join them temporarily together. Take off the wire from terminals 'WL', leave it free, but connect an accurate voltmeter to that terminal, and terminal 'E'.

(a) *Run the engine at 3000 rpm*

(b) *The voltmeter should read as given below*

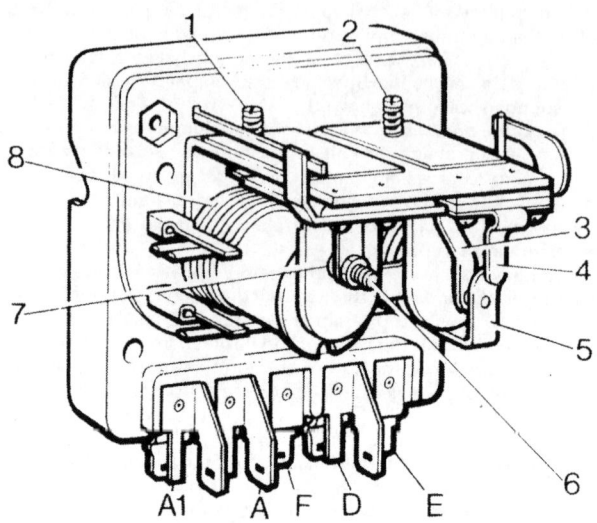

Fig. 10.6 The early (RB106/2) type control box (Sec 24)

1 Regulator adjustment screw	5 Armature tongue and moving contact
2 Cut-out adjustment screw	6 Regulator fixed contact screw
3 Fixed contact blade	7 Regulator moving contact
4 Stop arm	8 Regulator series windings

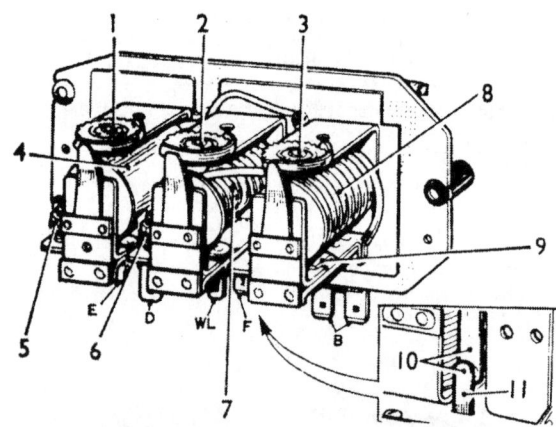

Fig. 10.7 The later (RB340) type control box (Secs 22 and 25)

1 Voltage adjustment cam	6 Current regulator contacts
2 Current adjustment cam	7 Current regulator
3 Cut-out adjustment cam	8 Cut-out relay armature
4 Voltage regulator	9 Backstop
5 Voltage regulator contacts	10 Cut-out contacts
	11 Fixed contact bracket

(c) *A reading that fluctuates more than 3 volts indicates dirty contacts*

(d) *If the reading is outside the limits adjust by turning the voltage adjustment cam anti-clockwise to raise or clockwise to lower the voltage (photo)*

(e) *Check by stopping the engine, restarting and again running the engine at 3000 rpm*

(f) *The setting must be done quickly to prevent heat build-up altering the regulator temperature*

25.4 Adjusting the voltage regulator on the RB340 control box

26.6 The later type fuse box – note the two spare fuses

(g) The size of adjustment needed should only be to turn the cam about half one of the serrations
(h) Voltage regulator settings:

Ambient temperature	Voltage range allowed before resetting necessary	Voltage to aim for when setting
10°C (50°F)	14.5 – 15.8	14.9 – 15.5
20°C (68°F)	14.4 – 15.6	14.7 – 15.3
30°C (86°F	14.3 – 15.3	14.5 – 15.1
40°C (104°F)	13.9 – 15.1	14.3 – 14.9

5 Current regulator: Short out the voltage regulator by either clipping its terminals together, or wedging cardboard between the armature core end and the solenoid lever. The leads being already removed from terminal 'B' and joined together, connect an ammeter between these leads and the 'B' terminal.

(a) Confirm that no other loads are taken from the control box side of the ammeter
(b) Start the engine, and run it at 4000 rpm
(c) Turn on the headlamps, and other electrical lights and circuits
(d) The ammeter should register a steady reading of the maximum rated output of the dynamo (22 amps for the C40/1)
(e) Fluctuation of more than 1 amp indicates dirty contacts
(f) Turn the adjuster cam (on the centre armature) anti-clockwise to increase the maximum current and clockwise to reduce it

6 Cut-out: The points of the cut-out should close at 13 volts. To check this, take off the lead from the 'WL' terminal; leave all other leads in place. Connect a voltmeter from the 'WL' terminal to earth.

(a) Start the engine
(b) Switch on the headlamps
(c) Watching the voltmeter, gradually speed up the engine
(d) The voltage will rise steadily as speed increase raises the dynamo voltage, then it will drop back slightly as the cut-out points close. At the moment before this drop back, voltage should be 13 volts

26 Fuses – general

1 On earlier models, two fuses are fitted to a separate fuse holder positioned adjacent to the control box.
2 The fuse marked 'A1 – A2' protects the electrical items such as the horn and lights, which function irrespective of whether the ignition is on or not.
3 The fuse marked 'A3 – A4' protects the ignition system and items which only operate when the ignition system is switched on (ie the stoplights, fuel gauge, flasher unit, and windscreen wiper motor).
4 If either of these fuses blow due to a short circuit or similar trouble, trace and rectify the cause before renewing the fuse.
5 On later models a 10 amp fuse is fitted in the sidelight and tail

light circuit and is fitted in a tube located in the wiring loom beneath the regulator. To expose the fuse, twist and press in one end and then pull the assembly apart and remove the fuse.
6 Later models have four fused circuits (photo). The circuits protected by the four fuses varies with individual models and you should refer to the wiring diagrams at the end of this Chapter for specific details. However the sort of thing you will find, depending on the equipment fitted, is as follows:

(a) Fuse 1 to 2: One side or parking lamp, one tail lamp, one number plate lamp and, on USA models, one front and rear side marker lamp
(b) Fuse 3 to 4: As in (a) above, but in respect of the lamps, on the other side of the car
(c) Fuse 5 to 6: Those circuits operated only when the ignition switch is on, such as direction indicators, windscreen wipers, brake stop lamps, reversing lamps and, where fitted, seat belt warning
(d) Fuse 7 to 8: Those circuits which can be operated independently of the ignition switch such as horns, interior and luggage compartment lamps, headlamp flasher, and where fitted, brake failure warning lamp, door and seat belt audible warning, and the cigar lighter

7 In addition on later models there are more line fuses in individual circuits such as the radio supply, hazard warning and, on USA models, the running-on control valve.
8 These latest circuits use 17 amp continuous rated fuses (35 amp blow rated) and two spare fuses are contained in the fuse box. If you have need to use a spare fuse, make sure that it is replaced as soon as possible – you never know when you may need it again.

27 Direction indicator flasher unit and circuit – fault tracing and rectification

1 The direction indicator flasher unit is located behind the facia on the right-hand side. It is sealed in a metal container and, when the ignition switch is on, it is operated by the direction indicator switch. Usually, when it is faulty the direction indicator lights will not operate or they will stay on, on one side only.
2 If there is no operation and the fuse is sound, as indicated by the brake stop lamps working, the circuit can be checked by removing the two electrical leads from the flasher unit, after noting which fits where, shorting the two leads with a piece of wire and, with the ignition on, operating the direction indicator switch. If the lights come on (of course they won't flash), the flasher unit must be renewed, but if no lights come on the defect will probably be in the wiring or switch.
3 Check that current is reaching the switch by using a test lamp; the ignition must be on and the leads to the flasher shorted together. If current is reaching the switch, test its output with the test lamp. You

will need to study the wiring diagrams to identify the correct pick-up points.

4   If the direction indicator lamps work, but either too quickly or too slowly, check each bulb for a burnt out filament, and if these are sound check the earthing of each bulb. If one bulb is not working but is in good condition, use the test lamp and lead to trace the supply and identify the cause of failure.

5   Rectification consists of renewing the defective component, or making electrical joints sound if this is the cause. Refer to the appropriate Section for details of bulb renewal.

28 Windscreen wiper blades and arms – removal and refitting

1   The windscreen wiper blades should be renewed as soon as it is apparent that they are not wiping the windscreen efficiently. To remove a blade, lift the wiper arm off the windscreen, depress the spring clip under the blade retainer at the end of the arm, and slide the blade assembly off the arm. Refitting is the reverse procedure.

2   Before removing a wiper arm, turn the windscreen wipers on and off to ensure that the arms are in their normal parked position, then mark the position of the arm to be changed so that reassembly will be correct.

3   On early models hinge back the wiper arm and simply pull the arm and blade assembly off the splined driveshaft. On later cars slacken the screw, give the screw head a tap to release the locking wedge, and withdraw the assembly from the shaft (photos).

4   To refit a wiper arm assembly, first align it in its correct position as noted on dismantling and push it onto the splines. On later cars, tighten down the screw to draw the locking wedge into place.

5   It's a good idea to apply a few drops of glycerine to the drive spindle occasionally, especially in winter. If you wish to change the arc through which the wiper blades move, this is simply done by repositioning each arm in turn on its splined drive, but after doing this operate the wipers to make sure that they don't foul the windscreen edges.

29 Windscreen wiper mechanism – fault diagnosis and rectification

Early models (Lucas DR3 motor)

1   Should the windscreen wipers fail to park or should they park badly, check the limit switch on the gearbox cover.

2   Loosen the four screws retaining the cover and place the projection close to the rim of the limit switch in line with the groove on the gearbox cover. Rotate the limit switch anti-clockwise 25° and tighten the four retaining screws. If you wish the wipers to be parked on the other side of the windscreen, rotate the switch 180° clockwise before tightening the screws.

3   Should the wipers fail, or work only slowly, check the current consumption by connecting a 0 to 15 amps moving coil ammeter, or equivalent, into the circuit and switching on the wipers and ignition switches. Consumption should be between 2.7 and 3.4 amps.

4   If no current is passing and the rest of the car's electrical circuits are all right, check the windscreen wiper circuit for breaks or loose connections. If excessive current is being taken look for some cause of overloading. This can be lack of lubrication in the drive or driveshafts,

or a defect in the gearbox or motor. If only a very light current is passing, make sure that the battery is fully charged and, if this is all right, examine the wiper motor brush gear and springs, cleaning the commutator if this is dirty.

Later models (Lucas 14W motor)

5   If the wipers fail to operate check the fuse in position 5 to 6; this can be quickly done by turning on the ignition switch and operating the direction indicators or brake stop light. If the fuse has blown, identify the cause before refitting a new one.

6   If the fuse is sound and the wipers still do not work, or if they work slowly, check the circuit for loose connections and poor insulation. Further investigation will require removal of the motor, and possibly the drive and wheelboxes. Refer to the relevant Sections for details.

30 Windscreen wiper motor and gearbox – removal and refitting

Early models

1   Disconnect the battery earth lead and then remove the facia panel, referring to Chapter 12 fo details. The wiper motor and gearbox are located behind the facia on the passenger's side of the car.

2   Remove the wiper arms, referring to Section 28 for details, and disconnect the electrical connections from the motor. Undo the large nut which holds the drive tubing to the motor gearbox.

3   Undo the three nuts securing the motor to the bulkhead and remove the motor and gearbox. As you do this, pull the drive cable from the drive tubing; this will cause the drive spindle shafts to rotate.

4   Refitting is the reverse of the removal procedure. Use a good general purpose grease to lubricate the inner cable before inserting it in the drive tubing.

Later models

5   Disconnect the battery earth lead, and remove the wiper arms and blades as described in Section 28. The wiper motor is located under the bonnet forward of the left-hand side of the bulkhead (photo).

6   Unscrew the nut which secures the drive tubing to the motor gearbox, then disconnect the electrical multi-connector plug from the motor.

7   Undo and remove the two bolts and washers securing the motor clamp band to the bodywork.

8   Remove the clamp band, and then remove the motor, pulling the inner cable out of the drive tubing as you do so. Retrieve the motor mounting rubber and mounting plate.

9   Refitting is the reverse of the removal procedure, but make sure that, before you insert it into the drive tubing, the inner cable is lubricated with a good general purpose grease.

31 Windscreen wiper motor and gearbox – dismantling and reassembly

1   Before dismantling the motor and gearbox, consider renewing the complete assembly, as spares are not easy to get. Probably the only repair which can be undertaken effectively by the home mechanic is brush renewal, although cleaning and relubricating might be adequate to extend the life of the assembly.

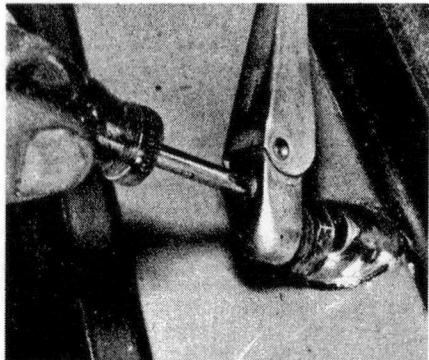
28.3a Slacken the screw ...

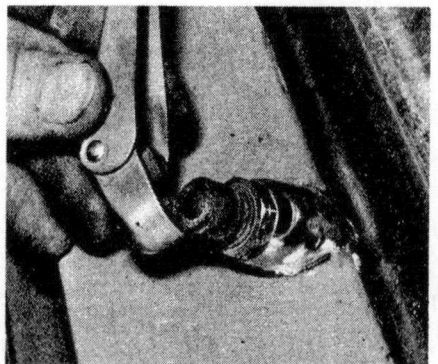
28.3b ... and remove the wiper arm

30.5 The location of the windscreen wiper motor (1275 cc car)

Early models (Lucas DR3 motor)

2   Undo and remove the four screws securing the gearbox cover and remove the cover. Undo and remove the two through-bolts from the commutator end cover and remove the cover.

3   Take a note of the location of the individual brushes so that, if they are suitable, they can be refitted in their original position, then lift out the brush gear retainer and remove the brush gear.

4   Clean the commutator with a petrol-dampened cloth; if necessary use a piece of fine glasspaper to remove persistent dirt or carbon deposits. Carefully examine the internal wiring for signs of chafing, deterioration or overheating. If you have a multi-meter, or can get an electrician to do it for you, check the resistance between adjacent commutator segments, which should be 0.34 to 0.41 ohm. Also check the field resistance, which should be 12.8 to 14.0 ohms. Anything lower than this indicates a short circuit and the need for renewal. Clean the assembly free of carbon dust and general dust.

5   Remove the circlip and washer from the gearbox cross-head connecting link pin, and remove the cross-head and cable assembly. Take careful note of the location of circlips, washers, spacers and other parts as you remove them. Remove the circlip and washer at the bottom of the final gear (worm wheel) shaft. Check that there is no burr on the circlip groove and then remove the gear shaft. The armature and worm drive can now be removed from the gearbox. Clean all parts free of grease and dirt and examine for wear and damage.

6   Reassembly is the reverse of the dismantling sequence, but ensure that the following lubrication is carried out:

(a)   Armature shaft self-aligning bearing: Immerse in clean engine oil for 4 hours before assembly

(b)   Armature bearings: Apply clean engine oil, but don't contaminate the commutator or brush gear

(c)   Gearbox felt lubricator: Apply clean engine oil

(d)   Wormwheel bearings, cross-head, guide channel, connecting rod, crankpin, worm, cable rack and wheelboxes, and the final gearshaft: liberally grease with good quality general purpose grease

Later models (Lucas 14W motor)

7   Remove the four gearbox cover retaining screws and remove the cover. Release the circlip and flat washer securing the connecting rod to the crankpin on the shaft and gear. Remove the connecting rod followed by the second flat washer.

8   Remove the circlip and washer securing the shaft and gear to the gearbox body. De-burr the gear shaft and remove the gear shaft, making a note of the location of the dished washer.

9   Scribe a mark on the yoke assembly and on the gearbox to ensure correct reassembly, and unscrew the two yoke bolts from the motor yoke assembly. Separate the yoke assembly including the armature from the gearbox body. As the yoke assembly has residual magnetism, keep it well away from metallic dust, iron filings, etc.

10   Unscrew the two screws securing the brush gear, and the terminal and switch assembly, and remove both assemblies.

11   Inspect the brushes for excessive wear. If the main brushes (the two directly opposite each other) are worn to the specified limit, or if the narrow section of the third brush is worn to the full width of the brush, fit a new brush gear assembly. Ensure that all brushes move freely in their boxes. Test the armature, or have it tested, for insulation, open or short circuits, renewing where necessary.

12   Clean and inspect all parts following the procedure for the earlier motor. Reassembly is the reverse of the dismantling procedure, and lubrication also follows that of the earlier motor. Tighten the yoke fixing bolts to their specified torque during reassembly, and adjust the armature endfloat to the specified clearance using the thrust screw and locknut.

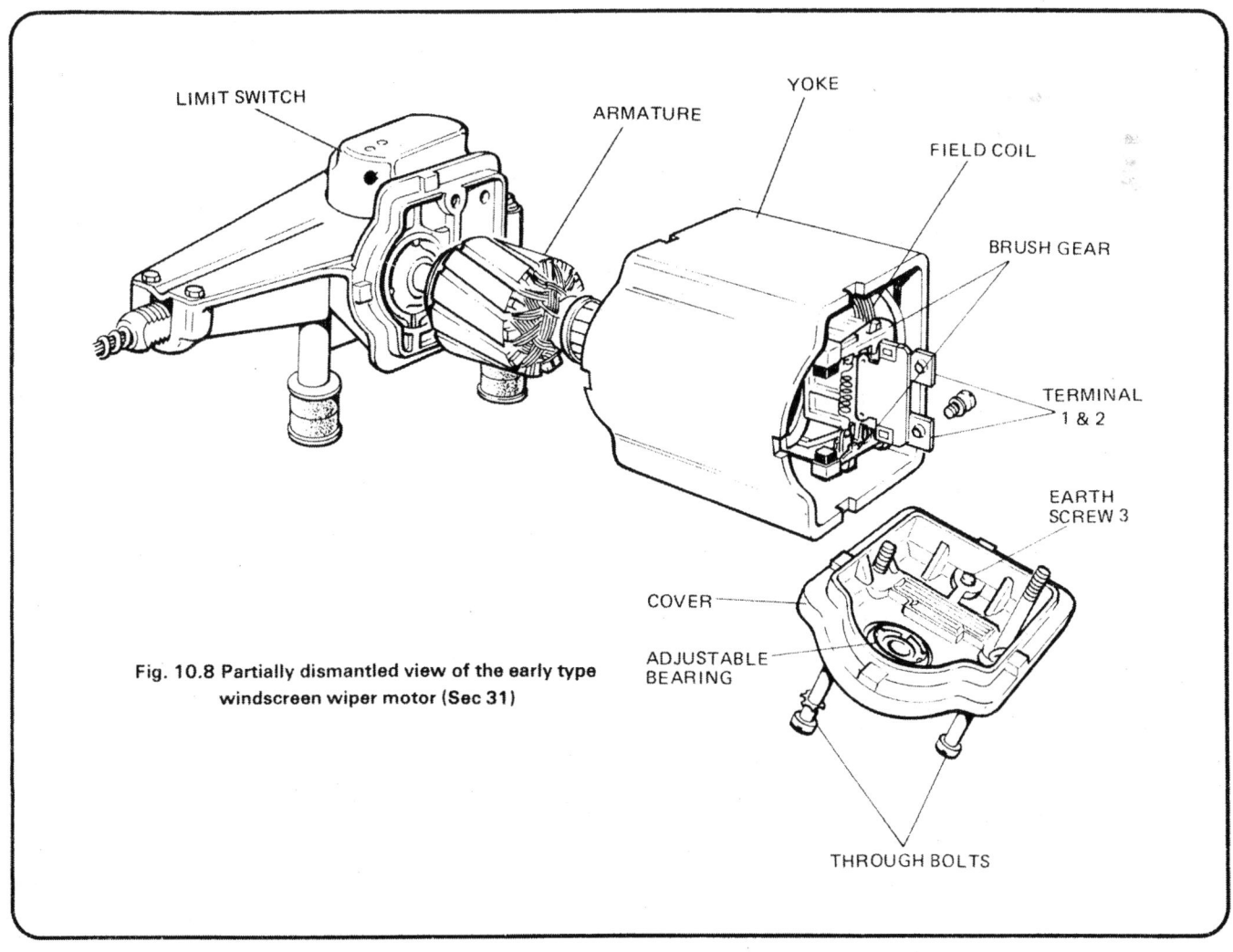

Fig. 10.8 Partially dismantled view of the early type windscreen wiper motor (Sec 31)

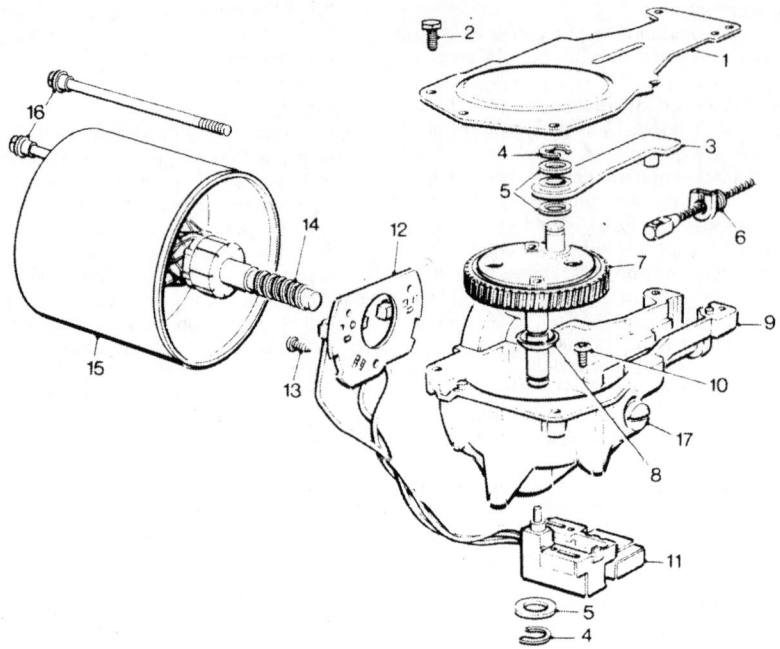

Fig. 10.9 Partially dismantled view of the later type of windscreen wiper motor (Sec 31)

1	Gearbox cover	6	Crosshead and inner cable	11	Limit switch assembly	15	Yoke assembly
2	Cover screw	7	Shaft and gear	12	Brush gear	16	Yoke bolts
3	Connecting rod	8	Dished washer	13	Brush gear screw	17	Armature endfloat
4	Circlip	9	Gearbox case	14	Armature		adjusting screw
5	Flat washers	10	Limit switch screw				

32 Windscreen wiper wheelboxes – removal and refitting

1   The windscreen wiper wheelboxes are located immediately under-neath the splined driveshafts on which the wiper arms fit. To gain access to these boxes on some cars, you may need to remove the facia, but it will depend on the model and standard of fit. It might even be necessary (for example when removing the right-hand wheelbox on the right-hand drive 1500 cc car) to remove the steering column as well. For information on these procedures refer to the relevant Chapters and Sections.

2   Remove the windscreen wiper blade and arm assemblies as described in Section 28. Then remove the windscreen wiper motor and gearbox together with the internal drive cable.

3   Once access has been gained to the wheelboxes, remove the two nuts securing the cover plate on the wheelbox concerned and remove the cover plate. Disengage the drive tube(s) from the wheelbox.

4   Remove the wiper drive spindle securing nut and remove the bush and washer to free the wheelbox, which can then be removed into the car.

5   The above is the recommended procedure, but you may find that you can remove the wheelboxes on your car without first removing the wiper motor and gearbox. This is more likely on the later cars, but removing the motor and gearbox makes the job easier.

6   Refitting is the reverse of the removal sequence but make sure that the wheelboxes are correctly lined up to accept the drive cables. Grease the wheelboxes and drive cable with a good general purpose grease during reassembly. Get the wheelbox(es) and drive tubing into position without tightening the fastenings. Use some putty sealant under the rubber washer under the spindle bush. Tighten the bush retaining nut and then the wheelbox retaining nuts. Before fitting the wiper arms operate the motor to ensure that they are fitted in the correct parked position.

33 Windscreen washer pump – removal and refitting

1   Disconnect the battery terminals and then remove the pump connecting wires (photo).

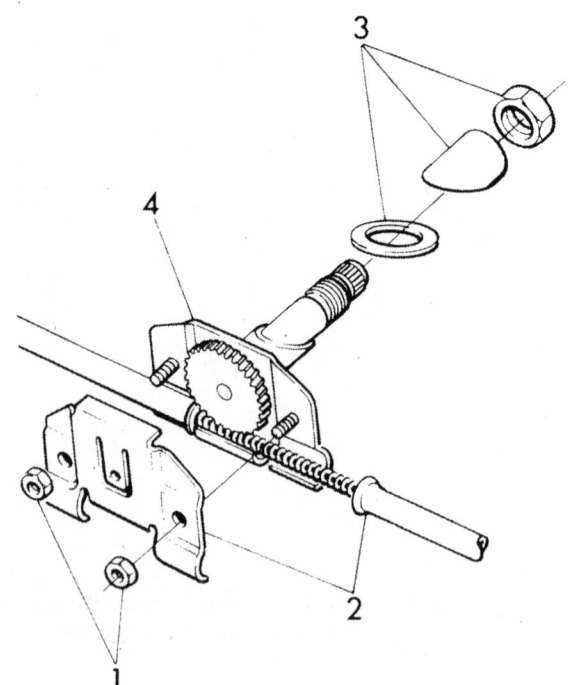

Fig. 10.10 Partially dismantled view of a windscreen wiper wheelbox (Sec 32)

1	Cover plate securing nuts	3	Wheelbox securing nut,
2	Cover plate and drive		bush and rubber washer
	cable tube	4	Wheelbox

2   Withdraw the water tubes from the pump, noting which tube fits to each connector, and then unscrew the two pump mounting screws. On some models the mounting screws may also secure other items of equipment such as piping. Note the details so that you can reassemble them correctly.

3   Refitting is the reverse of the removal procedure.

4   On some models the windscreen washer pump is manually operated by finger pressure and it is mounted on the facia. Removal simply involves undoing the bezel nut holding the pump to the facia, pushing the assembly forward and then disconnecting the two tubes, noting which tube fits to which connector. Refitting is the reverse of the removal procedure.

34 Horn(s) – fault tracing and rectification

1   If a horn (early models have only one horn) works badly or fails completely, first check the wiring lead to it for short circuits and loose connections. Also check that the horn is firmly secured and that there is nothing lying on the horn body (photo).

2   On early models the horn is protected by the fuse in the number 1 to 2 position, but on later models it is the one in number 7 to 8 position. If the fuse has failed the cause must be found. On the early models the fuse supplies only the horn, but on later models other circuits are supplied by the same fuse and these may need checking to identify the cause of failure. Refer to the wiring diagrams at the end of this Chapter.

3   The horn can be dismantled on early models and, if necessary, the interrupter contacts inside cleaned. Later horns cannot be dismantled, but they do have an adjuster to compensate for wear of the moving parts. To make an adjustment proceed as follows.

4   Identify the adjustment screw on the back of the horn case. Do not confuse it with the large screw and locknut in the centre which should not be disturbed. Turn the adjustment screw anti-clockwise until the horn just fails to sound. Then turn the screw a quarter of a turn clockwise, which is the optimum setting.

5   To eliminate the risk of the fuse blowing while resetting the adjustment in the car, you can *temporarily* use a piece of wire in place of the fuse, but *don't forget to refit the fuse* on completion.

6   On later models with twin horns, the horn which is not being adjusted should be disconnected while adjustment of the other takes place. Reconnect on completion.

7   Access to the horns on later models is obtained by removing the radiator grille.

35 Reversing lamp – bulb renewal

1   Later models incorporate a reversing lamp.

2   To renew a bulb, remove the two screws securing the lamp to the rear panel and withdraw the lens (photo).

3   Press the bulb downwards onto the lower sprung contact and withdraw it from the lamp.

4   Fit one end of the new bulb into the hole in the lower contact, and press in the top end of the bulb until it engages in the hole in the top contact. Refit the lens and the securing screws.

36 Reversing lamp switch – removal and refitting

1   Roll back the carpet from the left-hand side of the gearbox tunnel together with the felt.

2   From the same side of the tunnel at approximately $8\frac{1}{2}$ in (215 mm) from the front of the tunnel, peel back a $3\frac{1}{2}$ in (90 mm) square strip of sound insulation.

3   Through the tunnel aperture, disconnect the wiring and unscrew the reversing light switch from the gearbox, together with the spacing washer, if fitted.

4   Refit in the reverse order.

37 Headlight units – removal and refitting

1   First release the chrome securing ring. On early models this is retained with a screw whilst on later models, to remove the ring, simply lift it from the bottom and pull outwards (photo).

2   To remove the headlight unit, press the lens in and at the same time twist it slightly anti-clockwise and pull clear. With headlight clear, twist and pull off the bulb holder, and remove the bulb on the earlier models. On the later models, the fully sealed beam unit is removed by unscrewing the four retaining nuts, screws and washers to disconnect it from the body, and then pulling off the lead connection from the rear of the reflector (photo). Another type of assembly requires the headlamp wiring to be disconnected at snap connectors in the engine compartment, the wiring released from its clips and, after removing the headlamp rim, four screws, nuts and washers removed to release the headlamp assembly and rubber seal.

3   In all cases, refitting is the reverse of the removal sequence.

38 Headlight beam – adjustment

1   The headlight beams can be adjusted for both vertical and horizontal alignment by two screws located at right angles to each other in the headlamp mounting flange – one at the top and one at the side. These screws are accessible once the lamp rim has been removed (see previous Section). For vertical adjustment of the beam, use the top screw and for horizontal adjustment use the side screw.

2   The headlamp beams should be set so that, for full or high beam, the beams shine slightly below parallel on a level road surface and straight ahead. Do not forget that the beam position is affected by the way the car is located for night driving. Before adjusting the beams, make sure that the car is suitably loaded, if necessary.

3   Although this adjustment can be set approximately by the home mechanic, it should be regarded only as a temporary setting. Accurate adjustment should be entrusted to a garage where they will have the necessary apparatus to do the job with precision.

39 Sidelights and indicators (front) – bulb renewal

1   On the Mk I Sprite, peel back the outer rubber lip and remove the

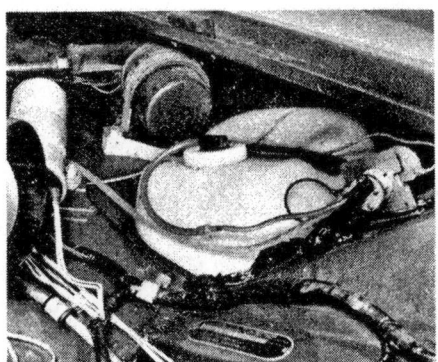
33.1 The windscreen washer motor to the right of the reservoir (1500 cc models)

34.1 View of the horns looking forward with the radiator removed

35.2 Removing a reversing light lens

37.1 Removing a headlamp rim

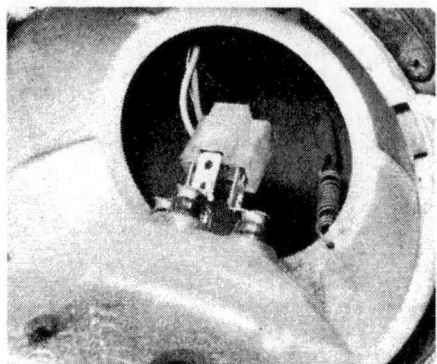

37.2 Removing the connector from a headlamp sealed beam unit

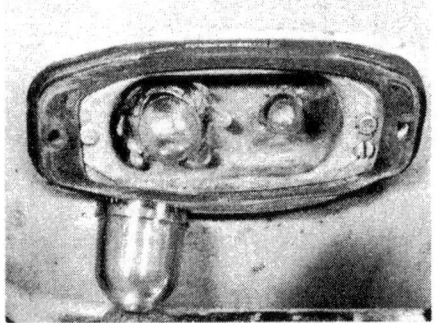

39.2 The front sidelight and indicator lens removed – note the indicator bulb cover also removed (1275 cc models)

39.3 Removing a front indicator bulb (1500 cc models)

40.1 The rear light assembly with lens removed

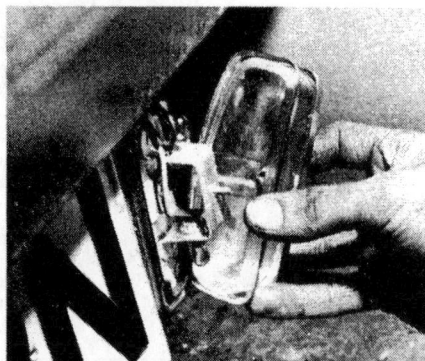

41.1 Removing a number plate light cover (1500 cc model shown)

41.2 A number plate light on later chrome bumpered cars

chrome finishing strip. Now peel back the inner lip and pull out the glass cover. The bulb may now be removed.
2　On later models of Sprite and Midget, the sidelight/indicator covers are removed after unscrewing the two retaining screws. The bulbs can then easily be inspected and renewed if required (photo). The indicator bulb cover (where fitted) simply pulls off to remove.
3　On the later models with rubber bumpers, the indicator light at the front is set into the bumper. To remove the light unit or renew a bulb, simply unscrew the lens retaining screws, and withdraw the lens. Access to the bulb and light unit retaining screws is now available as required (photo).
4　Reassemble in the reverse order but renew the rubber seal surround if it is perished or cracked. Later lens covers are marked 'TOP' to assist correct reassembly.

40 Tail light, stoplight and indicator light (rear) – removal, refitting and bulb renewal

1　The rear light cluster cover on the early models is secured to the body by a single screw, whilst on later models there are two screws (photo) to be removed to gain access to the bulbs.
2　To remove the cluster unit complete, disconnect the wiring snap connectors from inside the bodywork and unscrew the retaining nuts and washers from the inner body panel.
3　Refitting is the reversed sequence to removal.

41 Number plate light – removal, refitting and bulb renewal

1　On early models and 1500 cc models the single number plate light unit (two on 1500 cc models) is removed by first unscrewing the chrome cover (photo) retaining screw. The bulbs may now be inspected and renewed if required. To remove the complete unit unscrew the retaining nuts from the inner body panel or backing plate and disconnect the wiring snap connectors.
2　On later models with chrome bumpers, having the number plate lights located in the rear bumper (photo), the bulbs can be renewed after unscrewing and removing the lamp cover and lens retaining screw. If the unit is to be removed from the number plate, disconnect

the connecting wires at the snap connectors, and then unscrew the two nuts and washers retaining the lamp to the bumper.

3   On all models, refitting is the reverse of the removal procedure.

42 Brake pressure failure warning lamp – removal and refitting

1   To remove the brake pressure failure warning lamp from the facia it is first necessary to remove the instrument adjacent to it. Undo the knurled nut securing the bridge piece, remove the bridge piece and pull the instrument out of its location.

2   Reach through the aperture and remove the retaining clip from the back of the brake pressure failure warning lamp. Pull the lamp out of the facia and disconnect the electrical leads from the back of it.

3   To refit the lamp reverse the removal procedure.

43 Starter solenoid – removal and refitting

1   Disconnect the battery.

2   Remove the air intake hose from the heater and place aside.

3   Withdraw the rubber covers and unscrew the lead securing nuts and washers. Detach the leads from their respective terminals.

4   Remove the solenoid retaining screws, using a flexible drive cross-head screwdriver to unscrew the left-hand screw.

5   Slide the solenoid clear and disconnect the low tension leads, noting their respective terminal positions.

6   Refitting is the reverse procedure to removal.

44 Ignition/starter/(later) steering lock switch – removal and refitting

1   The procedure for removing and refitting the ignition switch varies with the model concerned. On the earliest cars the switch is mounted on the facia; on the later cars it is combined with the starter switch and steering lock, and when operated it controls the electrical supply to a number of other circuits. Before removing the ignition switch always disconnect the battery earth lead.

2   On the earliest models disconnect the electrical leads from the switch, unscrew the retaining nut, and remove the switch assembly from the facia, complete with its D-shaped lockwasher.

3   Later cars have a switch with a bezel ring instead of a nut and the ring is undone with a special tool in the slots provided. A pair of round-nosed pliers could be used instead, or a simple tool made up from a piece of scrap metal.

4   The locking barrel can be removed from the switch by inserting the key, turning the switch to 'ignition on' to line up the barrel retaining plunger with the small hole in the body, depressing the plunger and withdrawing the barrel.

5   Where the switch is combined with the steering lock, it can be removed from the steering lock by undoing the small retaining screw in the switch housing. After removal, note the positions of the individual leads before disconnecting them.

6   On some models it may be necessary to first dismantle the column cowl in order to get to the ignition switch. This procedure is covered in Section 54.

7   In all cases refitting a switch is the reverse of the removal procedure.

45 Hazard warning flasher unit or switch – removal and refitting

1   Disconnect the battery earth lead, then remove the eight screws and washers securing the centre console. Move the console to gain access to the inside.

2   To remove the warning switch, first disconnect the multi-connector plug, then detach the bulb holder complete with bulb and move it to one side. Depress the switch retaining catches and remove the switch; a special tool is provided to do this, but a blunt knife between the switch and facia achieves the same result.

3   The flasher unit is held in a metal clip. To remove it, first disconnect the multi-connector plug from the back of the flasher unit, then pull the unit out of its clip.

4   Refitting the switch or flasher unit is the reverse of the relevant removal procedure.

46 Seatbelt warning buzzer/timer module (USA models) – removal and refitting

1   Disconnect the battery terminals.

2   From inside the left-hand side of the facia panel, remove the module securing screw, press the small retaining catch and withdraw the wiring plug from the module.

3   The warning buzzer and timer module can now be removed from the car.

4   Refit in the reverse order.

47 Service interval warning lamp (USA models) – removal, refitting and bulb renewal

1   With the battery disconnected, unscrew the console retaining screws and then from inside the console withdraw the bulb holder from the warning lamp.

2   The bulb can now be removed and renewed if required.

3   To remove the lamp unit from the console, simply detach the retaining clip.

4   Refitting is the reversal of removal.

48 Courtesy lamp unit – removal, refitting and bulb renewal

1   To renew a bulb, simply undo the lens securing screws, and withdraw the lens. The bulb can now be renewed.

2   To remove the unit, unscrew the console retaining screws and from inside the console disconnect the wiring snap connectors. Then unscrew the unit retaining nuts and washers.

3   Refitting is the reverse of removal.

49 Stoplight switch – removal and refitting

1   Earlier models are fitted with a hydraulically operated stoplight switch fitted in the brake circuit in the engine compartment. Removal and refitting of this type is straightforward providing that suitable precautions are taken to avoid excessive loss of fluid. It will be necessary to bleed the system after completion – see Chapter 9. The stoplight switch on later models is operated by the brake pedal arm, and it is located on the clutch and brake pedal box. Disconnect the battery before starting to remove the switch.

2   On USA models, where fitted, first disconnect the service interval counter-to-gearbox drive cable by unscrewing the finger nut and pulling the drive free. Remove the service interval counter by undoing the two screws securing it to its mounting bracket, then move the counter to one side out of the way.

3   On all models, undo the eight screws which secure the pedal box to the car body and disconnect the electrical leads from the stoplight switch. Undo the switch locknut.

4   Carefully lift the pedal box and unscrew the stoplight switch.

5   Refitting is the reverse of the removal procedure. When screwing the switch into the pedal box, ensure that there is $\frac{1}{8}$ in (3 mm) free movement at the brake pedal before tightening the locknut (see Chapter 9). Check this measurement again after tightening the pedal box retaining screws and readjust if necessary.

50 Rocker switches – removal and refitting

1   First disconnect the battery.

2   From the inner facia panel, disconnect the wiring from the respective switch, and depress the plastic catches to withdraw the switch from the outside.

3   Refitting is the reverse of removal.

51 Tachometer – removal and refitting

1   Disconnect the battery before removing the tachometer.

2   On UK models ease the bulb holder out of the back of the

instrument and disconnect the electrical leads from the instrument. Undo and remove the two knurled nuts, washers and earthing cables on the bridge piece, then remove the bridge piece. Withdraw the tachometer and its sealing ring from the facia.

3   On USA models, first remove the two knurled nuts, washers, earth cables and clamps from the back of the instrument. Ease the instrument out of the facia, disconnect the electrical leads and remove the bulb holder from the back.

4   Refitting the instrument on either model is the reverse of the removal procedure.

52 Speedometer – removal and refitting

1   Disconnect the battery before removing the speedometer.

2   On UK models, disconnect the speedometer drive cable from the back of the instrument by either undoing the finger nut (early models) or depressing the clip and pulling the drive free (later models). Note their individual locations and ease the bulb holders out of the back of the instrument. Disconnect the wires from the voltage stabiliser. Remove the trip recorder reset retaining nut and withdraw the reset from its bracket. Undo and remove the two knurled retaining nuts, washers, and earthing cables, and the two retaining clamps. Depress the direction indicator switch down and towards the steering wheel and remove the speedometer together with its sealing ring from the facia.

3   On USA models, disconnect the speedometer drive cable by undoing the finger nut and pulling the drive out of the instrument. Lift the gearbox tunnel carpet, undo the console retaining screws and move the console back and towards the steering column. Undo and remove the two knurled retaining nuts, washers and clamps from the back of the instrument. Remove the trip remote control retaining nut and washer and lift the remote control out of its bracket. Ease the instrument out of the facia, pull out the bulb holder from the back and remove the speedometer from the car.

4   Refitting is the reverse of the removal procedure.

53 Fuel gauge – removal and refitting

1   Disconnect the battery before removing the fuel gauge.

2   *UK models:* Ease the bulb holder out of the back of the instrument and disconnect the electrical leads from the gauge. Undo and remove the knurled retaining nut, washer, earthing cables and bridge piece from behind the gauge. Remove the fuel gauge together with its sealing ring from the facia.

3   *USA models:* Disconnect the speedometer drive cable from the back of the speedometer. Lift the gearbox tunnel carpet, undo the console retaining screws and move the console back and towards the steering column. Remove the speedometer as described in the previous Section. Remove the knurled retaining nut, washer and bridge piece from the back of the fuel gauge. Move the gauge out of the facia, remove the bulb holder then disconnect the electrical leads from the back and remove the fuel gauge from the car.

4   Refitting is the reverse of the removal procedure.

54 Direction indicator multi-switch – removal and refitting

Early cars

1   On early cars the direction indicator switch is combined with the horn switch. To remove and refit the switch first disconnect the battery, then proceed as follows:

2   Unscrew the steering column pinch bolt and the three toe plate-to-steering column bolts.

3   Take note of the thickness and location of the upper column bracket flange-to-body packing washers. Now remove the three retaining bolts and nuts. Keep the packing washers in a safe place for reassembly. If the packing washers are mislaid, or if their positions are not recorded, the steering column will have to be aligned, as explained in Chapter 11, on reassembly.

4   Withdraw the steering column to enable the switch cowl to clear the facia, and unscrew the four cowl securing screws. Remove the cowl.

5   Unscrew and remove the direction indicator/horn switch-to-column securing screws. Disconnect the wiring multi-connector and remove the switch.

6   Refitting is the reversal of the removal sequence, but be sure to relocate the correct packing washers at the upper bracket flange bracket, as per paragraph 3 above. Tighten the three upper fixing bolts to their specified torque and tighten the pinion pinch bolt to its specified torque.

Later cars

7   On later UK models the direction indicator switch is combined with the headlight dip switch. Proceed as follows to remove and refit the switch.

8   Disconnect the battery.

9   Undo and remove the four screws securing the cowls to the steering column and remove the lower cowl. Move the upper cowl in an anti-clockwise direction round the steering column, depress the horn slip ring contact and ease the cowl off the column.

10   Remove the clip holding the switch wiring harness to the steering column and disconnect the multi-connector plug. Disconnect the horn slip ring contact terminal lead.

11   Undo and remove the two screws to release the switch assembly and the clamp and contact assembly from the steering column.

12   Refitting is a straightforward reversal of the removal procedure, but make sure that the locating tongue on the switch fits into the cut-away in the outer steering column before tightening the securing screws.

55 Heater unit, motor and fan – removal, dismantling, reassembly and refitting

Note: *The procedure described is applicable to the later type of heater with combined motor. The procedure for the earlier type of heater is straightforward and in many ways similar to that detailed below, the main difference being that the blower motor and fan are housed in a separate unit.*

1   Drain the cooling system (see Chapter 2) and disconnect the battery. Remove the battery and its tray.

2   Disconnect the air duct hose from the intake tube.

3   Shut the heater control valve, loosen the hose clips and disconnect the hoses from the heater (photos).

4   Disconnect the connecting leads at their snap connectors, and release the heater control cable from its bracket on the intake tube, and from the lever on the air intake on the heater.

5   On cars with manual choke, release the choke cable from the spring clips on the heater body.

6   Unscrew the unit retaining screws from the bulkhead noting the capillary tube retaining clip, and then lift the heater unit clear. Before dismantling the assembly, empty any residual coolant from the heater element.

7   Release the heater unit spring clips, and remove the cover. Do not damage the seal – renew if required.

8   Remove the heater element.

9   Unscrew the three screws retaining the fan and motor to the heater and disconnect. Note the position of the fan on its spindle, and remove the securing clip. Tap the spindle to withdraw it from the fan.

10   Refitting is the reversal of removal, but ensure that there is a good seal between the heater body and flange. If necessary, use a suitable sealant. Check the water hose connections to the heater on re-assembly for signs of leakage and open the heater control valve again if required.

56 Heater controls – removal and refitting

UK models

1   These cars have a combined fan switch and air flow control. The fan switch is operated by turning the control knob and the air flow by push-pull action of the same knob. To remove the control proceed as follows.

2   Disconnect the battery and disconnect the inner and outer control from the air valve and the heater casing intake tube.

3   Depress the plunger in the control knob shank and remove the knob and washer. Unscrew the control retaining ring using round-nosed pliers or a tool made up from scrap.

4   Remove the control from the facia and retrieve the spring washer. Disconnect the electrical cable connectors.

55.3a The heater hose connections on a 1275 cc car – note the heater control valve at the back of the rocker cover

55.3b The heater hose connections on a 1500 cc car – the heater control valve is at the bottom left

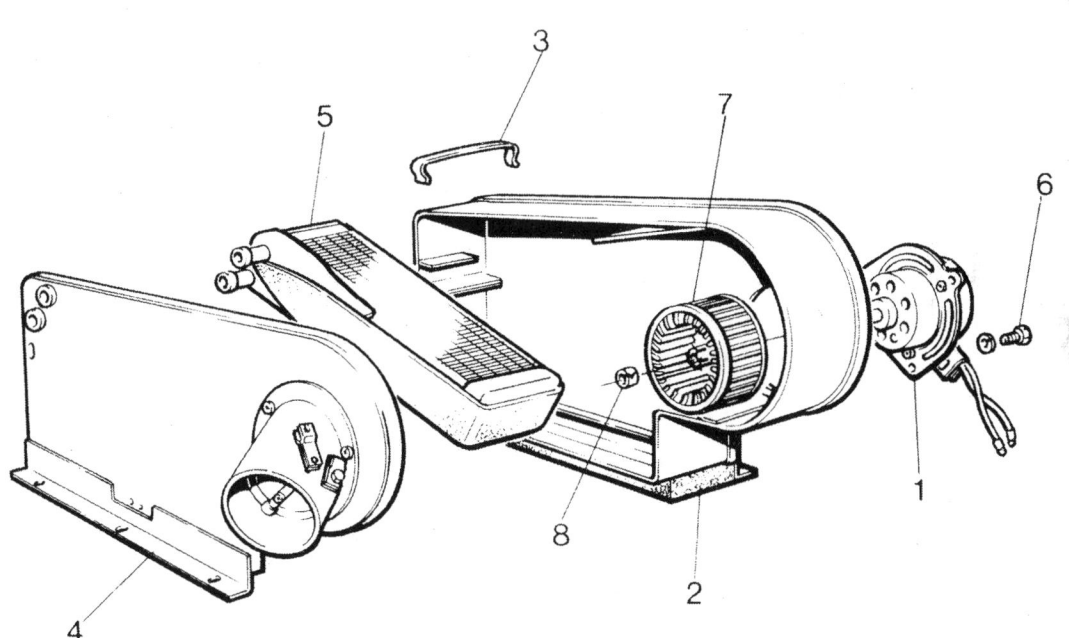

Fig. 10.11 Exploded view of the later heater unit (Sec 55)

1	Fan motor	3	Spring clip	5	Heater matrix	7	Fan
2	Heater unit case	4	Heater unit cover	6	Motor securing screw	8	Fan retaining clip

5   Unseat the grommet in the bulkhead holding the control cable and withdraw the control and cable assembly from the car.

6   Refitting is the reverse of the removal procedure. If necessary adjust the inner cable and outer sheath in their fastenings on the heater intake tube to achieve correct operation of the air intake valve when the control knob is moved.

USA models

7   These cars have an electrical rocker switch to control the heater fan and a separate control knob for the air flow.

8   The rocker switch has an illuminating lamp in it, but removal and refitting follows the procedure contained in Section 50.

9   To remove the air flow control depress the plunger retaining the control knob to its shaft and remove the knob.

10 Undo and remove the nut and two washers holding the control in the facia.

11 Undo the separate securing screws and release the inner cable and outer sheath from the control, then remove the control from the car.

12 Refitting is the reverse of the removal procedure but refer to paragraph 6 if adjustment is needed.

57 Radios and tape players – fitting (general)

A radio or tape player is an expensive item to buy, and will only give its best performance if fitted properly. It is useless to expect concert hall performance from a unit that is suspended from the dashpanel on string with its speaker resting on the floor! If you do not wish to do the installation yourself, there are many in-car entertainment specialists who will do the fitting for you.

Make sure the unit purchased is of the same polarity as the car, and ensure that units with adjustable polarity are correctly set before commencing the fitting operations.

It is difficult to give specific information with regard to fitting, as final positioning of the radio/tape player, speakers and aerial is entirely a matter of personal preference. However, the following paragraphs give guidelines to follow which are relevant to all fittings:

Radios

Most radios are a standardised size of 7 in wide by 2 in deep. This ensures that they will fit into the radio aperture provided in most cars. If your car does not have such an aperture, then the radio must be fitted in a suitable position either in or beneath the dashpanel. Alternatively, a special console can be purchased which will fit between the dashpanel and the floor or on the transmission tunnel. These consoles can also be used for additional switches and instrumentation if required. Where no radio aperture is provided, the following points should be borne in mind before deciding exactly where to fit the unit.

(a) *The unit must be within easy reach of the driver wearing a seat belt*

(b) *The unit must not be mounted in close proximity to an electronic tachometer, the ignition switch and its wiring, or the flasher unit and associated wiring*

(c) *The unit must be mounted within reach of the aerial lead, and in such a place that the aerial lead will not have to be routed near the components detailed in the preceding paragraph 'b'*

(d) *The unit should not be positioned in a place where it might cause injury to the car occupants in an accident; for instance under the dashpanel above the driver's or passenger's legs*

(e) *The unit must be fitted securely*

Some radios will have mounting brackets provided, together with instructions; others will need to be fitted using drilled and slotted metal strips, bent to form mounting brackets. These strips are available from most accessory shops. The unit must be properly earthed by fitting a separate earthing lead between the casing of the radio and the vehicle frame.

Use the radio manufacturer's instructions when wiring the radio into the vehicle's electrical system. If no instructions are available, refer to the relevant wiring diagram to find the location of the radio feed connection in the vehicle's wiring circuit. A 1 to 2 amp in-line fuse must be fitted in the radio's feed wire; a choke may also be necessary (see the next Section).

The type of aerial used and its fitted position, is a matter of personal preference. In general, the taller the aerial the better the reception. It is best to fit a fully retractable aerial; especially if a mechanical car-wash is used or if you live in an area where cars tend to be vandalised. In this respect, electric aerials which are raised and lowered automatically when switching the radio on or off are convenient, but are more likely to give trouble than the manual type.

When choosing a site for the aerial, the following points should be considered:

(a) *The aerial lead should be as short as possible; this means that the aerial should be mounted at the front of the car*

(b) *The aerial must be mounted as far away from the distributor and HT leads as possible*

(c) *The part of the aerial which protrudes beneath the mounting point must not foul the roadwheels, or anything else*

(d) *If possible, the aerial should be positioned so that the coaxial lead does not have to be routed through the engine compartment*

(e) *The plane of the panel on which the aerial is mounted should not be so steeply angled that the aerial cannot be mounted vertically (in relation to the end-on aspect of the car). Most aerials have a small amount of adjustment available*

Having decided on a mounting position, a relatively large hole will have to be made in the panel. The exact size of the hole will depend upon the specific aerial being fitted, although generally, the hole required is of $\frac{3}{4}$ in (19 mm) diameter. On metal bodied cars, a tank-cutter of the relevant diameter is the best tool to use for making the hole. This tool needs a small diameter pilot hole drilled through the panel, through which the tool clamping bolt is inserted. (On GRP bodied cars, a hole-saw is the best thing to use. Again, this tool will

require the drilling of a small pilot hole). When the hole has been made the raw edges should be de-burred with a file and then painted to prevent corrosion.

Fit the aerial according to the manufacturer's instructions. If the aerial is very tall, or if it protrudes beneath the mounting panel for a considerable distance, it is a good idea to fit a stay beneath the aerial and the vehicle frame. This stay can be manufactured from the slotted and drilled metal strips previously mentioned. The stay should be securely screwed or bolted in place. For best reception, it is advisable to fit an earth lead between the aerial and the vehicle frame; this is essential for GRP bodied cars.

It will probably be necessary to drill one or two holes through bodywork panels in order to feed the aerial lead into the interior of the car. Where this is the case, ensure that the holes are fitted with rubber grommets to protect the cable and to stop possible entry of water.

Positioning and fitting of the speaker depends mainly on its type. Generally, the speaker is designed to fit directly into the aperture already provided in the car (usually in the doors, or footwell walls). Where this is the case, fitting the speaker is just a matter of removing the protective grille from the aperture and screwing or bolting the speaker in place. Take great care not to damage the speaker diaphragm whilst doing this. It is a good idea to fit a gasket beneath the speaker frame and the mounting panel. In order to prevent vibration, some speakers will already have such a gasket fitted.

If a pod type speaker was supplied with the radio, the best acoustic results will normally be obtained by mounting it behind the rear seat. The pod can be secured to the mounting panel with self-tapping screws.

When connecting a rear mounted speaker to the radio, the wires should be routed through the vehicle beneath the carpets or floor mats, preferably the middle, or along the side of the floorpan where they will not be trodden on by the passenger. Make the relevant connections as directed by the radio manufacturer.

By now you will have several yards of additional wiring in the car; use PVC tape to secure this wiring out of harm's way. Do not leave electrical leads dangling. Ensure that all new electrical connections are properly made (wires twisted together will not do) and completely secure.

The radio should now be working, but before you pack away your tools it will be necessary to trim the radio to the aerial. If specific instructions are not provided by the radio manufacturer, proceed as follows. Find a station with a low signal strength on the medium-wave band, slowly turn the trim screw of the radio in or out until the loudest reception of the selected station is obtained – the set is then trimmed to the aerial.

Tape players

Fitting instructions for both cartridge and cassette stereo tape players are the same, and in general the same rules apply as when fitting a radio. Tape players are not usually prone to electrical interference like radios, although it can occur, so positioning is not so critical. If possible, the player should be mounted on an even keel. Also it must be possible for a driver wearing a seat belt to reach the unit in order to change or turn over tapes.

For the best results from speakers designed to be recessed into a panel, mount them so that the back of the speaker protrudes into an enclosed chamber within the car (eg door interiors or the boot cavity).

To fit recessed type speakers in the front doors, first check that there is sufficient room to mount a speaker in each door without it fouling the latch or window winding mechanism. Hold the speaker against the skin of the door and draw a line around the periphery of the speaker. With the speaker removed, draw a second cutting line within the first to allow enough room for the entry of the speaker back, but at the same time providing a broad seat for the speaker flange. When you are sure that the cutting-line is correct, drill a series of holes around its periphery. Pass a hacksaw blade through one of the holes and then cut through the metal between the holes until the centre section of the panel falls out.

De-burr the edges of the hole and then paint the raw metal to prevent corrosion. Cut a corresponding hole in the door trim panel, ensuring that it will be completely covered by the speaker grille. Now drill a hole in the door edge and a corresponding hole in the door surround. These holes are to feed the speaker leads through, so fit grommets. Pass the speaker leads through the door trim, door skin and out through the holes in the side of the door and door surround. Refit

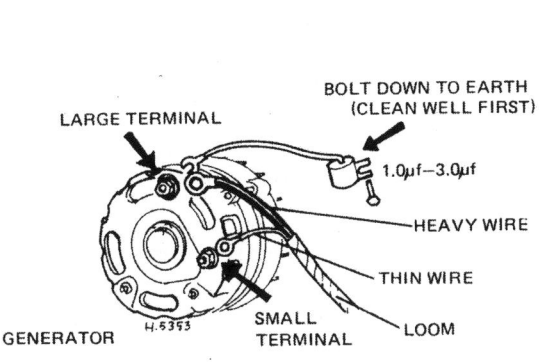

Fig. 10.12 The correct way to connect a capacitor to a generator (Sec 58)

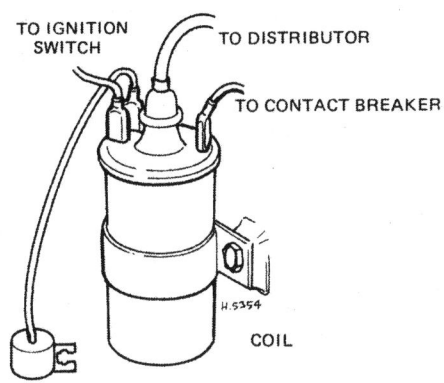

Fig. 10.13 The capacitor must be connected to the ignition switch side of the coil (Sec 58)

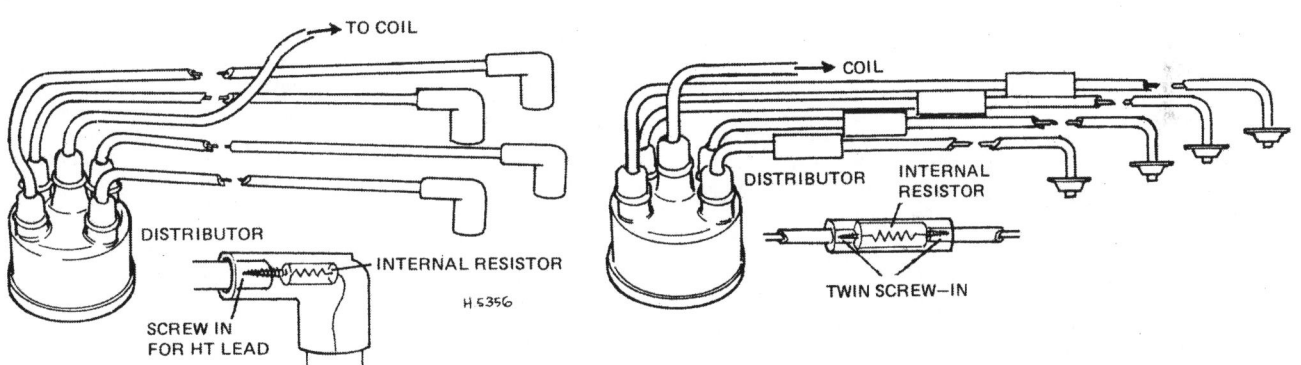

Fig. 10.14 Ignition HT lead suppressors (Sec 58)

Resistive spark plug caps   *'In-line' suppressors*

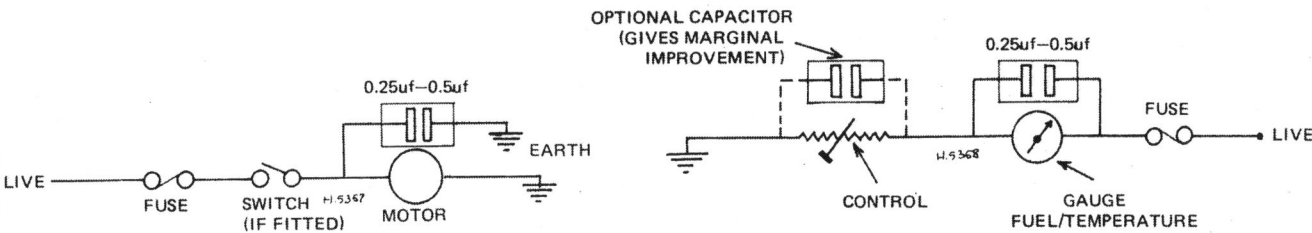

Fig. 10.15 Correct method of suppressing electric motors (Sec 58)

Fig. 10.16 Method of suppressing gauges and their control units (Sec 58)

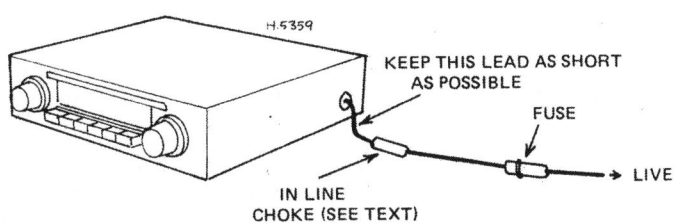

Fig. 10.17 An 'in-line' choke should be fitted into the live supply lead as close to the unit as possible (Sec 58)

the door trim panel and then secure the speaker to the door using self-tapping screws. **Note**: *If the speaker is fitted with a shield to prevent water dripping on it, ensure that this shield is at the top.*

Pod type speakers can be fastened behind the seats, or anywhere else offering a corresponding mounting point on each side of the car. If the pod speakers are mounted behind the seat. it is a good idea to drill several large diameter holes through to the boot cavity beneath each speaker – this will improve the sound reproduction. Pod speakers sometimes offer a better reproduction quality if they face the rear window -- which then acts as a reflector – so it is worthwhile to do a little experimenting before finally fixing the speaker.

58 Radios and tape players – suppression of interference (general)

To eliminate buzzes and other unwanted noises costs very little and is not as difficult as sometimes thought. With a modicum of common sense and patience, and following the instructions in the following paragraphs, interference can be virtually eliminated.

The first cause for concern is the generator. The noise this makes over the radio is like an electric mixer and the noise speeds up when you rev up (if you wish to prove the point, you can remove the drivebelt and try it). The remedy for this is simple; connect a $1.0 \mu f$ to $3.0 \mu f$ capacitor between earth, probably the bolt that holds down the generator base, and the *large* terminal on the dynamo or alternator. This is most important for if you connect it to the small terminal, you will probably damage the generator permanently (see Fig. 10.12).

A second common cause of electrical interference is the ignition system. Here a 1.0 f capacitor must be connected between earth and the 'switch' terminal on the coil (see Fig. 10.13). This may stop the tick-tick-tick sound that comes over the speaker. Next comes the spark itself.

There are several ways of curing interference from the ignition HT system. One is to use carbon fibre HT leads, but these have a tendency to 'snap' inside and you don't know then why you are firing on only half your cylinders. So the second, and more successful method is to use resistive spark plug caps (see Fig. 10.14) of about 10 000 ohm to 15 000 ohm resistance. If due to lack of room these cannot be used, an alternative is to use 'in-line' suppressors (Fig. 10.14). If the interference is not too bad, you may get away with only one suppressor in the coil to distributor line. If the interference does continue (a 'clacking' noise), then doctor all HT leads.

At this stage it is advisable to check that the radio is well earthed, also the aerial and to see that the aerial plug is pushed well into the set and that the radio is properly trimmed (see preceding Section). In addition, check that the wire which supplies the power to the set is as short as possible and does not wander all over the car. At this stage it is a good idea to check that the fuse is of the correct rating. For most sets this will be about 1 to 2 amps.

At this point, the more usual causes of interference have been suppressed. If the problem still exists, a look at the cause of interference may help to pinpoint the component generating the stray electrical discharges.

The radio picks up electromagnetic waves in the air. Some are made by radio stations and other broadcasters and some, which we do not want, are made by the car itself. The home made signals are produced by stray electrical discharges floating around in the car. Common producers of these signals are electric motors, ie the windscreen wipers, electric screen washers, electric window winders, heater fan or an electric aerial if fitted. Other sources of interference are electric fuel pumps, flashing turn signals and instruments. The remedy for these cases is shown in Fig. 10.15 for an electric motor whose interference is not too bad and Fig. 10.16 for instrument suppression. Turn signals are not normally suppressed. In recent years, radio manufacturers have included in the live line of the radio, in addition to the fuse, an in-line choke. If your circuit lacks one of these, put one in as shown in Fig. 10.17.

All the foregoing components are available from radio shops or accessory stores. If you have an electric clock fitted, this should be suppressed by connecting a $0.5 \mu f$ capacitor directly across it as shown for a motor in Fig. 10.15.

If after all this you are still experiencing radio interference, first assess how bad it is, for the human ear can filter out unobtrusive unwanted noises quite easily. But if you are still adamant about eradicating the noise, then continue.

As a first step, a few experts seem to favour a screen between the radio and the engine. This is OK as far as it goes, literally! The whole set is screened anyway and if interference can get past that then a small piece of aluminium is not going to stop it.

A more sensible way of screening is to discover if interference is coming down the wires. First, take the live lead; interference can get between the set and the choke (hence the reason for keeping the wires short). One remedy here is to screen the wire and this is done by buying screened wire and fitting that. The loudspeaker lead could be screened also to prevent pick-up getting back to the radio although this is unlikely.

Without doubt, the worst source of radio interference comes from the ignition HT leads, even if they have been suppressed. The ideal way of suppressing these is to slide screening tubes over the leads themselves. As this is impractical, we can place an aluminium shield over the majority of the lead areas. In a vee or twin-cam engine this is relatively easy but for a straight engine, the results are not particularly good.

Now for the really impossible cases, here are a few tips to try out. Where metal comes into contact with metal, an electrical disturbance is caused, which is why good clean connections are essential. To remove interference due to overlapping or butting panels, you must bridge the join with a wide braided earth strap (like that from the frame to the engine/transmission). The most common moving parts that could create noise and should be strapped are, in order of importance:

(a) *Silencer to frame*
(b) *Exhaust pipe to engine block and frame*
(c) *Air cleaner to frame*
(d) *Front and rear bumpers to frame*
(e) *Steering column to frame*
(f) *Bonnet and boot lids to frame*
(g) *Hood frame to bodyframe on soft tops*

These faults are most pronounced when (1) the engine is idling or (2) labouring under load. Although the moving parts are already connected with nuts, bolts, etc, these do tend to rust and corrode, thus creating a high resistance interference source.

If you have a ragged sounding pulse when mobile, this could be wheel or tyre static. This can be cured by buying some anti-static powder and sprinkling it liberally inside the tyres.

If the interference takes the shape of a high pitched screeching noise that changes its note when the car is in motion and only comes now and then, this could be related to the aerial, especially if it is of the telescopic or whip type. This source can be cured quite simply by pushing a small rubber ball on top of the aerial as this breaks the electric field before it can form; but it would be much better to buy yourself a new aerial of a reputable brand. If, on the other hand, you are getting a loud rushing sound every time you brake, then this is brake static. This effect is most prominent on hot dry days and is cured only by fitting a special kit, which is quite expensive.

In conclusion, it is pointed out that it is relatively easy and therefore cheap, to eliminate 95 per cent of all noise, but to eliminate the final 5 per cent is time and money consuming. It is up to the individual to decide if it is worth it. Please remember also, that you cannot get a concert hall performance out of a cheap radio.

Finally at the beginning of this Section are mentioned tape players; these are not usually affected by interference but in a very bad case, the best remedies are the first three suggestions, plus using a 3 to 5 amp choke in the 'live' line, and in extreme cases, screening the live and speaker wires.

Note: *If your car is fitted with electronic ignition, then it is not recommended that either the spark plug resistors or the ignition coil capacitor be fitted as these may damage the system. Most electronic ignition units have built in suppression and should, therefore, not cause interference.*

See overleaf for 'Fault diagnosis' – electrical system

59 Fault diagnosis – electrical system

Symptom	Reason(s)
Starter motor fails to turn engine	
No current at starter motor	Battery discharged
	Battery defective internally
	Battery terminal leads loose or earth lead not securely attached to body
	Loose or broken connections in starter motor circuit
	Starter motor switch or solenoid faulty
Faulty motor	Starter motor pinion jammed in mesh with ring gear
	Starter brushes badly worn, sticking, or brush wires loose
	Commutator dirty, worn, or burnt
	Starter motor armature faulty
	Field coils earthed
Starter motor turns engine very slowly	
Electrical defects	Battery in discharged condition
	Starter brushes badly worn, sticking, or brush wires loose
	Loose wires in starter motor circuit
Starter motor operates without turning engine	
Dirt or oil on drivegear	Starter motor pinion sticking on screwed sleeve
Mechanical damage	Pinion or ring gear teeth broken or worn
Electrical defect	Discharged battery
Starter motor noisy or excessively rough engagement	
Lack of attention or mechanical damage	Pinion or ring gear teeth broken or worn
	Starter drive main spring broken
	Starter motor retaining bolts loose
Battery will not hold charge for more than a few days	
Wear or damage	Battery defective internally
	Electrolyte level too low or electrolyte too weak due to leakage
	Plate separators no longer fully effective
	Battery plates severely sulphated
	Drivebelt slipping
Insufficient current flow to keep battery charged	Battery terminal connections loose or corroded
	Dynamo or alternator not charging properly
	Short in lighting circuit causing continual battery drain
	Regulator unit not working correctly (dynamo)
Ignition light fails to go out battery runs flats in a few days	
Dynamo not charging	Drivebelt loose and slipping, or broken
	Brushes worn, sticking, broken or dirty
	Brush springs weak or broken
	Commutator dirty, greasy, worn, or burnt
	Armature badly worn or armature shaft bent
	Commutator bars shorting
	Dynamo bearings badly worn
	Field coil burnt, open or short circuited
Regulator or cut-out not working correctly	Regulators incorrectly set
	Cut-out incorrectly set
	Open circuit in wiring of regulators or cut-out circuits
Alternator not charging	Drivebelt slipping or broken
	Alternator internal defect
Wipers	
Wiper motor fails to work	Blown fuse
	Wire connections loose, disconnected or broken
	Brushes badly worn
	Armature worn or faulty
	Field coils faulty
Wiper motor works very slowly and takes excessive current	Commutator dirty, greasy, or burnt
	Drive to wheelboxes too bent or unlubricated
	Armature bearings dry or unaligned
	Armature badly worn or faulty

Symptom	Reason(s)
Wiper motor works slowly and takes little current	Brushes badly worn Commutator dirty, greasy, or burnt Armature badly worn or faulty
Wiper motor works but wiper blades remain static	Driving cable rack disengaged or faulty Wheelbox gear and spindle damaged or worn Wiper motor gearbox parts badly worn

Horn

Horn operates all the time	Horn push either earthed or stuck down Horn cable to horn push earthed
Horn fails to operate	Blown fuse Cable or cable connection loose, broken or disconnected Horn as an internal fault
Horn emits intermittent or unsatisfactory noise	Cable connections loose Horn incorrectly adjusted

Lights

Lights do not come on	If engine not running, battery discharged Light bulb filament burnt out or bulbs broken Wire connections loose, disconnected or broken Light switch shorting or otherwise faulty
Lights come on but fade out	If engine not running battery discharged
Lights give very poor illumination	Lamp glasses dirty Reflector tarnished or dirty Lamps badly out of adjustment Incorrect bulb with too low wattage fitted Existing bulbs old and badly discoloured Electrical wiring too thin, not allowing full current to pass
Lights work erratically – flashing on and off especially over bumps	Battery terminals or earth connections loose Lights not earthing properly Contacts in light switch faulty

Wiring diagrams commence overleaf

Key to Figs. 10.18 to 10.28 inclusive. Not all items are fitted to all models

1 Dynamo/alternator
2 Control box
3 Battery
4 Starter solenoid or switch
5 Starter motor
6 Lighting switch
7 Headlamp dipswitch
8 RH headlamp
9 LH headlamp
10 High beam warning lamp
11 RH parking lamp
12 LH parking lamp
13 Panel lamp switch
14 Panel lamps
15 Number plate illumination lamp
16 RH stop and tail lamp
17 LH stop and tail lamp
18 Stop-lamp switch
19 Fuse unit
20 Interior courtesy lamp
21 RH door switch
22 LH door switch
23 Horn(s)
24 Horn push
25 Flasher unit
26 Direction indicator switch or combination direction indicator/headlamp flasher/dipswitch/horn push switch
27 Direction indicator warning lamp
28 RH front flasher lamp
29 LH front flasher lamp
30 RH rear flasher lamp
31 LH rear flasher lamp
32 Heater or fresh-air motor switch
33 Heater or fresh-air motor
34 Fuel gauge
35 Fuel gauge tank unit
36 Windscreen wiper switch
37 Windscreen wiper motor
38 Ignition/starter switch
39 Ignition coil
40 Distributor
41 Fuel pump

42 Horn relay
43 Oil pressure gauge
44 Ignition warning lamp
45 Speedometer
46 Coolant temperature gauge
49 Reverse lamp switch
50 Reverse lamp
57 Cigar lighter – illuminated
60 Radio
64 Bi-metal instrument voltage stabilizer
65 Luggage compartment lamp switch
66 Luggage compartment lamp
67 Line fuse
77 Windscreen washer pump
94 Oil filter switch
95 Tachometer
105 Oil filter warning lamp
118 Combined windscreen washer and wiper switch
152 Hazard warning lamp
153 Hazard warning switch
154 Hazard warning flasher unit
159 Brake pressure warning lamp and lamp test push
160 Brake pressure failure switch
168 Ignition key audible warning buzzer
169 Ignition key audible warning door switch
170 RH front side-marker lamp
171 LH front side-marker lamp
172 RH rear side-marker lamp
173 LH rear side-marker lamp
198 Driver's seat belt buckle switch
199 Passenger's seat belt buckle switch
200 Passenger seat switch
201 Seat belt warning gearbox switch
202 'Fasten belts' warning light
203 Line diode

Colour code for all wiring diagrams

B Black
G Green
K Pink
LG Light green
N Brown
O Orange

P Purple
R Red
S Slate
U Blue
W White
Y Yellow

When a cable has two colour code letters, the first denotes the main colour and the second denotes the tracer colour

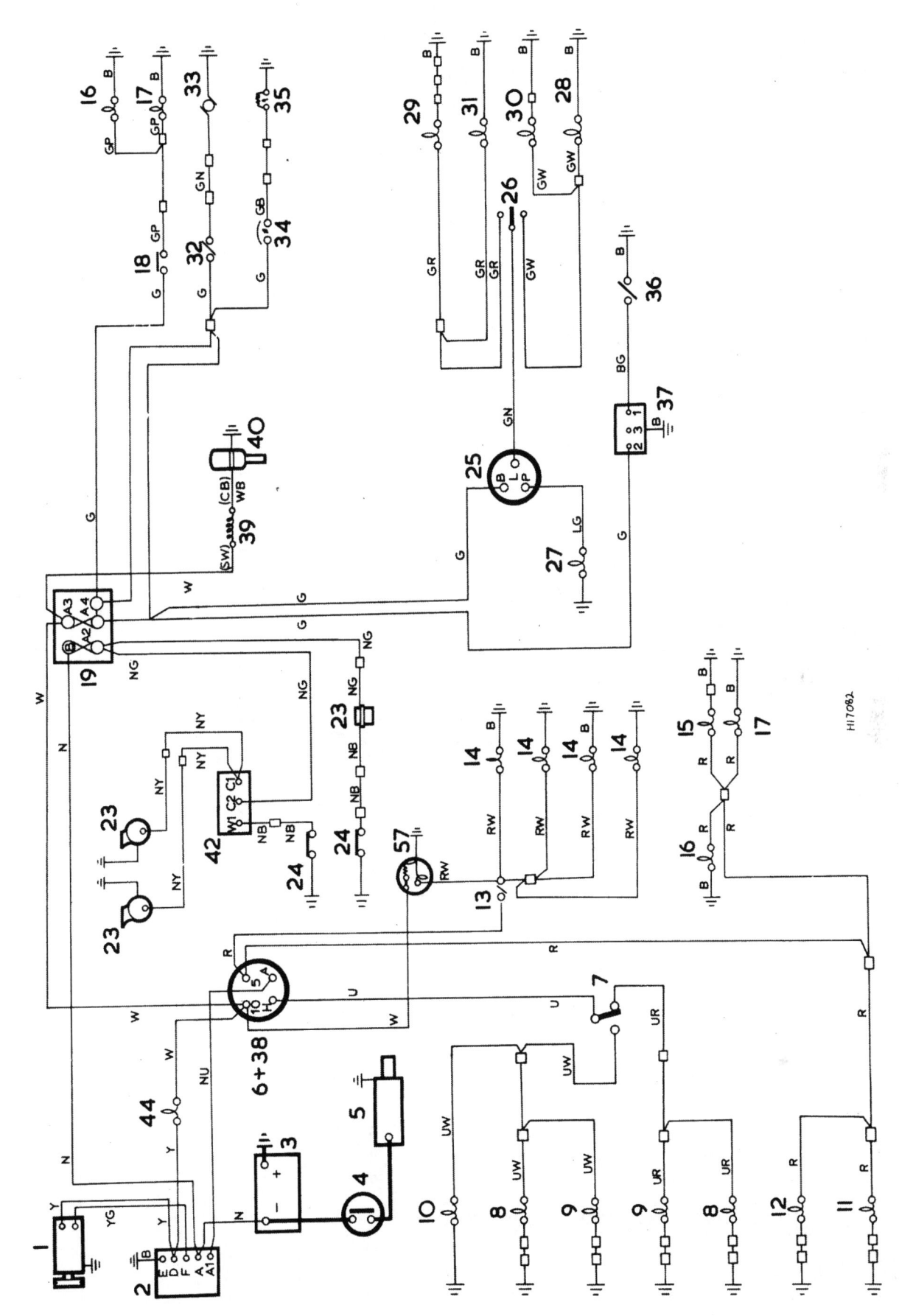

Fig. 10.18 Wiring diagram – Sprite Mk I

HI 7082

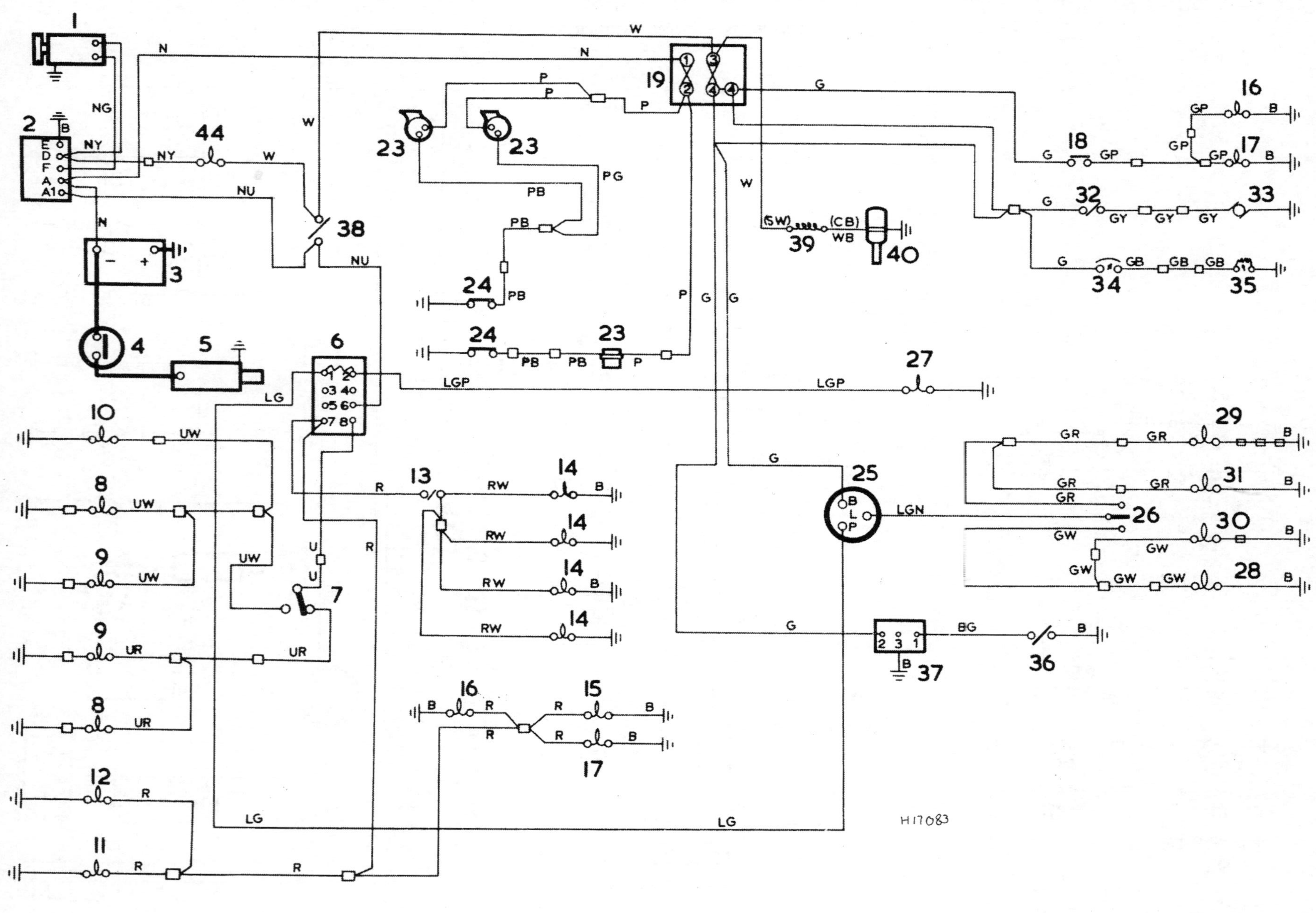

Fig. 10.19 Wiring diagram – Sprite Mk II, Midget Mk I (948 cc)

H17083

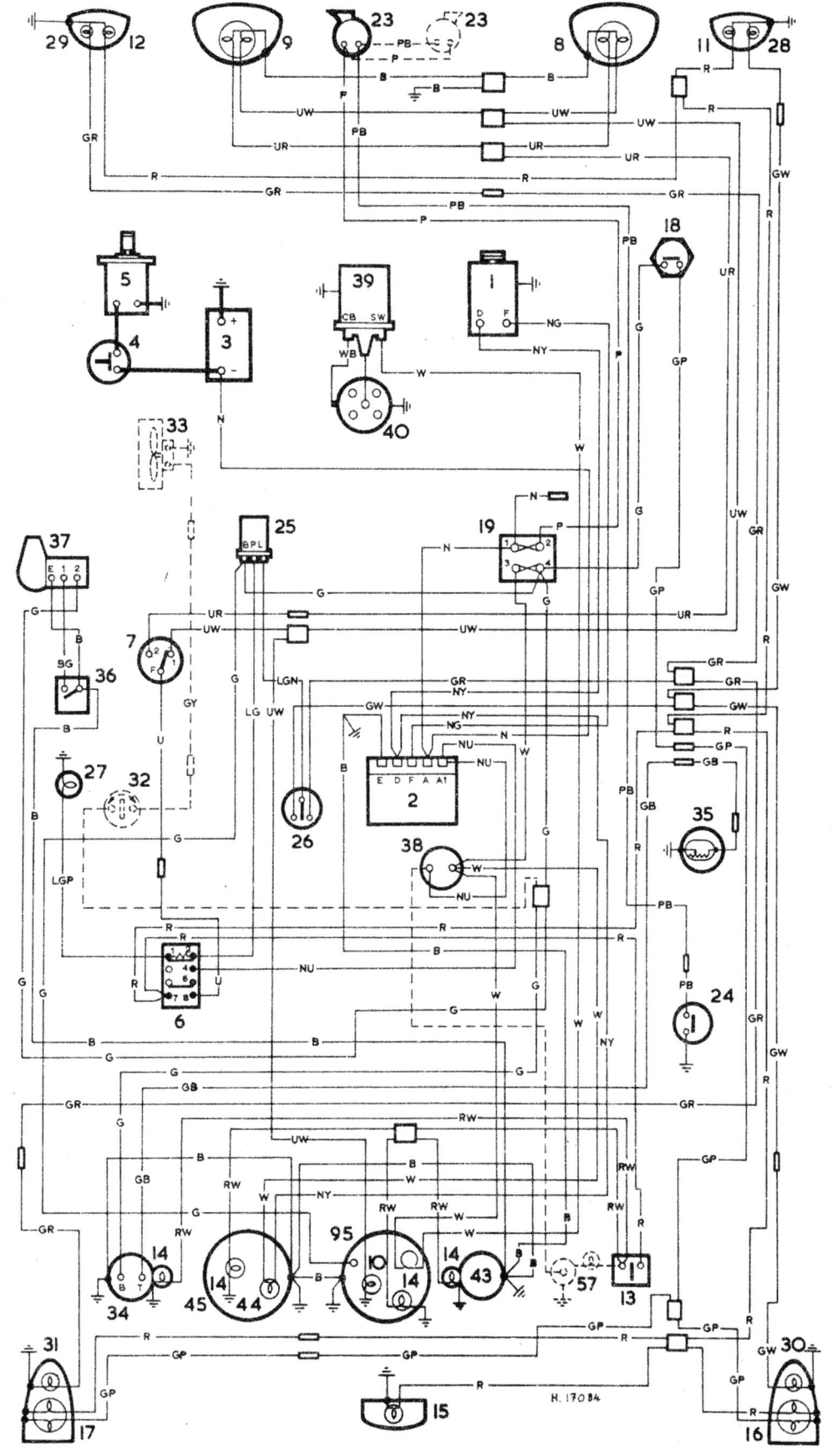

Fig. 10.20 Wiring diagram – Sprite Mk II, Midget Mk I (948 cc) & Sprite Mk III,
Midget Mk II (1098 cc)

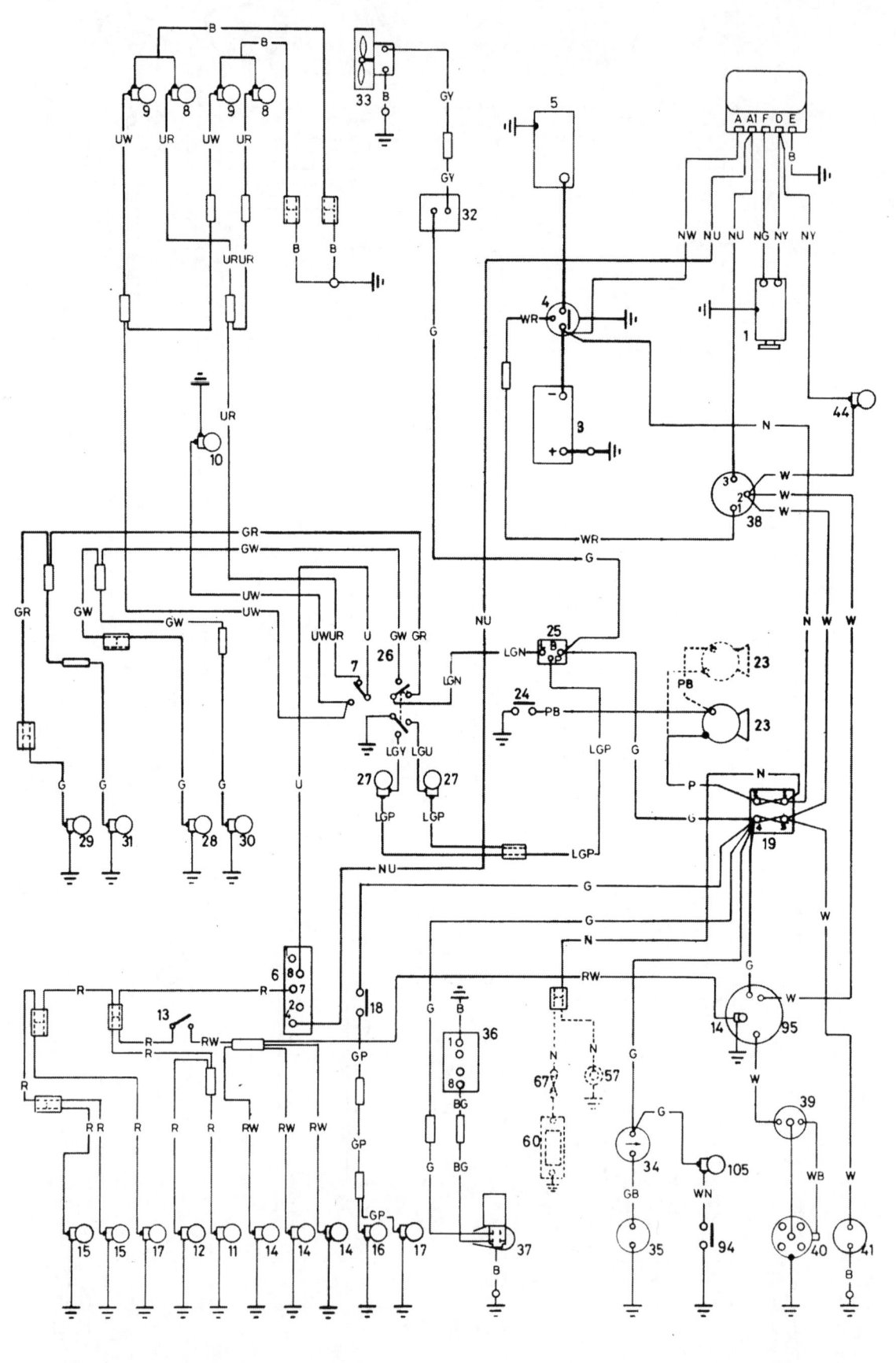

Fig. 10.21 Wiring diagram (UK models) – Sprite Mk IV, Midget Mk III (1275 cc, positive earth)

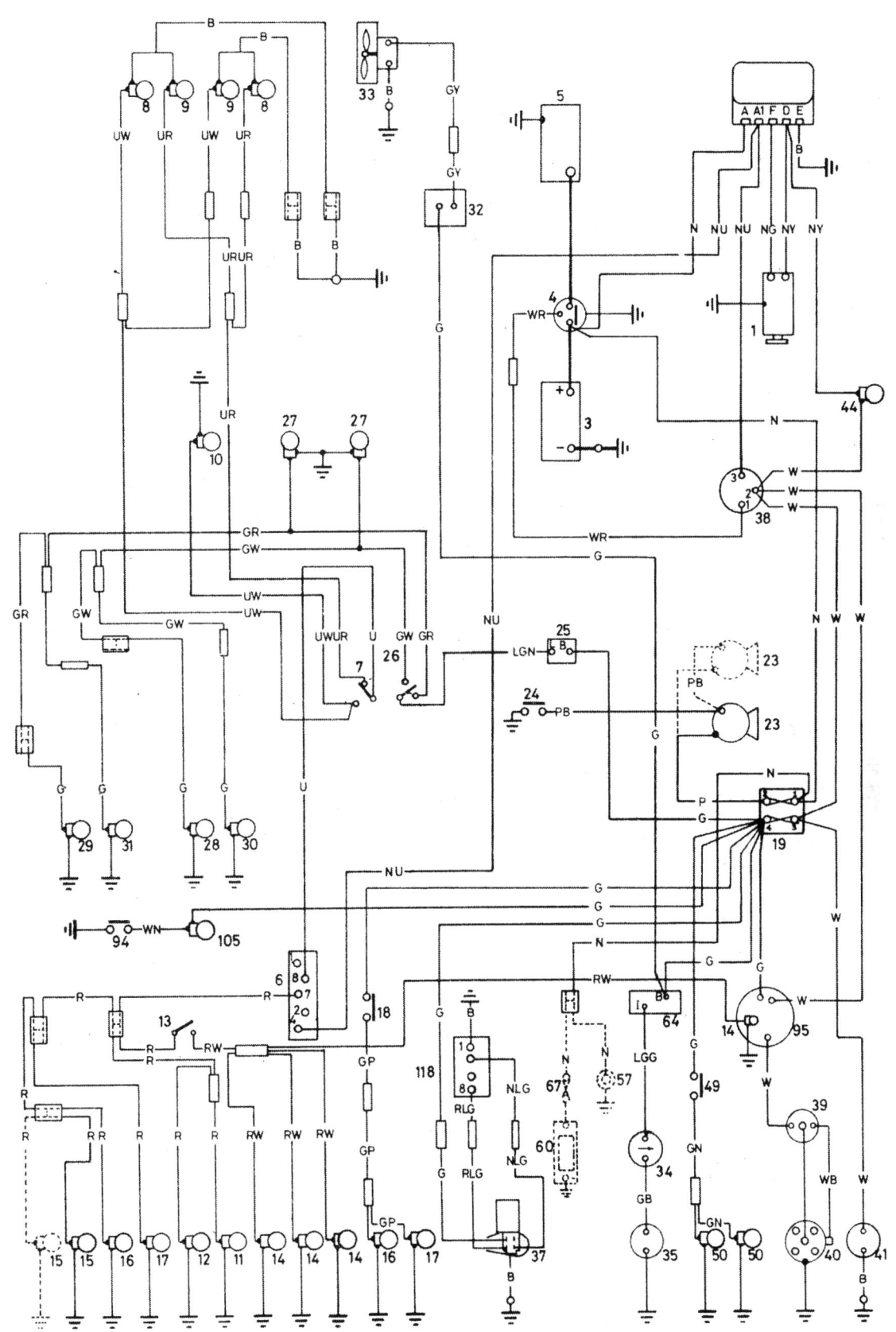

Fig. 10.22 Wiring diagram (UK models) – Sprite Mk IV (car nos H – AN9 – 72041 to H – AN10 – 85286), Midget Mk III
(car nos. G – AN4 – 60460 to G – AN5 – 74885, G – AN4 – 74901 to
G – AN4 – 74947, G – AN4 – 75701 to 75735)

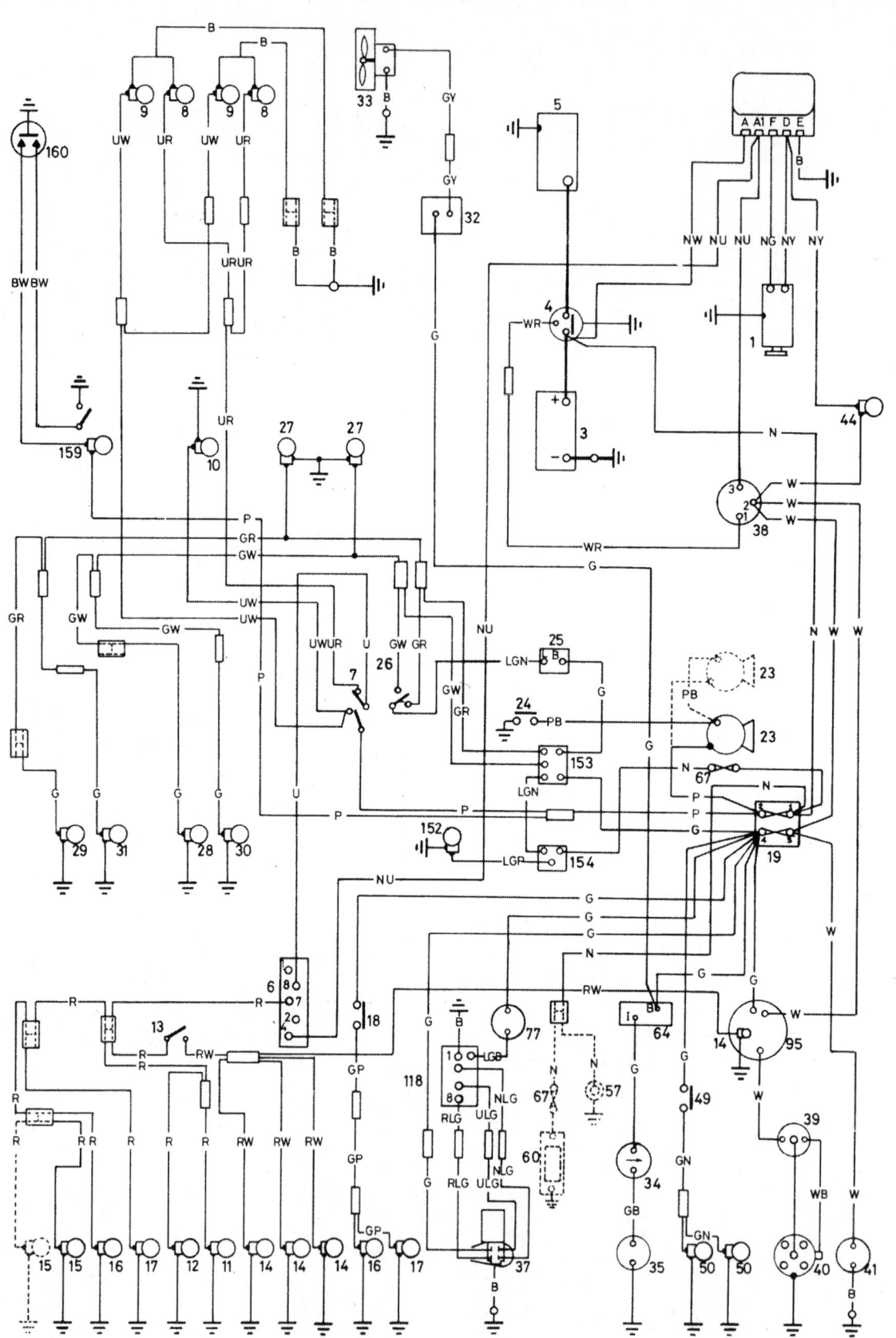

Fig. 10.23 Wiring diagram (USA models) – Sprite Mk IV (car nos. H – AN9 – 72041 to H – AN9 – 77590), Midget Mk III
(car nos. G – AN4 – 60460 to G – AN4 – 66225)

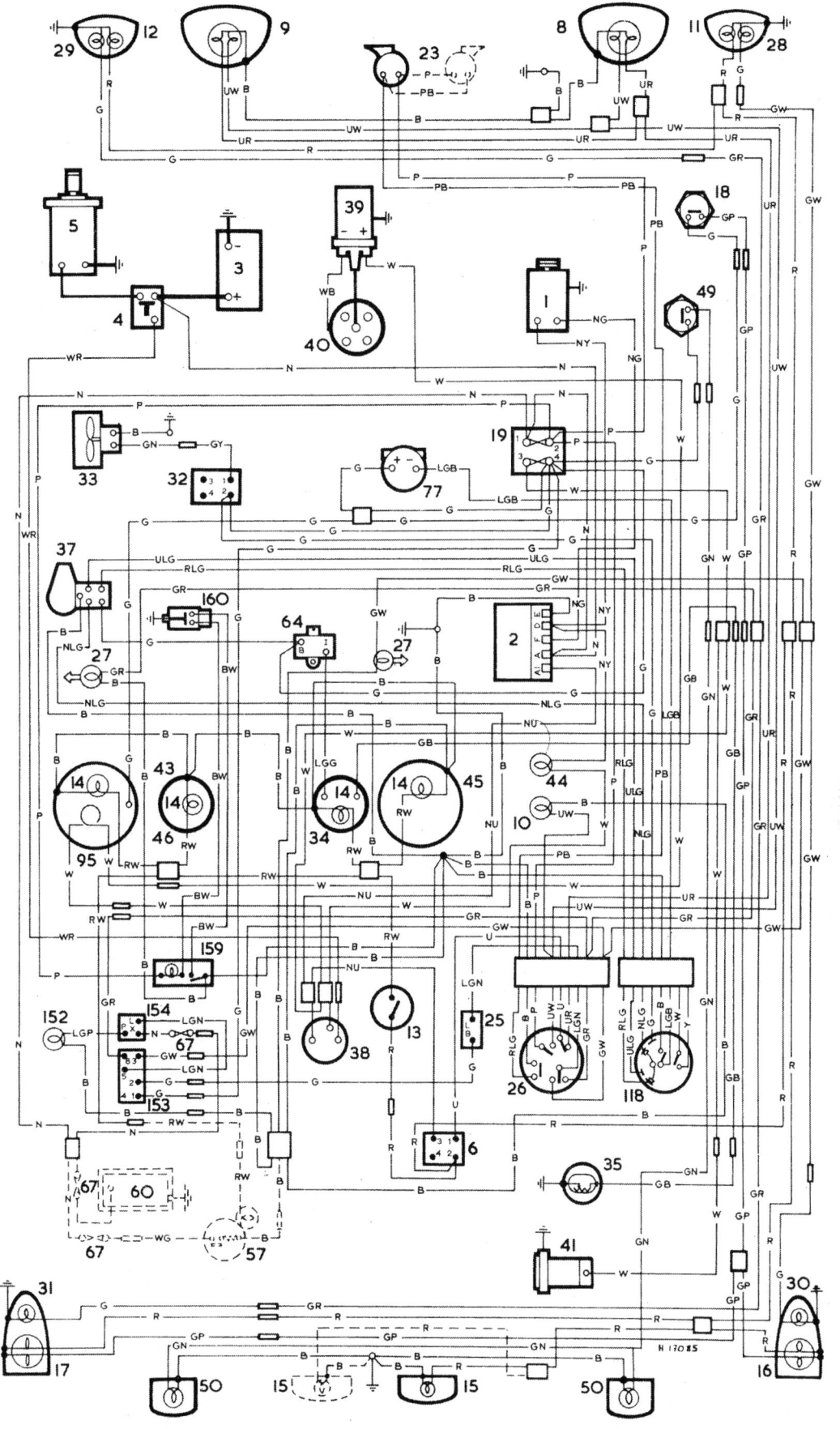

Fig. 10.24 Wiring diagram (USA models) – Sprite Mk IV (car nos. H – AN9 – 77591 onwards), Midget Mk III (car nos. G – AN4 – 66226 to G – AN5 – 74885, G – AN4 – 74901 to G – AN4 – 74947, G – AN4 – 75701 to 75735)

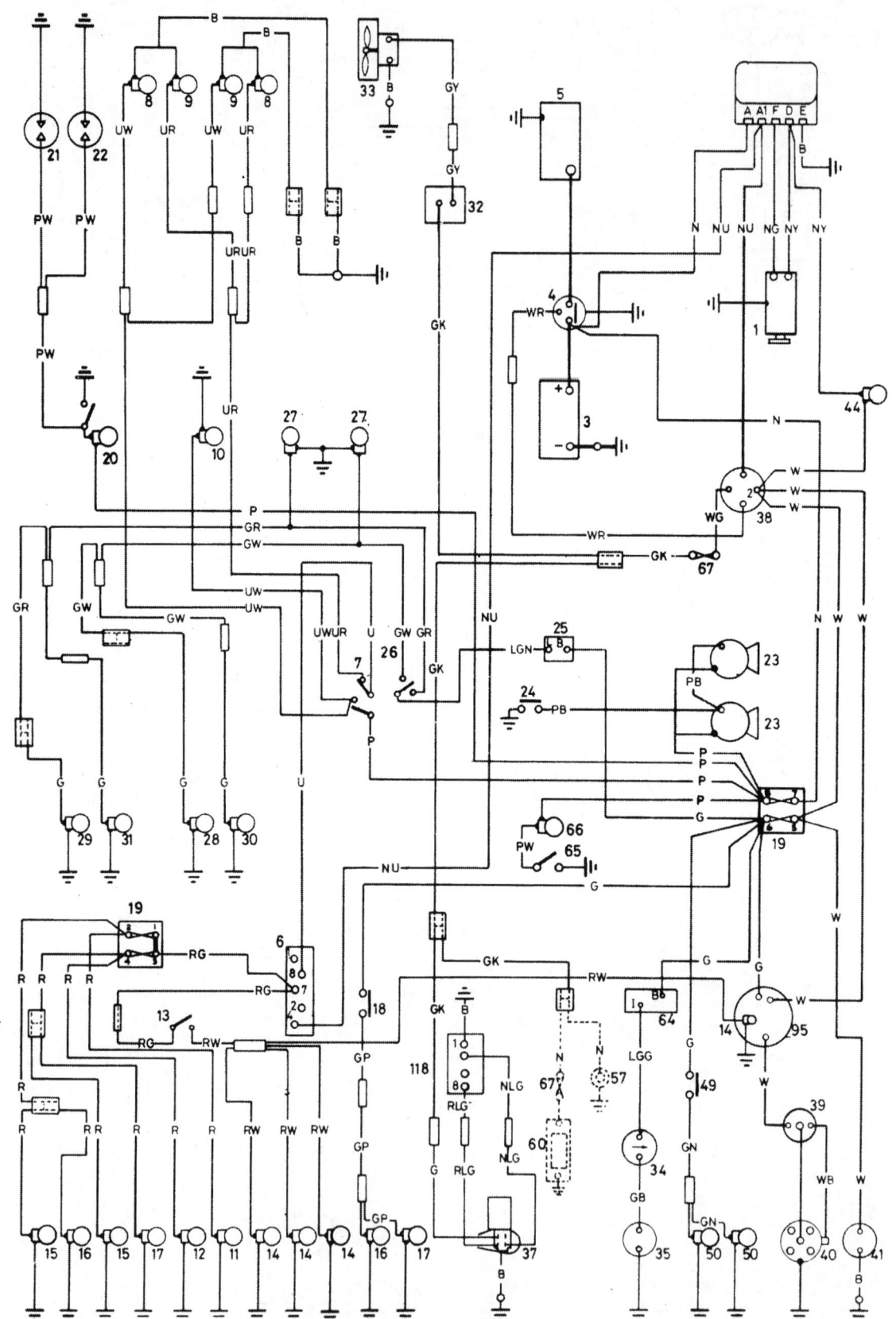

Fig. 10.25 Wiring diagram (UK models) – Sprite Mk IV (car no. H – AN10 – 85287 onwards), Midget Mk III (car nos. G – AN5 – 74886 to G – AN5 – 105500)

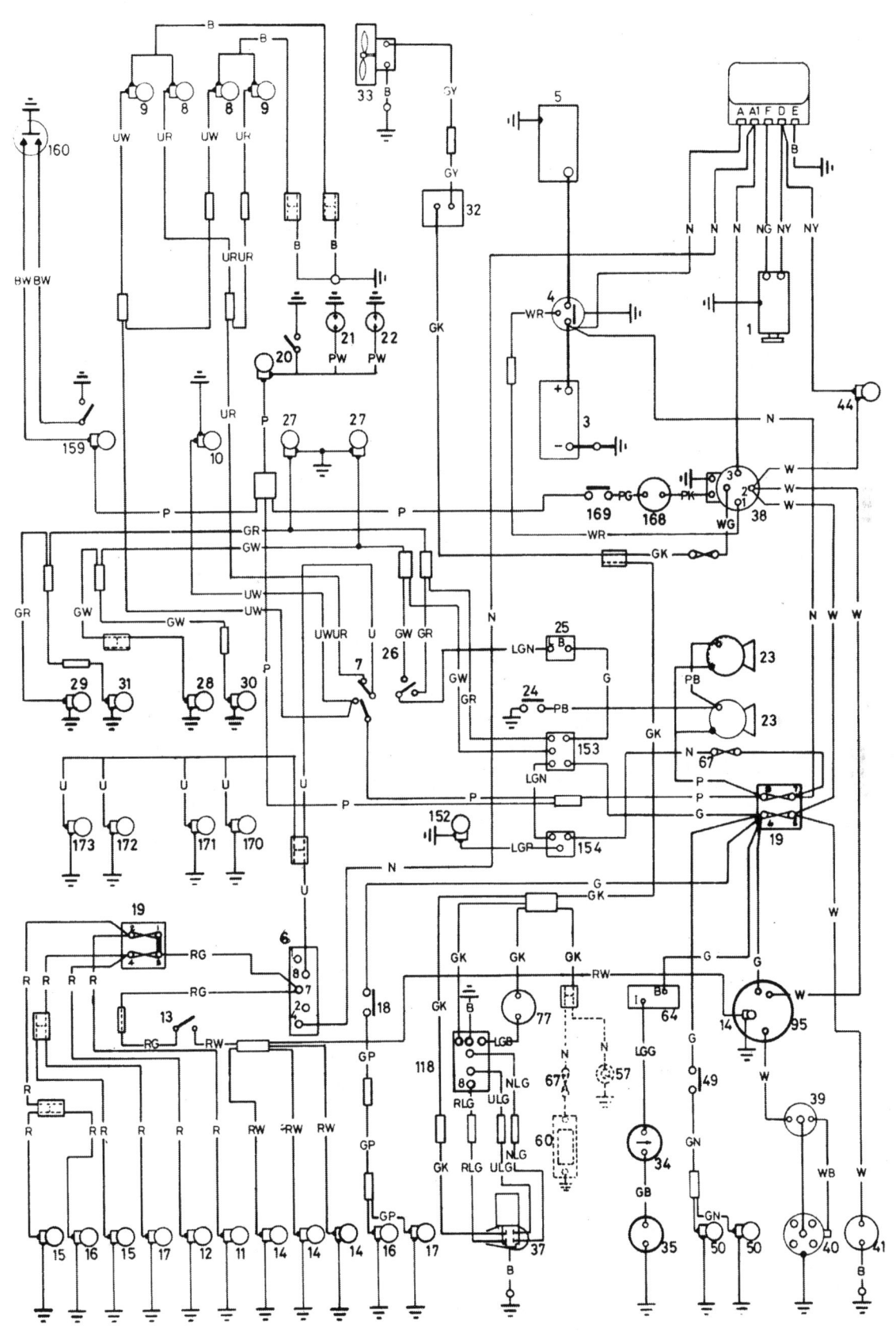

Fig. 10.26 Wiring diagram (USA models) – Midget Mk III (car nos. G – AN5 – 74886 to
G – AN5 – 105500)

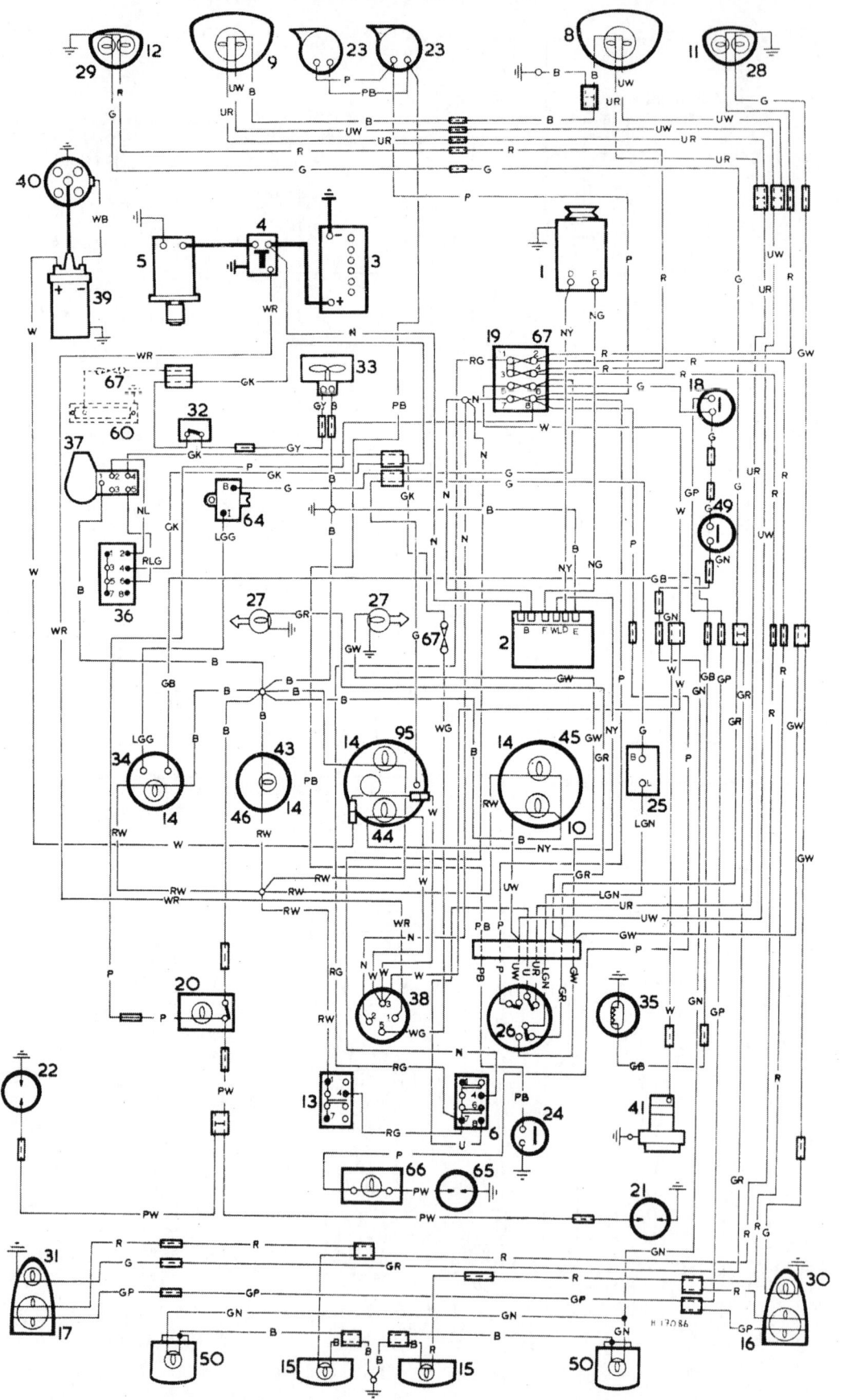

Fig. 10.27 Wiring diagram (UK models) – Midget Mk III (car no. G – AN5 – 105501 onwards, except 1500 models)

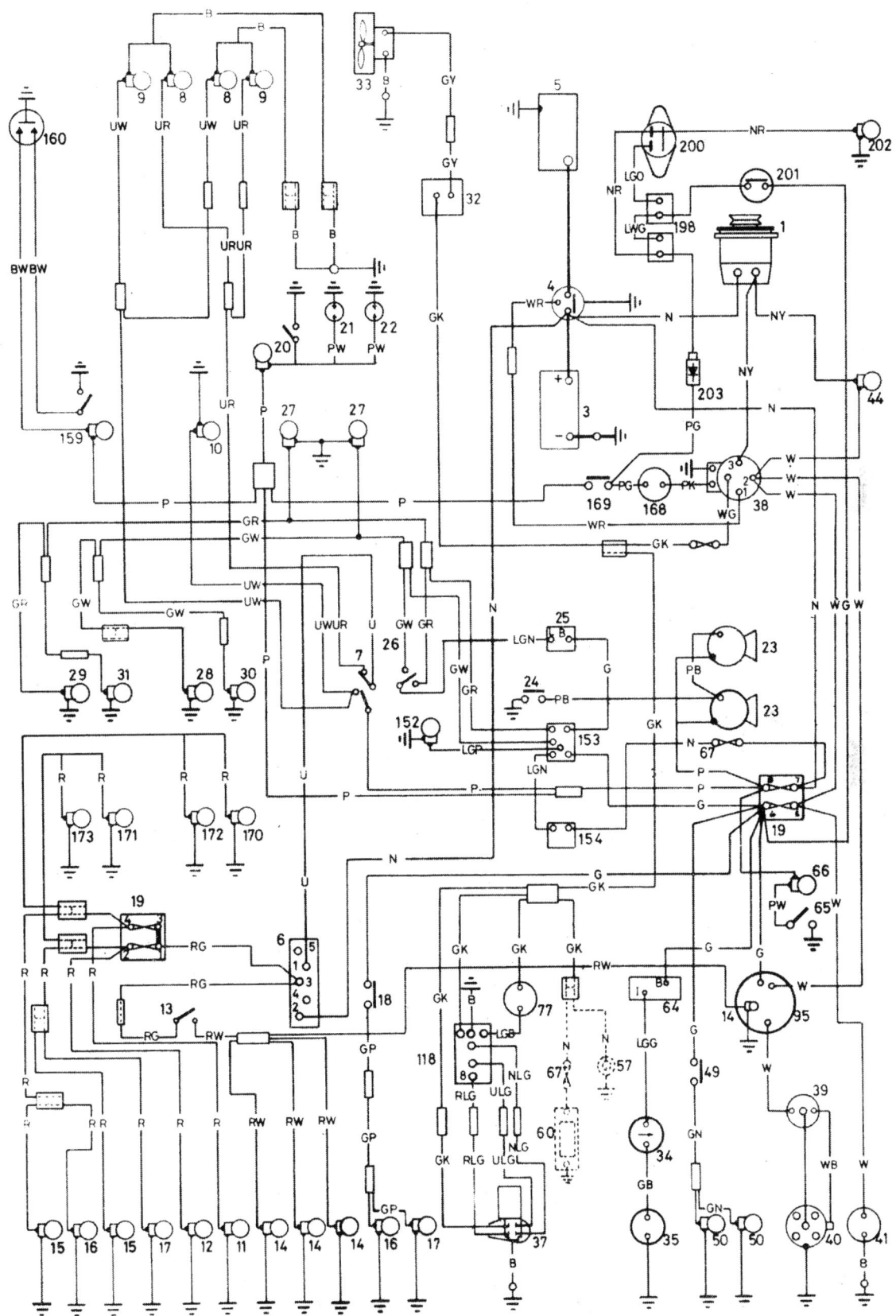

Fig. 10.28 Wiring diagram – Midget Mk III, USA (car no. G – AN5 – 105501 onwards to end of 1977 production), Midget Mk III, UK (1500 models to end of 1977 production)

Key to Fig. 10.29. Optional equipment shown dotted

1 RH front side marker lamp
2 Reverse lamps switch
3 Stop lamp switch
4 RH front flasher lamp
5 Horn push
6 Horn
7 Oil pressure switch
8 Service interval counter for EGR valve
9 Diode for EGR valve service interval counter
10 Diode for brake warning
11 Diode for catalytic converter service interval counter – if fitted
12 Service interval counter for catalytic converter – if fitted
13 RH rear side-marker lamp
14 RH rear flasher lamp
15 RH tail lamp
16 Stop-lamp
17 RH parking lamp
18 Headlamp main beam
19 Headlamp dip beam
20 Direction indicator switch
21 Headlamp dipswitch
22 Headlamp flasher switch
23 Windscreen washer pump
24 Running-on control valve oil pressure switch
25 Running-on control valve
26 Coolant temperature transmitter
27 Line fuse for running-on control valve
28 Flasher unit
29 Brake pressure failure switch
30 Time delay buzzer
31 Fuel gauge tank unit
32 'CATALYST' warning light – if fitted
33 Reverse lamp
34 Combined windscreen washer and wiper switch
35 Instrument voltage stabilizer
36 Hazard warning switch
37 Handbrake switch
38 Interior courtesy lamp door switch
39 EGR valve warning light

40 Number plate illumination lamp
41 Windscreen wiper motor
42 Fuse unit
43 Direction indicator warning lamp
44 Handbrake warning lamp
45 Ignition/starter switch
46 Switch illumination lamp
47 Driver's seat belt buckle switch
48 Interior courtesy lamp
49 Distributor
50 Alternator
51 Resistor – distributor
52 Oil pressure warning light
53 Ignition warning lamp
54 'FASTEN BELTS' warning lamp
55 Luggage compartment lamp
56 Ignition coil
57 Panel lamp
58 Fuel gauge
59 Lighting switch
60 Luggage compartment lamp switch
61 LH parking lamp
62 LH front flasher lamp
63 Starter solenoid
64 Headlamp main beam warning lamp
65 Oil pressure gauge
66 Hazard warning flasher unit
67 Ignition key audible warning door switch
68 Cigar lighter
69 Cigar lighter illumination lamp
70 LH front side-marker lamp
71 Battery
72 Starter motor
73 Heater motor
74 Heater motor switch
75 Tachometer
76 Heater control illumination lamp
77 Panel lamp switch
78 Line fuse for hazard warning
79 Line fuse for radio (if fitted)
80 Radio (if fitted)
81 LH rear flasher lamp
82 LH tail lamp
83 LH rear side-marker lamp

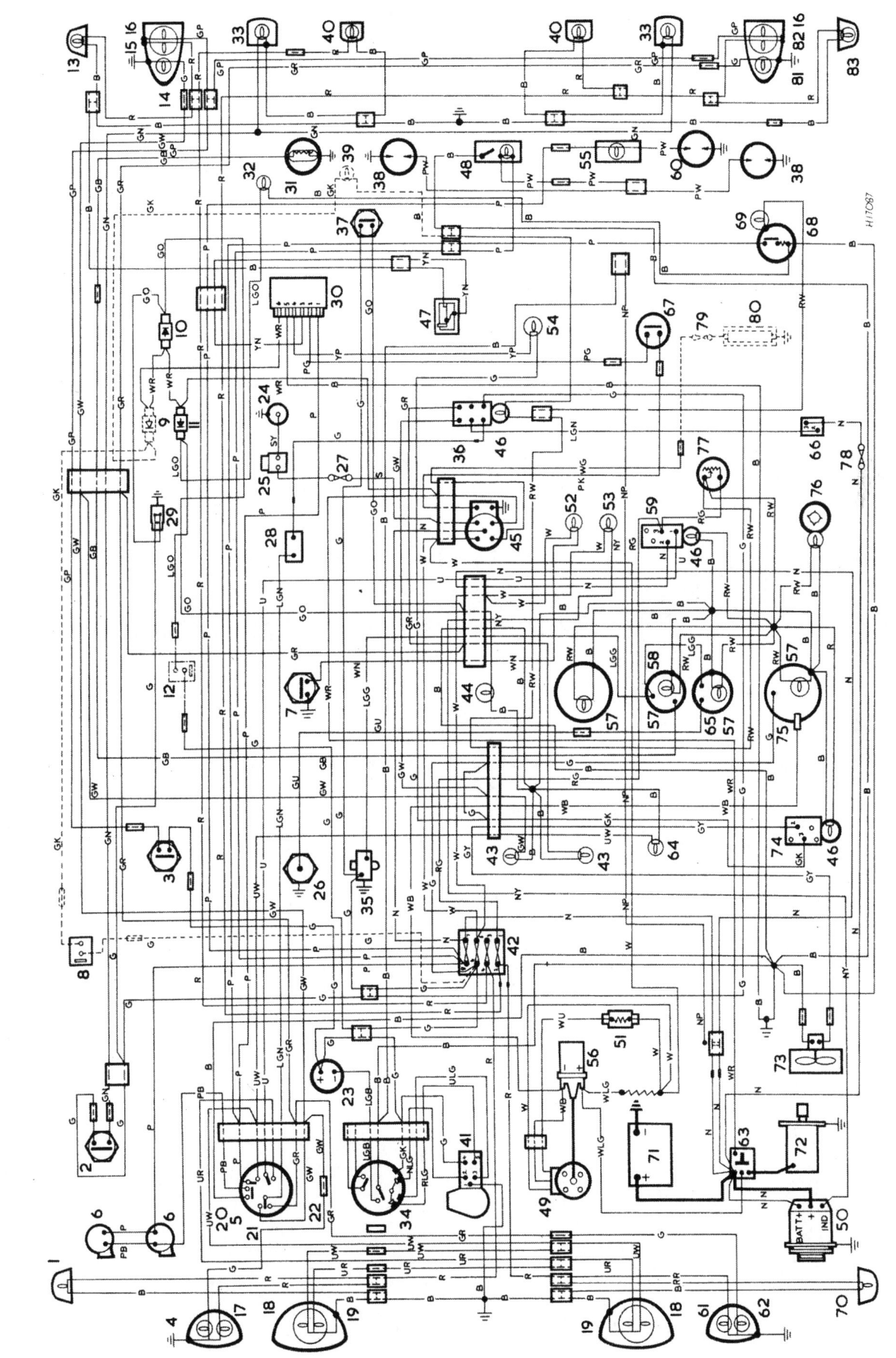

Fig. 10.29 Wiring diagram (California) — 1978 onwards

Key to Fig. 10.30. Optional equipment shown dotted

1 RH front side-marker lamp
2 Reverse lamp switch
3 Stop-lamp switch
4 RH front flasher lamp
5 Horn push
6 Horn
7 Oil pressure switch
8 Diode for brake warning
9 RH rear side-marker lamp
10 RH rear flasher lamp
11 RH tail lamp
12 Stop-lamp
13 RH parking lamp
14 Headlamp main beam
15 Headlamp dip beam
16 Direction indicator switch
17 Headlamp dipswitch
18 Headlamp flasher switch
19 Windscreen washer pump
20 Coolant temperature transmitter
21 Flasher unit
22 Brake pressure failure switch
23 Time delay buzzer
24 Fuel gauge tank unit
25 Reverse lamp
26 Combined windscreen washer and wiper switch
27 Instrument voltage stabilizer
28 Hazard warning switch
29 Handbrake switch
30 Interior courtesy lamp door switch
31 Number-plate illumination lamp
32 Windscreen wiper motor
33 Fuse unit
34 Direction indicator warning lamp
35 Handbrake warning lamp
36 Ignition/starter switch
37 Switch illumination lamp
38 Driver's seat belt buckle switch
39 Interior courtesy lamp
40 Distributor
41 Alternator
42 Resistor – distributor
43 Oil pressure warning light
44 Ignition warning lamp
45 'FASTEN BELTS' warning lamp
46 Luggage compartment lamp
47 Ignition coil
48 Panel lamp
49 Fuel gauge
50 Lighting switch
51 Luggage compartment lamp switch
52 LH parking lamp
53 LH front flasher lamp
54 Starter solenoid
55 Headlamp main beam warning lamp
56 Coolant temperature gauge
57 Hazard warning flasher unit
58 Ignition key audible warning door switch
59 Cigar-lighter
60 Cigar-lighter illumination lamp
61 LH front side-marker lamp
62 Battery
63 Starter motor
64 Heater motor
65 Heater motor switch
66 Tachometer
67 Heater control illumination lamp
68 Panel lamp switch
69 Line fuse for hazard warning
70 Line fuse for radio
71 Radio
72 LH rear flasher lamp
73 LH tail lamp
74 LH rear side-marker lamp

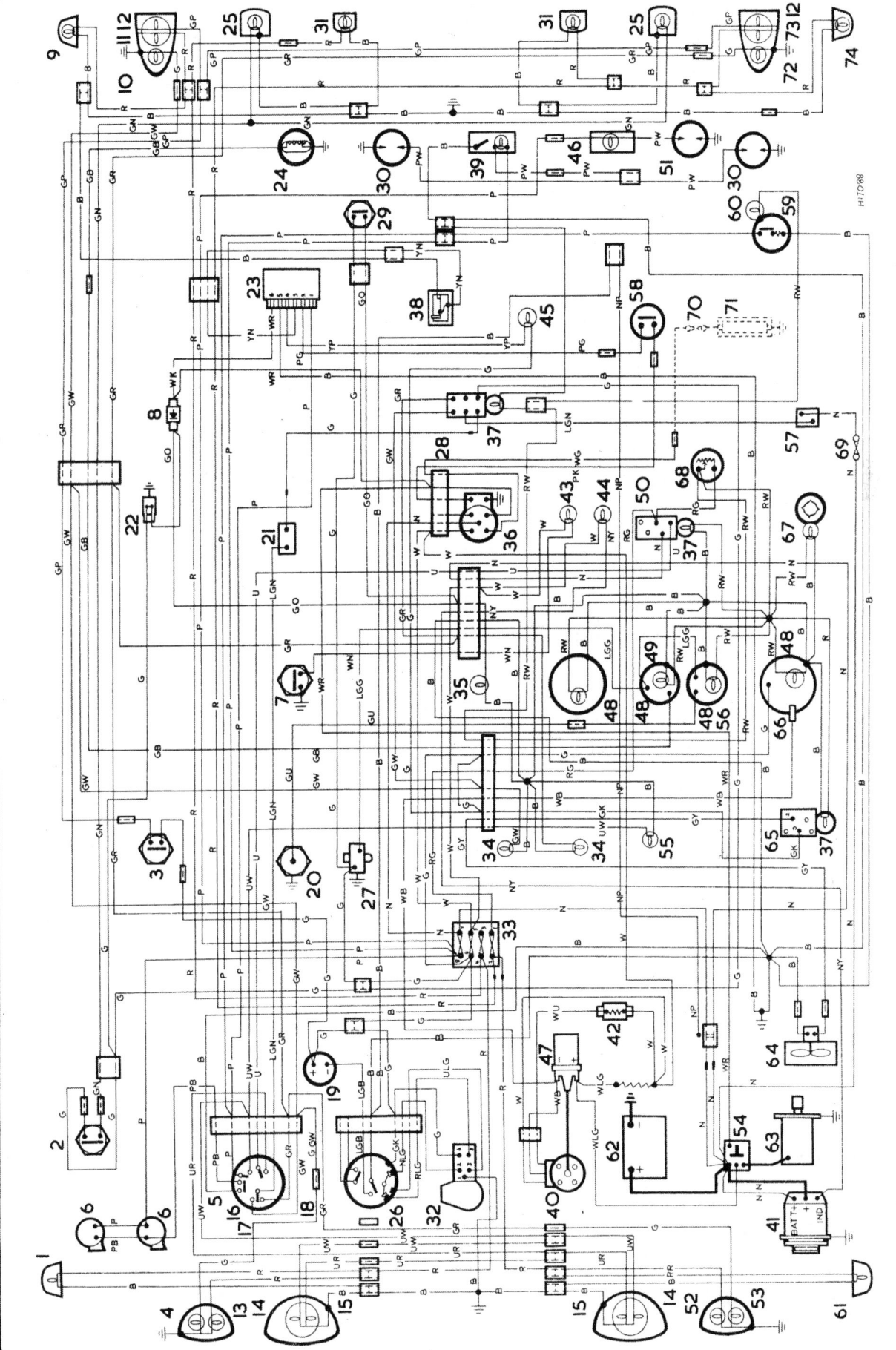

Fig. 10.30 Wiring diagram (USA and Canada, except California) – 1978 onwards

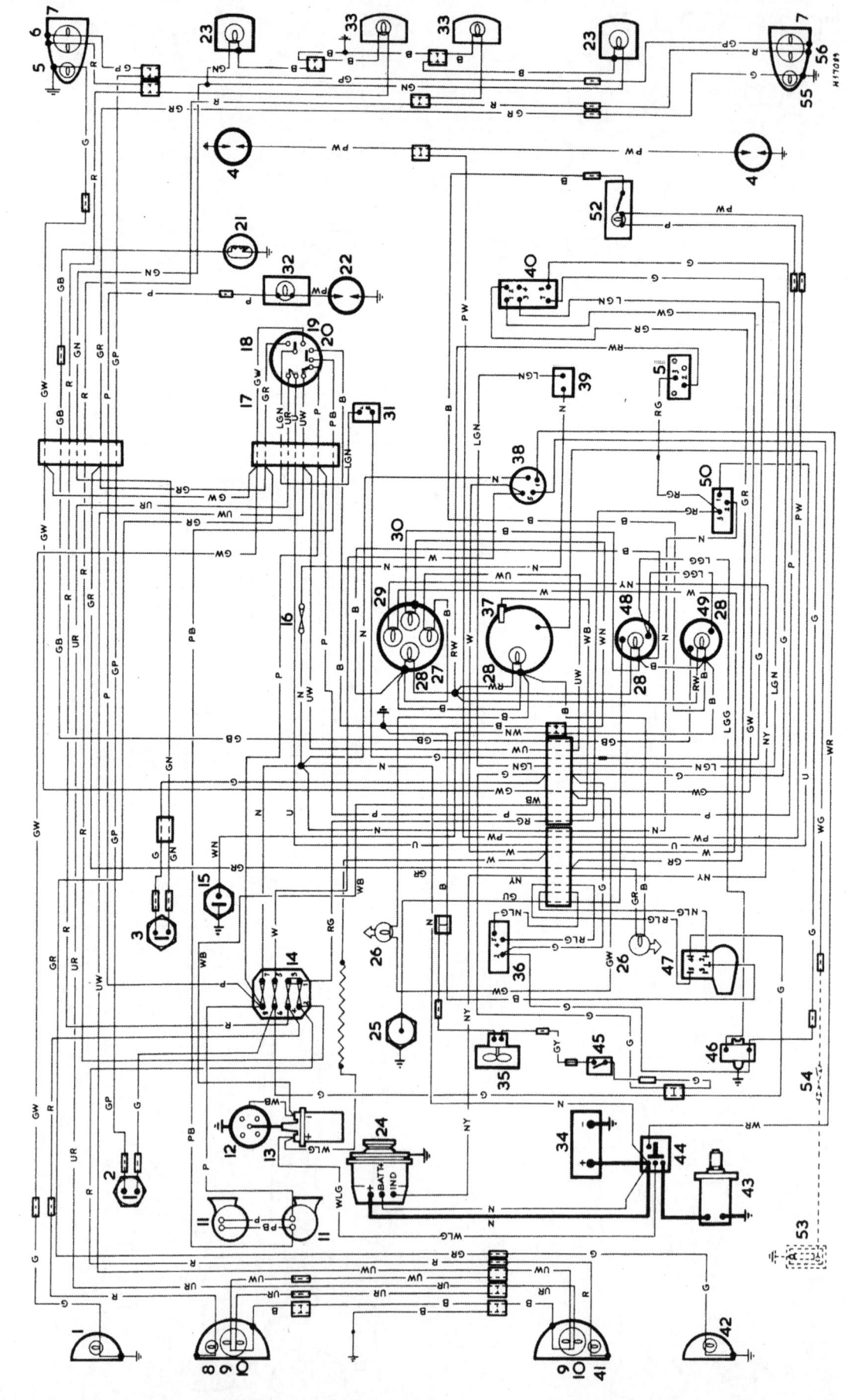

Fig. 10.31 Wiring diagram (UK) – 1978 models

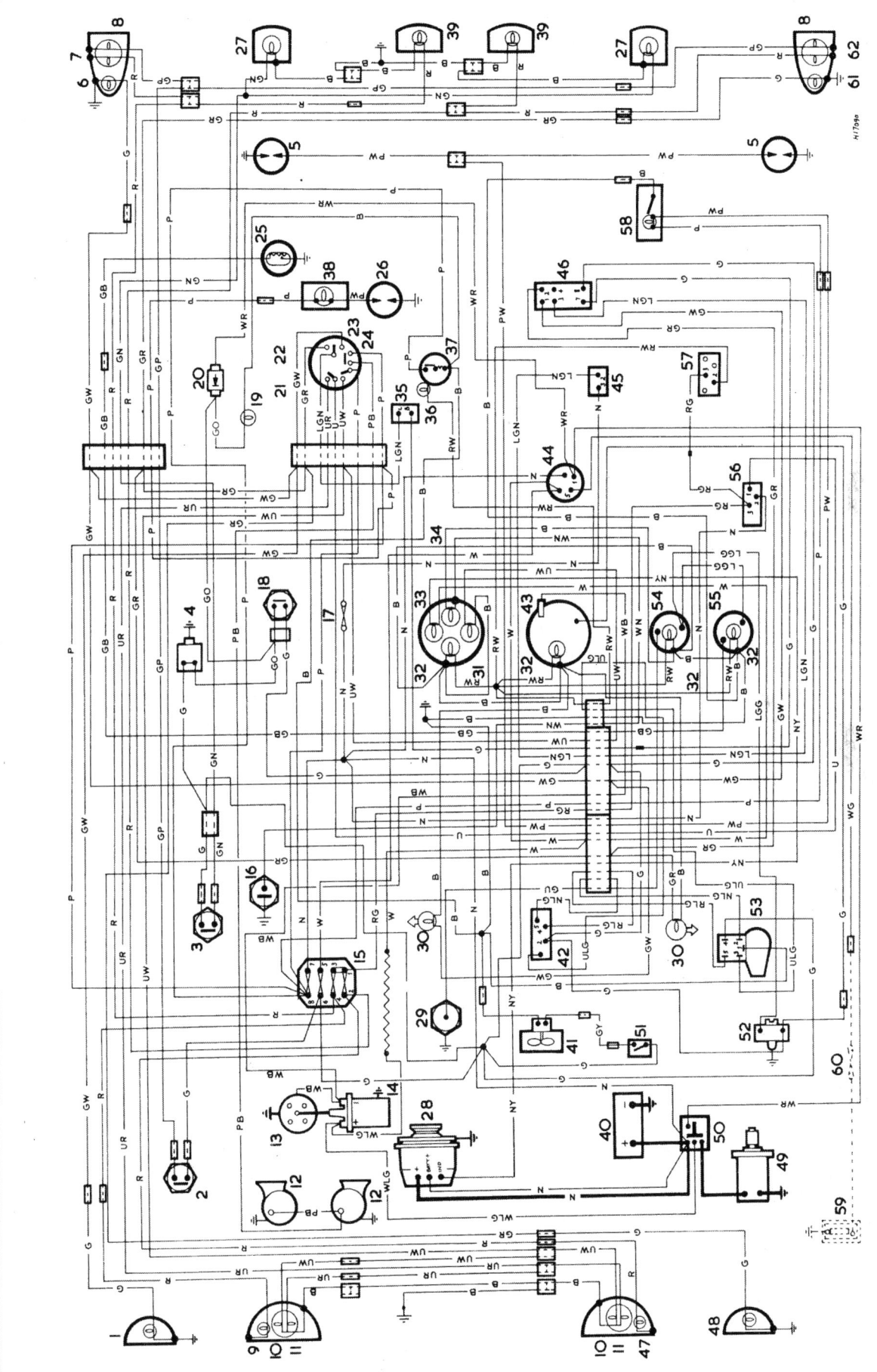

Fig. 10.32 Wiring diagram (UK) – 1979 models onwards

Key to Fig. 10.31. Optional equipment shown dotted

1 RH front direction indicator lamp
2 Stop-lamp switch
3 Reverse lamp switch
4 Interior lamp door switches
5 RH rear direction indication lamp
6 RH tail lamp
7 Stop-lamps
8 RH sidelamp
9 Headlamp main beam
10 Headlamp dip beam
11 Horn
12 Distributor
13 Ignition coil
14 Fuse unit (4-way)
15 Oil pressure switch
16 Line fuse for hazard warning
17 Headlamp flasher switch
18 Direction indicator switch
19 Horn push
20 Headlamp dipswitch
21 Fuel gauge tank unit
22 Luggage compartment lamp switch
23 Reverse lamps
24 Alternator
25 Coolant temperature transmitter
26 Direction indicator warning lamps
27 Main beam warning light
28 Panel lamp
29 Ignition warning light
30 Oil pressure warning light
31 Flasher unit
32 Luggage compartment lamp
33 Number plate illumination lamp
34 Battery (12 volt)
35 Heater or fresh air motor
36 Windscreen wiper switch
37 Tachometer
38 Ignition/starter switch
39 Hazard warning flasher unit
40 Hazard warning switch
41 LH sidelamp
42 LH front direction indicator
43 Starter motor
44 Starter solenoid
45 Heater or fresh air motor switch
46 Instrument voltage stabilizer
47 Windscreen wiper motor
48 Coolant temperature gauge
49 Fuel gauge
50 Lighting switch
51 Panel lamp switch
52 Interior courtesy lamp
53 Radio
54 Line fuse for radio
55 LH rear direction indicator lamp
56 LH tail lamp

Key to Fig. 10.32. Not all items are fitted to all models. Optional equipment shown dotte

1 RH front direction indicator lamp
2 Stop-lamp switch
3 Reverse lamp switch
4 Brake pressure failure switch
5 Interior lamp door switches
6 RH rear direction indicator lamp
7 RH tail lamp
8 Stop-lamps
9 RH sidelamp
10 Headlamp main beam
11 Headlamp dip beam
12 Horn
13 Distributor
14 Ignition coil
15 Fuse unit (4-way)
16 Oil pressure switch
17 Line fuse for hazard warning
18 Handbrake switch
19 Brake warning lamp
20 Diode for brake warning
21 Headlamp flasher switch
22 Direction indicator switch
23 Horn push
24 Headlamp dipswitch
25 Fuel gauge tank unit
26 Luggage compartment lamp switch
27 Reverse lamps
28 Alternator
29 Coolant temperature transmitter
30 Direction indicator warning lamps
32 Panel lamp
33 Ignition warning light
34 Oil pressure warning light
35 Flasher unit
36 Cigar lighter illumination lamp
37 Cigar lighter
38 Luggage compartment lamp
39 Number plate illumination lamp
40 Battery (12 volt)
41 Heater or fresh air motor
42 Windscreen wiper switch
43 Tachometer
44 Ignition/starter switch
45 Hazard warning flasher unit
46 Hazard warning switch
47 LH sidelamp
48 LH front direction indicator
49 Starter motor
50 Starter solenoid
51 Heater or fresh air motor switch
52 Instrument voltage stabilizer
53 Windscreen wiper motor
54 Coolant temperature gauge
55 Fuel gauge
56 Lighting switch
57 Panel lamp switch
58 Interior courtesy lamp
59 Radio
60 Line fuse for radio
61 LH rear direction indicator lamp

Chapter 11 Suspension and steering

Contents

Specifications

Front suspension

Type .... Independent with coil springs, wishbones and lever arm hydraulic shock absorbers

Springs

Free length
    Sprite Mk I & Mk II, Midget Mk I .... 9.4 in (238 mm)
    Sprite Mk III & Mk IV, Midget Mk II & Mk III (except 1500
    models) .... 9.59 in (244 mm)
    Midget Mk III (1500 models) .... 9.85 in (250 mm)
Spring rate .... 271 lbf/in (3.127 kgf/m)

Rear suspension

Type
    Sprite Mk I & Mk II, Midget Mk I .... Live axle with quarter-elliptic leaf springs and lever arm hydraulic shock absorbers
    All other models .... Live axle with semi-elliptic leaf springs and lever arm hydraulic shock absorbers

Springs

Number of leaves
    Sprite Mk I & Mk II, Midget Mk I 15
    Sprite Mk III & Mk IV, Midget Mk II & Mk III (except 1500
    models) 5
    Midget Mk III (1500 models) 6

Steering

Type .... Rack-and-pinion

Toe-in .... 0 to $\frac{1}{8}$ in (0 to 3.2 mm)

Steering pinion endfloat .... 0.010 in (0.25 mm)

Tyres

Type .... 5.20 x 13S Crossply or 145SR x 13 Radial

Tyre pressures lbf/in^2 (kgf/cm^2 / bar)

	Crossply tyres		Radial tyres	
	Front	*Rear*	*Front*	*Rear*
Normal car load	18 (1.27 / 1.24)	20 (1.4 / 1.38)	22 (1.54 / 1.52)	24 (1.68 / 1.66)
Maximum car load	18 (1.27 / 1.24)	24 (1.68 /1.66)	22 (1.54 / 1.52)	26 (1.82 / 1.79)
Sustained high speed driving	22 (1.54 / 1.52)	28 (1.96 / 1.93)	28 (1.96 / 1.93)	30 (2.1 / 2.07)

Wheels
Type
Pressed spoked .... 4½JSL x 13
Pressed disc .... 3.5D x 13
Wire .... 4J x 13

Lubrication
Lubricant type/specification
Tie-rod end balljoints (not later models) .... General purpose grease (Duckhams LB 10)
Steering and suspension grease nipples .... General purpose grease (Duckhams LB 10)
Steering rack:
    Early models .... Hypoid gear oil, viscosity SAE 140EP (Duckhams Hypoid 140S)
    Later models .... General purpose grease (Duckhams LB 10)

Torque wrench settings

	lbf ft	kgf m
Steering column top fixing bolts	12 to 17	1.66 to 2.35
Steering column pinch bolt	9 to 12	1.24 to 1.66
Steering rack housing clamp bolts	20 to 22	2.77 to 3.04
Steering rack mounting bracket bolts	17 to 18	2.35 to 2.49
Tie-rod balljoint nut	28 to 32	3.87 to 4.42
Tie-rod end assembly locknut	30 to 35	4.15 to 4.84
Tie-rod to rack locknut	80	11.06
Front and rear damper bolts	25 to 30	3.5 to 4.1
Front hub castellated nut		
Drum brakes	55 to 65	7.6 to 8.98
Disc brakes	46	6.4
Front hub and disc bolts	43	6
Steering arm bolts	39	5.4
Trunnion retaining nut	40	5.5
Steering wheel nut	37	5.11
Roadwheel nuts	44 to 46	6.0 to 6.4

1 General description

The independent front suspension is of the coil spring, lower wishbone and single upper link type. On the Sprite Mk I and II and the MG Midget Mk I the live rear axle is located by quarter-elliptic springs secured to the chassis at their front ends. Later models make use of semi-elliptic springs. The suspension, front and rear, is fitted with Armstrong double-acting lever type hydraulic shock absorbers, the levers of the two shock absorbers at the front acting as the top suspension link on each side of the car. Rack-and-pinion steering is used.

The rack-and-pinion steering gear is held in place behind the radiator and above the front frame crossmember by a clamp at each end of the rack housing. Tie-rods from each end of the steering rack housing operate the steering arms via exposed and rubber gaiter enclosed balljoints. The upper splined end of the helically-toothed pinion protrudes from the rack housing and engages with the splined end of the steering column. The pinion spline is grooved and the steering column is held to the pinion by a clamp bolt which partially rests in the pinion groove.

Caution: *All work undertaken on the steering mechanism must be to the highest standard. It is vitally important to maintain the integrity of the system and you must always use the right fasteners with correct locking devices where appropriate. Adjustments must be within specifications and spare parts must be new or in faultless condition. You life, and that of others, could depend on these points, and if you are in any doubt at all concerning what to do or how to do it, you should get professional advice or have the job done by an expert.*

2 Steering, suspension and shock absorbers – examination for wear

1   To check for wear in the outer balljoints of the tie-rods, place the car over a pit, or lie on the ground looking at the balljoints, and get a friend to rock the steering wheel from side to side. Wear is present if there is visible play in the joints.
2   To check for wear in the rubber and metal bushes, jack up the front of the car until the wheels are clear of the ground. Hold each wheel in turn, at the top and bottom, and try to rock it. If the wheel rocks, continue the movement at the same time inspecting the upper trunnion link rubber bushes, and the rubber bushes at the inner ends of the wishbone for play.

3   If the wheel rocks and there is no side movement in the rubber bushes, then the kingpins and metal bushes will be worn. Alternatively, if the movement occurs between the wheel and the brake backplate, then the hub bearings require renewal.
4   The rubber bushes can be renewed by the owner but, if there is play between the lower end of the kingpin and the wishbone, then it will be necessary to renew the fulcrum pin, and if movement is still evident, to purchase an exchange wishbone with new threaded bushes, as it is not possible to rebush the wishbone.
5   Sideplay, vertical or horizontal movement of the upper link or shock absorber arm relative to the shock absorber body is best checked with the outer end of the shock absorber arm freed from the upper trunnion link. If play is present the shock absorber bearings are worn and a replacement shock absorber should be purchased. How well the shock absorber functions can be checked by bouncing the car at each corner. After each bounce the car should return to its normal ride position within 1 to 1¼ up-and-down movements. If the car continues to move up-and-down in decreasing amounts, it means that either the shock absorbers require topping up, or, if they are already full, that the shock absorbers are worn and must be renewed.
6   The shock absorbers cannot be adjusted without special tools, and therefore must not be dismantled, but exchanged at your local BL agent for replacement units.
7   Excessive play in the steering gear will lead to wheel wobble, and can be confirmed by checking if there is any lost movement between the end of the steering column and the rack. Rack-and-pinion steering is normally very accurate and lost motion in the steering gear indicates considerable wear or lack of lubrication.
8   The outer balljoints at either end of the tie-rods are the most likely items to wear first, followed by the rack balljoints at the inner end of the tie-rods.
9   Check the rear spring leaves for signs of distortion or breakage (photo), and renew if necessary.

3 Anti-roll bar – removal and refitting

1   Jack up the car at the front, ensuring that the handbrake is on, and place stands or supports under the front suspension.
2   Undo and remove the screws and nuts in the end stops adjacent to the anti-roll bar supporting brackets and remove the stops.
3   Undo and remove the bolts and washers from each of the two brackets retaining the anti-roll bar to the car structure.

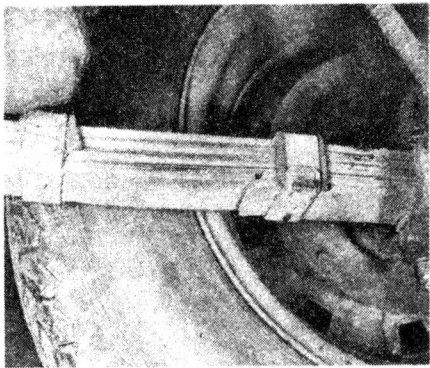

2.9 A broken leaf in the rear spring unit

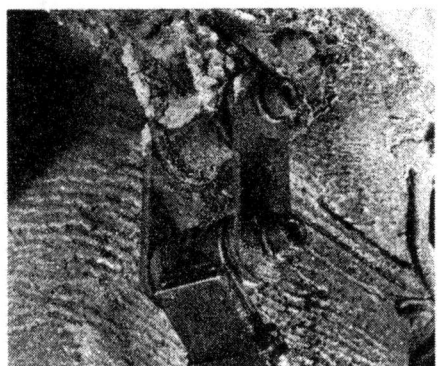

6.3a Removing the rear shackle nuts and pins

6.3b The rear spring front securing bracket

6.3c The U-bolt nuts removed

6.4a Removing the spring rubber bushes

6.4b The rear spring front location bracket, pin and washers

4   Undo and remove the two nuts securing the ends of the anti-roll bar to the links and remove the anti-roll bar from the car.
5   Refitting is the reverse of the removal procedure.

4 Coil springs – removal and refitting

Note: *Removal of one of the front springs is not difficult but it requires the use of two high tensile steel nuts and bolts not less than 4½ in (114 mm) long, the bolts being threaded their entire length. The bolts must be of the same diameter as the spring seat-to-wishbone bolts.*
1   Loosen the nuts on the roadwheel, place a block of wood about 1⅛ in (30 mm) thick between the underside of the shock absorber arm and the rubber stop and jack up the front of the car. The purpose of the block of wood is to keep the arm off the rubber stop. Support the car body on stands or blocks and apply the handbrake.
2   Remove the roadwheel and two diametrically opposed bolts from the spring seat. Insert the long bolts in the two empty holes in the spring seat and screw down the nuts. Remove the two remaining standard nuts, bolts and washers, and then unscrew the two nuts on the long bolts equally, two turns at a time.
3   As these two bolts are undone the spring seat will come away from the wishbone under the pressure of the coil spring and towards the end of the thread on the long bolts the spring will be fully extended. Unscrew the bolts from the nuts and release the seat and coil springs.
4   Refitting is a reverse of the removal procedure. The spring and seat are offered into position, the two long bolts inserted between the wishbone and the spring seat, and the long bolt nuts tightened down equally, compressing the spring. When the seat is flush against the wishbone the two ordinary nuts, bolts and spring washers can be inserted in the two empty holes and tightened up, the long bolts removed, and the remaining two ordinary nuts, bolts, and spring washers fitted. Finally, check that all four bolts are firmly tightened down, and don't forget to remove the block of wood from under the damper arm when the car is on the ground. Tighten the wheel nuts to their specified torque.

5 Rear quarter-elliptic springs – removal and refitting

1   Jack up the rear of the car, chock the front wheels front and rear, and then place a further jack or block underneath the differential to give support to the rear axle when the springs are removed. Do not raise the jack under the rear axle so that the springs are flattened, but allow them to hang fully suspended with the total weight of the axle just taken by the jack.
2   Remove the shackle pins at the axle end of the springs, remove the U-bolts and the bolts which pass upwards at the front end of the spring into the spring attachment plate. Pull the spring out rearwards from its chassis mounting.
3   Refitting is a direct reversal of the removal procedure. To help when fitting the U-bolts remove the axle check strap. Make the final tightening of all bolts when the weight of the car is on the springs.

6 Rear semi-elliptic springs – removal and refitting

1   Follow the instructions given in paragraph 1 of Section 5.
2   Unscrew and remove the bolts securing the axle check strap and lift away the strap.
3   Remove the rear shackle nuts, pins, and plates, the front bracket securing setscrews and nuts, and the four nuts and washers from the U-bolts which hold the spring to the rear axle and shock absorber anchorage plate. Lift away the plate and lower the spring (photos).
4   Refitting is the reverse order to removal but note the following:

(a) *Before refitting clean all mating parts thoroughly*
(b) *Renew the rubber bushes in the spring 'eye' at the rear if they are worn or perished (photo)*
(c) *Ensure that the corresponding washers are refitted to their respective positions when assembling the front spring bracket (photo)*
(d) *On completion lower the car to the ground and tighten the nuts and bolts with the car's weight on the springs*

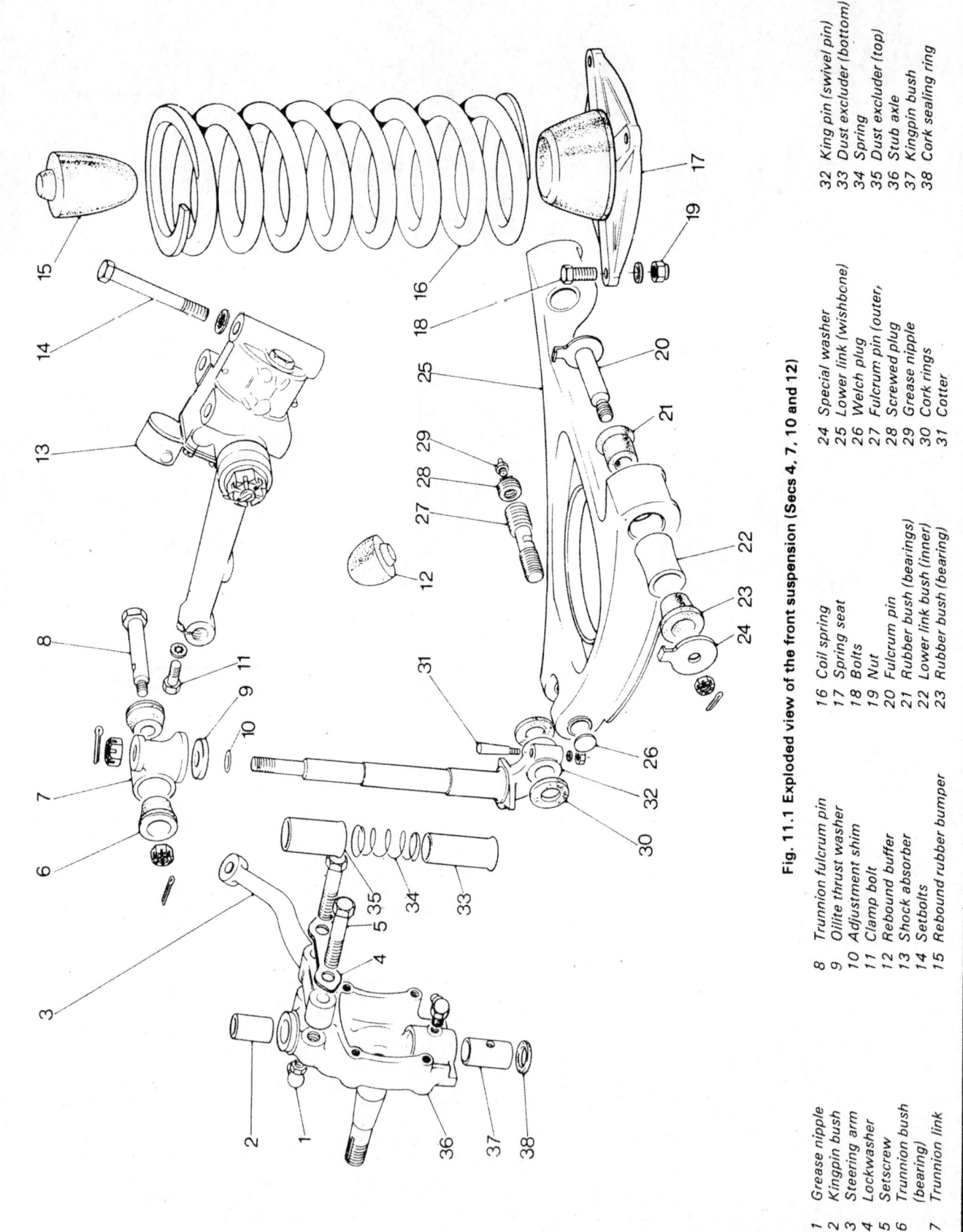

Fig. 11.1 Exploded view of the front suspension (Secs 4, 7, 10 and 12)

1 Grease nipple
2 Kingpin bush
3 Steering arm
4 Lockwasher
5 Setscrew
6 Trunnion bush (bearing)
7 Trunnion link
8 Trunnion fulcrum pin
9 Oilite thrust washer
10 Adjustment shim
11 Clamp bolt
12 Rebound buffer
13 Shock absorber
14 Setbolts
15 Rebound rubber bumper
16 Coil spring
17 Spring seat
18 Bolts
19 Nut
20 Fulcrum pin
21 Rubber bush (bearings)
22 Lower link bush (inner)
23 Rubber bush (bearing)
24 Special washer
25 Lower link (wishbone)
26 Welch plug
27 Fulcrum pin (outer,
28 Screwed plug
29 Grease nipple
30 Cork rings
31 Cotter
32 King pin (swivel pin)
33 Dust excluder (bottom)
34 Spring
35 Dust excluder (top)
36 Stub axle
37 Kingpin bush
38 Cork sealing ring

7 Front shock absorbers – removal and refitting

1   Loosen the roadwheel securing nuts, apply the handbrake and jack up the front of the car. Support the car on stands or blocks.
2   Remove the wheel and jack up the outer end of the wishbone until the shock absorber arm is clear of its rebound rubber.
3   Unscrew the clamp bolt and lockwasher from the roadwheel end of the shock absorber.
4   Pull out the split pin and unscrew the castellated nut from the trunnion fulcrum pin.
5   Remove the trunnion fulcrum pin and the trunnion rubber bushes.
6   Unscrew and remove the three setbolts and lockwashers which hold the shock absorber in place.
7   Lift away the shock absorber assembly. With the shock absorber removed, do not remove the jack from the outer end of the wishbone as undue strain will be put on the steering linkages, and the spring may slip from its top mounting.
8   Refitting is a straightforward reversal of the removal sequence. Renew the rubber bushes if they are worn, perished, or slack.
9   Tighten the shock absorber retaining bolts and wheel nuts to their specified torques.

8 Rear shock absorbers – removal and refitting

1   It is necessary to jack up the rear of the car for removal of the rear shock absorbers if a pit or ramp is not available. With the jack in position firmly support the rear of the car with axle stands or blocks, and chock the front wheels, front and rear.
2   To remove a shock absorber unscrew the nut and spring washer from the bolt which holds the shock absorber arm to the link arm; remove the two nuts and spring washers from the shock absorber securing bolts and remove the bolts; thread the lever over the link arm bolt and so remove the shock absorber.
3   Keep the shock absorber upright to prevent air getting into the operating chamber. Refitting is a straightforward reversal of the removal procedure, but tighten the shock absorber retaining bolts to their specified torque.

9 Front hubs – removal, overhaul and refitting

Note: *The front hubs are not adjustable, and if wear is detected (play between the roadwheels and backplate), the hubs will have to be removed and new bearings fitted. A hub extractor is required for this job and your local BL agent will probably be willing to lend or hire you one, but specify if you have wire or pressed wheels.*
1   Slacken the roadwheel nuts, jack up the car, apply the handbrake, support the car on stands then remove the roadwheel.
2   On drum braked cars, unscrew the drum retaining screw and pull off the drum. In the case of disc braked cars, remove the caliper assembly as described in Chapter 9, and support it on a block so the hydraulic hose is not stretched, which could cause damage.
3   Lever the hub dust cap, extract the split pin, and unscrew and remove the castellated nut and locating washer.
4   Use a hub extractor to pull the complete hub assembly off the stub axle. If the inner bearing remains on the stub axle shaft it must be pulled off with a hub bearing remover. Frequently, the inner race of the inner bearing is left in position and if this occurs, it is easiest to remove the brake backplate on drum braked cars to ease the removal of the race.
5   Carefully tap out the tapered distance piece and outer bearing with a suitable drift, and then drift out the inner bearing and oil seal from the inside of the hub. On later models, remove the brake disc by unscrewing the retaining bolts. The hub is now completely dismantled.
6   Reassembly and refitment is a reversal of the removal sequence, but the following points should be noted:

   (a) The bearings and the space between them must be lubricated with general purpose grease
   (b) If the THRUST markings are on the bearing **outer** *races, the markings must face each other. If the markings are on the* **inner** *races, they must point away from each other. (The position of the markings may vary according to the bearing manufacturer)*

   (c) The oil seal lip should face the inner bearing; lubricate the seal with engine oil on assembly
   (d) The castellated nut should be tightened to the specified torque wrench setting or the nearest split pin hole
   (e) The maximum run-out of the brake disc is 0.006 in (0.152 mm). Reposition the disc on the hub or renew, if necessary, to obtain this tolerance. The disc to hub retaining bolts must be tightened to the specified torque wrench setting
   (f) Wipe away excess grease and do not fill the hub dust cap before refitting
   (g) Tighten the wheel nuts to their specified torque

10 Front suspension rubber bushes – removal and refitting

Note: *If the rubber bushes on the inner ends of the wishbone or the rubber bushes in the trunnion link are worn on either side of the car, they can be renewed fairly easily by the owner. To renew the bushes in the trunnion link, follow the instructions given in Section 7. The bushes in the inner ends of the lower wishbone can be removed in the following manner:*
1   Remove the coil spring as detailed in Section 4.
2   With a pair of pliers, extract the split pins from the castellated nuts on the inner end of the wishbone mounting. **Note**: *Some models use Nyloc self-locking nuts which must not be re-used once removed.*
3   Tap out the fulcrum pins and remove the rubber bushes.
4   Reassembly is a reversal of the removal procedure. New bushes can be made to fit more easily if they are lubricated with hydraulic fluid prior to assembly.

11 Tie-rod balljoints – removal and refitting

1   If the tie-rod outer balljoints are worn, it will be necessary to renew the whole balljoint assembly, as they cannot be dismantled.
2   Prior to removal of the balljoint, mark the position of the locknut on the tie-rod accurately, to ensure a fairly accurate toe-in on reassembly.
3   Free the balljoint from the steering lever by removing the retaining nut, and break the balljoint taper by using an extractor.
4   Slacken off the balljoint locknut, and, holding the tie-rod by its flat with a spanner to prevent it from turning, unscrew the complete balljoint assembly from the rod. Refitting is a reversal of the removal procedure. Check and adjust the front wheel alignment as described in Section 13.

12 Front stub axle and kingpin – dismantling and reassembly

Note: *If the kingpin bushes are worn, the fitting of new bushes is a job for your local BL agent as it involves the use of special tools. In addition, new bushes have to be reamed in position in the stub axle. If the bushes are badly worn, check the kingpin for ovality with a micrometer and renew the pin if necessary. To remove and refit the stub axle and kingpin, proceed as follows:*
1   Slacken the roadwheel nuts, jack up the front of the car, support it on stands or blocks and apply the handbrake. Remove the road-wheel.
2   On early cars remove the brake drum, wheel hub, and brake assembly, including the backplate. On later cars remove the brake caliper, wheel hub, brake disc and dust shield. In either case refer to Chapter 9 for brake information, and to Section 9 of this Chapter for hub removal details.
3   Refer to Section 4 and remove the suspension coil spring.
4   Undo the nut on the steering rod-to-steering arm balljoint; earlier models have a split-pinned nut in this position. Remove the balljoint from the steering arm by tapping the steering rod or by using a balljoint separator.
5   Where fitted, disconnect the anti-roll bar by undoing the nut securing the link to the suspension lower arm.
6   Disconnect the shock absorber arm from the suspension trunnion link as detailed in Section 7 and remove the bushes.
7   Remove the nuts, special washers, fulcrum pins and rubber bushes from the lower suspension arm inboard pivots, and then remove the stub axle and lower suspension arm assembly from the car.
8   Clean off all road dirt and, with the assembly on a bench, remove

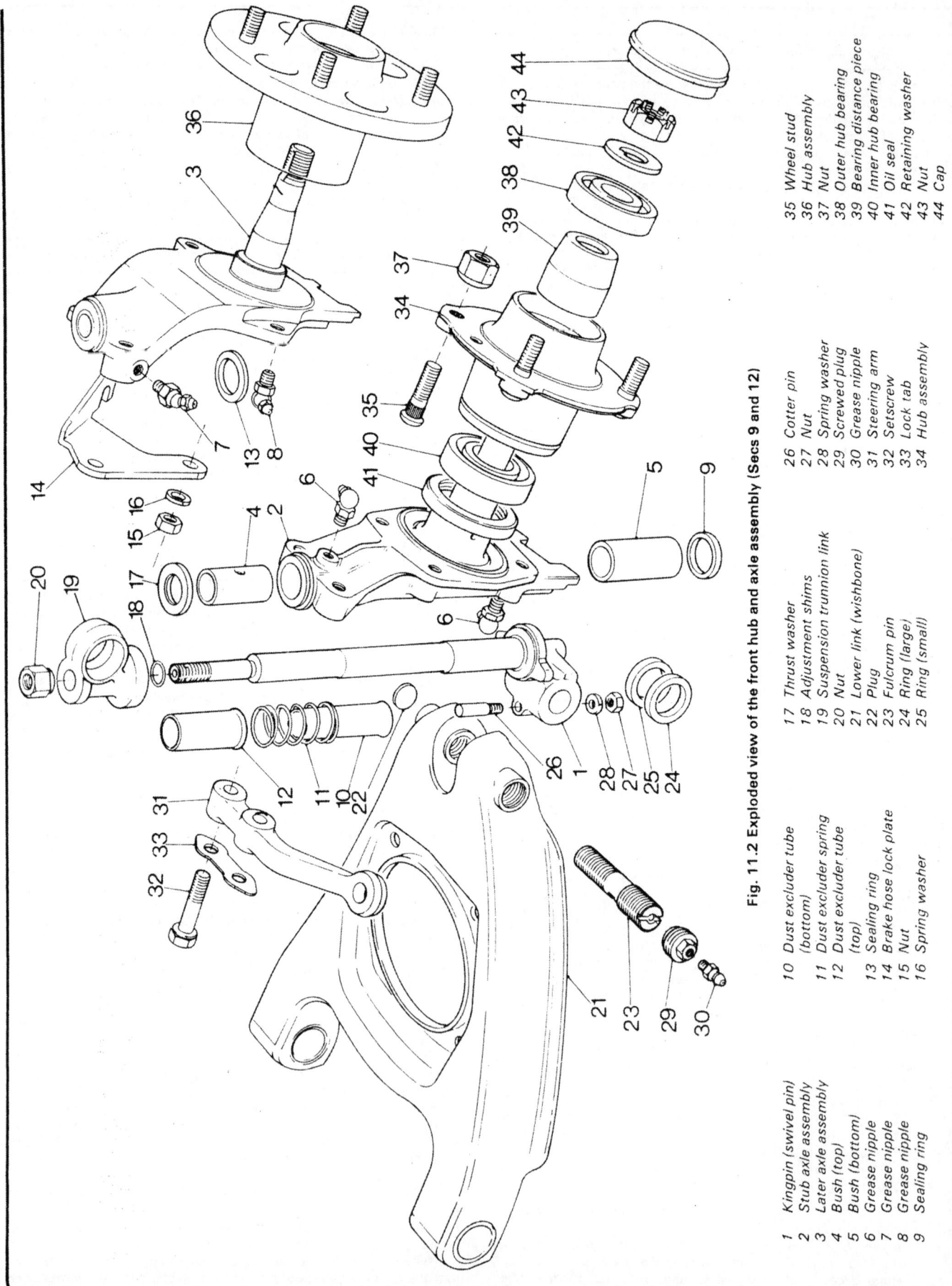

Fig. 11.2 Exploded view of the front hub and axle assembly (Secs 9 and 12)

1 Kingpin (swivel pin)
2 Stub axle assembly
3 Later axle assembly
4 Bush (top)
5 Bush (bottom)
6 Grease nipple
7 Grease nipple
8 Grease nipple
9 Sealing ring
10 Dust excluder tube (bottom)
11 Dust excluder spring
12 Dust excluder tube (top)
13 Sealing ring
14 Brake hose lock plate
15 Nut
16 Spring washer
17 Thrust washer
18 Adjustment shims
19 Suspension trunnion link
20 Nut
21 Lower link (wishbone)
22 Plug
23 Fulcrum pin
24 Ring (large)
25 Ring (small)
26 Cotter pin
27 Nut
28 Spring washer
29 Screwed plug
30 Grease nipple
31 Steering arm
32 Setscrew
33 Lock tab
34 Hub assembly
35 Wheel stud
36 Hub assembly
37 Nut
38 Outer hub bearing
39 Bearing distance piece
40 Inner hub bearing
41 Oil seal
42 Retaining washer
43 Nut
44 Cap

the split pin and the slotted nut at the top end of the swivel pin. Remove the trunnion link, thrust washer and shims, noting the sequence of assembly. Store the shims in a safe place.

9 Slide the stub axle off the swivel pin. Lift the bottom dust excluder to compress the spring and remove the two tubes and spring.

10 Undo the nut, but before removing it, tap the cotter pin loose from the swivel pin bottom fulcrum. When loose remove the nut, cotter pin and spring washer.

11 Unscrew the fulcrum pin plug from the suspension lower arm and unscrew the fulcrum pin. Remove the swivel pin and its two sealing washers. Remove the O-ring seal from the swivel pin and discard it, as a new one should be fitted on reassembly.

12 Clean all parts thoroughly, removing all old grease and road dirt. Inspect for wear, damage and corrosion, renewing parts where necessary. Check that grease nipples and passages are unobstructed.

13 Reassembly is the reverse of the dismantling procedure, but the following points should be noted:

(a) Lubricate all parts during assembly, and on completion use a grease gun to charge the grease nipples. Wipe off all surplus grease

(b) If the steering arm was removed, use a new lockwasher on reassembly, and tighten the bolts to their specified torque

(c) Use new sealing washers when assembling the swivel pin to the lower link arm fulcrum

(d) Use a new cotter pin to secure the fulcrum pin

(e) Before fitting a new sealing washer in the bottom of the swivel axle, soak the washer in oil

(f) After fitting the trunnion link, tighten the nut to its specified torque and, if necessary, align it with the next split pin hole. Test the movement of the swivel axle on the swivel pin. It should move freely, but with a slight resistance, and no vertical movement. If necessary add or remove shims under the trunnion link to achieve the correct fit and feel. Finally lock the nut with a new split pin

13 Front wheel alignment – checking and adjusting

1 Accurate front wheel alignment is essential for good steering and minimum tyre wear. Adjusting the front wheel alignment on these cars consists of altering the amount of toe-in, ie the amount by which the wheels point inwards at the front. Correct results are more likely to be obtained from using the special equipment held by BL garages, but this is not normally available to the average home mechanic. There are several types of tracking gauge available in car accessory shops, and if one of these can be obtained to do the checking, the adjusting of the alignment is relatively simple. In the absence of a checking gauge, a competent enthusiast could devise a means of measuring the amount of toe-in at the wheel rims at axle centre height, but it is emphasised that accuracy is essential and it is recommended that, in all cases of non-professional checking and adjusting, the results should be considered only adequate to get to a dealer, where a precision check can be made.

2 Where appropriate equipment is available and can be used with confidence, proceed as follows. Check that the tyres are correctly inflated, that the front wheels are not damaged, the hub bearings are not worn and that the steering mechanism is in good order, without slackness or wear at the joints; refer to Section 2 for examination procedures.

3 The car must be unladen and the steering positioned with the wheels in the straight-ahead position. Using the alignment checking equipment in accordance with the maker's instructions, take a series of measurements and average them to obtain the existing toe-in, if any. **Note**: *Only move the car forwards during this procedure, as rearwards movement will produce incorrect indications.*

4 Where adjustment is required, slacken the locknuts at the outer ends of each tie-rod and slacken the clips securing the rubber gaiters at the inner ends of the rods. Both rods have right-hand threads and each must be rotated in the required direction *by an equal amount* to correct the misalignment. It is important that the tie-rods are adjusted to exactly equal length.

5 Tighten the locknuts to their specified torque, holding the balljoints with another spanner, and then tighten the rubber gaiter clips. On completion recheck the front wheel alignment and readjust if necessary.

14 Steering rack – removal and refitting

1 Owing to differences in the steering mechanisms, it is necessary to deal separately with three broad categories: early cars, that is those pre-Mk IV Sprites and Mk III Midgets; later UK cars, ie right-hand drive cars; and finally USA and Canada cars, ie left-hand drive cars.

Early cars

2 Remove the radiator as described in Chapter 2. Centralise the steering and loosen the front roadwheel nuts.

3 Jack up and support the front of the car on stands or blocks. Apply the handbrake and remove the front roadwheels.

4 Unscrew the nut and remove the bolt from the clamp on the lower end of the steering column. Make alignment marks on the clamp to assist correct reassembly.

5 Remove the split pins and slotted nuts from the two balljoints joining the tie-rods to the steering arms. Tap the balljoints or use a balljoint separator to disengage them from the steering arms.

6 Undo and remove the setscrews securing the steering rack brackets to the front crossmember. Remove the rack complete with mounting brackets, disengaging the steering column clamp from the pinion at the same time.

7 Refitting is the reverse of the removal procedure. If, during overhaul or repair, the mounting brackets on the rack housing were disturbed, do not tighten the bolts securing the housing to the brackets until the assembly has been refitted to the car. This will ensure correct alignment of the steering column and rack pinion shaft. On completion check and adjust the front wheel alignment as described in the previous Section.

Later UK models (right-hand drive cars)

8 Prepare the car as indicated in paragraphs 2 to 5 inclusive.

9 Undo and remove the two bolts in the steering column upper attachment fitting and retrieve the shim between the fitting and structure. Carefully pull the column up to disengage the clamp at the bottom from the steering rack pinion and temporarily tie the column up to support it.

10 Make alignment marks on the steering rack and the brackets bolted to the crossmember to facilitate refitting. Undo and remove the two bolts and spring washers in each of the two clamps which secure the steering rack to the brackets, and remove the steering rack.

11 To refit the steering rack, position it on the brackets on the crossmember, fit the clamps and the bolts and washers, but don't tighten the bolts at this stage.

12 Make sure that the steering rack is in the straight-ahead position and that the flat on the pinion shaft is uppermost. Also ensure that the steering column is positioned straight-ahead with the slot in the clamp uppermost.

13 Engage the steering column clamp with the pinion shaft as far as it will go, then fit and tighten the bolts and washers in the steering column upper attachment fitting.

14 Turn the steering wheel through a complete turn to the left and back, then through a complete turn to the right and back. Check that the marks made on the rack and brackets during removal are aligned as originally, then fit the two bolts and washers in each of the two clamps and tighten the bolts to their specified torque. Note that if the marks are not aligned, or if new brackets are being fitted to the crossmember, the steering rack will have to be aligned as described in Section 16.

15 Tighten the steering column clamp-to-rack pinion bolt to its specified torque.

16 Complete the refitting by reversing the procedure in paragraphs 2 to 5 inclusive, noting that the tie-rod balljoint nuts should be tightened to their specified torque. On completion check and adjust the front wheel alignment as described in the previous Section.

Later USA and Canada models (left-hand drive cars)

17 The procedure for these cars broadly follows that contained in paragraphs 8 to 13 inclusive for UK cars. However, during removal, after removing the steering column clamp pinch bolt (paragraph 4) remove the three bolts and washers from the toe plate mid-way down the steering column. Then slacken the three bolts in the column upper attachment fitting before pulling the column back just enough to disengage the clamp at the bottom.

18 On refitting, proceed as for UK cars (paragraphs 11 to 13

inclusive), but after tightening the steering column upper attachment bolts, fit and tighten the three toe plate bolts. Complete the refitting as for UK cars

15 Steering rack mounting brackets – removal and refitting

1   Remove the radiator as described in Chapter 2.
2   Undo and remove the two bolts and washers securing each of the two steering rack clamps to the mounting brackets.
3   Undo and remove the three bolts and washers securing each of the two mounting brackets to the structural crossmember.
4   Remove the mounting brackets but take care to retrieve any packing washers which may be fitted between the mounting bracket, located at the pinion end of the rack, and the crossmember. This packing is essential for refitting.
5   Refitting the brackets is the reverse of the removal procedure. However, if new brackets are being fitted, or if the original packing washers are not available for refitting, or if the rack is being refitted after repair damage, the rack will have to be realigned on USA and Canada models, or on Midget Mk III cars from number GAN5-114643 and 1500 cc cars. Realignment procedure is described in the next Section. When tightening the bracket attachment bolts, don't exceed their specified torque, and similarly tighten the rack clamp fixing bolts to their specified torque.

16 Steering rack and column – alignnment

1   Assuming that the steering rack is being refitted after removal, and that the steering column is already in position but not secured, proceed as follows.
.2   Fit the steering rack mounting brackets to the rack using the clamps, bolts and washers. Tighten the clamp bolts and then loosen each of them one turn. Position the rack assembly in the car.
3   Fit the two front bolts and the top bolt with their washers to the bracket which is furthest from the steering rack pinion, but don't tighten the bolts just yet.
4   Check that the steering rack is in the straight-ahead position with the flat on the pinion shaft facing up. Similarly check that the steering column is in the straight-ahead position with the clamp slot facing up. Then engage the steering column sleeve with the pinion shaft as far as it will go.
5   *UK models only:* Fit the steering column upper support bolts.
6   *USA and Canada models only:* Fit the two topmost bolts into the steering column upper fixing bracket and tighten them, by hand only, until the weight of the column is just taken and the gap between bracket and body fitting flanges is parallel and equal at both bolt positions. At the same time check that the column is central in the hole in the toe plate. Measure the gaps between flanges at the upper fixing bolt positions, then remove the two bolts, fit packing washers to the measured size in the gaps, refit the bolts and tighten them again by hand until the washers are just pinched. Fit the securing ring and sealing washer at the toe plate, then fit and tighten the three bolts.
7   *All models:* Fit the pinch bolt to the clamp at the bottom of the steering column and tighten it to its specified torque.
8   With the help of an assistant turn the steering wheel one full turn to the left and back, followed by one full turn to the right and back, and note any movement of the steering rack assembly in relation to the chassis crossmember. Carefully turn the steering in both directions until the neutral point is reached, that is where no movement of the rack assembly is obvious.
9   Measure the gap between the front face of the crossmember and the adjacent face of the rack mounting bracket at the pinion end of the rack. Fit metal packing to fill this gap, then fit the two front bolts and the top bolt, tightening them to their specified torque.
10 Tighten the steering rack housing clamp bolts to their specified torque, doing those nearest to the pinion first.
11 *USA and Canada models only:* Measure the gap at the third (lowest) bolt position on the steering column upper attachment bracket, fit packing washers to fill the gap, then fit the bolt but tighten it by hand to just pinch the washers.
12 Undo and remove the pinch bolt from the steering column clamp, and also the three toe plate bolts.
13 Check that the steering column slides up and down freely on the rack pinion by pushing and pulling on the steering wheel. If the

movement is stiff or tight the alignment procedure will have to be repeated.
14 When the alignment is satisfactory, refit the steering column pinch bolt at the bottom end and tighten it to its specified torque. Refit the three toe plate bolts and tighten them. Finally tighten the three bolts in the steering column top fixing bracket to their specified torque.
15 Complete the reassembly as described in Section 14.

17 Steering rack rubber gaiters – renewal

1   If a steering rack rubber gaiter is found to be damaged with subsequent loss of lubricant, it is essential that the steering rack is removed for dismantling, cleaning and inspection; no attempt should be made to renew the gaiter alone in such cases. However, if the gaiter gets damaged during other work on the car, or if it is wished to renew a gaiter that has not leaked lubricant or has not allowed dirt to contaminate the inner balljoint, the work can be done without removing the steering rack.
2   Jack up the front of the car, support it on stands or blocks, and apply the handbrake. Clean all road dirt off the parts to be worked on.
3   Mark the position of the balljoint assembly locknut on the tie-rod concerned to facilitate reassembly, then slacken the nut.
4   Remove the split pin and nut securing the balljoint to the steering arm on the axle assembly. Use a balljoint separator to disconnect the balljoint from the steering arm and unscrew the balljoint and its locknut from the tie-rod:
5   Loosen the clips securing the gaiter to the rack and manoeuvre the large clip onto the rack body. Slide the gaiter off the rack assembly.
6   Closely inspect the inner balljoint on the rack for contamination by dirt or water. If any is found the rack must be removed from the car for servicing. If all appears well, apply about 2 oz (60 gm) of a good general purpose grease to the balljoint and rack teeth.
7   Fit a new rubber gaiter to the rack and fit the large end clip. Fit the protective shield and clip to the small end of the gaiter and tighten the clips.
8   Complete the reassembly by reversing the removal procedure, and finally check the front wheel alignment as described in Section 13.

18 Steering rack (early models) – dismantling and reassembly

1   Mark the position of the locknuts on the tie-rods so that the toe in will be approximately correct on reassembly.
2   Release the locknuts and unscrew the tie-rods from the balljoints.
3   Unscrew the clips holding the rubber gaiters to the rack housing and tie-rods, drain the oil from the housing and remove the gaiters.
4   Unscrew and remove the damper cap, spring, plunger, and shim.
5   Unscrew and remove the secondary damper cap, spring, plunger, and washer.
6   Unscrew and remove the two bolts, from the pinion housing, and remove the housing, shims, pinion, and bottom thrust washer.
7   Each inner tie-rod balljoint is locked to a slot in the end of the rack by means of tabs on a lockwasher and also in three places to the ball housing. Prise out these tabs to free the tie-rod balljoint housing.
8   Unscrew the balljoint from the rack with a self-gripping wrench or the special BL tie-rod C-spanner if this can be borrowed. To examine the condition of the joint, unscrew the balljoint cap from the ball housing. Ensure the shims are kept with the correct joint.
9   Examine the condition of the ball on the end of the tie-rod, and the cup, which should be renewed if worn.
10 Remove the lockwashers and extract the rack from the pinion end of the rack housing. Clean the rack and pinion and carefully examine the condition of the teeth. If they are worn, pitted, or chipped, new items should be fitted. Renew the rubber gaiters if they are cracked, split, or perished.
11 On reassembly, which is a straightforward reversal of the dismantling sequence, use new lockwashers, adjust the backlash and endfloat (see appropriate Sections), and check that the rack balljoints fit tightly but are free to move. If they are excessively loose or tight, adjustment can be made by varying the thickness of the shims between the balljoint cap and the ball housing. The shims are available in 0.002, 0.003, 0.005 and 0.010 in (0.05, 0.076, 0.13 and 0.254 mm) thicknesses.
12 After fitting the steering rack in place, fill it with 10 fl oz (280 cc) of SAE 140 extreme pressure oil.

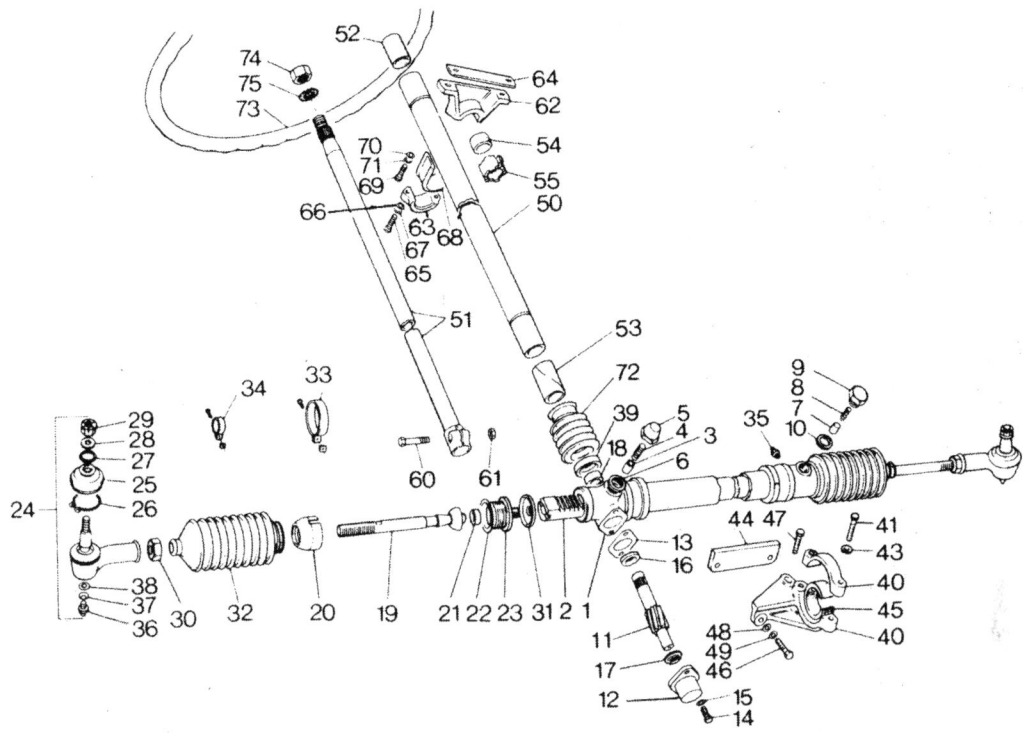

Fig. 11.3 Exploded view of the early pattern rack-and-pinion gear and steering column (Sec 18 and 23)

1	Rack housing	18	Pinion seal	36	Grease nipple	55	Clip
2	Rack	19	Tie-rod	37	Dished washer	60	Bolt
3	Damper plunger	20	Balljoint cap	38	Fibre washer	61	Nut
4	Damper pad spring	21	Ball cup	39	Retainer	62	Bracket
5	Damper pad cap	22	Shim	40	Bracket and cap assembly	63	Bracket cap
6	Shim	23	Ball housing	41	Setscrew	64	Shim
7	Secondary damper plunger	24	Ball socket assembly	43	Spring washer	65	Setscrew
8	Secondary damper spring	25	Boot	44	Seating	66	Plain washer
9	Secondary damper cap	26	Clip	45	Packing	67	Spring washer
10	Housing washer	27	Ring	46	Setscrew	68	Seating
11	Pinion	28	Plain washer	47	Setscrew	69	Setscrew
12	Pinion bearing	29	Nut	48	Plain washer	70	Plain washer
13	Shim	30	Locknut	49	Spring washer	71	Spring washer
14	Setbolt	31	Lockwasher	50	Outer column	72	Draught excluder
15	Spring washer	32	Rubber gaiter	51	Inner column tube	73	Steering wheel
16	Pinion thrust washer (top)	33	Clip (inner)	52	Felt bearing (top)	74	Nut
17	Pinion thrust washer (bottom)	34	Clip (outer)	53	Felt bearing	75	Shakeproof washer
		35	Grease nipple	54	Felt bearing (bottom)		

19 Steering rack (later models) – dismantling and reassembly

Note: *This Section is applicable to cars numbered GAN5-114643 onwards, and 1500 models.*

1 Remove the steering rack as described in Section 14 and the tie-rod balljoints as in Section 11. Clean off all external road dirt before dismantling the assembly.

2 Loosen the gaiter clips and slide the gaiters off the rack together with their clips and protective shields.

3 Slacken the locknuts behind each internal balljoint assembly and unscrew the balljoints from the rack.

4 Remove the springs in the ends of the rack (where fitted) and remove the locknuts. Be careful to keep the parts of each assembly together so that they are not mixed, and note the sequence of assembly as well as which way round parts fit.

5 Dismantle each inner balljoint by undoing the tabwasher and unscrewing the sleeved nut from the cup nut. Remove the tab washer, shims and cup.

6 Unscrew the grease plug in the end of the pinion preload plunger retaining cap, then unscrew and remove the cap, being careful to

retrieve the shims fitted to it. Withdraw the spring and plunger located under the cap.

7 Extract the circlip which retains the pinion shaft in the rack housing and carefully remove the pinion assembly, taking care not to lose the loose dowel. Note the sequence of the assembled parts, then remove the retaining ring, shims, pinion shaft bush and thrust washer from the pinion shaft. Remove and discard the O-ring seal from the groove in the retaining ring.

8 Slide the rack from the pinion end of the housing and then remove the thrust washer from the pinion housing bore.

9 If it is intended to renew the pinion lower bush, turn the rack housing over so that the bottom of the pinion housing is uppermost and, with a suitable drift, drive out the endplug and lower bush.

10 Thoroughly clean all components, taking care to keep separate assemblies together and avoiding mixing similar parts. Inspect for wear damage, cracks and signs of deterioration. In particular examine the teeth of the rack and pinion, balljoints and bearings. Having got to this stage it is sensible to discard all rubber components and renew them. Similarly renew tabwashers, and of course any defective part.

11 Before starting the reassembly soak the pinion bushes and the plunger in clean engine oil, heated to 100°C (212°F), for two hours

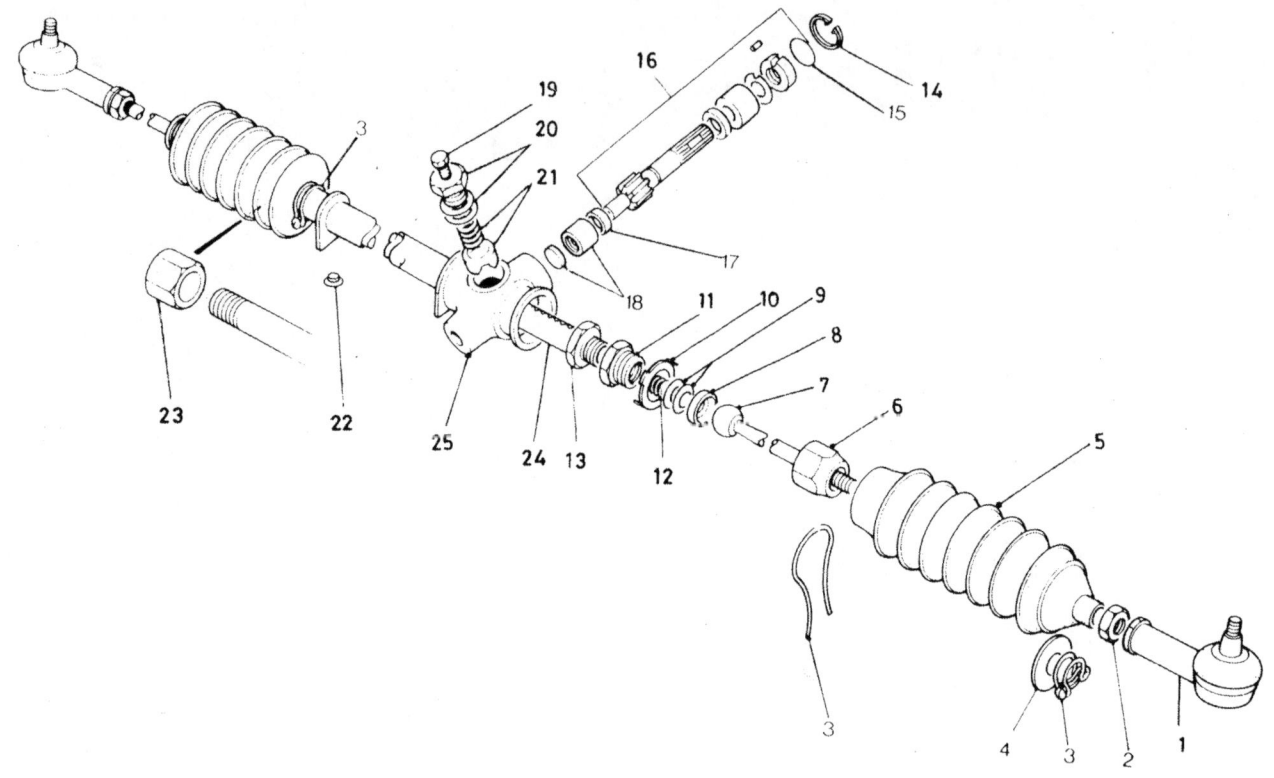

Fig. 11.4 Exploded view of the steering rack-and-pinion on cars from GAN5-114643 and 1500 models; note that a left-hand drive assembly is shown but right-hand drive is similar (Sec 19)

1 Balljoint assembly	8 Cup	14 Circlip	20 Cap and shims
2 Locknut	9 Shims	15 O-ring seal	21 Spring and plunger
3 Gaiter retaining clips	10 Tab washer	16 Pinion assembly	22 Location plug
4 Protective shield	11 Sleeve nut	17 Thrust washer	23 Locknut (longer)
5 Gaiter	12 Spring (only fitted with	18 Bush and endplug	24 Rack
6 Cap nut	steel cups)	19 Grease plug	25 Housing
7 Tie-rod ball	13 Locknut		

and leave the parts in the oil to allow them to cool. This procedure charges the porous metal, of which these parts are made, with lubricant. Be careful when heating the oil as it is easy to start a fire; it only needs to be as hot as boiling water.

12 Use the pinion shaft to fit the bottom bush. First fit the endplug into the recess in the bush, and with the bush on the shaft and using oil for lubricant, press the bush into the rack housing, keeping the shaft central in its bore. Remove the pinion shaft and then fit the thrust washer over the bush with its chamfer uppermost, ie towards the pinion teeth when that's fitted.

13 Use a good general purpose grease and liberally grease the rack and its teeth before inserting it into the rack housing from the pinion end. Position it so that 3.5 in (89 mm) of the toothed end protrudes fro the housing. Take this measurement from the internal face in the housing against which the balljoint locknut would come into contact (Fig. 11.5). The flat on the rack registers with the locating plug which is held in position by the rack mounting bracket. Note that when the rack is in the straight-ahead position with the pinion assembled, the flat on the pinion must be within 30° either side of the pinion housing centre line on the plunger cap side.

14 Refer to Section 22 for details of assembling the pinion shaft and of checking and adjusting the pinion endfloat.

15 Refer to Section 20 for details of assembling the preload plunger and of checking and adjusting the preload or, in other words, the rack-and-pinion backlash.

16 To obtain the correct assembled fit of each balljoint you will need additional shims to make the initial measurement. You can use the shims from the opposite balljoint to do this, but make sure that you don't get them mixed as they should be retained with their original assemblies. Smear the ball end of the tie-rod with graphited grease and fit the cup nut over the tie-rod onto the ball and fit the cup. Fit a

new tab washer to the sleeve nut and then fit the shim pack plus the additional ones after measuring their total thickness. Screw the sleeve nut into the cup nut and, using feeler gauges, measure the gap between the tab washer and the nut. This dimension plus 0.002 in (0.05 mm) is the amount by which the shim pack must be reduced to obtain the correct assembled fit. Dismantle the balljoint, noting down the required thickness of the shim pack, and repeat the procedure on the other balljoint using the combined shims again. Then dismantle that joint and fit to each joint the correct shim pack thickness. Shims are available in 0.002 in (0.05 mm) and 0.010 in (0.25 mm) thicknesses. Reassemble the balljoints and lock the tab washers over the cup and sleeve nuts on each assembly.

17 Slip the retaining clip for the rubber gaiter onto the small diameter end of the housing.

18 Thread the locknuts onto each end of the rack, checking that there is a distance of 23.20 in (590 mm) between their inner faces. Note that the smaller of the two nuts fits to the pinion end of the rack. Balljoints with nylon cups have no springs, but where the cups are steel fit the two springs into the recesses in the ends of the rack and then screw each balljoint and tie-rod assembly onto the rack as far as possible up to the locknuts. Tighten each locknut to the specified torque, maintaining the correct set distance.

19 Slide the rubber gaiters onto the tie-rods and fit the protective shields to the tie-rod ends of the gaiters. Lubricate each balljoint and the rack including teeth with about 2 oz (60 gm) of good quality general purpose grease, and then fit the inner ends of the rubber gaiters to the rack housing. Fit and tighten all the gaiter clips.

20 Screw the balljoint locknuts onto the tie-rods and then fit the balljoints, ensuring that the distance between pin centres is 42.7 in (1084 mm). Tighten the locknuts to their specified torque and recheck the pin centre distance measurement.

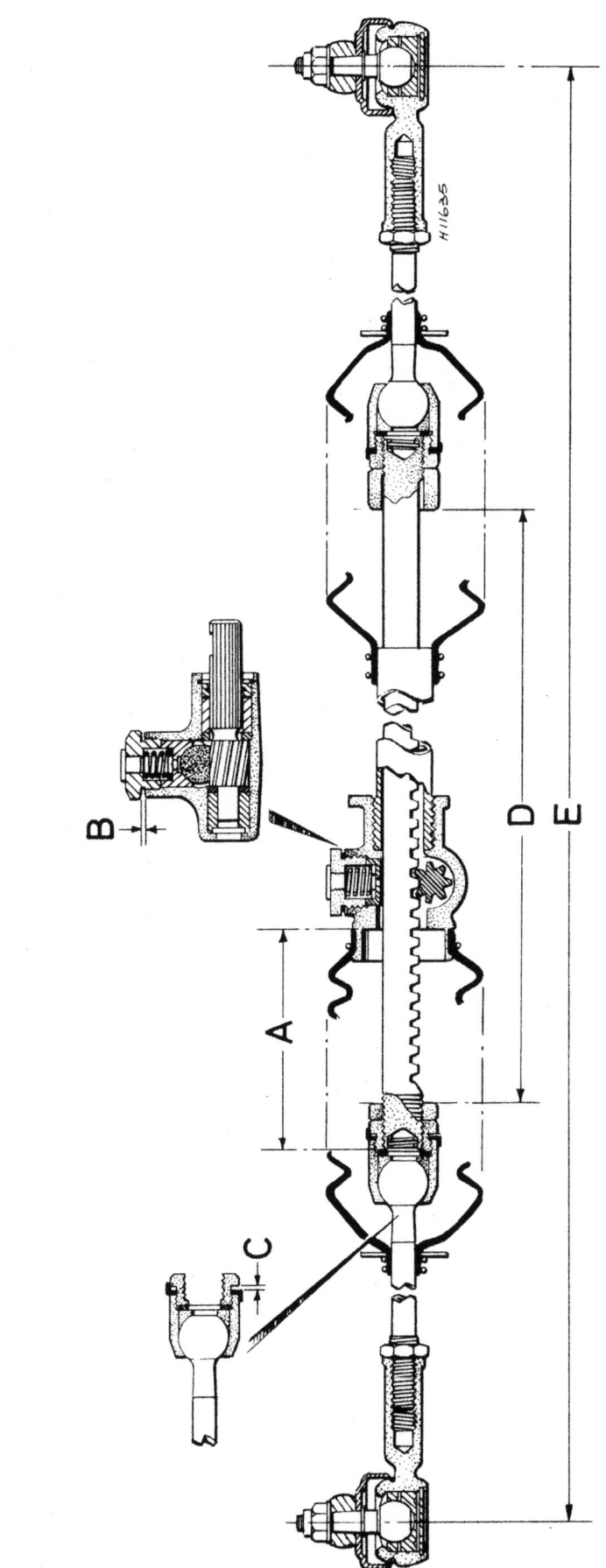

Fig. 11.5 Cross-sectional view of the later rack-and-pinion showing adjustments (Secs 19 and 20)

A   3.5 in (89 mm)
B   Add 0.004 in (0.1 mm) to this measurement to determine thickness of shim pack
C   Add 0.002 in (0.05 mm) to this measurement to determine amount by which trial shim pack must be reduced
D   23.20 in (590 mm) between locknuts
E   42.7 in (1084 mm) between ball pin centres

20 Rack-and-pinion backlash (plunger preload) – checking and adjusting

1   Backlash between the pinion and the rack is controlled by shims under the preload plunger (damper) cap. If backlash exists, check and adjust as follows:
2   Where the steering rack is installed in the car disconnect, but don't remove, the outer balljoints from the axle steering arms as described in Section 11.
3   Unscrew the plunger cap and remove the spring and the shims.
4   With the rack installed in the car or on the bench fit the plunger and cap but without the spring and shims. Tighten the cap until all backlash has been eliminated.
5   Using feeler gauges measure the gap between the underside of the cap and the rack housing (photo) making sure that no burrs affect the measurement. Then remove the cap and plunger, smear the plunger with grease and refit it together with the spring into the housing.
6   Shims are available in thicknesses of 0.002 in (0.05 mm), 0.004 in (0.10 mm) and 0.010 in (0.25 mm). Using at least one shim of 0.004 in (0.10 mm) make up the thickness to equal the gap measured under the cap plus an additional 0.004 in (0.1 mm).
7   Assemble the shims on the cap and then fit and tighten the cap.
8   Fit a grease nipple to the cap, after removing the plug, if fitted, and use a grease gun to inject $\frac{1}{2}$ to $\frac{3}{4}$ oz (14 to 21 gm) of a good quality general purpose grease. Remove the nipple and refit the plug, wiping off any surplus grease.
9   Where the rack is installed in the car reassemble, following the procedure in Section 11.

21 Pinion endfloat (early models) – checking and adjusting

1   This work is normally done during overhaul of the steering rack, but if it is installed, disconnect the steering column and tie-rod balljoints and proceed as follows:
2   Unscrew the bolts retaining the pinion bearing housing in place and remove the shims. Refit the bearing housing and bolt it down without the shims so that there is no pinion endfloat.
3   Measure the gap between the pinion bearing housing and the rack housing with a feeler gauge and add to this figure between 0.002 to 0.005 in (0.05 to 0.13 mm). The total figure represents the thickness of the shims that must be fitted between the pinion and rack housings. Shims are available in thicknesses of 0.003, 0.005 and 0.010 in (0.08, 0.13 and 0.25 mm).

22 Pinion endfloat (later models) – checking and adjusting

1   This Section is applicable to the Midget Mk III from car number GAN5-114643, and 1500 cc models. The work involved is normally done during reassembly of the steering rack after overhaul. With the assembly dismantled and cleaned as described in Section 19 proceed as follows:
2   Fit the thrust washer, bush and retaining ring to the splined part of the pinion shaft. The lubricating groove on the bush, must face to the thrust washer. Then insert the pinion unit into its housing with the flat on the pinion facing towards the plunger boss.
3   Insert the circlip.
4   With a dial gauge mounted on the rack housing, push the pinion down and then zero the gauge.
5   Now raise the pinion until the retaining ring butts against the circlip. Note the gauge reading.
6   Remove the dial gauge and circlip. Then withdraw the pinion unit. Remove the retaining ring and fit the new O-ring into its groove.
7   To the reading taken in paragraph 5, add 0.010 in (0.25 mm) to give the correct endfloat. Make up shims to this final figure. Shims of 0.005 in (0.13 mm) and 0.010 in (0.25 mm) are available.
8   With the shims and retainer fitted to the pinion shaft, lubricate it with a general purpose grease and insert the pinion shaft unit into position in the pinion housing. Ensure that the flat on the pinch bolt is adjacent to the plunger boss. Align the respective components and insert the dowel pin. Fit the circlip to retain the unit, ensuring that the gap of the inserted circlip is opposed to the dowel pin.

20.5 Measuring the gap beneath the plunger cap to determine shim requirements

23 Steering column (early models) – removal and refitting

1   Disconnect the battery by removing the earth lead.
2   Disconnect the wire from the horn at its snap connector under the facia.
3   Unscrew and remove the three setscrews behind the facia panel which hold the steering column surround in place between the facia and the steering wheel.
4   Unscrew and remove the two bolts which hold the steering column bracket cap in place.
5   Unscrew and remove the nut and bolt from the clamp on the lower end of the steering column.
6   Remove the inner and outer column from the facia by pulling on the steering wheel.
7   The inner and outer columns can be separated by removing the steering wheel. See Section 24.
8   Refitting is a reverse of the removal procedure.

24 Steering column (later models) – removal and refitting

1   Disconnect the battery earth lead.
2   If it improves access, remove the car heater intake hose then undo and remove the pinch bolt and nut securing the bottom end of the steering column to the steering rack pinion.
3   Disconnect the steering column wiring connectors beneath the facia including the ignition switch.
4   Remove the two or three bolts, depending on model, securing the upper attachment to the car body and retrieve the shim packing if any is fitted. It is important to keep this packing for re-use on assembly.
5   Where fitted remove the three bolts and washers securing the toe plate fixing ring to the steering column.
6   Withdraw the steering column assembly complete with wheel from the car.
7   Refitting is the reverse of the removal procedure but the following points should be noted:

   (a) *If a new steering column assembly is being fitted, it must be aligned on left-hand drive models or on Midget Mk III cars from number GAN5-114643 and 1500 cc cars as explained in Section 16*

   (b) *Tighten the steering column upper fixing bolts to their specified torque and tighten the clamp pinch bolt and nut to its specified torque*

25 Steering column lock – removal and refitting

1   Remove the steering wheel and column as described in Sections 23 and 24. Undo the retaining screws and remove the cowls over the switch gear.
2   With the ignition key set in the 'I' position, and the lock disengaged, drill out, or remove with a suitable tool, the retaining shear bolts from the lock clamp.
3   The steering lock and ignition switch can then be removed.
4   Refitting is the reverse of the removal procedure, but note the following:

   (a) *Tighten the new shear bolts initially to 6 lbf ft (0.8 kgf m) and then check the operation of the steering lock*
   (b) *If the lock operation is satisfactory, further tighten the shear bolts until they shear at the waists*

26 Steering column bush – removal and refitting

If there is any play in the top of the steering column, it will be necessary to renew the felt or nylon bush which is fitted between the top of the inner and outer steering columns. The bush is renewed after removing the steering wheel and prising the old bush out. The new bush should be soaked in heavy oil and slid into place.

27 Steering wheel – removal and refitting

1   Unscrew and remove the small screw from the side of the steering wheel boss, where this is fitted, and prise off the motif cap from the centre of the steering wheel with a small screwdriver. On some models a bayonet type fitting is used; this needs to be pressed in and turned, to release it. With a suitable socket spanner, unscrew the nut which retains the wheel to the steering column.
2   Remove the nut, and on later models the retaining washer under it, and pull the wheel off the splines on the column. The wheel should not be tapped or driven from the column, or the column collapsible section on later models may be damaged. Refitting is a simple reversal of this process. On left-hand drive models set the cancelling trip with the formed ridge facing the direction indicator switch, and when fitting the steering wheel ensure that the tongues engage in the slots of the cancelling trip.
3   Finally tighten the steering wheel retaining nut to its specified torque.

28 Wheels and tyres – maintenance

1   While the roadwheels are removed it is sound advice to clean the inside of each wheel to remove the accumulation of dirt and, in the case of the front ones, disc pad dust.
2   Wire wheels can be cleaned more easily by applying a grease solvent with a brush and then cleaning off with a high pressure hose or a stiff brush and clean water.
3   Check the general condition of the wheels for signs of rust and repaint if necessary.
4   Check the spokes (where applicable) for looseness, cracks or breakage. Loose spokes can be re-tensioned by tightening the adjustment nuts at the wheel rim with an open-ended spanner. Only the loose spokes should be tightened, and the wheel should be checked for truth by a wheel specialist. Do not overtighten the spokes, and if loose spokes are found to be badly rusted, they must be renewed.
5   Examine the wheel stud holes and, if elongated, or the dished recesses in which the nuts seat have worn, or become over-compressed, then the wheel will have to be renewed.
6   Likewise, badly buckled wheels must be renewed.
7   Clean and check the hub splines of spoke wheels. If showing signs of wear, have them checked and renewed if necessary.
8   Check the general condition of the tyres and pick out any embedded flints from the tread. Check that the tread depth complies with the legal requirement and renew as necessary.
9   Periodical interchanging of the roadwheels may be worthwhile providing that the wheels are correctly balanced, (independent of the car). The spare wheel should be interchanged also.
10 If the wheels have been balanced on the car, then they must not be interchanged, as the balance of the wheel, tyre and hub will be upset. The exact fitting position must be marked before removing a roadwheel so that it can be refitted to its balanced position.
11 Wheels should be balanced halfway through the life of a tyre to compensate for the loss of tread.
12 Ensure that the tyres, including the spare, are kept inflated to their recommended pressures. Tyre pressures should be checked when tyres are cold.

29 Fault diagnosis – suspension and steering

Symptom	Reason(s)
Steering feels vague, car wanders and floats at speed	Tyre pressures uneven Shock absorbers worn or require topping up Spring clips broken Steering gear balljoints badly worn Suspension geometry incorrect Steering mechanism free play excessive Front suspension and rear axle mounting points out of alignment
Stiff and heavy steering	Tyre pressures too low No grease in kingpins No lubricant in steering gear No grease in steering balljoints Front wheel toe-in incorrect Suspension geometry incorrect Steering gear incorrectly adjusted too tightly Steering column misaligned
Wheel wobble and vibration	Wheel nuts loose Front wheels and tyres out of balance Irregular tyre wear Steering balljoints badly worn Hub bearings badly worn Steering gear free play excessive Front springs loose, weak or broken

Chapter 12 Bodywork and fittings

Contents

1 General description

Since the Midget Mk 1 (Sprite Mk II) was introduced in 1961, the arrangement of the bodywork has been broadly maintained up to, and including, the 1500 which is the last of the line. The combined body and underframe is of all-steel welded construction, making a strong and torsionally rigid shell.

Following conventional two-seater sports car practice, the engine is forward mounted with a luggage compartment at the rear. The two doors each have a wind-down window and a quarterlight, with outside key locking and inside locking levers, on all except very early models. The same key also locks the luggage compartment.

The folding hood can be stowed in the rear compartment behind the two seats (or on early models in the luggage compartment). An optional hardtop is available which can be fitted instead of the folding hood.

2 Maintenance – bodywork and underframe

1 The general condition of a car's bodywork is the thing that significantly affects its value. Maintenance is easy but needs to be regular. Neglect, particularly after minor damage, can lead quickly to further deterioration and costly repair bills. It is important also to keep watch on those parts of the car not immediately visible, for instance the underside, inside all the wheel arches and the lower part of the engine compartment.

2 The basic maintenance routine for the bodywork is washing – preferably with a lot of water, from a hose. This will remove all the loose solids which may have stuck to the car. It is important to flush these off in such a way as to prevent grit from scratching the finish. The wheel arches and underframe need washing in the same way to remove any accumulated mud which will retain moisture and tend to encourage rust. Paradoxically enough, the best time to clean the underframe and wheel arches is in wet weather when the mud is thoroughly wet and soft. In very wet weather the underframe is usually cleaned of large accumulations automatically and this is a good time for inspection.

3 Periodically, it is a good idea to have the whole of the underframe of the car steam cleaned, engine compartment included, so that a thorough inspection can be carried out to see what minor repairs and renovations are necessary. Steam cleaning is available at many garages and is necessary for removal of the accumulation of oily grime which sometimes is allowed to become thick in certain areas. If steam cleaning facilities are not available, there are one or two excellent grease solvents available which can be brush applied. The dirt can then be simply hosed off.

4 After washing paintwork, wipe off with a chamois leather to give an unspotted clear finish. A coat of clear protective wax polish will give added protection against chemical pollutants in the air. If the paintwork sheen has dulled or oxidised, use a cleaner/polisher combination to restore the brilliance of the shine. This requires a little effort, but such dulling is usually caused because regular washing has been neglected. Always check that the door and ventilator opening drain holes and pipes are completely clear so that water can be drained out. Bright work should be treated in the same way as paintwork. Windscreens and windows can be kept clear of the smeary film which often appears, by adding a little ammonia to the water. If they are scratched, a good rub with a proprietary metal polish will often clear them. Never use any form of wax or other body or chromium polish on glass.

3 Maintenance – upholstery and carpets

1 Mats and carpets should be brushed or vacuum cleaned regularly to keep them free of grit. If they are badly stained remove them from the car for scrubbing or sponging and make quite sure they are dry before refitting. Seats and interior trim panels can be kept clean by a wipe over with a damp cloth. If they do become stained (which can be more apparent on light coloured upholstery) use a little liquid detergent and a soft nail brush to scour the grime out of the grain of the material. Do not forget to keep the head lining clean in the same way as the upholstery. When using liquid cleaners inside the car do not over-wet the surfaces being cleaned. Excessive damp could get into the seams and padded interior causing stains, offensive odours or even rot. If the inside of the car gets wet accidentally it is worthwhile taking some trouble to dry it out properly, particularly where carpets are involved. *Do not leave oil or electric heaters inside the car for this purpose.*

4 Minor body damage – repair

Repair of minor scratches in the car's bodywork

If the scratch is very superficial, and does not penetrate to the metal of the bodywork, repair is very simple. Lightly rub the area of the scratch with a paintwork renovator, or a very fine cutting paste, to remove loose paint from the scratch and to clear the surrounding bodywork of wax polish. Rinse the area with clean water.

Apply touch-up paint to the scratch using a thin paint brush; continue to apply thin layers of paint until the surface of the paint in the scratch is level with the surrounding paintwork. Allow the new paint at least two weeks to harden: then blend it into the surrounding paintwork by rubbing the paintwork, in the scratch area, with a paintwork renovator or a very fine cutting paste. Finally, apply wax polish.

Where the scratch has penetrated right through to the metal of the bodywork, causing the metal to rust, a different repair technique is required. Remove any loose rust from the bottom of the scratch with a penknife, then apply rust inhibiting paint to prevent the formation of rust in the future. Using a rubber or nylon applicator fill the scratch with bodystopper paste. If required, this paste can be mixed with cellulose thinners to provide a very thin paste which is ideal for filling narrow scratches. Before the stopper-paste in the scratch hardens, wrap a piece of smooth cotton rag around the top of a finger. Dip the finger in cellulose thinners and then quickly sweep it across the surface of the stopper-paste in the scratch; this will ensure that the surface of the stopper-paste is slightly hollowed. The scratch can now be painted over as described earlier in this Section.

Repair of dents in the car's bodywork

When deep denting of the car's bodywork has taken place, the first task is to pull the dent out, until the affected bodywork almost attains its original shape. There is little point in trying to restore the original shape completely, as the metal in the damaged area will have stretched on impact and cannot be reshaped fully to its original contour. It is better to bring the level of the dent up to a point which is about $\frac{1}{8}$ in (3 mm) below the level of the surrounding bodywork. In cases where the dent is very shallow anyway, it is not worth trying to pull it out at all. If the underside of the dent is accessible, it can be hammered out gently from behind, using a mallet with a wooden or plastic head. Whilst doing this, hold a suitable block of wood firmly against the outside of the panel to absorb the impact from the hammer blows and thus prevent a large area of the bodywork from being 'belled-out'.

Should the dent be in a section of the bodywork which has double skin or some other factor making it inaccessible from behind, a different technique is called for. Drill several small holes through the metal inside the area – particularly in the deeper section. Then screw long self-tapping screws into the holes just sufficiently for them to gain a good purchase in the metal. Now the dent can be pulled out by pulling on the protruding heads of the screws with a pair of pliers.

The next stage of the repair is the removal of the paint from the damaged area, and from an inch or so of the surrounding 'sound' bodywork. This is accomplished most easily by using a wire brush or abrasive pad on a power drill, although it can be done just as effectively by hand using sheets of abrasive paper. To complete the preparation for filling, score the surface of the bare metal with a screwdriver or the tang of a file, or alternatively, drill small holes in the affected area. This will provide a really good 'key' for the filler paste.

To complete the repair see the Section on filling and re-spraying.

Repair of rust holes or gashes in the car's bodywork

Remove all paint from the affected area and from an inch or so of the surrounding 'sound' bodywork, using an abrasive pad or a wire brush on a power drill. If these are not available a few sheets of abrasive paper will do the job just as effectively. With the paint removed you will be able to gauge the severity of the corrosion and therefore decide whether to renew the whole panel (if this is possible) or to repair the affected area. New body panels are not as expensive as most people think and it is often quicker and more satisfactory to fit a new panel than to attempt to repair large areas of corrosion.

Remove all fittings from the affected area except those which will act as a guide to the original shape of the damaged bodywork (eg headlamp shells etc). Then, using tin snips or a hacksaw blade, remove all loose metal and any other metal badly affected by corrosion. Hammer the edges of the hole inwards in order to create a slight depression for the filler paste.

Wire brush the affected area to remove the powdery rust from the surface of the remaining metal. Paint the affected area with rust inhibiting paint; if the back of the rusted area is accessible treat this also.

Before filling can take place it will be necessary to block the hole in some way. This can be achieved by the use of zinc gauze or aluminium tape.

Zinc gauze is probably the best material to use for a large hole. Cut a piece to the approximate size and shape of the hole to be filled, then position it in the hole so that its edges are below the level of the surrounding bodywork. It can be retained in position by several blobs of filler paste around its periphery.

Aluminium tape should be used for small or very narrow holes. Pull a piece off the roll and trim it to the approximate size and shape required, then pull off the backing paper (if used) and stick the tape over the hole; it can be overlapped if the thickness of one piece is insufficient. Burnish down the edges of the tape with the handle of a screwdriver or similar, to ensure that the tape is securely attached to the metal underneath.

Bodywork repairs – filling and re-spraying

Before using this Section, see the Sections on dent, deep scratch, rust holes and gash repairs.

Many types of bodyfiller are available, but generally speaking those proprietary kits which contain a tin of filler paste and a tube of resin hardener are best for this type of repair. A wide, flexible plastic or nylon applicator will be found invaluable for imparting a smooth and well contoured finish to the surface of the filler.

Mix up a little filler on a clean piece of card or board – measure the hardener carefully (follow the maker's instructions on the pack) otherwise the filler will set too rapidly or too slowly.

Using the applicator apply the filler paste to the prepared area; draw the applicator across the surface of the filler to achieve the correct contour and to level the filler surface. As soon as a contour that approximates the correct one is achieved, stop working the paste – if you carry on too long the paste will become sticky and begin to 'pick up' on the applicator. Continue to add thin layers of filler paste at twenty-minute intervals until the level of the filler is just proud of the surrounding bodywork.

Once the filler has hardened, excess can be removed using a metal plane or file. From then on, progressively finer grades of sandpaper should be used, starting with a 40 grade production paper and finishing with 400 grade wet-and-dry paper. Always wrap the abrasive paper around a flat rubber, cork, or wooden block – otherwise the surface of the filler will not be completely flat. During the smoothing of the filler surface the wet-and-dry paper should be periodically rinsed in water. This will ensure that a very smooth finish is imparted to the filler at the final stage.

At this stage the dent should be surrounded by a ring of bare metal, which in turn should be encircled by the finely 'feathered' edge of the good paintwork. Rinse the repair area with clean water, until all of the dust produced by the rubbing-down operation has gone.

Spray the whole repair area with a light coat of primer – this will show up any imperfections in the surface of the filler. Repair these imperfections with fresh filler paste or bodystopper, and once more smooth the surface with abrasive paper. If bodystopper is used, it can be mixed with cellulose thinners to form a really thin paste which is ideal for filling small holes. Repeat this spray and repair procedure until you are satisfied that the surface of the filler, and the feathered edge of the paintwork are perfect. Clean the repair area with clean water and allow to dry fully.

The repair area is now ready for final spraying. Paint spraying must be carried out in warm, dry, windless and dust free atmosphere. This condition can be created artificially if you have access to a large indoor working area, but if you are forced to work in the open, you will have to pick your day very carefully. If you are working indoors, dousing the floor in the work area with water will help to settle the dust which would otherwise be in the atmosphere. If the repair area is confined to one body panel, mask off the surrounding panels; this will help to minimise the effects of a slight mis-match in paint colours. Bodywork fittings (eg chrome strips, door handles etc) will also need to be masked off. Use genuine masking tape and several thicknesses of newspaper for the masking operations.

Before commencing to spray, agitate the aerosol can thoroughly, then spray a test area (an old tin, or similar) until the technique is mastered. Cover the repair area with a thick coat of primer; the thickness should be built up using several thin layers of paint rather than one thick one. Using 400 grade wet-and-dry paper, rub down the surface of the primer until it is really smooth. While doing this, the work area should be thoroughly doused with water, and the wet-and-dry paper periodically rinsed in water. Allow to dry before spraying on more paint.

Spray on the top coat, again building up the thickness by using several thin layers of paint. Start spraying in the centre of the repair area and then, using a circular motion, work outwards until the whole repair area and about 2 inches of the surrounding original paintwork is covered. Remove all masking material 10 to 15 minutes after spraying on the final coat of paint.

Allow the new paint at least two weeks to harden, then, using a paintwork renovator or a very fine cutting paste, blend the edges of the paint into the existing paintwork. Finally, apply wax polish.

5 Major body damage – repair

Where serious damage has occurred or large areas need renewal due to neglect, it means almost certainly that completely new sections or panels will need welding in, and this is best left to professionals. If the damage is due to impact it will also be necessary to completely check the alignment of the body shell structure. Due to the principle of construction the strength and shape of the whole car can be affected by damage to one part. In such instances the services of a BL agent with specialist checking jigs is essential. If a body is left mis-aligned, it is first of all dangerous as the car will not handle properly, and, secondly, uneven stresses will be imposed on the steering, engine and transmission, causing abnormal wear or complete failure. Tyre wear may also be excessive.

6 Bonnet – removal and refitting

1   On the Austin Healey Sprite Mk I, the bonnet and wings lift off together as one unit. First, disconnect the wiring harness to the lights and direction indicators at the snap connectors. Remember to mark each side of each connection, otherwise it is easy to reconnect them incorrectly and find that the headlamps flash when the flashing direction indicator switch is turned on, and so on. The wiring harness must also be disconnected from its securing clip located on the right-hand hinge. Remove the screw at the top of each of the two telescopic bonnet supports and, with the aid of an assistant, lift the bonnet away. The bonnet is too heavy and cumbersome to be lifted away by one person only.
2   On later models, disconnect the bonnet stay at one end where this is the self-supporting type. Mark the position of the hinges with a pencil in relation to the bonnet. Unscrew and remove the bonnet hinge retaining setscrews from the underside of the bonnet, and with the help of an assistant, lift it clear of the car.
3   Refitting is a reverse of removal, but before fully tightening the setscrews, check that the bonnet is correctly positioned to the pencil lines, and that when closed it is fully retained by its catch.

7 Bonnet lock and release cable – removal and refitting

1   Lift and support the bonnet.
2   Compress the lock spring and loosen the locking nut, then unscrew the bonnet lock pin to remove.
3   To remove the release cable, undo the cable clamp setscrew from the catch plate arm, and from inside the car pull the catch knob and cable through. If the outer cable is to be removed, undo and remove its retaining clip on the inner panel of the nearside front wing and from the bulkhead, unscrew its retaining nut from the location bracket. Pull it clear, guiding it carefully through the rubber grommet in the front panel.
4   Refit in the reverse order, but ensure that the cable clamp setscrew is fully tightened and check its operation prior to shutting the bonnet.
5   Adjust the bonnet lock by tightening the lock pin, to compress the spring and retaining thimble to suit, and retain in position by tightening the locknut.

8 Bonnet safety catch – removal and refitting

1   To remove the bonnet safety catch, raise and support the bonnet.
2   Withdraw the split pin from the retaining pin. Pull the pin through and remove the catch lever complete with spring.

Fig. 12.1 Boot lid lock showing retaining nuts and bolts (Sec 10)

3   Refit in the reverse order, and check the action prior to closing the bonnet.

9 Boot lid – removal and refitting

1   Raise and support the boot lid. On later models, disconnect the boot lid stay at one end. Mark the position of the hinges to the lid to assist realignment on assembly.
2   Undo the hinge setscrews and remove the lid. The striker plate may be removed by unscrewing the retaining screws.
3   Refit in the reverse order

10 Boot lid lock – removal and refitting

1   Lift the lid and unscrew the two nuts retaining the handle unit to the lid.
2   Then remove the two bolts and nuts to withdraw the handle and lock unit from the lid.
3   Refitting is the reverse procedure.

11 Padded crash roll – removal and refitting

1   To remove the padded crash roll (where fitted), take off the facia panel as detailed in Section 17, and then unscrew the rail fixing screws and nuts and lift the crash roll away.
2   Refitting is the reversal of this procedure.

12 Front bumpers (chrome type) – removal and refitting

1   The bumpers are removed by unscrewing the bumper bracket setbolts (nuts and washers at the front) from the body, and the bumpers lifted away complete with brackets.
2   Refitting is the reverse procedure to removal.

13 Front bumper ('rubber' type) – removal and refitting

1   Remove the earth strap from the battery, then disconnect the sidelight wires from their connections under the bonnet and pull them through to hang free under the wings.
2   Unscrew and remove the four nuts and washers retaining the inner bumper brackets to the car (photo), and then remove the bumper outer brackets retaining nuts/washers from inside each front wing. The bumper unit can now be lifted clear of the car. Remove the inner bumper brackets.
3   The number plate can be easily removed together with its bracket by unscrewing the retaining bolts. To remove the sidelights unscrew the lens retaining screws, and remove the lens. Then unscrew the light unit retaining screws from the bumper and withdraw the unit.
4   Refitting is the direct reversal of removal, but ensure that the side

13.2 Retaining bolts and bracket on the later type 'rubber' front bumper

light lenses are refitted the correct way up, with the drain slots downwards.

14 Rear bumpers – removal and refitting

1   The earliest models have one-piece bumpers, and removal consists of undoing and removing the bumper bracket securing setscrews and removing the bumper complete with its brackets.
2   Later models have a two piece rear bumper with the rear number plate lamps inset at the inner ends of the two parts of the bumper. To remove a half bumper, first disconnect the battery earth lead, then disconnect the electrical supply to the rear number plate lamp at the connectors inside the car adjacent to the lamp and pull the leads free. Undo and remove the securing nuts and washers and remove the half bumper.
3   The latest models have a one-piece 'rubber' bumper which can be removed by undoing and removing the four securing nuts and eight washers, and then removing the bumper.
4   In each case refitting is the reverse of the removal procedure.

15 Radiator grille – removal and refitting

1   Raise and support the bonnet.
2   Unscrew and remove the grille-to-body retaining bolts and nuts, and self-tapping screws, and lift the grille clear of the body.
3   Refitting is the reverse of removal.

16 Windscreen – removal and refitting

1   Remove the windscreen wiper arms and blades. referring to Chapter 10 for details if necessary.
2   On the earlier models, except the Sprite Mk II and Midget Mk II, the windscreen in removed by unscrewing the five cross-head screws from each of the windscreen pillars and lifting the windscreen away. The pillars can be removed after unscrewing the cross-head screw and cross-head bolt whose nut is accessible with the door open.
3   On the Sprite Mk III and IV, Midget Mk II and III, it is first necessary to remove the facia as described in Section 17. The windscreen to A-post setscrews, and the centre stay setscrew should then be removed and the windscreen lifted out. Refitting in both cases is a reversal of the removal procedure.
4   On later Midgets and 1500 models, remove the sun visors and the rear view mirror, and then disconnect the battery. Now remove the facia panel just far enough to gain access to the windscreen pillar retaining bolts (photo). Disconnect the wiper arms and blades and loosen the windscreen wiper wheelbox nuts to release the bottom seal.

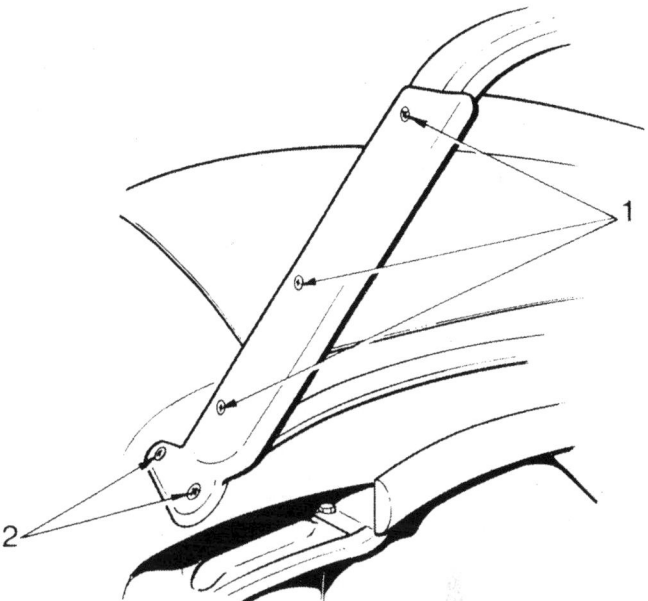

Fig. 12.2 Windscreen frame retaining screws on early models (Sec 16)

1   Windshield-to-pillar screws   2   Pillar-to-body screws

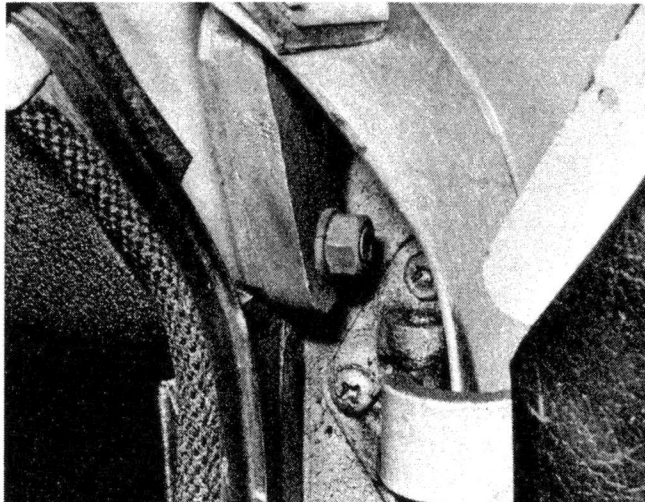

16.4 The windscreen side pillar location bolt retaining nut and spring washer, which are accessible through the door hinge channel

5   Remove the windscreen centre stay bolts from the body. With the windscreen side pillars removed together with the shims, the windscreen can be lifted clear.
6   Refit in the reverse order, but in each case, ensure that the hood fits the top of the windscreen correctly before fully tightening the side pillar bolts, and that the shims are refitted to their correct location.

17 Dashboard/facia panel – removal and refitting

Sprite Mk I and II and Midget Mk I
1   Remove the steering wheel by prising off the centre motif cap after unscrewing the retaining screw in the boss of the steering wheel (where fitted), and then with a suitable socket spanner unscrew the nut which holds the wheel to the steering column, and pull the wheel off the steering column splines.
2   The facia panel is held by a series of nuts and bolts along its top edge, and cross-head screws along the bottom edge and behind the steering column surround.

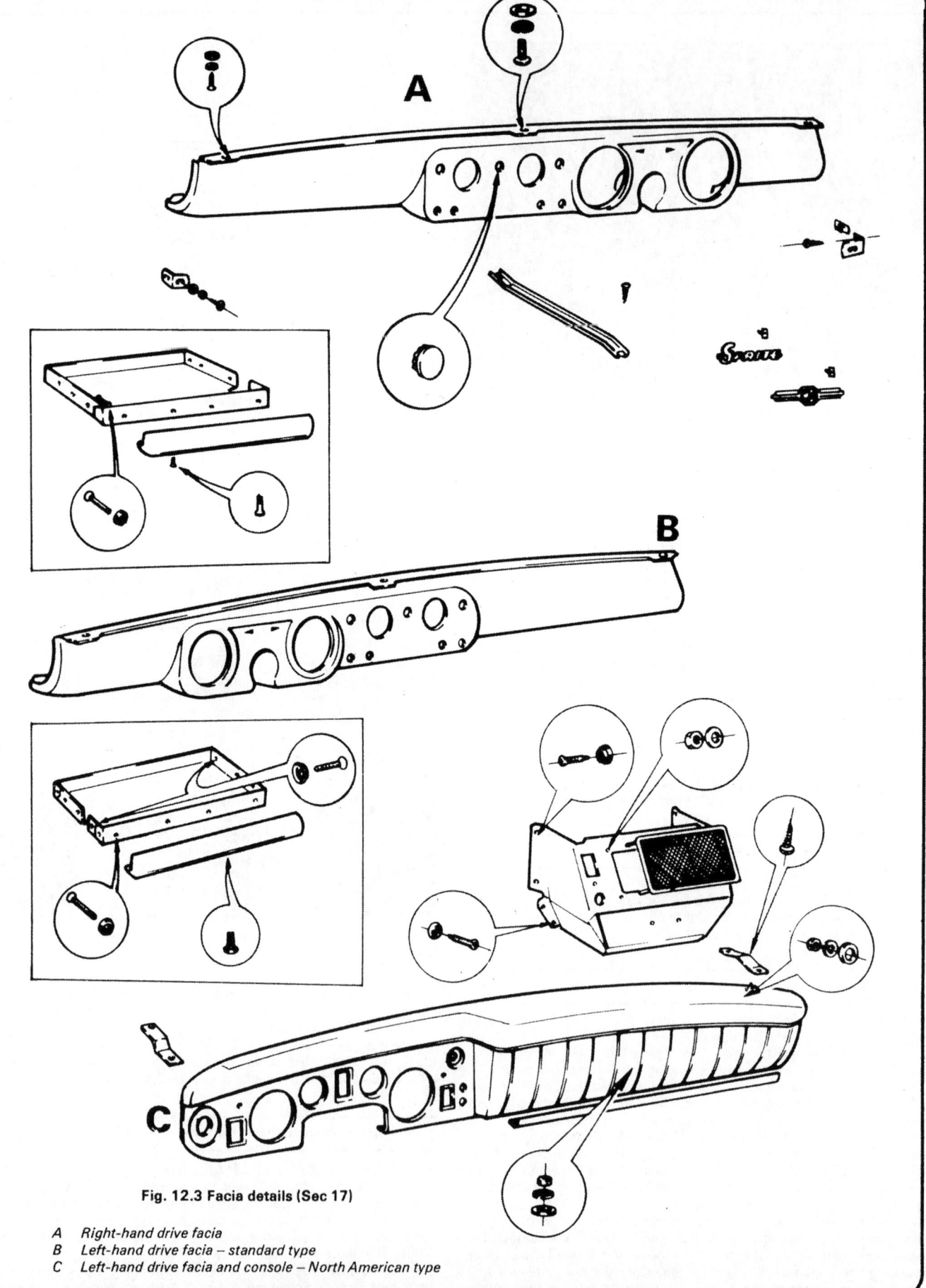

Fig. 12.3 Facia details (Sec 17)

A Right-hand drive facia
B Left-hand drive facia – standard type
C Left-hand drive facia and console – North American type

3   Unscrew the oil pressure pipe from its union with the combined oil pressure/water temperature gauge, and free the water temperature gauge pipe at its connection with the radiator. Unscrew the unions holding the tachometer and speedometer drives in place and release the starter and choke cables.

4   It is now possible to pull the facia into the interior where further dismantling can be carried out as required.

5   Refit in the reverse order of removal.

Sprite Mk III and Midget Mk II

6   Unscrew the steady bracket securing setscrews, the setscrews at each end of the facia panel, and the setscrew under the crash roll.

7   Free the steering column as detailed in Chapter 11, and lower the column and wheel. The facia can then be dropped to give access to the connections to the instruments and controls. With these disconnected the facia can be lifted away.

8   Refit by reversing the removal procedure.

Later models and 1500

9   Disconnect the earth lead from the battery.

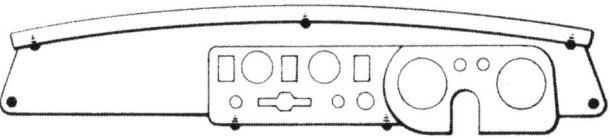

Fig. 12.4 Standard facia retaining screw positions (Sec 17)

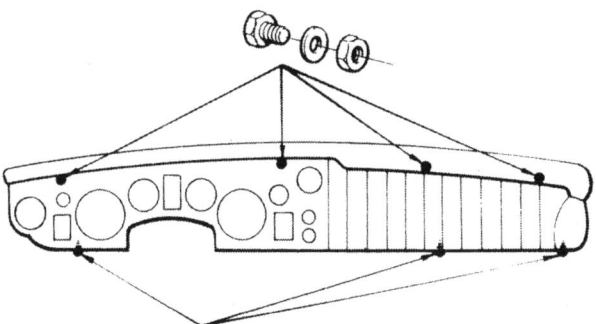

Fig. 12.5 Retaining screw positions on the North American type facia (Sec 17)

19.3 Removing the window winding handle after removing the central screw – later model

10   On models without an electrical coolant temperature gauge, drain the coolant system (See Chapter 2) then remove the thermostat housing, and release the capillary tube clips retaining it to the water pipe, inlet manifold and bulkhead. Straighten the tube and push it through the bulkhead grommet.

11   Disconnect the flasher switch top and bottom cowls and remove.

12   Remove the choke cable from the carburettor and under the rubber strap securing the cable to the heater body. Withdraw the choke cable rubber cover.

13   Withdraw the steering column as described in Chapter 11.

14   Press the heater control knob plunger to remove the knob and washer. Then unscrew the lock rings from both the heater control and windscreen washer control. Withdraw the respective control units from behind the facia.

15   Remove the two screws and washers securing the bottom end of the facia, and then the two stay support screws.

16   Support the facia from underneath and unscrew the upper retaining screws/nuts from the top inside edge, and carefully lower the facia unit and tilt to give access to the interior. Further dismantling of other components from the facia can now be achieved. If disconnecting the oil pressure pipe from the gauge, be careful not to spill oil onto the carpets, and retain the pipe sealing washer.

17   If disconnecting the complete wiring harness from the facia take note of the various positions to make reassembly easier.

18   Refitting is a reversal of removal, but check the wiring connections prior to reconnecting the battery.

USA and Canada models

19   Disconnect the battery and then undo the centre console retaining screws and move the console aside towards the steering column. Remove the screws securing the facia support plates to the bulkhead.

20   Remove the heater control knob after depressing the plunger in its shank, then undo the securing nut and remove the washers to enable the control to be withdraw from the facia. Let the control hang behind the facia.

21   Undo the clamps securing the tachometer, remove it from the facia and disconnect its wiring.

22   Undo the four nuts and washer holding the top of the facia, partly remove it and disconnect the two multi-connectors and the single snap connector. Undo the speedometer drive from the back of the instrument and pull the facia forward.

23   Further dismantling will depend on particular requirements. Carefully note details of wiring connections, instrument locations, switch and light bulb locations, etc before disconnecting or removing them so that correct refitting can be achieved.

24   Refitting is the reverse of the removal procedure.

18 Seats – removal and refitting

1   Slide the seat forward and from the rear end of the seat runners, unscrew the retaining bolts and washers.

2   The nuts and washers at the front end of the runners are removed from underneath the car.

3   If fitted, disconnect the seat belt warning cables, and lift the seat clear.

4   Refitting is the reverse of removal.

19 Interior door handles – removal and refitting

1   The door handle is held in place by a central cross-head screw. Remove this screw and the handle can be pulled off. Refitting is a direct reversal of this procedure.

2   To withdraw the window winding handle from its shaft, expose the pin holding the handle in place by pushing back the disc and drive out the pin. The handle can now be pulled off.

3   On later models, the handles are retained by a cross-head screw. Remove in the same way as that for the door handles (photo).

20 Door trim – removal and refitting

Sprite Mk III and IV, Midget Mk II and III, and 1500 models

1   Remove the window winder and interior door handles, and then

20.2 Removing the door lock escutcheon

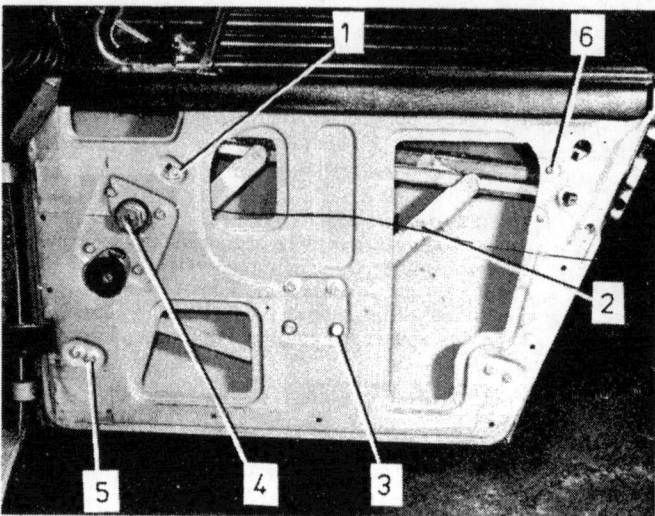

25.2 The door fittings revealed with the trim removed

1   Winding mechanism arm stop
2   Winding mechanism arm
3   Winding mechanism securing bolts
4   Winding mechanism handle spindle
5   Door glass front channel bottom securing bolts

unscrew the door pull retaining screws. On later models (Midget Mk III GAN5-105501 on), the door pull retaining screws are enclosed within the end caps, which can be levered away to give access to the screws.
2   On later models, remove the door handle and then the two escutcheon retaining screws, and lift clear (photo).
3   The door trim can now be carefully prised away from the door panel. The trim should be pulled downwards to clear the upper trim moulding. The top moulding can be removed by unscrewing the two nuts and washers from the inner panel.
4   Refit in the reverse order.

21   Exterior door handle – removal and refitting

All models from Sprite Mk II and Midget Mk II
1   To remove the exterior door handle, first wind up the window, then remove the interior door and window winding handles, and the door trim as detailed in previous Sections. The exterior handle is held in place by a nut and screw and four washers. These should now be undone, and the handle is then easily removed.
2   To refit a door handle, first position it on the door with its washers located correctly, and check the clearance between the lock contactor on the lock and the plunger bolt on the handle. If necessary loosen the locknut and adjust the length of the plunger bolt to achieve a minimum clearance of 0.030 in (0.79 mm) then tighten the locknut. Refitting is then the reverse of the removal procedure; check operation on completion.

22   Door locks – removal and refitting

All models from Sprite Mk III and Midget Mk II
1   Fully wind up the window.
2   Remove the interior door and window winder handles and the door trim.
3   Undo the remote control securing screws and move the control inwards to disengage its stud from the operating lever before withdrawing the assembly.
4   Undo the door lock retaining screws and remove the assembly.
5   Refitting is the reverse of the removal procedure but note the following points:
   (a)   Move the lock contactor so that the latch is in the open position before positioning it in the door, and ensure that the locking lever engages the private lock operating fork. Fit and tighten the retaining screws noting that, where two screws are used, the short screw fits the lower hole
   (b)   Position the remote control assembly in the door so that its stud engages the operating lever, loosely fit the securing screws, move the assembly towards the lock until the lock operating lever is against its stop, and then tighten the screws
   (c)   Check operation on completion of refitting

23   Door – removal and refitting

1   Each door is held in place by two hinges and a check strap. To remove a door, first unscrew the two setscrews from the check strap coupling bracket located on the inside of the door pillars. Then open the door fully and unscrew the three cross-head screws from the body end of each of the two hinges and lift off the door complete with hinges.
2   The hinges are secured to the door itself by two horizontal cross-head screws on each hinge. The holes in which these screws lie are noramlly covered by rubber plugs.
3   Refitting is a direct reversal of this procedure. Check and, if necessary, adjust the striker as explained in the next Section.

24   Door striker plates – removal and refitting

1   If the striker plate has to be removed, first mark its position on the door pillar so that the new plate can be fixed in the correct position.
2   Unscrew the setscrews retaining the plate to the door pillar, lift the plate away and retrieve the shim(s).
3   On refitting, position the striker and original shim(s) with the screws just holding them in place. Close the door and check the clearance between the faces of the striker and the lock. This should be between 0.03 in (0.8 mm) and 0.06 in (1.6 mm). If necessary alter the shim(s) to achieve the correct clearance; spare shims are available in thicknesses of 0.03 in (0.8 mm) and 0.06 in (1.6 mm). Tighten the screws, recheck the clearance and check the door closing action. Finally check the door lock operation.

25   Ventilator assembly (quarterlight) – removal and refitting

All models from Sprite Mk III and Midget Mk II on
1   Remove the door trim as described in Section 20.
2   Remove the winding mechanism arm stop located just above the window winder spindle (photo).
3   Remove the two ventilator securing bolts in the front edge of the door and the two nuts and washers inside the top of the door towards the front.
4   Remove the two bolts securing the bottom end of the glass front channel, which are located near the door check strap. Tilt the ventilator assembly forward and remove the bracket from the bottom end of the

glass front channel. Lift the ventilator assembly clear of the door.
5   Refitting is the reverse of the removal procedure.

26 Window winder mechanism – removal and refitting

All models from Sprite Mk III and Midget Mk II on
1   Remove the ventilator (quarterlight) assembly as described in the previous Section.
2   Remove the four winder mechanism securing bolts located near the winder spindle, and also the four bolts located in the centre of the door.
3   Wind the mechanism to the rear of the door glass, tilt the glass rearwards and release the mechanism from the glass bottom channel.
4   Lift the glass up and remove the mechanism from the door.

5   Refitting is the reverse of the removal procedure. Check the operation of the winder mechanism before refitting the door trim.

27 Window glass – removal and refitting

All models from Sprite Mk III and Midget Mk II on
1   Follow the procedure listed in the previous Section as far as releasing the winder mechanism from the glass bottom channel (paragraph 3).
2   Push the door weather strip on the inner face of the glass down into the door and remove it together with its securing clips.
3   Lift the door glass up and remove it from the door by tilting it inwards.
4   Refitting is the reverse of the removal procedure.

Conversion factors

Length (distance)

Inches (in)	X	25.4	=	Millimetres (mm)	X	0.0394	= Inches (in)
Feet (ft)	X	0.305	=	Metres (m)	X	3.281	= Feet (ft)
Miles	X	1.609	=	Kilometres (km)	X	0.621	= Miles

Volume (capacity)

Cubic inches (cu in; in³)	X	16.387	=	Cubic centimetres (cc; cm³)	X	0.061	= Cubic inches (cu in; in³)
Imperial pints (Imp pt)	X	0.568	=	Litres (l)	X	1.76	= Imperial pints (Imp pt)
Imperial quarts (Imp qt)	X	1.137	=	Litres (l)	X	0.88	= Imperial quarts (Imp qt)
Imperial quarts (Imp qt)	X	1.201	=	US quarts (US qt)	X	0.833	= Imperial quarts (Imp qt)
US quarts (US qt)	X	0.946	=	Litres (l)	X	1.057	= US quarts (US qt)
Imperial gallons (Imp gal)	X	4.546	=	Litres (l)	X	0.22	= Imperial gallons (Imp gal)
Imperial gallons (Imp gal)	X	1.201	=	US gallons (US gal)	X	0.833	= Imperial gallons (Imp gal)
US gallons (US gal)	X	3.785	=	Litres (l)	X	0.264	= US gallons (US gal)

Mass (weight)

Ounces (oz)	X	28.35	=	Grams (g)	X	0.035	= Ounces (oz)
Pounds (lb)	X	0.454	=	Kilograms (kg)	X	2.205	= Pounds (lb)

Force

Ounces-force (ozf; oz)	X	0.278	=	Newtons (N)	X	3.6	= Ounces-force (ozf; oz)
Pounds-force (lbf; lb)	X	4.448	=	Newtons (N)	X	0.225	= Pounds-force (lbf; lb)
Newtons (N)	X	0.1	=	Kilograms-force (kgf; kg)	X	9.81	= Newtons (N)

Pressure

Pounds-force per square inch (psi; lbf/in²; lb/in²)	X	0.070	=	Kilograms-force per square centimetre (kgf/cm²; kg/cm²)	X	14.223	= Pounds-force per square inch (psi; lbf/in²; lb/in²)
Pounds-force per square inch (psi; lbf/in²; lb/in²)	X	0.068	=	Atmospheres (atm)	X	14.696	= Pounds-force per square inch (psi; lbf/in²; lb/in²)
Pounds-force per square inch (psi; lbf/in²; lb/in²)	X	0.069	=	Bars	X	14.5	= Pounds-force per square inch (psi; lbf/in²; lb/in²)
Pounds-force per square inch (psi; lbf/in²; lb/in²)	X	6.895	=	Kilopascals (kPa)	X	0.145	= Pounds-force per square inch (psi; lbf/in²; lb/in²)
Kilopascals (kPa)	X	0.01	=	Kilograms-force per square centimetre (kgf/cm²; kg/cm²)	X	98.1	= Kilopascals (kPa)
Millibar (mbar)	X	100	=	Pascals (Pa)	X	0.01	= Millibar (mbar)
Millibar (mbar)	X	0.0145	=	Pounds-force per square inch (psi; lbf/in²; lb/in²)	X	68.947	= Millibar (mbar)
Millibar (mbar)	X	0.75	=	Millimetres of mercury (mmHg)	X	1.333	= Millibar (mbar)
Millibar (mbar)	X	0.401	=	Inches of water (inH₂O)	X	2.491	= Millibar (mbar)
Millimetres of mercury (mmHg)	X	0.535	=	Inches of water (inH₂O)	X	1.868	= Millimetres of mercury (mmHg)
Inches of water (inH₂O)	X	0.036	=	Pounds-force per square inch (psi; lbf/in²; lb/in²)	X	27.68	= Inches of water (inH₂O)

Torque (moment of force)

Pounds-force inches (lbf in; lb in)	X	1.152	=	Kilograms-force centimetre (kgf cm; kg cm)	X	0.868	= Pounds-force inches (lbf in; lb in)
Pounds-force inches (lbf in; lb in)	X	0.113	=	Newton metres (Nm)	X	8.85	= Pounds-force inches (lbf in; lb in)
Pounds-force inches (lbf in; lb in)	X	0.083	=	Pounds-force feet (lbf ft; lb ft)	X	12	= Pounds-force inches (lbf in; lb in)
Pounds-force feet (lbf ft; lb ft)	X	0.138	=	Kilograms-force metres (kgf m; kg m)	X	7.233	= Pounds-force feet (lbf ft; lb ft)
Pounds-force feet (lbf ft; lb ft)	X	1.356	=	Newton metres (Nm)	X	0.738	= Pounds-force feet (lbf ft; lb ft)
Newton metres (Nm)	X	0.102	=	Kilograms-force metres (kgf m; kg m)	X	9.804	= Newton metres (Nm)

Power

Horsepower (hp)	X	745.7	=	Watts (W)	X	0.0013	= Horsepower (hp)

Velocity (speed)

Miles per hour (miles/hr; mph)	X	1.609	=	Kilometres per hour (km/hr; kph)	X	0.621	= Miles per hour (miles/hr; mph)

Fuel consumption*

Miles per gallon, Imperial (mpg)	X	0.354	=	Kilometres per litre (km/l)	X	2.825	= Miles per gallon, Imperial (mpg)
Miles per gallon, US (mpg)	X	0.425	=	Kilometres per litre (km/l)	X	2.352	= Miles per gallon, US (mpg)

Temperature

Degrees Fahrenheit = (°C x 1.8) + 32   Degrees Celsius (Degrees Centigrade; °C) = (°F - 32) x 0.56

It is common practice to convert from miles per gallon (mpg) to litres/100 kilometres (l/100km), where mpg (Imperial) x l/100 km = 282 and mpg (US) x l/100 km = 235

Index

produktsicherheit@kolibri360.de

Zeitfracht Medien GmbH
Ferdinand-Jühlke-Straße 7
99095 Erfurt, Deutschland
produktsicherheit@kolibri360.de